FOOD

Readings from
SCIENTIFIC AMERICAN

FOOD

with introductions by
Johan E. Hoff and Jules Janick
Purdue University

W. H. Freeman and Company
San Francisco

Library of Congress Cataloging in Publication Data

Hoff, Johan E.   comp.
  Food: readings from Scientific American.

  1. Food—Addresses, essays, lectures.   I. Janick, Jules, 1931–   joint comp.   II. Scientific American.
III. Title.
TX353.H53   641.3′008   73-3138
ISBN 0-7167-0876-0
ISBN 0-7167-0875-2 (pbk)

Most of the SCIENTIFIC AMERICAN articles in *Food* are available as separate Offprints. For a complete list of more than 900 articles now available as Offprints, write to W. H. Freeman and Company, 660 Market Street, San Francisco, California 94104

Copyright © 1950, 1951, 1952, 1953, 1954, 1956, 1958, 1959, 1960, 1961, 1963, 1964, 1965, 1966, 1967, 1969, 1970, 1971, 1972, 1973 by SCIENTIFIC AMERICAN, INC.

No part of this book may be reproduced by any mechanical, photographic, or electronic process, or in the form of a phonographic recording, nor may it be stored in a retrieval system, transmitted, or otherwise copied for public or private use without written permission from the publisher.

Printed in the United States of America

9 8 7 6 5 4 3 2 1

PREFACE

Seldom in recent times has the importance of our food and food supply been brought so strongly to our attention as today. We are constantly being exposed to ominous headlines about world famine, food poisonings, mass malnutrition, and carcinogens and toxic materials being spewed into the environment. Are these in fact real problems, or are they exaggerated distortions? An emotional and hysterical reaction must not be allowed to color the judgment required to assess each situation. Reasoned decisions are necessary to solve the present-day problems of food and to ensure a plentiful and wholesome food supply for all people. In order to make progress in this area, we must first know what our foods are, what their functions are in the human body, how they are produced, and what the prospects are of securing their continued supply.

The twenty-eight articles presented here were selected in an attempt to lay the foundation for such a reasoned judgment. They appeared in SCIENTIFIC AMERICAN between 1950 and 1972. We cannot hope in these relatively few articles to cover adequately the varied and exciting spectrum of activities in food research today. Yet each article tells a story that comes direct from the author's research or experience, and, although recent discoveries and events have dated some of the developments here described, the stories come to us fresh and compelling. The compilation serves to highlight the enormous progress that has occurred over a span of relatively few years, and at the same time to emphasize the great and growing problems that remain. We hope this collection will prove of interest to all seriously concerned with the well-being of mankind, now and in the future, and in particular to students in food science, nutrition, agriculture, and ecology.

February 1973

JOHAN E. HOFF
JULES JANICK

CONTENTS

I NUTRITION AND MALNUTRITION

		Introduction 1
HAAGEN-SMIT	1	Smell and Taste 8
MARGARIA	2	The Sources of Muscular Energy 13
MAYER	3	Appetite and Obesity 21
FRUTON	4	Proteins 27
KRETCHMER	5	Lactose and Lactase 35
YOUNG AND SCRIMSHAW	6	The Physiology of Starvation 44
TROWELL	7	Kwashiorkor 52
WOODWARD	8	Biotin 57
GILLIE	9	Endemic Goiter 63
WOODWELL	10	Toxic Substances and Ecological Cycles 72
GOLDWATER	11	Mercury in the Environment 80

II CONVENTIONAL SOURCES AND RESOURCES

		Introduction 88
MANGELSDORF	12	Wheat 94
MANGELSDORF	13	Hybrid Corn 105
PATTON	14	Milk 115
PHILLIPS	15	Cattle 123
WILSON	16	Poultry Production 131
HOLT	17	The Food Resources of the Ocean 139
KERMODE	18	Food Additives 153
ROSE	19	Beer 160
AMERINE	20	Wine 169

III THE FUTURE: FEAST OR FAMINE?

		Introduction 183
DEEVEY	21	The Human Population 189
SCRIMSHAW	22	Food 197
BROWN	23	Human Food Production as a Process in the Biosphere 205
BOERMA	24	A World Agricultural Plan 215
PIRIE	25	Orthodox and Unorthodox Methods of Meeting World Food Needs 229
PINCHOT	26	Marine Farming 238
HARPSTEAD	27	High-lysine Corn 245
CHAMPAGNAT	28	Protein from Petroleum 254

Bibliographies 261
Index 265

Note on cross-references: References to articles included in this book are noted by the title of the article and the page on which it begins; references to articles that are available as Offprints, but are not included here, are noted by the article's title and Offprint number; references to articles published by SCIENTIFIC AMERICAN, but which are not available as Offprints, are noted by the title of the article and the month and year of its publication.

FOOD

I
NUTRITION AND MALNUTRITION

I

NUTRITION AND MALNUTRITION

INTRODUCTION

Man's food has many dimensions. The quantitative dimension is obvious; insufficiency leads progressively from mild discomfort to severe hunger and ultimately to death. But there is also a qualitative aspect. Improper diets lead to malnutrition, obesity, or disease. Food affects health, life span, physical fitness, body size, and mental development.

Food also has a cultural dimension. Our food habits are part of our cultural and emotional life, and our preferences are ingrained. We cling to our food habits; they have become rituals and patterns in our daily routine. Satisfactory dining soothes both body and soul and is a major factor in quality of life.

For the dietician, good nutrition reduces to an accounting of calories, amino acids, vitamins, and a few minerals. The list of essential nutrients is a modest one. Approximately forty substances are included, and although there is no assurance that a few essential substances may not still remain undiscovered, it is reasonable to assume that the list is almost complete. Our requirements of these nutrients can be met in many ways, yet it still is not clear what combination of foods is optimal. It does seem clear, however, that there is no universal food that will satisfy all our requirements. Among the hundreds of thousands of living species of plants and animals that compete with man for space and resources, we seek out those relatively few that are edible, that have been found through experience to be tolerable, or of more benefit than harm. The species that we eat were not made for that purpose, but for the purpose of sustaining themselves. Moreover, we must consume a variety of these species, for no single one can provide us with the full spectrum of our complex needs.

Our body, from one point of view, is a thermodynamic system that receives mass and energy from the environment: mass for growth, replacement of worn parts, and for reproduction; energy to fuel the chemical processes that take place in the body and for work. Both are provided for in our food. And when this human system operates under steady-state conditions—i.e., without a net gain or loss of mass or energy—then the expenditures are balanced by the intake, the demand by the supply. Deviations from the steady-state condition are dangerous. Too little intake leads to hunger and starvation; too much, to obesity and heart failure. Looked at in this way, food and feeding seem very simple and straightforward phenomena indeed. In reality, they are very complex, and are the subject of study by scientists in a battery of disciplines—medicine, biology, biochemistry, and psychology, just to mention a few. The articles contained in this section were selected to illustrate some of the areas that are under intensive investigation in the varied and exciting spectrum of activities in food research of today.

The essay by A. J. Haagen-Smit, "Smell and Taste," deals with the body's responses to the initial contact with food, a subject that has intrigued scholars since the time of Plato and which challenges the skills of today's chemists and physiologists. Although Haagen-Smit's article is now considerably dated, his description of the phenomena is still valid. It is interesting to note that in comparison with the cumbersome methods of 1952, in which thousands of pounds of foodstuff were required for the isolation and identification of a few odor components, the elegant techniques in use today require only a few milliliters (a thimble full) of an air sample taken from the vicinity of the food in order to identify dozens of components. Indeed, the recent advances in this field, the domain of the flavor chemist, are due mainly to the revolution in laboratory instrumentation that has taken place over the past two decades. The gas chromatograph (an instrument that analyzes mixtures of volatiles), without which a modern flavor chemist would be helpless, was not yet invented when Haagen-Smit wrote his article. The application of the mass spectrograph (an instrument which makes possible the determination of organic-compound structure) to anything but inorganic materials had not yet been attempted, and today's most powerful tool—the marriage of these two instruments—had not even been imagined. Innovation in instrumentation has in a similar manner kindled impressive advances in our understanding of the sensory perception of tastes and odors—the physiology of the chemical senses. Here we see that developments in automatic recording instruments and vastly improved and miniaturized sensing transducers have made possible studies that would have been inconceivable only twenty years ago. In addition to those mentioned by Haagen-Smit, new olfactory theories have come and gone, none of which have increased our understanding of the mechanisms of odor perception. The era of olfactory theories, which started with Linneus in the eighteenth century, seems now to be fading, and a realization is growing that the explanation has to be sought on the level of molecular biology.

The physiology of taste and odor perception on the microscopic level is in the meantime progressing rapidly. The physiologist is concerned with the way nerve impulses are generated and transmitted and is from necessity sometimes forced to seek out rather unusual creatures for experimentation, such as the humble blow fly (see "Taste Receptors" by Edward S. Hodgson, SCIENTIFIC AMERICAN, May 1961) because they possess features of unique design. Progress in experimental physiological techniques has now made possible the study of olfactory and taste responses in more conventional laboratory animals, such as rabbits, dogs, cats, and even in humans. The reader who might be particularly interested in these aspects of food research should consult modern texts (see Bibliography).

The energy requirement of the animal body is customarily divided into two functional classifications: the energy requirement for basal metabolism and that for active work. The former includes energy expenditures for such processes as respiration, circulation, digestion, thermal equilibrium; in humans it amounts to roughly one-half of the total energy intake for a moderately active person. The other half is the subject of Rodolfo Margaria's article "The Sources of Muscular Energy." The human body does not function as a heat machine, such as a steam engine or an internal combustion engine, both of which convert stored chemical fuel energy into heat and translate the heat energy into mechanical energy by expansion of hot gases under high pressure. The human body operates in a more sophisticated way by converting the bound chemical energy in food to other forms of chemical energy for temporary storage and later conversion upon demand to mechanical energy by chemical processes. The nature of these processes is just beginning to be unraveled. Margaria's article is concerned with the physiology and biochemistry of the various energy-storage forms, the way these are mobilized when required, and the resulting effects of combustion products and oxygen utilization on the body.

The basal metabolic requirements of human beings have been found to be surprisingly predictable. As one might expect, they depend on the size of a person—i.e., upon the biological mass that has to be sustained in thermal steady-state equilibrium and supplied with oxygen and nutrients by circulation and breathing. A close correlation has been found to exist between the surface area of a person and the number of calories required for basal metabolism. If this requirement for a certain person amounts to 1200 kilocalories, an excess in intake beyond this level has to be expended through physical (and mental) activity if this person is to maintain his weight. The requirements for physical exercise and activity are highly variable. People who lead a sedentary life and who are either indolent or abhor exercise in any form, may, in extreme cases, require no more than 500 kilocalories. On the other hand, individuals engaged in heavy physical activity, such as logging, may require ten times that amount. The excess in intake, which is not utilized, is stored in the form of fat in the adipose tissue. An imbalance between intake and utilization indicates that something is wrong, that the signal devices of appetite and satiety do not function properly.

"Appetite and Obesity" by Jean Mayer addresses itself to the various causes that make this control system malfunction, and to the identification of the control center of the system, the hypothalamus. Much progress has been made since Mayer's pioneering studies. For example, it is now known that imbalanced diets—food intakes that are deficient in one or more essential factors—may cause overeating in terms of caloric intake as the body makes an effort to obtain adequate amounts of the deficient factor. It is further indicated that several genetic factors, not necessarily related to the function of the hypothalamus, may be involved. Thus, the study of fat mobilization receives very intensive attention today. It has been found that individuals differ greatly in their ability to convert stored fat in the adipose tissue back to metabolizable substances in the blood. It is thought that the syndrome of "fat babies" is due to genetic defects in the fat-mobilization system. Curiously enough, but perhaps not very surprising, such studies have been greatly assisted by research in animal husbandry done for an entirely different reason. For example, investigations into differences in the fat-storing ability of different strains of swine have shown that fat mobilization is controlled partly by the endocrine glands and partly by unknown factors in the adipose tissue itself and in the blood. The involvement of hormones in this control suggests that obesity in man is also a psychosomatic condition, and, indeed, the evidence is mounting that psychological factors are operating in a great number of cases. It appears that some people experience an "emotional hunger" that results from the deprivation of affection or from either boredom or frustration and which may be satisfied by eating. The interdisciplinary area between psychology and physiology has in the study of obesity one of its most fruitful and promising fields.

The major organic constituent of the human body is protein. It forms the very basis of the cell, the unit from which the body is constructed. Protein has a myriad of forms and functions, including highly inert and resistant materials such as those that make up fingernails and hair, contractile elements such as those in muscle, impulse-conducting elements such as those in nervous tissue, and enzymes such as those in digestive juices. In fact we know today that we are not dealing with a single substance, but with thousands of different substances that have in common the characteristic of being composed of some combination of twenty amino acids—no more, but sometimes less. Most of these amino acids, the building blocks of proteins, can be synthesized in the human body from other material, but eight (for adults) or ten (for the young) of them are not synthesized in adequate amounts to support the protein construction needed for growth and replacement of dead tissue. These are the so-called essential amino acids, which must be provided through the diet. It follows that a good and adequate diet must contain the essential amino acids in amounts and proportions corresponding to our needs. Further, they must be provided together! Protein malnutrition is probably the most formidable problem facing mankind today. There are many reasons for the difficulty in finding adequate sources of full-value protein. Plant proteins are never fully satisfactory in this respect, for of their essential amino acids, one or more will occur in concentrations that are less than optimal in terms of nutritional responses, such as growth of the young. The deficient amino acid may be identified if improved growth is observed when a particular amino acid is added to diets restricted to a single source. Most cereal proteins are deficient in the amino acid lysine (see "High Lysine Corn" in section III) and most legume (peas, beans) protein is deficient in the amino acid methionine. A diet containing a mixture of cereals and legumes has a tendency to reduce the deficiency of both of these amino acids and have an improved "biological value" in comparison with diets of either component alone.

Few areas within the biological sciences have undergone a more rapid development than the decipherment of protein structure and function. Joseph S. Fruton, in his essay "Proteins," records the beginning of the revolution that started in the 1950's. (Also refer to "Proteins" by Paul Doty, SCIENTIFIC AMERICAN, September 1957.) Initiated by X-ray crystallographers such as Crick in England and Ramachandran in India, the efforts of protein chemists have culminated in the complete architectural description of some 25 enzymes and of numerous structural proteins (keratin, collagen) and carrier proteins (hemoglobin, myoglobin, cytochromes). (See *The Structure and Action of Proteins* by Dickerson and Geis, Harper and Row, 1969.) This task was at the time of Fruton's article considered an almost impossible one considering the immense number of spatial arrangements that could be constructed from the individual amino acids, the building blocks of proteins. The consequences of this revolution cannot yet be fully appreciated. But visions of synthetic enzymes, enzyme analogs, specific enzyme inhibitors and their manifold applications in industry, medicine, and nutrition are not too unrealistic. All of these aspects are of interest to the food scientist. Not only must he concern himself with the sufficiency of essential amino acids in the diet, but also with the way they are utilized, with factors present in the diet that may interfere with their utilization, and with inborn genetic defects or genetic "metabolic errors" that may prevent their utilization.

An example of factors that interfere with the utilization of proteins are the "protease inhibitors," which are found in legumes and in a great many other vegetables, including the common potato. Proteases are enzymes that digest the proteins in the food and reduce them to amino acids and small peptides that may be absorbed through the wall of the intestinal tract. When protease inhibitors are present (they are themselves proteins), the enzymes are unable to perform their proper function, and the proteins in the food remain undigested. Proper processing or cooking of the food will, however, render the protease inhibitors inactive and, furthermore, susceptible to enzyme attack. Processing achieves two effects: detoxification of food and increase of nutritional value.

An example of the sort of metabolic error that prevents utilization of dietary components is the inborn inability to handle the supply of phenylketonuria; individuals suffering from this disease can only survive on diets low in phenylalanine. The recent finding that a large part of mankind is unable to tolerate lactose is an astonishing example of inborn genetic "defects." In "Lactose and Lactase" Norman Kretchmer relates the ability of adults to digest lactose to the extent to which animal husbandry is being practiced in various regions of the world. It seems puzzling that the awareness of this phenomenon was so late in developing in view of the large shipments of dried milk that have gone to underdeveloped countries in an effort to fight malnutrition during recent decades. It is tempting to speculate that other regional preferences and avoidances in diets may have their base in physiological requirements, as in the example of milk and lactose.

Just as an oversupply (overeating) may lead to unhappy consequences, so will, of course, an undersupply. Mankind is all too familiar with hunger and starvation. They have been its constant companions throughout recorded history and are still with us today, as we recall the recent tragedies in Bangladesh and Biafra. Yet few investigators have been tempted to choose this scourge of mankind as a subject of study: the cure and prevention of the afflictions seem all too obvious. Nevertheless, as is pointed out in the article "The Physiology of Starvation" by Vernon Young and Nevin Scrimshaw, much of practical significance can be learned from such studies. The nutritional needs of the body, particularly the overriding requirement of the brain for glucose, are vividly demonstrated on fasting subjects. New information has been obtained on the appropriate composition of reducing diets and of diets for maximizing the chance of survival and rate of recovery of starvation victims. Of particular importance is the advance in understanding of the starvation disease marasmus and the protein-deficiency disease described in the article "Kwashiorkor" by Hugh C. Trowell. These nutritional diseases, which primarily afflict children in underdeveloped countries and are directly attributable to an insufficient and improper food supply, are certainly not unique to our times. But the fact that millions of children are today allowed to exist under conditions of insufficiency seems oddly incongruous. There is considerable evidence that such early nutritional experiences adversely affect intellectual development.

Deficiency diseases due to lack of nutrients required in very small amounts (micro- or trace nutrients) were recognized relatively early, although the identity of the essential factors missing were unknown. The cure and prevention of scorbut (scurvy), caused by Vitamin C deficiency, was known in the British navy in the eighteenth century (the curative use of lime gave rise to the nickname "limey" for the British sailor). Beriberi, once a dreaded endemic disease in Southeast Asia, was essentially eliminated when it was recognized in the 1880's that removal of the thiamine-rich bran layer from rice by efficient industrial operations was responsible for the deficiency. Similarly, the cure and prevention of rickets became known during World War I, when the deficiency disease was traced to lack of milk products in the diet and prevention was accomplished with a fat-soluble fraction present in high concentration in cod liver oil. But the isolation and identification of the essential growth factors, the vitamins, did not take place until the 1930's, when organic chemistry had progressed to a state of great sophistication. The list of known vitamins has not undergone any major changes since that time, and there is a tendency to consider this a fully explored field. Yet the problems of vitamin biosynthesis, their relationship to enzyme systems, and their mode of action, continue to pose important and challenging questions. It is curious that SCIENTIFIC AMERICAN has reported on only one of these very exciting substances, and then on one that almost never occurs at deficiency levels in the diet. But the story on "Biotin," as told by John D. Woodward, is in many respects typical of that of many of the other vitamins. The input from microbiology in terms of recognition of essential growth factors, the input from animal nutrition in recognition of deficiency symptoms, and finally the approach taken in the study of its mode of action in enzyme systems are essentially common themes. Another aspect of vitamins, which may be of equal importance to that of the dramatic elimination of deficiency diseases, is now recently emerging. The controversy over the effect of Vitamin C in massive doses on the prevention and cure of the common cold (see *Vitamin C and the Common Cold* by Linus Pauling, W. H. Freeman and Company, 1970) may spur a re-evaluation of the requirements of this and other nutrients in our diet. Especially meaningful may be the concept of individual differences in requirements, which suggests that individual deficiencies may exist widely in a population which is otherwise considered to exist on an adequate diet. (The average American diet may be deficient in Vitamin A and iron.)

The human body also requires a certain amount of so-called trace elements in the diet. The requirement of one of these, iodine, is vividly demonstrated in the article "Endemic Goiter" by R. Bruce Gillie. Goiter, an abnormal growth due to hypertrophic thyroid, can be traced to a lack of iodine in the diet. When this element is deficient in the environment and the disease reaches persistent and endemic proportions, a high incidence of cretinism results. Thanks to one of the most successful endeavors in physiological chemistry, we are now in the possession of a rather complete understanding of why iodine needs to be present in the diet and how deficiencies can be cured. We have in the process learned much about the way in which the iodine-containing hormone thyroxin operates, and we have become aware of goitrogenic substances in our food supply, substances which prevent the incorporation of iodine into thyroxin. It is especially tragic that hundreds of millions of people probably still suffer from endemic goiter in spite of this knowledge; another illustration of how difficult it is to change our ingrained food habits. The studies that led to an understanding of the function of the thyroid have also made us aware of a potential danger associated with atomic explosions and radioactive fallout. The realization that the radioactive isotope of iodine (^{131}I) would accumulate in the thyroid, and the potential disastrous consequences that this poses for the human race, probably had a major effect upon the decision by the atomic powers to ban the testing of atomic weapons.

The two last articles in this section deal with the future—the ominous future. Nobody need be told these days about the degradation of our environment, of pollution and waste threatening to affect our very existence. What is the truth in all this? How serious is the threat? The way certain persistent pesticides, such as DDT, behave in the environment, how they move upwards in the food cycle and accumulate in alarming concentrations in the higher species, is described by G. M. Woodwell in "Toxic Substances and Ecological Cycles." The evidence seems clear that certain species of birds, and perhaps fishes, are in danger of becoming extinct. But it is less clear whether this represents a threat to man or to his food supply, and evidence of another type is mounting. Industrial chemicals such as PCB's (polychlorinated biphenyls) have been in use for a long time (over forty years for PCB), but have only recently been found to show up in the food cycle and undergo the same concentration process as DDT. It seems reasonable to ask how many other chemicals are being and have been poured into the environment that will later be found in our food supply and then found to be toxic. The frequently observed synergism demonstrated by some pesticides, wherein mixtures of compounds are effective at concentrations far below the concentrations at which either required compound would be effective by itself, suggests that similar synergistic effects may eventually be found to exist between contaminants in our diet. The thought that widespread genetic effects may show up in subsequent generations when it is much too late to do much about it is thoroughly disquieting. Of this we know precariously little, and we find ourselves in a dilemma in decision making. On the one hand, we know that the use of pesticides is a *sine qua non* for the high efficiency of modern agriculture and that the large and growing human population could not be fed without them. On the other hand, we know also that unless we change our ways, the consequences may be uncomfortable or lethal. In this situation, the wisest attitude is probably one dictated by expediency and common sense: to ban the chemicals that are found to be culprits and discontinue practices that are found to be harmful. This was the attitude taken and the motivation behind the voluntary curtailment of PCB production.

The article "Mercury in the Environment" by Leonard J. Goldwater demonstrates these principles particularly well. Mercury compounds in industrial wastes released into inland waters were found to constitute a real danger in contaminating fish for food, and the use of mercury in agricultural chemicals caused severe incidents of mercury poisoning when accidentally ingested. The action that followed was logical and reasonable. Industries in question were ordered to reduce sharply the amounts of mercury wastes they released, and mercurials were banned in agriculture. The initial public reaction, however, went much further, and the presence of mercury found anywhere was assumed to be the product of man's activities. A more balanced view emerged when all the data were in. Mercury appears to be a natural component of the environment, and naturally moves up the food chain to attain high concentrations in predatory fishes, such as swordfish. The resulting ban on the sale of swordfish should be looked upon as a beneficial by-product of the concern that was expressed, not as an indictment of man's industrial activities.

Any attempt to look into the future is bound to give one numerous reasons for concern. Our food supply may be in danger of becoming unwholesome due to man-made contamination, and the population may outgrow our food-producing potential. But precious little is gained by taking precipitous and premature action, and much may be lost. Yet there is good and valid reason for vigilance, and research efforts must be increased in order to guarantee good and safe nutrition for all.

1

SMELL AND TASTE

A. J. HAAGEN-SMIT
March 1952

Two of the five senses depend upon chemical stimuli rather than physical. The chemistry of the substances that these senses can detect and differentiate are important clues to their mechanism

OUR SENSES of taste and smell constitute a most astonishing chemical laboratory. In a fraction of a second they can identify the chemical structure of compounds it would take a chemist days to analyze by the usual laboratory methods. A trained nose can recognize, for example, nearly every member of a series of homologous alcohols, aldehydes or acids. Moreover, from exceedingly small amounts of material it can analyze not only single compounds but complex mixtures of them in food.

Our chemical senses are of great importance for our well-being. They determine our reaction to foods and set the stage for digestion. The odor of broiled steak has an immediate effect on metabolism: it starts secretions of saliva and stomach juices even before eating begins. By setting up a favorable condition for digestion the flavor factors in food play a role in nutrition comparable to those of vitamins and hormones.

The science of nutrition has gone through successive phases in which there was great concern about the body's needs of calories, carbohydrates, fats and proteins, vitamins and, lately, amino acids. Now it seems to be flavor's turn. Nutritionists are paying more and more attention to our nearly forgotten senses of smell and taste. But to put the improvement of flavor on a scientific basis we need to know what substances are responsible for the various tastes.

This is a complex problem. The chemist must start with thousands of pounds of raw material to isolate weighable quantities of the pure essences that our senses of smell and taste can detect in such small traces. This difficult analytical work has been carried out in only a few foods, mostly fruits such as strawberry, apple, raspberry and pineapple. When the juices of these fruits are distilled, the residue, consisting mainly of sugars and fruit acids, has a taste which is usually not very characteristic of the original flavor. All of the odor substances, and some of those responsible for the taste, are in the volatile part that is distilled away. This volatile part consists of various alcohols, aldehydes, acids and esters.

The natural ingredients do not entirely account for the flavors of the products we eat and drink. New flavors are added when the raw material is cooked or processed. For example, the flavor of wine is due not only to substances originally present in the grapes but also to compounds produced by fermentation through the aid of microorganisms. More than 50 substances have already been identified as contributors to the flavor of wine, and there are undoubtedly a great many more. Frying or roasting adds new flavors to food by breaking down proteins and carbohydrates. The chemical complexity of an elaborate flavor system such as that of Soy sauce is indicated by the involved process by which this condiment is manufactured: various fungi are inoculated into a mixture of rice and grain; the broth they produce is then heated, and the mixture is fermented again and again, alternately in the presence of dissolved oxygen and in the absence of oxygen. On the other hand, our chemical senses readily recognize and enable us to reject substances produced by other organisms that spoil or rot the food. We have learned to associate these foul smells and bad tastes with adverse reactions of our digestive system. Actually the substances responsible for the bad flavors are harmless in the concentrations in which they generally occur, but they serve as warning signals against dangerous toxins the organisms produce at the same time.

OUR perception of flavor depends on both taste and smell; indeed, it is often difficult to distinguish between the parts that odor and taste play in our food. Of the two, the sense of smell is by far the more sensitive, and it may be stimulated at a great distance. R. W. Moncrieff, in his classic book on the chemical senses, recounts how a female Great Peacock moth hatched in the laboratory attracted the same evening about 40 male specimens, which must have traveled several miles, because these insects were rare in the neighborhood. As everyone knows, the odor of a skunk is noticeable several hundred feet from where its glands are emptied. Because of the distances at which odors are perceived, some think the stimulation cannot be entirely chemical, on the ground that the odor substances must be too diluted when they reach the olfactory receptors; it has therefore been suggested that physical vibrations are responsible for odor. But it can be shown that in a barely perceptible dilution of an odoriferous substance a single sniff still contains many millions of molecules. When the molecules arrive at the olfactory hairs and cells in the upper part of the nose, they must produce a reaction in the cells, giving rise to electrical impulses which are transmitted to the olfactory lobe of the brain.

To be smellable a substance apparently must fulfill two conditions: it must be volatile at ordinary temperature and must be soluble in fat solvents. All the known odor substances either are gases or have a high vapor pressure, boiling below about 300 degrees Centigrade. Most inorganic substances, being salts of very low vapor pressure, have no discernible odor. Among the minority that do are the halogens (fluorine, chlorine, iodine, bromine), phosphorus, ozone and certain compounds such as hydrogen sulfide, sulfur dioxide, nitrogen oxides and ammonia. Their odor is usually rather unpleasant and often irritating.

In organic chemistry the situation is very different; the organic compounds are much more likely to be odoriferous and their odors have a vastly greater range. Of nearly half a million synthetic compounds listed in a well-known encyclopedia of organic substances, a large proportion have a high enough vapor pressure to make them odoriferous.

CAROLUS LINNAEUS, the father of taxonomy, who in the 18th century began to establish laws of order in the living world by cataloguing plants, also attempted to classify substances according to their odors. But his classifications were necessarily subjective, and early odor taxonomists were severely handicapped by the lack of an assortment of pure organic chemicals to serve as standards of comparison. In 1895 Hendrik C. Zwaardemaker, one of Linnaeus' followers, devised a system in which all odors were reduced to nine main types, with subdivisions in each type:

1. Ethereal—fruits, resins, ethers.
2. Aromatic—camphor, cloves, lavender, lemon, bitter almonds.
3. Balsamic or fragrant—flowers, violet, vanilla, coumarin.
4. Ambrosial—amber, musk.
5. Alliaceous—hydrogen sulfide, arsine, chlorine.
6. Empyreumatic—roast coffee, benzene.
7. Caprylic—cheese, rancid fat.
8. Repulsive—deadly nightshade, bedbug.
9. Nauseating or fetid—carrion, feces.

It is possible even today to agree on the proper place of a substance in this system, but it is also clear that the system does not reduce odors to their fundamental elements. As is well known, odor receptors in the nose soon become used to a particular odor and cease to notice it—this is called fatigue. Consequently it should be possible to find out by a fatigue test whether one odor is essentially the same as another (*i.e.*, stimulates the same receptors). Such experiments have shown that the odors of camphor and of cloves, for example, produce fatigue for each other; hence they belong in the same subclass. As a result of these experiments some of Zwaardemaker's classes have been changed.

In recent years Ernest C. Crocker and Lloyd F. Henderson of the Arthur D. Little laboratories have reduced odors to four elementary classes, corresponding to four kinds of receptors. According to their system, all known odors are composites of these types: 1) fragrant or sweet, 2) acid or sour, 3) burnt or empyreumatic, 4) caprylic or goaty. Any odor is described by a formula which gives the strength of each component on a scale from one to eight: thus the odor of a rose is represented by 6423, meaning that it is strong in the fragrant component, has some acid odor and also has a little of the burnt and caprylic odors. The system describes ethyl alcohol as 5414 and vanillin as 7122. The authors of this system maintain that a trained observer can recognize to a certain extent the degree in which the four postulated basic odors are present. To try to describe the vast array of odors in terms of just four basic types may be an oversimplification, but the system has the virtue of emphasizing that every odor is a combination of impressions.

Once we are aware of this fact, we find that we are able to perform such

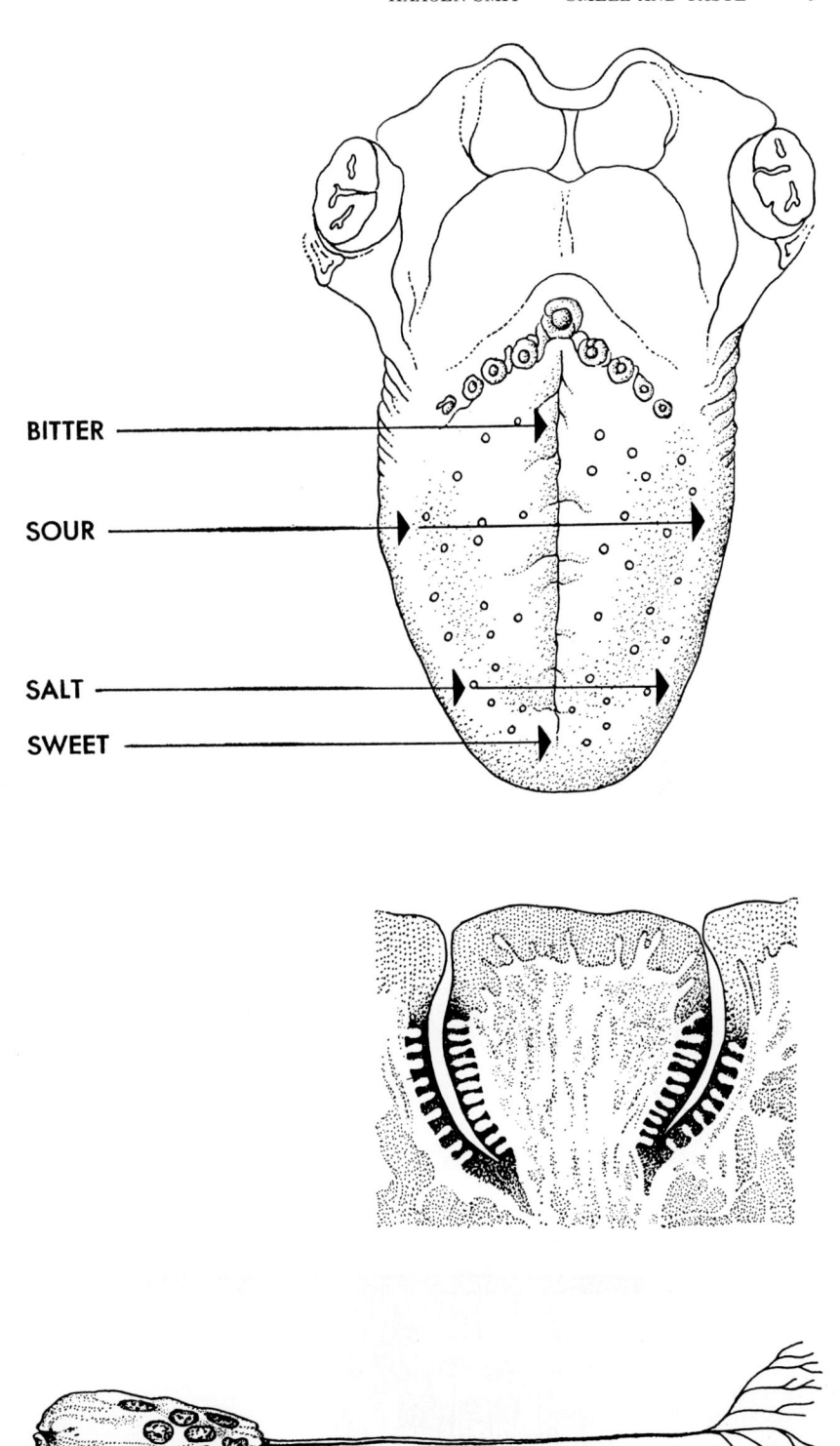

TASTE RECEPTORS are located in the tongue, the top of which is shown in the drawing at the top of this illustration. On the surface of the tongue are numerous round structures called papillae; the larger of these are indicated by the small circles in the drawing. A cross section of one of the largest papillae is shown in the drawing at the middle of the illustration. The small white structures adjoining the fissure around the papilla are the taste buds. An individual taste bud (*left*) and its nerve fiber (*right*) are shown in the drawing at the bottom. Some areas of the tongue are more sensitive to certain tastes than others; these areas are indicated by the arrows on the top drawing.

analyses in our minds. It is then possible to overcome the difficulty that no substance smells exactly like another, and we can find the dominant odor for proper classification. In the numerous substances that have now been synthesized by the organic chemist we have material to test the different classification systems, and since the substances' chemical nature is well known, a search for correlations between chemical structure and odor is possible.

Let us concentrate on two distinctive and well-defined odors—those of camphor and mint. There are more than 200 known compounds with a camphorlike odor and nearly as many with the mint odor. In each group chemists have found a certain common characteristic of structure; when they synthesize a compound with this building principle in its structure, there is a fair certainty that the product will have the odor in question. For instance, one can produce a substance with a mint odor by building a molecule resembling menthol, the main constituent of the oil of peppermint. It is not necessary to follow the whole plan of the menthol molecule; apparently only a small part of its structure is responsible for the mint smell. The requirement seems to be a short carbon chain, with branches preferably not more than two or three carbon atoms long (*see diagrams on opposite page*).

The camphor odor is closely related to that of mint; one can be converted to the other by slight changes in the molecule. Apparently the critical difference that transforms a minty compound into a camphorlike one is the substitution of a methyl group (CH_3) for one hydrogen atom in the mintlike substance. On the other hand, the odor reverts to mint when an ethyl group is substituted for one of the methyl groups in the camphor structure.

In general we observe that the camphor odor is characteristic of compounds which have a number of small groups crowding around a carbon atom. These do not necessarily have to be methyl groups; halogens and nitro groups are equally effective.

Closely related to the mint and camphor odors are those of cedar, wood, peach, musk and civet. As the number of carbon atoms is increased in the series of ring ketones, for example, the odor gradually changes from camphor to cedar to musk to civet. The odor evidently is governed by the size of the carbon ring. In a similar series of lactones, musk odor develops when the molecules reach a size corresponding to that of the cyclic ketones of musk odor. The typical musk smell is largely due to the structure of the carbon skeleton, and to a lesser degree to the oxygen atom.

These and similar considerations lead to the conclusion that for mint, camphor, turpentine, cedar, lemon, cineole, peach, musk and civet, the hydrocarbon part of the molecule is of dominant importance, and that there is reason to classify all these odors in one group, which corresponds to Zwaardemaker's classes of aromatic and ambrosial odors and to Crocker's class of "fragrant."

WE SEE, therefore, that chemical structure can account for the various classes of odors. This explains the failure of the many odor theories based on some general principle such as the reactivity, oxidizability or vibrational characteristics of odoriferous substances. It is reasonable to assume that for each class of odorous materials there is a specific receptor mechanism in the smelling apparatus. For the class to which camphor and mint belong, the mechanism must enable us to detect small differences in the carbon skeleton of a large number of compounds. Just as a specific antibody meshes with an antigen in the body, so the active part of an odorous molecule may fit some part of a protein structure in the nasal receptors, thereby altering cell reactions and giving rise to electric impulses. This theory would account for the fact that only a part of the

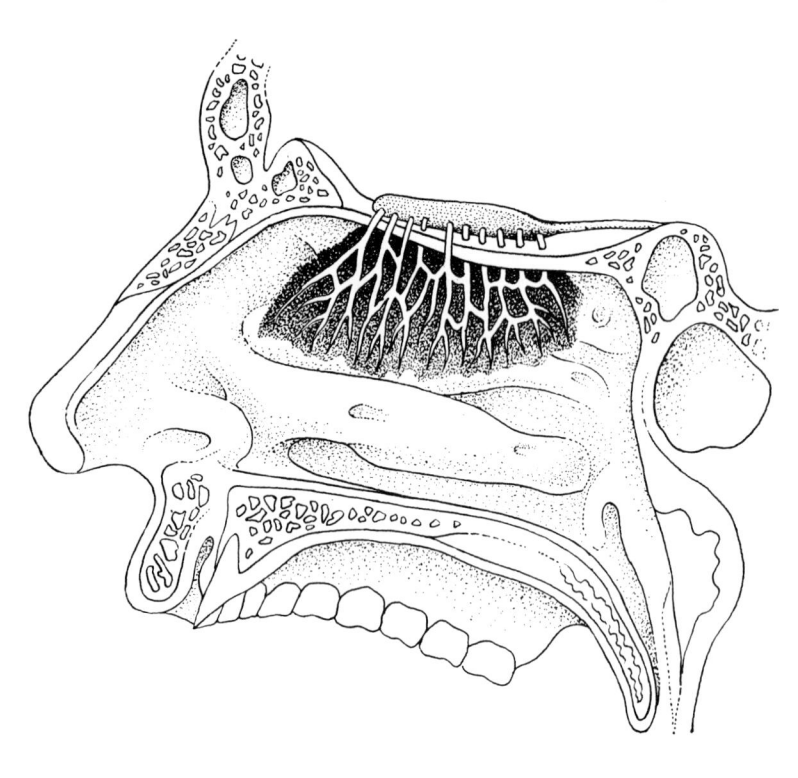

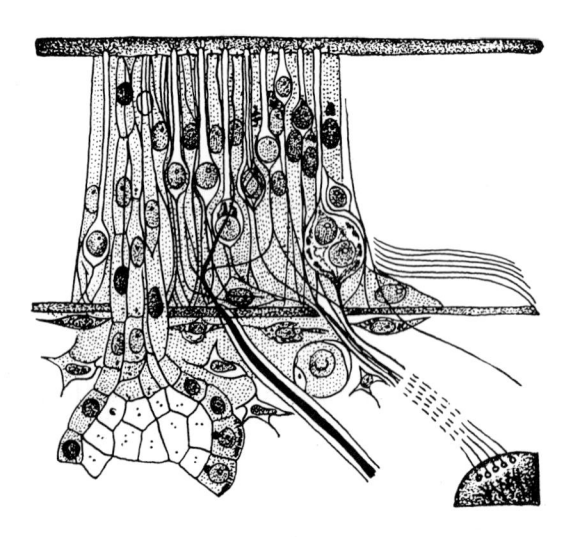

SMELL RECEPTORS are in a spongy region at the top of the nasal cavity, a cross section of which is shown at the top of this illustration. At the bottom is a microscopic cross section of the cells in the olfactory mucous membrane.

MOLECULAR STRUCTURE of substances that smell like mint or camphor is similar. At the right is the molecular diagram of camphor. Second from the right is the diagram of another substance that smells like camphor. The remaining diagrams are of substances that smell like mint. Similar structures are in color.

molecule is of dominant importance for the smell impression. The grouping of odors in classes according to similarity of chemical structure, or, in other words, the fact that small changes in the active part of the molecule produce only slight alterations in the odor sensation, may be explained by the assumption that the various substances in a class fit the receptor molecules more or less closely.

The consulting chemist Jerome Alexander and George B. Kistiakowsky of Harvard University have suggested that odoriferous substances act by interfering with enzyme-catalyzed reactions in the odor receptors. Since enzymes are affected in their action by exceedingly small amounts of a variety of substances, this theory plausibly explains the high sensitivity of our sense of smell and the wide range of compounds that possess odors. The well-known reversibility of inhibitory effects on enzymes would account for the rapid recovery of the reception system to normal, thus enabling it to register new odor impressions.

A$ $S HAS BEEN mentioned, odor strongly affects the flavor of food. We are suddenly reminded of this when a cold inactivates our olfactory system. The food tastes flat, since we are dependent on our sense of taste alone. We are left with a distinction between bitter, sweet, salt and sour.

The sensory apparatus of taste is located chiefly on the upper surface of the tongue, at the soft palate, on the epiglottis and at the beginning of the gullet. Here lie the so-called taste buds, estimated to number about 9,000. It is fairly certain that different tastes are located at different places. The bitter sensations are definitely located at the back of the tongue, whereas the sweet and salt receptors are at the tip and edges. It is generally accepted that we possess four different taste senses—bitter, sweet, salty and sour.

We taste things only when they are dissolved in water. To detect a substance by taste we need a far greater amount than we can detect by smell—about 3,000 times as much in some cases.

As in the odor field, attempts have been made to find the chemical relation among the members of each of the four taste groups. The sour taste is related to the acidity of the solution, though not in direct proportion; for example, a 1/200 normal solution of acetic acid tastes just as sour as a 1/800 normal solution of HCl, which is four to five times as acid.

Salty tastes are produced by inorganic salts. The anions of chlorine, bromine, SO_4 and NO_3 are especially effective in producing this saline taste when combined with the proper metal ions. For example, sodium chloride is salty, whereas cesium chloride has a dominating bitter taste.

The sweet taste is given by sugars, saccharin, dulcin and beryllium chloride. It is difficult to see what these substances have in common. As in the cases of odor substances, minor changes in these compounds do not remove the sweet taste. For example, compounds somewhat related to glucose, such as glycerol, are sweet.

The bitter taste, similarly, is exhibited by a wide variety of compounds—many alkaloids, certain glucosides, bile salts, magnesium and ammonium salts.

Bitter and sweet are closely related, and a slight modification of the molecule is sometimes enough to produce strongly bitter substances instead of the expected sweet ones. For example, when the oxy-

STRUCTURAL SIMILARITY of a steroid molecule (*left*) and that of a ketone (*right*) causes them to have the same musky odor. The carbon chain of the steroid molecule is cross-linked (*colored lines*); the carbon chain of the ketone is not. The effect of the two molecules on the smell receptors is nonetheless much the same.

gen in the sweet material dulcin is replaced by sulfur, we get the bitter compound p-ethoxy-phenylthiocarbamide.

This substance, and the material from which it is derived (phenyl thiourea), brings out an interesting point: just as people may have color blindness, some people have certain kinds of "taste blindness." To three or four out of ten people, this substance is not bitter but tasteless. Apparently it is a hereditary taste deficiency, which started among Caucasians and spread to other races. Since the discovery of this particular type of "taste blindness," many more substances have been found to exhibit similar taste properties. Sodium benzoate, tasteless to most people, tastes either sweet or bitter to one out of four. Such experiments demonstrate vividly the truth of the saying "*De gustibus non est disputandum.*"

A search for a common factor that would account for the similarity in taste of the bitter-or-sweet substances is not likely to be successful. As in the odor field, we have to turn our attention to the receptor cells to find the mechanism of taste perception. Here, too, an enzyme theory seems to be the most promising approach. An investigator of the taste mechanism is in a more fortunate position than those studying the odor receptors, because the four basic tastes, though subjective, are a great deal more sharply defined than the basic odor types. In addition, experimental work is aided by the fact that the taste buds are more accessible and are located in different places for the four tastes. This allows one to carry out reactions on the tissues and to study the influence of a number of taste substances on the cell mechanism. By such histochemical methods it has been shown that the skin overlying the taste buds contains relatively high concentrations of certain enzymes such as alkali phosphatases and esterases, and that these enzymes are inhibited by substances having a well-defined taste and are not inhibited by others.

In the past, studies of odor and taste reception have concentrated on the stimulants and attempted to deduce the nature of the reception mechanism from them. At best such deductions will be vague and uncertain. For a real understanding of the basic processes, we must study the happenings in the receptor cells themselves. The enzyme theory and the other new working hypotheses about the tasting and smelling processes illustrate this shift in emphasis. They may stimulate the exceedingly difficult experimental work that is necessary before solutions of the odor and taste problems can be found.

SWEET SUBSTANCES have molecular structures apparently with little in common. From top to bottom these molecular diagrams represent sucrose (sweetness arbitrarily taken as 100), dulcin (sweetness 265), saccharin (sweetness 675) and 4-nitro-2-amino phenyl propyl ether (sweetness 3300).

THE SOURCES OF MUSCULAR ENERGY

RODOLFO MARGARIA
March 1972

The immediate source is adenosine triphosphate (ATP). The ultimate sources are the combustion of food and the breakdown of glycogen. The time relations of these processes offer some practical hints.

A muscle can be regarded as an engine, and like any engine it obtains its energy essentially from the "burning" of fuel. Its performance, or capacity for work, depends on the nature and availability of the source of energy. In the case of an artificial engine the energy input is easily identified and measured: it is simply the rate of consumption of the supplied fuel. The muscle engine, however, is much more complex. It uses several different fuels, and it regenerates some of them itself. As a result the evaluation of the factors involved in muscle performance is far from a simple matter. It requires detailed, quantitative analysis of each of the sources of energy and their relative timing and collaboration. Through systematic investigations over the past few years a reasonably comprehensive picture of the operation of the energy sources in muscular exercise has been obtained, and it has become possible to suggest rational regimes for employing muscles most efficiently. The new knowledge should be widely applicable in athletics and in physical work, thus improving the productive capacity, comfort and health of people engaged in such activities.

The direct source of energy for a muscle's activity is adenosine triphosphate (ATP); the release of energy from the splitting of ATP into adenosine diphosphate (ADP) and phosphoric acid is what powers muscle contractions. The ATP must be synthesized continuously, as there is no appreciable store of it in the muscle. It is actually resynthesized from its products as soon as it is broken down. The energy needed for the recombination of ADP and phosphoric acid into ATP is supplied by another energy-yielding reaction in the cells: the splitting of creatine phosphate. This auxiliary "phosphagen" is likewise in short supply in the muscle and needs to be resynthesized continuously. There are, in turn, two ultimate sources of energy for the resynthesis of the phosphagens: (1) combustion of food, measured by the consumption of oxygen, and (2) glycolysis, the breakdown of glycogen resulting in the formation of lactic acid. The second of these processes is reversible: with an input of energy from food combustion, lactic acid is reconstituted to glycogen.

The system, then, consists of five reactions, three of which (phosphagen-splitting, food combustion and glycolysis) yield energy and two of which (phosphagen and glycogen resynthesis) absorb energy [*see top illustration on page 15*]. We need to obtain a measure of each of these five quantities in order to compute the net total of energy and power (energy per unit of time) available to the muscle for given levels of performance.

How can we disentangle the factors for separate measurement? Fortunately we can set up experimental conditions in which some of the factors can be disregarded. For example, it is known that during moderate exercise (that is, below a certain level of exertion) the muscles do not produce lactic acid; therefore glycolysis and the reverse do not enter into the equation. Furthermore, if the exercise is maintained at a constant level of energy consumption, the splitting and resynthesis of the phosphagens soon balance out in energy terms, so that we can disregard those quantities also. In exercise under these conditions the net expenditure of energy can be calculated simply from the consumption of oxygen. It has been known for some time that the energy yield from food combustion in the muscles is five calories per milliliter of oxygen consumed. Hence it is easy to calculate that during exercise at a constant, submaximal level the energy employed for the given work load is a number of calories amounting to five times the number of milliliters of oxygen consumed. This formula has been known and employed in physiological studies for many years. In such studies the work load is commonly measured on an ergometer such as a treadmill or a bicycle.

When exercise is raised to a strenuous level at which energy can no longer be provided in sufficient quantity through oxidation (because of the limit on the rate of delivery of oxygenated blood to the tissues), the muscles begin to supplement the energy supply by means of glycolysis. The quantitative details of this process are difficult to get at and have only recently been determined.

Let us consider a maximal effort such as a runner's sprint of 100 or 400 meters at top speed. Within a few seconds his muscles' energy requirement has established an equilibrium between the splitting and the resynthesis of phosphagen and also has passed the limit of production of energy by oxidation. The only variable, then, is the amount of energy generated by glycolysis. Can this be estimated from measurement of the amount of lactic acid (the breakdown product) in the blood? If glycogen were resynthesized from lactic acid about as rapidly as it is broken down, such a measurement would be meaningless. Actually, however, the resynthesis is very slow; it takes about 15 minutes, by exponential increase, to reach half its maximal rate. Therefore in a test of strenuous exercise lasting only a few seconds or a few minutes the amount of resynthesis is so small it can be disregarded and the concentration of lactic acid in the blood can be

AFTER A HARD RUN an athlete may be near exhaustion because his muscles have depleted their supply of ATP, and oxidation and glycolysis have not yet been able to replenish the muscles with their primary source of energy. Here the kneeling runner, comforted by one of his Adelphi University teammates, has just finished running the fourth half-mile leg of a two-mile relay at the Wanamaker Millrose Games, which were held at Madison Square Garden, New York, in January 1972. His team finished fourth.

taken as a good indication of the energy contribution of glycolysis beyond what is supplied by oxidation. For a given subject the production of lactic acid per minute should vary directly with the magnitude of the energy requirement or with the length of time a given requirement is imposed on the muscles.

Of course, the subject's blood cannot be sampled while he is running. Furthermore, a sample taken during the exercise would be misleading, because it takes time for the lactic acid to diffuse from the muscles into the body fluids. As a result the drawing of the blood samples can conveniently be postponed until two or three minutes after the run, and the lactic acid concentration in the blood at that time can be considered a reasonably accurate representation of the total quantity of lactic acid formed as a result of the exercise.

Experiments have proved these assumptions to be correct. Subjects were tested in runs on a treadmill, tilted at different inclinations to call for different intensities of exercise, and the exercise levels were strenuous enough to lead to exhaustion in one minute to 10 minutes. Measurement of the lactic acid concentration in the blood after the run indicated that the amount of glycolysis for a given work load did indeed increase linearly with time, as the premises predicted [see bottom illustration at right]. On the basis of assumptions about the diffusion of lactic acid to the various tissues and organs of the body it was possible to calculate how much lactic acid the muscles produced in relation to the body's total weight. This calculation likewise showed that the amount of lactic acid produced per minute per kilogram of body weight varied in direct proportion to the energy requirement [see illustration on following page].

The measurements established several interesting facts. They confirmed that in steady exercise the body meets its energy needs exclusively by means of oxidation up to a certain level of requirement for energy, and they showed that ordinarily the maximum provided by oxidation is about 220 calories per minute per kilogram of body weight. The production of lactic acid usually began when the energy requirement passed that level. Furthermore, the amount of lactic acid produced in relation to the energy need indicated that the energy yield from glycolysis is about 230 calories per gram of lactic acid produced. This determination of the energy yield

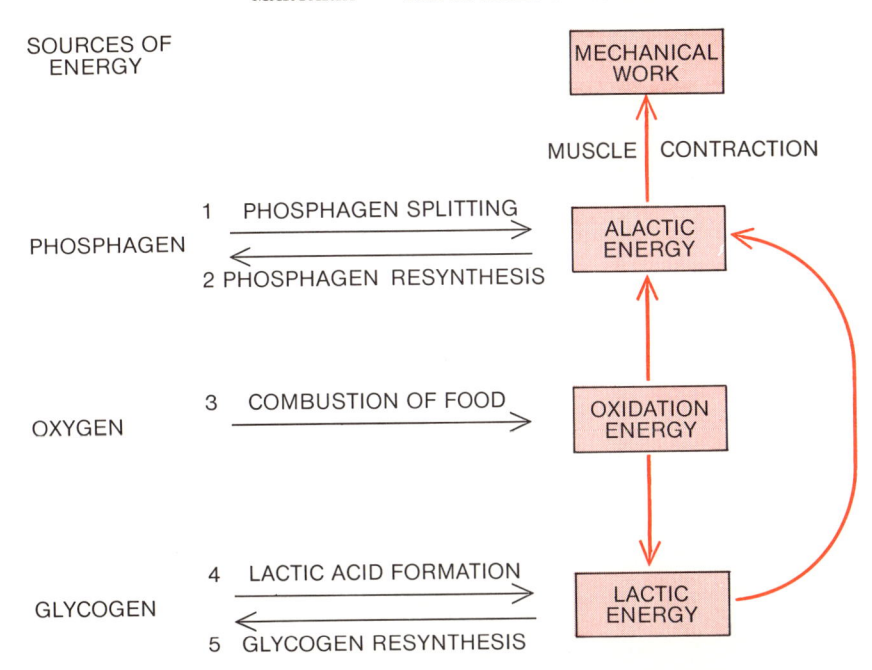

RELATIONS OF SOURCES of muscular energy are outlined. "Phosphagen," the direct source of energy, is a general term for the high-energy phosphates such as ATP and creatine phosphate (CP) that are found in cells. Energy is released by the splitting of phosphagen molecules. The split phosphagen is almost immediately resynthesized. Energy for the recombination is supplied by the two secondary energy sources: the combustion of food and the breakdown of glycogen, a carbohydrate stored in the muscle, into lactic acid. Glycogen in turn is resynthesized from lactic acid with energy from oxidation. The overall cycle consists of five reactions, three of which release energy and two of which absorb it.

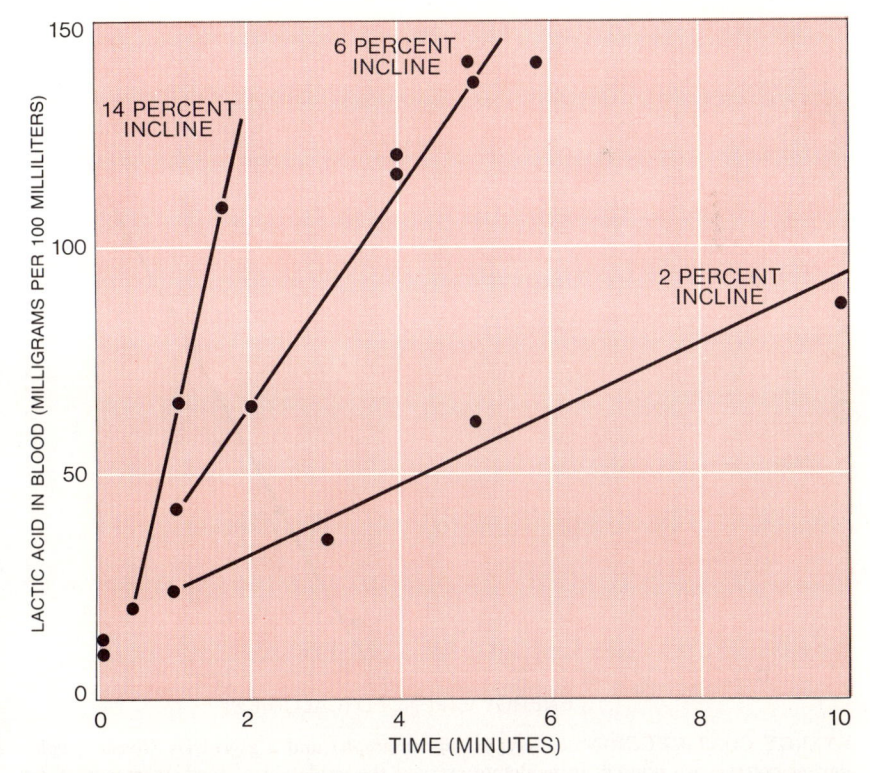

HEAVY EXERCISE leads to the formation of lactic acid. For a given work load the concentration of lactic acid in the blood increases linearly with the duration of the exercise. The exercise consisted in running to exhaustion at a constant speed of 12 kilometers per hour on a treadmill tilted at inclines of 2, 6 or 14 percent. At these work loads the rate of increase of lactic acid, indicated by the slope of the curves on the graph, is proportional to the intensity of the exercise. Blood samples were taken a few minutes after the exercise to allow the lactic acid from the muscles to become uniformly distributed throughout the body.

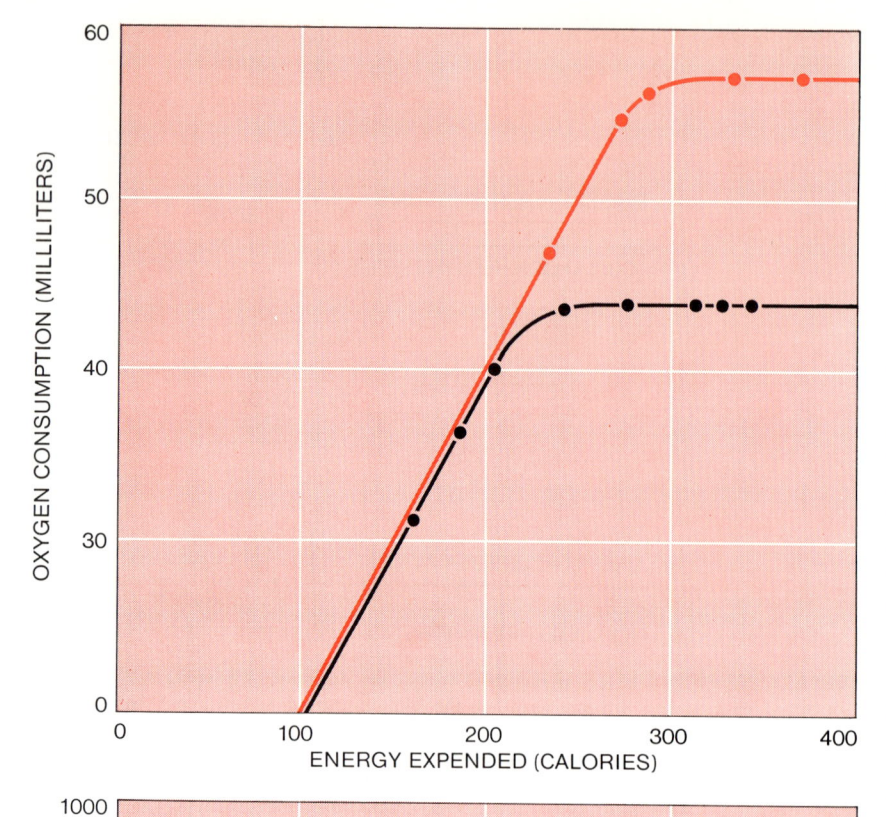

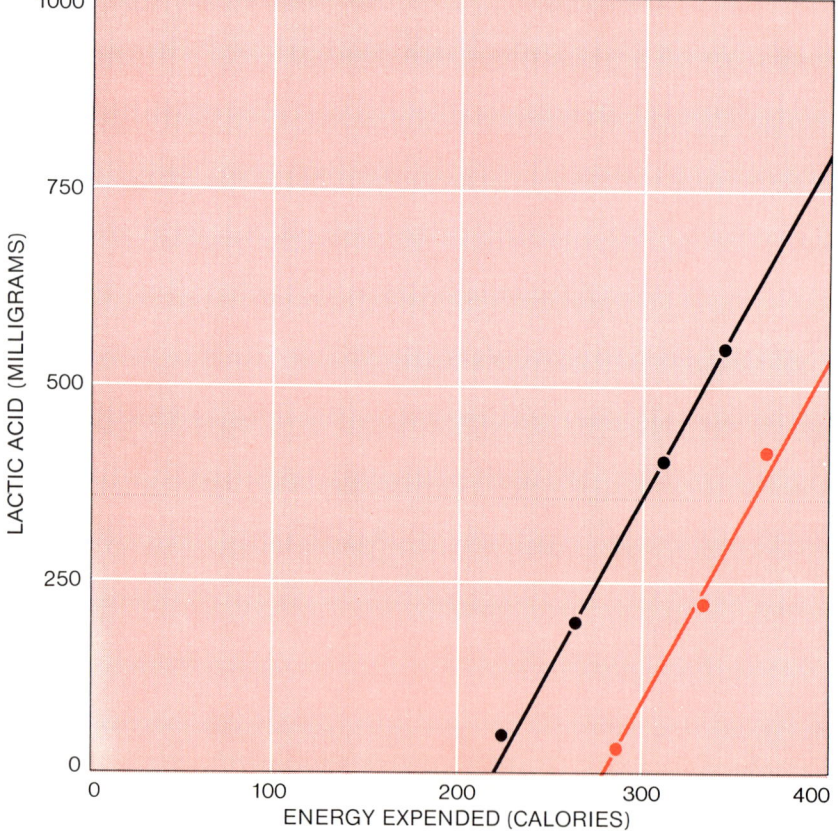

could be considered a close approximation of the true value, since it was obtained in vivo with the subjects showing an entirely normal physiological state in terms of their body temperature and the physical characteristics of their body fluids. Moreover, the energy yield was the same in trained athletes as it was in other persons.

Another significant finding is that trained athletes (middle-distance runners) were able to obtain an unusually large share of their energy need from oxygen consumption, so that lactic acid production began at a somewhat higher level of exertion than it does in nonathletes. The same effect was obtained by nonathletes by their breathing oxygen during exercise. Breathing oxygen before the performance, however, apparently is not helpful, and there is no physiological basis for believing it should be (although it is sometimes resorted to by athletes). Oxygen respiration during a performance is useful because it provides an extra current supply for the continuing need for chemical energy; by the same token, air with a subnormal content of oxygen, such as the athletes had to contend with at the high altitude of Mexico City in the Olympic Games of 1968, understandably must reduce performance.

As the trained athletes' performances in our tests indicated, people differ in their capacity for performing work without resorting to glycolysis. When we tested subjects with different capacities in this respect on the same work load, we found that individuals differ in the rate of lactic acid production. A person with a low capacity for oxygen consumption produces considerably more lactic acid.

What, then, is the total contribution glycolysis can make to the muscle machine? Measurements of the lactic acid concentration in the blood after strenuous exercise have shown that the maximum increase in this content is about 1.5 grams per liter, or about 1.12 grams per kilogram of body weight. Putting the yield per gram at about 230 calories, we can compute that the maximum amount of energy obtainable from the formation of lactic acid is about 260 calories per kilogram of body weight.

Obviously the rate at which lactic acid can be produced must have an upper limit, just as there is a limit on the rate of oxygen consumption by the tissues. In the case of lactic acid the limit is imposed by the rate of the chemical processes involved in its production. We find that increasing the intensity of ex-

ENERGY CONTRIBUTIONS of oxygen (*upper graph*) and a glycolysis (*lower graph*) during exercise are plotted. In moderate exercise the oxidation of food, as measured by increased oxygen consumption (in milliliters per minute per kilogram of body weight), provides virtually all of the energy requirement (shown on the abscissa in calories per minute per kilogram of body weight). When the energy requirement surpasses the upper limit of oxygen consumption, the additional energy is provided by formation of lactic acid (in milligrams per minute per kilogram of body weight) from glycogen. Athletes (*colored curves*) have a higher oxygen-consumption capacity, which delays the formation of lactic acid.

ercise raises the rate of lactic acid production only to a certain level; beyond that the speed of its production cannot be pushed further. The maximal rate is about 1.7 grams per kilogram of body weight per minute, which corresponds to a power output of 390 calories per kilogram per minute. Thus the power available from glycolysis turns out to be about 50 percent higher than the power from oxidation (220 calories per kilogram per minute).

Consider now the physiological debts the body contracts in strenuous exercise that leads quickly to exhaustion, say within 35 seconds, when lactic acid production has reached its maximal rate. We know that in exercise of such intensity there is for the first 15 seconds or so no energy contribution from glycolysis. The oxidative mechanism also is rather sluggish and in the first 15 seconds it contributes only a small portion of the energy, although its contribution rises at an exponential rate. On the basis of these known facts we can calculate the energy contributions made in exhausting exercise by each of the three energy-yielding mechanisms: oxygen consumption, lactic acid production and phosphagen-splitting, the last called the "alactic" mechanism [*see illustration on following page*].

The calculation on this basis indicates that theoretically the maximal contribution of phosphagen-splitting itself (the alactic source) would be about 200 calories per kilogram of body weight, which would amount to the splitting of almost all the available phosphagen. We find in experiments that the amount of split phosphagen at the end of a maximal aerobic exercise (exercise that can be supported by energy from oxidations only) is only about half this theoretical quantity; the amount corresponds to an energy yield of about 100 calories per kilogram of body weight instead of 200 calories. At the end of supramaximal exercise that involves energy from anaerobic sources and leads to exhaustion in a short time, the energy yield from phosphagen breakdown may go up to 150 calories per kilogram of body weight; this has been found recently by Pietro di Prampero and others in my laboratory in measurements of the alactic oxygen debt. Under no conditions, however, did they find that the energy yield from phosphagen reaches 200 calories per kilogram of body weight, which would be the case if all the phosphagen in the muscle had been broken down.

In spite of this experimental finding in strenuous supramaximal exercise to exhaustion, I believe practically all the available phosphagen has actually been split. The reason the experiments show otherwise probably lies in the fact that the theoretical estimate of the energy balance overstates the amount of contribution by glycolysis during the exercise. It overlooks the fact that some of the lactic acid is produced afterward during the early period of the muscles' recovery. This production of lactic acid represents an energy debt that is used to pay a corresponding amount of the alactic debt. In other words, a fraction of the alactic debt is shifted into a lactacid debt. That such a process of anaerobic recovery (contributing energy for phosphagen resynthesis by a means other than oxidation) takes place after exercise was observed many years ago in studies of the isolated frog muscle by the author and Gianni Moruzzi and more recently in our laboratory at the University of Milan by Paolo Cerretelli. It is estimated now that during recovery from very strenuous exercise the delayed production of lactic acid may contribute about 50 calories per kilogram of body weight to the resynthesis of phosphagen, which would explain why Prampero did not find complete breakdown of phosphagen at exhaustion.

In short, the "oxygen debt" that the British physiologist A. V. Hill first described in the 1920's has two aspects: oxygen is needed for the dual functions of (1) reconstituting glycogen from lactic acid (as Hill observed) and (2) providing energy directly on its own account for the resynthesis of phosphagen (as H. T. Edwards, D. B. Dill and I found later in studies at the Harvard Fatigue Laboratory). We call these aspects the lactacid oxygen debt and the alactic oxygen debt.

From the standpoint of provision of energy we can distinguish three phases in the operation of the muscle engine in strenuous exercise. During the first phase, lasting only a few seconds, all the energy is provided solely by the splitting of phosphagen, as the oxidative and glycolytic reactions have not yet got under way. How much power can be provided by this alactic mechanism? We can obtain a measure of the maxi-

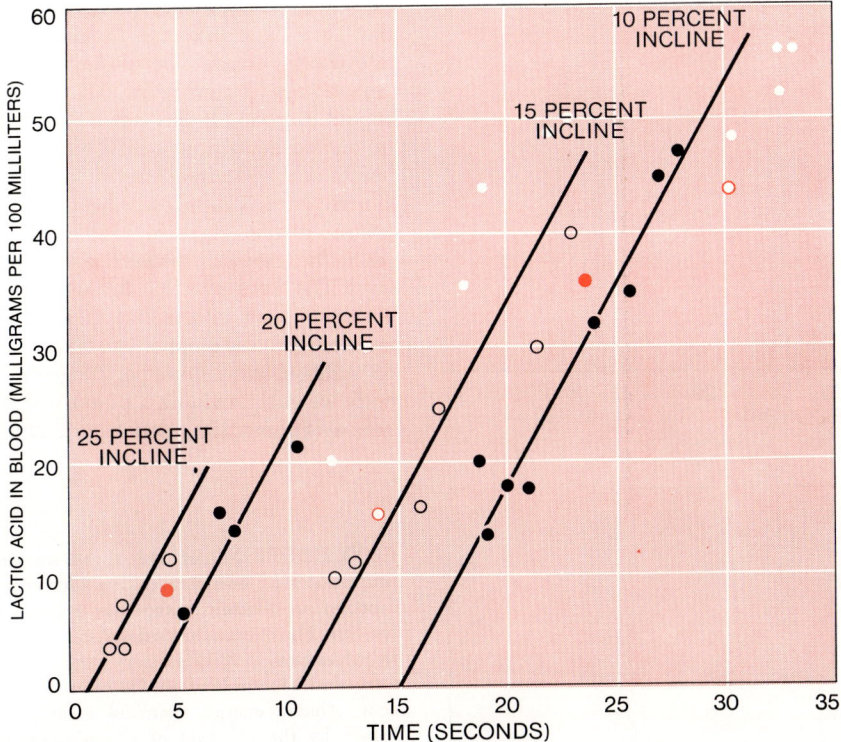

SUPEREXERTION pushes the rate of lactic acid formation to its upper limit, after which increasing the intensity of the exercise no longer affects the rate, as is indicated by the parallel slope of the curves in the graph. The work load consisted in running to exhaustion at a constant speed of 18 kilometers per hour on a treadmill tilted at inclines of 10, 15, 20 or 25 percent. The point of exhaustion (*colored dots and colored circles*) is reached more rapidly as the exercise becomes more strenuous. Although rate of lactic acid production does not change, the more strenuous the exercise, the more quickly formation of lactic acid begins.

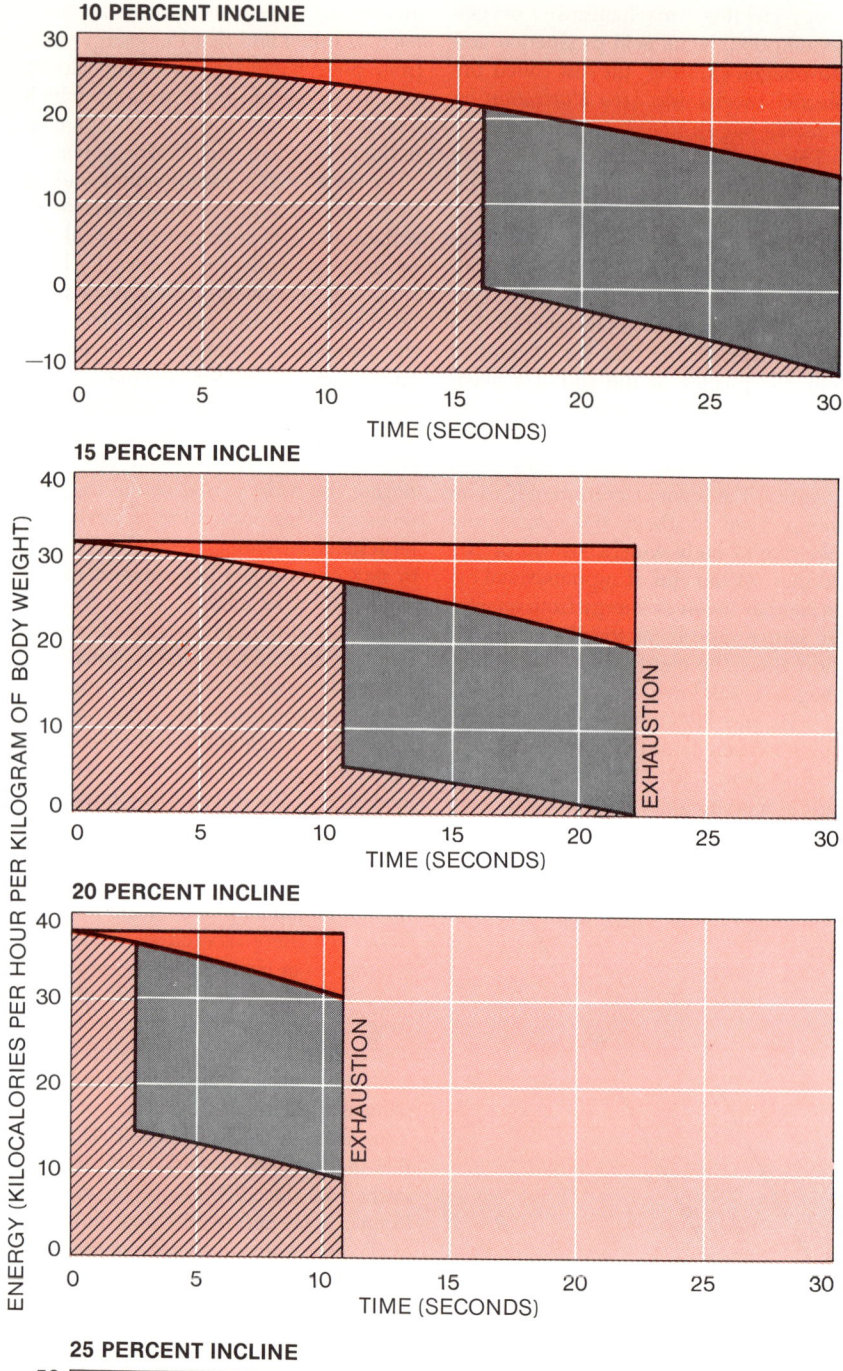

mum output by using an exercise in which the subject climbs stairs two steps at a time at top speed. The maximum speed is reached within three seconds and is maintained for one or two seconds after that. Since the work consists almost entirely in lifting the body, it can be calculated as the kilogram-meters of rise per second per kilogram of body weight. The maximum efficiency in the use of muscle energy by a man running uphill has been found to be about 25 percent. Dividing the work performed in the tests by this figure, we calculate that the maximum of muscular power obtainable from the splitting of phosphagen is about 800 calories per minute per kilogram of body weight. (Of course, this test tells us only about the power in the muscles of the lower limbs; work involving mainly the arms might give a different figure.)

The second phase in the energy economy, chronologically speaking, is the arrival of oxidation as a source of energy for resynthesizing phosphagen. The maximum power available from this contribution too can conveniently be measured experimentally. The rate of the heartbeat gives a sufficiently accurate measure of the rate of oxygen consumption by the body, and it has been found that there is a maximum for the heart rate during exercise, depending on the person's age. A convenient and well-accepted exercise for this test is stepping up on and down from a stool of a given height at a given frequency dictated by a metronome. The subject's heart rate is measured after three or four minutes, when the rate has reached a constant level. The test shows that this rate in an average young man indicates a maximum oxygen consumption of about 40 to 45 milliliters per minute per kilogram of body weight, providing a power contribution of about 220 calories per minute

CONTRIBUTIONS of the three energy sources during exercises calling for superexertion are plotted in the four graphs at the left. The exercises consisted in running to exhaustion at 18 kilometers per hour on a treadmill inclined at 10, 15, 20 or 25 percent. Alactic energy (*hatched areas*), released by the splitting of phosphagen, is both the initial and the major source of energy during superexertion. Energy from the oxidation of food (*colored area*) increases exponentially from the onset of strenuous exercise, but the mechanism is sluggish and provides only a small portion of the required energy during the first few seconds. The remaining energy is provided by breakdown of glycogen into lactic acid (*gray area*).

per kilogram, as we have already noted.

The third energy contribution for exercise, which enters only after oxidation is no longer able to keep up with the muscles' needs, is glycolysis. I have already mentioned that the maximum quantity of lactic acid produced in strenuous exercise is about 1.12 grams per kilogram of body weight, corresponding to an energy production of about 260 calories per kilogram. In recent studies Jan Karlsson and Bengt Saltin of the Gymnastic School in Stockholm found that on the average human muscle contains about 10 grams of glycogen per kilogram of muscle tissue, which suggests that only about a third of the glycogen in the muscles is broken down to lactic acid to furnish energy for work. These general characteristics are not very significant for judging an individual's capacity for exercise, however, because people vary greatly in the glycogen content of their muscles. The glycogen content depends on the state of the individual's nutrition; obviously, then, an athlete or anyone engaging in strenuous exercise should pay careful attention to nutrition.

The measurements I have described give us a balance sheet showing the capacity and power of each of the three contributing mechanisms and some information about the contraction and repayment of the alactic and lactacid oxygen debts. We are interested, however, not just in the overall balance sheet but, more important, in the timing of the respective processes for supplying energy. From the various experiments and analyses we can now sketch a rough, well-confirmed picture of the energy events that take place during exercise and the following recovery period.

In exercise that calls for maximal consumption of oxygen but no glycolysis, the oxygen consumption rises exponentially to its limit (40 milliliters per minute per kilogram of body weight) and then, at the end of the exercise, falls back exponentially to the rate of a resting muscle. The oxygen debt contracted is entirely alactic; it amounts to about 20 milliliters and is quickly paid off. Only half of the phosphagen content of the muscle is split during the peak period of activity, and all of this is resynthesized by means of energy from oxidation in the brief recovery period [see top illustration on following page].

The picture in exercise that requires the additional input of energy from glycolysis is considerably more complex and has only recently been traced out. When the energy requirement is twice as great as what can be furnished by oxidation (that is, when the requirement is equivalent to an oxygen consumption of 80 milliliters per minute per kilogram of body weight), oxygen consumption rises to its maximum rate in half the time, and the formation of lactic acid, apparently triggered by the splitting of 50 percent of the muscle phosphagen, begins at that point. If the exercise proceeds to exhaustion, presumably the remaining 50 percent of the muscle phosphagen is split. The alactic oxygen debt at the onset of the recovery period after exhaustion amounts to about 40 milliliters per kilogram of body weight, the lactacid oxygen debt depends on the amount of lactic acid built up during the exercise. In the recovery period of the alactic energy debt 30 milliliters are paid by energy from oxidation and about 10 milliliters by energy from the delayed production of lactic acid through glycolysis [see bottom illustration on following page].

What does all of this tell us about how to make efficient use of the muscle engine? Obviously it is advisable to avoid, if possible, driving the muscle to the pitch of incurring a lactacid debt. The payment of that debt is a very slow process, taking more than an hour after the exercise has been concluded, and the lactic acid in the body induces a state of acidosis that hampers muscle performance, causes great discomfort and produces other disagreeable symptoms. On the other hand, if the oxygen debt is only alactic, there is no acidosis and the debt is paid off in a few minutes.

Because there is always a certain period of delay in the onset of lactic acid production, even in highly strenuous exercise, one can avoid this production by limiting the activity period to a short enough time. This suggests that, in the case of exercise or work that may push the energy requirements beyond what can be furnished by oxidation, the muscles can be used most effectively by adopting a schedule of intermittent activity and rest, each activity period being short enough to forestall lactic acid production and each rest period long enough to pay off the alactic oxygen debt contracted during the period of strenuous activity.

We have conducted experiments that

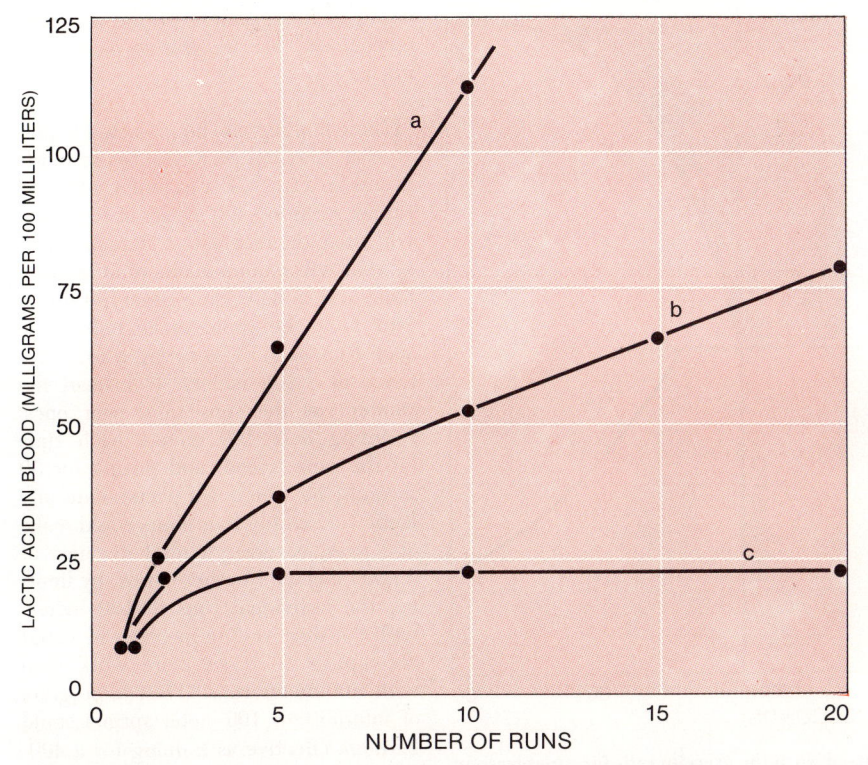

REST INTERVALS between sessions of strenuous running can greatly reduce the production of lactic acid and increase the total distance that can be run. The exercise consisted in running on a treadmill at 18 kilometers per hour for 10 seconds followed by a rest period. When the rest period was 10 seconds (a), the runner could complete 10 cycles before exhaustion. When the rest period was 20 seconds (b), exhaustion occurred after 20 cycles. With a rest period of 30 seconds between runs (c) the lactic acid level remained constant and the exercise could be continued indefinitely. Athletes in training can increase the amount of strenuous exercise they can perform by judicious timing of rest periods.

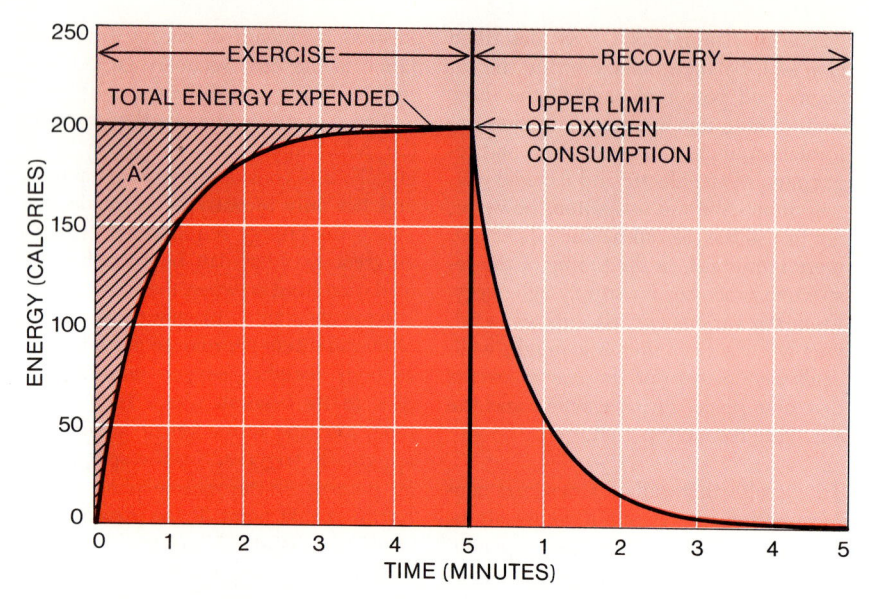

ALACTIC OXYGEN DEBT is created by muscles drawing energy from phosphagen-splitting (*hatched area A*) while the oxidation mechanism is being activated. In moderate exercise that does not lead to the formation of lactic acid, oxygen consumption quickly rises to its upper limit of about 40 milliliters (equivalent to 200 calories) per minute per kilogram of body weight and provides all of the energy required by the muscles. At the end of the exercise additional oxygen is consumed (*colored area B*) to repay the alactic oxygen debt (*A*). The repayment energy is used to resynthesize the phosphagens that were split.

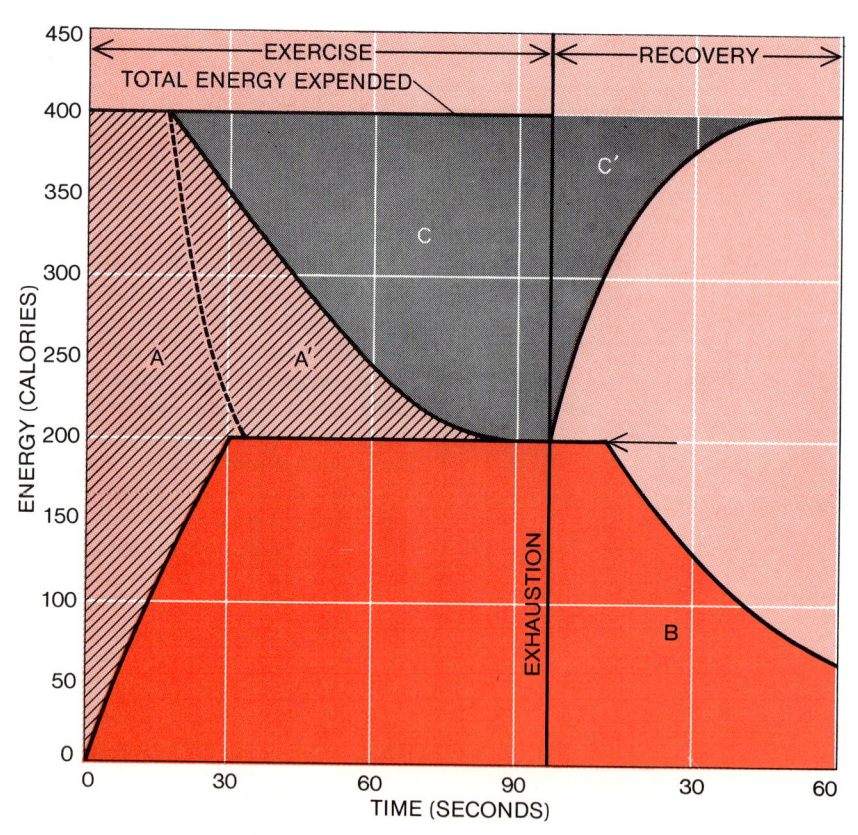

ALACTIC AND LACTACID DEBTS are incurred when the exercise calls for superexertion to exhaustion. The alactic oxygen debt (*hatched areas A and A'*) is formed by the muscles obtaining energy from phosphagen-splitting while energy from oxygen consumption (*colored area*) is rising to its upper limit (*arrow*). The lactacid oxygen debt (*gray area C and C'*) is the result of energy obtained from the formation of lactic acid. During recovery from superexertion oxygen consumption remains at a high level for 15 to 20 seconds and then begins to drop. Energy from the delayed oxygen consumption (*colored area B*) pays the greater part (*area A*) of the alactic oxygen debt. Continued production of lactic acid (*C'*) after the exercise is over provides energy to pay the fraction *A'* of the alactic debt.

strikingly demonstrate the value of this tactic. The test consisted in running on a treadmill at a speed and incline that would lead to exhaustion in about 35 seconds if it were continued without rest. We limited the run to 10 seconds at a time and varied the experiment by trying rest periods of different lengths between the runs. The object of the test was to find out how many 10-second runs could be accomplished (in effect, how much distance could be covered in total) before exhaustion.

When the rest period was 10 seconds, the subjects could run about 10 cycles (totaling 100 seconds of exercise) and cover a distance corresponding to 500 meters. The lactic acid in the blood at the end of the performance amounted to 1.15 grams per liter. When the rest period was increased to 20 seconds, the subjects accumulated less lactic acid and covered a considerably greater distance. With a rest period of 30 seconds between runs the subjects were able to go on with runs indefinitely and showed a lactic acid content in the blood of only about .2 gram per liter; this content could be attributed to the fact that leg muscles usually generate a little lactic acid at the beginning of exercise because of sluggishness of the oxidative mechanism [*see illustration on preceding page*].

These findings can be projected to predict potential performances in sports events on a track. For example, a trained runner sprinting 400 meters at top speed will finish the race with a state of acidosis that will require a rest of at least an hour and a half for recovery; thus in four hours he could make only three such runs at most, covering a total distance of 1,200 meters. If instead the runner cut the runs to shorter ones, sprinting only 100 meters each time (at the same speed) and resting for 30 seconds, he would not accumulate any lactic acid and in four hours could make 360 runs, covering a total distance of 36,000 meters. In other words, by limiting the individual runs to 100 meters with the short resting intervals he could accomplish 30 times more work than with 400-meter runs. Thus a program of intermittent 100-meter sprints could be more effective as training for a 400-meter runner than 400-meter sprints.

The same principle very probably applies to any kind of muscular work that can be taxing for the worker. By proper pacing of the work and the intervals of rest a person can produce more work than by driving himself relentlessly.

3

APPETITE AND OBESITY

JEAN MAYER
November 1956

It is often said that obesity is caused simply by overeating. But what causes people to overeat? The answer to the question is sought by the physiological experiments described herein

Obesity has been called the "Number 1 Nutrition Problem," if not the "Number 1 Health Problem," in Western countries at the present time. All recent statistical studies agree that overweight is associated with a shortening of life. For example, Louis I. Dublin found that among men and women insured with the Metropolitan Life Insurance Company, overweight persons show a 50 per cent greater than normal mortality between the ages 20 and 64. The mortality rate among them increases with the degree of overweight: deaths among moderately obese men, for example, are 42 per cent above the standard risk, and among the markedly obese, 79 per cent. By and large their higher death rate reflects a greater susceptibility to "degenerative" diseases, notably diabetes, cirrhosis of the liver, and heart, kidney and

RAT EXERCISES on a treadmill in the author's laboratory at the Harvard University School of Public Health. It was discovered that exercising rats in this manner two hours a day prevented the progressive obesity usually suffered by rats confined in small cages.

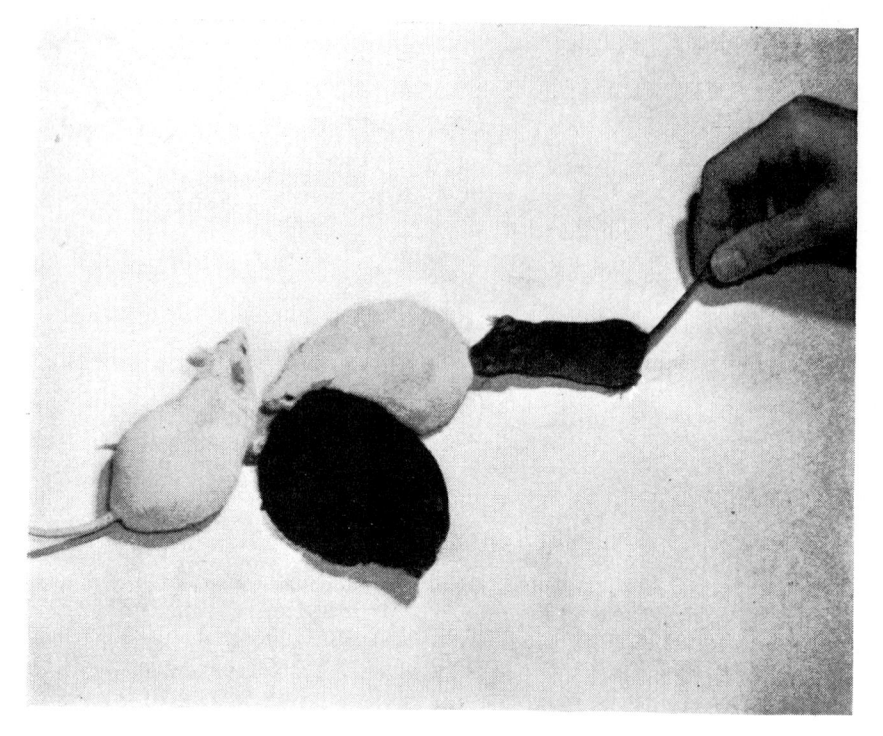

THREE FAT MICE demonstrate obesity due to three different causes. At the right is a normal black mouse for purposes of comparison. The other black mouse is the littermate of the normal mouse; it is fat because it carries the hereditary obese-hyperglycemic gene. The white mouse at the left became obese after a lesion was surgically made in its hypothalamus. The other white mouse became obese after it was injected with gold thioglucose.

STEREOTACTIC APPARATUS is used to make experimental lesions at exactly the same place in the brains of several animals. Animals of a standard size are used. The head of the anesthetized animal is fixed in the frame at the left side of the apparatus. The lesion is made by an electrode which is accurately located in the brain by turning the three upper knobs.

circulatory diseases. Overweight increases the risk of death from cardiovascular or kidney disease by more than 50 per cent. (On the other hand, the death rates from tuberculosis, ulcers and suicide are actually lower than average among obese persons.)

Unhappily the underlying causes of obesity are still largely unknown. To say that obesity is due to overeating is not much more illuminating than to say that alcoholism is caused by overdrinking.

The real question is: Why do people overeat? What factor (or factors) disturbs the mechanism of regulation of food intake in such a way that the balance between intake and energy output is tipped in favor of excessive consumption? This article summarizes some of the recent efforts to discover the disturbances that lead to obesity in animals and in man.

The first problem to be tackled is to get a clearer concept of how appetite is normally regulated. A number of years ago the most popular theory, advanced by the late Walter B. Cannon of Harvard University and Anton J. Carlson of the University of Chicago, held that contractions of the stomach were the main signal arousing the sensation of hunger (sometimes in the form of the so-called "hunger pangs"). While there is no doubt that such contractions exist and may play a part in awareness of hunger, the notion that they played a basic role had to be abandoned when it was demonstrated that denervation of the stomach or even its total removal by surgery did not fundamentally alter the regulation of food intake. The influence of bulk in the diet, of "filling up the stomach" as such, was shown to be minor. It may delay hunger pangs but it does not eliminate the over-all feeling of hunger.

Carlson made the interesting suggestion that a low level of sugar in the blood was the cause of stomach contractions, but this was discarded when several workers failed to find any regular relation between sugar level and hunger sensations. The well-known ravenous appetite of diabetics with high blood sugar also seemed to invalidate the idea.

The first productive clue to how food intake is regulated came in the early 1940s when S. W. Ranson and his colleagues at Northwestern University discovered that animals became obese after destruction of the central area of the hypothalamus, an important part of the mid-brain. John R. Brobeck and an associate at Yale University then showed that destruction of side areas of the hypothalamus caused animals to refuse food. José M. Delgado, working at Yale on monkeys, and Stig Larsson, working at the University of Stockholm on goats, found that electric stimulation of the same area induced their animals to eat.

Pursuing these findings in our laboratory in the department of nutrition at the Harvard University School of Public Health, we began with a systematic exploration of how the regulatory centers in the hypothalamus operated. We used the very convenient technique developed by the Harvard psychologist B. F. Skinner for measuring animal responses and behavior. The essential feature of the method is that the animal itself produces a reward (*e.g.*, a small pellet of food) by pressing a lever, and the strength of the rewarding effect, or the intensity of the animal's desire, is measured by the frequency with which it presses the lever [see "Pleasure Centers in the Brain," by James Olds; SCIENTIFIC AMERICAN Offprint 30]. In our experience the animal had to press the lever a certain number of times to obtain a food pellet, and a record of its behavior was registered automatically by an electrical recorder.

Application of this method showed that the feeding behavior of normal animals exhibits a clear-cut daily cycle. The animal feeds rapidly and frequently for several hours; there follows a "satiety period" during which it eats very much less and in a desultory fashion. However, if the central area of the animal's hypothalamus is destroyed, it does not taper off in this way but goes on eating at the same high rate. Our experiments demonstrated that the central area of the hypothalamus is a satiety center which normally acts as a brake on the lateral area, where stimulation to eat is constantly present. In other words, what is "regulated" is not hunger but satiety.

The next question was: How do the satiety centers in the hypothalamus determine when the body's hunger for food has been satisfied? It appeared improbable that they could use as an index the body's content of fat or protein, which between meals declines by only a very small amount in proportion to the total.

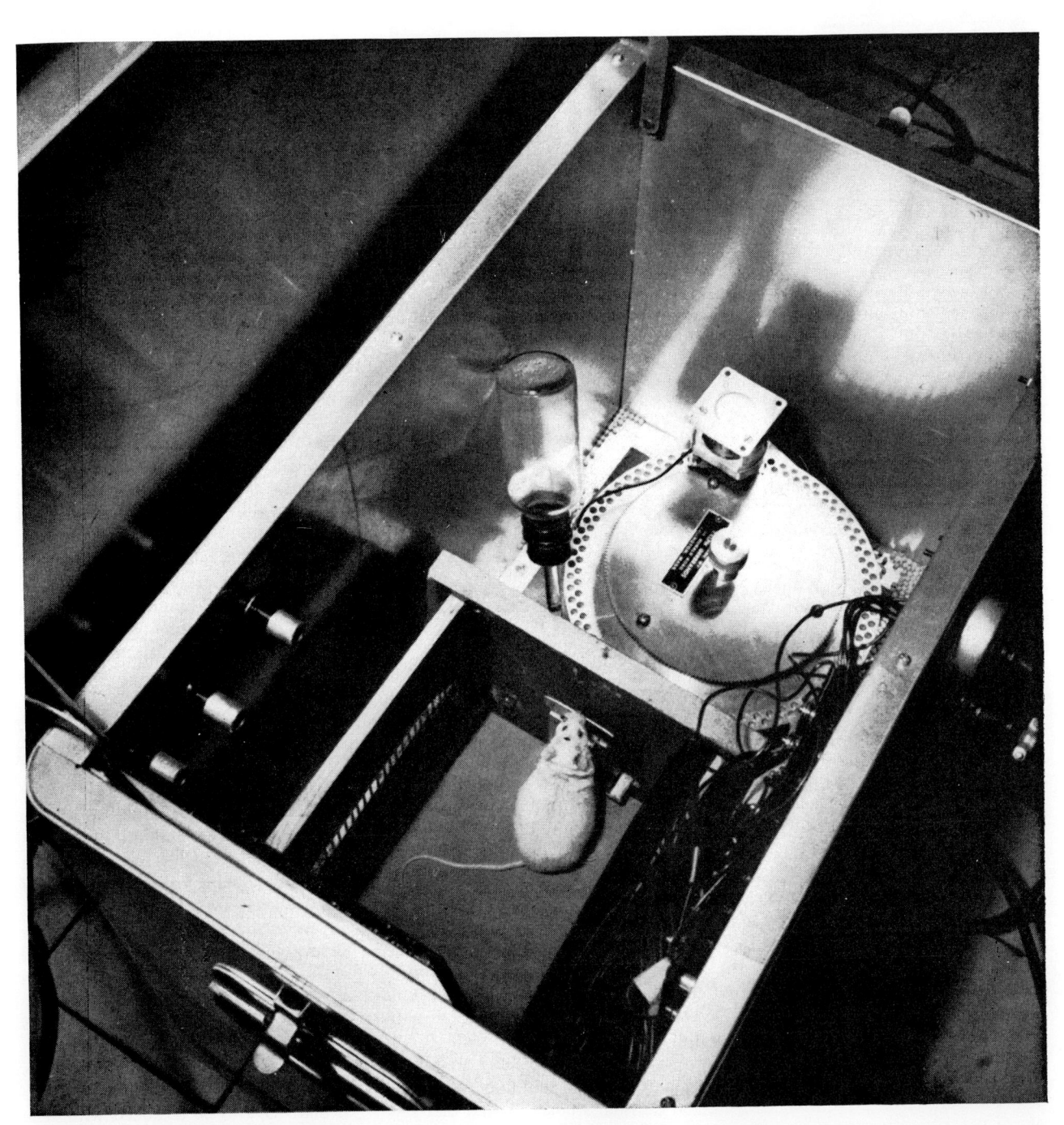

OBESE MOUSE PRESSES A LEVER in a special cage designed to study the feeding behavior of small animals. The large disk at the upper right is part of an automatic feeder that discharges pellets of food into a tray at the right of the mouse whenever it presses the lever a predetermined number of times. To the left of the lever is a tube from the water bottle suspended above the disk.

INTAKE OF FOOD by an animal in the cage on page 23 may be continuously recorded on a strip of paper. The curve shows the number of times the animal pressed the food lever.

The sugar reserves, on the other hand, would provide a sensitive index. The stores of sugars carried by the organs of the body are limited. In the liver of man, for example, the content of glycogen after a meal amounts to only about 300 calories (a moderately active man spends 3,000 calories of energy a day). Furthermore sugar, in the form of glucose, is the sole fuel of the central nervous system. It seemed reasonable to assume, therefore, that the satiety centers of the central hypothalamus might be sensitive to the availability of sugar from the blood, and that their utilization of sugar might be a measure of hunger.

An elaborate program of experiments was carried out to test this hypothesis. In the first series of experiments we found that the rate of food intake by animals did indeed correlate well with the rate of utilization of sugar by the body as a whole. Next we conducted tests with human subjects, using as a measure of sugar utilization the difference between the sugar level in arteries and in veins. The results further supported the hypothesis: the subjects' feelings of hunger appeared appeased when the rate of sugar utilization fell. These observations were confirmed and extended by Albert Stunkard of Cornell University. He studied "hunger" contractions of the stomach, employing a stomach balloon technique of Cannon and Carlson. Stunkard found that when the difference between the sugar levels in the arteries and veins was small (indicating reduced availability of sugar), the subject showed contractions of the stomach and had subjective feelings of hunger, while a large difference (indicating appreciable reserves of sugar) accompanied satiety. Very recently two findings have brought convincing confirmation of our hypothesis concerning the role of sugar. Stunkard and a colleague found that administration of glucagon, a pancreatic hormone, which raises the blood sugar level without decreasing utilization of sugar, invariably eliminated gastric contractions and hunger feelings. A particularly striking illustration of this effect was given by a patient who had lost the use of his brain cortex after an accident and whose central nervous system was therefore reduced to the lower centers of the midbrain. The only treatment (aside from intake of food) that eliminated hunger contractions of the stomach in this patient was glucagon, raising the level of available sugar.

The other recent finding gives a more direct "proof" of the theory. My associate Norman Marshall and I experimented on mice and rats with a chemical called gold thioglucose—a compound of glucose and gold linked together by a "sulfur bridge." A single dose of gold thioglucose induces overeating and obesity in animals. We established that the substance selectively destroys the satiety area of the central hypothalamus. Compounds of gold with other substances, even very similar to glucose, did not produce these effects. It appears, therefore, that gold thioglucose exerted its destructive effect because the gold was "dragged in" by glucose, for which the satiety cells have a special affinity. The experiment demonstrates that these cells do indeed act as sensitive receptors of glucose.

Once the cells have taken in glucose, they must translate this fact into an electrical signal to other centers in the central nervous system. Tracer studies show that potassium generally accompanies glucose into cells, and the passage of potassium ions into the glucose-receiving cells may account for the generation of electrical impulses.

The impulses from the hypothalamus satiety cells, on reaching the cerebral cortex, are interpreted there and translated into sensations of satiety or hunger. But other factors—psychological as well as physiological—may intervene to modify appetite, at least temporarily. Conditioned reflexes and habits, in particular, have to be reckoned with. The whole scheme is one of great complexity, and therefore it is to be expected that any one of a number of dysfunctions may cause a person to overeat. The dysfunction may affect either the regulatory centers or the general metabolism of the body. Hence we conclude that there are both "regulatory" and "metabolic" roads to obesity.

Thinking in terms of first causes, we can trace obesity to three sources: heredity, injury and unfavorable external factors (*i.e.*, relating to nutrition or exercise).

Genetic obesity has been studied in particular in the mouse. There is a form called "yellow" obesity, because it is associated with a yellowish coat color. This mutation has been known for half a century, and it affects a dominant gene; only when a yellow mouse is mated to a nonyellow one do the offspring survive. Those offspring of the mating that inherit a yellow coat also become obese. Another interesting form of obesity in the mouse was discovered five years ago at the Jackson Memorial Laboratory in Bar Harbor by Margaret M. Dickie and has been studied intensively in our laboratory. These mice weigh three to five times more than normal ones, are inactive and have poor resistance to cold. Their distinguishing marks are high levels of sugar and cholesterol in the blood. Even when restricted to the same amount of food as their normal littermates, they manufacture more fat; reduced to an insufficient diet, they lose mainly protein rather than fat. This last trait, incidentally, is characteristic of the "metabolic" forms of obesity. We have been able to elucidate the primary mechanism responsible for the overeating and obesity of these mice: they secrete unusual amounts of the two hormones produced by the pancreas—insulin and glucagon. Their hypersecretion of these hormones has been substantiated by measurements made in collaboration with the Toronto laboratory of Charles H. Best, the codiscoverer of insulin.

Other forms of genetic obesity have been found in mice, rats, the Shetland shepherd dog and a strain of chickens. And of course certain strains of domestic animals, hogs in particular, have been bred for centuries because of their tendency to obesity. The evidence for genetic obesity in man is far less clear-cut, but a number of studies very strongly suggest that children of overweight parents exhibit a much greater tendency to obesity than children of normal-weight persons, and that this is not entirely due to factors of upbringing.

Traumatic obesity has been produced in the laboratory by several different

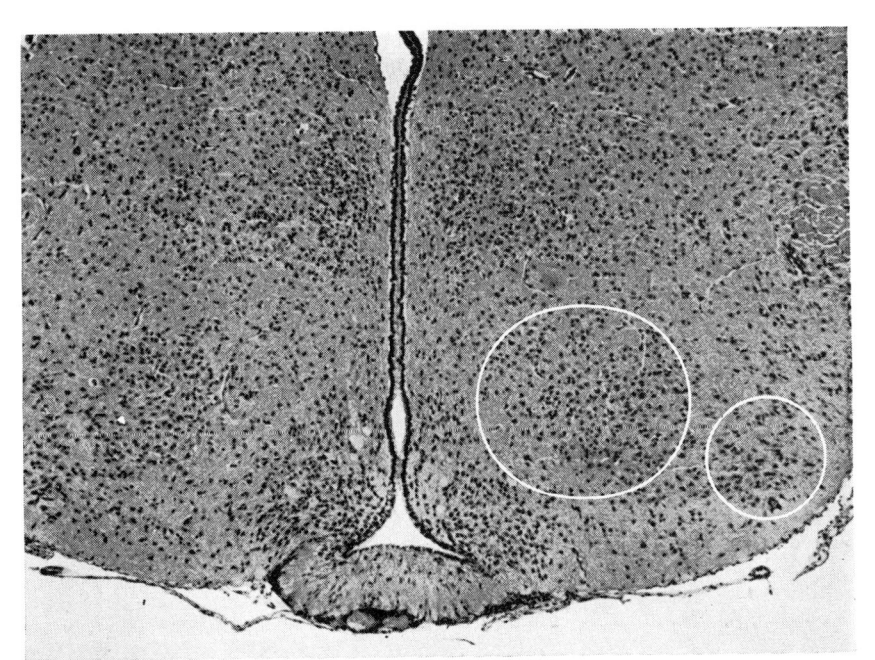

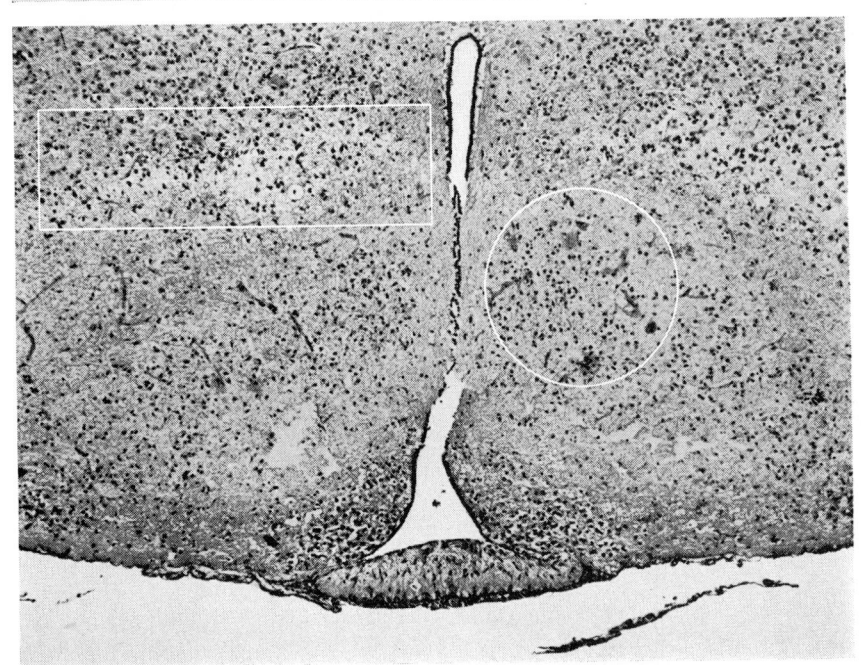

HYPOTHALAMUS of the mouse brain is shown in these photomicrographs of sections through the brain. The larger loop in the photomicrograph at the top surrounds the ventromedial nucleus, which is the center of the "satiety" cells. The smaller loop surrounds the lateral area, which contains the "feeding" centers. If the cells in the ventromedial nucleus are destroyed, the animal becomes obese. If the lateral areas of both brain hemispheres are destroyed, the animal stops feeding. The photomicrograph at the bottom shows the hypothalamus of a mouse which three days earlier had been injected with gold thioglucose. Many cell nuclei (*black dots*) have disappeared; the whole area is disorganized and "thinned" due to the death of cells and edema. The small blots in the circle at the right are hemorrhages. The rectangle shows the line of demarcation between normal and abnormal tissue.

means. We have induced it in the mouse by destroying centers in the hypothalamus, by implanting specialized tumors and by injecting, or causing the animals to secrete, excessive doses of certain hormones. In the type of obesity caused by destruction of the regulatory centers, the animal synthesizes an excessive amount of fat only if it is allowed to overeat. If it is underfed, its body composition becomes normal when it has been reduced to normal weight. We have studied metabolic obesities in rats in collaboration with Jacob Furth, of the Children's Cancer Research Foundation in Boston. Injection of tumorous tissue from the pituitary gland will induce such an obesity; it is traceable to excessive secretion of the pituitary hormone ACTH. In some species of animals it is possible to induce obesity by injecting long-lasting insulin, alone or in combination with a substance that depresses the activity of the thyroid gland. Castration, as is well known, also may lead to obesity.

Besides these "constitutional" obesities—genetic or traumatic—obesity can be produced by tampering with the environment. Paul Fenton of Brown University has shown that certain strains of mice become very obese when placed on high fat diets. Olaf Mickelsen at the National Institutes of Health in Bethesda, Md., observed the same effect with a strain of rats.

The influence of exercise is important. We found that exercising rats on a treadmill for two hours a day prevented the progressive "creeping" obesity which is typical of normal animals restricted in small cages. Exercise on the treadmill also cut down considerably the rate of weight gain of mice with a traumatic or hereditary tendency to obesity. An amusing natural illustration of this point is furnished by the "waltzing mouse"—a breed with a gene which causes it to turn constantly in its cage, as if it were chasing its tail. If this type is crossed with a genetically obese mouse, the offspring never reach anything like the weight of the fat parent: their exercise holds their weight down to only 30 per cent above normal, instead of the potential three or four times normal weight.

Our studies have shown that the effect of exercise also applies to human beings. Many overweight youngsters eat no more than their contemporaries of normal weight, but are characterized by a very limited spontaneous physical activity, if not total avoidance of exercise. The same is true of adults. People who do not exercise usually eat as much as those who are moderately active.

We are still a long way from understanding all the complexities of the mechanism regulating appetite, or from being able to cure a basic tendency to overweight or underweight (which may be even more dangerous than obesity). It can safely be said, however, that progress in the last decade has been highly encouraging and that advances of our knowledge in this important field should take place even more rapidly in the near future.

PROTEINS

JOSEPH S. FRUTON
June 1950

The large molecules characterized by nitrogen are synonymous with life. Their structure and function are fundamental problems of chemistry

There is present in plants and in animals a substance which . . . is without doubt the most important of all the known substances in living matter, and, without it, life would be impossible on our planet. This material has been named Protein.

SO WROTE Gerard Johannes Mulder, a Dutch agricultural chemist, in 1838. It was in his scientific papers that the word "protein," from the Greek *proteios*, meaning of the first rank, made its first public appearance. The word had been suggested to him by the great Swedish chemist Jöns Jacob Berzelius (who also introduced to chemistry "catalysis," "polymer" and other important terms). Mulder and his great German contemporary Justus von Liebig thought that protein was a single substance—a basic structural unit existing in the same form in materials as diverse as egg white and blood fibrin. This was soon shown to be an error; the number and variety of proteins was found to be legion. But Mulder has certainly been proved correct in his emphasis on the importance of proteins to life.

The proteins are one of the three principal organic constituents of living matter (the fats and carbohydrates are the others), but in the importance and diversity of their biological functions they stand alone. They represent nearly one half of the body's dry matter. (About 70 per cent of the body is water.) Of the total body protein, more than a third is found in the muscles: the protein myosin forms the fibers that are the fundamental contractile elements in muscular movement. The bones and cartilage account for another 20 per cent; here the protein collagen contributes to the structural stability of the skeleton. And the skin has about 10 per cent of the body protein, the skin protein keratin serving to protect the interior tissues against attack from the external environment.

Perhaps the most important of the proteins are the enzymes. These substances are present in only minute amounts in comparison with myosin, collagen or keratin, but they are indispensable for the promotion and direction of the body's myriad chemical reactions. Thus the digestion of foodstuffs in the stomach and the intestine depends on the continuous activity of protein enzymes such as pepsin or trypsin. It is the synchronized action of a series of enzymic proteins that enables the body cells to use oxygen to oxidize the carbon and hydrogen in food and thereby provide the major portion of the chemical energy required for vital functions. This energy is used not only for muscular movement but also to counteract the wear and tear of living tissues by the continuous regeneration of body constituents, including the proteins, under the specific directive influence of a host of other enzymes.

The hormones also are proteins. These remarkable products of the secretory activity of the endocrine organs are carried by the blood in infinitesimal amounts to the tissues, where they play a decisive role in the regulation of the pace and direction of metabolism. Still other proteins are the antibodies of the blood, which defend the organism against viruses, which are themselves proteins, and the harmful substances produced by disease-causing bacteria. Finally the genes, the basic units of heredity, are believed to contain a particular type of protein called nucleoproteins.

Where there is such diversity of function, there must be a corresponding diversity of chemical structure. The number of identified proteins is extremely large, and growing rapidly. To learn what proteins are present in living systems, to examine their chemical structure, to explain their biological functions in terms of their structure—these are among the most fundamental problems of modern biochemistry. When the answers to them have been found, we shall have a much more precise definition of what has been termed "the physical basis of life."

The Problem

To study the chemical structure of a particular protein it is necessary to destroy the cellular organization characteristic of life and to extract the protein with a suitable solvent, such as a dilute salt solution. This procedure inevitably brings into solution many of the other proteins present in the cell, and the task of separating the desired protein from the unwanted materials becomes a test of the experimenter's skill and, very frequently, of his good fortune. Proteins are extremely fragile chemical structures. This imposes serious restrictions upon the kind of laboratory procedures the chemist may use in separating them from one another. Delicate techniques for separating proteins have, however, been worked out during the past 25 years in fundamental researches by a number of great biochemists, especially Sven P. L. Sörensen of Denmark, Otto Warburg of Germany, and John H. Northrop, Moses Kunitz, Edwin J. Cohn and Carl F. Cori of the U. S.

By careful control of factors such as salt concentration, alcohol concentration, acidity and temperature, fairly selective precipitation of a given protein may be achieved; today it is often possible to isolate a single protein from the dozens or even hundreds present in a tissue extract. Many individual proteins have been obtained in the form of crystals which may be recrystallized at will, thus leading to further purification. Although crystallinity *per se* is not a satisfactory criterion of a protein's purity, the availability of crystalline proteins has for the first time given to the biochemist reproducible material for the study of the chemical nature of these substances.

All proteins are made principally of carbon, hydrogen, oxygen, and nitrogen. It is the nitrogen, representing from 12

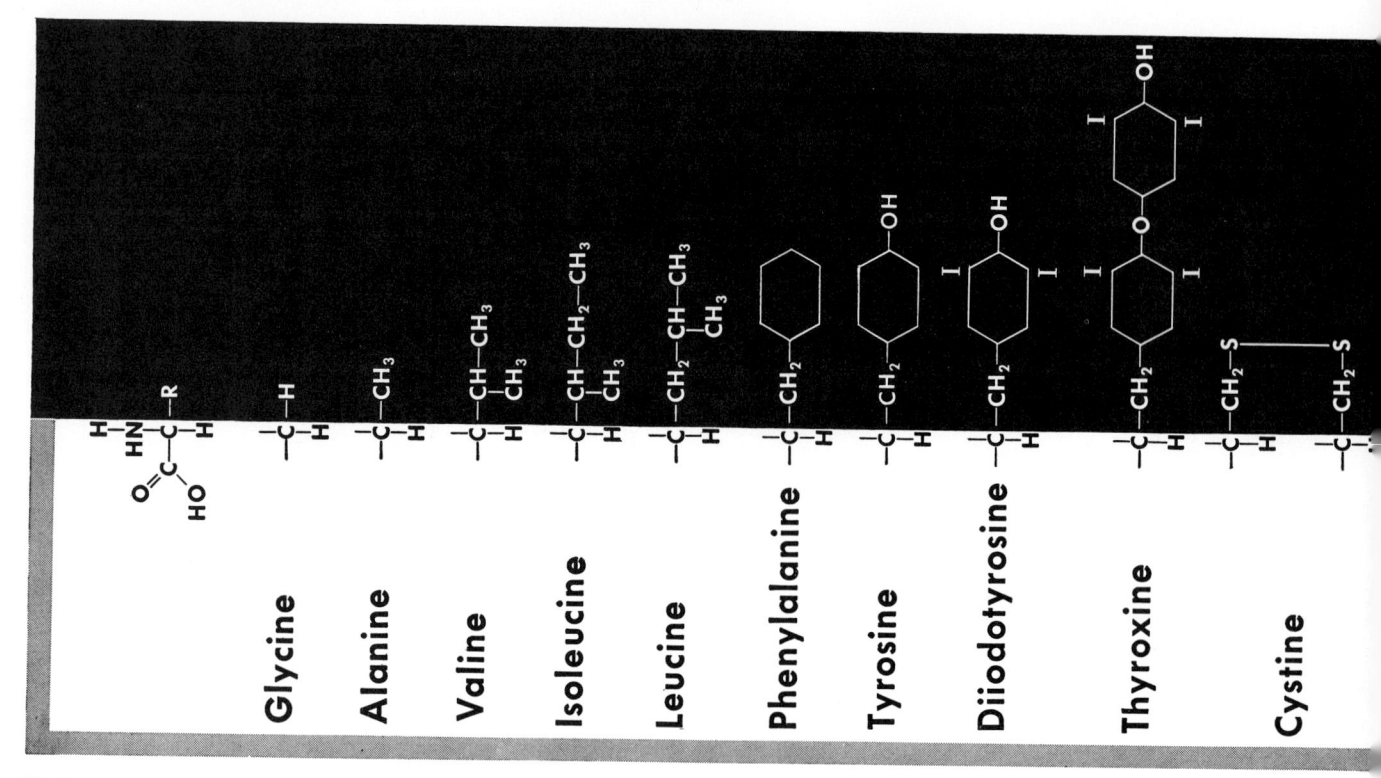

THE AMINO ACIDS are the molecular constituents of proteins. Shown in this chart are all 22 of the amino acids that have been obtained by breaking down proteins (*see diagram on page 38*). At the far left is the

to 19 per cent of the molecule, that is the special mark of a protein. Most proteins also contain small amounts of sulfur, and many have some phosphorus. Over a century ago Mulder, noting these very small proportions of sulfur and phosphorus in his crude protein preparations, concluded that the protein molecule must be huge, since each molecule had to contain at least one atom of these elements. Proteins, in other words, are "macromolecules." Not until modern methods of measuring their molecular weights were developed, however, was it possible to determine just how large they are.

The most reliable and convenient method is to whirl them in an ultra high speed centrifuge, a technique devised by the Swedish physical chemist, The Svedberg. The proteins are spun in a centrifuge at speeds up to 70,000 revolutions per minute, which develops a centrifugal force as much as 400,000 times that of gravity. In such a field the large protein molecules move outward from the center of rotation with selective speeds: the larger they are, the faster their motion. An ingenious optical apparatus measures the rate of this molecular sedimentation, and the molecular weight can then be calculated.

Their Size

Now these measurements show that the smallest known protein is about 13,000 times as heavy as a hydrogen atom, *i.e.*, its molecular weight is about 13,000. The largest known proteins have molecular weights of the order of 10 million. To determine the structure of molecules of such sizes is obviously quite a formidable problem. One can get some idea of how formidable it is by comparing a protein with a nonprotein organic molecule. A particularly complex example of the latter is one of the penicillins, which has a molecular weight of 334 and the formula $C_{16}H_{18}O_4N_2S$. This molecule is simplicity itself in comparison with the typical milk protein lactoglobulin, whose molecular weight is about 42,000 and whose approximate formula is $C_{1864}H_{3012}O_{576}N_{468}S_{21}$.

The structure of the penicillin molecule was worked out only after years of joint labor by the great chemists of the U. S. and England. The usual method of attacking such a task in organic chemistry is (1) to establish the proportions of the various elements in it, (2) to develop a working hypothesis about the arrangement of these atoms by a process of trial and error, and finally (3) to test the hypothesis by trying to synthesize the molecule from known substances by known chemical reactions. By this classical procedure organic chemists within the past 100 years have found the formulas of about 500,000 organic compounds, including many that are made by living organisms. But in a protein the number of atoms is so large that it has not been possible to establish its molecular structure by this method.

What the protein chemist can do at present is to cleave the protein molecule into the smaller molecules of which it is composed—the amino acids. The protein is cleaved by treatment with acids or alkalis; because water enters into the reaction, the process is called hydrolysis. When the protein has been broken down into its amino acids, the chemist can then obtain some clues to its composition, because the atomic structures of the amino acids themselves have all been determined by the classical methods of organic chemistry.

The amino acids formed by hydrolysis of a protein have certain structural features in common: each has an acidic carboxyl group (COOH) and a basic amino group (NH_2) or imino group (NH). Both the acidic and basic groups are attached to the same carbon atom, the so-called alpha-carbon. Since a carbon atom has four chemical bonds, this same alpha-carbon has two other units linked to it. One of these is invariably a hydrogen atom. What distinguishes the amino acids from one another is the fourth group attached to the alpha-carbon. This group, the so-called side chain, differs in each amino acid.

Isolating Amino Acids

The simplest amino acid, glycine, was isolated in 1820 by the French chemist Henri Braconnot. He obtained it by acid hydrolysis of gelatin. The list of known amino acids from proteins has now grown to 22. It is not likely that many new ones will be added to it. Every protein amino acid except glycine can exist in two geometrical forms, one the mirror image of the other; by convention

basic chemical structure common to all amino acids. In the shaded area are the characteristic structures of the various amino acids. The amino acids are here arranged in the order of their similarities in structure.

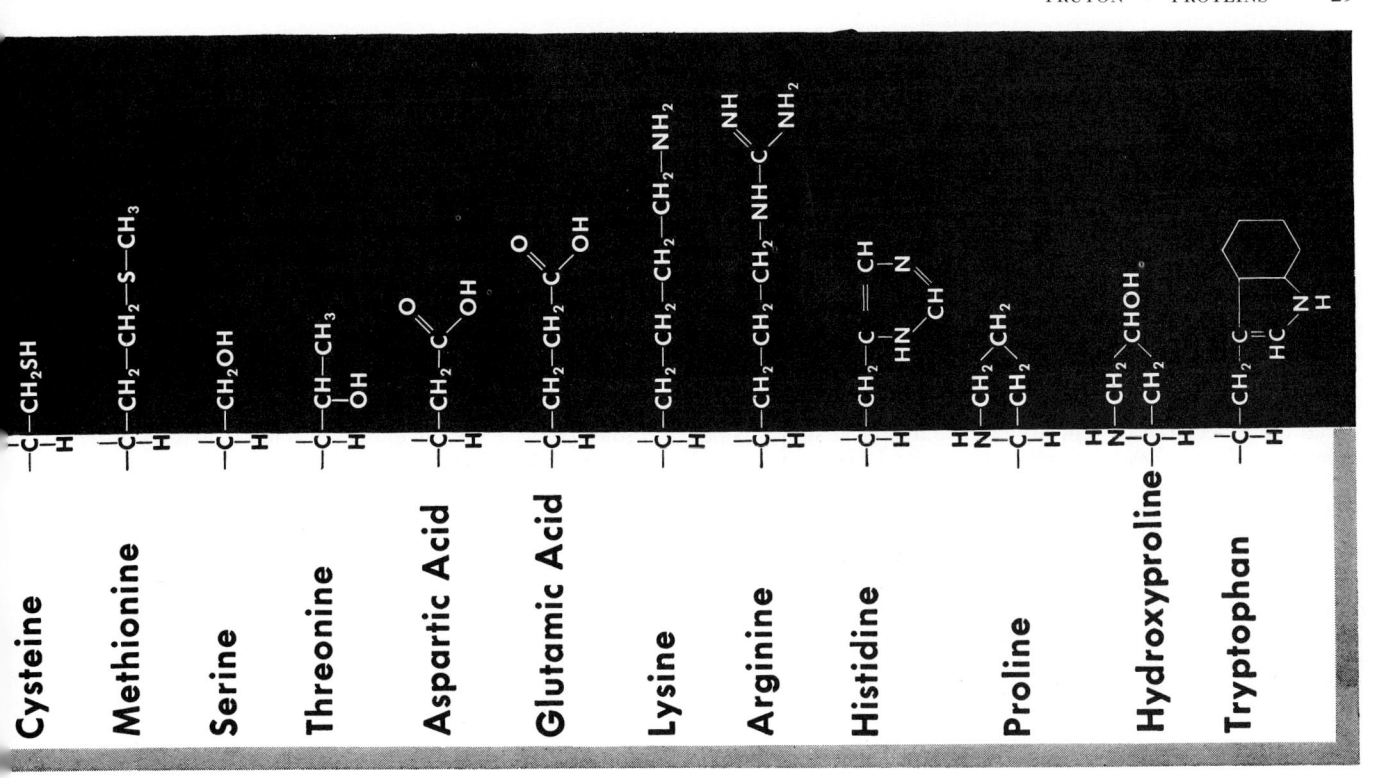

these are designated the "L" and "D" forms. Only the "L" type of the amino acids is obtained by the hydrolysis of proteins.

During the past 80 years an intensive effort has been devoted to the development of experimental methods for the accurate quantitative determination of the relative amounts of the various amino acids formed by hydrolysis of a protein. All the great names associated with the recent history of protein research have been linked with ingenious techniques designed to solve this problem. Among them are those of the German chemists Albrecht Kossel and Emil Fischer, Thomas Burr Osborne of the Connecticut Agricultural Experiment Station, and Max Bergmann and Donald D. Van Slyke of the Rockefeller Institute for Medical Research.

Because the various amino acids are structurally similar in all respects except the nature of the side-chain group, the problem has been to find chemical processes that will select and isolate them on the basis of this rather subtle mark of identification. Until about a decade ago the main effort was concentrated on a search for specific chemical reagents which in each case would precipitate completely a single amino acid from the complex mixture produced by the hydrolysis of a protein. A few amino acids were actually determined by this method, but eventually it became clear that it was hopeless to try to separate all the amino acids in this way.

Several years ago Erwin Brand of Columbia University, by dint of much labor and the use of a number of different techniques, finally accomplished the first complete analysis of a protein into its constituent amino acids. There was still needed, however, a single reliable analytical method. In the past few years this goal has been achieved, and it is now possible to say that the problem of protein analysis has been solved, at least in principle.

The most valuable contribution to the solution was the development of new chromatographic techniques for the separation of amino acids. Chromatography itself was invented by the Russian botanist Michael Tswett in 1906. It got its name from the fact that it was first used to separate pigments. Tswett was interested in isolating the chlorophyll pigments of green leaves. He conceived the idea that they might be separated quickly by taking advantage of their differing rates of adsorption by an adsorbing material. As he himself described it, "if a petroleum ether solution of chlorophyll is filtered through a column of an adsorbent (I use mainly calcium carbonate which is stamped firmly into a narrow glass tube), then the pigments . . . are resolved from top to bottom into various colored zones, since the more strongly absorbed pigments displace the more weakly absorbed ones and force them farther downwards. This separation becomes practically complete if, after the pigment solution has flowed through, one passes a stream of pure solvent through the adsorbent column. Like light rays in the spectrum, so the different components of a pigment mixture are resolved on the calcium carbonate column . . . and can be estimated on it qualitatively and quantitatively. Such a preparation I term a chromatogram and the corresponding method, the chromatographic method."

Tswett realized that "the adsorption phenomena described are not restricted to the chlorophyll pigments, and one must assume that all kinds of colored and colorless chemical compounds are subject to the same laws." It was many years before this brilliant intuition of Tswett was appreciated. Since 1930 chromatographic techniques have been developed to separate colorless as well as colored chemical compounds. It was the English chemists A. J. P. Martin and R. L. M. Synge who found a way to apply the technique to the separation of amino acids. They introduced the use of a starch column as the adsorbent. From this idea William H. Stein and Stanford Moore of the Rockefeller Institute for Medical Research later worked out a beautiful method for the precise quantitative analysis of all the amino acids formed when a protein is hydrolyzed.

In their method a carefully prepared starch column in a tall glass tube is treated with an organic solvent such as butyl alcohol. To this column then is added the amino-acid mixture that is to be analyzed, this mixture also being diluted with the same solvent. After this, more of the solvent is passed through the column. The individual amino acids move down the column, each at a different rate that depends largely on the nature of its side chain. Under favorable circumstances, these differences in rate may be so great that each of the amino acids emerges from the column separately. Thus it is possible to follow accurately the successive appearance of the separate amino acids and to determine the amount of each.

So far only a few proteins have been studied by this method, but the results attained are sufficient to indicate its great importance in protein chemistry. Nevertheless, it has not by any means solved the problem of protein structure. What this advance has accomplished is to bring the proteins to the historical stage reached by the simpler organic molecules a century ago, when it became possible to calculate the relative proportions of the atoms constituting an organic compound. From this, organic chemists were able to go on to discover the arrangement of the atoms in an organic molecule. In the same way protein chemists are now in a position to proceed with greater confidence to consider the spatial arrangement of amino acids in a protein molecule.

How Amino Acids Are Linked

The next question concerns the nature of the linkages between the individual amino acids. The most widely accepted hypothesis is one proposed independently by Emil Fischer and the German biochemist Franz Hofmeister in 1902. They suggested that the amino group attached to the alpha-carbon of one amino acid is joined to the carboxyl group attached to the alpha-carbon of another. This union is accompanied by the elimination of the elements of water from the molecules that unite. It is this bond that is broken when the elements of water are introduced in acid hydrolysis. The bond is called a "peptide linkage," and the Fischer-Hofmeister hypothesis is known as the peptide theory.

The theory has been supported by so much experimental evidence that its essential truth seems highly probable. Support for the theory came from work on artificially synthesized peptides, *i.e.*, groups of amino acids linked together by peptide bonds. In this Fischer was the pioneer; he pointed out that "if one wishes to attain clear results in this difficult field, one must first discover a method which will permit the experimenter to join the various amino acids to one another in a stepwise manner and with well-defined intermediary products." Much research has been done during the past half-century, and is still continuing, to develop methods for the laboratory synthesis of peptides. One of the greatest achievements came in 1932 with the invention of the "carbobenzoxy" method by a distinguished pupil of Fischer, Max Bergmann, who was then director of the Kaiser Wilhelm Institute for Leather Research in Dresden and later came to the Rockefeller Institute for Medical Research.

In living systems proteins are hydrolyzed by enzymes such as pepsin, trypsin and chymotrypsin. These catalysts act to speed up the hydrolytic reactions, thus making it possible for them to take place at the ordinary temperatures and under the normal acidity conditions of the organism. According to the peptide theory, these enzymes cause the hydrolysis of peptide bonds. If this theory is correct, then the same enzymes should hydrolyze simple peptides synthesized in the laboratory. For a long time protein chemists made intensive but vain efforts to create synthetic compounds that could be hydrolyzed by the enzymes, and their failure was interpreted by some as evidence against the peptide theory. In 1937, however, the author, working in Bergmann's laboratory at the Rockefeller Institute and using the carbobenzoxy method of peptide synthesis, succeeded in forming synthetic compounds which were specifically hydrolyzed at their peptide bonds by these enzymes. This finding strongly supported the Fischer-Hofmeister theory.

The Peptides

An additional support for the peptide theory is the finding that when the hydrolysis of protein is interrupted before the protein is entirely converted to amino acids, peptides can occasionally be isolated. The isolation of peptides obviously is not easy, for we have here the same difficulty of separating the components of a complex mixture that we encounter in the case of amino acids. The problem is, if anything, even more complicated, because the number of different peptides into which a protein may be split is considerably larger than the number of possible amino acids, and the amount of each peptide is very small. The new methods of chromatography appear well suited to the fractionation of peptides, and many investigators are now using them. Another valuable new approach to the problem has recently been provided by Lyman C. Craig of the Rockefeller Institute. He has developed a separation method based on the same general principles as are the familiar laboratory procedures for the extraction of a chemical substance from one solvent, such as water, by another solvent, such as ether. With this method Craig has demonstrated that preparations of several of the antibacterial agents, such as gramicidin, which were thought to be pure peptides, actually are mixtures of several distinct but closely related peptides. It is to be expected that this promising technique and the chromatographic method will form the main experimental lines of attack in the investigation of peptides obtained from proteins.

The brilliant work now being done by the British chemist Frederick Sanger at Cambridge University provides further grounds for optimism. Sanger is studying the structure of the important protein hormone insulin. He has subjected insulin to the action of the reagent dinitrofluorobenzene, a substance that combines readily with the alpha-amino groups at the ends of insulin's peptide chains. The result of this combination is a compound called dinitrophenylinsulin (DNP-insulin). All the end alpha-amino groups in the compound are occupied by dinitrophenyl (DNP) groups. When the protein is subjected to hydrolysis by strong acid, all the peptide bonds are cleaved, but the linkages between the DNP group and the alpha-amino groups of the end amino acids are essentially unaffected. In other words, each end amino acid remains linked to a DNP group. Since the DNP group confers upon any compound in which it is present a distinctive yellow color, the DNP-amino acids can readily be separated by means of chromatography, and their structure can be determined.

By this method of analysis Sanger has shown that the basic structural unit of insulin is composed of four peptide chains, of which two have glycine and two have phenylalanine as the end amino acids. He has also offered strong evidence for the idea that the four peptide chains are held together by bridges consisting of two sulfur atoms; when these disulfide bridges are broken by a relatively mild chemical treatment, the peptide chains are separated from one another. The next step, which is now occupying Sanger's attention, is to determine the sequence of the amino acids in each of these four chains. For this purpose the four DNP-peptides are subjected to partial, rather than complete, acid hydrolysis of the peptide bonds. The result is a series of yellow DNP-peptides that can be separated by chromatography. If the elucidation of the structure of these peptides, now under way, is successful, the next step will be to attempt to construct a picture of the insulin molecule from the nature of the fragments.

Portrait of a Protein

The studies discussed thus far suggest that the protein molecule is a threadlike structure of several hundred amino acids, linked to one another through peptide bonds and strung out to form a chain (or several chains joined by disulfide bridges) of considerable length. There is good evidence that this description actually applies to insoluble proteins such as keratin or silk fibroin and to a few soluble ones, notably the myosin of muscle and the fibrinogen of blood.

But most of the known proteins are not threadlike or fibrous. The enzymes,

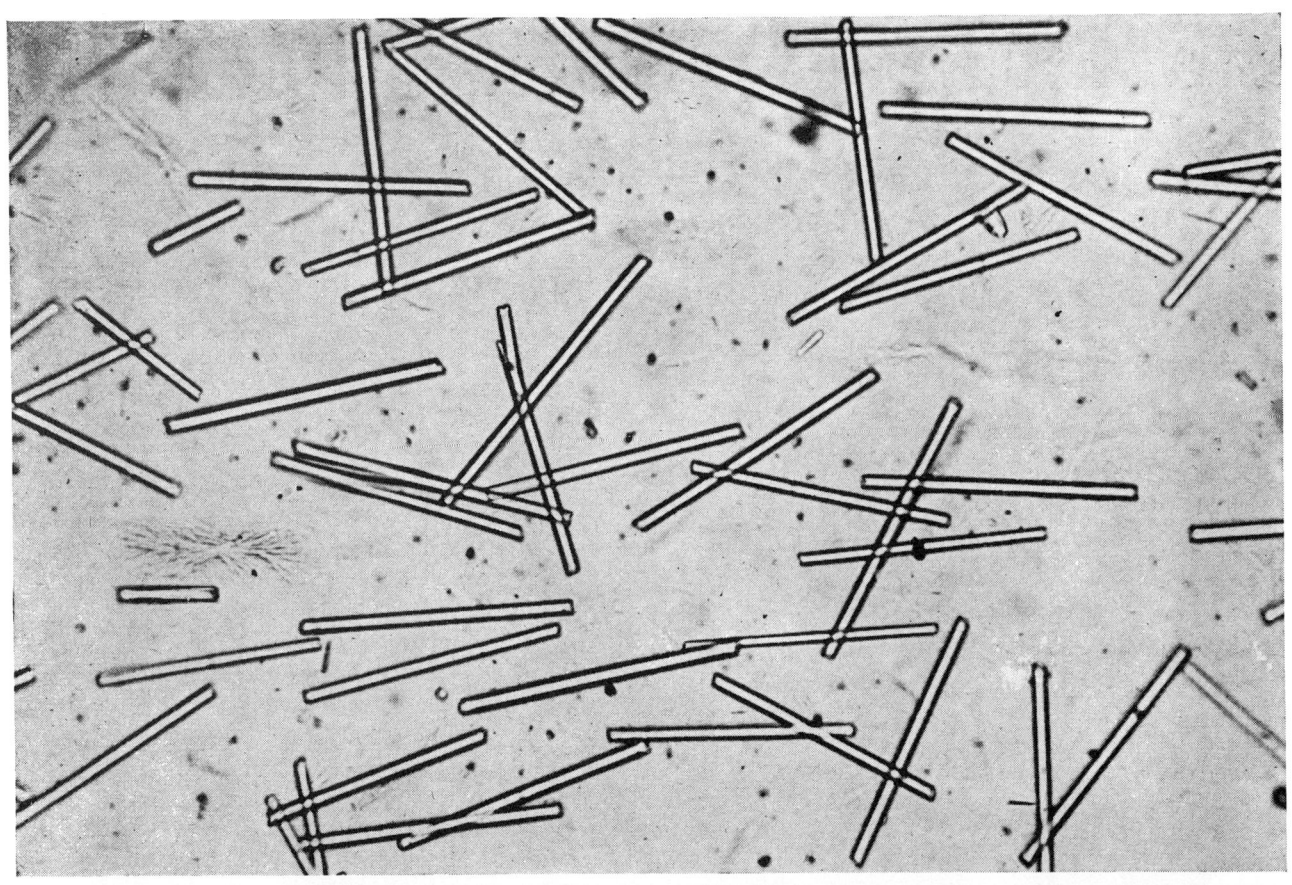

THE ENZYME PHOSPHORYLASE, like other enzymes, is a protein. These phosphorylase crystals, magnified 270 times, were isolated by Arda Alden Green and Gerty T. Cori of Washington University at St. Louis.

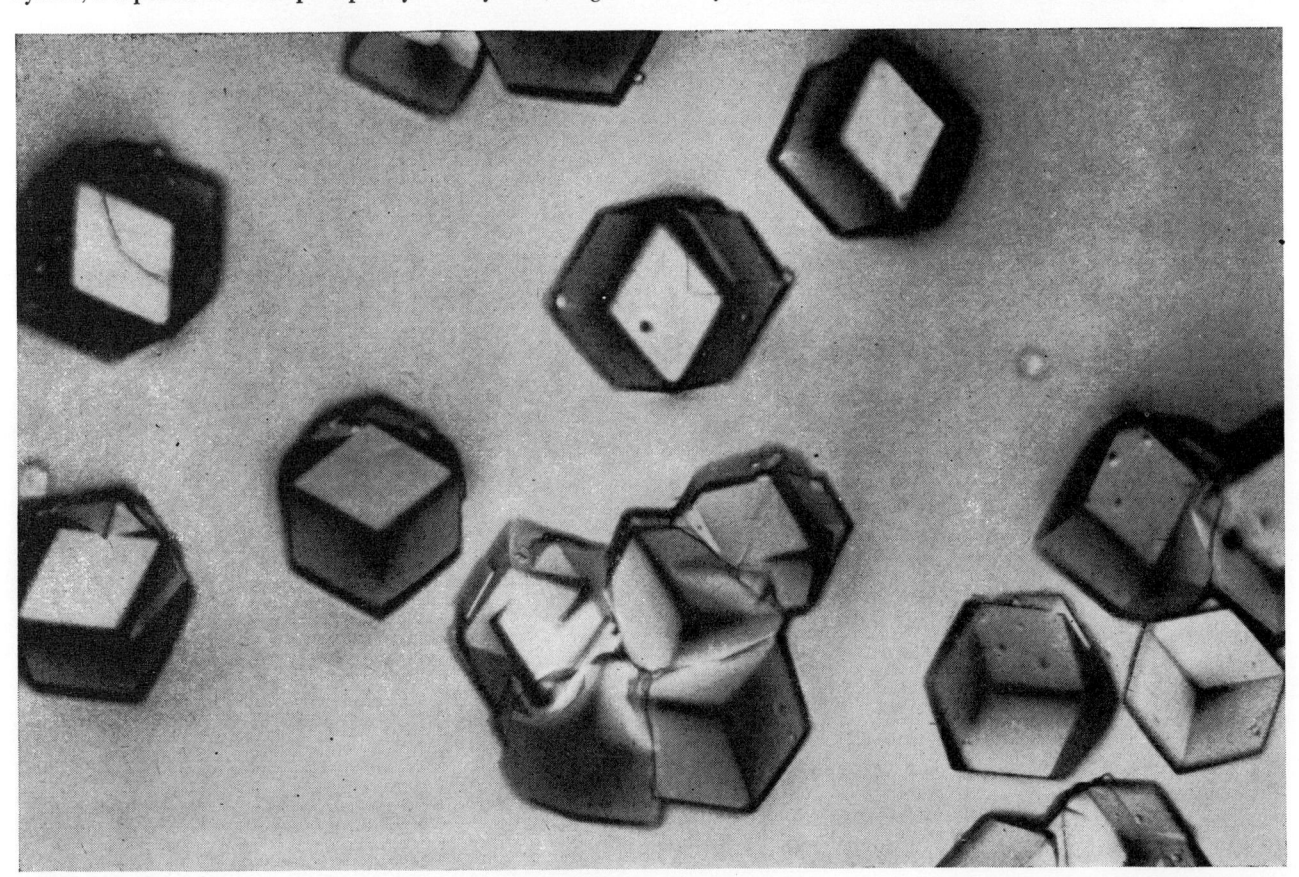

THE BUSHY STUNT VIRUS, like other viruses, is also a protein. These bushy stunt virus crystals, magnified 336 times, were isolated by Wendell M. Stanley, then of the Rockefeller Institute for Medical Research.

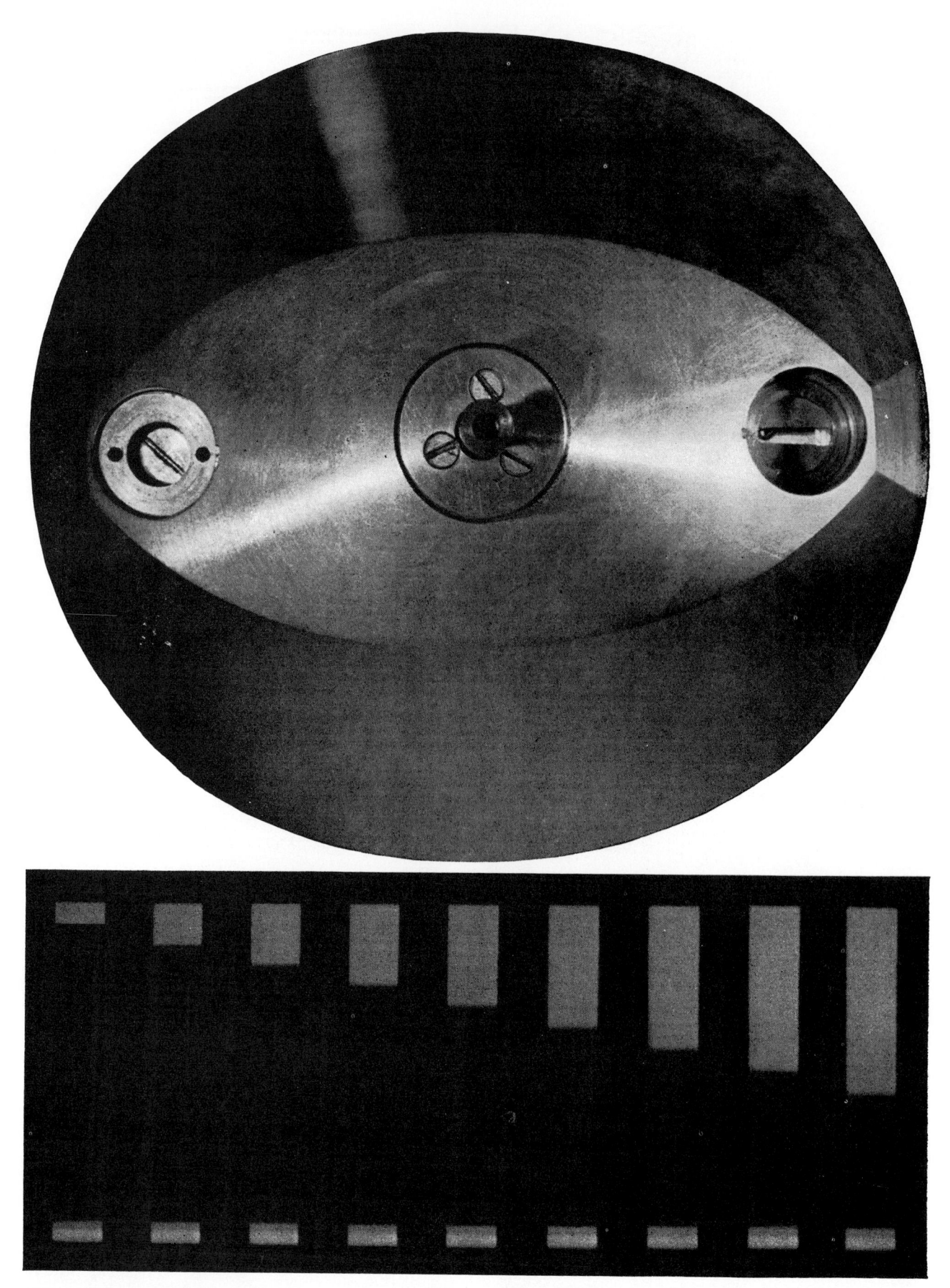

THE ULTRACENTRIFUGE is used to determine the molecular weight of proteins. At the top is a rotor from the ultracentrifuge at the Rockefeller Institute. At the bottom is a series of photographs made by E. G. Pickels, now of the Specialized Instruments Corporation, showing the sedimentation of a protein in an ultracentrifuge.

the protein hormones and all the blood proteins except fibrinogen are globular. They are soluble in water or salt solutions, but this characteristic solubility may readily be lost or decreased by subjecting the proteins to relatively small increases in temperature (up to 140 degrees Fahrenheit) or to mild acidity. This alteration in solubility is referred to as "denaturation." When the shape of such altered proteins is studied, it is found that they now approximate more closely the fibrous proteins. The denaturation of an enzyme or of a hormone usually deprives it of its characteristic biological activity. In some cases, if the exposure of the protein to the unfavorable conditions is not prolonged unduly, its denaturation can be reversed by restoring normal conditions. The protein then regains its characteristic solubility and its biological activity simultaneously.

It is obvious, therefore, that protein denaturation is associated with the conversion of a globular molecule to a rather fibrous one, and that this transformation is accompanied by the loss of some of the important biological properties of the protein. A natural deduction from these facts is that the peptide chains in the globular protein are coiled in a very specific way and that this characteristic folding is made possible by specific bonds between parts of the peptide chains. We can also make a deduction about the relative strength of these bonds. They must be much easier to rupture than ordinary peptide bonds, because the conditions required for denaturation are quite mild compared with those necessary for the cleavage of peptide bonds.

The nature of these special bonds has been the subject of much stimulating speculation. Among the several theories is one offered in 1936 by Alfred E. Mirsky of the Rockefeller Institute for Medical Research and Linus Pauling of the California Institute of Technology. They suggested that a major factor in conferring upon the extended peptide chain of a protein its characteristic folding is the presence of "hydrogen bonds." This hypothesis has been successful in accounting for many of the known differences in the properties of "native" and denatured proteins. According to the theory, there are a multitude of bonds formed by the "sharing" of a hydrogen atom of an amino group with an oxygen atom of a carboxyl group. Taken individually these hydrogen bonds are weak, but in a protein molecule with several hundred amino-nitrogen atoms and a correspondingly large number of carboxyl-oxygen atoms, these weak bonds reinforce one another so that a stable structure results.

To the concept of the protein molecule as a long polypeptide chain or chains composed of many amino acids must

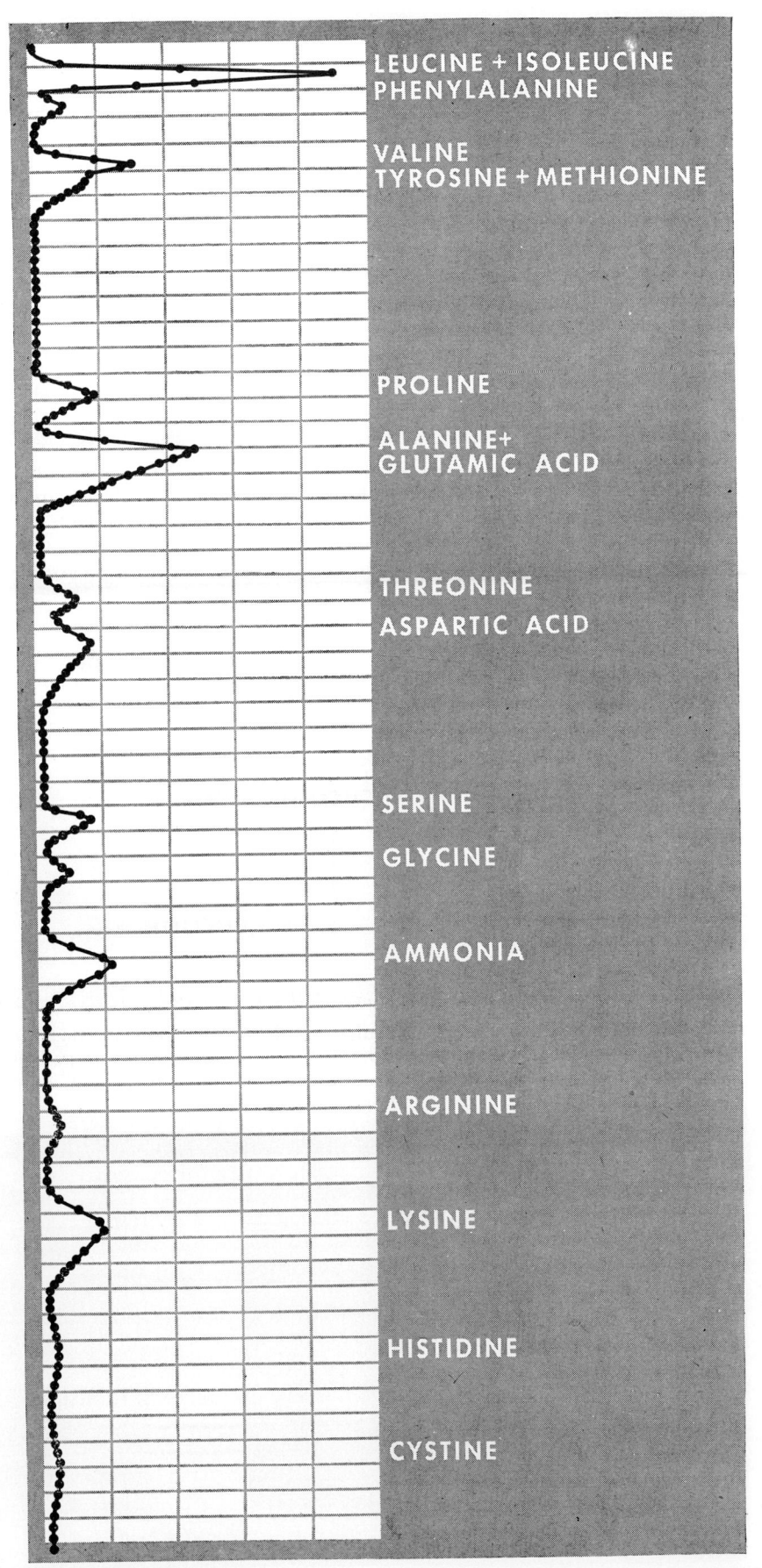

CHROMATOGRAPHY reveals amino acid content of decomposed protein beta-lactoglobulin. Vertical coordinate: amount of solvent passed through chromatographic tube; horizontal, concentration of amino acid in solvent.

HYDROGEN BONDS between parallel polypeptide chains have been postulated as one of the forces holding together a highly organized native protein molecule. Here the hydrogen bonds are indicated by dotted lines. In the hydrogen bond a hydrogen atom is shared by amino acids in each of the parallel polypeptide chains.

END GROUPS of insulin were identified by allowing them to combine with reagent (*upper left*). When insulin was broken down, end groups were still attached to reagent. Such work showed that insulin has four peptide chains joined by disulfide bonds (-S-S- *at right*). Two chains end in glycine (G) and two in phenylalanine (P).

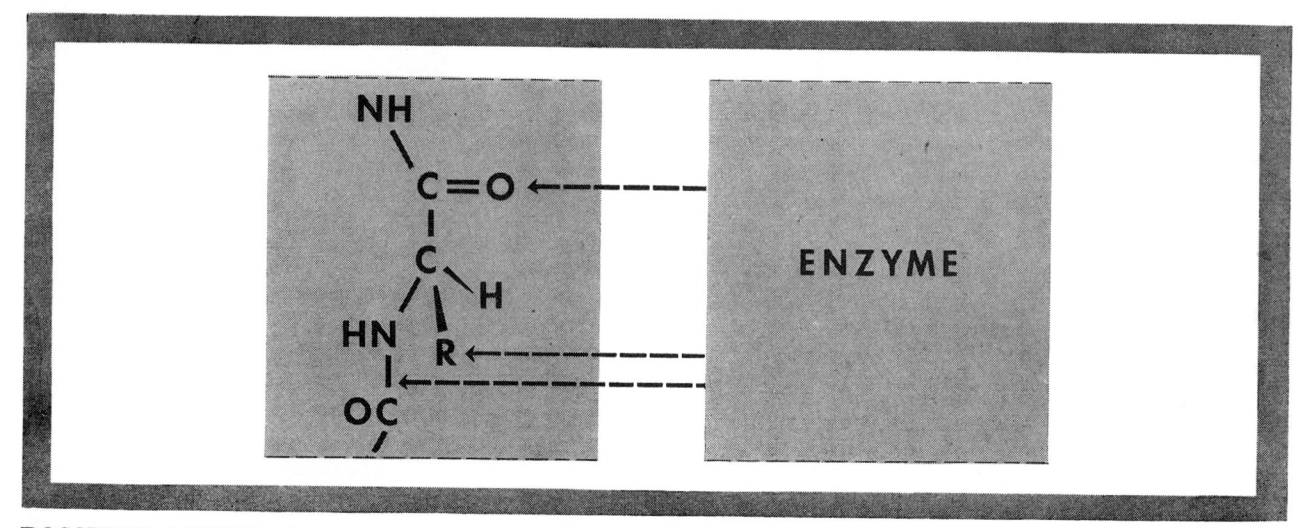

POSSIBLE ACTION of a protein-splitting enzyme is illustrated in this drawing. The enzyme molecule comes in contact with certain parts (*arrows*) of the protein molecule (*left*) in such a way as to make the sensitive peptide bond (*between C and NH at upper left*) more reactive. Only a segment of the protein molecule is shown.

therefore be added the idea that in each kind of protein the parts of the peptide chain have a characteristic internal arrangement which is responsible for that molecule's particular chemical and biological properties. Consequently the problem of protein structure involves not only the already formidable task of establishing the arrangement of the amino acids in the peptide chain, but even more difficult questions as to the nature and position of the bonds that are broken during denaturation.

Although the artificial creation of a protein molecule still lies beyond the powers of the chemist, it is no problem at all for the living organism. The living cell, whether of an amoeba or of a mammalian liver, performs the task of protein synthesis with rapidity and precision. Many organisms can use proteins foreign to their make-up, break them down to the component amino acids or peptides, and use the fragments to create their own characteristic proteins. Moreover, the proteins of a living organism are not laid down and kept intact throughout its life; rather there is a ceaseless breakdown and resynthesis of body proteins. In a sense, therefore, the problem of life is the problem of how living systems make proteins and how they constantly counteract the tendency toward protein degradation. Thus the study of the mechanisms by which cells synthesize proteins is perhaps the most challenging task of biochemistry.

The Making of a Bond

A logical starting point for this investigation is the comparatively simple question of how living systems put two amino acids together to form a peptide bond. Many laboratories in this country are actively engaged in the exploration of this question. Although no clear-cut answer can yet be given, there are several hints as to its possible solution.

Among the views that have been entertained is the theory that in living cells the formation of peptide bonds is effected by the same enzymes that cause the breakdown of the peptide bonds after death. The principal support for this hypothesis has come from the demonstration that protein-splitting enzymes can indeed link two amino acids together to form a peptide bond. But this process will occur only under certain specific conditions. The most important of these is the necessity of counteracting the natural tendency of the protein-splitting enzymes to effect the hydrolysis of peptide bonds. A simple experimental procedure for achieving this reversal of hydrolysis is to choose a reaction which will result in formation of an insoluble peptide that comes out of solution as fast as it is formed. By taking advantage of this fact, it is possible to show without question that protein-splitting enzymes

AMINO ACIDS are symbolized with acidic (*pointed*), neutral (*flat*) and basic (*notched*) ends. They are thus acidic (*left*), neutral (*center*) or basic.

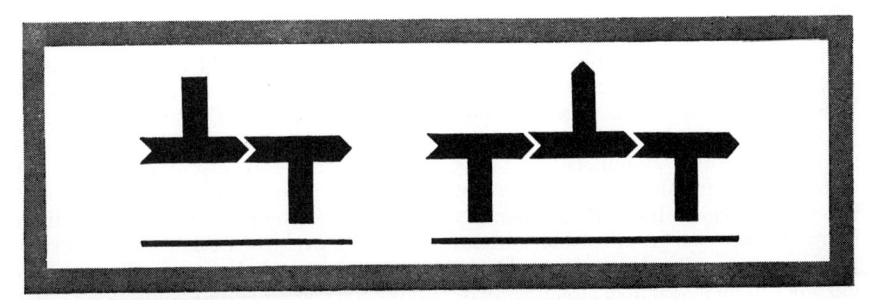

PEPTIDES are chains of amino acids joined acidic end to basic. Line below each peptide is a symbol for a longer chain of amino acids (*see below*).

FIBROUS PROTEIN is constructed of polypeptide chains (*parallel lines*). Some of the chains are joined by linkages between amino acid side chains.

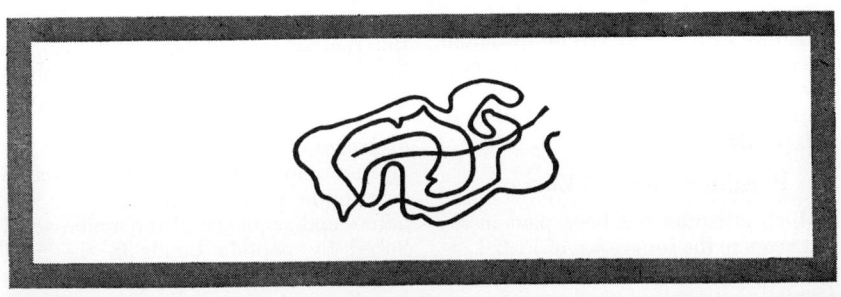

DENATURED GLOBULAR PROTEIN is a disorganized skein of polypeptide chains. The structure of the protein in its native state is thus destroyed.

NATIVE GLOBULAR PROTEIN is made up of organized polypeptide chains. The organization, here shown in two dimensions, occupies three.

can catalyze the synthesis of peptide bonds.

The attractive feature of the theory is the fact that these enzymes exhibit a striking specificity of action on peptide linkages. In the case of the protein-splitting enzymes, the specificity of enzyme action depends largely on the nature of the amino acids that participate in the formation of the peptide bond. What is more, these enzymes act only at peptide linkages that involve amino acids of the L-type, which we noted earlier to be characteristic of the protein constituents. For example, one enzyme may catalyze peptide synthesis only when the amino acid that contributes the alpha-carboxyl group for formation of a peptide is L-tyrosine or L-phenylalanine. Replacement of either of these two amino acids by any other amino acid, as far as tests made so far show, prevents action by the enzyme. Indeed, biochemists know of no other group of biocatalysts that compares with the protein-splitting enzymes in their selective action on peptide bonds. By virtue of this sharp specificity, therefore, these enzymes are well fitted to direct, precisely and reproducibly, the complex sequence of successive peptide syntheses required for the formation of a protein.

To observe their synthetic action, however, it is necessary to remove the product from the reaction. In other words, work must be put into the system to counteract the natural tendency of the enzyme to hydrolyze the product after it is synthesized. It follows that if enzymes do actually perform peptide synthesis in cells, this process must be coupled to another reaction that provides the necessary chemical energy. There is excellent reason for believing that the chemical energy comes from the breakdown of foodstuffs such as glucose by oxidation or fermentation, but it has not been possible as yet to demonstrate that the breakdown of glucose is linked directly with peptide-bond synthesis in cells.

Possible Sources of Energy

Much attention has been paid in recent years to the suggestion of Fritz Lipmann of the Massachusetts General Hospital that peptide bond synthesis involves the intermediate formation of amino-acid derivatives of phosphoric acid. The source of these phosphoric-acid intermediates, according to Lipmann's theory, is a "high energy" phosphate carrier such as adenosinetriphosphate. The latter substance has been shown to play a decisive role in the exchanges of chemical energy that occur during the metabolic breakdown of sugars. Work in several laboratories during recent years has provided experimental evidence that phosphate-containing intermediates may indeed be involved in the biological formation of certain amides, such as hippuric acid or glutamine. These amides are closely related structurally to the peptides; they differ from the latter only in that the CO-NH bond links an amino acid to a non-amino acid group. The intervention of adenosinetriphosphate in the synthesis of the amide bond of glutamine, first demonstrated by the late John F. Speck of the University of Chicago, is of especial interest because this glutamic acid derivative is widely distributed in the tissues and fluids of animals and plants.

Although the experimental data offered in support of the Lipmann theory are impressive, they do not yet present a picture that would account satisfactorily for the specificity of peptide-bond formation. Each of the two theories discussed above thus contributes to a different, but equally essential, facet of the problem; it may well be that the two theories are complementary, rather than mutually exclusive. Such a view is supported by work begun in Bergmann's laboratory in 1937 and continued by the author at Yale University. These experiments have shown that protein-splitting enzymes will catalyze the hydrolysis and synthesis of peptide bonds. They have also shown that the same enzymes will cause reactions in which one of the two components contributing to a peptide bond may be replaced by another, without the need for the introduction of appreciable chemical energy but with the same specificity exhibited in synthesis and hydrolysis.

If these results should prove to have general significance, it would mean that an amide containing an amino acid derivative linked to ammonia (*e.g.*, glutamine) could exchange the ammonia for an amino acid or even a peptide. The energy for this process would come from the synthesis of glutamine, which, as Speck has shown, may involve a phosphate-containing intermediate. The specificity of the enzyme that catalyzes the exchange of the amide-nitrogen for the alpha-amino nitrogen of an amino acid or peptide would then determine the nature and sequence of the amino acids linked by peptide bonds in the final product. As a further consequence of this hypothesis, it would follow that a simple peptide composed of two or three amino acids would be transformed, in the presence of a suitable enzyme, into a longer chain by the replacement of one of the amino acids by a peptide. Energy would be required for the formation of the simple initial peptide, perhaps via a phosphate-containing intermediate, but the further course of peptide synthesis would be under the directive control of the highly specific enzymes that act at peptide bonds.

Another avenue of approach to the problem of how peptide bonds are formed is to seek out biological systems that exhibit unusual requirements for certain peptides, as compared with their demand for the individual amino acids of which these peptides are composed. If a bacterial cell, for example, uses a peptide for growth more efficiently than it does the amino acids, that would suggest that the rate of synthesis of the peptide controls the rate of utilization of the amino acids for protein formation. This approach is being explored in studies of the bacterial metabolism of peptides at Yale University by Sofia Simmonds in collaboration with the author. They may be expected to provide valuable biological material for the unequivocal testing of the various hypotheses relating to the mechanism of peptide-bond formation.

Nature's Noblest Structure

From all this it must be abundantly evident that the decisive discoveries in the study of the biological synthesis of proteins still lie in the future. Whatever the answer concerning the enzymatic mechanism of peptide-bond formation turns out to be, clearly it will provide only a part of the picture of the total process. What, for example, is the nature of the forces that confer upon the biologically interesting proteins, such as the enzymes and hormones, their characteristic physical, chemical and physiological properties? A denatured insulin molecule, though rendered inactive as a hormone, presumably still contains the same amino acids as the active molecule, and the peptide linkages that join these amino acids apparently have not been broken measurably. How, then, is the peptide chain molded in the living cell so as to form an active hormone with its specific attributes? Are we dealing here with an intricate mechanism whereby a model of the finished product is available as a matrix upon which the fragments are assembled?

These questions cannot be answered as yet, but it is well to remember that biochemistry is a relative newcomer among the scientific disciplines. Its growth has been meteoric, and it is exerting a decisive influence on the future development of all aspects of biology and their applications to medicine and agriculture. In the last analysis all the problems of biology meet in the unsolved problems concerning the structure and the mode of action of proteins. In groping for new experimental avenues into this great unknown, the protein chemist is thus probing into the basic questions of life. Whether he succeeds or not, he cannot help being filled with a sense of awe and humility in the face of what has justly been called the noblest piece of architecture produced by Nature—the protein molecule.

LACTOSE AND LACTASE

NORMAN KRETCHMER
October 1972

Lactose is milk sugar; the enzyme lactase breaks it down. For want of lactase most adults cannot digest milk. In populations that drink milk the adults have more lactase, perhaps through natural selection

Milk is the universal food of newborn mammals, but some human infants cannot digest it because they lack sufficient quantities of lactase, the enzyme that breaks down lactose, or milk sugar. Adults of all animal species other than man also lack the enzyme—and so, it is now clear, do most human beings after between two and four years of age. That this general adult deficiency in lactase has come as a surprise to physiologists and nutritionists can perhaps be attributed to a kind of ethnic chauvinism, since the few human populations in which tolerance of lactose has been found to exceed intolerance include most northern European and white American ethnic groups.

Milk is a nearly complete human food, and in powdered form it can be conveniently stored and shipped long distances. Hence it is a popular source of protein and other nutrients in many programs of aid to nutritionally impoverished children, including American blacks. The discovery that many of these children are physiologically intolerant to lactose is therefore a matter of concern and its implications are currently being examined by such agencies as the U.S. Office of Child Development and the Protein Advisory Group of the United Nations System.

Lactose is one of the three major solid components of milk and its only carbohydrate; the other components are fats and proteins. Lactose is a disaccharide composed of the monosaccharides glucose and galactose. It is synthesized only by the cells of the lactating mammary gland, through the reaction of glucose with the compound uridine diphosphate galactose [*see illustrations on next page*]. One of the proteins found in milk, alpha-lactalbumin, is required for the synthesis of lactose. This protein apparently does not actually enter into the reaction; what it does is "specify" the action of the enzyme galactosyl transferase, modifying the enzyme so that in the presence of alpha-lactalbumin and glucose it catalyzes the synthesis of lactose.

In the nonlactating mammary gland, where alpha-lactalbumin is not present, the enzyme synthesizes instead of lactose a more complicated carbohydrate, N-acetyl lactosamine. Test-tube studies have shown that alpha-lactalbumin is manufactured only in the presence of certain hormones: insulin, cortisone, estrogen and prolactin; its synthesis is inhibited by the hormone progesterone. It is when progesterone levels decrease late in pregnancy that the manufacture of alpha-lactalbumin, and thus of lactose, is initiated [*see the article "Milk," by Stuart Patton, beginning on page 117*].

The concentration of lactose in milk from different sources varies considerably. Human milk is the sweetest, with 7.5 grams of lactose per 100 milliliters of milk. Cow's milk has 4.5 grams per 100 milliliters. The only mammals that do not have any lactose—or any other carbohydrate—in their milk are certain of the Pinnipedia: the seals, sea lions and walruses of the Pacific basin. If these animals are given lactose in any form, they become sick. (In 1933 there was a report of a baby walrus that was fed cow's milk while being shipped from Alaska to California. The animal suffered from severe diarrhea throughout the voyage and was very sick by the time it arrived in San Diego.) Of these pinnipeds the California sea lion has been the most intensively studied. No alpha-lactalbumin is synthesized by its mammary gland. When alpha-lactalbumin from either rat's milk or cow's milk is added to a preparation of sea lion mammary gland in a test tube, however, the glandular tissue does manufacture lactose.

In general, low concentrations of lactose are associated with high concentrations of milk fat (which is particularly useful to marine mammals). The Pacific pinnipeds have more than 35 grams of fat per 100 milliliters of milk, compared with less than four grams in the cow. In the whale and the bear (an ancient ancestor of which may also be an ancestor of the Pacific pinnipeds) the lactose in milk is low and the fat content is high.

Lactase, the enzyme that breaks down lactose ingested in milk or a milk product, is a specific intestinal beta-galactosidase that acts only on lactose, primarily in the jejunum, the second of the small intestine's three main segments. The functional units of the wall of the small intestine are the villus (composed of metabolically active, differentiated, nondividing cells) and the crypt (a set of dividing cells from which those of the villus are derived). Lactase is not present in the dividing cells. It appears in the differentiated cells, specifically within the brush border of the cells at the surface of the villus [*see illustrations on page 38*]. Lactase splits the disaccharide lactose into its two component monosaccharides, glucose and galactose. Some of the released glucose can be utilized directly by the cells of the villus; the remainder, along with the galactose, enters the bloodstream, and both sugars are metabolized by the liver. Neither Gary Gray of the Stanford University School of Medicine nor other investigators have been able to distinguish any qualitative biochemical or physical difference among the lactases isolated from the intestine of infants, tolerant adults and intolerant adults. The difference appears to be

LACTOSE, a disaccharide composed of the monosaccharides glucose and galactose, is the carbohydrate of milk, the other major components of which are fats, proteins and water.

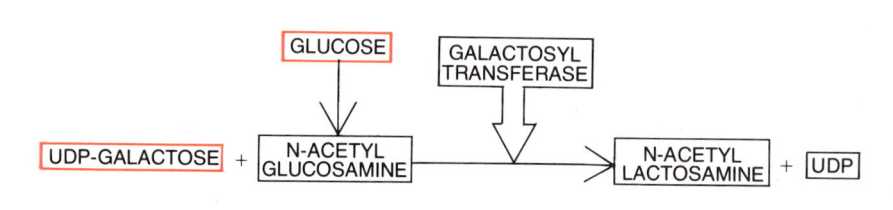

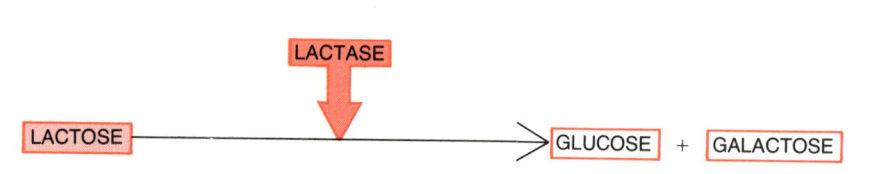

SYNTHESIS OF LACTOSE in the mammary gland begins late in pregnancy when specific hormones and the protein alpha-lactalbumin are present. The latter modifies the enzyme galactosyl transferase, "specifying" it so that it catalyzes the synthesis of lactose from glucose and galactose (*top*). In the nonlactating gland the glucose takes part in a different reaction (*middle*). In intestine lactase breaks down lactose to glucose and galactose (*bottom*).

merely quantitative; there is simply very little lactase in the intestine of a lactose-intolerant person. In the intestine of Pacific pinnipeds, Philip Sunshine of the Stanford School of Medicine found, there is no lactase at all, even in infancy.

Lactase is not present in the intestine of the embryo or the fetus until the middle of the last stage of gestation. Its activity attains a maximum immediately after birth. Thereafter it decreases, reaching a low level, for example, immediately after weaning in the rat and after one and a half to three years in most children. The exact mechanism involved in the appearance and disappearance of the lactase is not known, but such a pattern of waxing and waning activity is common in the course of development; in general terms, one can say that it results from differential action of the gene or genes concerned.

Soon after the turn of the century the distinguished American pediatrician Abraham Jacobi pointed out that diarrhea in babies could be associated with the ingestion of carbohydrates. In 1921 another pediatrician, John Howland, said that "there is with many patients an abnormal response on the part of the intestinal tract to carbohydrates, which expresses itself in the form of diarrhea and excessive fermentation." He suggested as the cause a deficiency in the hydrolysis, or enzymatic breakdown, of lactose.

The physiology is now well established. If the amount of lactose presented to the intestinal cells exceeds the hydrolytic capacity of the available lactase (whether because the lactase level is low or because an unusually large amount of lactose is ingested), a portion of the lactose remains undigested. Some of it passes into the blood and is eventually excreted in the urine. The remainder moves on into the large intestine, where two processes ensue. One is physical: the lactose molecules increase the particle content of the intestinal fluid compared with the fluid in cells outside the intestine and therefore by osmotic action draw water out of the tissues into the intestine. The other is biochemical: the glucose is fermented by the bacteria in the colon. Organic acids and carbon dioxide are generated and the symptoms can be those of any fermentative diarrhea, including a bloated feeling, flatulence, belching, cramps and a watery, explosive diarrhea.

At the end of the 1950's Paolo Durand of the University of Genoa and Aaron Holzel and his colleagues at the University of Manchester reported detailed studies of infants who were unable to digest lactose and who reacted to milk sugar with severe diarrhea, malnutrition and even death. This work stimulated a revival of interest in lactose and lactase, and there followed a period of active investigation of lactose intolerance. Many cases were reported, including some in which lactase inactivity could be demonstrated in tissue taken from the patient's intestine by biopsy. It became clear that intolerance in infants could be a congenital condition (as in Holzel's two patients, who were siblings) or, more frequently, could be secondary to various diseases and other stresses: cystic fibrosis, celiac disease, malnutrition, the ingestion of certain drugs, surgery and even non-specific diarrhea. During this period of investigation, it should be noted, intolerance to lactose was generally assumed to be the unusual condition and the condition worthy of study.

In 1965 Pedro Cuatrecasas and his colleagues and Theodore M. Bayless and Norton S. Rosensweig, all of whom were then at the Johns Hopkins School of Medicine, administered lactose to American blacks and whites, none of whom had had gastrointestinal complaints, and reported some startling findings. Whereas only from 6 to 15 percent of the whites showed clinical symptoms of intolerance, about 70 percent of the blacks were intolerant. This immediately suggested that many human adults might be unable to digest lactose and, more specifically, that there might be significant differences among ethnic groups. The possibility was soon confirmed: G. C. Cook and S. Kajubi of Makerere University College examined two different tribes in Uganda. They found that only 20 percent of the adults of the cattle-herding Tussi tribe were intolerant to lactose but that 80 percent of the nonpastoral Ganda were intolerant. Soon one paper after another reported a general intolerance to lactose among many ethnic groups, including Japanese, other Orientals, Jews in Israel, Eskimos and South American Indians.

In these studies various measures of intolerance were applied. One was the appearance of clinical symptoms—flatulence and diarrhea—after the ingestion of a dose of lactose, which was generally standardized at two grams of lactose per kilogram (2.2 pounds) of body weight, up to a maximum of either 50 or 100 grams. Another measure was a finding of low lactase activity (less than two units per gram of wet weight of tissue) determined through an intestinal biopsy after ingestion of the same dose of lactose. A third was an elevation of blood glucose of less than 20 milligrams per 100 milliliters of blood after ingestion of the lactose. Since clinical symptoms are variable and the biopsy method is inconvenient for the subject being tested, the blood glucose method is preferable. It is a direct measure of lactose breakdown, and false-negative results are rare if the glucose is measured 15 minutes after lactose is administered.

By 1970 enough data had been accumulated to indicate that many more groups all over the world are intolerant to lactose than are tolerant. As a matter of fact, real adult tolerance to lactose has so far been observed only in northern Europeans, approximately 90 percent of whom tolerate lactose, and in the

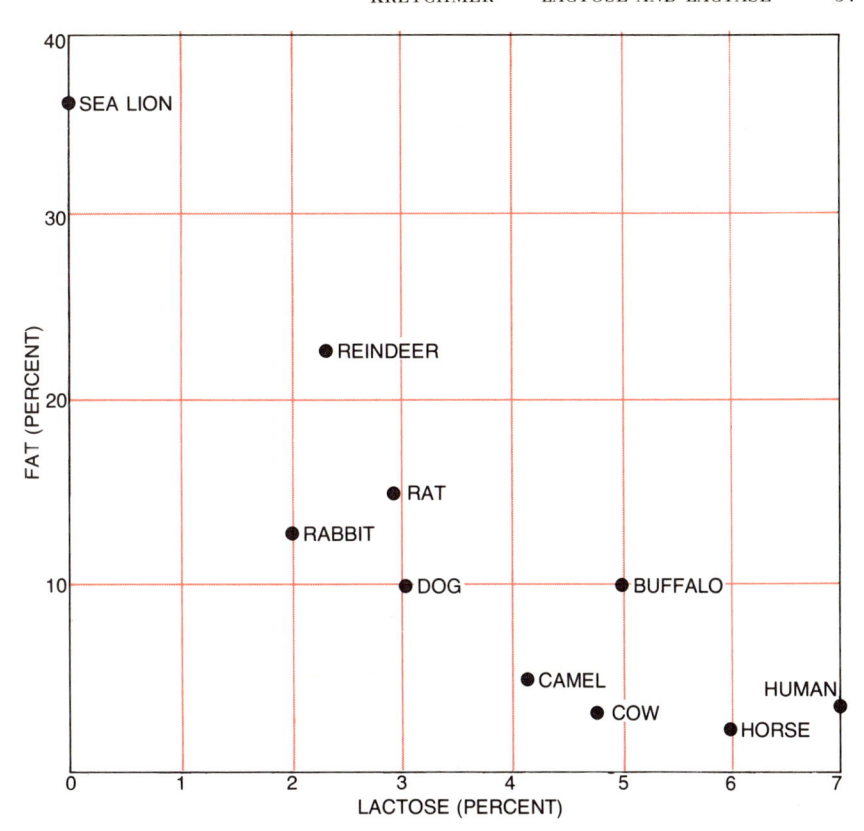

CONCENTRATION OF LACTOSE varies with the source of the milk. In general the less lactose, the more fat, which can also be utilized by the newborn animal as an energy source.

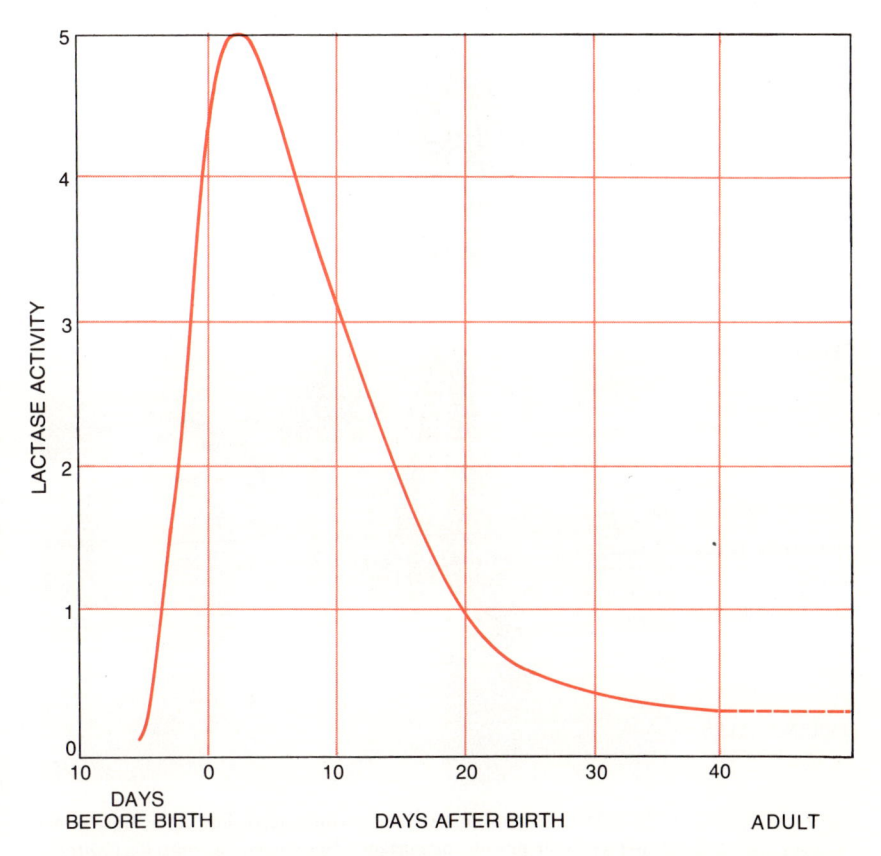

LACTASE is present in mammals other than man, and in most humans, in the fetus before birth and in infancy. The general shape of the curve of enzyme activity, shown here for the rat, is about the same in all species. Enzyme activity, given here in relative units, is determined by measuring glucose release from intestinal tissue in the presence of lactose.

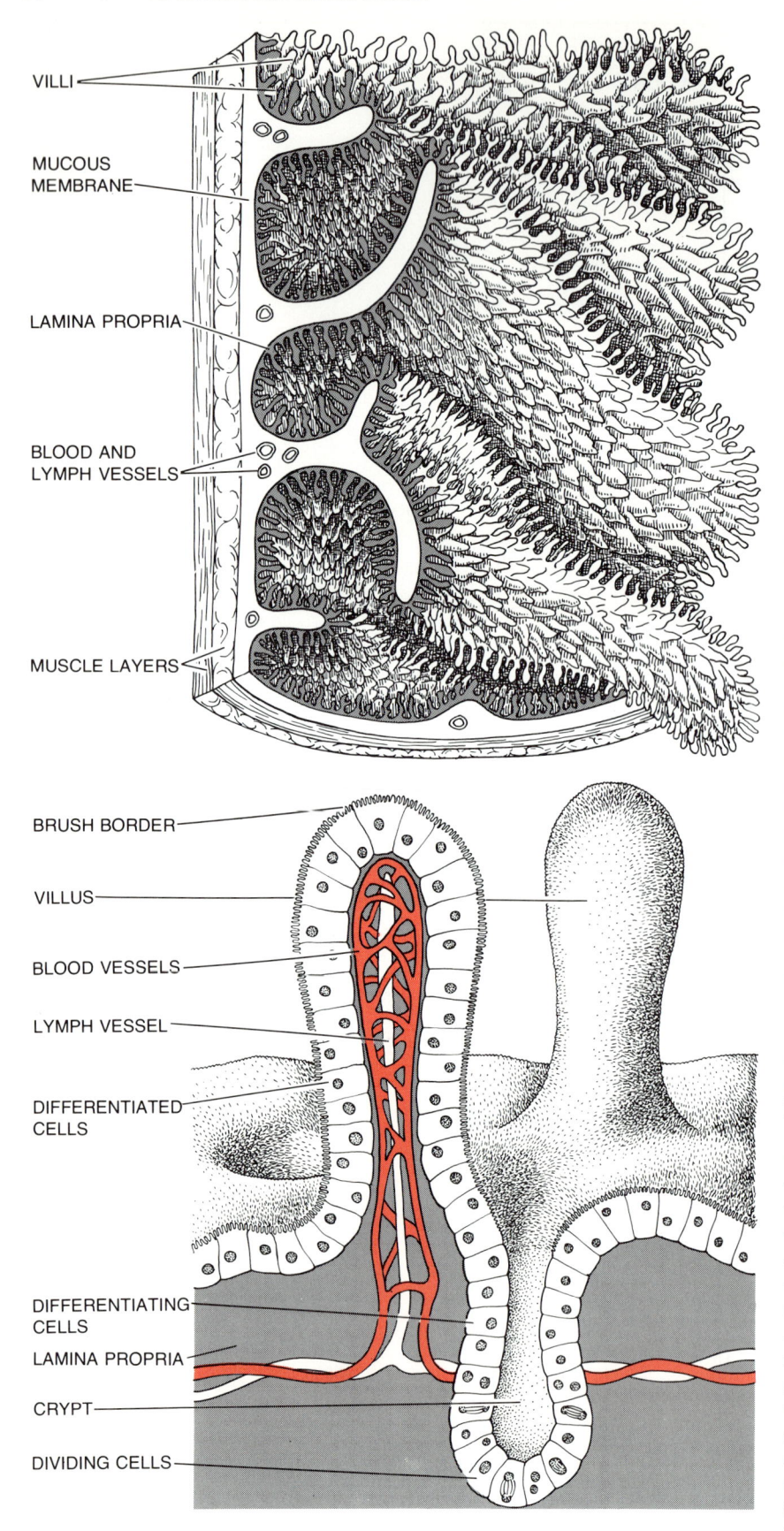

38   I · NUTRITION AND MALNUTRITION

members of two nomadic pastoral tribes in Africa, of whom about 80 percent are tolerant. Although many other generally tolerant groups will be found, they will always belong to a minority of the human species. In this situation it is clearly more interesting and potentially more fruitful to focus the investigation on tolerant people in an effort to explain adult tolerance, a characteristic in which man differs from all other mammals.

There are two kinds of explanation of adult tolerance to lactose. The first, and perhaps the most immediately apparent, originates with the fact that most people who tolerate lactose have a history of drinking milk. Maybe the mere presence of milk in the diet suffices to stimulate lactase activity in the individual, perhaps by "turning on" genes that encode the synthesis of the enzyme. Individual enzymatic adaptation to an environmental stimulus is well known, but it is not transferable genetically. The other explanation of tolerance is based on the concept of evolution through natural selection. If in particular populations it became biologically advantageous to be able to digest milk, then the survival of individuals with a genetic mutation that led to higher intestinal lactase activity in adulthood would have been favored. An individual who derived his ability to digest lactose from this classical form of Darwinian adaptation would be expected to be able to transfer the trait genetically.

These two points of view have become the subject of considerable controversy. I suspect that each of the explanations is valid for some of the adult tolerance being observed, and I should like to examine both of them.

The possibility of individual adaptation to lactose has been considered since the beginning of the century, usually through attempts to relate lactase activity to the concentration of milk in the diet of animals. Almost without exception the studies showed that although there was a slight increase in lactase activity when a constant diet of milk or milk products was consumed, there was no significant change in the characteristic curve reflecting the developmental rise and fall of enzymatic activity. Recently there have been reports pointing toward adaptation, however. Some studies, with human subjects as well as rats, indicated that continued intensive feeding of milk or lactose not only made it possible for the individual to tolerate the sugar but also resulted in a measurable increase in lactase activity. The discrepancy among the findings could be partly

WALL OF SMALL INTESTINE, seen in longitudinal section (*top*), has outer muscle layers, a submucosa layer and an inner mucous membrane. The mucous membrane (*bottom*) has a connective-tissue layer (lamina propria), which contains blood and lymph capillaries, and an inner surface of epithelial cells. The cells multiply and differentiate in the crypts and migrate to the villi. At what stage the lactase is manufactured is not known; it is found primarily in the microvilli, which constitute the brush border of the differentiated cells.

attributable to improvement in methods for assaying the enzyme activity.

On balance it would appear that individual adaptation may be able to explain at least some cases of adult tolerance. I shall cite two recent studies. John Godell, working in Lagos, selected six Nigerian medical students who were absolutely intolerant to lactose and who showed no physiological evidence of lactose hydrolysis. He fed them increasing amounts of the sugar for six months. Godell found that although the students did develop tolerance for the lactose, there was nevertheless no evidence of an increase of glucose in the blood—and thus of enzymatic adaptation—following test doses of the sugar. The conjecture is that the diet brought about a change in the bacterial flora in the intestine, and that the ingested lactose was being metabolized by the new bacteria.

In our laboratory at the Stanford School of Medicine Emanuel Lebenthal and Sunshine found that in rats given lactose the usual pattern of a developmental decrease in lactase activity is maintained but the activity level is somewhat higher at the end of the experiment. The rise in activity does not appear to be the result of an actual increase in lactase synthesis, however. We treated the rats with actinomycin, which prevents the synthesis of new protein from newly activated genes. The actinomycin had no effect on the slight increase in lactase activity, indicating that the mechanism leading to the increase was not gene activation. It appears, rather, that the presence of additional amounts of the enzyme's substrate, lactose, somehow "protects" the lactase from degradation. Such a process has been noted in many other enzyme-substrate systems. The additional lactase activity that results from this protection is sufficient to improve the rat's tolerance of lactose, but that additional activity is dependent on the continued presence of the lactose.

Testing the second hypothesis—that adult lactose tolerance is primarily the result of a long-term process of genetic selection—is more complicated. It involves data and reasoning from such disparate areas as history, anthropology, nutrition, genetics and sociology as well as biochemistry.

As I have noted, the work of Cuatrecasas, of Bayless and Rosensweig and of Cook and Kajubi in the mid-1960's pointed to the likelihood of significant differences in adult lactose tolerance among ethnic groups. It also suggested that one ought to study in particular black Americans and their ancestral populations in Africa. The west coast of Africa was the primary source of slaves for the New World. With the objective of studying lactose tolerance in Nigeria, we developed a joint project with a group from the University of Lagos Teaching Hospital headed by Olikoye Ransome-Kuti.

The four largest ethnic groups in Nigeria are the Yoruba in western Nigeria, the Ibo in the east and the Fulani and Hausa in the north. These groups have different origins and primary occupations. The Yoruba and the Ibo differ somewhat anthropometrically, but both are Negro ethnic groups that probably came originally from the Congo Basin; they were hunters and gatherers who became farmers. They eventually settled south of the Niger and Benue rivers in an area infested with the tsetse fly, so that they never acquired cattle (or any other beast of burden). Hence it was not until recent times that milk appeared in their diet beyond the age of weaning. After the colonization of their part of Nigeria by the British late in the 19th century, a number of Yoruba and Ibo, motivated by their intense desire for education, migrated to England and northern Europe; they acquired Western dietary habits and in some cases Western spouses, and many eventually returned to Nigeria.

The Fulani are Hamites who have been pastoral people for thousands of years, originally perhaps in western Asia and more recently in northwestern Africa. Wherever they went, they took their cattle with them, and many of the Fulani are still nomads who herd their cattle from one grazing ground to another. About 300 years ago the Fulani appeared in what is now Nigeria and waged war on the Hausa. (The Fulani also tried to invade Yorubaland but were defeated by the tsetse fly.) After the invasion of the Hausa region some of the Fulani moved into villages and towns.

As a result of intermarriage between the Fulani and the Hausa there appeared a new group known as the town-Fulani or the Hausa-Fulani, whose members no longer raise cattle and whose ingestion of lactose is quite different from that of the pastoral Fulani. The pastoral Fulani do their milking in the early morning and drink some fresh milk. The milk reaches the market in the villages and towns only in a fermented form, however, as a kind of yogurt called *nono*. As the *nono* stands in the morning sun it becomes a completely fermented, watery preparation, which is then thickened with millet or some other cereal. The final product is almost completely

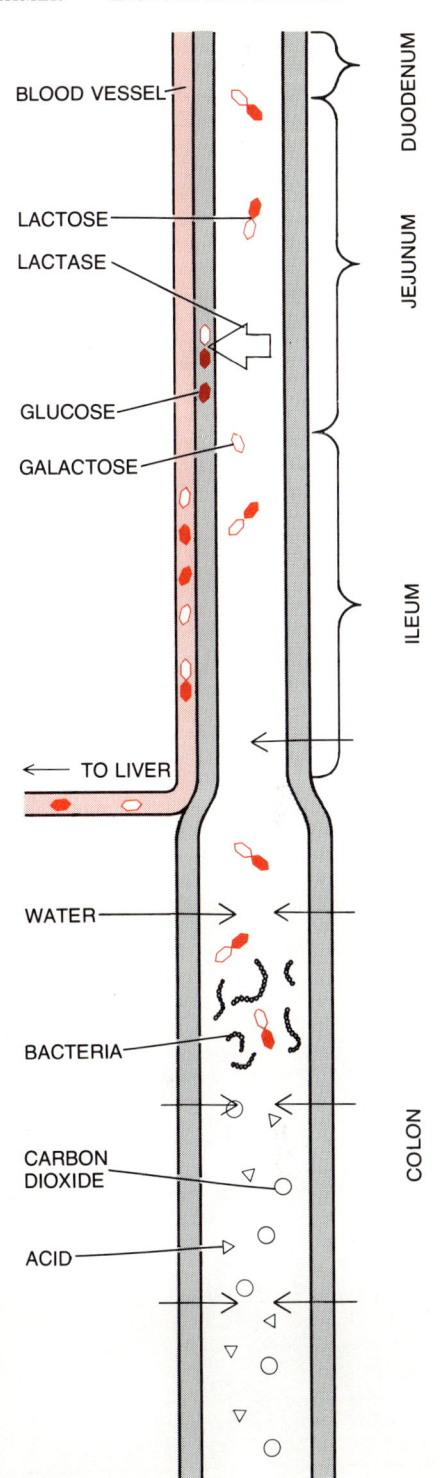

DIGESTION OF LACTOSE is accomplished primarily in the jejunum, where lactase splits it into glucose and galactose. Some glucose is utilized locally; the rest enters the bloodstream with the galactose and both are utilized in the liver. In the absence of enough lactase some undigested lactose enters the bloodstream; most goes on into the ileum and the colon, where it draws water from the tissues into the intestine by osmotic action. The undigested lactose is also fermented by bacteria in the colon, giving rise to various acids and carbon dioxide gas.

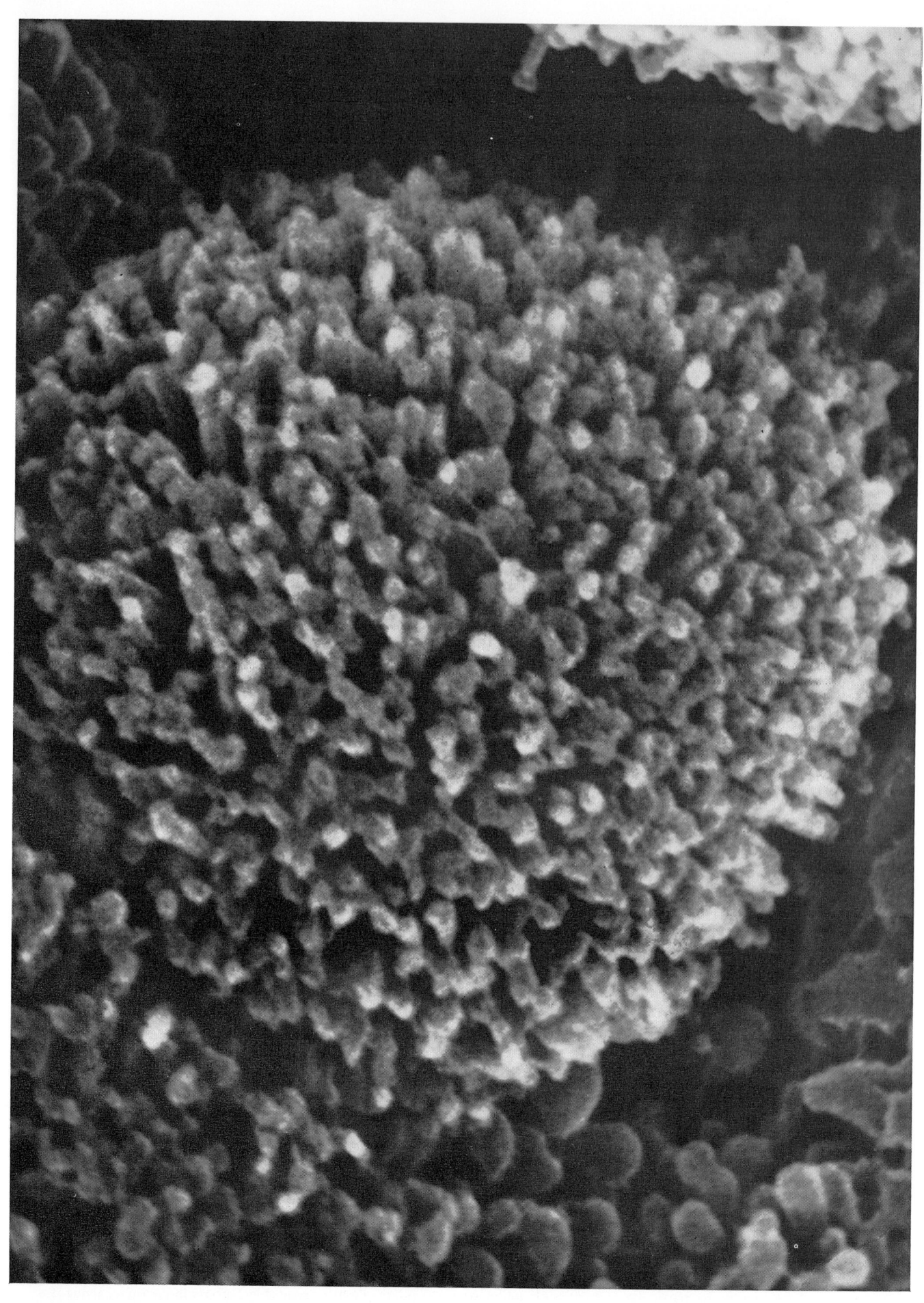

LACTOSE IS DIGESTED BY LACTASE in the intestine, a single epithelial cell of which is enlarged 37,500 diameters in this scanning electron micrograph made by Jeanne M. Riddle of the Wayne State University School of Medicine. The cell, on the surface of one of the finger-like villi that stud the lining of the intestine, is in turn covered by innumerable fine processes called microvilli.

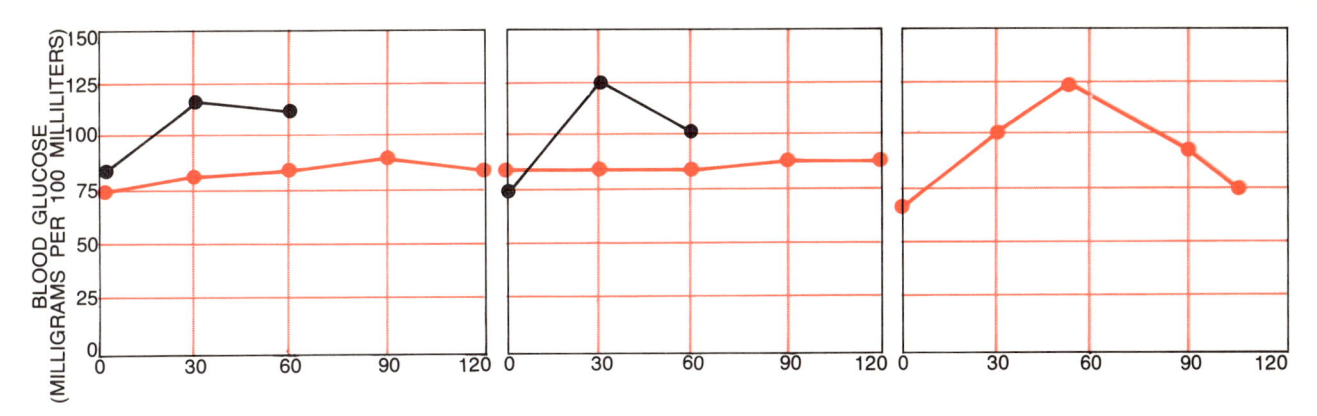

LACTOSE INTOLERANCE is determined by measuring blood glucose after ingestion of lactose. The absence of a significant rise in blood glucose after lactose ingestion (color) as contrasted with a rise in blood glucose after ingestion of sucrose, another sugar (black), indicates that a Yoruba male (left) and an American Jewish male (middle) are lactose-intolerant. On the other hand, the definite rise in blood glucose after ingestion of lactose in a Fulani male (right) shows that the Fulani is tolerant to lactose.

free of lactose and can be ingested without trouble even by a person who cannot digest lactose.

We tested members of each of these Nigerian populations. Of all the Yorubas above the age of four who were tested, we found only one person in whom the blood glucose rose to more than 20 milligrams per 100 milliliters following administration of the test dose of lactose. She was a nurse who had spent six years in the United Kingdom and had grown accustomed to a British diet that included milk. At first, she said, the milk disagreed with her, but later she could tolerate it with no adverse side effects. None of the Ibos who were studied showed an elevation of glucose in blood greater than 20 milligrams per 100 milliliters. (The major problem in all these studies is determining ethnic purity. All the Yorubas and Ibos who participated in this portion of the study indicated that there had been no intermarriages in their families.) Most of the Hausa and Hausa-Fulani

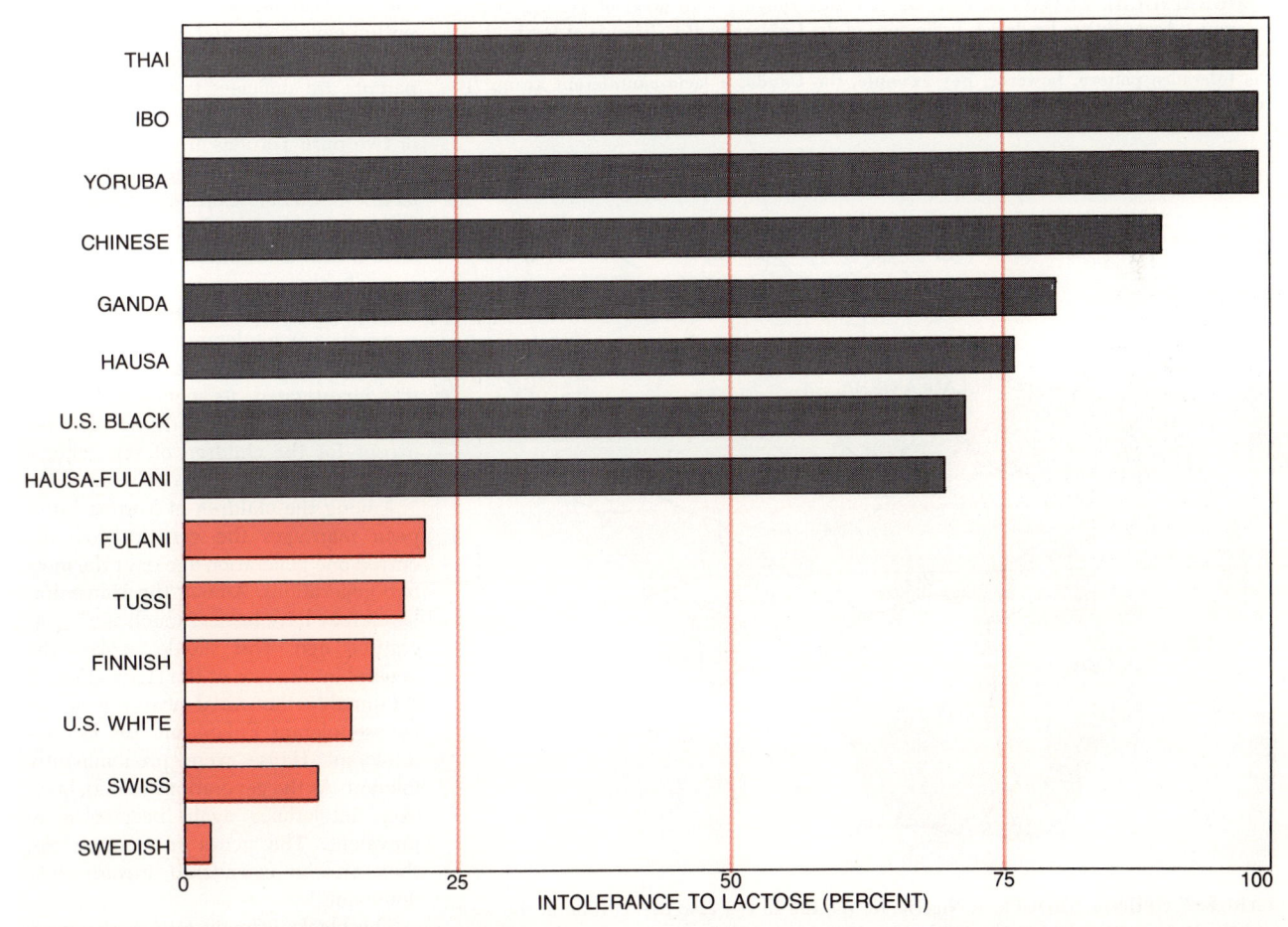

INTOLERANCE VARIES WIDELY among populations. The bars are based on tests conducted by a number of investigators by different methods; they may not be strictly comparable or accurately reflect the situation in entire populations. Among the groups studied to date lactose intolerance is prevalent except among northern Europeans (and their descendants) and herders in Africa.

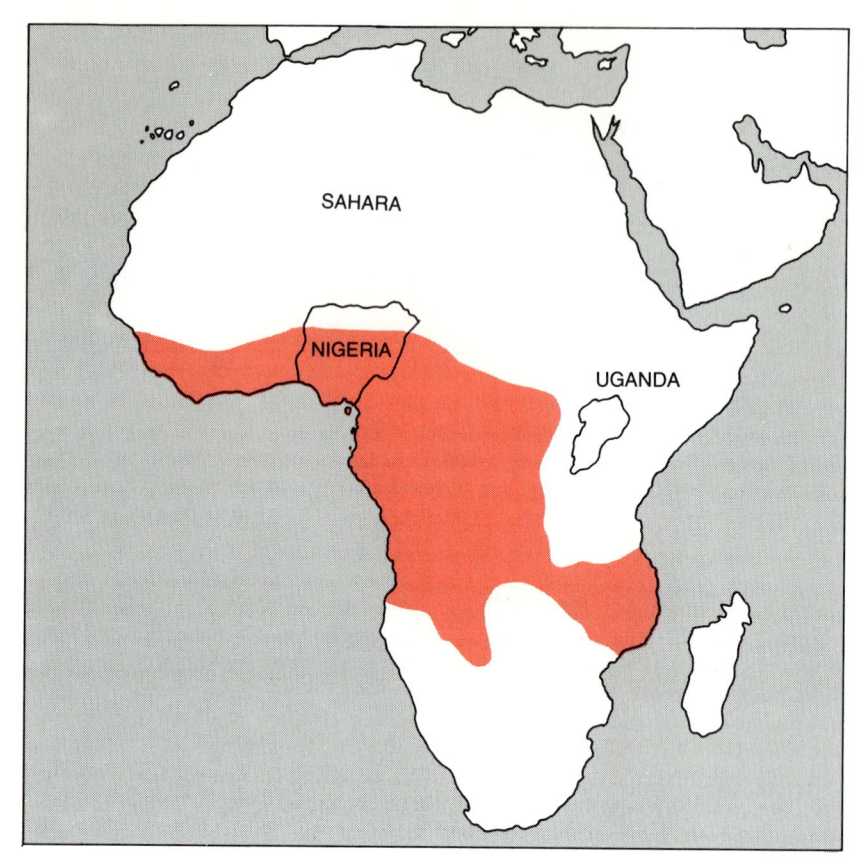

GEOGRAPHICAL EXTENT of dairying coincides roughly with areas of general lactose tolerance. According to Frederick J. Simoons of the University of California at Davis, there is a broad belt (*color*) across Africa in which dairying is not traditional. Migrations affect the tolerance pattern, however. For example, the Ganda, a lactose-intolerant group living in Uganda, came to that milk-drinking region from the nonmilking central Congo.

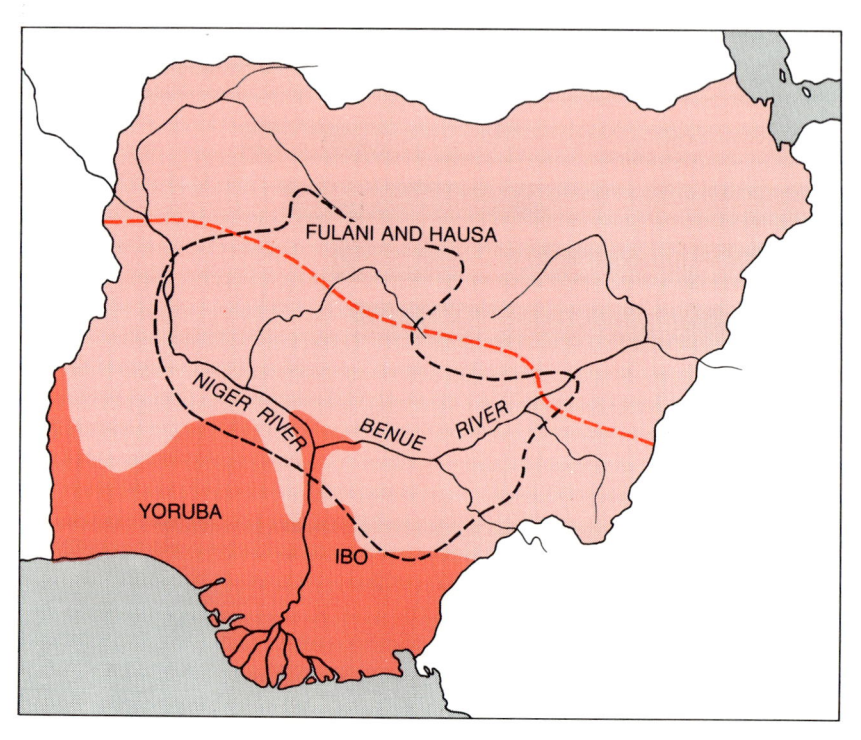

LARGEST ETHNIC GROUPS in Nigeria are the Ibo in the east, the Yoruba in the west and the Hausa and Fulani in the north. Map shows regions of mangrove swamp or forest (*dark color*) and grassland or desert (*light color*). Southern livestock limit (*broken colored line*) is set by climate, vegetation and tsetse fly infestation (*broken black line*).

(70 to 80 percent) were intolerant to lactose. In contrast most of the nomadic Fulani (78 percent) were tolerant to it. In their ability to hydrolyze lactose they resembled the pastoral Tussi of Uganda and northern Europeans more than they resembled their nearest neighbors.

Once the distribution of lactose intolerance and tolerance was determined in the major Nigerian populations, we went on to study the genetics of the situation by determining the results of mixed marriages. One of the common marriages in western Nigeria is between a Yoruba male and a British or other northern European female; the reverse situation is less common. Our tests showed that when a tolerant northern European marries a lactose-intolerant Yoruba, the offspring are most likely to be lactose-tolerant. If a tolerant child resulting from such a marriage marries a pure Yoruba, then the children are also predominantly tolerant. There is no sex linkage of the genes involved: in the few cases in which a Yoruba female had married a northern European male, the children were predominantly tolerant.

On the basis of these findings one can say that lactose tolerance is transmitted genetically and is dominant, that is, genes for tolerance from one of the parents are sufficient to make the child tolerant. On the other hand, the children of two pure Yorubas are always intolerant to lactose, as are the children of a lactose-intolerant European female and a Yoruba male. In other words, intolerance is also transmitted genetically and is probably a recessive trait, that is, both parents must be lactose-intolerant to produce an intolerant child. When the town-dwelling royal line of the Fulani was investigated, its members were all found to be unable to digest lactose—except for the children of one wife, a pastoral Fulani, who were tolerant.

Among the children of Yoruba-European marriages the genetic cross occurred one generation ago or at the most two generations. Among the Hausa-Fulani it may have been as much as 15 generations ago. This should explain the general intolerance of the Hausa-Fulani. Presumably the initial offspring of the lactose-tolerant Fulani and the lactose-intolerant Hausa were predominantly tolerant. As the generations passed, however, intolerance again became more prevalent. The genes for lactase can therefore be considered incompletely dominant.

The blacks brought to America were primarily Yoruba or Ibo or similar West African peoples who were originally intolerant to lactose. American blacks have been in this country for between 10 and 15 generations, in the course of which a certain complement of white northern European genes has entered the black population. Presumably as a result lactose intolerance among American blacks has been reduced to approximately 70 percent. One can speculate that if this gene flow eventually stopped, lactose intolerance would approach 100 percent among American blacks.

What events in human cultural history might have influenced the development of tolerance to lactose in the adults of some groups? Frederick J. Simoons of the University of California at Davis has proposed a hypothesis based on the development of dairying. It would appear that the milking of cattle, sheep, goats or reindeer did not begin until about 10,000 years ago, some 100 million years after the origin of mammals and therefore long after the mammalian developmental pattern of lactase activity had been well established. Man presumably shared that pattern, and so adults were intolerant to lactose. When some small groups of humans began to milk animals, a selective advantage was conferred on individuals who, because of a chance mutation, had high enough lactase activity to digest lactose. A person who could not digest lactose might have difficulty in a society that ingested nonfermented milk or milk products, but the lactose-tolerant individual was more adaptable: he could survive perfectly well in either a milk-drinking or a non-milk-drinking society.

The genetic mutation resulting in the capability to digest lactose probably occurred at least 10,000 years ago. People with the mutation for adult lactase activity could be members of a dairying culture, utilize their own product for food (as the Fulani do today) and then sell it in the form of a yogurt (as the Fulani do) or cheese to the general, lactose-intolerant population. These statements are presumptions, not facts, but they are based soundly on the idea that tolerance to lactose is a mutation that endowed the individual with a nutritional genetic advantage and on the basic assumption, which is supported by fact, that lactose intolerance is the normal genetic state of adult man and that lactose tolerance is in a sense abnormal.

FULANI WOMAN offers *nono*, a yogurt-like milk drink, for sale in the marketplace of a town in northern Nigeria. The pastoral Fulani drink fresh milk. The partially fermented *nono*, with reduced lactose content, is tolerated by villagers who could not digest milk.

What are the implications of all of this for nutrition policy? It should be pointed out that many people who are intolerant to lactose are nevertheless able to drink some milk or eat some milk products; the relation of clinical symptoms to lactose ingestion is quantitative. For most people, even after the age of four, drinking moderate amounts of milk has no adverse effects and is actually nutritionally beneficial. It may well be, however, that programs of indiscriminate, large-scale distribution of milk powder to intolerant populations should be modified, or that current moves toward supplying lactose-free milk powder should be encouraged.

6

THE PHYSIOLOGY OF STARVATION

VERNON R. YOUNG AND NEVIN S. SCRIMSHAW
October 1971

How does the human body adapt to prolonged starvation? Studies of fasting subjects indicate how best to utilize food when food is scarce and also how protein and calorie requirements are related

The human body has a remarkable capacity for surviving without food for long periods. There is the well-authenticated case of Terence MacSwiney, the Irish revolutionist and mayor of Cork, who in his famous hunger strike in a British prison in 1920 survived for 74 days before dying of starvation. It has been shown many times that a fast for the biblical period of 40 days and 40 nights is well within the capability of a healthy adult. Recent tests of total fasting by obese persons for weight reduction have yielded remarkable results. Some obese individuals have gone without food for as long as eight months and emerged from the ordeal in good condition.

How does the body accommodate itself to prolonged starvation? Although a knowledge of how to survive though hungry could not do much to ameliorate the chronic hunger and the famines that afflict a large portion of mankind as a result of poverty and droughts and wars, the question does not lack practical importance. From investigation of the body's responses to food deprivation we can learn much about its specific nutritional needs. Studies of the physiological and biochemical adaptations to starvation have also thrown light on a wide range of other questions, from appropriate diets for reducing weight to more effective regimes of food use during a food-shortage emergency. Moreover, they have advanced the understanding of the starvation disease called marasmus, which is increasing in many developing countries because mothers are giving up prolonged breast-feeding and their infants are not receiving an adequate substitute diet during a critical time in development.

Experimental studies of the effects of food deprivation over very long periods began around the turn of the century. One classic study was conducted in 1915 by F. G. Benedict of the Carnegie Nutrition Laboratory in Boston; he studied a volunteer subject who fasted for 31 days. In the 1940's Ancel Keys and his collaborators at the University of Minnesota tested a group of volunteer subjects kept on a semistarvation diet (about 1,600 calories per day) for 168 days. These experiments have been followed by trials of abstinence from food for the treatment of obesity, pioneered by Garfield G. Duncan of the University of Pennsylvania School of

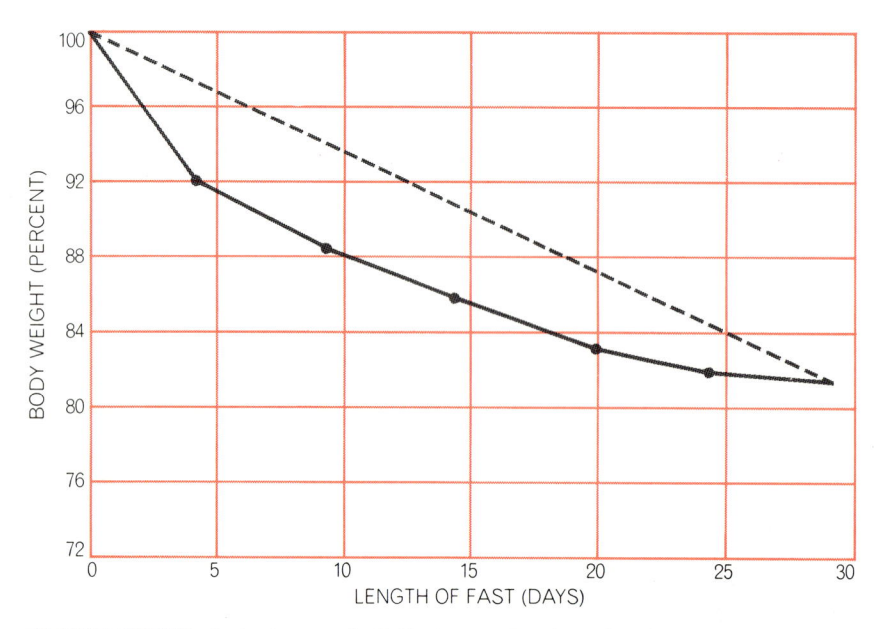

CLASSIC STUDY of a fasting man by L. Luciani in 1890 shows how body weight decreases with fasting time. The decrease is not linear (*broken curve*) but slows with time (*solid curve*). When subject began fast, he weighed 139.5 pounds; after 29 days he weighed 113.

Medicine and Walter Lyon Bloom of Piedmont Hospital in Atlanta.

A large number of obese patients have now undergone the total-fasting treatment for extensive periods under careful observation at centers in North America and Europe, and in almost all cases there have been no serious complications. The longest reported fasts were by two women treated by T. J. Thompson and his co-workers at the Stobhill General Hospital and Ruchill Hospital in Glasgow. One was a 30-year-old woman who ate no food for 236 days and reduced her weight from 281 pounds to 184; the other patient, a 54-year-old woman, fasted for 249 days and reduced from 282 pounds to 208. Of 13 fasting patients in Thompson's group none showed any significant adverse side effects that could be attributed to lack of food.

There have been several deaths elsewhere among fasting obese patients, but in all but one case the deaths apparently were due to preexisting medical conditions that had been aggravated by the obesity rather than by the fasting itself. The one exception was a 20-year-old girl who in 30 weeks of total fasting cut her weight from 260 pounds to 132 pounds. On the seventh day after she had resumed eating, her heartbeat became irregular, and she died of ventricular fibrillation on the ninth day. E. S. Garnett and his co-workers at the General Hospital in Southhampton, England, found that this patient not only had lost fatty tissue but also had consumed, during her fast, half of the lean-tissue mass in her body, including part of the fibrous tissue of the heart muscle.

To explain the body's ability to mobilize its inner resources for survival in the absence of food intake we must begin with a review of its chemical needs. The primary need, of course, is fuel to supply energy for the vital functions. Normally the principal fuel is glucose, and its most critical user is the brain, for which glucose is fully as essential as oxygen. A rapid drop of the sugar level in the blood, which must continuously deliver glucose to the brain, brings about behavioral changes, confusion, coma and, if prolonged, structural damage to the brain resulting in death. In the body at rest the brain consumes about two-thirds of the total circulating glucose supply (compared with about 45 percent of the oxygen supply). Most of the remaining third of the glucose supply goes to the skeletal muscles and the red blood cells.

The human brain requires between

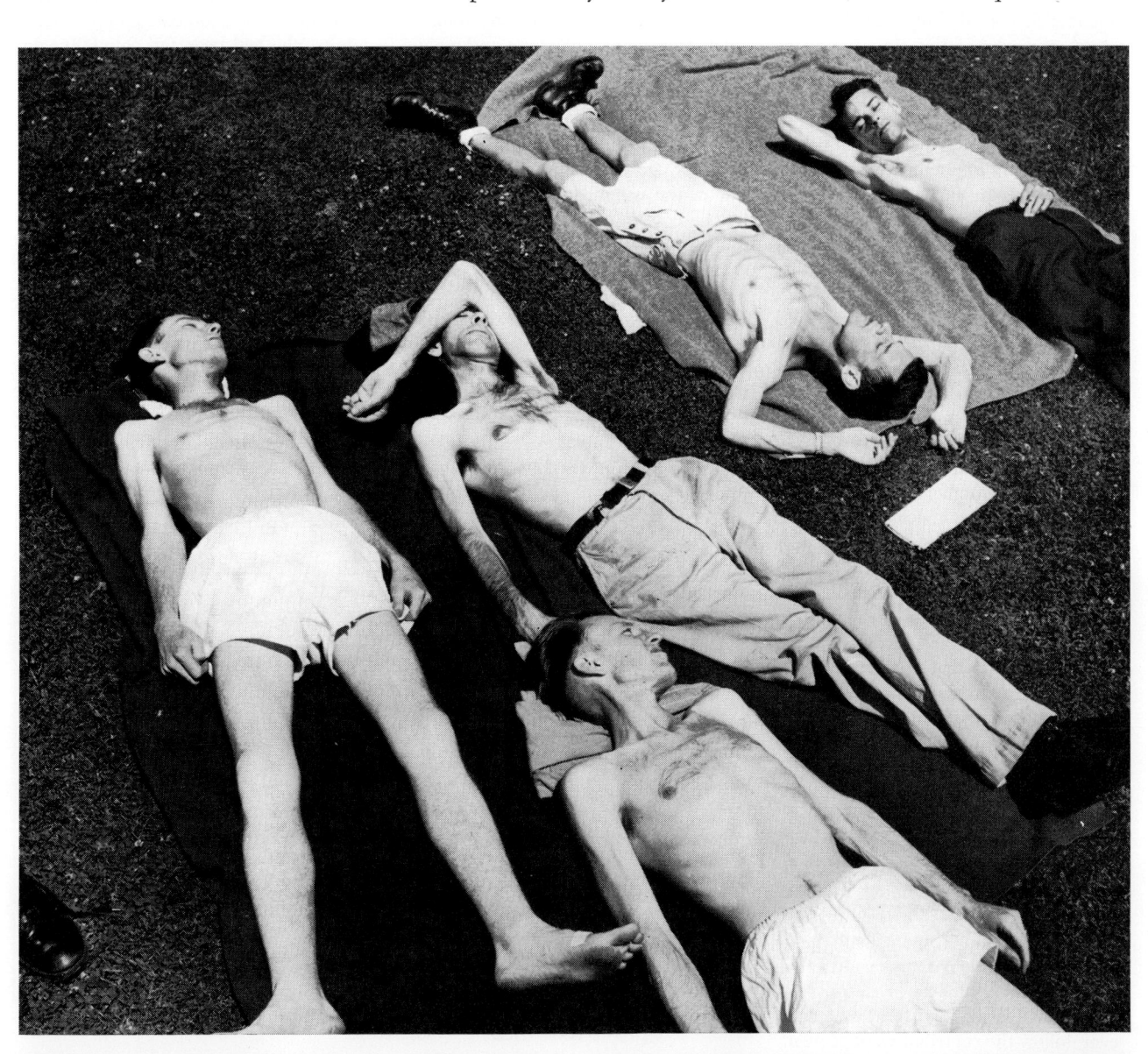

SEMISTARVED VOLUNTEER SUBJECTS rest in sun during an experiment undertaken in 1944 by Ancel Keys and his colleagues at the University of Minnesota. Volunteers were conscientious objectors of World War II. Their fast was only partial; they received a ration of 1,600 calories per day for 168 days. This photograph was made by Wallace Kirkland of *Life* and is copyrighted by Time Inc.

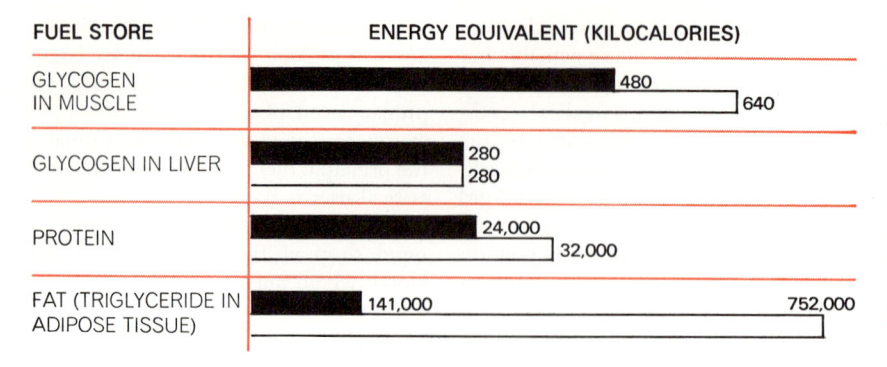

FUEL STORE	ENERGY EQUIVALENT (KILOCALORIES)
GLYCOGEN IN MUSCLE	480 / 640
GLYCOGEN IN LIVER	280 / 280
PROTEIN	24,000 / 32,000
FAT (TRIGLYCERIDE IN ADIPOSE TISSUE)	141,000 / 752,000

FUEL STORES in normal adult (*black bars*) and obese adult (*white bars*) are compared. Each pair of bars is on a different scale. The main store is fat, and in obese people this store is five or six times larger than in normal people. The data are from George F. Cahill, Jr.

100 and 145 grams of glucose (equivalent to about 400 to 600 calories) per day. The body's main reserve of glucose, in the form of glycogen in the liver, amounts to considerably less than 100 grams, and part of this store is not ordinarily available because the liver tends to conserve some glycogen for stressful emergencies the body must be prepared to meet. As a result the liver's store of fuel can supply the brain's need for only a few hours. In fact, the stored glucose is not sufficient for the duration of the overnight fast between dinner and breakfast. Between meals the liver begins to draw on the tissues of the body for materials to synthesize the required glucose. We have found by examination of subjects in our laboratory at the Massachusetts Institute of Technology that after a person has eaten a meal at 10:00 P.M. certain amino acids that are precursors for the synthesis of glucose begin to accumulate in the blood plasma by 1:00 A.M., and they continue to increase until breakfast. The rise in amino acids is an indication that proteins in the skeletal muscles are being broken down to provide material for the production of glucose by the liver. Analysis of the blood also shows that at the same time the blood contains free fatty acids, which are derived from the breakdown of triglycerides in the fatty tissues and are capable of supplying energy to tissues other than those of the nervous system.

Clearly if the breakdown of protein continued at the initial rate, the skeletal muscles would rapidly waste away and the body could not survive for long. As starvation is prolonged, other sources of energy for the brain come into play, as we shall see. Let us first, however, follow the contribution of protein.

During the early period of starvation the body of an average man (143 pounds) synthesizes about 160 grams of glucose per day. Most of this is produced by the liver, but the kidney cortex also synthesizes an appreciable amount of glucose. The loss of protein involved and substantial losses of body minerals (such as calcium, potassium and magnesium) cause a loss of the water associated with these substances in the body, and this is mainly responsible for the initial loss of weight. As starvation continues, however, a progressively greater proportion of the weight loss is accounted for by the consumption of body fat. Gram for gram, fat is much richer in energy than other nutrients are: fat represents about nine calories per gram of weight in the body, whereas protein in the body carries only two calories per gram and carbohydrate one calorie per gram. Thus each unit of consumption of body fat donates much more energy to the starved body. This is probably a major factor in slowing the loss of weight as starvation is prolonged [*see illustration on page 44*]. Eventually the fat consumed during continued loss of weight in obese people provides for essentially all the energy needed by the body.

There is an interesting question concerning what the weight loss means in terms of cells. Does the loss take the form of shrinkage of the cells' size or reduction of their number? Animal studies have shown that total or nearly total starvation can reduce the number of cells or fibers in the skeletal muscles. Little direct study of this question has been conducted in man. Radiographs of the chest in persons on a starvation diet have indicated that the heart shrinks in size, but not whether this is due to a reduction of the cells' size or of their number. Jules Hirsch of Rockefeller University obtained somewhat more definite information. He studied a group of obese adults who had been fed only 600 calories per day and had lost upward of 100 pounds of body weight. Examining cells of their fatty tissues aspirated through a hypodermic needle, he found that the cells had shrunk by about 45 percent in size. The number of cells had not changed appreciably, however, except in a few people who had achieved particularly large losses of body fat.

George F. Cahill, Jr., of the Elliott P. Joslin Research Laboratory of the Diabetes Foundation, the leading investigator of the biochemical aspects of starvation in man, has looked into the changes in metabolism of obese people during fasting. Analyzing the blood's content of metabolites from skeletal muscle, he

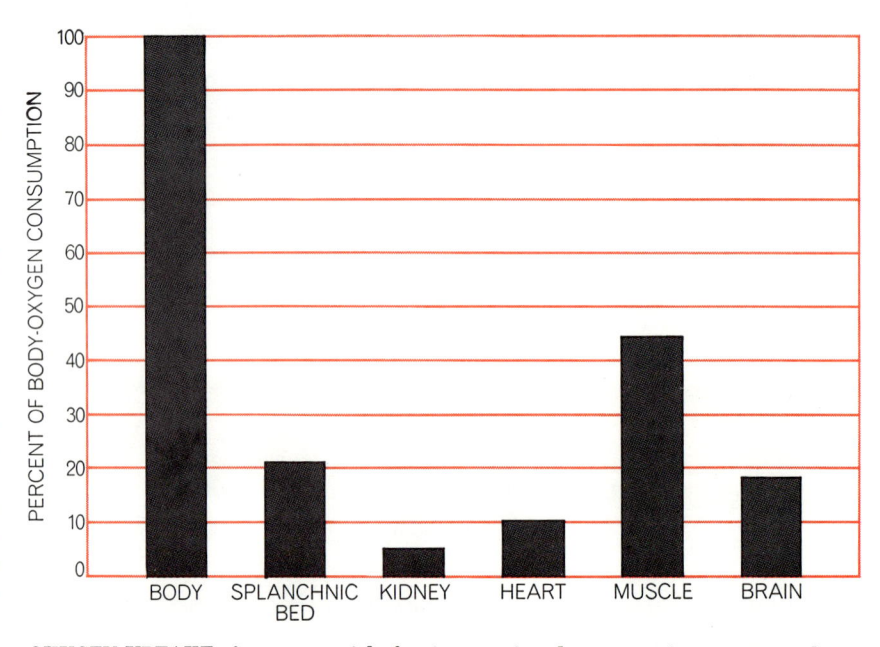

OXYGEN UPTAKE after an overnight fast is apportioned among various organs as shown by bars at right. "Splanchnic bed" refers to viscera, mainly the liver. Pattern of oxygen uptake is quite different from that of glucose uptake (*see illustration on opposite page*).

finds that at the beginning of fasting (not long after a meal has been digested and absorbed) the blood shows an increase of amino acids released from the muscle cells. Of these amino acids, which provide the supply of substrate for the liver's synthesis of glucose, the principal one is alanine. Furthermore, it turns out that alanine given by injection can increase the production of glucose, as shown by a rise of the glucose level in the blood.

The amount of alanine released from the muscle cells is surprising, because alanine makes up only 7 percent of the total content of amino acids in the cell proteins. It appears that most of the alanine discharged from the cells during fasting is not produced directly from protein breakdown but must be synthesized from alanine's immediate precursor, pyruvic acid, by the addition of an amino group furnished by other amino acids liberated by the breakdown of protein.

Cahill has proposed a cycle for the conversion of alanine to glucose and reconversion to alanine; it is somewhat analogous to the Cori cycle for lactate [*see illustration on page 50*]. According to Cahill's model, the alanine cycle, like Cori's, merely recycles a fixed supply of glucose. In addition, however, the alanine cycle offers an efficient means of transporting to the liver the nitrogen derived from the amino acids liberated by the breakdown of muscle protein.

As starvation continues, a number of general factors come to the aid of the organism. The basal metabolic rate slows, and the body's need for calories is further reduced by the loss of metabolically active tissue. The starving person engages in less spontaneous activity and becomes more sparing in the expenditure of energy, so that he uses his available energy more efficiently in accomplishing a given work load. His ability to survive will also depend, of course, on individual variables such as his body size and his stores of fat, and on environmental ones such as temperature and humidity.

Paramount, however, is the matter of the expenditure of protein. The starving body soon resorts to strong measures to preserve its integrity. It is confronted with two seemingly irreconcilable demands. The brain still requires a daily supply of energy equivalent to at least 100 grams of glucose; yet the synthesis of glucose at that rate would quickly exhaust the protein on which life depends. The triglycerides of fatty tissue provide a source of synthesis for glucose, but they can furnish only about 16 grams per day. In order to obtain the rest of the daily glucose requirement, some 90 grams, the body would have to break down about 155 grams of muscle protein. This would involve a daily loss of 25 grams of nitrogen. The nitrogen content in the body of an adult amounts to about 1,000 grams, and a loss of more than 50 percent of that amount is lethal. Hence a starving man could not live longer than three weeks if he had to expend his nitrogen at that rate.

Actually the body takes steps to control its loss of protein. The skeletal-muscle cells reduce their release of alanine, and the liver's synthesis of glucose declines. Cahill and an associate, Oliver E. Owen, found that by the fifth or sixth week of an obese adult's fast the liver and kidney were producing only 24 grams of glucose per day, and that essentially all of this glucose was going to the brain.

Where and how did the brain obtain the rest of the energy it required? Cahill discovered that the deficit was made up by a substitute source of energy derived from the fatty tissues. The blood of the starved obese subjects showed an accumulation of ketone bodies: acetoacetic acid and two derivatives from it, acetone and beta-hydroxybutyric acid. These substances yield energy on oxidation, and the brain evidently had adapted to using them as energy substrates in place of glucose.

Ordinarily the metabolism of fatty acids does not create ketones. In response to starvation, however, fatty acids are released from the fat depots and are oxidized in the liver to acetoacetic acid, which is then transported by the blood to other tissues to provide them with energy. The accumulation of ketones in the blood during starvation—and indeed in people on a high-fat diet—has been known for some time as the condition called ketosis. It is now clear that the ketosis of starvation signals a response to depletion of the body's supply of glucose, as Hans A. Krebs of the University of Oxford suggested some years

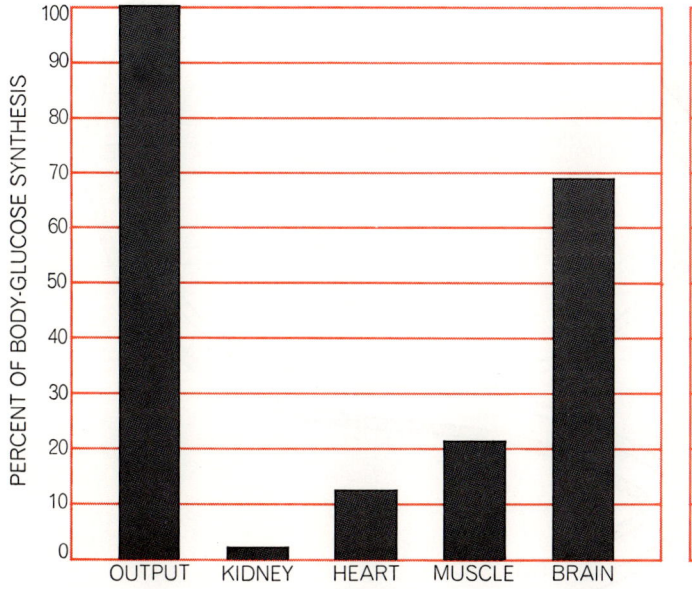

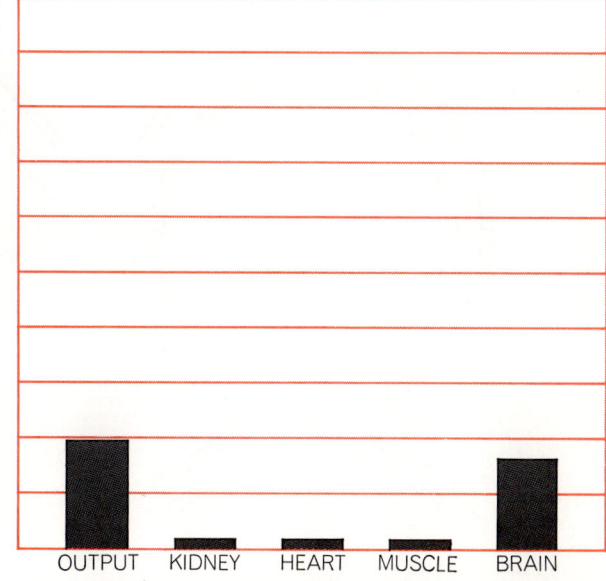

GLUCOSE OUTPUT AND UPTAKE after overnight fast (*bars at left*) and after five weeks' starvation (*bars at right*) are compared. "Output" is glucose synthesis; the other bars indicate the uptake of glucose by various organs. After the overnight fast glucose comes mainly from the liver; after the five weeks' starvation it comes 50 percent from the liver and 50 percent from the kidneys.

48 I • NUTRITION AND MALNUTRITION

ago. The evidence indicates that the brain promptly adopts the ketone bodies, particularly beta-hydroxybutyrate, as a substitute energy source, possibly within the first week of starvation. The Oxford group has recently shown (in studies conducted with experimental animals) that the brain has the enzymatic machinery to utilize ketone bodies. Their studies suggest that the human brain can probably begin to utilize ketone bodies for meeting its energy needs as soon as these metabolites in the blood supplying the brain reach a high enough level.

The breakdown of body protein is not completely eliminated. Even in prolonged starvation nitrogen in the form of urea and ammonia continues to be excreted in the urine. It reflects the basic turnover of proteins in the body that goes on at all times. In our laboratory we estimated the amount of this basic turnover by measuring the urinary-nitrogen output of subjects who were fed a diet containing no protein but adequate in calories. Comparing their daily nitrogen loss with that reported for starved subjects in the fourth week without food, we find that the starved obese subjects' loss is not markedly higher. This could mean that the starved subjects were producing some five more grams of glucose per day than can be obtained through the basic turnover of body protein. The body cannot do entirely without glucose, because most tissues need it for replenishing the tricarboxylic acid (TCA) cycle, which among other things synthesizes the energy-rich adenosine triphosphate (ATP) on which so much of the body's chemistry depends. Nevertheless, the very small extra loss of protein shown by obese people during prolonged starvation indicates that, thanks to the substitution of ketones for energy, their need

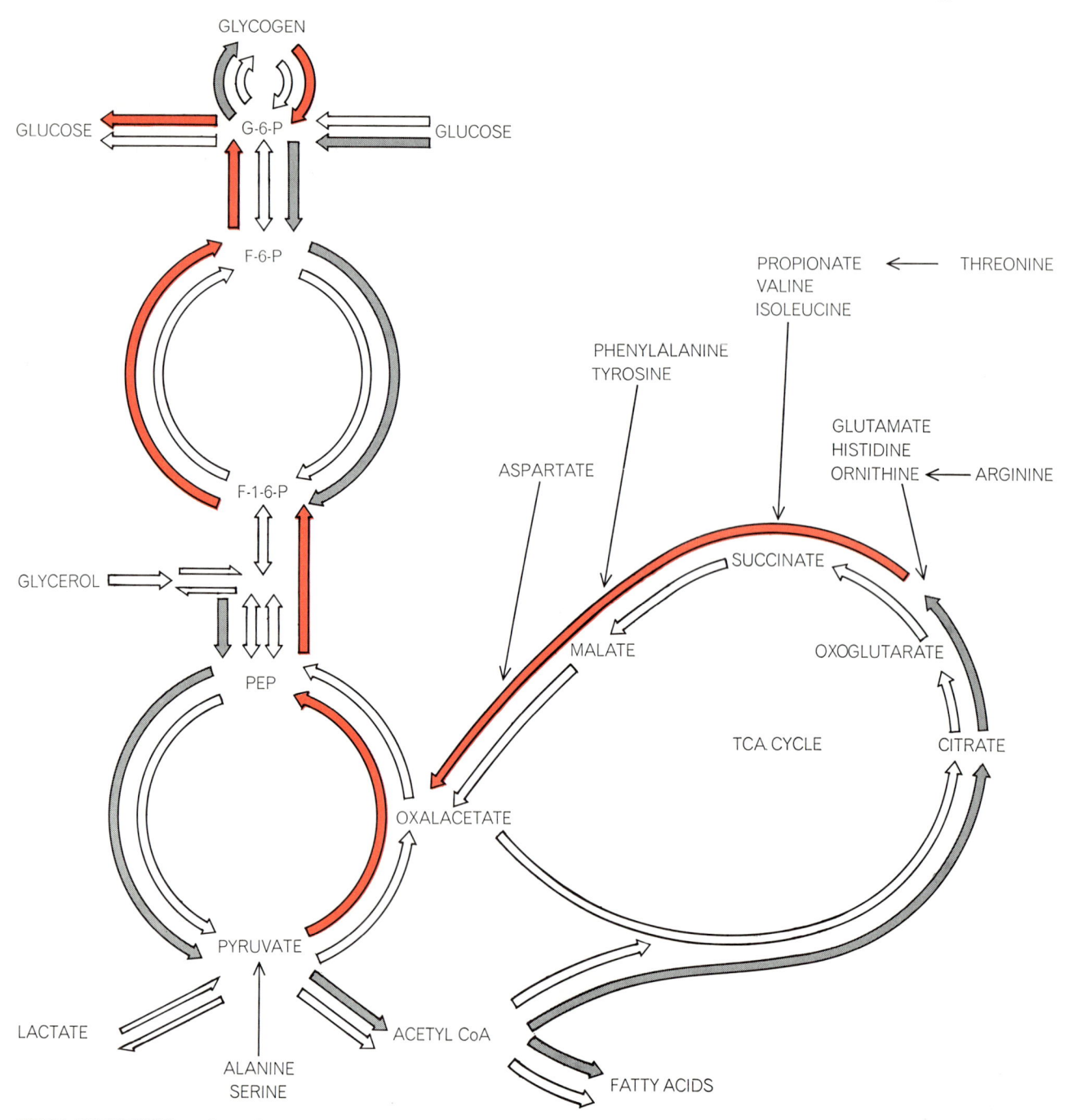

MAIN PATHWAYS in the utilization and production of carbohydrate in the liver are outlined in starvation (*dark-colored arrows*) and nonstarvation (*gray arrows*). "G-6-P" stands for glucose-6-phosphate; "F-6-P," for fructose-6-phosphate; "F-1-6-P," for fructose-1-6-diphosphate; "PEP," for phosphoenolpyruvate; "CoA," for coenzyme A, and "TCA cycle," for tricarboxylic acid cycle.

for glucose is limited to not much more than is provided by the ordinary turnover of protein in the body.

One of the consequences of the body's conservation of protein during starvation is that urination for the excretion of nitrogen is reduced. Hence a starving man needs less water intake. If his loss by sweating is minimal, a cup of water a day is sufficient to maintain his body's water balance.

What are the mechanisms that bring about the adaptive changes in metabolism during prolonged starvation? This question remains to be explored. No doubt hormones will be found to play an important part. It is known that the pancreatic hormone insulin is an important regulator of chemical activity in the body's ordinary daily cycle of eating and fasting. During the digestion of a meal the absorption of glucose and amino acids from the intestinal tract stimulates the secretion of insulin; the hormone in turn stimulates the synthesis of fat and inhibits its breakdown, promotes the uptake of glucose and amino acids by the muscle cells and inhibits the synthesis of glucose by the liver. After the meal has been absorbed the insulin level in the blood falls, and during prolonged starvation it stands at a level lower than normal. Cahill has found that during prolonged starvation glucagon, the pancreatic hormone whose effect is opposite to that of insulin, is at a higher level in relation to insulin. Glucagon normally acts to stimulate the liver's synthesis of glucose. It is possible, therefore, that the alteration in the balance between the two hormones in the blood during starvation serves to heighten the activity of the liver in forming glucose and in metabolizing fats. The possible participation of other hormones, notably the growth hormone of the anterior pituitary gland and the glucocorticoid hormones of the adrenal gland, is being investigated, but so far it does not appear that these play primary roles in the metabolic adaptation to starvation.

There is a striking change in the role of the cortex of the kidney during prolonged starvation. It is promoted from a relatively minor partner of the liver in the synthesis of glucose to the main producer; by the sixth week of an obese person's fast the kidney cortex is synthesizing more glucose from amino acids than the liver is. This shift is believed to be attributable, at least in part, to the change in the acid-base balance in the blood caused by the increase in the body's production of ketone bodies.

The ability of an adult to survive pro-

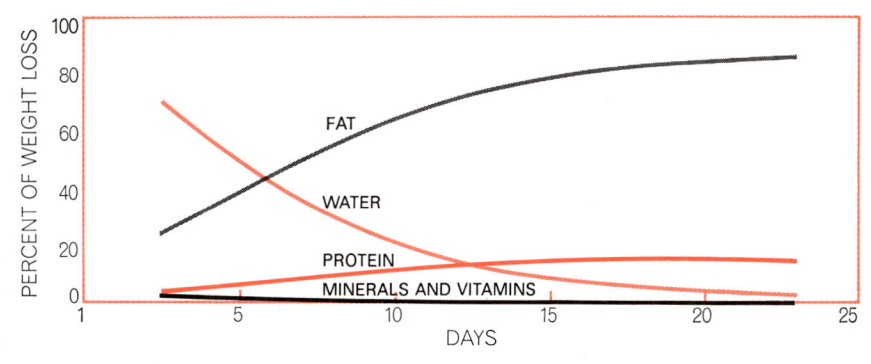

DAILY WEIGHT LOSS in prolonged starvation is analyzed by constituents of the body. Data are from Josef Brožek, Ancel Keys and their co-workers at University of Minnesota.

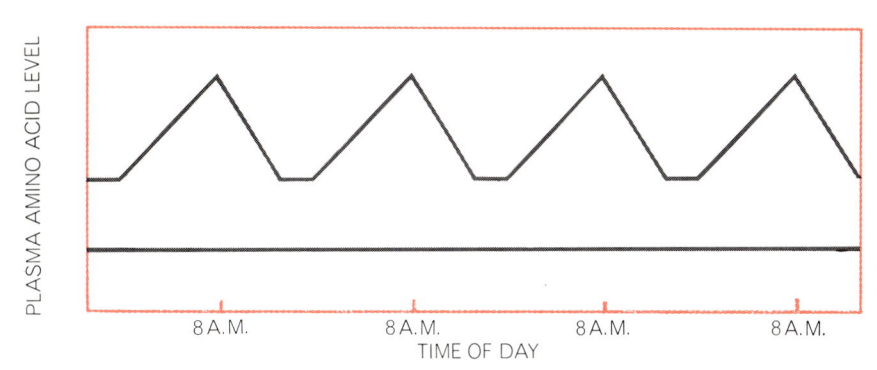

LEVELS OF AMINO ACIDS IN THE BLOOD normally follow these generalized curves. The level of certain amino acids (for example tryptophan, leucine and valine) rises and falls daily (*top curve*). The level of others (for example aspartic acid) remains steady.

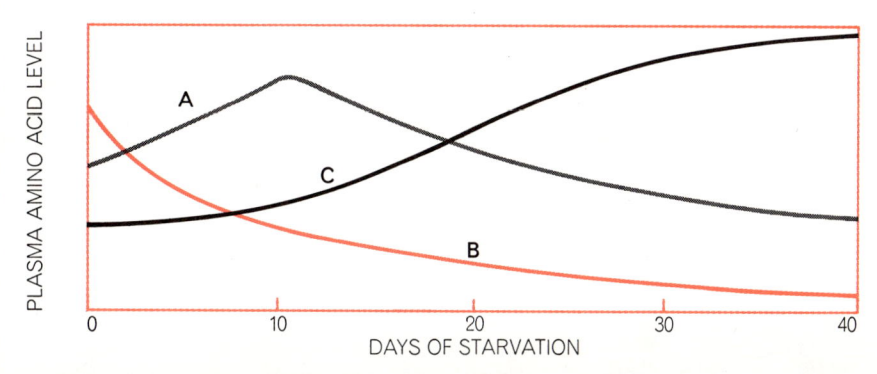

LEVELS OF AMINO ACIDS IN STARVATION follow different curves. Certain of the amino acids (for example valine) rise and then fall (*A*). Other amino acids (for example alanine) fall steadily (*B*). Still others (for example glycine) show a delayed rise (*C*).

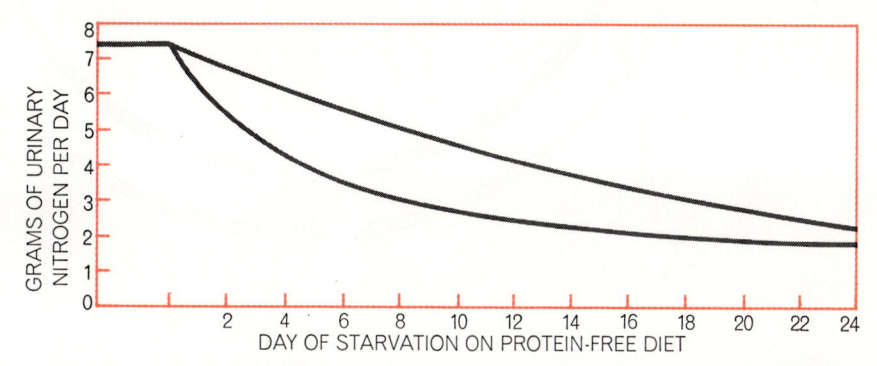

NITROGEN LOST IN URINE by starved subjects (*top curve*) and by subjects fed a protein-free but otherwise adequate diet (*bottom curve*) are compared. The difference between curves reflects starved person's need to synthesize glucose out of his own protein.

longed starvation is not shared by children, particularly very young children. In a child deprived of food growth stops almost immediately, because of the high requirement of energy necessary to build protein. The child develops the emaciated condition known as marasmus. In cases where a deficiency of protein is more pronounced than a deficiency of calories the child shows the symptoms of the disease called kwashiorkor. A child who has suffered undernourishment very early and for an appreciable length of time will never reach normal size for his age, even though he is later fed well enough to restore a normal rate of growth. This is part of the reason for the small body size of many people in impoverished countries.

Particularly critical is the first year or so of life, the "preweaning" period. Because the brain is still growing and developing during this time, underfeeding is likely to result in permanent physical stunting of the central nervous system. Myron Winick of the Cornell University Medical Center in New York City found in experimental studies of rats, and in analysis of the brains of children who had died of marasmus, that the underfed brain had a subnormal content of DNA. Starvation had interfered with cell division and left the animal or child with a permanent deficit in the number of cells in the brain. Winick's experiments with rats also showed that when the mother was underfed during pregnancy, malnutrition of the offspring after birth had an even more devastating effect on the brain.

In the burgeoning cities of the less developed countries many mothers in low-income families are now abandoning breast-feeding early, either in order to go to work or in imitation of the more affluent classes. As a result infantile marasmus is becoming common in a number of countries. A particularly well-documented report of this trend, and the cause, has been made by Fernando Mönckeberg of the University of Chile, who studied the situation in that country.

What useful conclusions can we draw from the studies conducted so far on the body's adaptations to starvation? First, let us consider the best way of coping with emergency situations in which the food supplies are very limited.

A little food, of course, is better than

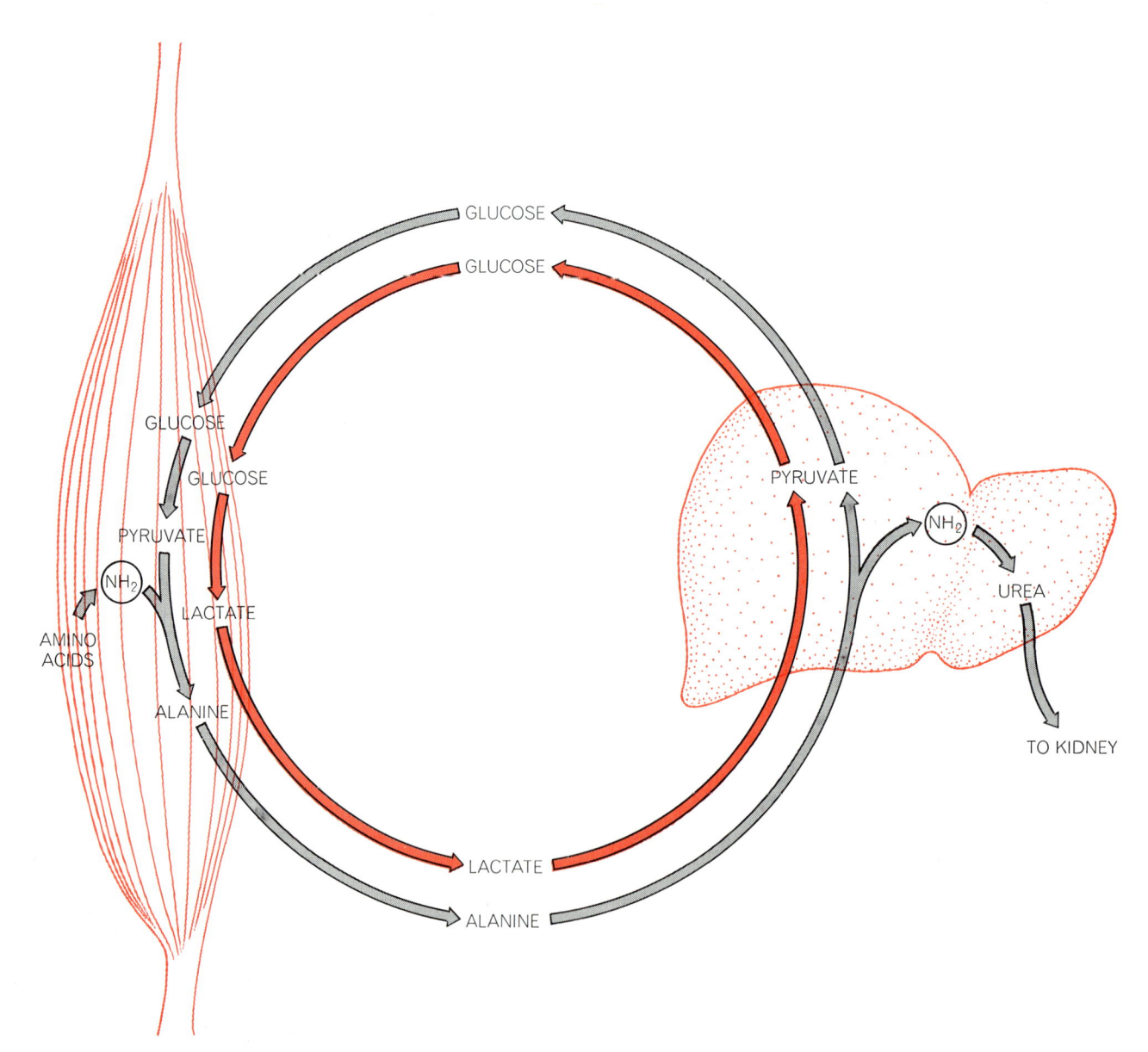

TWO METABOLIC-SUBSTRATE CYCLES operate between muscles (*left*) and the liver (*right*) through the blood. Lactate cycle worked out by Carl F. Cori (*color*) results in a net gain for muscle of two molecules of adenosine triphosphate (ATP). Alanine cycle proposed by Cahill would also facilitate the removal of nitrogen from amino acids liberated by the breakdown of muscle protein.

no food at all. Yet there is a paradox here. The edema of famine is hardly ever seen in cases of total starvation but develops often in semistarvation. Moreover, a semistarved person's survival time may actually be shortened if he tries to subsist on a diet consisting mainly of carbohydrate and deficient in protein. In such circumstances a child may quickly fall victim to kwashiorkor. Why is it that, although a person can be stricken with this disease when he eats a little food, it never shows up in total starvation, when the person gets no protein intake at all?

The typical clinical signs of kwashiorkor are apathy, loss of appetite, edema and changes in the skin and hair. On close examination of the blood and other tissues it is found that there is a marked drop in the concentration and activity of key enzymes. In the light of the known facts about the body's adjustment to a lack or shortage of food we can deduce the reason for the enzyme deficiency. In a semistarved child or adult the brain probably continues to depend mainly on glucose for energy. With some glucose being supplied by way of food, the need to synthesize glucose from body proteins would be reduced. Consequently there is only a modest release of amino acids from skeletal muscle into the bloodstream. If the semistarved individual is receiving little or no protein in his food, the amount of free amino acid in the blood is not sufficient for the body's synthesis of essential enzymes and other tissue proteins. Therefore the body shows the devastating results of protein deficiency. This is precisely what was observed during the recent famine in Biafra. The population was subsisting almost solely on the starchy roots of the cassava plant. Edema and other symptoms of acute protein deficiency were most conspicuous in the children. A high frequency of kwashiorkor is now being found among the East Pakistan refugees in India because many of the young children are not receiving protein foods.

We are seeing in such phenomena an indication of the conditions that gave rise to the evolution of man's present metabolic resources. In the hunting and plant-gathering phase of his early history his hungry periods took the form of general undernourishment, and the body evolved adaptations to improve metabolic efficiency for that contingency. It is only recently that human populations have come to depend heavily on a single cultivated plant staple for food—a situation with which the human body is not prepared to cope.

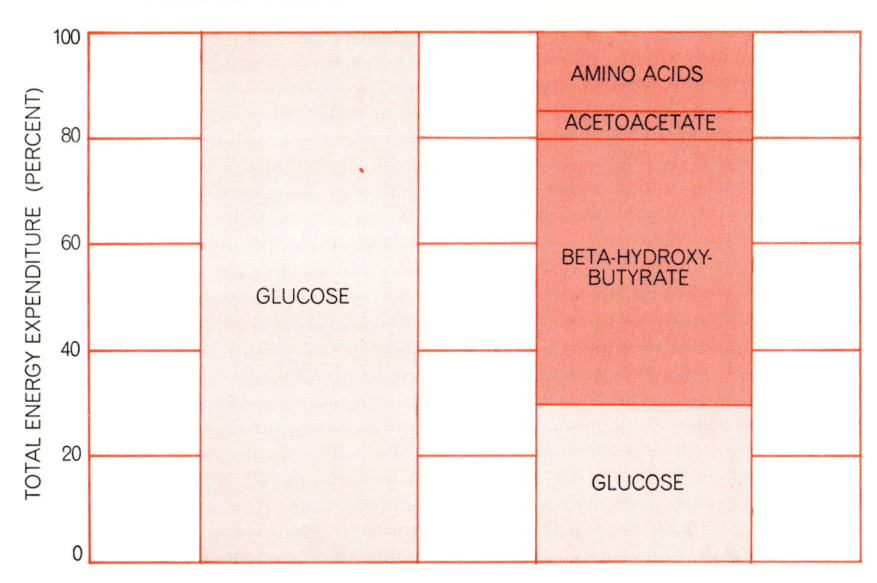

ENERGY NEEDS OF THE BRAIN are met differently in normal circumstances (*bar at left*) and after five to six weeks of starvation (*bar at right*). Glucose normally suffices, but in starvation it can meet only 30 percent of the requirement and other substances fill in.

We do not yet have precise knowledge about the mechanisms that cause the brain to switch from glucose to ketone bodies as its main energy source to induce this switch artificially for preservation of the body's integrity. All that can be suggested is that in a food-shortage emergency it may be best to spread out the consumption of the limited supply of protein and/or carbohydrate over the day, taking nibbles at frequent intervals, so that the periods of fasting and consequent breakdown of body protein for glucose synthesis will be shortened.

More information of practical usefulness is available on dieting for weight reduction, since most of the studies of adaptation to starvation have been carried out in obese subjects. It is quite clear that there is no way of achieving a permanent weight reduction without reducing the intake of calories to less than the outgo. The greater the difference between the intake and the expenditure of caloric energy, the faster one will lose weight. What about the various special diets that have become popular?

A high-protein or high-carbohydrate diet in theory should tend to minimize the body's loss of protein. It has also been argued that part of the protein and carbohydrate intake is spent in generating body heat after a meal and therefore does not go into the building of body fat. In practice, however, these considerations are probably too small in effect to be significant in preserving health or reducing weight.

On the whole it must be said that bizarre reducing diets have no scientific basis; any apparent success they may have appears to be due solely to their poor palatability or, as in the case of low-carbohydrate, high-protein diets, a rapid initial weight loss due to loss of body water. The best diet for reducing is still one that is balanced in food ingredients and sufficiently low in total calories to produce weight loss at the desired rate.

From a purely biochemical standpoint the most efficient way to lose weight, as the starvation tests have shown, is complete fasting into the stage where body fat is being consumed as the main source of energy for the brain and other tissues. Total fasting for an extensive length of time can be dangerous, however. It should not be prescribed for high-risk patients, and in all cases one must take care to avoid too much exercise in the initial phases and refrain from continuing the fast too long. Duncan of the University of Pennsylvania School of Medicine, who has perhaps had the most experience with this method of dealing with obesity, has treated fasting patients in a total of more than 1,300 hospital admissions without a fatality. Each fast has been limited to 10 days or two weeks, with patients returning for repeated fasts at varying intervals. Duncan cautions that any total fast for more than two weeks should still be considered in the category of a research enterprise. It must be emphasized that no one should undertake total fasting for weight reduction without prior medical screening, hospitalization and continuous medical supervision.

7

KWASHIORKOR

HUGH C. TROWELL
December 1954

This word borrowed from an African tribe refers to the most severe and common nutritional disorder of man. Only recently discovered, it is caused by a deficiency of protein in the diet.

In 1929 an English woman physician working among tribes in the Gold Coast of West Africa encountered a puzzling disease. It seemed to attack only young children, and it was usually fatal. The victim slowly lost energy and appetite, lay miserably in bed, ate very little and passed loose stools containing undigested food; eventually his face and legs became swollen with fluid, his hair lost its color and curl, rashes broke out on his skin and death soon followed.

Because the victims were most often babies that had been weaned from the mother's breast to an unbalanced diet, the physician, Dr. Cicely Williams, judged that the disease was due to malnutrition. She described it as a new form not previously known to the medical profession, and she attributed it to the people's unsatisfactory diet of potatoes, yams, cassava and bananas. Dr. Williams named the disease *kwashiorkor*, as the Ga tribe called it.

When she reported her discovery to European authorities, many were skeptical; they considered it hardly likely that African peasants could have recognized a disease which had escaped the notice of Western medicine. One nutritional expert in London decided, on the basis of the rash, that the disease was pellagra. But Dr. Williams, though unable to continue her study because she had to leave the Gold Coast to go to Malaya, insisted that it was a new disease, and defended her view with great vigor. Time was to prove her right. It was also to show that kwashiorkor afflicts a great deal more of the world than just the Gold Coast of Africa.

In 1930 I encountered this disease in the Kenya Colony in East Africa, but I did not hear of Dr. Williams' reports until several years later. Then I unfortunately listened to the experts and decided that it was a curious mixture of pellagra and nutritional edema; I called it "infantile pellagra." At about that time it was discovered that pellagra was due to a deficiency of nicotinic acid. Some of this vitamin was sent to me. It came; it was tried; almost all the patients nonetheless died.

I returned to England to hunt in the medical libraries of London. There I found, in independent accounts published by various tropical workers in obscure journals, one report after another of a disease very similar to kwashiorkor. The names and circumstances were different, but slowly it became apparent that L. Normet's cases of *bouffissure* ("swelling") *d'Annam* in Indo-China (1926) were much the same as A. Castellanos' cases of *pelagroide beriberico* in Cuba (1935). The earliest descriptions of this disease were given in 1906 by A. Czerny and A. Keller in Germany and J. P. Correa in Mexico. Altogether the search of the literature yielded some 40 different names for what was evidently the same disease.

The investigators often recognized that the symptoms were those of malnutrition. Yet the patients did not respond as expected to feeding. About half of them died even though they were fed whole milk combined with liver extracts and all the known vitamins. Some of the observers therefore concluded that the disease must be some kind of infection: malaria, hookworm or an attack by some other tropical bug that caused the victims to waste away.

I clung, somewhat obstinately, to the idea that the disease was due to malnutrition. Perhaps kwashiorkor was an advanced, incurable stage of this condition. I suggested that it should be called "malignant malnutrition," for I was still losing a third of my patients. Soon afterward kwashiorkor stopped being "malignant" and became curable. The cure was discovered quite by accident. Workers in Uganda, where milk is scarce, had sent to England for milk powder to treat kwashiorkor patients. By mistake the

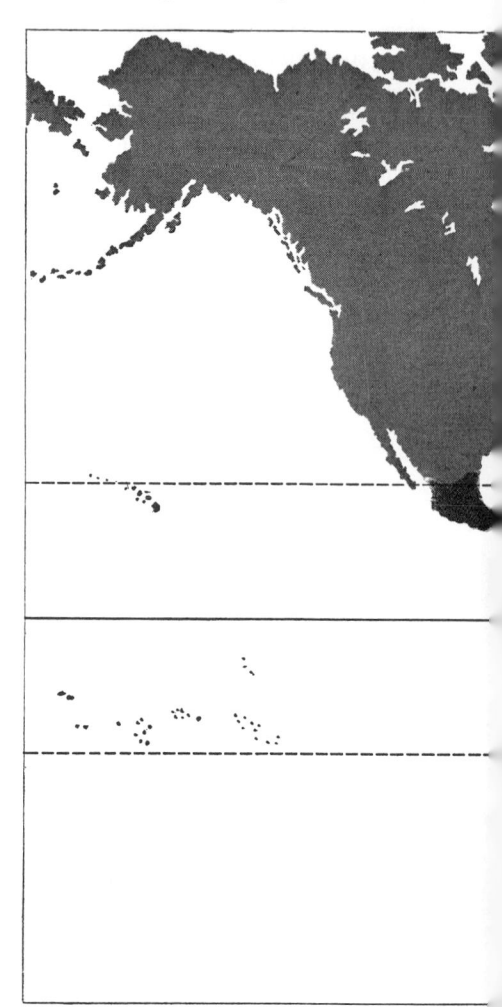

GEOGRAPHICAL AREAS reporting kwashiorkor are outlined in color on this

British sources sent not powdered whole milk but powdered skim milk. It was given to the patients anyway, and miraculously most of them recovered from the disease. The reason for the superiority of skim milk to full-cream milk was at once apparent: skim milk seldom produced diarrhea, which suggested that it was digested better than whole milk.

By this time we had begun to have a good notion of the true cause of kwashiorkor. The Uganda workers, and others in Central America, had learned that the blood of patients with the disease was low in protein (serum albumin). And there were other clues that also pointed in the protein direction.

One of the difficulties in analyzing the disorder had been that victims show almost no abnormalities on post-mortem examination. The only thing unusual about their organs is a fatty liver, but this condition is present in many fatal diseases. During World War II, however, we in Africa began to hear reports of some extremely interesting findings by nutrition investigators in Canada, Britain and the U. S. Several experimenters there had produced fatty livers in animals by feeding them a diet deficient in the amino acid methionine (a component of protein) or lacking choline (a fraction of the vitamin B complex).

Attempting to enlist the help of U. S. workers on my kwashiorkor problem, I sent them post-mortem liver samples and X-rays of the intestines of victims of the disease. Unfortunately these were impounded by the censor as possible avenues of illegal communication! I had better luck with samples sent to Harold (now Sir Harold) Himsworth, secretary of the Medical Research Council of Great Britain. Himsworth decided that the effects of kwashiorkor on the liver were the same as those he had produced in animals by certain diet experiments. He became greatly interested in the kwashiorkor problem, and has been the main support of our work on this disease at the Mulago Hospital in Uganda.

Shortly after Himsworth's report supporting the idea that kwashiorkor was a dietary disease, still more conclusive confirmation came from a series of brilliant investigations carried out by the brothers Joseph and Theodore Gillman of Johannesburg. They developed an instrument with which it is possible to remove safely a thread of liver tissue from a living patient. By this means they were able to study the effects of various diets on kwashiorkor patients and to determine which diets would cause fat to disappear from the liver. Their tests left no doubt that the disease is due to malnutrition.

Until recently we have not heard much about protein deficiency. In the temperate regions of the world, where most hospitals and biological research are concentrated, malnutrition has been considered synonymous with deficiencies of vitamins rather than proteins. This is understandable, since the chief staple in the temperate belts is grain—a food relatively well endowed with protein but poor in certain vitamins. Diseases such as scurvy and rickets, now known to be due to deficiencies of vitamins, have been recognized for thousands of years

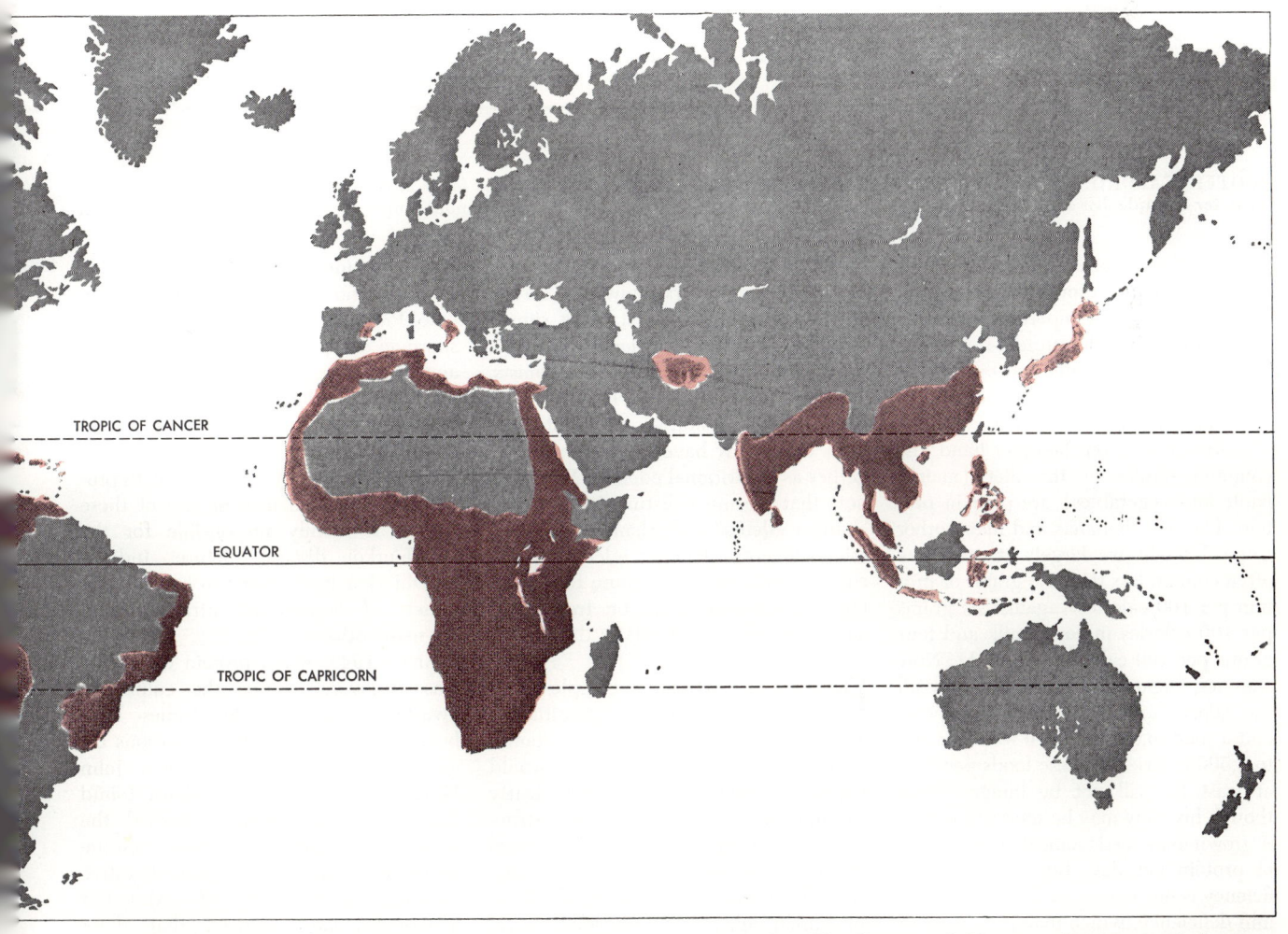

map. The information on which the map is based was gathered by the World Health Organization and the Food and Agriculture Organization. The disease probably occurs in every tropical country of the Americas, Africa and Asia and in many temperate countries.

54   I • NUTRITION AND MALNUTRITION

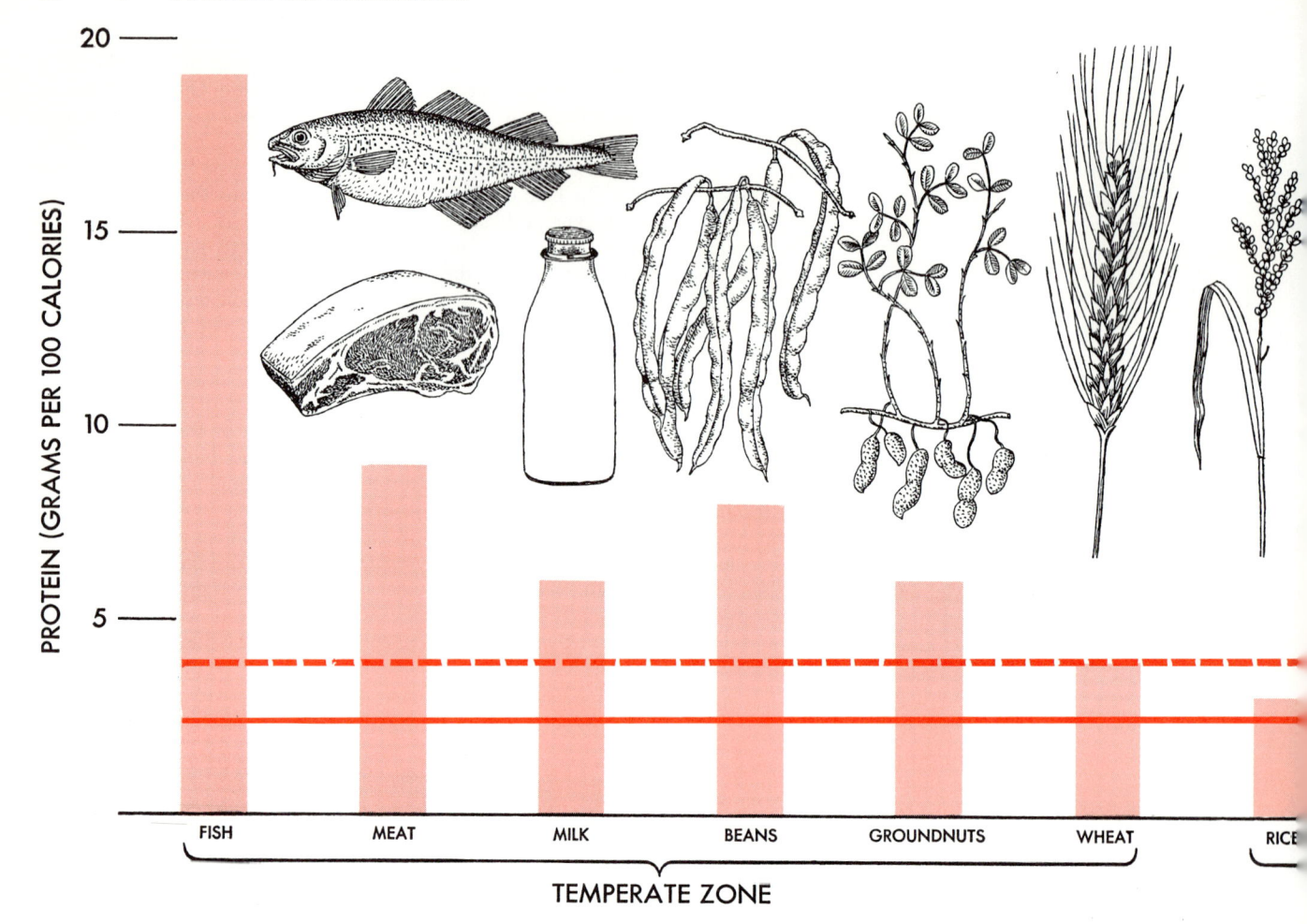

PROTEIN-CALORIE RATIOS of various foods are compared. Meat, for example, has a high ratio of protein to calories; banana, a low ratio. The staple foods of the temperate zone are bracketed at the left; those of the moist tropic zone, at the right. It will be seen

in the civilized world. Protein deficiency has gone unnoticed for at least two good reasons: (1) in the temperate regions the ordinary diet includes protein-rich foods, such as fish, meat, milk and beans, and (2) protein deficiency is difficult to distinguish from plain starvation.

In the tropics, on the other hand, the common staples of the diet (mainly fruits and vegetables) are poor in protein. Potatoes, bananas and many other tropical foods are largely starch; they often contain less than 1.5 grams of protein per 100 calories (against six grams per 100 calories in cow's milk and four grams per 100 calories in wheat). Now starches, sugars and fats can supply all the calories and energy a person needs, and a man may seem well fed on 2,500 to 3,500 calories of these foods per day; at least he will not be hungry, even though his body may be short of protein. A grown man needs some 65 to 80 grams of protein per day. But a protein deficiency is not so easy to detect as a vitamin deficiency, which manifests itself in certain specific and well-recognized symptoms. The most conspicuous symptom of acute protein malnutrition is edema. The same accumulation of fluid and swelling occurs, however, in an undernourished person starving simply from lack of enough calories. It is this parallelism that has misled nutritionists. Protein malnutrition has hitherto been confused with simple undernutrition; both conditions have been lumped together as "nutritional edema." We know now that we must distinguish between "hunger edema" and edema due to protein deficiency. Hunger edema can be cured merely by giving more food. Protein malnutrition must be treated by adding protein-rich foods to the diet.

Proteins are extremely complex substances. Whereas it is possible to write the chemical formula of a vitamin on a small sheet of note paper, it would require several volumes to depict clearly and in complete detail the atomic structure of some proteins. Moreover, these complex structures are not static; the proteins, forming the building blocks of all animal cells, are in constant movement and flux—they group, break apart and group again. And this is not all. Each protein requires a certain combination of amino acids. A deficiency of a single amino acid may produce a disease. Probably in kwashiorkor there is a shortage of many essential amino acids, and these deficiencies may differ according to the specific diet. Further complexity arises from the fact that certain vitamins and growth factors (*e.g.*, vitamin B_{12}) are closely associated with protein: possibly the lack of one of these factors is mainly responsible for the kwashiorkor disease picture. Indeed, kwashiorkor itself seems to be only one variety of protein malnutrition; there are many others.

Since 1944, when protein deficiency was discovered to be the culprit in kwashiorkor, systematic studies have been made of its effects on various organs and tissues of the body. John Davies, who joined me in Africa, found that protein malnutrition caused the secretory granules to disappear from the pancreas, so that no pancreatic digestive enzymes were produced; Margaret Thompson later showed that these enzymes reappeared in the intestines when milk protein was fed to patients. Rex Dean discovered certain peculiar

| MAIZE | POTATO | BANANA | YAM | CASSAVA | SUGAR | BUTTER AND FATS |

TROPIC ZONE

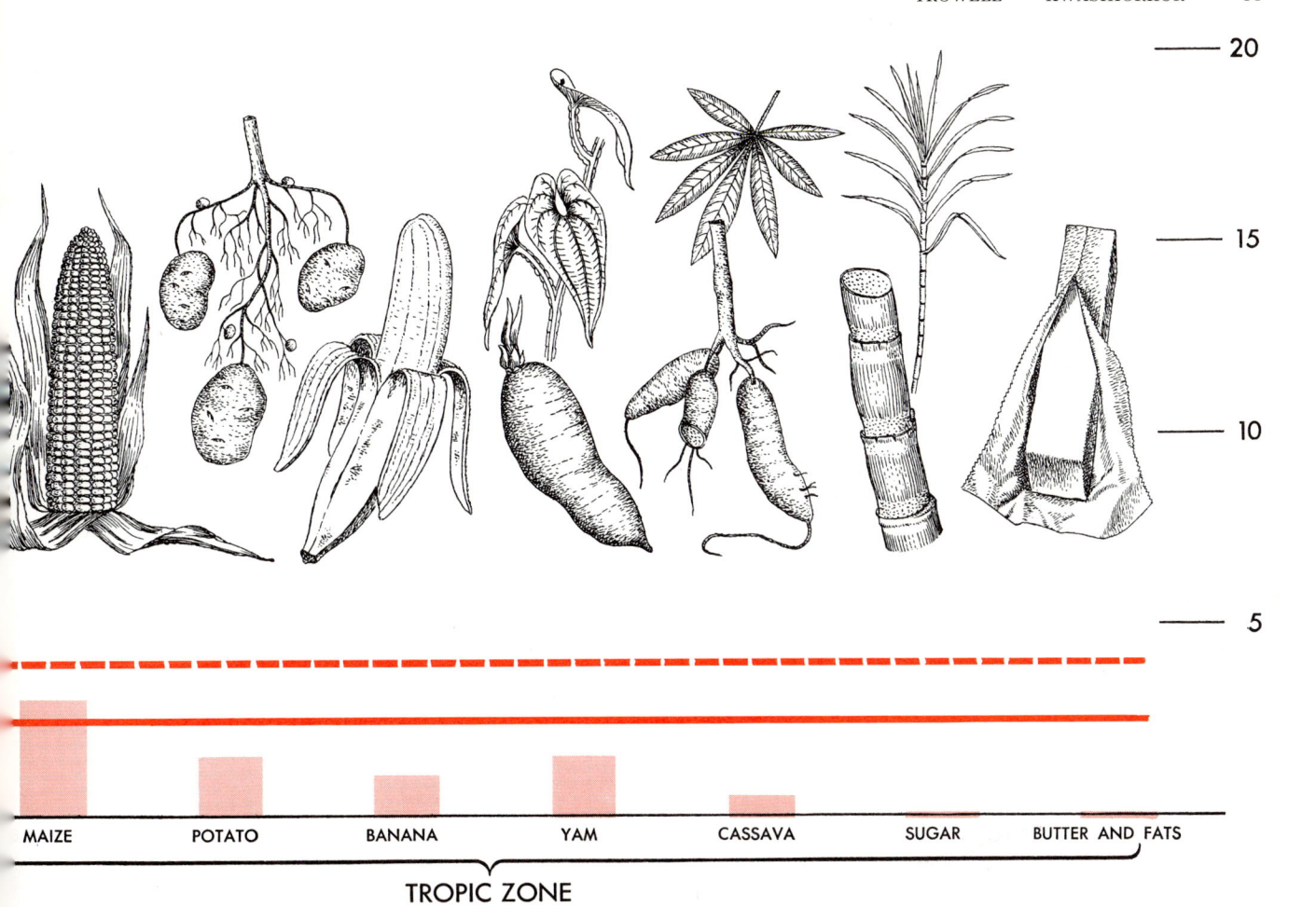

that the staples of the temperate zone are protein-rich and those of the tropic zone protein-poor. Adults require a dietary minimum of about 2.5 grams of protein per 100 calories (*solid horizontal line*); infants, about 4 grams of protein per 100 calories (*dotted line*).

changes in the blood and tissues of patients suffering from kwashiorkor. Protein enters into the composition of all body cells, all hormones and all enzymes. It is probable that many of these are affected by protein malnutrition, even when the deficiency is not serious enough to cause acute illness. There is a growing body of evidence that chronic protein deficiency may cause cirrhosis of the liver and predispose to cancer in that organ. At the moment a good deal of interest is directed to investigation of the endocrine glands of adults who have been subject to protein malnutrition.

How widespread is protein malnutrition over the world? Is it confined to the tropics? Is it almost exclusively a childhood disease or do many adults also suffer from it? A series of surveys and conferences, initiated largely by the World Health Organization and the Food and Agriculture Organization, has made it possible to say something about the geographical distribution of the disease. Kwashiorkor probably occurs in every country in the tropical belt around the world, and now that the disease has become more widely recognized, cases of it have recently been reported in Rome, Barcelona, Santiago, cities of Japan and many other cities in temperate regions.

Severe cases, which are easy to diagnose, are uncommon; even in the most seriously affected regions and at the most susceptible age (the second year of life) it is doubtful that more than 1 per cent of the children become obviously ill. It is likely, however, that in many parts of the world the majority of young children suffer some protein malnutrition. In almost all backward regions children grow extremely well during the first few months of life while they are nursing, but after that their growth is retarded, they cease to be lively, black curly hair becomes soft and brown and they show slight signs of kwashiorkor. Doubtless other deprivations and infections play their parts, but many experts now believe that the principal cause of this failure of growth of body and development of intelligence is an inadequate intake of protein.

As for adults, in most parts of the world the common diet seems to meet the minimum protein requirement—roughly estimated to be about 2.5 grams of protein per 100 calories. But in the moist and warm tropics there are many areas where the protein content of the diet is marginal or below par. Occasionally in adults one sees a clinical picture somewhat like that of kwashiorkor in childhood, or intermediate between kwashiorkor and hunger edema. Work carried out by Eric Holmes in our hospital has indicated that to correct chronic protein malnutrition in adults requires many months of very high protein feeding—as much as 150 grams of protein a day.

It should not be supposed from the foregoing that protein malnutrition is generally prevalent among either children or adults in all tropical countries. People of good income and education eat enough protein, even in the tropics. So do many of the poorer classes in areas of uncrowded population and dry climate, where some cereals are grown and animals are kept. It is rather in the moister tropics, where grains store poorly and the staple articles of diet are protein-poor, that kwashiorkor is common in childhood and protein malnutrition is probably chronic in many adults.

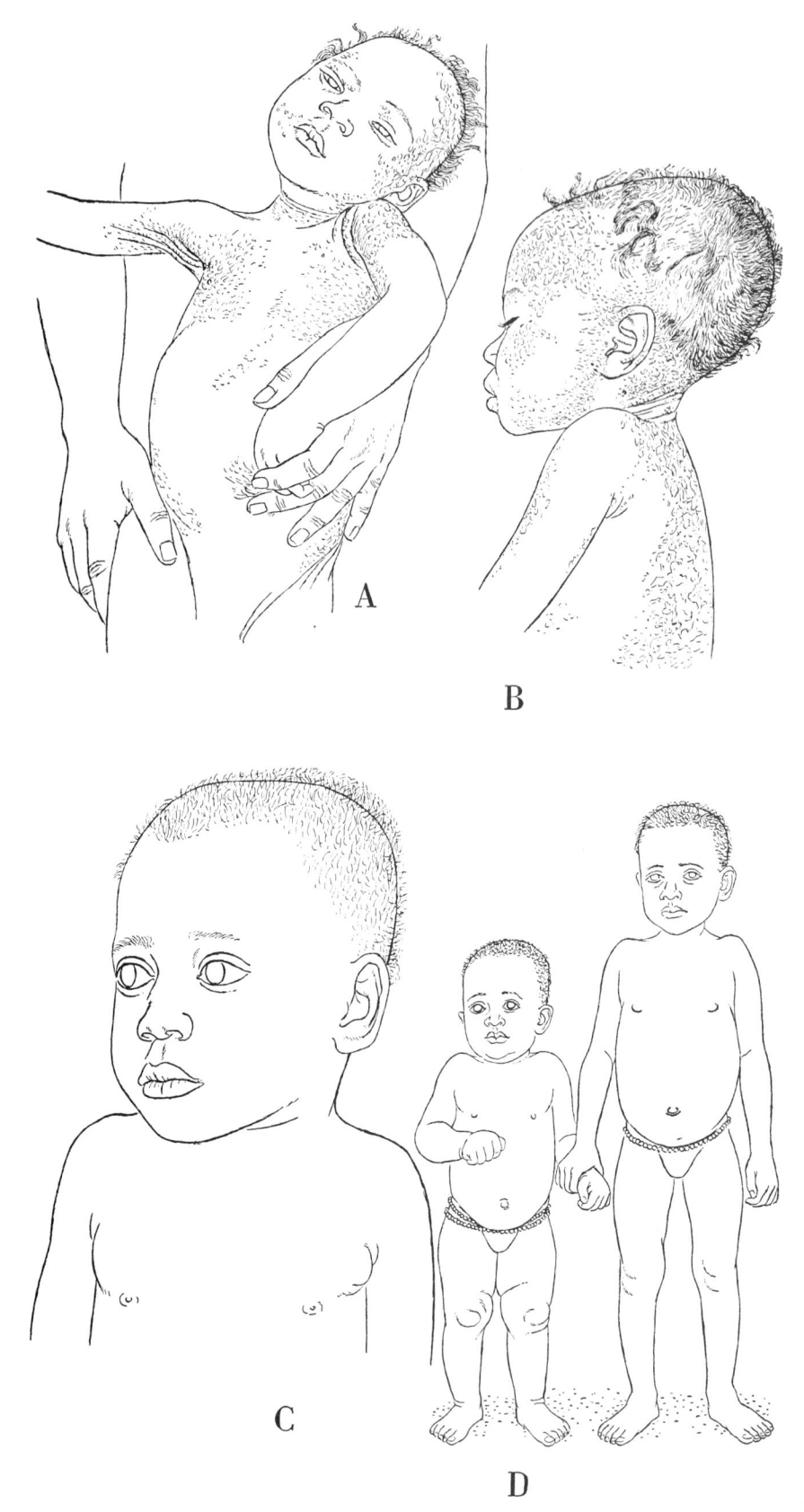

In these areas the prevention of the disease demands action along many lines. Firstly, all medical personnel and their ancillary services in nursing and public health should be instructed concerning kwashiorkor. This is no small problem. Secondly, the general public must be instructed in the disease. Thirdly, more protein-rich foods should be made available, especially to young children and pregnant and lactating women. It should not be forgotten that vegetable protein is probably almost as good as animal protein, and it will always be far cheaper. In really poor parts of the world everything should be done to increase the production and consumption of a varied diet containing much vegetable protein. It would be a great help if the large surplus of skim milk left from the manufacture of butter in the temperate regions of the world could be reduced to a preservable powder and sent to the tropics. To prepare, pack, transport, distribute and market this powder where it is needed will not be easy. Much will depend on the price and on how well powdered skim milk can compete in prestige and palatability with local sources of vegetable protein.

The treatment of severe cases of kwashiorkor has improved greatly in recent years. It is now clearly understood that whole cow's milk is digested poorly and often provokes a fatal attack of diarrhea. Small feeds of skim milk powder, mixed with a little water and mashed banana and sugar, are often well tolerated. If the patient is not doing well, pure milk protein may be given for a few days, until appetite has returned and digestion has recovered. Intravenous injection of protein or amino acids has not proved successful, for very little protein can be given in this manner. Severe cases are often fed by a tube passed down the gullet into the stomach.

Treated thus in hospital, 90 per cent of the cases of kwashiorkor now recover. I can remember the time when more than half of our patients died. Almost all severe cases still die if they cannot get hospital treatment. This still remains the disease of the poor infants of the world—a disease barely recognized, mentioned in few textbooks, demonstrated to few medical students. Of kwashiorkor Jack Chisholm of the Capetown Medical School and M. Autret, of the Food and Agriculture Organization reported to the WHO in 1952: "It is the most severe and widespread nutritional disorder known to medical science."

SYMPTOMS of kwashiorkor were observed in African children. In one severe case (A) they were a rash, wasting of the limbs and mental apathy. In another (B) these symptoms were accompanied by large areas of peeling skin. In a third case (C) the hair of the patient was pale, soft and scanty. At the lower right (D) a normal child of eight months is compared with her sister who is three years of age and suffering from kwashiorkor. The younger child weighed 19 pounds; the older one was only slightly larger and weighed 23 pounds.

BIOTIN

JOHN D. WOODWARD
June 1961

This little known but remarkably potent member of the family of B vitamins has been a biochemical puzzle for three decades. The details of its functions are only now beginning to emerge

Hardly anyone who is not a biologist or a biochemist will have heard of biotin. The name of this vitamin does not appear on the labels of tonics and vitamin pills; dietitians do not compile lists of foods that contain it. Perhaps there has never been a case of natural biotin deficiency. Yet anyone deprived of the minute traces of the substance that are required by probably every cell of the body would surely die.

The requirement is extremely small, and biotin is widely distributed. From the point of view of nutrition it can safely be ignored. Nevertheless the amazingly potent vitamin has fascinated biochemists for many years. Since the turn of the century different workers have "discovered" it at least three times and given it half a dozen names. About 20 years ago the diverse lines of research were finally brought together, and the names were shown to apply to a single substance. The chemical structure of biotin was worked out soon afterward. But the job of discovering its essential function, or functions, in the chemistry of living cells has barely begun.

The story goes back to 1901 and some experiments of the Belgian microbiologist E. Wildiers on the culture of yeast cells. His simple medium contained all the nutrients then thought to be essential, but the cells often grew poorly. He found he could obtain normal growth by adding small amounts of brewer's wort (an extract of ground malt) or extracts of dead yeast cells. The extracts evidently contained an unknown nutrient; Wildiers named it "Bios."

It was many years before Wildiers's observations gained general acceptance. Eventually it became clear that his hypothetical material represented not one but a number of distinct growth factors—water-soluble B vitamins including the now familiar thiamin (B_1), riboflavin (B_2), pyridoxine (B_6) and nicotinic acid (pellagra-preventive factor). One of the Bios fractions, unlike the others, was readily adsorbed by charcoal and so could be separated, at least partially, from the rest of the complex.

In the early 1930's this fraction, designated IIb, attracted the attention of Fritz Kögl, an organic chemist at the University of Utrecht. Up to that time all the known sources of Bios IIb contained it in exceedingly tiny amounts, so Kögl began by looking for a richer raw material. Egg yolk was one of the best sources he could find. By 1936 Kögl and B. Tönnis succeeded in isolating about a milligram (less than .00004 ounce) of "beautiful crystals" that strongly promoted the growth of yeast. This scarcely visible quantity they had extracted, in a series of 16 different and tedious steps, from 550 pounds of dried duck-egg yolks. With so small a sample they could do little more than determine the melting point of the crystals. The great biological activity of the substance in yeast cultures, however, convinced the chemists that they had found the active principle of Bios IIb. They called the elusive compound biotin.

At about the time that Kögl was beginning his research, Franklin E. Allison and his colleagues in the Bureau of Chemistry and Soils of the U. S. Department of Agriculture embarked on a study of another microorganism, the nitrogen-fixing bacterium *Rhizobium trifolii*. They found that the growth and respiration of this organism were stimulated by extracts from various organic sources. Because they believed that an unknown factor in the extracts acted in conjunction with an enzyme, they called the factor coenzyme R (for "respiration").

Philip M. West and P. W. Wilson at the University of Wisconsin noted a similarity between the growth-promoting effects of coenzyme R and of biotin. This suggested that they might be the same substance hiding behind different names. By then Kögl had improved his extraction methods and had a larger supply of crystalline biotin. A test of the material on a culture of *Rhizobium* was made by R. Nilsson, G. Bjälfe and D. Burström of the University of Uppsala in Sweden; they found it to have exactly the same stimulating effects as coenzyme R. In this respect, at least, the two were identical.

The next chapter of the story is drawn from the field of animal nutrition. It opens with a flashback to 1916, when W. G. Bateman of Yale University made the casual observation that raw egg white in the diet of animals had a toxic effect. Nothing came of this until 11 years later, when Margaret A. Boas at the Lister Institute of Preventive Medicine in London happened on the same phenomenon. She was using raw egg white as a source of protein in the diet of rats. After a few weeks the animals developed dermatitis and hemorrhages of the skin; their hair fell out; their limbs became paralyzed; they lost considerable weight and eventually they died. Only raw or cold-dried egg white produced the symptoms. Cooking made it harmless. Subsequent investigation showed that the effects of raw egg white could be alleviated or prevented by any one of a variety of foodstuffs. The action was thought to be due to a substance, common to all these foods, that was dubbed protective factor X.

The search for the protective factor was taken up by Paul György, originally at the University of Heidelberg and later at the University of Cambridge and

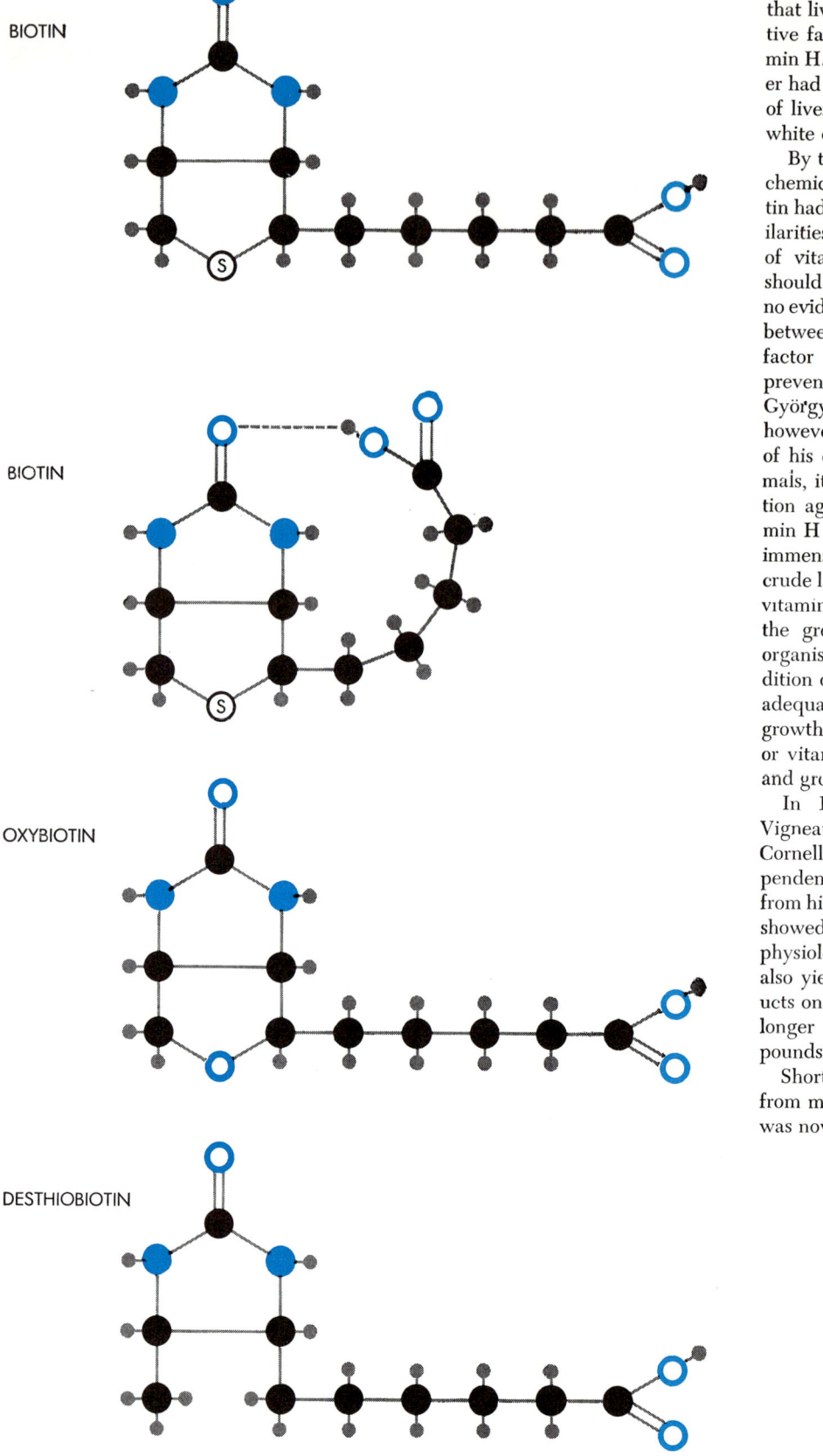

BIOTIN

BIOTIN

OXYBIOTIN

DESTHIOBIOTIN

- HYDROGEN
- CARBON
- OXYGEN
- NITROGEN
- SULFUR

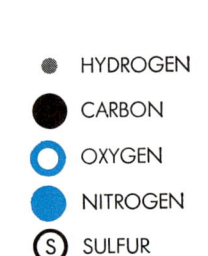

BIOTIN AND RELATED COMPOUNDS are depicted in these structural diagrams. The second biotin molecule is hypothetical; it shows side chain twisted so that a hydrogen bond (*broken line*) forms between oxygen and hydrogen. This might change the configuration of the molecule and thus activate the nitrogen atoms. Oxybiotin resembles biotin in biological activity; its molecule contains an oxygen atom instead of a sulfur atom. Desthiobiotin lacks the sulfur atom; it is probably the immediate precursor of biotin.

Western Reserve University. He learned that liver is a good source of the protective factor, which he had named "vitamin H." Concentrates prepared from liver had more than 3,000 times the power of liver itself to protect rats on an egg-white diet.

By that time preliminary work on the chemical and physical properties of biotin had turned up some provocative similarities between biotin and concentrates of vitamin H. On the other hand, it should be remembered that there was no evidence of a physiological connection between the two. Biotin was a growth factor for microorganisms; vitamin H prevented egg-white injury in animals. György now suspected a connection, however, and asked Kögl for a sample of his crystalline biotin. Tested on animals, it showed the same protective action against egg-white injury that vitamin H did. In fact, the pure biotin was immensely more potent than the rather crude liver extracts of vitamin H. Would vitamin H concentrates in turn support the growth of biotin-requiring microorganisms? They did. Moreover, the addition of raw egg white to an otherwise adequate culture medium prevented the growth of these organisms. More biotin or vitamin H overcame the toxic effect and growth resumed.

In 1940 György and Vincent du Vigneaud and his colleagues at the Cornell University Medical College independently isolated crystalline vitamin H from highly active liver concentrates and showed that it matched Kögl's biotin in physiological and physical properties. It also yielded the same breakdown products on chemical analysis. There was no longer any doubt that the two compounds were one and the same.

Shortly afterward, biotin was isolated from milk. With so plentiful a source it was now possible to accumulate enough

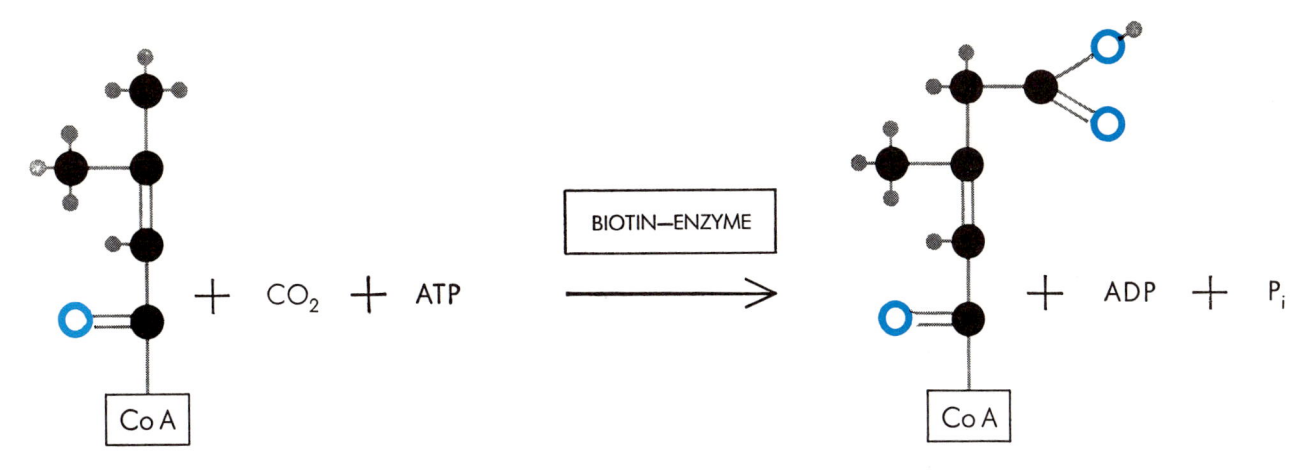

BETA-METHYL-CROTONYL-CoA

BETA-METHYL-GLUTACONYL-CoA

CARBON DIOXIDE TRANSFER is effected by an enzyme that contains biotin. Adenosine triphosphate (ATP) supplies energy for many cellular reactions. The biotin-enzyme directs the union of carbon dioxide and beta-methyl-crotonyl-CoA to give beta-methyl-glutaconyl-CoA, adenosine diphosphate (ADP) and inorganic phosphate (P_i). Proposed details of this reaction are shown below.

PROPOSED SEQUENCE OF REACTIONS to account for the transfer of carbon dioxide is diagramed. In the first step ATP reacts with the biotin-enzyme. In the second step carbon dioxide combines with the biotin-enzyme. The carbon dioxide is transferred to beta-methyl-crotonyl-CoA in the third step, producing beta-methyl-glutaconyl-CoA. CoA is an abbreviation for coenzyme A.

of the vitamin for a concerted attack on its chemical structure. Du Vigneaud and others proceeded to dissect the molecule and by 1942 were able to write its complete structural formula [see illustration on page 58]. The next year Stanton A. Harris and his colleagues at the research laboratory of Merck & Co., Inc., clinched this part of the problem when they synthesized a substance with the proposed structure. It was identical with natural biotin, both chemically and in its physiological action.

So closed a most satisfying chapter in biological research. Bios IIb, coenzyme R, protective factor X, vitamin H and biotin had been shown to be the same substance—an essential preliminary to any attempt to understand its biochemical function.

Today biotin is known to be very widely distributed. In fact, it is probably an essential constituent of all living cells, both plant and animal. Yet its potency is so great that no cell contains more than a trace of it. Liver, one of the richest sources, contains less than one part of biotin per million. Kögl spent five years accumulating 70 milligrams of the crystalline material. He estimated that he would have needed 360 tons of yeast or about $175,000 worth of eggs (1937 prices) to extract one gram.

Kögl's refined material was not free biotin but its methyl ester, in which the final hydroxyl (OH) of the carboxyl group (COOH) is replaced by a methyl group (CH_3). In tissues biotin is also often found in combination with other compounds rather than free. Proteins are a common partner, and the compounds the two substances form have been named bioto-proteins. The toxic material in egg white is the protein avidin. It combines with biotin in a complex that the digestive enzymes of higher animals cannot split apart and that is

60   I • NUTRITION AND MALNUTRITION

not absorbed from the alimentary canal. Thus raw egg white exerts its toxic action by inducing a deficiency of biotin. Cooking or any heat treatment denatures avidin, destroying its power to combine with biotin. Moreover, the avidin-biotin complex readily breaks down when it is heated.

Under normal circumstances human beings and other mammals do not suffer biotin deficiency even when the vitamin is eliminated from the diet. The intestines contain bacteria that synthesize biotin for themselves and incidentally for their host. Therefore the deficiency can be induced in test animals only by feeding them avidin or by eliminating the intestinal flora with antibacterial drugs. Using these techniques various workers have studied biotin deficiency in many species of higher animal, including rats, mice, hamsters, dogs, cattle, pigs, monkeys and even man. A biotin-free diet alone can induce deficiency symptoms in chickens, presumably because of the low bacterial content of their alimentary tract.

The precise symptoms of biotin deficiency vary from species to species, but skin lesions, dermatitis, loss of hair and nervous disorders usually characterize the disease. Human volunteers at the University of Georgia School of Medicine, put on a diet containing about half a pound of dried egg white a day, developed a scaling dermatitis and a peculiar

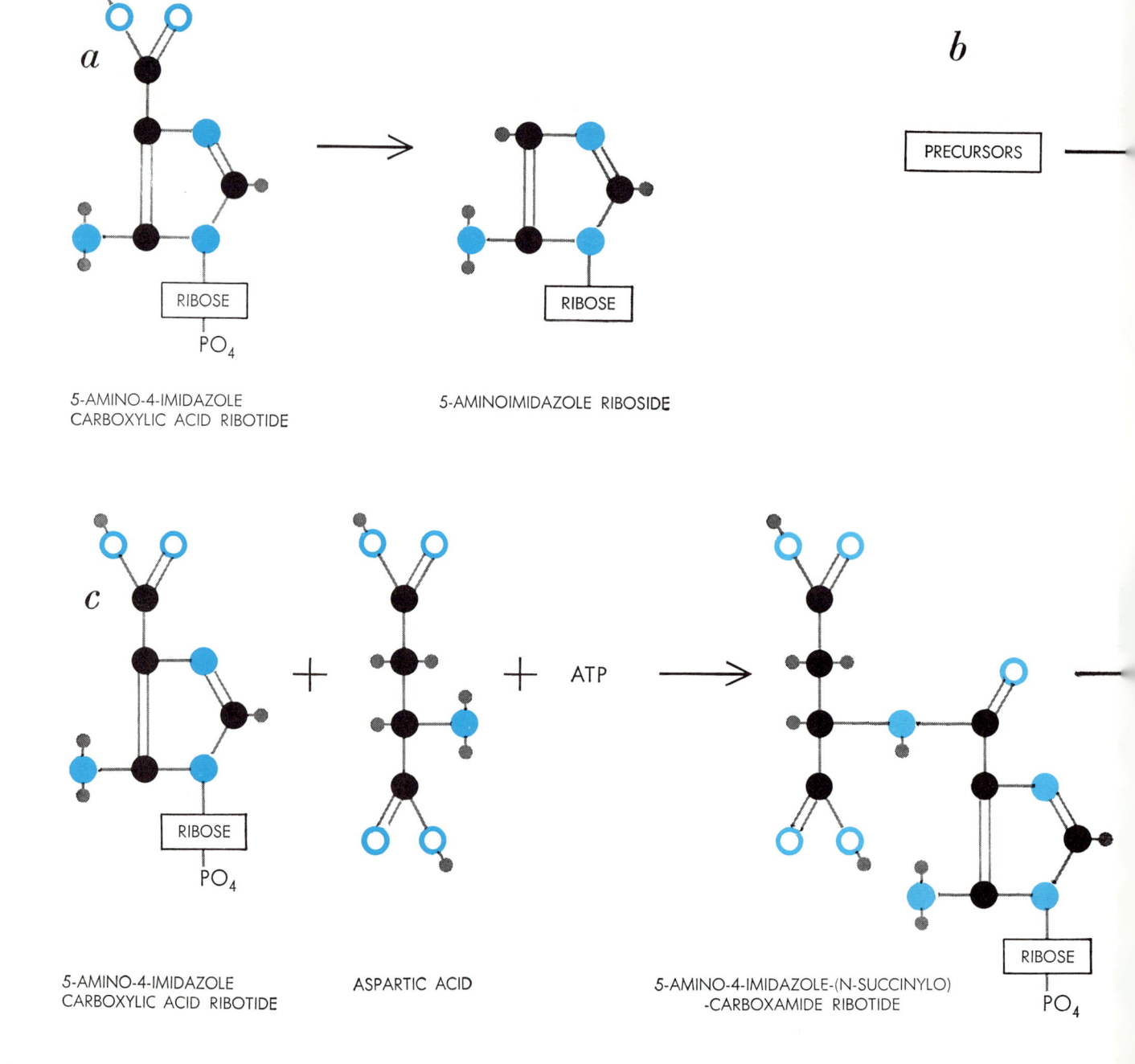

SYNTHESIS OF PURINES depends on biotin. When yeast is deprived of biotin, the synthesis stops with the intermediate shown at left in *a*. This, in turn, breaks down spontaneously to 5-aminoimidazole riboside, which accumulates in the culture medium. The stoppage is caused by a lack of aspartic acid, which is made with the aid of biotin (*b*). When biotin, or aspartic acid, is fed to

gray pallor. Lassitude, mental depression and muscle pains accompanied these symptoms. Administration of biotin promptly relieved the condition.

Of course, the observation of such gross effects cannot by itself elucidate the biochemical role of biotin. Experiments now under way in many laboratories, on a wide variety of cells and tissues, are directed at two fundamental problems: the precise function of biotin in the cell and the way in which it is synthesized by the organisms that manufacture it.

One difficulty in understanding how biotin works is that it seems to play a number of different roles. Almost all the other B vitamins, which are "cousins" of biotin, have been shown to have unique and specific functions at the cellular level. Biotin participates in many different biochemical reactions and transformations: it helps convert carbon dioxide to carbohydrates; it acts in removing amino (NH_2) groups from certain amino acids and the carboxyl group from certain other organic acids that are key intermediates in the breakdown of carbohydrates; it plays an essential part in the synthesis of aspartic acid and of fatty acids; there is evidence that it is involved in glucose oxidation and the metabolism of pyruvic acid. The list shows that biotin participates in the metabolism of the three principal constituents of living organisms: carbohydrates, fats and proteins. This apparent diversity of function suggests that biochemists have been unable to see the forest for the trees. The role of biotin may be more subtle than has been supposed. Perhaps the vitamin acts to synthesize specific enzymes rather than to assist in their chemical function, serving as a toolmaker rather than as a tool.

Some evidence for a fundamental role of this sort has come out of experiments in our laboratory at the University of Birmingham in England. In the course of investigation of biotin deficiency in yeast D. Peter Lones, Cyril Rainbow and I found an unexpected compound accumulating in the culture medium. It was a material now known to be an intermediate in the synthesis of purines by cells. The purines, essential components of nucleic acids and other cell constituents, are compounds having a common double-ring framework of carbon and nitrogen atoms [see illustration on these two pages]. Largely through the elegant studies of John M. Buchanan at the Massachusetts Institute of Technology and G. Robert Greenberg, then at Western Reserve University, each step in the biosynthesis of purines has been delineated.

About halfway along this cellular assembly line aspartic acid is incorporated into the growing framework of the molecule. Biotin-deficient yeast is unable to manufacture enough aspartic acid to keep pace with the purine assembly process. This results in a pile-up of the unfinished purine intermediate, which eventually spills out of the cells into the surrounding medium. If aspartic acid itself is included in the medium, the bottleneck is broken, the assembly line starts moving again and the intermediate compound no longer accumulates. Other recent work indicates that biotin can also function as a coenzyme, as Allison originally supposed. Whereas some of the enzymes for which biotin was once thought to be a cofactor have now been shown to be active without it, Salih J. Wakil at the University of Wisconsin has obtained an enzyme, involved in the synthesis of fatty acids, that does require the vitamin. The activity of the enzyme preparation is proportional to its biotin content. Moreover, the activity disappears with the addition of avidin and reappears when more biotin is added. A similar biotin-containing enzyme has been described by Feodor Lynen of the Max Planck Institute for Cell Chemistry in Munich. Both this enzyme and Wakil's seem to effect the uptake of carbon dioxide through the intermediate formation of an active "carboxylated" biotin. Lynen has provisionally identified such an intermediate, in which carbon dioxide is attached at one of the nitrogen atoms of the biotin molecule. He suggests that there are many biotin-containing enzymes that transfer carbon dioxide in different reactions.

W. Traub of the University of London has suggested a mechanism by which the nitrogen atoms in the biotin molecule may be enabled to participate in these reactions. Examining the spatial arrangement of the molecule, he found that under certain conditions the keto (C-O) oxygen of the ring and one oxygen of the carboxyl group in the side chain may come close enough to each other for a special kind of intramolecular bond—the hydrogen bond—to form between them. This would distort the molecule in such a way that it would increase the chemical reactivity of the nitrogen atoms in the ring.

As for the synthesis of biotin by living cells, the process has not yet been traced very far. The immediate precursor of the vitamin is probably desthiobiotin, which lacks only the sulfur atom of the biotin molecule [see illustration on page 58]. Part of the carbon skeleton is thought to be supplied by pimelic acid, a seven-carbon compound. In fact, pimelic acid acts like biotin in certain microorganisms and stimulates the production of biotin in others.

Here matters stand as these lines are written. The story, which nicely illustrates the trend in modern biology, began with the recognition of an undefined principle in brewer's wort and it closes

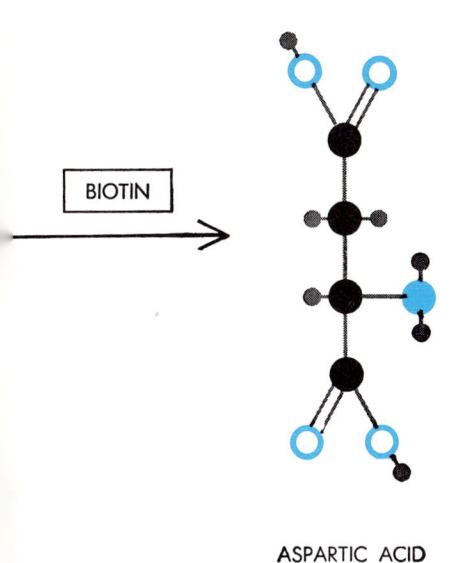

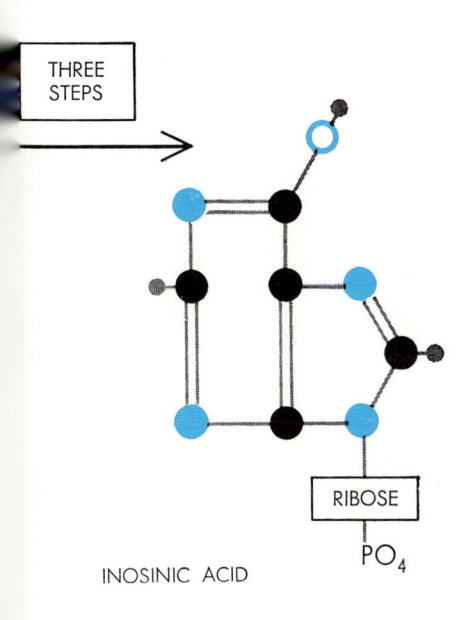

the yeast, the assembly line resumes. Inosinic acid, which is one of the purines, is the end product of this particular process.

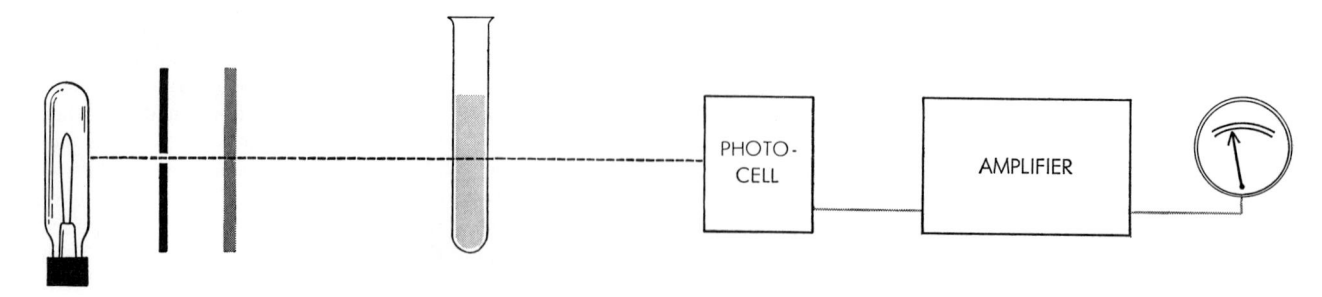

MICROBIOLOGICAL ASSAY OF BIOTIN employs cultures of yeast cells. It can detect a biotin concentration of only one part in 500,000 million. More yeast cells appear in a culture as the concentration of biotin rises, making the suspension more turbid. A light (*left*) shines through a diaphragm, a filter and the culture in the test tube until it hits a photocell, which detects changes in light intensity. The amount of light transmitted by the culture registers on the ammeter at right, giving the measure of the concentration of biotin. With a compound as active as biotin such a method of quantative measurement is essential to the understanding of its functions.

with the consideration of individual atoms in a precisely known molecular structure. There is still a lot to learn, and biotin is very much a "hot" topic today. By the time this article is published the chances are that someone will have made a further important contribution to the understanding of this unfamiliar but vital substance.

ENDEMIC GOITER

R. BRUCE GILLIE
June 1971

The disorder has a long record because its principal sign is so apparent. It is now a disease of the poor, because an unbalanced diet often cannot correct for a deficiency of iodine in the soil

The "regular and rounded neck" with which Maria de' Medici was endowed by Rubens [*see illustration on page 68*] is a goiter, or compensatory hypertrophy of the thyroid gland. The thyroid is a pinkish pad of tissue wrapped partly around the trachea and esophagus; it is a ductless gland of vertebrates that secretes into the blood the hormones that regulate the rate of development and metabolism. Goiter is an unusually obvious manifestation of an endocrine disorder, and as such it has drawn attention, sometimes admiring and sometimes fearful, since man's earliest days.

There are many different causes of goiter: disease, developmental defects and environmental conditions. Endemic goiter, so designated because it affects a significant proportion of a given population, is almost always the result of a dietary deficiency of iodine, an essential substrate for the synthesis of the thyroid hormones thyroxine and tri-iodothyronine. Iodine-deficiency goiter is now easily prevented or cured by the ingestion of minute quantities of iodine, but over the centuries it has been one of the most persistent and ubiquitous diseases of mankind. As recently as 1960, 200 million people were still afflicted with it.

The secretion of thyroid hormones is a link in one of the exquisitely balanced feedback systems that regulate the internal environment of vertebrate organisms [see "The Thyroid Gland," by Lawson Wilkins; SCIENTIFIC AMERICAN, March, 1960]. Impulses from the nervous system cause the hypothalamus at the base of the brain to release a neurosecretion, the thyrotropin-releasing factor (TRF), into portal veins leading directly to the pituitary, the pea-sized master gland that regulates the activity of the thyroid and other endocrine glands. The thyrotropin-releasing factor stimulates the pituitary to secrete into the blood thyrotropin, or thyroid-stimulating hormone (TSH), which in turn causes the thyroid to synthesize and secrete its hormones. The system is self-regulating: an excess of thyroid hormones in the blood suppresses hypothalamus and pituitary activity and reduces the secretion of the thyroid-stimulating hormone; when the thyroid hormone concentration is too low, the pituitary responds by secreting more thyroid-stimulating hormone to restore the normal thyroid-hormone level [*see illustration on page 66*].

If the thyroid is healthy and there is enough iodide (ionic iodine) in the blood, the thyroid-stimulating hormone steps up the trapping of iodide by the thyroid and in other ways abets the synthesis of thyroxine and tri-iodothyronine within the follicles of the thyroid gland [*see illustration on page 8*]. In the absence of sufficient iodide thyroxine synthesis is inhibited; the flow of thyroid-stimulating hormone is unchecked and its effect is to increase the number and change the shape of the cells that form the follicles; in time the follicles become distended. This compensatory proliferation of cells and distension of the follicles, which constitute goiter, may restore thyroid-hormone production to a satisfactory level for normal life.

A Chinese document from about 3000 B.C. is the earliest known record of goiter. Remarkably, it not only described the symptoms but recommended an effective cure: the ingestion of seaweed and burned sponge, which contain large amounts of iodine. Speculating on the causes of what was apparently a common affliction, Chinese scholars listed poor quality of drinking water, mountainous terrain and emotional vicissitudes, all of which are indeed associated with a higher incidence of goiter. The Chinese even administered desiccated thyroid glands of deer as a treatment for goiter. (Nowadays extracts of beef, sheep or hog thyroid are given for hypothyroidism.)

The Ebers Papyrus of Egypt, dating from about 1500 B.C., described two possible treatments for goiter: surgical removal of the gland (which must have been a high-risk procedure if it was ever attempted) and the ingestion of salt (presumably containing iodine) from a particular site in lower Egypt.

Hippocrates blamed goiter on the drinking water in certain places. Juvenal, Vitruvius and Julius Caesar were impressed by the enlarged neck of residents of some alpine regions; Caesar, in fact, believed that the large neck was a national characteristic of the Gauls. The word "goiter," incidentally, is from the Latin *guttur*, or "throat."

Roman physicians noticed that even in a normal person the size of the thyroid may fluctuate somewhat during times of physiological stress such as puberty, menstruation and pregnancy. They noticed in particular that the physical and emotional circumstances surrounding the initial sexual activity of a bride brought about a slight swelling of her thyroid. The Romans thereupon originated the ritual of measuring the circumference of a bride's neck with a ceremonial ribbon before and after her first week of marriage. If the circumference increased, the marriage was considered consummated.

Because moderate goiter is quite compatible with normal life, causing no pain and often no impairment, it was not necessarily perceived as an affliction; if in some cultures it was considered a divine stigma, in others it was a mark of beauty. In Europe it was often attributed to some serious religious or social transgression—robbing the graves of saints, for example. In Germany during the Middle

Ages it was thought that the condition could be caused by strenuous work, including childbirth. That was the rationale for a now forgotten custom of tying a cord around the neck of a woman in labor. In India inhaling the odor of people dying of malaria was said to cause goiter. At one time or another the condition has been blamed on indolence, drunkenness and debauchery. In 1867 a French student of the matter named J. Saint Leger listed more than 40 different possible causes then being cited—among them a lack of electricity in the atmosphere, incest, alcoholism and coitus interruptus.

Cures were not so easy to find. A procedure that appears to have persisted for many centuries was piercing the thyroid gland with a red-hot needle. That presumably created an inflammation, and the resulting fibrosis may well have reduced the size of the gland. Actual surgery could not have been effective until the end of the 19th century. One reason is that the thyroid is so richly supplied with blood vessels that in the early days of surgery an incision would have resulted in excessive and uncontrollable bleeding. Even after the advent of satisfactory techniques surgical removal was dangerous at best before the discovery of the parathyroid glands. These tiny glands, nesting on the surface of the thyroid lobes, regulate the concentration of calcium in the blood, and their inadvertent removal along with the goitrous thyroid would threaten life.

The first attempt at an epidemiological survey was made at the request of Napoleon I, who was impressed (as Caesar had been) by the many cases he saw in the course of his alpine campaigns. Napoleon was also disturbed by the loss of potential recruits who had to be rejected because the military uniform would not fit their goitrous necks.

The basic mystery surrounding goiter, of course, was the function of the thyroid gland in health. The early anatomists were impressed by the gland's large blood supply and puzzled by the fact that (like the other endocrine glands) it had no duct and therefore, it seemed to them, could have no secretory function. In the Middle Ages some anat-

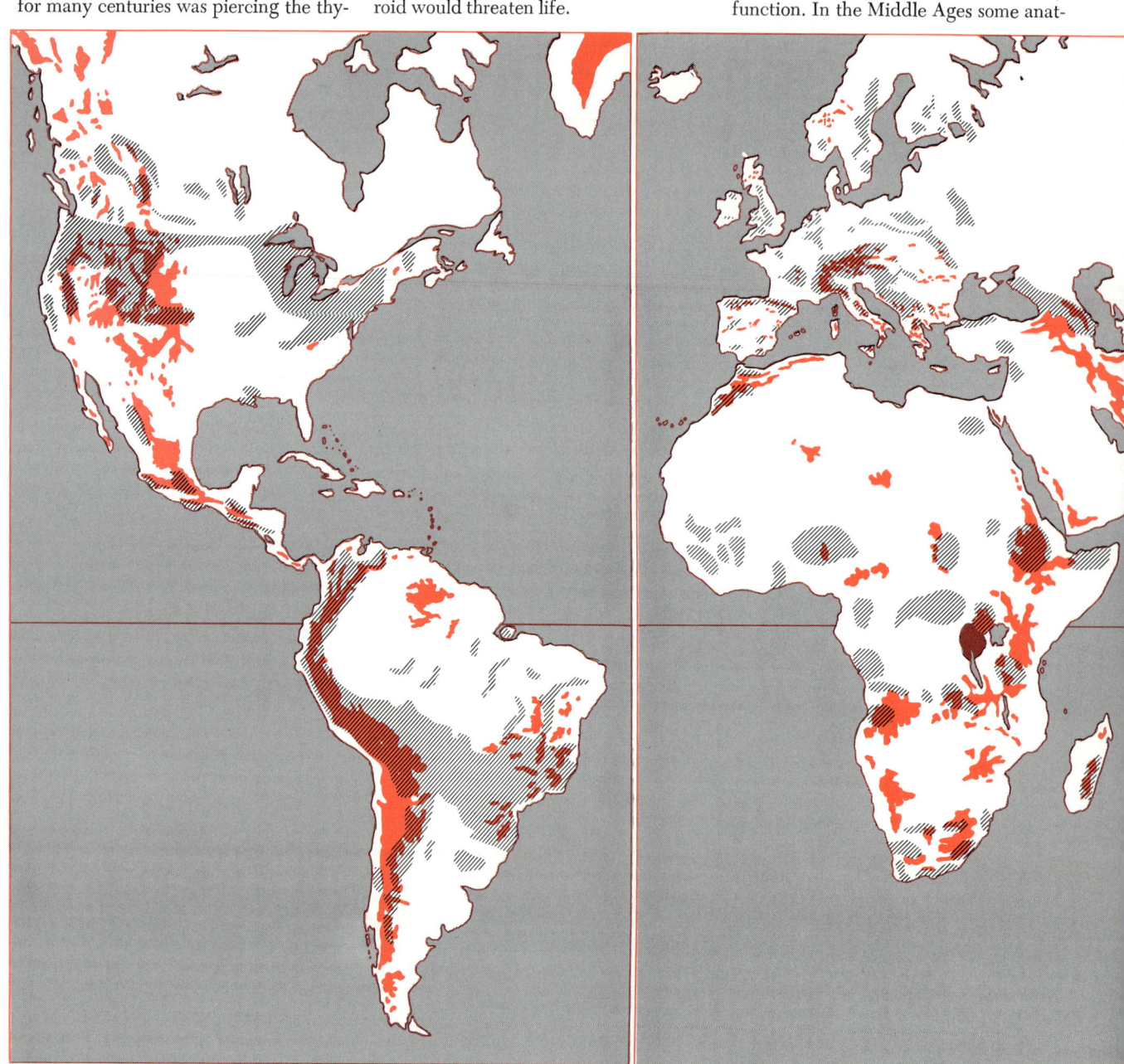

REGIONS OF ENDEMIC GOITER and the mountainous terrain with which it is often associated were mapped by the World Health Organization. Areas where iodine-deficiency goiter is endemic are indicated by the black hatching. Populations near seacoasts are sel-

omists thought of the thyroid as the seat of the soul. Others were more practical. The Italian anatomist Giulio Casserio wrote in 1600: "Kind nature has especially beautified the gentle female sex with many sorts of ornaments. And not the least among them is this one, that the empty spaces which exist around the larynx being filled up, they show to our eyes, to the great joy of our sight, a regular and rounded neck." Paintings by artists of the time, including Dürer and Rembrandt, suggest that Casserio's view was the general one, since madonnas and other female subjects are often depicted with moderately goitrous necks.

In 1656 the British anatomist Thomas Wharton wrote a complete description of the thyroid and also named it after the Greek word for a large oblong shield: *thyreos*. Wharton agreed with Casserio that it served to beautify the neck ("particularly in females to whom for this reason a larger gland has been assigned"), but he suggested that it might also keep the tracheal cartilages warm, since they were "rather of a chilly nature," and lubricate the larynx, rendering the voice more melodious. Other students believed the thyroid shunted blood away from the brain to protect it from sudden changes in blood pressure, or that it was a cushion to support and protect the structures of the larynx.

It was not until 1895, after surgeons had seen the effects of removal of the thyroid gland and after treatment with thyroid extract had been attempted, that Adolf Magnus-Levy of Germany demonstrated that the thyroid regulated the basal metabolic rate: the rate at which the cells of the body consume oxygen, which is to say the rate at which they convert nutrients into the energy of life. In the same year the German biochemist Eugen Baumann learned that the thyroid is particularly rich in iodine. It was a serendipitous discovery. Baumann was trying to analyze the protein content of thyroid tissue, and his usual procedure was to precipitate the protein from an extract with sulfuric acid. One day, reaching for the sulfuric acid on a shelf above his workbench, he picked up a bottle of nitric acid instead, and before he had realized his mistake he had added some of its contents to the extract. To his astonishment the characteristic brownish-purple fumes of iodine gas swirled up from the preparation. Baumann went on to describe the role of iodine in thyroid physiology. In 1914 Edward C. Kendall of the Mayo Foundation first crystallized some thyroid hormone. It was a large and difficult task: the 37 grams of crystallized hormone that Kendall subsequently obtained were derived from three and a quarter tons of pig thyroid! Finally in 1927 Charles Robert Harington of the University College Hospital Medical School in London and George Barger of the University of Edinburgh established the definitive structure of thyroxine, confirming Baumann's observations. Well before that time Baumann's work had led on the one hand to the understanding that endemic goiter was the result of environmental iodine deficiency and on the other to simple and effective iodine therapy.

As investigators looked into the ecology of goitrous populations they first found a correlation between goiter and the accessibility of a population to the sea and thus to a seafood diet rich in iodine. A map compiled by the World Health Organization makes it clear that it is in inland areas, particularly mountainous ones, that goiter may be endemic [*see illustration on these two pages*]. The Alps, the Pyrenees, the Himalayas and the Andes are strikingly goitrous. So are inland plains regions in Italy, in the Congo and in the Great Lakes basin of North America.

The geography of goiter is not simple, however. Many inland and mountainous regions do not support goitrous populations, and there are coastal areas that unpredictably have goitrous populations. A factor that is more closely correlated with the incidence of endemic goiter than mere distance from the ocean is the

dom affected because of the iodine content of seafood. Not all inland areas are equally affected; the geology and remoteness of mountainous regions (*color*) make them most susceptible.

iodine content of the soil. As long as the soil content of iodine is adequate, enough iodine (about 100 to 200 micrograms per person per day) will be ingested in locally grown produce to prevent the onset of goiter. Although the iodine content of soils is generally higher in coastal regions than it is inland, soil content is determined by more complex factors than distance from the ocean alone. The most seriously depleted soils are in areas that were subjected to the most intense glaciation. Such glaciation did two things. By crushing virgin igneous rocks that had never been exposed to atmospheric iodine, it left behind vast amounts of new, iodine-poor topsoil, and it leached the soluble iodine salts out of the original soil.

Leaching may also make soils along the shores of rivers that periodically overflow their banks deficient in iodine. An interesting example of this process was noted in a study of two villages on opposite banks of the Congo River in an area where heavy rain and periodic flooding had reduced the iodine content of the soil. On one bank the village population was 80 percent goitrous; on the alluvial soil of the opposite bank the population was hardly goitrous at all. Iodine being leached by the heavy rain out of land upstream was being redeposited in the alluvial soil around the second village, making the iodine concentration there just sufficient to prevent goiter.

The steady replenishment of iodine in terrestrial soils from atmospheric iodine tends in time to reverse the effects of glaciation. The degree of replenishment is complexly affected by the distance of an area from the ocean, the prevailing wind conditions and the amount of iodine in the precipitation. In addition some areas of the world have natural terrestrial iodine deposits that may also help to determine the iodine content of the local soil. In other words, the ecology of a human society as well as its principal staple diet is a major factor in the etiology of endemic goiter.

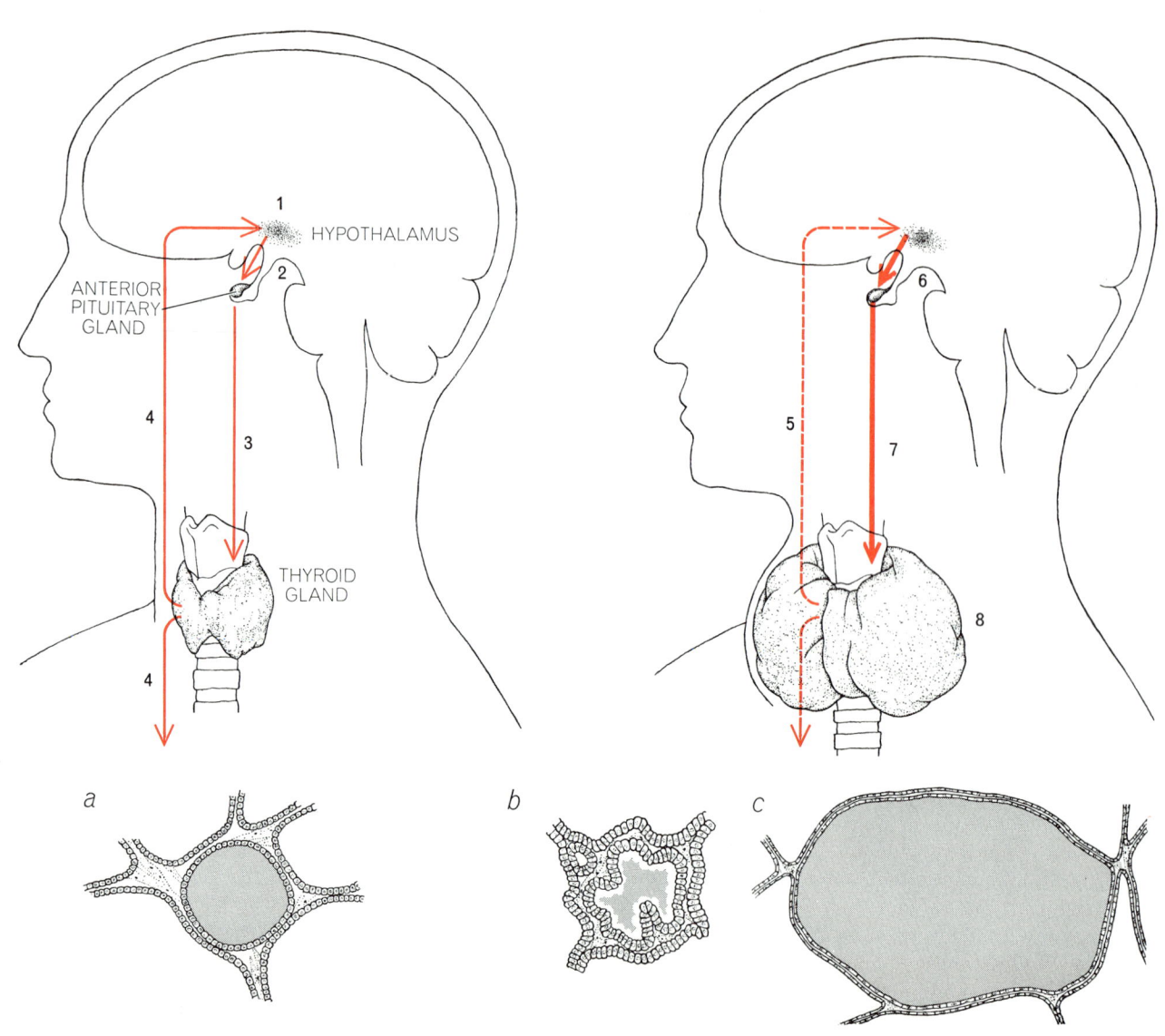

NEGATIVE-FEEDBACK SYSTEM controlling production of thyroid hormones begins with the neurosecretion from the hypothalamus (1) of thyrotropin-releasing factor (TRF), which goes directly to the pituitary (2) and causes it to release thyrotropin, or thyroid-stimulating hormone (TSH), into the bloodstream (3). In the thyroid gland TSH acts to bring about the synthesis and secretion into the circulation of the thyroid hormones thyroxine and tri-iodothyronine (4); the amount of thyroid hormones reaching the hypothalamus in turn controls the secretion of TSH, completing the negative-feedback loop. In the absence of iodine, an essential substrate for thyroid hormones, not enough hormone is produced (5) to "turn off" the system; excessive TRF (6) and TSH (7) are secreted, stimulating the iodine-depleted thyroid tissue to grow (8). A normal thyroid follicle, in which hormones are synthesized and stored, consists of an envelope of cells containing a colloid, thyroglobulin (a). In the absence of iodine TSH causes the cells to proliferate and become more columnar (b) and then to produce more colloid, so that the follicles become distended (c), forming a goiter.

Beginning in 1907 the extensive investigations of David Marine and O. P. Kimball of the Western Reserve University School of Medicine with laboratory animals provided the first direct experimental evidence that endemic thyroid hypertrophy is caused by iodine deficiency. These workers subsequently carried out the first large-scale program of goiter prophylaxis in Akron, Ohio. The study, completed in 1920, involved 4,500 schoolgirls between the fifth and the 12th grade. Half of them received two grams of iodized salt twice a year and the other half served as untreated controls. At the end of two and a half years 65.4 percent of the treated group showed regression of goiter and only five treated girls evinced thyroid enlargement. Meanwhile only 13.8 percent of the girls in the untreated group showed a regression of goiter and 495 untreated girls had developed thyroid hypertrophy. The study was a dramatic demonstration of the efficacy of iodine in the treatment and the prevention of simple goiter.

When these findings were published, many individuals and groups of health enthusiasts took to consuming iodine to the extent of a fetishism. Some people even hung around their neck little bottles of iodine from which they would occasionally take a swig. Iodine became the magic ingredient in the nostrums of certain charlatans. To everyone's surprise, rather than preventing goiter, iodine sometimes served to stimulate it. This apparently paradoxical effect of iodine on the etiology of goiter was later explained by Jan Wolff and Israel L. Chaikoff of the School of Medicine of the University of California at Berkeley, who found that very high iodine concentrations in the blood plasma inhibit the biosynthesis and secretion of thyroid hormone. This aspect of thyroid physiology, together with increasing reports of severe iodine toxicity and the fear that iodine might lead to toxic hyperthyroidism, elicited strenuous opposition to the iodization of table salt by many medical experts, lay people and politicians. The political and ethical controversy over the incorporation of iodine into table salt was even more intense than the present-day controversy over the fluoridation of water. It was not until the mid-1920's that iodine prophylaxis was generally accepted.

Although the idea that some positive agent in food or drink was responsible for goiter had antedated the discovery of iodine deficiency as a cause, it was not until 1941 that a goitrogenic substance was identified. Curt P. Richter and Kathryn H. Clisby of the Johns Hopkins University School of Medicine were investigating the effects of certain rat poisons. When they fed laboratory rats the drug thiourea, they observed to their surprise that the rats survived but their thyroid began growing and soon became goitrous. At about the same time Julia B. and Cosmo G. MacKenzie, in another laboratory at Johns Hopkins, were studying the effect of a new sulfonamide drug on the bacterial flora of the rat intestine. They observed the same phenomenon: the thyroid of their treated rats became hypertrophic, as if the animals had been maintained for several weeks on an iodine-deficient diet. The drugs were apparently preventing the proper utilization of iodine, which was present in normal concentrations in the animals' food and water. Since that time many additional antithyroid compounds have been discovered.

Theoretically these drugs could act by any of three different mechanisms. First, they could operate at the intestinal level

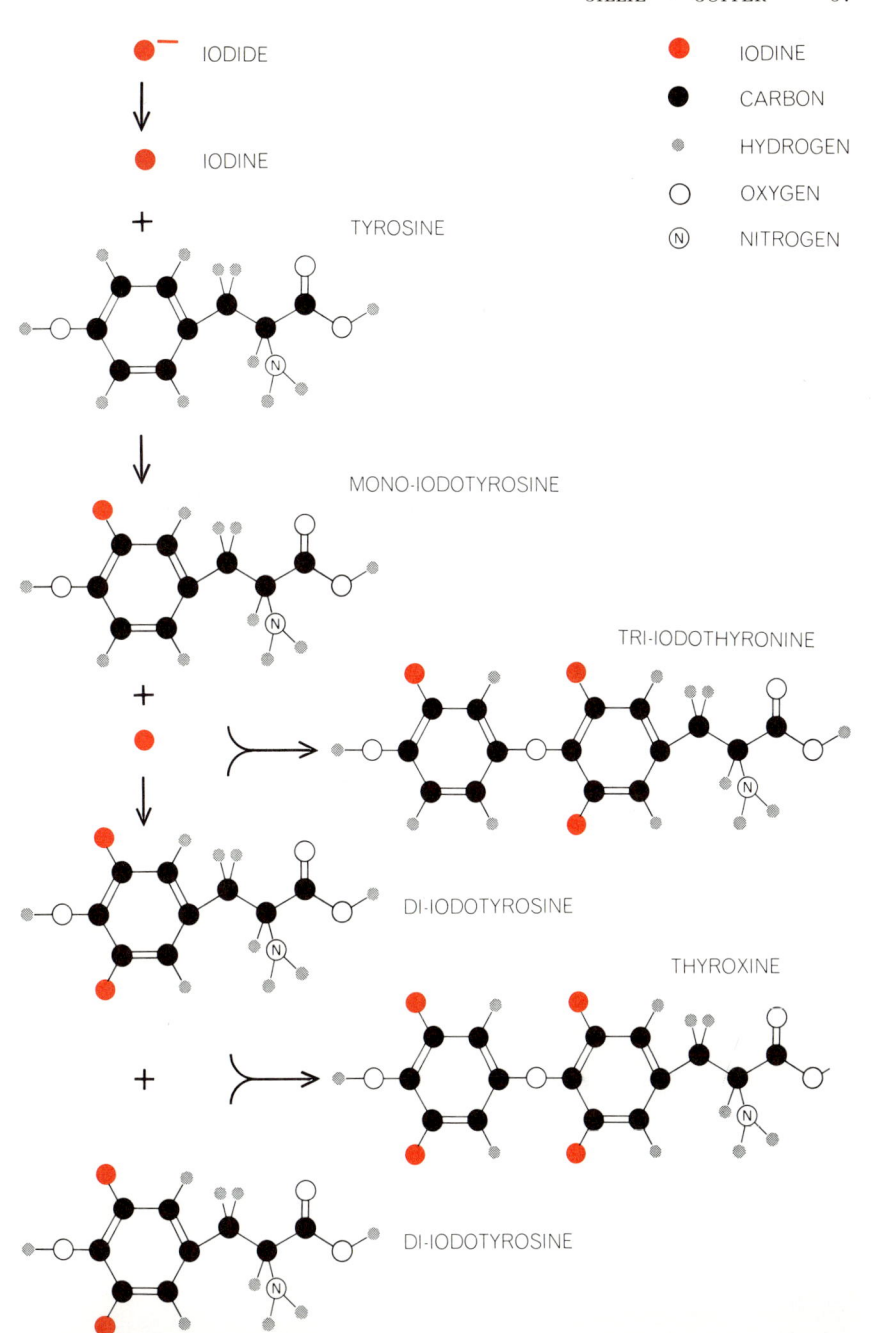

BIOSYNTHESIS of the thyroid hormones depends on the presence of ionic iodine, primarily as sodium iodide. The iodide is oxidized to elemental iodine and combines with the amino acid tyrosine to form mono-iodotyrosine and di-iodotyrosine. Two molecules of di-iodotyrosine may combine to form thyroxine, or mono- and di-iodotyrosine molecules may combine to form tri-iodothyronine. (Only hormone products are shown, not by-products.)

MODERATE GOITER is evident in this detail from a portrait of Maria de' Medici, wife of Henry IV of France. It was painted in 1625 by Rubens and now hangs in the Prado in Madrid. Moderate goiter was considered an adornment in the late Renaissance.

to chelate, or sequester, iodine and so prevent its normal absorption into the bloodstream. Second, they could act at the surface of the thyroid epithelial cell to inhibit the selective absorption of iodine from the blood passing through the gland. (This trapping of iodine ions is an amazingly efficient process: the thyroid concentrates the ions to a level several hundred times higher than their concentration in the plasma.) Third, the goitrogenic compounds could gain admission to the cells of the thyroid and there inhibit the biosynthetic pathway at any of several crucial steps or prevent the release of thyroxine from its storage form in the follicles. It appears that the last two mechanisms are the significant ones. Thiocyanate and perchlorate inhibit the active transport processes of the iodide trap, thiouracil blocks the oxidation of iodide to iodine by certain peroxidase enzymes, and sulfonamides interfere with the incorporation of tyrosine [see *illustration below*].

Soon after the discovery of these goitrogenic compounds it was found that goiter endemic to some areas was a result of similar, naturally occurring compounds in local foods. Soybeans and members of the genus *Brassica*, which includes Brussels sprouts, cabbages, turnips and other vegetables, are among the foodstuffs containing significant amounts of goitrogenic compounds. In a nutritionally varied diet such foods do no harm, but they are a more serious matter in societies that survive on less varied diets.

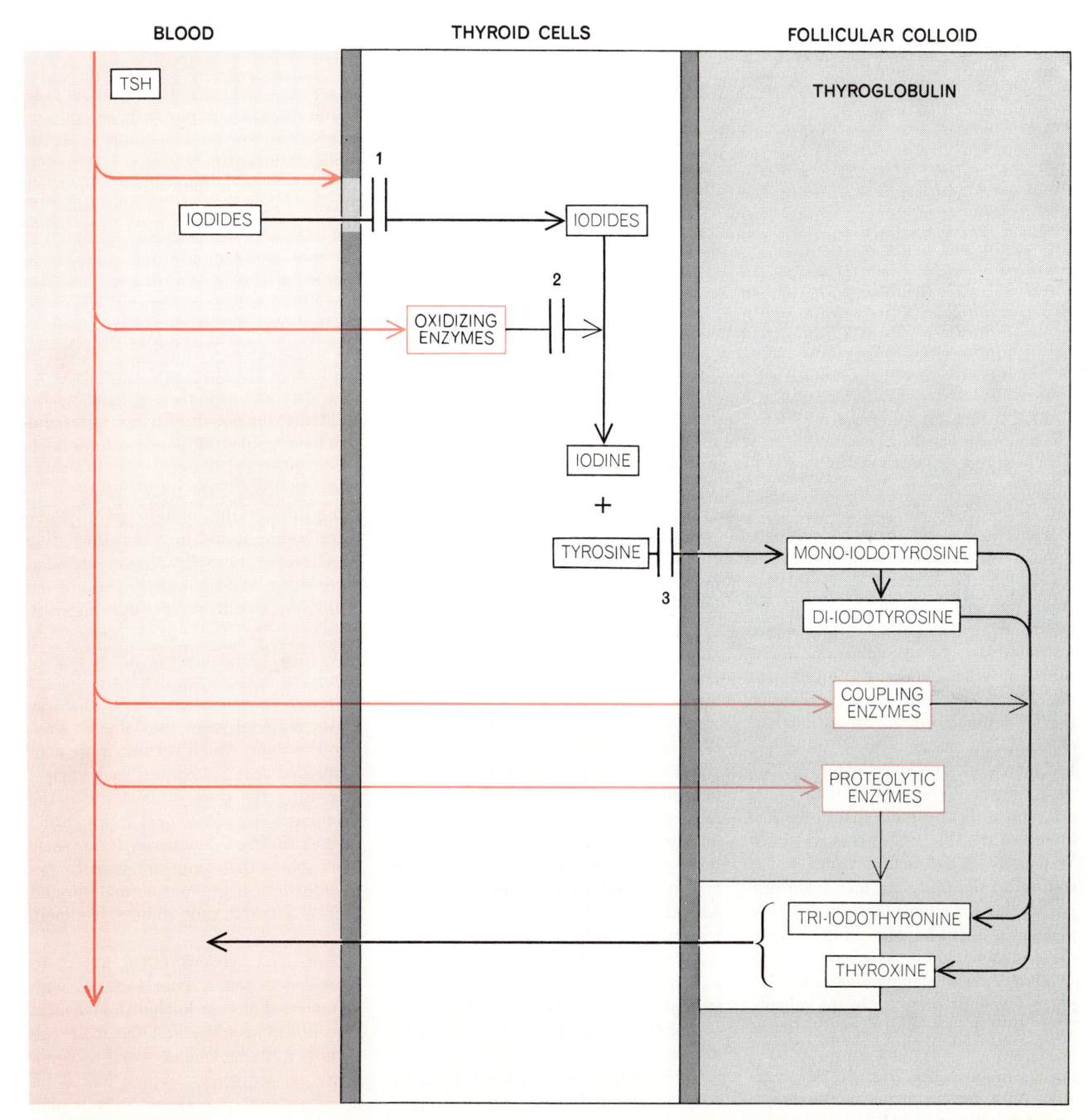

THYROID ACTIVITY is diagrammed schematically. Iodide trapped by thyroid-follicle cells is converted by oxidizing enzymes in the cells into iodine, which combines with tyrosine to form the thyroid hormones. The hormones are stored attached to thyroglobulin; on demand they are freed by proteolytic enzymes and pass into the blood. TSH stimulates hormone production by acting to abet iodide-trapping and the activity of three sets of enzymes. Goitrogenic substances interfere with hormone production. Thiocyanates and perchlorates block the iodide trap (*1*), thiouracil the oxidizing enzymes (*2*), sulfonamides the combination with tyrosine (*3*).

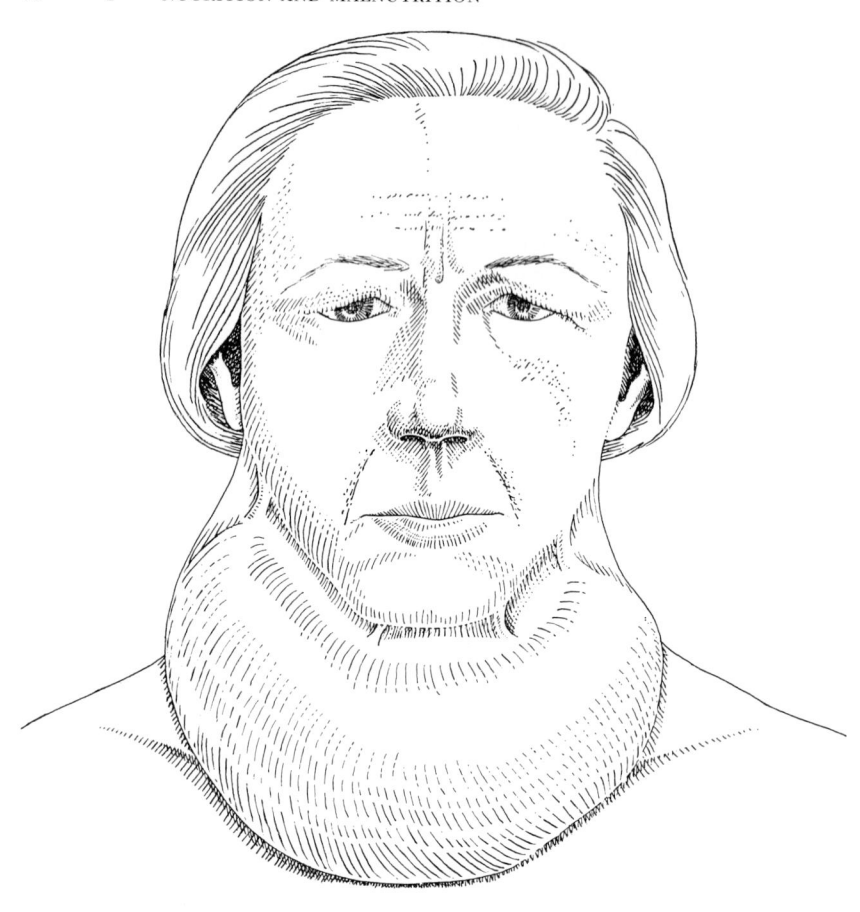

LARGE GOITER is seen frequently in regions where iodine-deficiency goiter is endemic. The drawing is based on a photograph made in the Alps near Innsbruck in Austria. Goiters have been reported that weighed four or five pounds, sometimes hanging below the chest.

The effect of the *Brassica* goitrogen was demonstrated not long ago in Tasmania, off the coast of southern Australia. The island was an area of endemic goiter, and so in 1949 a program was instituted to supply iodine-containing tablets to schoolchildren up to 16 years old. Five years later a survey revealed that the incidence of goiter in these children had not decreased; indeed, it had increased. The investigators verified their data and reevaluated their methods, and still they found that goiter had increased. F. W. A. Clements and J. W. Wishart, who had been instrumental in setting up the program, thereupon proposed that something other than iodine deficiency might be promoting goiter in these schoolchildren. As it happened, in 1950 the Australian government had begun a free-milk program in the schools. The increased demand for milk forced local dairies to keep their cows at pasture during seasons when grass was not available. As a consequence the cows were eating marrow-stem kale, which is more frost-resistant than grass and grows well all year. Marrow-stem kale is a member of the genus *Brassica* and contains a large amount of the goitrogenic compound. Further study revealed that this compound, present unaltered in the milk, was blocking utilization of the iodine being supplied in the tablets.

Clearly there are dangers inherent in administering to patients drug preparations that contain significant amounts of potentially goitrogenic compounds or elemental iodine. Although it is not common in this country, iatrogenic goiter—goiter caused by medical treatment—is becoming a more significant factor. Sulfonamides prescribed for urinary-tract infections, thiouracil drugs given routinely for the relief of hyperthyroidism and many iodine-containing compounds administered as expectorants in the treatment of asthma are potentially goitrogenic. The unborn infants of pregnant mothers who take these drugs have in some instances been killed *in utero* by goiters that develop when the drugs diffuse across the placenta and enter the fetal circulation. Because these drugs are concentrated in the lactating breast they may also induce goiter in a nursing infant. The most serious effect of these drugs in pregnancy is that they decrease the availability of maternal thyroxine to the early fetus, and thyroxine is of fundamental importance in the physical and mental development of the baby.

Several epidemiological surveys have indicated that goiter can arise spontaneously in a society, persist for a short time and then regress, all without any apparent change in the food or living habits of the people. The possibility of an infectious origin of goiter has been proposed to explain such epidemics, but no instance of this has been proved. It does seem possible that a strain of iodine-trapping bacteria could become resident among the normal flora of the intestine and decrease the availability of dietary iodine for absorption.

There is at least one documented case of goiter related to bacteria, although in a different way. While studying goitrous populations in the Himalayas in 1906, Robert McCarrison visited several neighboring villages in the valley of the Gilgit River. He was immediately impressed by the fact that whereas the village that was farthest upstream showed a low incidence of goiter (12 percent), as he moved downstream the incidence increased in each village, until in the lowest village more than 45 percent of the population had goiter. An isolated village that was near the river but whose residents did not drink river water did not have goiter. McCarrison undertook a controlled experiment with 30 volunteers divided into two groups. One group drank the muddy river water after boiling it and the other (including McCarrison himself) drank unboiled river water. Within a month most of the people in McCarrison's group began to develop goiter; those in the other group did not. He concluded from the experiment that bacteria were to blame for the goiter. Poor sanitation meant that the waste material from the villages went into the river, which became more contaminated as it flowed past each village, increasing the dose of bacteria in the drinking water of villagers in proportion to their distance downriver. It has since been shown that some strains of *Escherichia coli*, a bacterium normally found in fecal material, can produce thiouracil.

There is a vicious circle aspect to endemic goiter. Poor societies with an unvaried diet are likely to be the most susceptible to goiter and the most vulnerable to its biological, social and economic consequences. Where iodine-deficiency goiter is endemic in a human population domestic animals will probably be hypothyroid too. Goitrous sheep often produce less wool; goiter in cattle causes sterility, poor milk production and sickly calves; horses do less work;

hens with decreased thyroid activity produce eggs with insufficient calcium in the shell, leading to egg breakage and higher chick mortality. A poor society can scarcely afford to have these serious handicaps afflict the animals on which its survival may depend.

Long-standing endemic goiter has had particularly serious consequences in some remote communities, such as alpine valleys, where inbred populations have persisted for many generations in an iodine-deficient environment. Familial goitrous hypothyroidism can lead to a high incidence of individuals with the severe developmental defects of cretinism. Cretins manifest varying degrees of idiocy and are also physically dwarfed and often malformed. The mental retardation is believed to result from a deficiency of thyroxine during the first three months of pregnancy, when it must be supplied by the mother; the physical anomalies are probably due to a deficiency of the baby's own thyroxine during maturation.

The role of mountainous topography and isolation in cretinism is evident. There are many goitrous regions that do not show a high incidence of cretinism; the "goiter belt" in the Great Lakes region is an example. Presumably population mobility through this channel of westward migration supplied enough biological and social diversity so that cretinism did not develop.

The cretin is only the most extreme example of the consequences of decreased availability of thyroxine during the developmental stages of life. Because all the residents of a community affected by endemic goiter are potentially exposed to a suboptimal supply of thyroxine during their development, there may be serious but subtle effects on the quality of the society at large. Motivation, spontaneity, creativity and native intelligence may be diminished, and the resulting social stagnation may lead to further inbreeding.

Medical science and public health will eventually eliminate iodine-deficiency goiter as an endemic affliction. One must hope that this age-old and benign disorder will not be replaced by a different, nuclear-era thyroid dysfunction resulting from the ingestion of large amounts of radioactive iodine isotopes from nuclear fallout. The iodine is concentrated in the thyroid gland, where the radioactivity may damage cells irreversibly. The study of endemic goiter demonstrates the seriousness of this potential hazard and the effects it might have on the course of human evolution.

10

TOXIC SUBSTANCES AND ECOLOGICAL CYCLES

GEORGE M. WOODWELL
March 1967

Radioactive elements or pesticides such as DDT that are released in the environment may enter meteorological and biological cycles that distribute them and can concentrate them to dangerous levels

The vastness of the earth has fostered a tradition of unconcern about the release of toxic wastes into the environment. Billowing clouds of smoke are diluted to apparent nothingness; discarded chemicals are flushed away in rivers; insecticides "disappear" after they have done their job; even the massive quantities of radioactive debris of nuclear explosions are diluted in the apparently infinite volume of the environment. Such pollutants are indeed diluted to traces—to levels infinitesimal by ordinary standards, measured as parts per billion or less in air, soil and water. Some pollutants do disappear; they are immobilized or decay to harmless substances. Others last, sometimes in toxic form, for long periods. We have learned in recent years that dilution of persistent pollutants even to trace levels detectable only by refined techniques is no guarantee of safety. Nature has ways of concentrating substances that are frequently surprising and occasionally disastrous.

We have had dramatic examples of one of the hazards in the dense smogs that blanket our cities with increasing frequency. What is less widely realized is that there are global, long-term ecological processes that concentrate toxic substances, sometimes hundreds of thousands of times above levels in the environment. These processes include not only patterns of air and water circulation but also a complex series of biological mechanisms. Over the past decade detailed studies of the distribution of both radioactive debris and pesticides have revealed patterns that have surprised even biologists long familiar with the unpredictability of nature.

Major contributions to knowledge of these patterns have come from studies of radioactive fallout. The incident that triggered worldwide interest in large-scale radioactive pollution was the hydrogen-bomb test at Bikini in 1954 known as "Project Bravo." This was the test that inadvertently dropped radioactive fallout on several Pacific islands and on the Japanese fishing vessel *Lucky Dragon*. Several thousand square miles of the Pacific were contaminated with fallout radiation that would have been lethal to man. Japanese and U.S. oceanographic vessels surveying the region found that the radioactive debris had been spread by wind and water, and, more disturbing, it was being passed rapidly along food chains from small plants to small marine organisms that ate them to larger animals (including the tuna, a staple of the Japanese diet).

The U.S. Atomic Energy Commission and agencies of other nations, particularly Britain and the U.S.S.R., mounted a large international research program, costing many millions of dollars, to learn the details of the movement of such debris over the earth and to explore its hazards. Although these studies have been focused primarily on radioactive materials, they have produced a great deal of basic information about pollutants in general. The radioactive substances serve as tracers to show the transport and concentration of materials by wind and water and the biological mechanisms that are characteristic of natural communities.

One series of investigations traced the worldwide movement of particles in the air. The tracer in this case was strontium 90, a fission product released into the earth's atmosphere in large quantities by nuclear-bomb tests. Two reports in 1962—one by S. Laurence Kulp and Arthur R. Schulert of Columbia University and the other by a United Nations committee—furnished a detailed picture of the travels of strontium 90. The isotope was concentrated on the ground between the latitudes of 30 and 60 degrees in both hemispheres, but concentrations were five to 10 times greater in the Northern Hemisphere, where most of the bomb tests were conducted.

It is apparently in the middle latitudes

FOREST COMMUNITY is an integrated array of plants and animals that accumulates and reuses nutrients in stable cycles, as indicated schematically in black. DDT participates in parallel cycles (*color*). The author measured DDT residues in a New Brunswick forest in which four pounds per acre of DDT had been applied over seven years. (Studies have shown about half of this landed in the forest, the remainder dispersing in the atmosphere.) Three years after the spraying, residues of DDT were as shown (in pounds per acre).

73

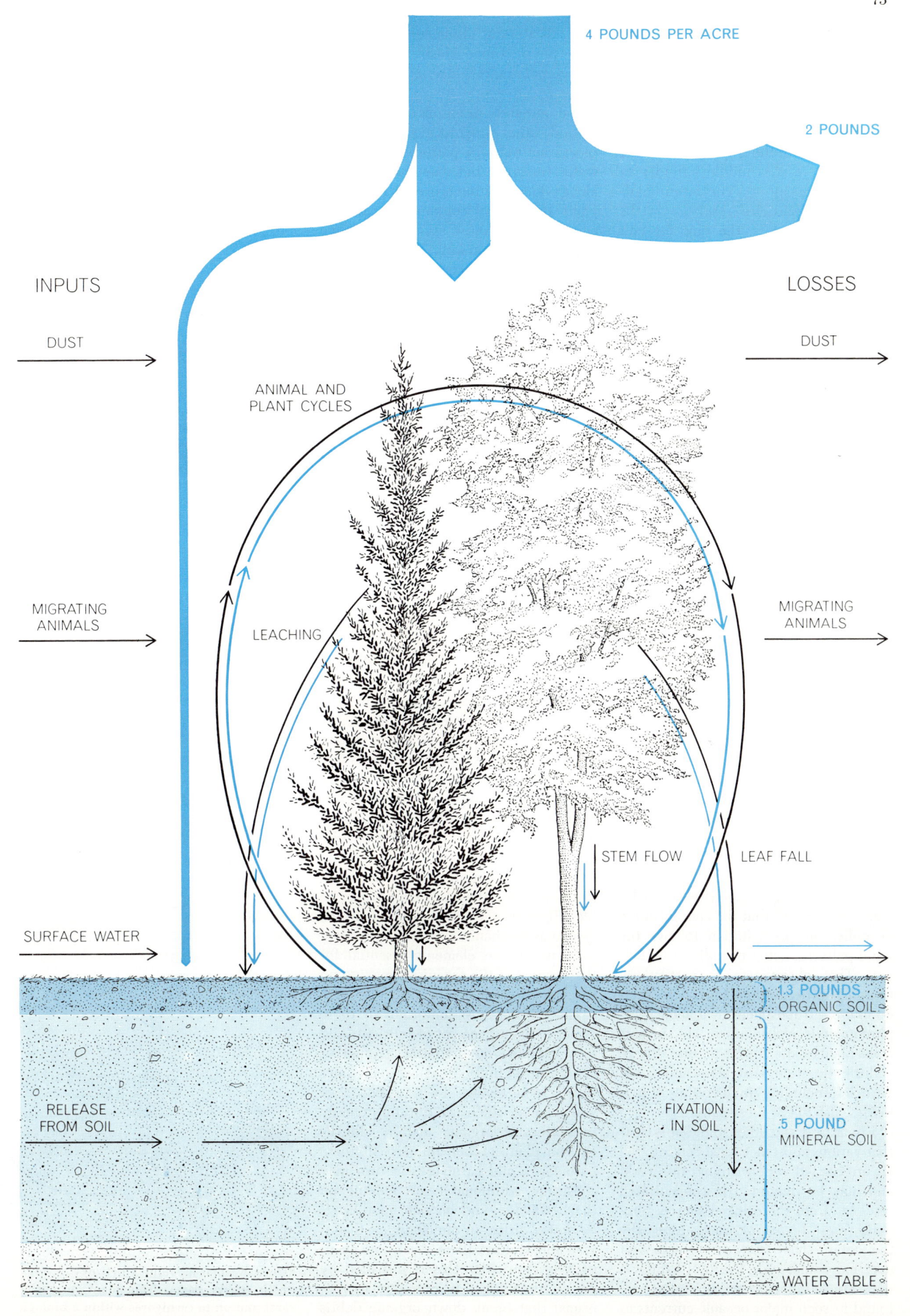

4 POUNDS PER ACRE

2 POUNDS

INPUTS

DUST

ANIMAL AND PLANT CYCLES

MIGRATING ANIMALS

LEACHING

SURFACE WATER

LOSSES

DUST

MIGRATING ANIMALS

STEM FLOW

LEAF FALL

1.3 POUNDS ORGANIC SOIL

RELEASE FROM SOIL

FIXATION IN SOIL

.5 POUND MINERAL SOIL

WATER TABLE

that exchanges occur between the air of upper elevations (the stratosphere) and that of lower elevations (the troposphere). The larger tests have injected debris into the stratosphere; there it remains for relatively long periods, being carried back into the troposphere and to the ground in the middle latitudes in late winter or spring. The mean "half-time" of the particles' residence in the stratosphere (that is, the time for half of a given injection to fall out) is from three months to five years, depending on many factors, including the height of the injection, the size of the particles, the latitude of injection and the time of year. Debris injected into the troposphere has a mean half-time of residence ranging from a few days to about a month. Once airborne, the particles may travel rapidly and far. The time for one circuit around the earth in the middle latitudes varies from 25 days to less than 15. (Following two recent bomb tests in China fallout was detected at the Brookhaven National Laboratory on Long Island respectively nine and 14 days after the tests.)

Numerous studies have shown further that precipitation (rain and snowfall) plays an important role in determining where fallout will be deposited. Lyle T. Alexander of the Soil Conservation Service and Edward P. Hardy, Jr., of the AEC found in an extensive study in Clallam County, Washington, that the amount of fallout was directly proportional to the total annual rainfall.

It is reasonable to assume that the findings about the movement and fallout of radioactive debris also apply to other particles of similar size in the air. This conclusion is supported by a recent report by Donald F. Gatz and A. Nelson Dingle of the University of Michigan, who showed that the concentration of pollen in precipitation follows the same pattern as that of radioactive fallout. This observation is particularly meaningful because pollen is not injected into the troposphere by a nuclear explosion; it is picked up in air currents from plants close to the ground. There is little question that dust and other particles, including small crystals of pesticides, also follow these patterns.

From these and other studies it is clear that various substances released into the air are carried widely around the world and may be deposited in concentrated form far from the original source. Similarly, most bodies of water—especially the oceans—have surface currents that may move materials five to 10 miles a day. Much higher rates, of course, are found in such major oceanic currents as the Gulf Stream. These currents are one more physical mechanism that can distribute pollutants widely over the earth.

The research programs of the AEC and other organizations have explored not only the pathways of air and water transport but also the pathways along which pollutants are distributed in plant and animal communities. In this connection we must examine what we mean by a "community."

Biologists define communities broadly to include all species, not just man. A natural community is an aggregation of a great many different kinds of organisms, all mutually interdependent. The basic conditions for the integration of a community are determined by physical characteristics of the environment such as climate and soil. Thus a sand dune supports one kind of community, a freshwater lake another, a high mountain still another. Within each type of environment there develops a complex of organisms that in the course of evolution becomes a balanced, self-sustaining biological system.

Such a system has a structure of interrelations that endows the entire community with a predictable developmental pattern, called "succession," that leads toward stability and enables the community to make the best use of its physical environment. This entails the development of cycles through which the community as a whole shares certain resources, such as mineral nutrients and energy. For example, there are a number of different inputs of nutrient elements into such a system. The principal input is from the decay of primary minerals in the soil. There are also certain losses, mainly through the leaching of substances into the underlying water table. Ecologists view the cycles in the system as mechanisms that have evolved to conserve the elements essential for the survival of the organisms making up the community.

One of the most important of these cycles is the movement of nutrients and energy from one organism to another along the pathways that are sometimes called food chains. Such chains start with plants, which use the sun's energy to synthesize organic matter; animals eat the plants; other animals eat these herbivores, and carnivores in turn may constitute additional levels feeding on the herbivores and on one another. If the lower orders in the chain are to survive and endure, there must be a feedback of nutrients. This is provided by decay organisms (mainly microorganisms) that break down organic debris

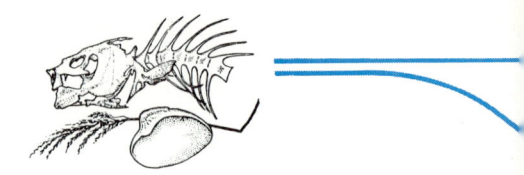

ORGANIC DEBRIS
MARSH 13 POUNDS PER ACRE
BOTTOM .3 POUND PER ACRE

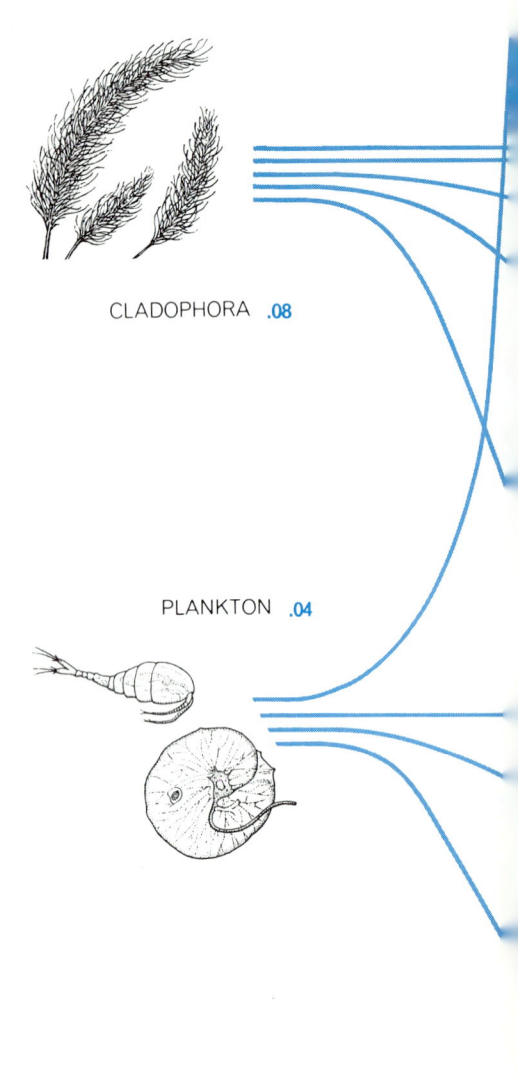

CLADOPHORA .08

PLANKTON .04

MARSH PLANTS
SHOOTS .33
ROOTS 2.80

FOOD WEB is a complex network through which energy passes from plants to herbivores and on to carnivores within a biologi-

BAY SHRIMP .16

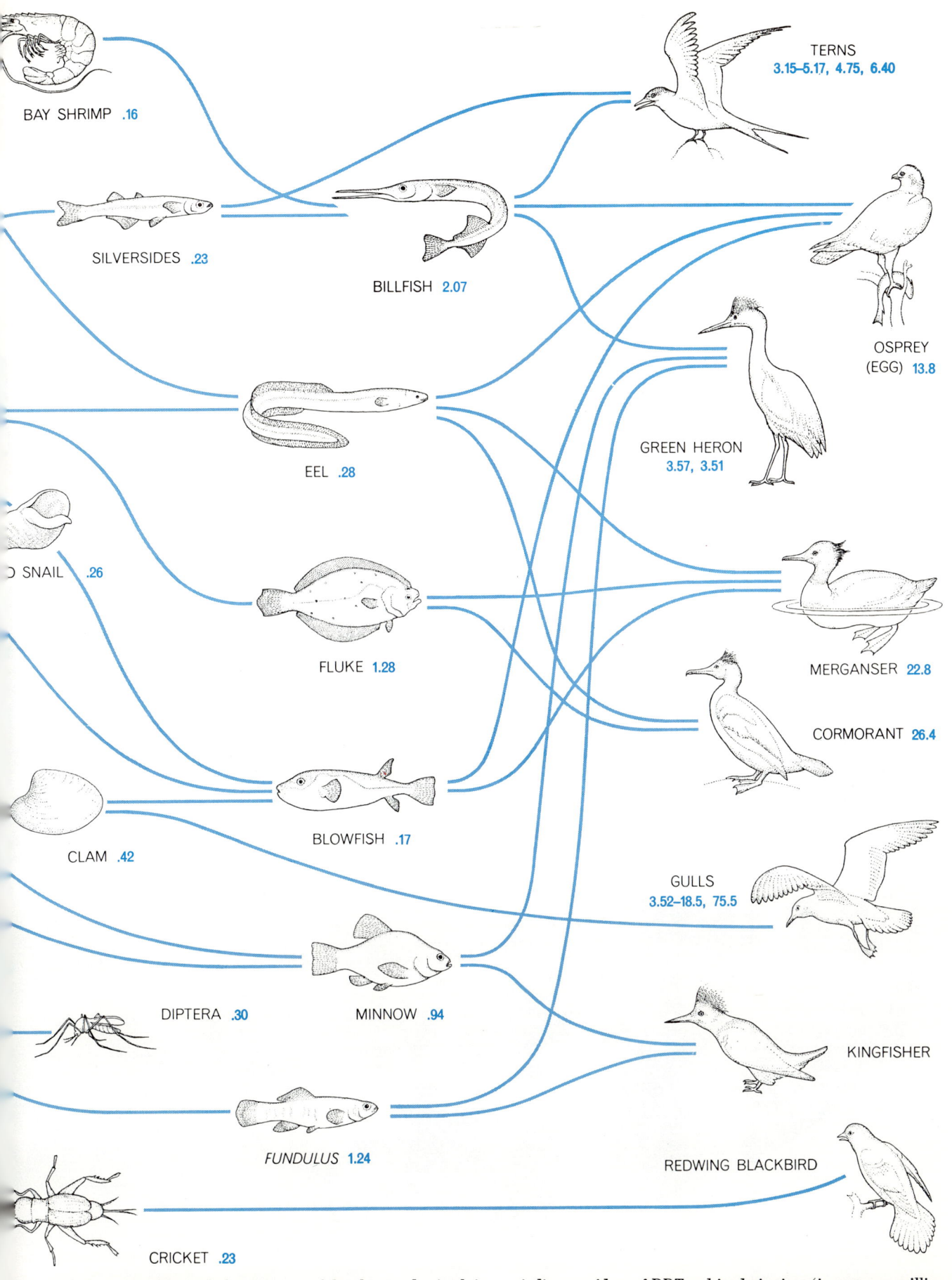

SILVERSIDES .23

BILLFISH 2.07

TERNS
3.15–5.17, 4.75, 6.40

OSPREY
(EGG) 13.8

EEL .28

GREEN HERON
3.57, 3.51

SNAIL .26

FLUKE 1.28

MERGANSER 22.8

CORMORANT 26.4

CLAM .42

BLOWFISH .17

GULLS
3.52–18.5, 75.5

DIPTERA .30

MINNOW .94

KINGFISHER

FUNDULUS 1.24

REDWING BLACKBIRD

CRICKET .23

cal community. This web showing some of the plants and animals in a Long Island estuary and along the nearby shore was developed by Dennis Puleston of the Brookhaven National Laboratory. Numbers indicate residues of DDT and its derivatives (in parts per million, wet weight, whole-body basis) found in the course of a study made by the author with Charles F. Wurster, Jr., and Peter A. Isaacson.

into the substances used by plants. It is also obvious that the community will not survive if essential links in the chain are eliminated; therefore the preying of one level on another must be limited.

Ecologists estimate that such a food chain allows the transmission of roughly 10 percent of the energy entering one level to the next level above it, that is, each level can pass on 10 percent of the energy it receives from below without suffering a loss of population that would imperil its survival. The simplest version of a system of this kind takes the form of a pyramid, each successively higher population receiving about a tenth of the energy received at the level below it.

Actually nature seldom builds communities with so simple a structure. Almost invariably the energy is not passed along in a neatly ordered chain but is spread about to a great variety of organisms through a sprawling, complex web of pathways [see illustration on preceding two pages]. The more mature the community, the more diverse its makeup and the more complicated its web. In a natural ecosystem the network may consist of thousands of pathways.

This complexity is one of the principal factors we must consider in investigating how toxic substances may be distributed and concentrated in living communities. Other important basic factors lie in the nature of the metabolic process. For example, of the energy a population of organisms receives as food, usually less than 50 percent goes into the construction of new tissue, the rest being spent for respiration. This circumstance acts as a concentrating mechanism: a substance not involved in respiration and not excreted efficiently may be concentrated in the tissues twofold or more when passed from one population to another.

Let us consider three types of pathway for toxic substances that involve man as the ultimate consumer. The three examples, based on studies of radioactive substances, illustrate the complexity and variety of pollution problems.

The first and simplest case is that of strontium 90. Similar to calcium in chemical behavior, this element is concentrated in bone. It is a long-lived radioactive isotope and is a hazard because its energetic beta radiation can damage the mechanisms involved in the manufacture of blood cells in the bone marrow. In the long run the irradiation may produce certain types of cancer. The route of strontium 90 from air to man is rather direct: we ingest it in leafy vegetables, which absorbed it from the soil or received it as fallout from the air, or in milk and other dairy products from cows that have fed on contaminated vegetation. Fortunately strontium is not usually concentrated in man's food by an extensive food chain. Since it lodges chiefly in bone, it is not concentrated in passing from animal to animal in the same ways other radioactive substances may be (unless the predator eats bones!).

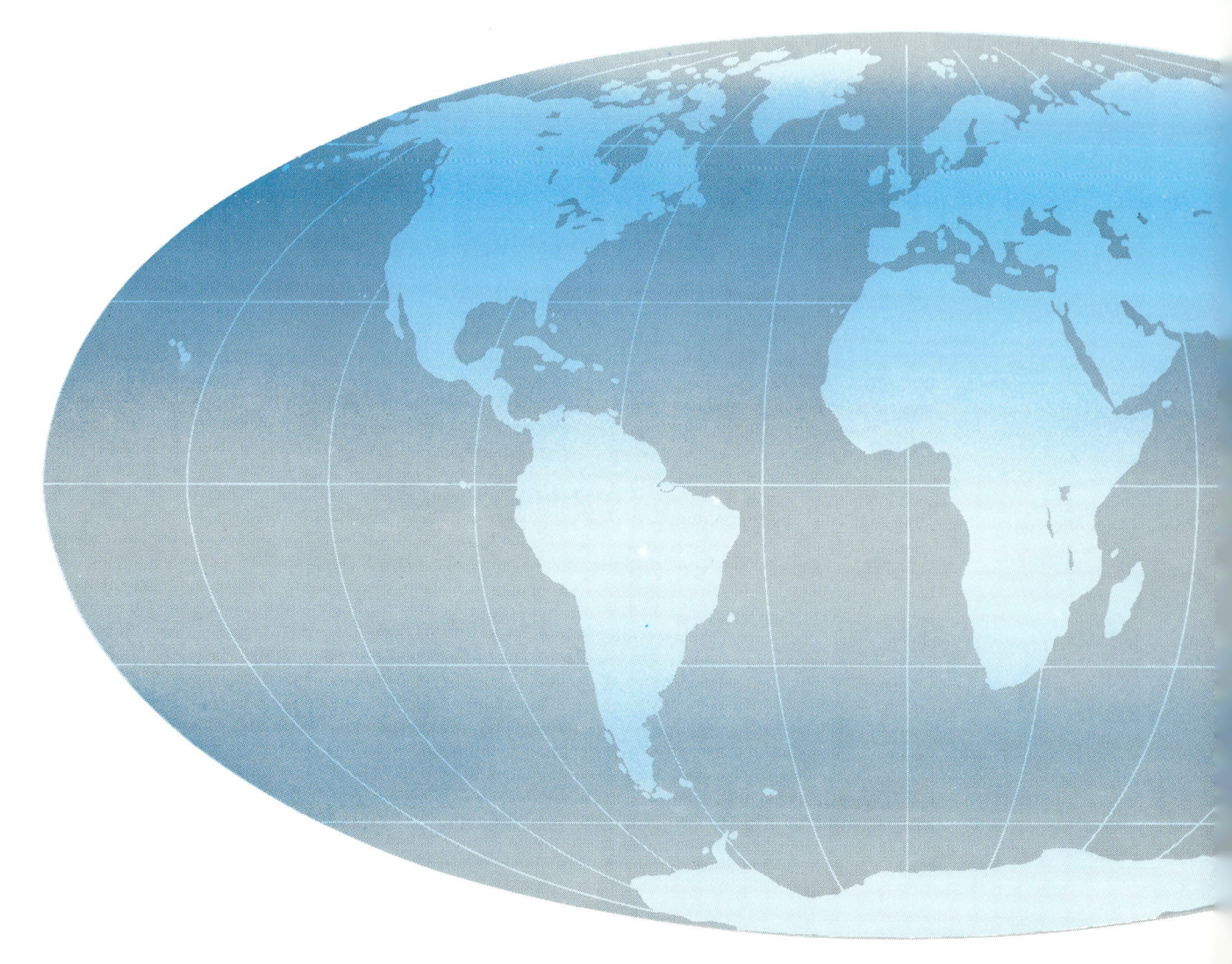

FALLOUT is distributed around the earth by meteorological processes. Deposits of strontium 90, for instance, are concentrated between 30 and 60 degrees north, as shown by depth of color on the map and by the curve (right). Points on the chart represent individual samples. The data are from a study made in 1963 and 1964 by Robert J. List and colleagues in several U.S. agencies. Such

Quite different is the case of the radioactive isotope cesium 137. This isotope, also a fission product, has a long-lived radioactivity (its half-life is about 30 years) and emits penetrating gamma rays. Because it behaves chemically like potassium, an essential constituent of all cells, it becomes widely distributed once it enters the body. Consequently it is passed along to meat-eating animals, and under certain circumstances it can accumulate in a chain of carnivores.

A study in Alaska by Wayne C. Hanson, H. E. Palmer and B. I. Griffin of the AEC's Pacific-Northwest Laboratory showed that the concentration factor for cesium 137 may be two or three for one step in a food chain. The first link of the chain in this case was lichens growing in the Alaskan forest and tundra. The lichens collected cesium 137 from fallout in rain. Certain caribou in Alaska live mainly on lichens during the winter, and caribou meat in turn is the principal diet of Eskimos in the same areas. The investigators found that caribou had accumulated about 15 micromicrocuries of cesium radioactivity per gram of tissue in their bodies. The Eskimos who fed on these caribou had a concentration twice as high (about 30 micromicrocuries per gram of tissue) after eating many pounds of caribou meat in the course of a season. Wolves and foxes that ate caribou sometimes contained three times the concentration in the flesh of the caribou. It is easy to see that in a longer chain, involving not just two animals but several, the concentration of a substance that was not excreted or metabolized could be increased to high levels.

A third case is that of iodine 131, another gamma ray emitter. Again the chain to man is short and simple: The contaminant (from fallout) comes to man mainly through cows' milk, and thus the chain involves only grass, cattle, milk and man. The danger of iodine 131 lies in the fact that iodine is concentrated in the thyroid gland. Although iodine 131 is short-lived (its half-life is only about eight days), its quick and localized concentration in the thyroid can cause damage. For instance, a research team from the Brookhaven National Laboratory headed by Robert Conard has discovered that children on Rongelap Atoll who were exposed to fallout from the 1954 bomb test later developed thyroid nodules.

The investigations of the iodine 131 hazard yielded two lessons that have an important bearing on the problem of pesticides and other toxic substances released in the environment. In the first place we have had a demonstration that the hazard of the toxic substance itself often tends to be underestimated. This was shown to be true of the exposure of the thyroid to radiation. Thyroid tumors were found in children who had been treated years before for enlarged thymus glands with doses of X rays that had been considered safe. As a result of this discovery and studies of the effects of iodine 131, the Federal Radiation Council in 1961 issued a new guide reducing the permissible limit of exposure to ionizing radiation to less than a tenth of what had previously been accepted. Not the least significant aspect of this lesson is the fact that the toxic effects of such a hazard may not appear until long after the exposure; on Rongelap Atoll 10 years passed before the thyroid abnormalities showed up in the children who had been exposed.

The second lesson is that, even when the pathways are well understood, it is almost impossible to predict just where toxic substances released into the environment will reach dangerous levels. Even in the case of the simple pathway followed by iodine 131 the eventual destination of the substance and its effects on people are complicated by a great many variables: the area of the cow's pasture (the smaller the area, the less fallout the cow will pick up); the amount and timing of rains on the pasture (which on the one hand may bring down fallout but on the other may wash it off the forage); the extent to which the cow is given stored, uncontaminated feed; the amount of iodine the cow secretes in its milk; the amount of milk in the diet of the individual consumer, and so on.

If it is difficult to estimate the nature and extent of the hazards from radioactive fallout, which have been investigated in great detail for more than a decade by an international research program, it must be said that we are in a poor position indeed to estimate the hazards from pesticides. So far the studies have not been made for pesticides but it appears that DDT may also be carried in air and deposited in precipitation.

CARNIVORE 2

CARNIVORE 1

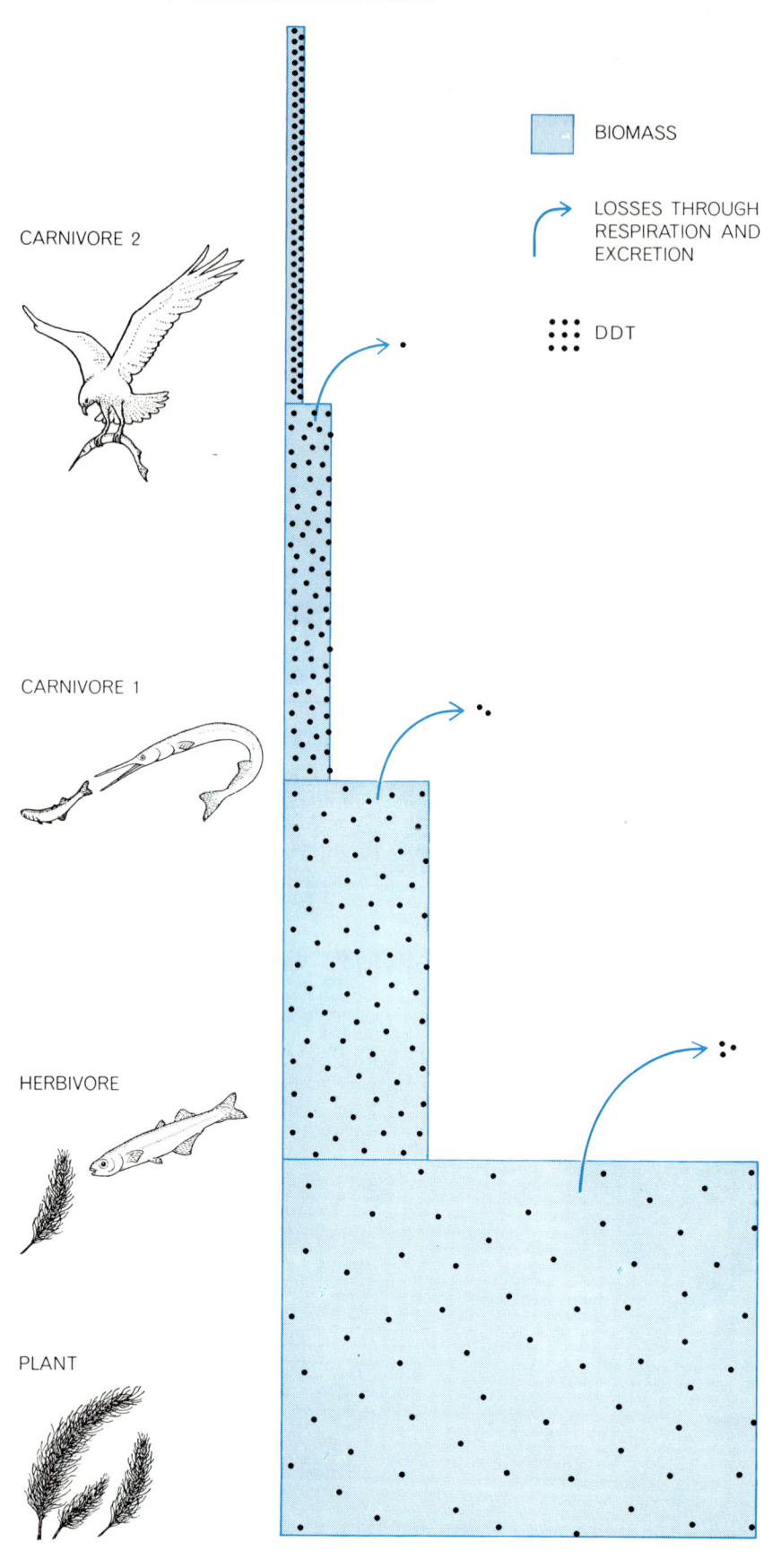

HERBIVORE

PLANT

BIOMASS

LOSSES THROUGH RESPIRATION AND EXCRETION

DDT

CONCENTRATION of DDT residues being passed along a simple food chain is indicated schematically in this diagram. As "biomass," or living material, is transferred from one link to another along such a chain, usually more than half of it is consumed in respiration or is excreted (*arrows*); the remainder forms new biomass. The losses of DDT residues along the chain, on the other hand, are small in proportion to the amount that is transferred from one link to the next. For this reason high concentrations occur in the carnivores.

amount of research effort given to the ecological effects of these poisons has been comparatively small, although it is increasing rapidly. Much has been learned, however, about the movement and distribution of pesticides in the environment, thanks in part to the clues supplied by the studies of radioactive fallout.

Our chief tool in the pesticide inquiry is DDT. There are many reasons for focusing on DDT: it is long-lasting, it is now comparatively easy to detect, it is by far the most widely used pesticide and it is toxic to a broad spectrum of animals, including man. Introduced only a quarter-century ago and spectacularly successful during World War II in controlling body lice and therefore typhus, DDT quickly became a universal weapon in agriculture and in public health campaigns against disease-carriers. Not surprisingly, by this time DDT has thoroughly permeated our environment. It is found in the air of cities, in wildlife all over North America and in remote corners of the earth, even in Adélie penguins and skua gulls (both carnivores) in the Antarctic. It is also found the world over in the fatty tissue of man. It is fair to say that there are probably few populations in the world that are not contaminated to some extent with DDT.

We now have a considerable amount of evidence that DDT is spread over the earth by wind and water in much the same patterns as radioactive fallout. This seems to be true in spite of the fact that DDT is not injected high into the atmosphere by an explosion. When DDT is sprayed in the air, some fraction of it is picked up by air currents as pollen is, circulated through the lower troposphere and deposited on the ground by rainfall. I found in tests in Maine and New Brunswick, where DDT has been sprayed from airplanes to control the spruce budworm in forests, that even in the open, away from trees, about 50 percent of the DDT does not fall to the ground. Instead it is probably dispersed as small crystals in the air. This is true even on days when the air is still and when the low-flying planes release the spray only 50 to 100 feet above treetop level. Other mechanisms besides air movement can carry DDT for great distances around the world. Migrating fish and birds can transport it thousands of miles. So also do oceanic currents. DDT has only a low solubility in water (the upper limit is about one part per billion), but as algae and other organisms in the water absorb the substance in fats, where it is highly soluble, they make room for more DDT to be dissolved into the water. Accordingly water that never contains more than a trace of DDT can continuously transfer it from deposits on the bottom to organisms.

DDT is an extremely stable compound that breaks down very slowly in the environment. Hence with repeated spraying the residues in the soil or water basins accumulate. Working with Frederic T. Martin of the University of Maine, I found that in a New Brunswick forest where spraying had been discontinued in 1958 the DDT content of the soil increased from half a pound per acre to 1.8 pounds per acre in the three years between 1958 and 1961. Apparently the DDT residues were carried to the ground very slowly on foliage and decayed very little. The conclusion is that DDT has a long half-life in the trees and soil of a forest, certainly in the range of tens of years.

Doubtless there are many places in the world where reservoirs of DDT are accumulating. With my colleagues Charles F. Wurster, Jr., and Peter A. Isaacson of the State University of New York at Stony Brook, I recently sampled a marsh along the south shore of Long Island that had been sprayed with DDT for 20 years to control mosquitoes. We found that the DDT residues in the upper layer of mud in this marsh ranged up to 32 pounds per acre!

We learned further that plant and animal life in the area constituted a chain that concentrated the DDT in spectacular fashion. At the lowest level the plankton in the water contained .04 part per million of DDT; minnows contained one part per million, and a carnivorous scavenging bird (a ring-billed gull) contained about 75 parts per million in its tissues (on a whole-body, wet-weight basis). Some of the carnivorous animals in this community had concentrated DDT by a factor of more than 1,000 over the organisms at the base of the ladder.

A further tenfold increase in the concentrations along this food web would in all likelihood result in the death of many of the organisms in it. It would then be impossible to discover why they had disappeared. The damage from DDT concentration is particularly serious in the higher carnivores. The mere fact that conspicuous mortality is not observed is no assurance of safety. Comparatively low concentrations may inhibit reproduction and thus cause the species to fade away.

That DDT is a serious ecological hazard was recognized from the beginning of its use. In 1946 Clarence Cottam and Elmer Higgins of the U.S. Fish and Wildlife Service warned in the *Journal of Economic Entomology* that the pesticide was a potential menace to mammals, birds, fishes and other wildlife and that special care should be taken to avoid its application to streams, lakes and coastal bays because of the sensitivity of fishes and crabs. Because of the wide distribution of DDT the effects of the substance on a species of animal can be more damaging than hunting or the elimination of a habitat (through an operation such as dredging marshes). DDT affects the entire species rather than a single population and may well wipe out the species by eliminating reproduction.

Within the past five years, with the development of improved techniques for detecting the presence of pesticide residues in animals and the environment, ecologists have been able to measure the extent of the hazards presented by DDT and other persistent general poisons. The picture that is emerging is not a comforting one. Pesticide residues have now accumulated to levels that are catastrophic for certain animal populations, particularly carnivorous birds. Furthermore, it has been clear for many years that because of their shotgun effect these weapons not only attack the pests but also destroy predators and competitors that normally tend to limit proliferation of the pests. Under exposure to pesticides the pests tend to develop new strains that are resistant to the chemicals. The result is an escalating chemical warfare that is self-defeating and has secondary effects whose costs are only beginning to be measured. One of the costs is wildlife, notably carnivorous and scavenging birds such as hawks and eagles. There are others: destruction of food webs aggravates pollution problems, particularly in bodies of water that receive mineral nutrients in sewage or in water draining from heavily fertilized agricultural lands. The plant populations, no longer consumed by animals, fall to the bottom to decay anaerobically, producing hydrogen sulfide and other noxious gases, further degrading the environment.

The accumulation of persistent toxic substances in the ecological cycles of the earth is a problem to which mankind will have to pay increasing attention. It affects many elements of society, not only in the necessity for concern about the disposal of wastes but also in the need for a revolution in pest control. We must learn to use pesticides that have a short half-life in the environment—better yet, to use pest-control techniques that do not require applications of general poisons. What has been learned about the dangers in polluting ecological cycles is ample proof that there is no longer safety in the vastness of the earth.

LOCATION	ORGANISM	TISSUE	CONCENTRATION (PARTS PER MILLION)
U.S. (AVERAGE)	MAN	FAT	11
ALASKA (ESKIMO)			2.8
ENGLAND			2.2
WEST GERMANY			2.3
FRANCE			5.2
CANADA			5.3
HUNGARY			12.4
ISRAEL			19.2
INDIA			12.8-31.0
U.S. CALIFORNIA	PLANKTON		5.3
CALIFORNIA	BASS	EDIBLE FLESH	4-138
CALIFORNIA	GREBES	VISCERAL FAT	UP TO 1,600
MONTANA	ROBIN	WHOLE BODY	6.8-13.9
WISCONSIN	CRUSTACEA		.41
WISCONSIN	CHUB	WHOLE BODY	4.52
WISCONSIN	GULL	BRAIN	20.8
MISSOURI	BALD EAGLE	EGGS	1.1-5.6
CONNECTICUT	OSPREY	EGGS	6.5
FLORIDA	DOLPHIN	BLUBBER	ABOUT 220
CANADA	WOODCOCK	WHOLE BODY	1.7
ANTARCTICA	PENGUIN	FAT	.015-.18
ANTARCTICA	SEAL	FAT	.042-.12
SCOTLAND	EAGLE	EGGS	1.18
NEW ZEALAND	TROUT	WHOLE BODY	.6-.8

DDT RESIDUES, which include the derivatives DDD and DDE as well as DDT itself, have apparently entered most food webs. These data were selected from hundreds of reports that show DDT has a worldwide distribution, with the highest concentrations in carnivorous birds.

11

MERCURY IN THE ENVIRONMENT

LEONARD J. GOLDWATER
May 1971

The metal is widely distributed, mostly in forms that do no harm. The question is whether its concentration by industrial and biological processes now endangers animals and human beings

In the early 1950's fishermen and their families around Minamata Bay in Japan were stricken with a mysterious neurological illness. The Minamata disease, as it came to be called, produced progressive weakening of the muscles, loss of vision, impairment of other cerebral functions, eventual paralysis and in some cases coma and death. The victims had suffered structural injury to the brain. It was soon observed that Minamata seabirds and household cats, which like the fisherfolk subsist mainly on fish, showed signs of the same disease. This led to the discovery of high concentrations of mercury compounds in fish and shellfish taken from the bay, and the source of the mercury was traced to the effluent from a factory.

Since then there have been several other alarming incidents. In 1956 and 1960 outbreaks of mercurial poisoning involving hundreds of persons took place in Iraq, where farmers who had received grain seed treated with mercurial fungicides ate the seed instead of planting it. There were similar outbreaks later in Pakistan and in Guatemala. In Sweden, where poisoning of game birds and other wildlife, apparently by mercury-treated seeds, began to be noticed in 1960, the Swedish Medical Board in 1967 banned the sale of fish from about 40 lakes and rivers after it was found that fish caught in those waters contained high concentrations of methyl mercury. In 1970 alarm rose to a dramatic pitch in North America. Following the discovery of mercury concentrations in fish in Lake Saint Clair by a Norwegian investigator working in Canada, restrictions on fishing and on the sale of fish were imposed in many areas in the U.S. and Canada, and government agencies in both countries began to take action to control the discharge of mercury-containing wastes into lakes and streams.

Suddenly, almost overnight, mankind has become acutely fearful of mercury in the environment. The alarm is understandable. Quicksilver has always been regarded as being magical and somewhat sinister, in part because of its unique property as the only metal that is a liquid at ordinary temperatures. Mercury's peculiarities have been recognized since medieval times, when the alchemists took a keen interest in the element's fascinating properties. Its toxic properties became so well known that some mercury compounds came to be used as agents of suicide and murder. There are indications that Napoleon, Ivan the Terrible and Charles II of England may have died of mercurial poisoning, either accidental or deliberate. (Charles II experimented with mercury in his laboratory.) It has been suggested (incorrectly) that mercury is what made Lewis Carroll's Hatter mad (since it is used in the manufacture of felt hats). And it is authentically recorded that as early as 1700 a citizen of the town of Finale in Italy sought an injunction against a factory making mercuric chloride because its fumes were killing people in the town.

Nevertheless, although the recent incidents give us justifiable concern about the potential hazards of mercury in the environment, a panicky reaction would be quite inappropriate. Mercury, after all, is a rare element, ranking 16th from the bottom of the list of elements in abundance in the earth and comprising less than 30 billionths of the earth's crust. There are comparatively few places in the world where it occurs naturally in more than trace amounts, and the ore-bearing deposits of commercial value are so limited that a handful of mines scattered over the globe account for most of the world production. The uncompounded element in liquid form is not a poison; a person could swallow up to a pound or more of quicksilver with no significant adverse effects. Nor should it be forgotten that certain compounds of mercury have been used safely for thousands of years, and some are still prescribed, as effective medications for various infections and disorders. We need not shrink from mercury as an unmitigated threat. What is now required is detailed investigation of how mercury is being redistributed and concentrated in the environment by man's activities and in what forms and compounds it may be harmful to life. Extensive research on these questions is under way.

We consider first what might be called the normal distribution of mercury in nature. The element is found in trace amounts throughout the lithosphere (rocks and soil), the hydrosphere, the atmosphere and the biosphere (in tissues of plants and animals). In the rocks and

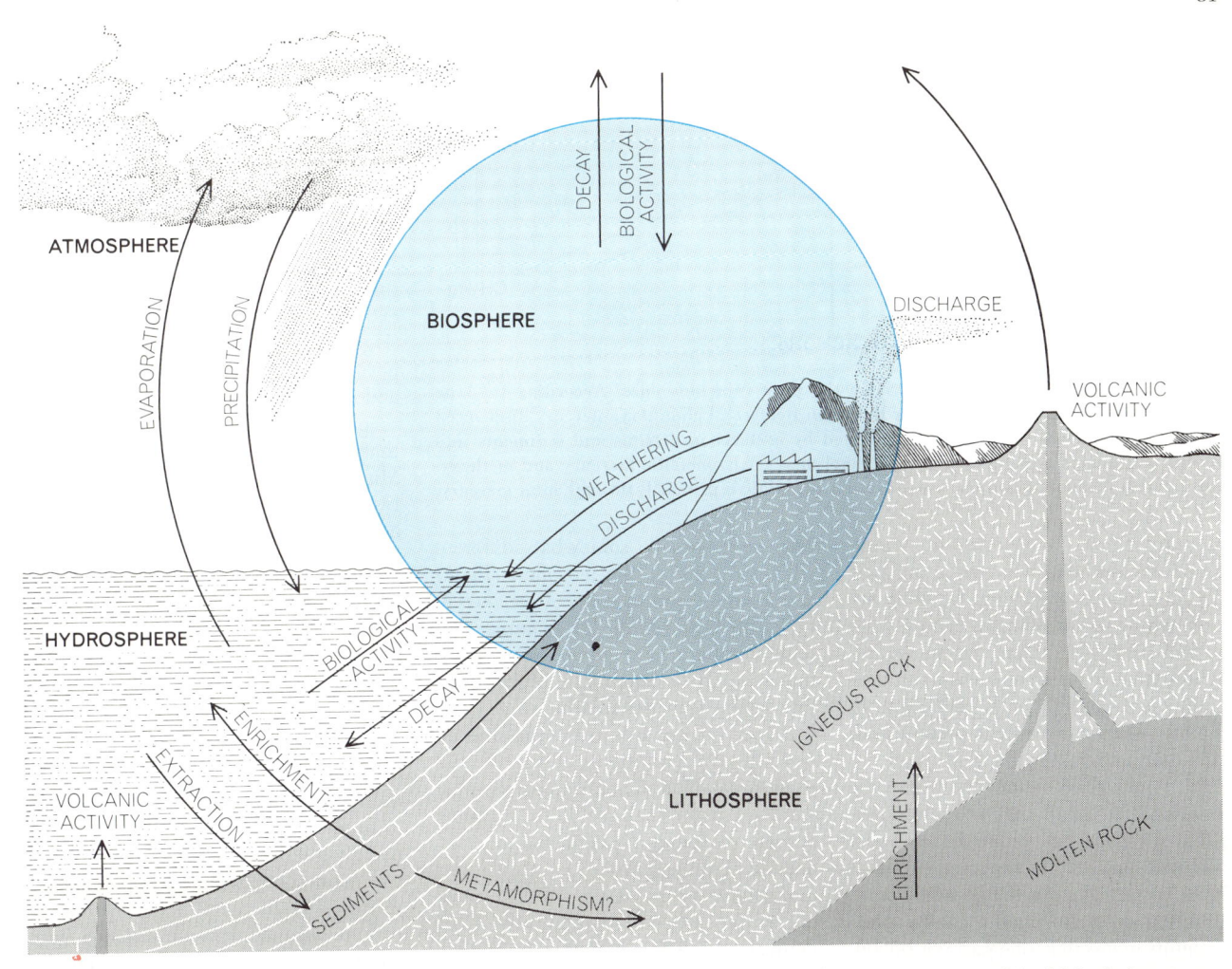

MERCURY CYCLE disperses the metal through the lithosphere, hydrosphere and atmosphere and through the biosphere, which interpenetrates all three. Mercury is present in all spheres in trace amounts, but it tends to be concentrated by biological processes. Man's activities, in particular certain industrial processes, may now present a threat by significantly redistributing the metal.

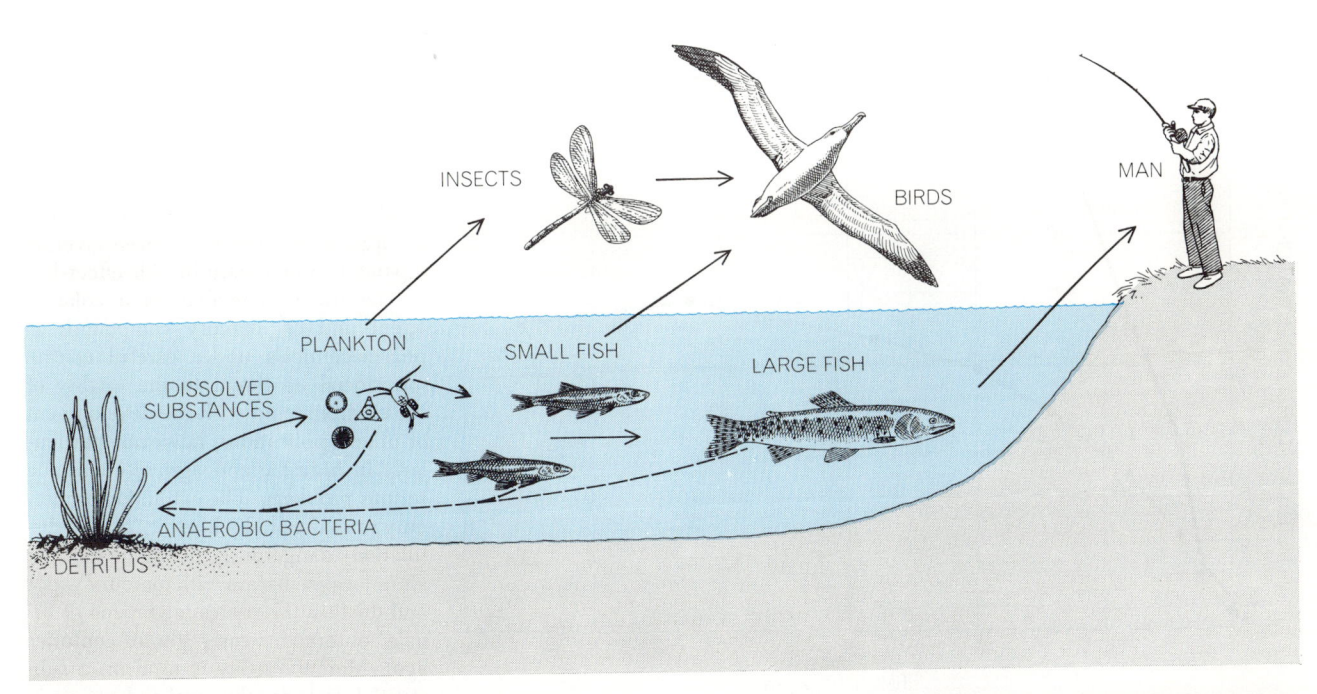

AQUATIC FOOD CHAIN is a primary mechanism by which mercury is concentrated. At each trophic level less mercury is excreted than ingested, so that there is proportionately more mercury in algae than in the water they live in, more still in fish that feed on the algae and so on. Bacteria and the decay chain (*broken arrows*) promote conversion of any mercury present into methyl mercury.

82   I • NUTRITION AND MALNUTRITION

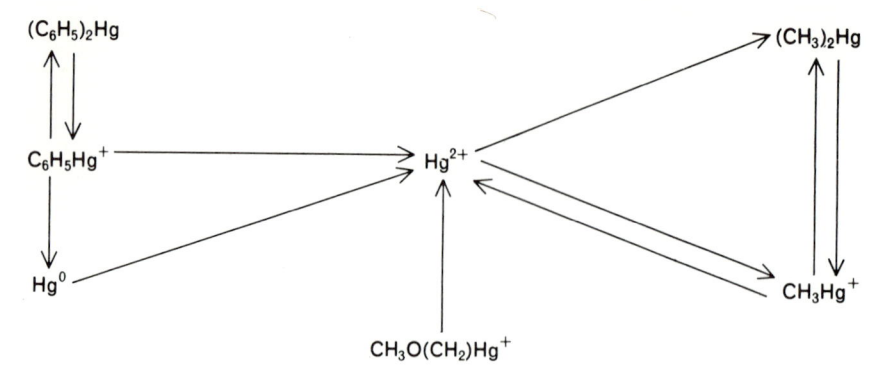

METHYL MERCURY COMPOUNDS are the most injurious ones. According to Arne Jernelöv of the Swedish Water and Air Pollution Research Laboratory, mercury discharged into water in various forms can be converted by bacteria in detritus and sediments into methyl and dimethyl mercury (*right*). Phenyl mercurials, metallic mercury and methoxyethyl mercury (*left and bottom*) are converted into methyls primarily through ionic mercury.

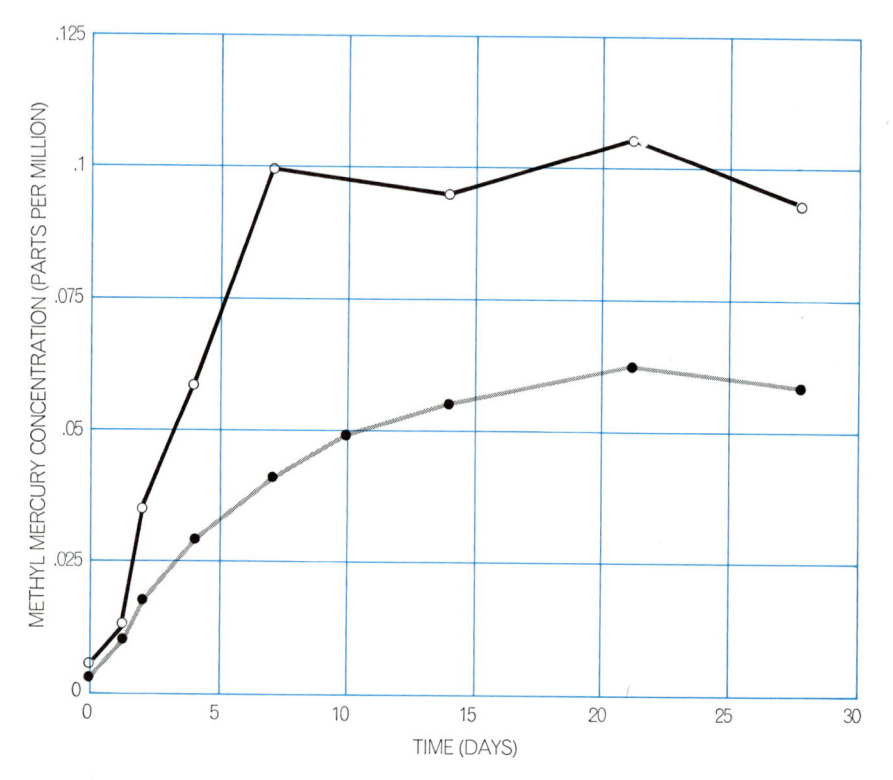

CONVERSION of inorganic into methyl mercury in sediment was measured by Sören Jensen and Jernelöv at intervals after the addition of 10 (*gray*) and 100 (*black*) parts per million of inorganic mercury. At lower mercury concentrations methylation may not occur.

soils (apart from ore concentrations) mercury is measured in fractions of one part per million, except in topsoils rich in humus, where the amount may run as high as two parts per million. In the hydrosphere (the seas and fresh waters) it generally occurs only in parts per billion. In the atmosphere mercury is present both as vapor and in the form of particles. Under natural conditions, however, the amount is so small that extremely sensitive methods are required to detect and measure it; the measurements that have been made at a few locations indicate that this atmospheric "background" amounts to less than one part per billion.

The situation is somewhat different when we come to the biosphere. Plants and animals tend to concentrate mercury; it has been found, for example, that some marine algae contain a concentration more than 100 times higher than that in the seawater in which they live, and one study of fish in the sea showed mercury concentrations of up to 122 parts per billion. There is considerable variation, as we shall see, in the amounts of mercury found in plants and animals, depending on circumstances. Under natural conditions, however, the concentration in the earth's vegetation (aside from cultivated plants) averages no more than a fraction of one part per million.

Thus the natural cycle of circulation of mercury on the earth [*see top illustration on preceding page*] disperses it widely through the habitable spheres in trace amounts that pose no hazard to life. How seriously has man altered its distribution?

The only ore containing mercury in sufficient concentration for commercial extraction is cinnabar, or mercuric sulfide (HgS). There are minable cinnabar deposits in many regions around the world, and man was attracted to its use as early as prehistoric times. There is evidence that cinnabar was mined in China, Asia Minor, the Cyclades and Peru at least two or three millenniums ago. Cinnabar, a brilliant red mineral, came into use at first as a pigment, but it was not until medieval times that physicians and other investigators became interested in extracting quicksilver from ore to produce medicines and other useful compounds. Hippocrates is believed to have prescribed mercury sulfide as a medication, and this was probably one of the first compounds of a metal to be employed therapeutically.

By the Middle Ages, when alchemists had synthesized chlorides, oxides and various other inorganic compounds and mixtures of mercury, its use in medications began to spread. Calomel (mercurous chloride, or HgCl) came into wide use as a cathartic, and in the 16th century mercury compounds were introduced as a treatment for syphilis. By the 19th century scores of mercurials were being employed in medicine. Many are still in the pharmacopoeias; the most useful ones today are the diuretics. It has been found that even among the organic compounds of mercury there are some that can be used safely. As much as 78.5 grams of mercury in the form of an organic compound has been given to a patient without harmful side effects!

The use of cinnabar as a coloring agent and of mercury compounds in pharmaceuticals under careful control introduced no threat to the quality of the environment. With the development of other applications, however, particularly in industry and agriculture, came serious problems. The extraction of mercury from the ore by heating (that is, distillation) dangerously contaminates the air in localized areas with mercury vapor and dust (as the protesting citizen of Finale observed nearly three centuries ago). Mercury today is used on a substantial scale in chemical industries, in the manufacture of paints and paper and in pesticides and fungicides for agriculture. The world production of mercury

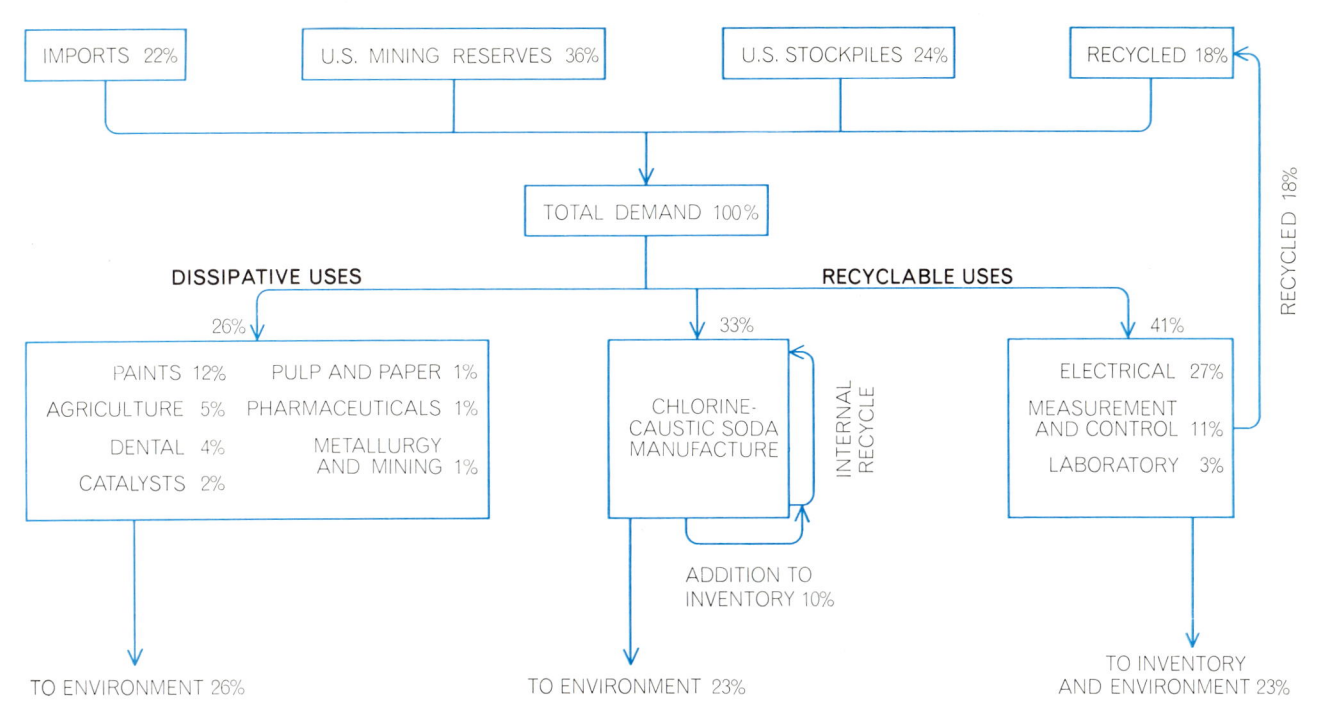

```
IMPORTS 22%   U.S. MINING RESERVES 36%   U.S. STOCKPILES 24%   RECYCLED 18%
                              │
                       TOTAL DEMAND 100%
         DISSIPATIVE USES              RECYCLABLE USES
              26%           33%              41%
   PAINTS 12%  PULP AND PAPER 1%    CHLORINE-        ELECTRICAL 27%
   AGRICULTURE 5%  PHARMACEUTICALS 1%  CAUSTIC SODA  MEASUREMENT
   DENTAL 4%   METALLURGY           MANUFACTURE      AND CONTROL 11%
   CATALYSTS 2%  AND MINING 1%                       LABORATORY 3%
                                    INTERNAL RECYCLE
                                    ADDITION TO
                                    INVENTORY 10%
                                                           RECYCLED 18%
   TO ENVIRONMENT 26%    TO ENVIRONMENT 23%      TO INVENTORY
                                                 AND ENVIRONMENT 23%
```

MERCURY FLOW through the U.S. is shown for 1968. The chart is based on one prepared by Robin A. Wallace, William Fulkerson, Wilbur D. Shults and William S. Lyon of the Oak Ridge National Laboratory. Major use of mercury has been as a cathode in the electrolytic preparation of chlorine and caustic soda. In this process a large inventory of mercury is continuously recycled, but in 1968 23 percent of total mercury demand still went to make up what was wasted. Another 10 percent went for start-up of new plants. Since then legislation and lawsuits have required manufacturers to increase recycling sharply, reducing emissions to the environment.

now amounts to about 10,000 tons per year, of which about 3,000 tons are used in the U.S. (The principal producers are Spain, whose mines at Almadén are the richest in the world, Italy, the U.S.S.R., China, Mexico and the U.S.) From the large-scale uses a considerable amount of mercury wastes is flowing into the air, the soil and streams, lakes and bays.

In agriculture, for example, corrosive sublimate (HgCl$_2$) is used to disinfect seeds and to control many diseases of tubers, corms and bulbs (including potatoes). The chlorides of mercury (both mercuric and mercurous) are also employed to protect a number of vegetable crops. In recent decades farmers in Europe and the U.S. have adopted the use of organic compounds of mercury, some of which are highly toxic, principally to prevent fungal diseases in seeds and in growing plants, fruits and vegetables. These chemicals may present a potential threat to health through the ingestion of treated seeds by birds (and people), through concentration in food plants and through percolation or runoff from the fields into surface waters. The U.S. Geological Survey, after analyzing the concentration of mercury in a number of U.S. rivers in 1970, reported that although the mercury content was only one part per 10 billion or less in most rivers and streams, "it may be several thousand times this concentration in some natural waters."

In order to evaluate the hazards of mercury in the environment we must examine the forms in which it occurs there and the relative toxicity of its various compounds. Liquid mercury itself, as we have already noted, is not ordinarily toxic to man. Inhalation of mercury vapor, however, can be injurious. In acute cases it causes irritation and destruction of the lung tissues, with symptoms including chills, fever, coughing and a tight feeling in the chest, and there have been reports of fatalities from such exposure. The acute exposures, however, usually come about not from the general environment but by accident, such as heating a household mercurial. More common is a chronic form of injury resulting from occupational exposure to mercury vapor, for example among mercury miners and workers in felt hat factories employing mercury nitrate for processing. These exposures, as we have found in examinations of miners, are not necessarily incapacitating; they produce tremors, inflammation of the gums and general irritability.

The soluble inorganic salts of mercury have long been known to be toxic. Mercury bichloride (corrosive sublimate), which has been used on occasion for suicide and homicide, produces corrosion of the intestinal tract (leading to bloody diarrhea), injury to the kidneys, suppression of urine and ultimately death from kidney failure when it is taken by mouth in a substantial dose. Its former use in moderate doses by mouth for treatment of syphilis did not, however, result in observable poisoning in most cases. Mercurous chloride is less soluble than the mercuric salt and therefore is less dangerous. It is still used medicinally, but some of its uses have been abandoned because it was found to cause painful itching of the hands and feet and other symptoms in children. Among other inorganic mercurials, some of the oxides, such as the red oxide used in antifouling paint for ship bottoms, may be potentially hazardous. In general, however, these inorganic mercurials are not important factors in contamination of the general environment.

What does cause us concern now with regard to the environment is the presence of some of the organic compounds of mercury, specifically the alkyls: the methyl and ethyl compounds. In Minamata Bay the substances that had poisoned the fish and people were identified as methyl mercurials. The grain that caused outbreaks of illness and death among the farmers of Iraq had been treated with ethyl mercury *p*-toluene sulfonanilide. And alkyls of mercury were similarly incriminated in Sweden and other places.

It has been known for some time that alkyl mercury can cause congenital mental retardation, and recent laboratory studies have shown that it can produce abnormalities of the chromosomes and, through "intoxication" of the fetus in the uterus, can bring about cerebral palsy. The alkyl mercurials attack the brain cells, which are particularly susceptible to injury by this form of mercury. The chemical basis of this effect seems to be mercury's strong affinity for sulfur, particularly for the sulfhydryl groups (S-H) in proteins (for which arsenic and lead have a similar affinity). Bound to proteins in a cell membrane, the mercury may alter the distribution of ions, change electric potentials and thus interfere with the movement of fluid across the membrane. There are also indications that the binding of mercury to protein disturbs the normal operation of structures such as mitochondria and lysosomes within the cell. Alkyl mercury appears to be especially dangerous because the mercury is firmly bonded to a carbon atom, so that the molecule is not broken down and may maintain its destructive action for weeks or months. In this respect it differs from the inorganic and phenyl (aryl) mercurials, and that may explain why it produces permanent injury to brain tissue, whereas the injury caused by inorganic and aryl mercurials is almost invariably reversible.

At one time it was thought that aryl mercurials (compounds based on the phenyl group) might act like the alkyls; however, in an extensive series of studies I initiated in 1961 at the Columbia University School of Public Health we found that chemical workers who continually handled phenyl mercurials and experienced exposures far above the supposedly safe limit did not show any evidence of toxic effects.

Having examined the nature of the mercury "threat" and its quantitative presence in the environment, we should now look at the other side of the equation: the extent of man's exposure and his response to this factor up to now.

Without question the major source of man's intake of mercury is his food. Alfred E. Stock in Germany initiated analyses of the mercury concentration in foods in the 1930's, and there have been several follow-up studies since then, including one by our group at Columbia in 1964. (Numerous further investigations are now in progress.) The measured concentrations in samples from various sources are in the range of fractions of one part per million [see illustration on next page], but the concentrations in fish in contaminated waters may run several hundred times higher than that. A joint commission of the Food and Agriculture Organization and the World Health Organization proposed in 1963 that the permissible upper limit for mercury in foods (except fish and shellfish) should be .05 part per million; there is as yet no firm basis, however, for determining what the safe standard ought to be. Perhaps the most significant conclusion that can be drawn from these sets of samplings is that in general the concentration of mercury in foods does not appear to have changed substantially over the past 30 years. The comparisons may not be entirely valid, however, because of differences in analytical methods.

In addition to food, there are other possible everyday sources of exposure to mercury. It is used fairly commonly in antiseptics, paint preservatives, floor waxes, furniture polishes, fabric softeners, air-conditioner filters and laundry preparations for suppression of mildew; no doubt there are other such exposures

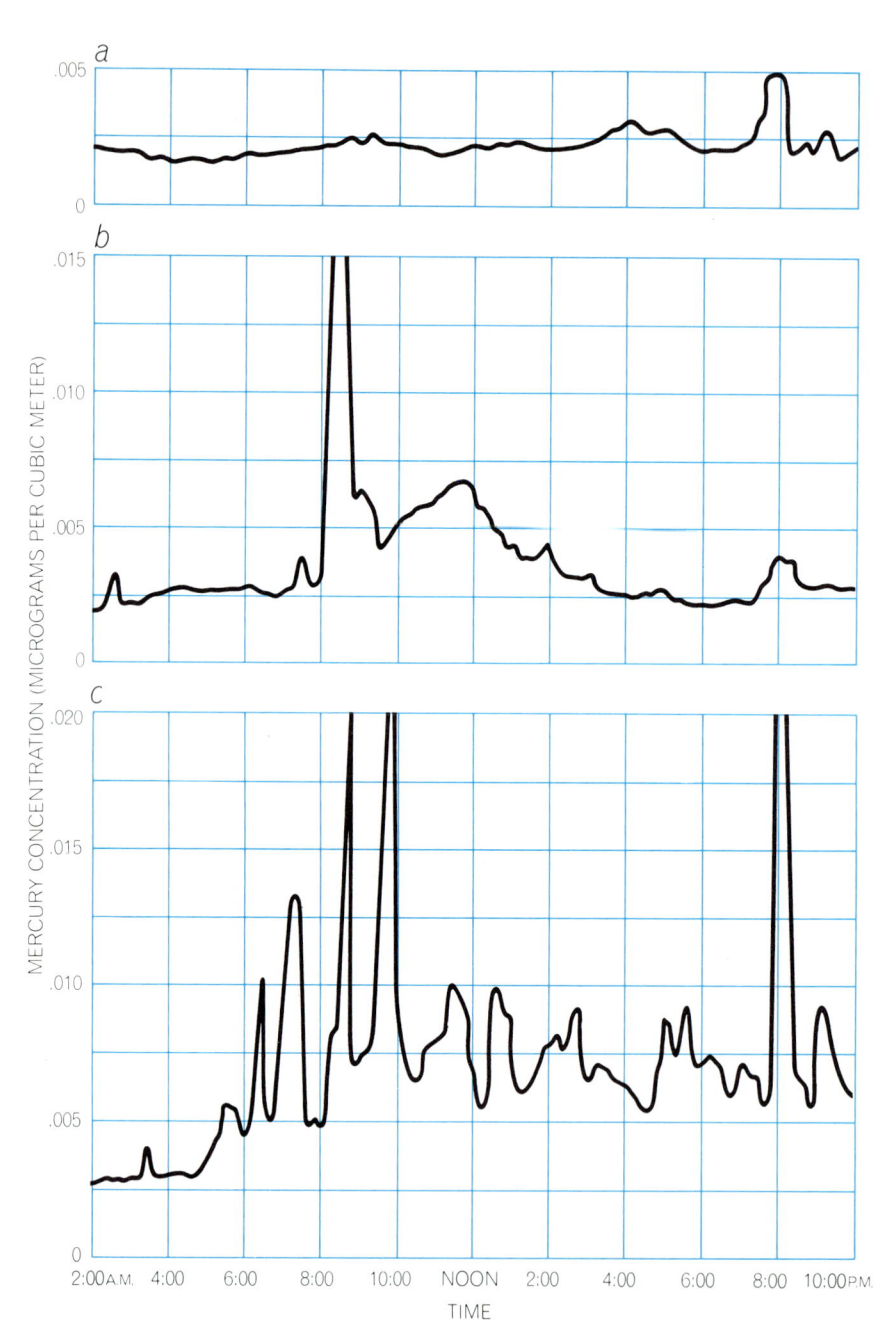

ATMOSPHERIC MERCURY LEVELS were measured by S. H. Williston at a station south of San Francisco. The concentration averaged about .0002 microgram of mercury per cubic meter of air when the wind blew from the Pacific (a) and was somewhat higher when the wind was from the generally nonindustrial southeast (b). The average was .008 microgram, with many peaks that went off the record at .02 microgram, when the wind was from the industrial area to the northeast (c). The mercury was often associated with dust particles.

of which we are not aware. In view of all these factors, it is not surprising to find that 20 to 25 percent of the "normal" population—persons who have apparently had no medicinal or occupational exposure to mercury—show easily measurable amounts of mercury in their body fluids. Several studies of this matter have been made, including a fairly extensive international investigation we carried out at Columbia in 1961–1963 as a joint project with the WHO. Analyzing 1,107 specimens of urine collected from "normal" subjects in 15 countries, we found that except in rare instances the mercury content in the urine ran no higher than about 20 to 25 parts per billion. A similar examination of blood samples showed that the highest mercury concentration in the blood among "normal" subjects was 30 to 50 parts per billion. And analyses of human tissues made at autopsy have indicated that similar traces of mercury are present in the body organs.

It is important to consider these findings in the context of the evolutionary relationship of life on our planet to the presence of mercury. Unquestionably the element has been omnipresent in the sea, where life originated, from the beginning, and presumably all plants and animals carry traces of mercury as a heritage from their primordial ancestry. Man as the top of a food chain must have added to that heritage by eating fish and other mercury-concentrating forms of food. Over the millions of years he presumably has built up an increased tolerance for mercury. (The development of tolerance for chemicals is of course well recognized today. It was put to use more than 2,000 years ago by Mithradates the Great, king of Pontus, who armed himself against poisoners by taking small and increasing doses of toxic agents.) Tolerance for a potent substance not infrequently grows into dependence on it, and it is reasonable to suppose that man, as well as other forms of life, may now be dependent on mercury as a useful trace element. Whether its effects are beneficial or harmful may be influenced decisively by the form in which it is incorporated in tissues, by the dose and probably by other factors. It has been found, for instance, that the highly toxic element arsenic is sometimes present in healthy shrimp in concentrations of close to 200 parts per million (dry weight) in the form of trimethylarsine. Methylation in this case apparently suppresses the element's toxicity. The biochemical behavior of mercury has much in common with that of arsenic, which suggests that there may be harmless forms of methyl mercury as well as toxic ones in fish.

Our concern, then, must be with any disturbance of the environment that alters the natural balance of mercury in relation to other substances or that generates virulent forms of mercurials. In the case of the fish in Minamata Bay apparently both factors were at work. The polluting effluent from the chemical plant itself contained methyl mercury, and elemental mercury in the effluent was methylated by microorganisms in the mud on the bottom of the bay. This conversion was fostered by the enrichment of the water with a high concentration of mercury and organic pollutants that promoted the growth of the methylating bacteria. The result was the accumulation in the fish of concentrations of methyl mercury as high as 50 parts per million (wet weight), which is 100 times the *total* mercury concentration currently accepted as "safe" in the U.S. and Canada. The effect on the fishermen and their families was compounded by the fact that their diet consisted largely of the bay fish and may have been deficient in some essential nutrients; dietary deficiencies are known to enhance the adverse effects of toxic agents.

The current journalistic outcry on the "mercury problem" has produced a state of public alarm approaching hysteria. "Protective" measures are being proposed and applied without basis in established knowledge. Research on mercury poisoning in the past has focused primarily on occupational hazards involving prolonged exposure, principally by way of inhalation. Mercury in the general environment, however, presents an almost entirely different problem. Discharge of mercury into the atmosphere, either as vapor or as particulate matter, is not likely to become a serious general hazard. The main threats to which we shall have to give attention are solid and liquid wastes that may ultimately enter bodies of water, thus threatening fish and eaters of fish, and agricultural uses of mercury that may dangerously contaminate food. We do not yet have enough information to estimate the magnitude of these threats or to establish realistic standards of control.

To begin with, we need a better understanding of what should be considered a toxic level of mercury in the human body. Analysis of the mercury con-

	A	B	C	D	E
MEATS	.001–.067	.005–.02	.0008–.044	.31–.36	.001–.15
FISH	.02–.18	.025–.18	.0016–.014	.035–.54	0–.06
VEGETABLES (FRESH)	.002–.044	.005–.035	0.	.03–.06	0–.02
VEGETABLES (CANNED)			.005–.025		.002–.007
MILK (FRESH)	.0006–.004	.0006–.004	.003–.007	.003–.007	.008
BUTTER	.002 (FATS)	.07–.28			.14
CHEESE	.009–.01				.08
GRAINS	.02–.036	.025–.035	.002–.006	.012–.048	.002–.025
FRUITS (FRESH)	.004–.01	.005–.035		.018	.004–.03
EGG WHITE				.08–.125	.01
EGG YOLK				.33–.67	.062
EGG (WHOLE)	.002	.002	0		
BEER	.00007–.0014	.001–.015			.004

CONCENTRATION IN FOODS was reported by Alfred E. Stock in Germany in 1934 (*A*) and 1938 (*B*), O. S. Gibbs in the U.S. in 1940 (*C*), Y. Fujimura in Japan in 1964 (*D*) and the author's group in the U.S. in 1964 (*E*). A listing of "0" means simply a concentration too low to be detected by the method used. The World Health Organization proposed a permissible upper limit of .05 part per million for foods other than fish; the U.S. Food and Drug Administration has set an upper limit of .5 part per million for fish.

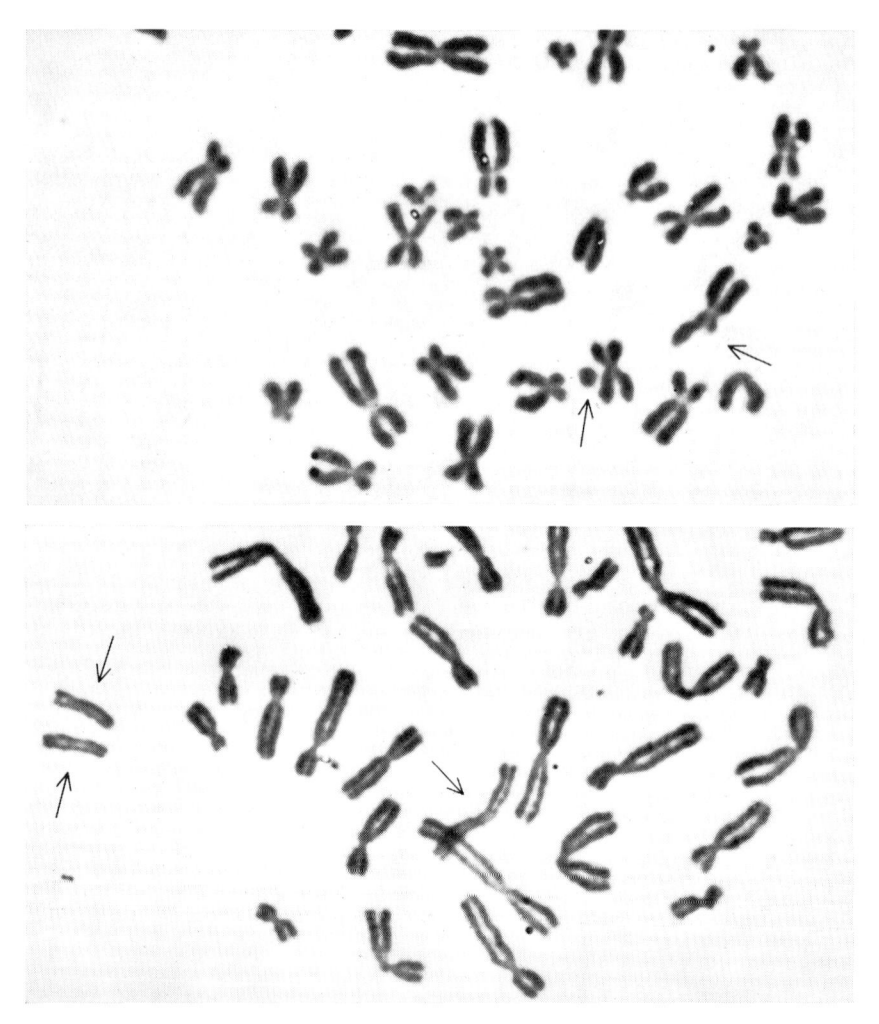

CHROMOSOME DAMAGE is found in persons with high blood levels of mercury after exposure to methyl mercury in fish. Photographs of lymphocytes made by Staffan Skerfving of the Swedish National Institute of Public Health show a broken chromosome and extra fragment (*top*) and three sister-chromatid fragments that lack centromeres (*bottom*).

centration in the urine or in the blood has not given much enlightenment on this point. Among workers exposed to mercury in their occupations it has been found that the mercury content in the urine varies greatly from day to day and from one individual to another. As a general rule the body's excretion of mercury does tend to reflect the amount of exposure, but recent studies of workers in the chemical industries have disclosed that individuals who have been exposed to mercury in high concentrations or for long periods often show no sign of adverse effects. Furthermore, high levels in the urine or the blood do not necessarily indicate poisoning; many cases have been observed in which the individual had a mercury concentration in the blood amounting to 10 to 20 times the "normal" upper limit and yet showed no indications of illness or toxic symptoms! All in all there is substantial evidence that host factors may be more important than the amount of exposure, up to a point, in determining the individual's response to mercury in the environment. In any case, urine or blood analysis is of no value for early diagnosis of mercury poisoning. Other possible indicators, such as disturbances of the blood enzyme system, are being investigated, but no reliable diagnostic test has yet been produced. Nor can we define a precise threshold for the toxic level, either for exposure to or for absorption of mercury.

A good deal of useful information is available, on the other hand, about the sources and avenues of possible danger. Mercury in one form or another can invade the human system by way of the lungs, the skin or the ingestion of food. (Incidentally, recent studies have shown that the mercury in dental fillings is not a hazard; most people with amalgam fillings have negligible amounts of mercury in their urine or blood.) Mercury in the air, as we have noted, is a local problem confined to certain industries. Attack by way of the skin is also a problem that does not apply to the general environment, although direct contact with organic mercurials can cause severe (second degree) local burns of the skin and can result in absorption of measurable quantities of mercury into the body from underclothing and bed linen.

With regard to food, we can identify the most important possible sources of trouble. There is abundant evidence that the inorganic compounds of mercury and the phenyl mercurials are relatively nontoxic compared with the alkyl mercurials. We need to be concerned, however, about the potential conversion of the inorganic forms and the phenyls to methyl mercury, which on the basis of the experience so far must be rated as the prime hazard in the environment. A number of alkyl mercury fungicides have already been eliminated, quite properly, from use on food crops. Government agencies are now beginning to move to ban other organic mercurials as well from any use that might contaminate our food or water.

A calm view of the present state of affairs regarding mercury in the environment suggests that the best way to deal with the problem is to apply the techniques of epidemiology, preventive medicine, public health and industrial hygiene that have been effective in meeting hazards in the past. A system should be set up for frequent monitoring of the environment for the detection of significant increases in mercury contamination. Research should be carried forward to establish measures for the levels and forms of mercurial pollution that signal a threat to health. Techniques for mass screening of the population to detect mercurial poisoning should be developed. Controls should be applied to stop the discharge of potentially harmful mercury wastes at the point of origin. Toxic mercurials in industry and agriculture should be replaced by less toxic substitutes. To implement such a program we shall need, of course, realistic education of the public and legislative action with adequate enforcement. And these measures should be applied to all contaminants that threaten man's environment, not only mercurials.

It would be foolish to declare an all-out war against mercury. The evolutionary evidence suggests that too little mercury in the environment might be as disastrous as too much. In the case of mercury, as in all other aspects of our environment, our wisest course is to try to understand and to maintain the balance of nature in which life on our planet has thrived.

II
CONVENTIONAL SOURCES AND RESOURCES

II

CONVENTIONAL SOURCES AND RESOURCES
INTRODUCTION

Man is omnivorous and obtains his food directly from plants or indirectly from them by consuming the flesh of animals, which ultimately derive their sustenance from plants. In that sense all flesh is grass, and ultimately the sun is the source of all food energy. When we harvest plants, we harvest solar energy. The efficiency of food production is based on the proximity of our foods to the solar source. The conversion of solar energy to energy stored by plants in the form of carbohyrates is about 1 or 2 percent. Each time this energy is transferred to another organism (such as when a steer grazes), a 90–95 percent loss occurs. (Most of the energy is walked off or wasted by the steer, and not all of the animal is consumed.) This, of course, is not as inefficient as it sounds, because a steer can use much plant material that is unused by humans. Nevertheless, the flow of energy through a succession of living organisms (a food chain or web) means that the further man's diet gets away from plants, the higher is the real cost. Put another way, when food gets scarce man must be a direct rather than an indirect consumer of plants.

The use of animal protein is of course very attractive. Animal protein is more complete than are the proteins of individual plant species; i.e., animal protein contains the 8 or 10 amino acids we require in a proportion close to our needs. To get an even approximate nutritive equivalent from plant protein, we must mix a number of sources and consume larger bulk because the essential amino acids must be consumed simultaneously and the concentration of protein in plants is lower. Finally, animal protein is a food source that many of us find very palatable.

One advantage of meat consumption is that a meat-eating society seldom has a food shortage. If meat is scarce, price dictates a shift to plant proteins (more cereal "filler" in the hamburger, more macaroni casseroles, less beefsteak). In essence, animal feed constitutes society's reserves. Where pressure of human population on land resources is great, animal protein satisfies only a small fraction of the human requirement; the plant food is virtually all consumed. When shortages occur, there may be no effective reserve, in which case food shortages quickly worsen to become famines. Ultimately, the key factors that determine adequacy of food supply are availability of sufficient arable land area per person and the level of technology used in converting this resource to food.

Civilization is based upon the complex relationships between man and a few other life forms known as crop plants and domestic animals. The technologies that make up agriculture, date back some 10,000 years to the transition from hunting and food gathering to cultivation and husbandry. This dramatic change is now known in the history of man as the Neolithic Revolution. Agriculture ensures a dependable food supply and build-up of surpluses which allows the release of specialists for other activities.

Although civilization has changed immensely with the passage of millenia, the plants and animals selected by our ancestors for sustenance have remained with us. But they have been changed to what are in fact new creatures, new species. Many no longer occur in wild form, and in their present state of dependency are incapable of surviving by themselves. The relationship is mutual, for there is no doubt that man is utterly dependent on his "creations." While individuals might survive without them, civilization as we know it could not. Out of the thousands of species that accompany man on this planet, the handful that have been chosen now seem irreplaceable. Modern man has uncovered no new potential crop plant or domesticable animal. Even our early explorers, in their search for new foods, uncovered only those crop plants already under cultivation by primitive man. It has always been more convenient to improve upon the base provided than to search out new forms.

The success of agriculture has been the discovery that certain plants are capable of high caloric output per unit area of land. Such plants include the grain crops plus potato, cassava, sugarcane, and banana. All great civilizations have been based on the cultivation of at least one of these great calorie producers in abundance.

World grain production today amounts to about 1.2 million tons per year, or about 1.6 pounds per capita per day, of which the triumvirate composed of wheat, rice, and corn accounts for about three quarters. The high world production of grains is based on many factors. Grains are a concentrated source of energy and are easily stored. Few other crops are capable of such high concentration of energy or nutrients per unit area of land. They are versatile and combine well with other foods. Finally, they can be transformed into other products through processing, cooking, and fermentation.

Wheat, source of our daily bread, "gift" of the Mother God Ceres (hence cereal), became the foundation of the civilizations of Egypt, Greece, Rome, and modern Europe. Its story ("Wheat") is chronicled by Paul C. Mangelsdorf, who shows that the modern crop plant (*Triticum aestivum* subspecies *vulgare*) is not a minor variation of a weed, but is a complex hybrid of several species selected for a peculiar characteristic. The seed of many primitive grasses is attached to a fragile stalk that "shatters" when mature to release the seed helter skelter. By a selection of types in which the seeds cling tenaciously to their stalk—a distinct disadvantage to a wild species—man has unknowingly ensured that the existence and future evolution of wheat is dependent upon man, just as much as man is dependent upon wheat.

It has been possible to elucidate the mysteries of the origin of wheat only because the building blocks are still extant. Many are still, in fact, cultivated. Since the appearance of this article twenty years ago, the rate of change in the evolution of wheat has accelerated. The never-ending race between plant breeders and a fungus that causes stem rust—the most serious scourge of wheat—has continued. The breeder is still ahead, if barely. The emergence of the more productive short-stemmed wheats has ushered in the Green Revolution. Another development, the introduction of cytoplasmic male sterility to convert a normally self-pollinated crop to a cross-pollinated crop, has made possible hybrid wheats—now in limited production. Finally, the first man-made crop species has appeared. Called "triticale," it is a result of hybridizing wheat (*Triticum*) and rye (*Secale*).

Crop plants have developed so slowly from wild plants that man has been essentially unconscious of his accomplishments as a plant breeder. Throughout history, man has chosen to look upon crop plants as gifts of the gods rather than things of his own creation. In this century, methods were discovered for directing and speeding up the process of evolution. Animal and crop breeding, once only arts, have become firmly established on the basis of genetics, and each is a science in its own right, contributing to the understanding of genetic principles.

This is well brought out in "Hybrid Corn," Paul Manglesdorf's second piece. The origins of hybrid corn derive from a study made early in this century of genetic variation in this crop plant. Hybrid corn is now produced by a system of genetic control within and between maize populations through inbreeding and cross-breeding, which makes possible a high-yielding, highly uniform population. The discovery of hybrid vigor has been essential to the mechanization of agriculture. The success of hybrid corn has also spawned the scientific approach to the breeding of many other crops and the mechanization of all grain production. The breeding principle has proved useful for a number of other seed-propagated crops (such as sorghum, onions, cole crops). The tedious hand-detassling operation to control the source of pollen in the production of hybrids has been successfully eliminated by the incorporation of male sterility based on a combination of nuclear genetic factors and nonnuclear factors carried in the cytoplasm and passed along only through the seed parent. This technique, mentioned in passing at the end of Manglesdorf's 1951 article, has been so successful that practically all of the United States corn crop has been so converted.

In 1969, however, a rather unusual event occurred. Plants with male-sterile cytoplasm were attacked, by a new (T) race of the fungus (*Helminthesporium maydis*), which causes the Southern Corn Blight disease. The 1970 epidemic was especially severe and reduced the United States corn crop by 15–20 percent (1 billion bushels worth more than a billion dollars)! This disaster jolted many into an appreciation of the biologic realities of our food supply. Extreme uniformity and refinement of our food crops makes them vulnerable to attack by pathogens or predators.

As man moved from food gathering to cultivation, hunting also gave way to husbandry. The dog, companion in the hunt, probably paved the way for an appreciation of the potential of domestication. It was cattle, however, that proved to be an ideal of a continued, reliable food supply, for they provided meat as well as milk (and in some cultures blood). Equally important to early agriculture was the use of cattle as beasts of burden, long before horse power was "harnessed" with the adoption of a nonchoking collar. The inedible parts of the animal (hide, bones, and fat) served a number of other valuable uses. Manure was found to be a good soil supplement in farming, and in some parts of the world serves as a convenient fuel supply. The use of animal by-products is still expanding; in modern applications, they are found to be valuable as a source of drugs (hormones, enzymes). For the nomads, and later for the farming communities, cattle were an efficient source of food, since the animals could sustain themselves on vegetation otherwise unsuitable for man. The conversion of grass to high-quality human food takes place by microbial fermentation in the compartmentalized stomachs of cattle (refer also to "The Metabolism of Ruminants," SCIENTIFIC AMERICAN, February 1958).

Milk production probably played a dominant part in the domestication of cattle, since the act of milking demands selection for docility and dependence. This product of the female mammal is the only food provided by nature for the specific purpose of nurturing young. The additional source of this vital food, made available through animal husbandry, greatly enhanced the survival rate of the human young and the infirm, and probably accounts for a great deal of the vitality exhibited by nomadic tribes and the impact they have had on civilizations throughout the history of mankind. Stuart Patton, in his essay "Milk," makes the interesting observation that the lactating mammary cell is second only to the photosynthetic cell as a factor in maintaining mammalian life. The processes that give rise to milk, this "liquid tissue," are incredibly complex. Production begins in the rumen (the cow is a walking fermentation tank with a capacity of up to 60 gallons), where microbes perform marvelous feats in converting otherwise indigestible compounds into such absorbable and utilizable compounds as glucose, amino acids, and vitamins. It continues in the mammary gland, where virtually all of the milk constitutents are synthesized, assembled, and finally excreted from precursors transported from the rumen via the blood stream. The result is a product ideally suited for the feeding of the young. This biosynthetic process has to be considered one of the finer examples of intricate specialization in nature.

Ralph W. Phillips' article "Cattle" traces the development of breeds as adaptions to specific environments—from the frigid north to the sweltering tropics. In addition to these temperature adaptions, there has been a selection of cattle for efficiency in meat and milk production. Animal improvement has continued with changing objectives. For example, high fat content, so highly prized in milk that its price is still pegged to the price of butter, is grudgingly giving way to selection for protein. Cross-breeding of cattle has led to types with increasing productivity and vigor—if inelegant appearance. The genetic improvement of cattle, coupled with advances in animal nutrition, have revolutionized animal agriculture in temperate areas. If animal husbandry could be better adapted to the tropics, necessary high-quality protein could be provided, but this would require improvements in breeding, animal nutrition, pasture management, and disease control, all of which remain to be accomplished.

Other warm-blooded animals, such as hogs, goats, and sheep, are used as sources of food (and fiber) in many parts of the world. The goat, however, is a destructive grazer and has been confined to marginal lands that can support no other use; overgrazing by goats has often led to ecological disaster. Sheep are widespread in various parts of the temperate climates, particularly because of the use of wool as a fiber. But sheep are ill-adapted to warm areas, and mutton is not a popular food in much of the world. Hogs are extremely efficient as converters of grain to meat protein—in fact, more efficient than cattle. But since pigs are nonruminants, they are direct competitors of man for high-energy foods.

Domestic fowl, including chicken, geese, ducks, turkey, and quail, are raised in many areas of the world, but production has long been based on a small-scale "cottage" industry approach, and, until recently, poultry products were relatively expensive foods. In the 1930's prosperity was defined in the United States as a chicken in every pot, and it is said in Brazil that when a farmer eats a chicken, one of the two is sick. The chicken, highly prized for its varied beauty by fanciers and its fighting ability by sportsmen, has become an example of the high potentiality of modern animal husbandry. This is the theme of Wilbur O. Wilson's article "Poultry Production." One of the many contributions of American agriculture in the past 20 years is the adaption of the chicken to mechanization and mass production. As production has become more efficient (egg yields have doubled in 30 years), prices have decreased. This technology has been exported to Europe, where traditional poultry-raising systems still make poultry more or less a luxury food.

Another conventional source of protein is provided through fishing, the aquatic equivalent of hunting. The ocean yields approximately 55 million metric tons of fish products per year, about one tenth that of animal agriculture. About half of the yields of the ocean are used as protein supplements for animal feed, much of which is exported by protein-deficient countries! Because fishing is a mining operation (there is no "planting"), enormous inputs have been put into the extractive machinery with—it must be admitted—profitable results, but little of consequence has been expended in guaranteeing continued productivity. The management of the ocean is complicated by the "Law of the Commons." Individual decisions (usually made, in the context of the example, by nations) are not compatible with optimum total productivity. Thus an individual decision to add a cow to a common pasture (or an additional vessel to the whaling fleet) may be marginally productive to the individual, but the future total yield may decline because of excessive exploitation. In "The Food Resources of the Ocean," S. J. Holt discusses the advances in fishery technology and charts the potential yield of the oceans (estimated as from two to four times the present production).

The problems of attaining and maintaining maximum return from the seas are political as well as technical in nature, and add a new dimension to food production. Overall efficiency of some fisheries can be increased merely by reducing the size of the fishing fleet or by increasing the mesh size of nets (leaving smaller fish free to breed). But international agreements to adopt, much less comply with, these common-sense concepts have been difficult to obtain. Management of our ocean resources requires emphasis on biological realities rather than political expediencies. The objective, as in land agriculture, must be sustained yield. Technology can increase ocean yields, but damage to our ocean resources by overexploitation, and increasingly by pollution, may reverse the trend toward greater productivity—perhaps permanently.

While man gets hungrier every day and the demand for food continues to increase, most foods continue to be seasonably produced. In the Temperate Zone the growing season is broken by winter, and even in the tropics there is usually a seasonal component that limits continuous production. Extending the supply, especially for rapidly deteriorating products, is essential. The arts of food preservation, the basis of many ancient and modern technologies, is basic to the story of foods. These techniques involve physical and chemical processes that sterilize foods or render them incapable of supporting the growth of microorganisms.

Canning and freezing, modern methods of food preservation, are relatively recent developments. Canning has been traced back to Napoleonic times, but has become a major method only in this century; freezing dates from the 1920's. These processes are routine and yet crucial to modern society. Interestingly, there are no articles on these types of food preservation in SCIENTIFIC AMERICAN, probably because they are taken for granted.

Other techniques for food preservation include drying, fermentation, and the use of various chemical additives. All have an ancient tradition. The origin of the spice trade, which gave incentive to early exploration, is related in large part to their use as chemical adjuncts to food: it has been said that the great value of spices was originally to mask the unpleasant flavors of spoiled foods. In "Food Additives," G. O. Kermode discusses the modern problems associated with this branch of the food art. Additives have long been prized by the food industry for food preservation as well as for changing flavor, enhancing color, and improving texture. They are invaluable in preventing deterioration and waste in many foods; in fact, they have become essential for so-called convenience foods. The question of safety and the misuse of additives, however, has been responsible for increasing controls on their use. With the rise of consumerism the subject has become controversial and highly emotional. It can probably be stated that the proliferation of additives (which still goes on in spite of the high cost of safety testing) is not always in the best interest of the consumer. The purist sees no need for ice creams of new and unique flavors, or for jams colored in various shades of red, or for stabilizers that enhance the shelf life of products up to several months when a few days used to be considered sufficient. But present-day society has become utterly dependent on the use of food additives. Without them the modern food industry would be unmanageable, mass distribution over whole continents would be impossible, and our food supply would again become highly seasonal.

The action of bacteria and yeast in decomposing carbohydrates anaerobically is known as fermentation. Microorganisms associated with decay can thus be utilized in food preservation by a process commonly known as pickling. Fermentation of grapes, honey, barley, and rice leads directly to products long prized by man—wine, mead, beer, saki. In "Wine," by Maynard A. Amerine, and in "Beer," by Anthony H. Rose, the sequence of operations developed through centuries of empirical development are explained in terms of biochemistry and microbiology. An understanding of the processes involved have made it possible for the winemaker and the brewmaster to control the operations so that the products are of consistent quality. Still, the subtleties of chemistry that distinguish the good from the exquisite elude the scientist.

The present-day fermentation industry, with its solid background of scientific input, is an example of the degree of sophistication and care in manufacturing that now prevails in the modern food industry. No other industry, with the exception of the pharmaceutical industry, is subject to so many regulations and such close control by public agencies. The public health aspects that now completely dominate the manufacturing and processing of foods in this country have not come easily. The early history of the industry is replete with incidents involving food-borne diseases caused by lack of sanitation or careless use of additives. But as the industry matured, as its scope expanded to provide processed food to virtually every person in the country every day of their lives, so did, of necessity, the regulatory machinery of Federal and local government. The huge production units and nationwide marketing of products by individual manufacturers require that officials entrusted by the public keep a watchful eye to ensure that the products are safe and wholesome. (Consumption of an unsafe product widely distributed could have terrible consequences.) The food industry has in turn been forced to develop manufacturing procedures, quality control methods, and standards that in a self-policing effort often go beyond the requirement set by law. Although food processing and the production industries are essentially based on ancient practices, the modern versions based on science and new technology bear little resemblance to techniques practiced only a few decades ago.

12

WHEAT

PAUL C. MANGELSDORF
July 1953

The grass that bears our daily bread is synonymous with European civilization. What is the basis of its usefulness, and what is the origin of modern wheat?

WHEAT is the world's most widely cultivated plant. The wheat plants growing on the earth may even outnumber those of any other seed-bearing land species, wild or domesticated. Every month of the year a crop of wheat is maturing somewhere in the world. It is the major crop of the U. S. and Canada and is grown on substantial acreages in almost every country of Latin America, Europe and Asia.

Apparently this grain was one of the earliest plants cultivated by man. Carbonized kernels of wheat were found recently by the University of Chicago archaeologist Robert Braidwood at the 6,700-year-old site of Jarmo in eastern Iraq, the oldest village yet discovered—a village which may have been one of the birthplaces of man's agriculture. Through the courtesy of Dr. Braidwood I have had an opportunity to study some of these ancient kernels and compare them with modern kernels, carbonized to simulate the archaeological specimens. The resemblance between the ancient and modern grains is remarkable. There were two types of kernels in the Jarmo site; one turned out to be almost identical with a wild wheat still growing in the Near East, and the other almost exactly like present-day cultivated wheat of the type called einkorn. Evidently there has been no appreciable change in these wheats in the 7,000 years since Jarmo.

When he domesticated wheat, man laid the foundations of western civilization. No civilization worthy of the name has ever been founded on any agricultural basis other than the cereals. The ancient cultures of Babylonia and Egypt, of Rome and Greece, and later those of northern and western Europe, were all based upon the growing of wheat, barley, rye and oats. Those of India, China and Japan had rice for their basic crop. The pre-Columbian peoples of America —Inca, Maya and Aztec—looked to corn for their daily bread.

What are the reasons for this intimate relation between the cereals and civilization? It may be primarily a question of nutrition. The grain of cereal grasses, a nutlike structure with a thin shell covering the seed, contains not only the embryo of a new plant but also a food supply to nourish it. Cereal grains, like eggs and milk, are foodstuffs designed by nature for the nutrition of the young of the species. They represent a five-in-one food supply which contains carbohydrate, proteins, fats, minerals and vitamins. A whole-grain cereal, if its food values are not destroyed by the over-refinement of modern processing methods, comes closer than any other plant product to providing an adequate diet. Man long ago discovered this fact and learned to exploit it. Guatemalan Indians manage to subsist fairly well on a diet which is 85 per cent corn. In India people sometimes live on almost nothing but rice. Such diets do not meet the approval of modern nutritionists, but they are better than those made up too largely of starchy root crops such as potatoes, sweet potatoes or cassava, or of proteinaceous legumes such as beans, peas and lentils.

Perhaps the relationship between cereals and civilization is also a product of the discipline which cereals impose upon their growers. The cereals are grown only from seed and must be planted and harvested in their proper season. In this respect they differ from the root crops, which in mild climates can be planted and harvested at almost any time of the year. Root-crop agriculture can be practiced by semi-nomadic peoples who visit their plantations only periodically. The growing of cereals has always been accompanied by a stable mode of life. Moreover, it forced men to become more conscious of the seasons and the movements of the sun, moon and stars. In both the Old World and the New the science of astronomy was invented by cereal growers, and with it a calendar and a system of arithmetic. Cereal agriculture in providing a stable food supply created leisure, and leisure in turn fostered the arts, crafts and sciences. It has been said that "cereal agriculture, alone among the forms of food production, taxes, recompenses and stimulates labor and ingenuity in an equal degree."

From Grain-chewing to Bread

Today wheat is the cereal *par excellence* for breadmaking, and it is used almost exclusively for that purpose. But it is quite unlikely that breadmaking, a complex and sophisticated art, came suddenly into full flower with the domestication of wheat. Man may have begun by merely parching or popping the grain to make it edible. Primitive wheats, like other cereals, were firmly enclosed in husks, called glumes. Heating makes the glumes easy to rub off and allows the kernel itself to be more easily chewed or ground into meal. The scorching and parching of grains is still practiced on unripened cereals in parts of the Near East. In Scotland until recently barley glumes were sometimes removed by setting fire to the unthreshed heads. The Chippewa Indians still prepare wild rice by heating the unhusked kernels and tramping on them in a hollow log.

Hard-textured cereal grains with a certain moisture content explode and escape from their glumes when heated. In America the first use of corn was undoubtedly by popping. The earliest known corn had small vitreous kernels, and archaeological remains of popped corn have been found in early sites in both North and South America. In India certain varieties of rice are popped by stirring the kernels in hot sand. Many villages in India have a village popper who performs this service for his neighbors and provides himself with food by taking his toll of the product.

The botanical as well as archaeological evidence, though meager, indicates that wheat was first used as a parched cereal. The dwellings at Jarmo contain ovens which prove that this primitive economy knew the controlled use of heat. All the very ancient prehistoric kernels so far found are carbonized as if they had been over-parched. In itself this evidence is not telling, since only carbonized grains would be preserved indefinitely, but it is in harmony with other evidence. Finally, the most ancient wheats are species whose kernels would not be removed from the husks merely by threshing. The simplest method of husking them to make them edible would have been parching.

Probably the second stage in progress was to grind the parched grains and soak the coarse meal in water to make a gruel. For the toothless, both old and young, this must have been a life-saving invention. Gruel or porridge is well known as a primitive form of food. A gruel prepared from parched barley was the principal food of the common people of ancient Greece. American Indians prepared a kind of porridge from corn, which has its modern counterpart in "mush" and "polenta."

A gruel allowed to stand for a few days in a warm dwelling would become infected with wild yeasts. Fermenting the small amounts of sugar in cereal, the yeasts would have produced a mild alcoholic beverage. This would have pointed the way to leavened bread. It is questionable which art developed first—brewing or breadmaking. Some students believe that brewing is older even than agriculture, but there is no supporting archaeological or historical evidence. On the contrary, the earliest Egyptian recipes for beer described a process in which the grain was first made into half-baked loaves, which then became the raw material for beer-making. There is no doubt that brewing and the making of leavened bread are closely related arts, both depending upon fermentation by yeasts.

Modern breadmaking, however, had to await the appearance of new types of wheat. It is as much a product of the evolution of wheat as it is one of human ingenuity.

From Wild Grass to Wheat

Wheat differs from most cultivated plants in the complexity of its variations. True, the other major cereals, rice and corn, are each differentiated into thousands of varieties, but these form a continuous spectrum of variation and hence are classed as a single botanical species. Wheat is separated into distinct groups which differ from one another in many ways and are therefore classified as separate species under the single Old World genus *Triticum*. The domesticated wheats and their wild relatives have been studied more intensively than any other group of plants, cultivated or wild, and from these studies, truly international in scope, a picture is beginning to emerge of the evolution of wheat under domestication.

Authorities differ on the number of distinct species of wheat. This article follows the classification of Nikolai Vavilov, the Russian geneticist and botanist who, with his colleagues, brought together for study more than 31,000 samples of wheat from all parts of the world. Vavilov recognized 14 species; other botanists have recognized fewer or more. All authorities agree, however, that the wheat species, whatever their number, fall into three distinct groups, determined by the number of chromosomes in their cells. The chromosome numbers (in the reproductive cells) of the three types are, respectively, 7, 14 and 21. They were discovered by T. Sakamura in Japan in 1918 and slightly later, but independently, by Karl Sax in the U. S. The numbers are closely associated with differences in anatomy, morphology, resistance to disease, productiveness and milling and baking qualities. It is interesting to note that August Schulz, a German botanist, had arranged the wheats into these three groups in 1913, well before their chromosome numbers were known.

The 14- and 21-chromosome wheats have all arisen from 7-chromosome wheat and related grasses, through hybridization followed by chromosome doubling. The cultivated wheats are the most conspicuous example of this "cataclysmic evolution," described by G. Ledyard Stebbins, Jr., in his article in SCIENTIFIC AMERICAN of April, 1951. It is the only known mechanism by which new true-breeding species can be created almost overnight.

Since different wild grasses have been involved in wheat's evolution, the species differ not only in the number but also in the nature of their chromosomes. Relationships of different sets of chromosomes are determined by studying the degree of chromosome pairing in the reproductive cells of hybrids. If the pairing is complete, or almost so, the chromosome sets (genoms) of the parents are regarded as identical or closely related. If there is no pairing, the parental genoms are considered to be distinct. Four different genoms, each comprising seven chromosomes, designated A, B, D

Wheat field and farm buildings

FOURTEEN SPECIES OF WHEAT are shown actual size. From left to right they are *Triticum aegilopoides* (wild einkorn), *T. monococcum* (einkorn), *T. dicoccoides* (wild emmer), *T. dicoccum* (emmer), *T. durum* (macaroni wheat), *T. persicum* (Persian wheat), *T. turgidum* (rivet wheat), *T. polonicum* (Polish wheat), *T.*

and G, are recognized in wild and cultivated wheats.

Another important difference in wheats is in their heads. Primitive cereals and many wild grasses have heads whose central stem is brittle and fragile, breaking apart when mature and providing a natural mechanism for seed dispersal. When such cereals are threshed, the heads break up into individual spikelets (clusters of one or more individual grass flowers) in which the kernels remain firmly enclosed in their husks. Under domestication this characteristic, so essential to perpetuation of the species in the wild, has been lost. New forms have evolved, not only in wheat but in other cereals, in which the stems are tough and the heads remain intact when mature. In such cereals threshing alone removes the kernels from their glumes. The cereals with free-threshing, naked grains are much more useful to man, especially for milling and baking, than those that cling stubbornly to their husks. In wheats, therefore, the naked varieties have almost completely superseded the primitive forms.

Ancestors

The 7-chromosome wheats, probably the most ancient, consist of two species: *T. aegilopoides* and *T. monococcum*, known as wild einkorn and einkorn. Carbonized kernels of both were found at Jarmo, but whether they are the only wheats occurring in this ancient village site remains to be seen. Both species of einkorn have fragile stems and firm-hulled seeds. Their spikelets contain but a single seed, hence their name. Each has the same set of chromosomes, genom A, and they hybridize easily together to produce highly fertile offspring. Cultivated einkorn has slightly larger kernels than the wild form and a slightly tougher stem. Its heads do not fall apart quite so easily when ripe. Except for these slight differences the two species are essentially identical, and einkorn is

timopheevi (which has no common name), *T. aestivum* (common wheat), *T. sphaerococcum* (shot wheat), *T. compactum* (club wheat), *T. spelta* (spelt) and *T. macha* (macha wheat). The first two species have 7 chromosomes; the following seven, 14 chromosomes; the last five, 21 chromosomes (*see table on next two pages*).

undoubtedly the domesticated counterpart of the wild species. Apparently little significant change has been wrought in them over the centuries.

Wild einkorn has its center of distribution in Armenia and Georgia of the Soviet Union, and in Turkey. It also occurs in the eastern Caucasus and in western Iran. Westward from Asia Minor it is a common grass on the sides of low hills in Greece and Bulgaria and a weed in the well-drained vineyards of southern Yugoslavia. Cultivated einkorn originated, according to Vavilov, in the mountains of northeastern Turkey and the southwestern Caucasus. However, if my identification of the kernels at Jarmo is correct, and if Jarmo represents the beginnings of agriculture, einkorn may have been domesticated first slightly farther south in eastern Iraq. Certainly it is an ancient cereal. Carbonized grains of it have been found in neolithic deposits of the lake-dwellers and in many other sites in central and northeastern Europe. Impressions of einkorn have been identified in neolithic pottery in Britain and Ireland. There are no records of its prehistoric occurrence in India, China or Africa.

Einkorn is still grown in some parts of Europe and the Middle East, usually in hilly regions with thin soils. Its yields are low, usually not more than 8 to 15 bushels per acre. A bread, dark brown in color but of good flavor, can be made from it if it is husked, but it is more commonly used as a whole grain, like barley, for feeding cattle and horses. Einkorn's importance lies not in its present use but in its progeny. It is the ancestor of all other cultivated wheats, with the possible exception of the type called emmer. Einkorn's descendants all have in common the set of seven chromosomes called genom A.

Second Stage

In the next stage of evolution are the 14-chromosome species, of which Vavilov recognized seven. All these have come from the hybridization and chromosome doubling of a 7-chromosome wheat with a 7-chromosome related wild grass. The wheat parent in each case was undoubtedly einkorn, or possibly in one instance its wild relative, since all the species possess the genom A. But the wild-grass parent remains to this day unidentified and is the chief botanical mystery in the origin of cultivated wheats. This parent contributed a genom B to all in the group except one species. Edgar McFadden and Ernest Sears of the U. S. Department of Agriculture have suggested that genom B may have been derived from a species of *Agropyron*, a genus of weedy grasses which includes the pernicious couch grass of the northeastern U. S. Only one of the 14-chromosome wheats is found wild. This species, which is called wild emmer, is indigenous to southern Armenia, northeastern Turkey, western Iran, Syria and northern Palestine.

Closely resembling wild emmer, and possibly derived directly from it by domestication, is emmer, the oldest of 14-chromosome cultivated wheats and once the most widely grown wheat of all. An alternative possibility, however, is that emmer is the product of hybridization between einkorn and a 7-chromosome wild relative. The fact that crosses of wild and cultivated emmer are sometimes partly sterile indicates that the two forms may not be closely related and that one may be the product of an ancient hybridization and the other of a more recent one. There is at least no doubt about the antiquity of emmer. Well-preserved spikelets scarcely different from those of modern emmer have been found in Egyptian tombs of the Fifth Dynasty. Emmer may well have been the chief cereal of the Near East from very early times to the Greco-Roman period, for until the Jarmo find it was the only wheat found archaeologically in early sites of that region. Remains or impressions of it have also been common in neolithic sites in continental Europe, Britain and Ireland.

Emmer, like einkorn, has a fragile stem and clinging hull. Good bread and fine cake and pastry can be made from it, but most emmer today is fed to livestock. Some varieties are quite resistant to stem and leaf rust, the principal diseases of wheat, and have been useful in plant breeding.

The 14-chromosome wheats were the first to produce species with tough stems and with kernels that thresh free from their glumes. Four such species are known: *durum* (macaroni), *persicum* (Persian), *turgidum* (rivet) and *polonicum* (Polish). All have a more recent history than einkorn or emmer. The oldest, durum, first appeared in the Greco-Roman period about the first century B.C. One of the most recent, Polish

wheat, unique for its massive heads and long, hard kernels, did not appear until the 17th century. None of these wheats except durum is of great commercial importance today. Durum wheat, the best variety for the manufacture of macaroni, spaghetti and other edible paste products, is grown fairly extensively in Italy, Spain and parts of the U. S. Rivet wheat is of some interest because it is the tallest-growing (four to six feet high) and under ideal conditions one of the most productive. However, its grains are soft, yielding a weak flour unsuitable for bread-making unless mixed with stronger wheats. One variety of rivet called "miracle" or "mummy" wheat, with massive branched heads, has been persistently exploited as a rare and valuable wheat claimed to have been propagated from prehistoric grains discovered in ancient Egyptian tombs, usually in the wrappings of a mummy. The story in all of its versions is a complete fabrication. Wheat kernels, like seeds of other plants, are living metabolic systems with a maximum life expectancy of about 10 years. Furthermore, there is no evidence that rivet wheat was ever known in ancient Egypt.

One additional 14-chromosome wheat, *T. timopheevi*, which has no common name, deserves mention. This species was discovered in this century by Russian botanists and is known only in western Georgia, where it is grown on a few thousand acres. The species is of botanical interest because its second set of seven chromosomes, designated genom G, is different from that of any of the other 14-chromosome wheats. It is also of great practical interest because it is resistant to virtually all diseases attacking other cultivated wheats, including rusts, smuts and mildews. In the hands of skilled wheat breeders it may become the ancestor of improved wheats for the next century.

Third Stage

The 21-chromosome wheats, of which there are five, are as a group the most recently evolved and the most useful today. All are cultivated; none has ever been known in the wild. All are products of the hybridization of 14-chromosome wheats containing the genoms A and B with a wild 7-chromosome relative of wheat (almost certainly a grass species of the genus *Aegilops*) containing the genom D. All are believed to have arisen from such hybridization after man, spreading the revolutionary art of agriculture, exposed his earlier cultivated wheats to hybridization with native grasses.

Two of the 21-chromosome wheats, *T. spelta* (spelt) and *T. macha*, are, like einkorn and emmer, hard-threshing species. *T. macha*, like *T. timopheevi*, is confined to western Georgia, where it is grown on not more than a few thousand acres. Spelt was once the principal wheat of central Europe. No archaeological remains of it have been found in the Near East or any part of Asia. There is no doubt about the hybrid origin of spelt, for it has now been synthesized by McFadden and Sears and independ-

LATIN NAME	COMMON NAME	CHROMOSOMES NUMBER	CHROMOSOMES GENOMS	GROWTH	GRA
T. AEGILOPOIDES	WILD EINKORN	7	A	WILD	HUL
T. MONOCOCCUM	EINKORN	7	A	CULTIVATED	HUL
T. DICOCCOIDES	WILD EMMER	14	AB	WILD	HUL
T. DICOCCUM	EMMER	14	AB	CULTIVATED	HUL
T. DURUM	MACARONI WHEAT	14	AB	CULTIVATED	NAI
T. PERSICUM	PERSIAN WHEAT	14	AB	CULTIVATED	NAI
T. TURGIDUM	RIVET WHEAT	14	AB	CULTIVATED	NAI
T. POLONICUM	POLISH WHEAT	14	AB	CULTIVATED	NAI
T. TIMOPHEEVI		14	AG	CULTIVATED	HUL
T. AESTIVUM	COMMON WHEAT	21	ABD	CULTIVATED	NAI
T. SPHAEROCOCCUM	SHOT WHEAT	21	ABD	CULTIVATED	NAI
T. COMPACTUM	CLUB WHEAT	21	ABD	CULTIVATED	NAI
T. SPELTA	SPELT	21	ABD	CULTIVATED	HUL
T. MACHA	MACHA WHEAT	21	ABD	CULTIVATED	HUL

SOME CHARACTERISTICS of the 14 species, as well as their distribution and antiquity, are given in this table. The genoms are sets of inherited charac-

ently by H. Kihara in Japan. In both cases the researchers concluded that the botanical characteristics to be sought in the unknown 7-chromosome parent of spelt were possessed by *Aegilops squarrosa*, a completely useless wild grass which grows as a weed in wheat fields from the Balkans to Afghanistan. Both researchers hybridized this wild grass with wild emmer. McFadden and Sears doubled the chromosome number by treatment with colchicine; Kihara was fortunate in discovering a case of natural doubling. The hybrid was highly fertile and similar in characteristics to cultivated spelt. As a final step in a brilliant piece of inductive reasoning and genetic experimentation, McFadden and Sears crossed their synthesized spelt with natural spelt and obtained fully fertile hybrids. The results leave no doubt that the wild grass used in this experiment is one of the parents of cultivated spelt, and they suggest strongly that the other four 21-chromosome wheats are likewise hybrids in which the genom D has been derived from the same grass or a species close to it.

These experiments suggest that cultivated spelt originated in the region where the species of wild grass and wild emmer overlap. But the primitive hulled form of spelt has not been found there. An alternate possibility is that the wild grass hybridized not with wild emmer but with the cultivated species, which has had a much wider distribution. Vavilov concluded that hulled spelt originated in southern Germany. Earlier Elisabeth Schiemann, Germany's leading student of cereals, had placed it in Switzerland and southwest Germany. Both centers are not far from the northeastern limits of the area in which cultivated emmer and the wild grass are known to have occurred together. Thus the botanical and historical evidence are not far apart in indicating a central European origin.

The remaining three species of 21-chromosome wheats are *T. aestivum* (common), *sphaerococcum* (shot) and *compactum* (club). They are the true bread wheats, accounting for about 90 per cent of all the wheat grown in the world today. The three are closely related and easily intercrossed. Whether they are the product of three different hybridizations between 14-chromosome wheats and wild grasses, or of three diverging lines of descent from a single hybridization, is not known. Club and shot wheat differ from common wheat in a number of details whose inheritance is governed by a relatively small number of genes. It is possible, therefore, that the three species are descended from a single hybrid ancestor. Common wheat or something very like it has recently been produced by Kihara by crossing 14-chromosome Persian wheat with the wild grass used to synthesize spelt. Its chromosome number has not yet been doubled, but its botanical characteristics are those of common wheat.

Where and when the modern bread wheat first occurred are still matters for conjecture. Since Persian wheat is known only in a limited area in northeastern Turkey and the adjoining states of the Soviet Union, common wheat very probably originated there. Kernels of shot wheat have been found at the most ancient site in India, Mohenjo-Daro, dated about 2500 B.C. A wheat found in neolithic store-chambers in Hungary has been identified as club wheat. Impressions of grains of bread wheat, either common or club, have been found in the neolithic Dolmen period, dated between 300 and 2300 B.C. The earliest archaeological wheat in Japan, dated in the third century, is regarded by Kihara as a bread wheat. And since the 14-chromosome wheats evidently are recent introductions in China, it is possible that the wheat described in the Chinese classics for the Chou period (about 1000 B.C.) is a 21-chromosome bread wheat. All these items, none in itself conclusive, indicate that the bread wheats originated before the time of Christ but later than einkorn or emmer. A conservative guess would put their origin at approximately 2500 B.C.

A Historic Explosion

Whether the bread wheats originated earlier than this or later, and whether they had one hybrid origin or three, they represent today the most rapid increase in geographical range and numbers of any species of seed-plant in history. They are now grown in all parts of the world from the Equator to the Arctic Circle. Originating probably not more than 5,000 years ago in the general region of Asia Minor, the new species have increased at an average rate of

GEOGRAPHICAL DISTRIBUTION	EARLIEST EVIDENCE
STERN IRAN, ASIA MINOR, GREECE, SOUTHERN YUGOSLAVIA	PRE-AGRICULTURAL
TERN CAUCASUS, ASIA MINOR, GREECE, CENTRAL EUROPE	4750 B. C.
STERN IRAN, SYRIA, NORTHERN PALESTINE, NORTHEASTERN TURKEY, ARMENIA	PRE-AGRICULTURAL
A, CENTRAL ASIA, NORTHERN IRAN, GEORGIA, ARMENIA, EUROPE, MEDITERRANEAN AREA, ABYSSINIA	4000 B. C.
TRAL ASIA, IRAN, MESOPOTAMIA, TURKEY, ABYSSINIA, SOUTHEASTERN EUROPE, U.S.	100 B. C.
GESTAN, GEORGIA, ARMENIA, NORTHEASTERN TURKEY	NO PREHISTORIC REMAINS
SSINIA, SOUTHERN EUROPE	NO PREHISTORIC REMAINS
SSINIA, MEDITERRANEAN AREA	17TH CENTURY
STERN GEORGIA	20TH CENTURY
RLD WIDE	NEOLITHIC PERIOD
TRAL AND NORTHWESTERN INDIA	2500 B. C.
JTHWESTERN ASIA, SOUTHEASTERN EUROPE, U.S.	NEOLITHIC PERIOD
TRAL EUROPE	BRONZE AGE
STERN GEORGIA	20TH CENTURY

teristics, or combinations of sets. The chromosome number is a clue to the evolution of wheat. The species with larger chromosome numbers descended from those with smaller by hybridization and chromosome doubling.

HEAD of common wheat is dissected to show the rachis (*lower right*) which bears the spikelets. Enclosing each kernel is a bearded glume. In some varieties the beard is absent. At lower left is a single spikelet of spelt, which during threshing remains intact and attached to a joint of the rachis.

about 75,000 acres per year until they now occupy almost 400 million acres. Their evolution and dispersal have been explosive phenomena in which man's principal part has been to recognize their usefulness and to open up new agricultural areas for their culture.

The particular value of the bread wheats lies not only in their productiveness and in their free-threshing, naked kernels, but in the peculiar quality of their gluten, the protein component. Of all the cereals only the bread wheats are capable of producing the light, fluffy, leavened breads we know today.

All known species of cultivated wheat, except einkorn and possibly emmer, came into existence spontaneously. Man played no part in their origin except as he spread their culture and their opportunities for natural hybridization over the earth. There is no evidence that ancient man gave much attention to selection of superior forms, or if he did, no evidence that he succeeded. The cultivated einkorn of today is scarcely different from the einkorn of millennia ago, and it, in turn, is no great improvement over wild einkorn. Essentially the same can be said about emmer. Consequently, to speak of primitive man as a plant breeder is to attribute more purposefulness to his activities than the evidence warrants.

Within the past century, especially since the rediscovery of Mendel's laws of inheritance in 1900, vast programs of wheat improvement have been undertaken in almost all the wheat-growing regions of the world. These have been especially successful in the U. S. and Canada, where a constant succession of new varieties has been introduced. Scarcely any state of the Union today grows extensively the principal varieties of wheat grown 50 years ago.

Early in the century the most common method of wheat breeding was "pure-line" selection as invented by Wilhelm Johannsen, a Danish botanist and geneticist. Johannsen had concluded from experiments on garden beans that self-fertilized plants such as beans, peas and cereals are racial mixtures of many pure lines, differing from one another in many characteristics but each genetically uniform. Continuous selection can have no effect in changing the characters of a genetically pure line, but a mixture of lines can be separated into its component parts and improvements effected by propagating the superior lines.

In practice the wheat breeder selects hundreds of individual heads from a variety, threshes each one separately and grows the progeny of each in a short row called a head row. In succeeding generations more and longer rows are grown, and the pure lines, each originating from a single head, are compared in productiveness and other characteristics. Among wheat breeders in the

U. S. It is standard procedure at this stage to use rows 16 feet long and one foot apart. Rows of this length and spacing simplify computation, since the yield of grain in grams can be converted to a bushel yield per acre by simply pointing off one decimal place. The more promising lines are increased still further in field plots and eventually one is chosen as the best, is named and is distributed to farmers.

The two outstanding U. S. varieties produced by pure-line selection are both Kansas products. The first, Kanred (Kansas Red), was selected by Herbert Roberts of the Kansas Agricultural Experiment Station from Crimean, a hard, red, winter-type wheat introduced from Russia by Mark Carleton. The first head selections were made in 1906, and the improved pure line first distributed for commercial growing in 1917. By 1925 Kanred wheat, the product of a single head only 19 years earlier, was grown on nearly five million acres in Kansas, Nebraska, Colorado, Oklahoma and Texas. The second Kansas wheat, Blackhull, is the product of a single head selection made in 1912 from a field of Turkey wheat by Earl Clark, a farmer and plant breeder. Blackhull, like Kanred, was first distributed in 1917. By 1929 it occupied almost six million acres, principally in Kansas and Oklahoma.

The Hybrid Wheats

Pure-line selection merely sorts out from a variety the superior lines already there; it creates no new genetic combinations. To form a new variety the breeder employs hybridization. He selects as parents two varieties with the characteristics he seeks to combine. For example, one parent may be chosen for its superior milling and baking qualities, the other for its resistance to disease. To cross these two the breeder first emasculates one of them by removing the anthers, the male pollen-containing organs, with delicate forceps when these organs are full-grown but not yet ripe. Then he covers the emasculated head with a small glassine bag to prevent uncontrolled pollination. A few days later, when its female organs, the stigmas, have become receptive, the operator pollinates them with ripe anthers taken from the second parent.

Such pollinations produce seeds that grow into first-generation hybrid plants. These are quite uniform and nothing is accomplished by practicing selection among them. But in the second and subsequent generations genetic segregation creates new combinations as numerous and diverse as the hands in a shuffled deck of cards. The opportunities for creative selection are enormous. It is in the early generations following a cross that the plant breeder shows his skill, for at this stage he must select for propagation those combinations which approach most closely the ideal wheat he has in mind and discard those which do not meet his specifications. Eventually genetic segregation produces pure lines.

One of the earliest and greatest achievements in hybrid wheat was the development of the Marquis strain. This variety, a hybrid of early-growing Hard Red Calcutta from India and Red Fife from Poland, was produced in Canada by Charles Saunders, cerealist for the Dominion from 1903 to 1922. The cross from which Marquis wheat was derived

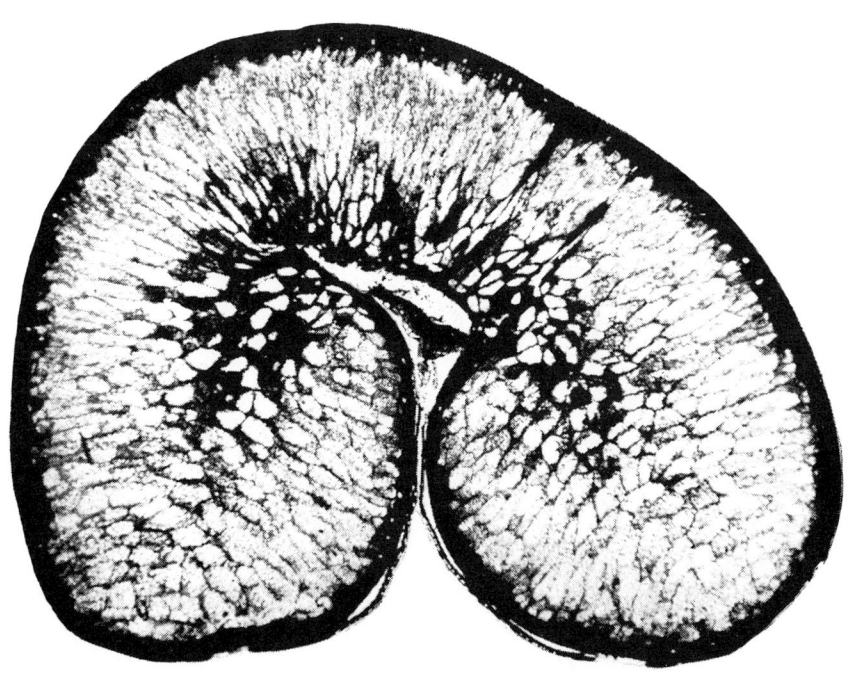

KERNEL of common wheat is photographed in cross section at the Northern Regional Research Laboratory of the U. S. Department of Agriculture. The interior of the kernel is the endosperm, from which flour is made.

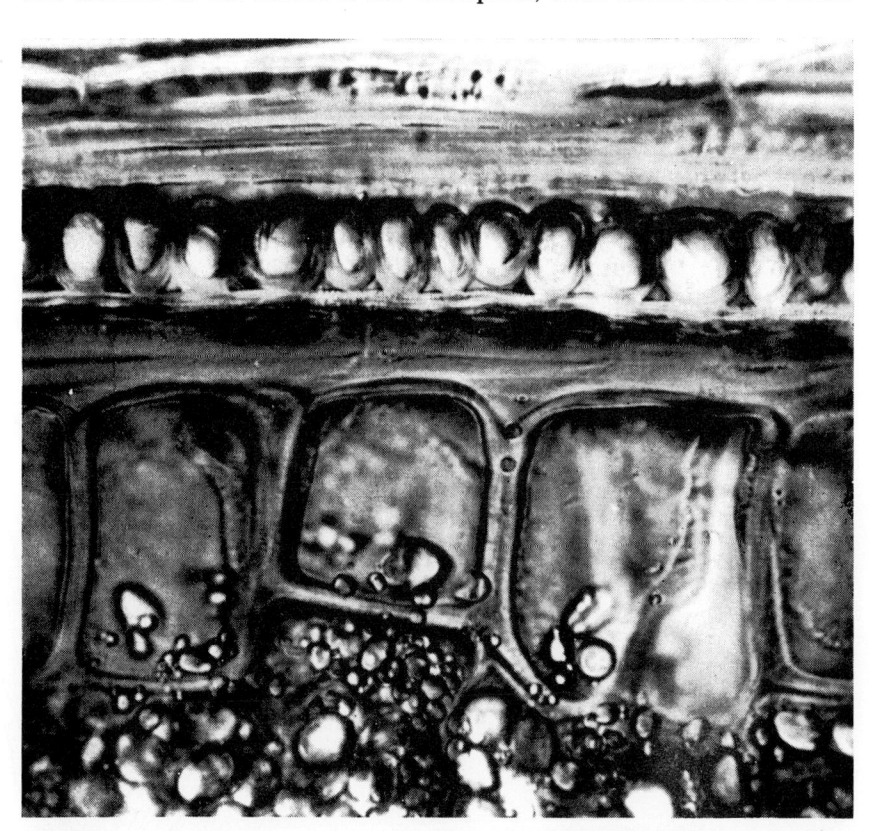

BRAN, or outer layer of the kernel, is shown in this photomicrograph made at the Northern Regional Research Laboratory. At the bottom of the photomicrograph, which enlarges these structures 600 times, is the endosperm.

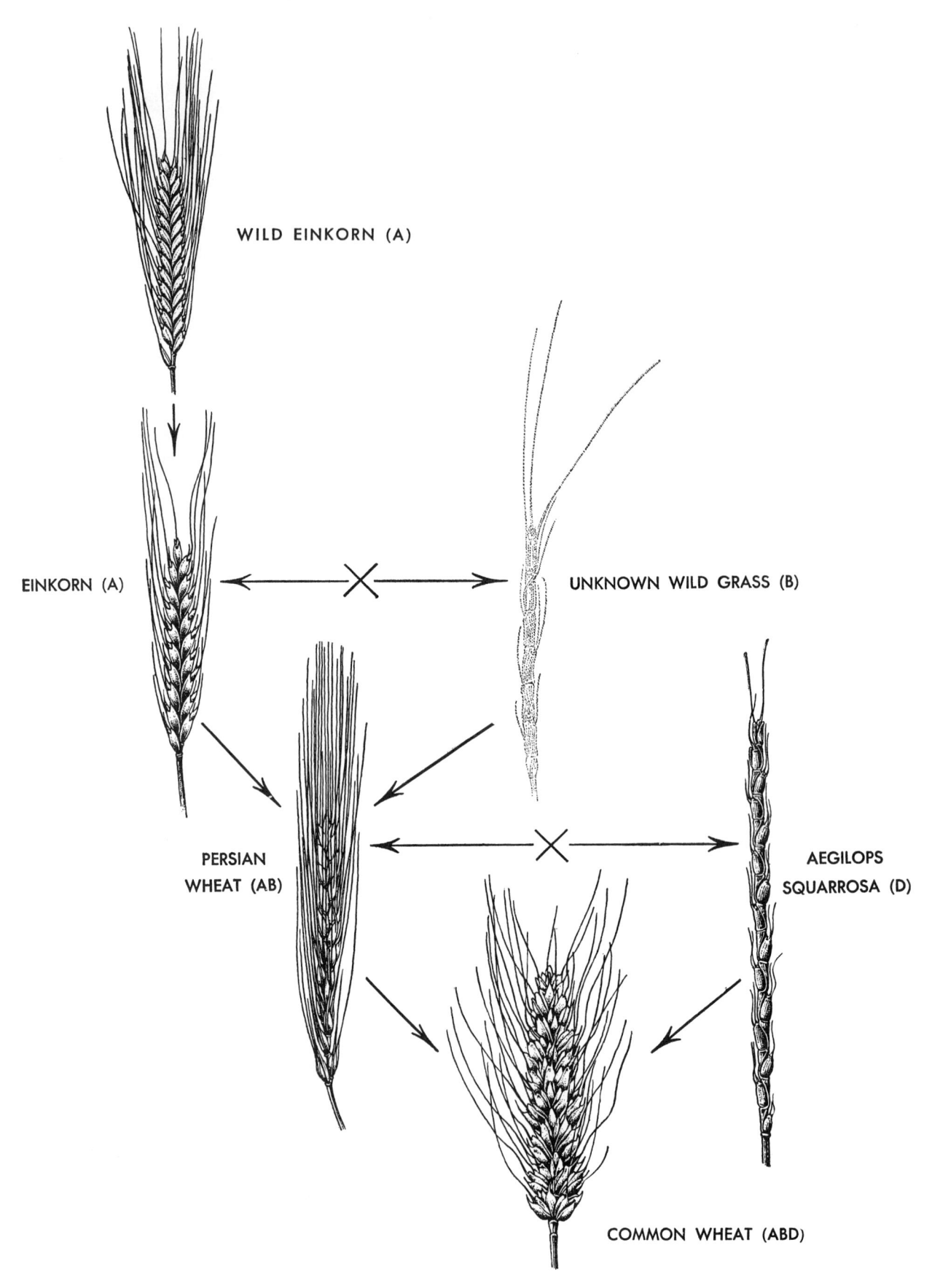

EVOLUTION of common wheat is outlined. Wild einkorn (7 chromosomes, genom A) evolved into einkorn, which, crossed with a wild grass (genom B), gave rise to Persian wheat (14 chromosomes, genom AB). When this wheat was crossed with another grass (genom D), common wheat (21 chromosomes, genom ABD) resulted.

had been made in 1892 by his brother Arthur under the direction of his father, William Saunders, who had been hybridizing wheats since 1888. The new hybrid was promising from the beginning. It was a few days earlier than the spring-planted varieties then commonly grown in Canada, thus often avoiding the first frosts. The grain yielded a cream-colored, strongly elastic dough with strong gluten and excellent baking qualities. Marquis wheat later set new standards for baking quality. By 1907, four years after the initial head selection, there were 23 pounds of seed. Distribution to farmers began in the spring of 1909. News of the new wheat spread swiftly from the prairie provinces down into our own spring-wheat belt. By 1913 Marquis seed was being imported into Minnesota and the Dakotas at the rate of 200,000 bushels per year. In 1918 more than 300 million bushels were produced, and the superiority of this variety over those previously grown was a factor in meeting the food shortage of World War I, just as 25 years later hybrid corn was a similar factor in World War II.

For 20 years Marquis was the "king of wheats" in Canada and the U. S., and during this period it served as a standard both in the field and in the milling and baking laboratory. Marquis was also used extensively as a parent in new hybrids and is the ancestor of many improved wheats, including Tenmarq, developed in Kansas by John Parker; Ceres, produced in North Dakota by L. R. Waldron, and Thatcher and Newthatch, bred by Herbert K. Hayes and his associates in Minnesota.

Today most new wheat varieties are produced by controlled hybridization rather than by pure-line selection, which is little used. The modern wheat breeder has many objectives. Usually his principal one is productiveness, but involved in this are many factors, including resistance to diseases and tolerance of unfavorable environmental conditions. To test new wheats for these characteristics, breeders have invented devices and methods for subjecting wheat to artificial drought, cold and epidemics of disease.

Breeders v. Fungi

Breeding for disease resistance is especially important because wheat is a self-fertilized plant which, except for natural hybridization and occasional mutations, tends to remain genetically uniform. A field of wheat of a single variety, especially one originating from a single head, contains millions of plants which are genetically identical. If the variety happens to be susceptible to a disease, it serves as a gigantic culture medium for the propagation of the disease organism, usually a fungus. Thus the growing of new varieties over large acreages increases the hazards from those diseases to which they are susceptible. The result is a never-ending battle between the wheat breeders and the fungi.

The breeding of wheat for resistance to stem rust, a devastating disease, is a prime example. There are many kinds of stem rust. Pathologists, led by Elvin Stakman of the University of Minnesota, have devised ingenious methods of identifying them by inoculation of different hosts. The wheat breeder then develops a new variety which is resistant to the predominating races of stem rust. This is distributed to farmers and its acreage increases rapidly. But while the wheat breeder is hybridizing wheats, nature is hybridizing rusts. The reproductive stage of stem rusts occurs not on wheat but on an alternate host, the common barberry. On this plant new races of rust are constantly created. Although most of them probably die out, one that finds susceptible wheat varieties may multiply prodigiously and in a few years become the predominating race. The wheat breeder then searches the world for wheats resistant to the new hazard and again goes through all the stages of producing a new hybrid variety. The competition between man and the fungi for the wheat crop of the world is a biological "cold war" which never ends.

A wheat breeder must seek not only disease resistance and productiveness but also milling and baking quality. In modern mass-production bakeries with high-speed mixing machinery, dough undergoes stresses and strains which it was never called on to endure when kneaded by hand in the home. As a result wheat breeders have been compelled to subject their new productions to elaborate milling and baking tests which simulate the processes of commercial bakeries. A new wheat that proves superior in the field may be rejected in the laboratory.

In spite of the difficulties involved, the development of more productive varieties of wheat is one of the surest ways of increasing the food supply and raising living standards. When Mussolini drained the Pontine swamp in Italy, the Italian wheat breeder Alzareno Strampelli produced new varieties of wheat which flourished in the fertile soils newly opened to cultivation. An important part of the well-publicized Etawah Village Improvement Program in India is the growing of improved varieties of wheat developed by British and Indian geneticists. Mexico's agricultural program, sponsored by the Rockefeller Foundation in cooperation with the Mexican Government, owes much of its success to new rust-resistant varieties of wheat. Crossing the old varieties of Mexican wheat with rust-resistant wheats from the U. S., South America, Australia and New Zealand, the U. S. breeder Norman Borlaug and his associates, working closely with Mexican technologists, have bred new varieties so resistant to rust that they can be grown in Mexico's summer rainy season as well as in the winter dry season, heretofore its only season for growing wheat. The bulk of Mexico's wheat acreage is now devoted to new hybrids developed since 1943, while acreage and production have expanded substantially.

Hybridization among wheats is usually confined to varieties of one species, but interspecific hybrids also are employed and sometimes are successful. A notable example is the development of Hope wheat by McFadden from a cross of Marquis with Yaroslav emmer, a 14-chromosome wheat extremely resistant to stem rust, leaf rust and several other diseases. From this hybrid, which was partly sterile, McFadden succeeded in developing a 21-chromosome wheat which has a high degree of resistance to many races of stem and leaf rust. Unfortunately Hope wheat has a grain somewhat lacking in milling and baking qualities and the variety has never become important commercially. It has, however, been the parent of many modern varieties of wheat which are commercially grown, including Newthatch in Minnesota, Austin in Texas and several of the new varieties developed in Mexico.

New Cereals

A future possibility in wheat breeding is the creation of wholly new types of cereals by species hybridization followed by artificial chromosome doubling, a man-made counterpart of wheat's earlier evolution in nature. In the U.S.S.R. and the U. S. wheat has been crossed with rye to produce a fertile, true-breeding hybrid cereal which combines the chromosomes of both. The hybrid, neither a wheat nor a rye, is more resistant to cold than wheat is, but less useful as a bread-making cereal. It has not become popular. Wheat has been crossed with a perennial wild grass to produce a new perennial cereal for which Russian agronomists have made fantastic claims. A field of this wheat, once planted, will, according to the Russians, yield a crop of grain year after year with little or no further attention except to gather the annual harvest. It turns out that this perennial "wheat" may have some promise as a forage grass for livestock, but so far little bread has been made from it and few people have been fed by it.

The idea of producing new cereal species by hybridization and chromosome doubling is, however, quite sound, and the possibilities inherent in it are far from exhausted. Some day new wheat species consciously created by man may replace those which arose spontaneously in nature.

13

HYBRID CORN

PAUL C. MANGELSDORF
August 1951

Vigorous new crosses of the ancient cultivated plant have revolutionized the agriculture of the Corn Belt. An account of their development and its consequences

HYBRID CORN, a man-made product developed during the past 25 years, may prove to be the most far-reaching contribution in applied biology of this century. With its accompanying improvements in farming methods, it has revolutionized the agriculture of the American Corn Belt. Because of it U. S. farmers are growing more corn on fewer acres than ever before in this country's history. The new abundance of food brought by hybrid corn played a significant role in World War II and in the rehabilitation of Europe after the war. Now this product, spreading to Italy, to Mexico and to other countries where corn is an important crop, promises to become a factor of considerable consequence in solving the world food problem.

What is hybrid corn and how has it made possible these substantial contributions to the world's food resources?

In a broad sense all corn is hybrid, for this plant is a cross-pollinated species in which hybridization between individual plants, between varieties and between races occurs constantly. Such natural, more or less accidental hybridization has played a major role in corn's evolution under domestication. But the hybrid corn with which we shall deal here is a planned exploitation of this natural tendency on a scale far beyond that possible in nature.

The biological basis of hybrid corn is a genetic phenomenon known as "hybrid vigor." It means simply that crossed animals or plants have greater vigor or capacity for growth than those produced by inbreeding. This fact has been known since Biblical times. The ancient Near Eastern peoples who mated the horse and the ass to produce a sterile hybrid, the mule, were creating and utilizing hybrid vigor. The mule is an excellent example of the practical advantages that often follow crossing. This animal, said to be "without pride of ancestry or hope of posterity," has greater endurance than either of its parents; it is usually longer-lived than the horse, less subject to diseases and injury and more efficient in the use of food. Hybrid corn resembles the mule (indeed, it used to be called "mule corn") in being more useful to man than either of its parents.

Early Experiments

The idea of crossing varieties of corn is as old as some of the early American Indian tribes, who regularly planted different kinds of corn close together to promote hybridization and increase yields. Cotton Mather, of witch-hunting fame, published in 1716 observations on the natural crossing of corn varieties, and James Logan, onetime Governor of Pennsylvania, in 1735 conducted experiments which demonstrated natural crossing between corn plants.

But it was Charles Darwin who made the important studies of hybrid vigor in plants which open the story of modern hybrid corn. He investigated the effects of self-pollination and cross-pollination in plants, including corn as one of his subjects. His were the first controlled experiments in which crossed and self-bred individuals were compared under identical environmental conditions. He was the first to see that it was the crossing between unrelated varieties of a plant, not the mere act of crossing itself, that produced hybrid vigor, for he found that when separate flowers on the same plant or different plants of the same strain were crossed, their progeny did not possess such vigor. He concluded, quite correctly, that the phenomenon occurred only when diverse heredities were united. These researches, together with his theory of evolution, inspired the studies on heredity which eventually led to the discovery of the principles underlying the production of hybrid corn.

Darwin's experiments were known, even before their publication, to the American botanist Asa Gray, with whom Darwin was in more or less constant communication. One of Gray's students, William Beal, became, like Gray, an admirer and follower of Darwin. At Michigan State College Beal undertook the first controlled experiments aimed at the improvement of corn through the utilization of hybrid vigor. He selected some of the varieties of flint and dent corn then commonly grown and planted them together in a field isolated from other corn. He removed the tassels—the pollen-bearing male flower clusters—from one variety before the pollen was shed. The female flowers of these emasculated plants then had to receive their pollen from the tassels of another variety. The seed borne on the detasseled plants, being a crossed breed, produced only hybrid plants when planted the following season.

The technique Beal invented for crossing corn—planting two kinds in the same field and removing the tassels of one—proved highly successful and is still essentially the method employed today in producing hybrid seed corn. But as a device for increasing corn yield his operation of crossing two unselected varieties, each of mixed inheritance, was ineffective: the gain in yield was seldom large enough to justify the time and care spent in crossing the plants. The missing requirement—the basic principle that made hybrid corn practicable—was discovered by George H. Shull of the Carnegie Institution.

His discovery was an unexpected by-product of theoretical studies on inheritance which he had begun in 1905. Shull's contribution grew from certain earlier studies made by two great scientists: Darwin's cousin Francis Galton and the Danish botanist Wilhelm Ludwig Johannsen. Galton had recognized that the result of the combination of parental heredity could take two forms: an "alternative" inheritance, such as the coat color of basset hounds, which came from one parent or the other but was not a mixture of both, and a "blended" inheritance, such as in human stature. He observed that children of very tall parents are shorter than their parents, on the average, while children of very short parents tend to be taller. These observations led Galton to the formulation of his "law of regression," which holds that the progeny of parents above

FIRST YEAR

DOUBLE CROSS made the experimental hybridization of corn a practical reality. First two pairs of inbred corn plants are crossed (*top*); then the process is repeated with their hybrid descendants (*bottom*). The second cross greatly multiplies the number of seeds produced by the first.

or below the average in any given characteristic tend to regress toward the average.

This regression is seldom complete, however, and Johannsen saw in that circumstance an opportunity for controlling heredity through the selection in successive generations of extreme variations. He tested the possibility by trying to breed unusually large and unusually small beans by selection. He found that, although selection apparently was effective in the first generation, it had no measurable effect whatever in later generations. Johannsen concluded that in self-fertilized plants such as the bean the progeny of a single plant represent a "pure line" in which all individuals are genetically identical and in which any residual variation is environmental in origin. He postulated that an unselected race such as the ordinary garden bean with which he started his experiments was a mixture of pure lines differing among themselves in many characteristics but each one genetically uniform. Johannsen's pure-line theory has been widely applied to the improvement of cereals and other self-fertilized plants. Many of the varieties of wheat, oats, barley, rice, sorghum and flax grown today are the result of sorting out the pure lines in mixed agricultural races and identifying and multiplying the superior ones.

Inbreeding

Shull's contribution was to apply the pure-line theory to corn, with spectacular, though unpremeditated, results. He started with the objective of analyzing the inheritance of quantitative or "blending" characteristics, and he chose the number of rows of kernels in an ear of corn as an inherited quantitative characteristic suitable for study. Through self-pollination he developed a number of inbred lines of corn with various numbers of rows of kernels. These lines, as a consequence of inbreeding, declined in vigor and productiveness and at the same time each became quite uniform. Shull concluded correctly that he had isolated pure lines of corn similar to those in beans described by Johannsen. Then, as the first step in studying the inheritance of kernel-row number, he crossed these pure lines. The results were surprising and highly significant. The hybrids between two pure lines were quite uniform, like their inbred parents, but unlike their parents they were vigorous and productive. Some were definitely superior to the original open-pollinated variety from which they had been derived. Inbreeding had isolated, from a single heterogeneous species, the diverse germinal entities whose union Darwin had earlier postulated as the cause of hybrid vigor.

Shull recognized at once that inbreed-

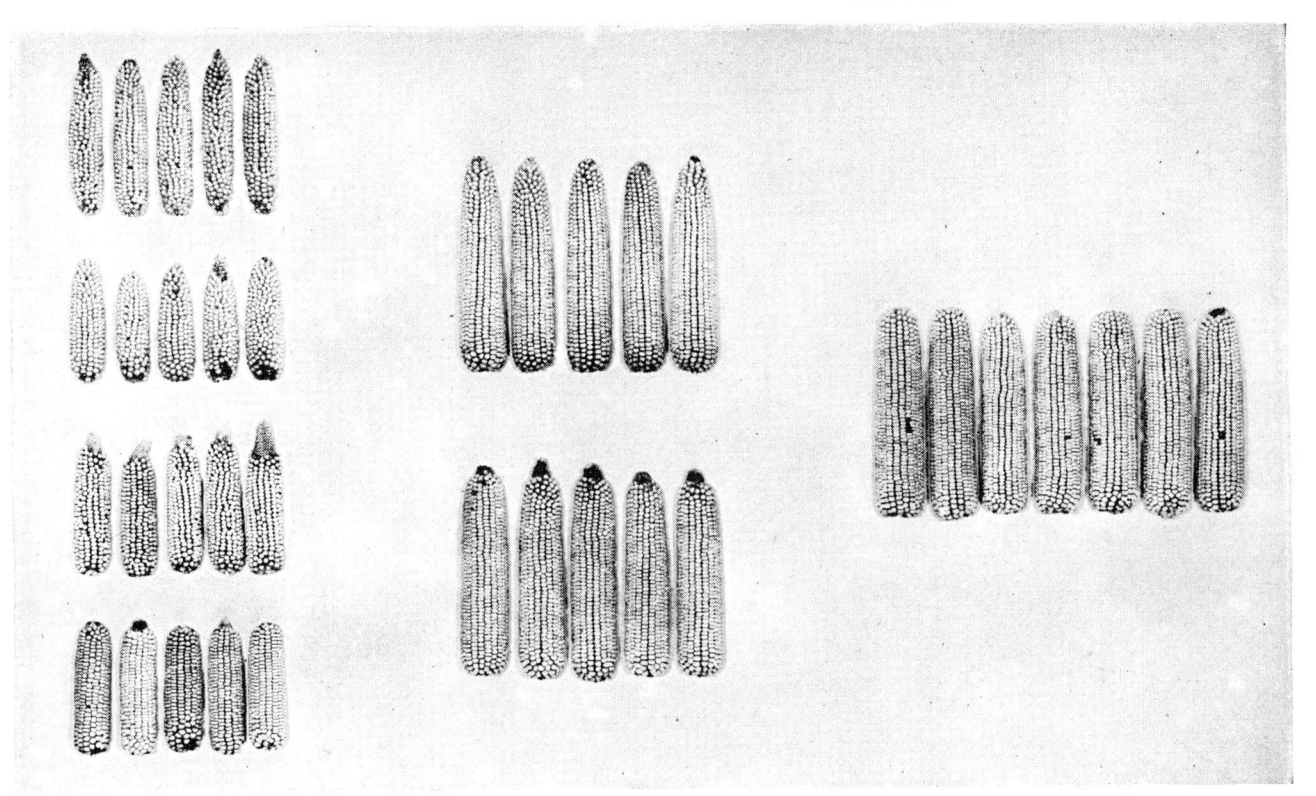

EARS of corn illustrate the effects of the double cross. At the left are the ears borne by the plants of four inbred strains. If the strains are divided into pairs, and one plant in each pair is allowed to pollinate the other, the latter bears ears like those shown in center. If a plant grown from a seed in one of the two center groups pollinates a plant grown from a seed in the other, the latter bears ears such as those on the right.

ing followed by crossing offered an entirely new method of improving the yield of corn. In two papers published in 1908 and 1909 he reported his results and outlined a method of corn breeding based upon his discoveries. He proposed the isolation of inbred strains as a first step and the crossing of two such inbred strains as a second. Only the first-generation cross was to be used for seed for crop production, because hybrid vigor is always at its maximum in the first generation. Shull's idea of growing otherwise useless inbred strains of corn solely for later crossing was revolutionary as a method of corn breeding, but it eventually won acceptance and is now the basis that underlies almost the entire hybrid seed-corn enterprise.

However, Shull's suggestion for the second step—the crossing of two weak inbred strains, known as a single cross—proved impractical as a method of seed production. Because the inbred strains are relatively unproductive, hybrid seed obtained in this way is too expensive except for certain special purposes.

The Double Cross

One further major development was needed to make hybrid corn practicable and the great boon to agriculture that it has become. This contribution came from the Connecticut Agricultural Experiment Station by the end of the second decade of this century. The story begins in 1906, when Edward M. East arrived there from the University of Illinois, where he had participated in corn-breeding experiments with some of Beal's former students. At the Connecticut Station, East began a series of studies of the effects of corn inbreeding and crossbreeding which were to continue to this day and yield a great deal of information about corn, including the effects of selection on its chemistry. It was East who called attention to the need for developing a more practical method for producing hybrid seed. It remained for Donald Jones, one of East's students, who assumed charge of the Connecticut experiments in 1915, to invent a method which solved the problem.

Jones' solution was simply to use seed from a double cross instead of a single cross. The double cross, which combines four inbred strains, is a hybrid of two single crosses. For example, two inbred strains, A and B, are combined to produce the single cross A×B. Two additional inbred strains, C and D, are combined to produce a second single cross C×D. All four strains are now brought together in the double cross (A×B) × (C×D). At first glance it may seem paradoxical to solve the problem of hybrid seed production by making three crosses instead of one. But the double cross is actually an ingenious device for making a small amount of scarce single-crossed seed go a long way. Whereas single-crossed seed is produced from undersized ears borne on stunted inbred plants, double-crossed seed is produced on normal-sized ears borne on vigorous single-cross plants. A few bushels of single-crossed seed can be converted in one generation to several thousand bushels of double-crossed seed. The difference in cost of the two kinds of seed is reflected in the units in which they are sold: double-crossed seed is priced by the bushel, single-crossed seed by the thousand seeds. Double-cross hybrids are never as uniform as single crosses, but they may be just as productive or more so.

Jones made a second important contribution to the development of hybrid corn by presenting a genetic interpretation of hybrid vigor. Shull and East had suggested that hybrid vigor was due to some physiological stimulation resulting from hybridity itself. Shull was quite certain that something more than gene action was involved. He thought that part of the stimulation might be derived from the interaction between the male nucleus and the egg cytoplasm. Jones proposed the theory that hybrid vigor is the product of bringing together in the hybrid the favorable genes of both parents. These are usually partly dominant. Thus if one inbred strain has the genes *AA BB cc dd* (to use a greatly oversimplified example), and the other has the genes *aa bb CC DD*, the first-generation hybrid has the genetic constitution, *Aa Bb Cc Dd*. Since the genes

MANY STRAINS OF CORN are tested for their value in hybridization. This photograph shows a field of the De Kalb Agricultural Association of De Kalb, Ill. On it are a number of strains illustrating the evolution of corn.

A, B, C and D are assumed not only to have favorable effects but to be partially dominant in their action, the hybrid contains the best genes of both parents and is correspondingly better than either parent. Jones' theory differs from a similar earlier theory in assuming that the genes involved are so numerous that several are borne on the same chromosome and thus tend to be inherited in groups. This explains why vigor is at its maximum in the first generation after crossing, and why it is impossible through selection in later generations to incorporate all of the favorable genes into a new variety as good or better than the first-generation hybrid. The ideal combination *AA DD CC EE*, which combines all of the favorable genes, is impossible to attain because of chromosomal linkage. For example, the genes *B* and *c* may be borne at adjacent loci on the same chromosome and thus be inseparably joined in their inheritance. Although Jones' theory is not universally accepted, and it now seems probable that hybrid vigor involves still other genetic mechanisms, it nevertheless gave great stimulus to practical hybrid corn breeding.

How It Is Produced

Historically, then, hybrid corn was transformed from Shull's magnificent design to the practical reality it now is when Jones' method of seed production made it feasible and his theory of hybrid vigor made it plausible. This combination proved irresistible to even the most conservative agronomists. Soon after 1917 hybrid corn-breeding programs were initiated in many states. By 1933 hybrid corn was in commercial production on a substantial scale, and the U. S. Department of Agriculture had begun to gather statistics on it. By 1950 more than three fourths of the total corn acreage of the U. S., some 65 million acres, was in hybrid corn.

This immense achievement stems from the work of many corn breeders, variously associated with the U. S. Department of Agriculture, state experiment stations and private industry. Among the pioneers in the breeding of corn were Henry A. Wallace, Herbert K. Hayes and Frederick D. Richey.

Hybrid corn is usually produced now by a process that involves three principal steps. To understand them we must consider briefly how corn produces progeny. The corn plant is unique among the major cereals in bearing its male and female flower clusters separately on the same plant. One cluster, the ear, bears only female flowers—several hundred or more enclosed in husks, each with its silk to receive the male pollen. The other, the tassel, bears only male flowers, usually more than a thousand in number. Each male flower contains three anthers, or pollen sacs, and each anther contains about 2,500 pollen grains. A single corn plant sheds several million pollen grains during its flowering period. These are so small and light and so easily carried by the wind that they seldom fall upon the silks of the same plant. As a consequence, under natural conditions cross-pollination is the rule. In experimental or seed-production plots special arrangements are made to control pollination. Experimental pollinations are usually made under bags. The young ears bearing the female flowers are covered with glassine or parchment bags before the silks have appeared. At the same time or a few days later the tassels also are bagged, for the collection of pollen. A single pollination produces an ear bearing several hundred seeds. A single bagged tassel produces enough pollen to pollinate several hundred ears.

The first step in the production of hybrid corn is the isolation of inbred strains. This is still accomplished, as in Shull's and East's experiments, by self-pollination. Hundreds of thousands of self-pollinations in corn are made each year, and tons of paper bags are consumed in the process. The manufacture of special corn-pollinating bags has become a recognized minor industry.

Self-pollination is a form of inbreeding approximately three times as intensive in its effects as matings between brothers and sisters in animals. The same plant is literally both the father and the mother of the offspring. Some plants—wheat, rice, barley and oats, for example—are naturally self-pollinated and suffer no deleterious effects from the process. But corn, a naturally cross-

LONG ROWS OF TASSELS stretch across a single-cross field of the Pioneer Hi-Bred Corn Company of Des Moines, Iowa. The tassels have been removed from two out of three rows; double-cross tassels are farther apart.

pollinated plant, responds to inbreeding with conspicuous effects. First, in the early generations many inherited abnormalities appear—defective seeds, dwarfs, albinos, stripes and a host of other chlorophyll deficiencies. These abnormalities were once supposesd to be the degenerative products of the "unnatural" process of inbreeding, but it is now known that inbreeding merely brings to light deleterious characters already present, which have previously remained hidden because they are recessive traits. Inbreeding actually helps the corn breeder, for it reveals hidden defects and allows the breeder to remove them permanently from his stocks.

After five or six generations of inbreeding the inbred strains have become remarkably uniform, much more uniform than any variety of corn occurring naturally. All the plants of a single strain are genetically identical, or almost so; and their genetic uniformity is reflected in a remarkable uniformity in all perceptible characteristics, physical and physiological. But even the best of these uniform strains yield no more than half as much as the open-pollinated varieties from which they were derived, and many yield much less. Their only value is as potential parents of productive hybrids.

Built-In Characteristics

Inbreeding accompanied by selection has given the corn breeder a remarkable degree of control over corn's heredity. Much of the breeding work today is aimed not only at greater yields but also at improvements in other characteristics. Almost all the corn now grown in the Corn Belt has been bred to possess stiff stalks that remain upright far into the fall—an important quality for mechanical harvesting. Some breeders, shaping the corn to the machines, are developing hybrids bearing two or three small ears instead of a single large one. Resistance to drought was recognized as an important characteristic during the hot dry summers of the 1930s and has been incorporated into many hybrids. Hybrid corn has also been bred for resistance to various diseases. Through selection corn varieties can even be developed to withstand the depredations of insects. Some inbred strains of corn are quite resistant to chinch-bug injury. Others are either unattractive to root worms or survive their assaults. The Southern corn breeder uses corn with long tight husks, which protect the ears against the inroads of ear worms and weevils. Corn breeders in Argentina claim to have isolated lines that contain a bitter substance rendering the foliage unattractive to grasshoppers. This same corn has been used in the U. S. in an attempt to develop new strains possibly resistant to the European corn borer. Strains resistant to corn-borer damage are frequently also unpalatable to aphids.

After inbreeding, the second step in the production of hybrid corn is the testing of the inbred lines in various crossing combinations to determine their hybrid performance. Usually the lines are first screened by crossing all to a common parent—an open-pollinated variety. This comparison allows the corn breeder to eliminate many of the poorer strains. The more promising ones are then tested further in single or double crosses. Of each hundred lines isolated, usually not more than one or two prove satisfactory for use in hybrids.

The final step in producing hybrid seed is to combine the selected strains into commercial hybrids. In sweet corn, especially for canning, where uniformity in the size and shape of the ears is a more important consideration than the cost of the seed, the product is usually a single cross. In field corn the cost of the seed is paramount, so all the seed produced for use is double-crossed. A given amount of land and labor will yield two to three times as much double-crossed seed as single-crossed.

Because the second-generation progeny of a hybrid decline markedly in yield and uniformity disappears, only one crop of corn is grown from the crossed seed. Hence the farmer must buy new hybrid seed each season. The production of hybrid seed corn has become a huge and highly specialized enterprise comparable to the pharmaceutical industry. Hundreds of different hybrids, adapted to a wide variety of soils and climates, are produced. Like

TASSELS ARE PULLED by mechanized hand labor near Vincennes, Ind. Here there are two rows of tassel plants and four rows of plants from which the tassels are removed by workers on a platform moved by tractor.

vaccines and serums, they cannot be identified by their appearance. It is their inherent genetic qualities that distinguish hybrids from one another, and farmers have learned to buy hybrid seed on the basis of these qualities.

The almost universal use of hybrid corn in the U. S., and the prospective wide adoption of it in other parts of the world, is not without its dangers. Chief among these is that farmers as a rule are no longer growing the open-pollinated varieties. These varieties, from which all inbred strains are ultimately derived, may therefore become extinct. Already more than 99 per cent of the corn acreage in several of the Corn Belt states is in hybrid corn; in Iowa it is 100 per cent hybrid. The loss of the original source of breeding material would mean not only that improvement of the present strains would be restricted but that new types of hybrid corn could not be developed to cope with new diseases or insect pests suddenly become rampant. Our corn would also lose the ability to adapt to climatic changes. Open-pollinated varieties of corn, in which cross-pollination is the rule, are admirably contrived for maintaining genetic plasticity and would be capable of surviving rather drastic changes in the environment. Hybrid corn, a small, highly selected sample of the original genetic diversity, has lost this capability.

The U. S. Department of Agriculture, recognizing the danger, has taken steps to maintain the open-pollinated varieties of the Corn Belt. It is also important, however, to preserve the indigenous corn varieties of other parts of the U. S. and of the countries of Latin America. Many of the U. S. varieties had their origin in Mexico, and Mexican corn in turn has ancient affinities with the corn of Central and South America. The indigenous varieties of the countries to our south may one day become of critical importance as sources of new genes to improve, or perhaps even to save, the corn of the U. S. The National Research Council is therefore planning, in cooperation with the Department of Agriculture, the State Department and other agencies, to collect and preserve the native corn varieties in the principal corn-growing countries of this hemisphere.

Future Development

What does the future hold for hybrid corn? To a large extent this will hinge on basic research in corn genetics. Unfortunately new discoveries have not kept pace with practical utilization. Corn breeders, like applied scientists in other fields, have been spending the accumulated capital of theoretical research of the past without taking adequate steps to create new capital. Still unsolved, for example, is the problem of the genetic basis of hybrid vigor, which is clearly of more than academic interest to the practical corn breeder.

Some advances can still be made by the application of present knowledge. Already a trend has begun toward developing highly specialized types of corn for particular purposes. There are special white corn varieties (lacking the pigment carotene) which are used for the manufacture of hominy; a "waxy" corn containing large amounts of the carbohydrate amylopectin has been developed for industrial purposes, including the making of tapioca; for feeding meat-animals breeders have produced a corn with a high protein content. It is possible that corn may be bred with a higher content of the pellagra-preventing vitamins of the B complex, especially niacin, in which corn is now notoriously deficient.

The methods of production no doubt also will be improved. Two techniques for creating uniform strains without prolonged inbreeding are under trial. One is now being tested by Sherret Chase at Iowa State College. This method involves the use of "haploid" plants, which contain only half of the normal number of chromosomes. Such plants occur spontaneously. Haploid plants are weak, often sterile and of no value in themselves. But their chromosomes can be doubled by treatment with the alkaloid colchicine, or they may double spontaneously. When this happens, they produce offspring containing the normal number of chromosomes. Since all the chromosomes come from a single original parental germ cell, plants derived in this way are completely pure for all of their genes and are even more uniform than strains resulting from inbreeding.

A second short-cut method for obtaining uniform strains has been suggested by Charles R. Burnham of the University of Minnesota. By treating seed with X-rays Burnham is attempting to produce an artificial stock of corn in which the chromosomes are broken and so "scrambled" that they will no longer form normal pairs with the chromosomes in normal plants when hybridized with them. Such hybrids, when self-pollinated, should produce three kinds of plants, of which one should have only normal chromosomes and be pure for all of its genes. Plants of the latter kind would be the equivalent of inbred strains.

The operation of detasseling as a prelude to crossing is also destined to be simplified. Detasseling has been called the "peskiest and most expensive" part of producing hybrid seed corn. Each summer the seed industry must find and train thousands of temporary workers, many of them high-school students, to perform this essential task. One firm alone employs more than 20,000 laborers during the detasseling season, and it has been estimated that on the peak day of the season some 125,000 persons in the U. S. are engaged in removing tassels from corn plants. Many attempts have been made to simplify this operation or eliminate it entirely, but until recently none was notably successful. Now what promises to be a partial solution to the problem has been discovered. It involves a certain form of sterility in corn which prevents the tassels from shedding pollen but which is transmitted only through the seeds. Marcus Rhoades of the University of Illinois has shown that this kind of sterility is inherited not through the chromosomes but through the cytoplasm of the germ cells. Jones and I have found that it can easily be incorporated into any inbred strain of corn by crossing, and that it is an excellent substitute for detasseling. A sterile inbred crossed to a fertile inbred produces a sterile single cross. A sterile single cross grown in a crossing field requires no detasseling. The resulting double cross also is sterile; that is, it produces no pollen. But it can be pollinated by planting it with a certain proportion of a comparable fertile double cross. Another method of obtaining a crop from it is to prevent the double cross from being sterile by incorporating in it an inbred strain carrying fertility-restoring genes. This scheme, which has proved completely successful in Jones' experimental cultures, is the last word in the biological manipulation of the corn plant. It employs hereditary factors in the cytoplasm to make corn sterile when sterility is a distinct asset, and uses hereditary factors on the chromosomes to make it fertile when fertility is essential. Hybrid seed produced in this way is being grown on a commercial scale for the first time in 1951.

Hybrid corn well illustrates the importance of the free interplay of theory and practice. The practical motive of improving corn has played its part, but the development of hybrid corn is due in even greater measure to fundamental research aimed only at increasing theoretical knowledge in genetics. Progress of the kind represented by this development is most likely to occur in a free society where truth is sought for its own sake and where there is no undue emphasis on utilitarian aspects. In the case of hybrid corn breeders actually had to go back before they went forward: the first step, inbreeding, led not to immediate improvement but to a drastic reduction in yield. To avoid having to defend this paradoxical procedure of "advancing backwards," corn breeders sometimes took the precaution of plant-

TASSEL IS REMOVED from "female" plant. Detasseling is one of the biggest jobs in growing hybrid seed. One firm employs 20,000 detasselers a season.

EAR IS BAGGED in an experimental plot. By bagging both the ear and the tassel on a small scale, experimenters can completely control pollination.

FERTILE TASSEL possesses many anthers, the pollen-bearing organs.

STERILE TASSEL has only aborted anthers, therefore sheds no pollen.

ing their experimental plots of stunted inbred corn in out-of-the-way places where the public was not likely to see them.

Impact on Food Supply

Hybrid corn's greatest significance lies in the contributions which it and similar developments in applied genetics can make to the world food supply. What hybrid corn has already accomplished toward this end is illustrated by two dramatic examples. During three war years, 1942 to 1944, the American farmer, though afflicted with an acute labor shortage and unfavorable weather, produced 90 per cent as much corn as he had during the previous four years of peace, themselves years of unprecedented production. In other words, hybrid corn enabled him to add a 20 per cent increase to the previous gains. Thanks to hybrid corn, the U. S. suffered no real food shortages at home, was able to ship vast quantities of food abroad to her Allies, and still had enough surplus grain to use large quantities in the manufacture of alcohol, synthetic rubber, explosives and other materials of war.

At the end of the war the American food surplus served a more peaceful but no less important purpose. In the year ending June 30, 1947, the U. S. shipped to hungry and war-torn Europe 18 million long-tons of food. Very little of this was corn, but the food actually sent represented, in terms of calories, the equivalent of 720 million bushels of corn. In the same year, through the use of hybrid corn, the corn crop of the U. S. had been increased by approximately 800 million bushels. That is, the U. S. gain in this one crop was sufficient to meet Europe's food deficit during the first postwar years, with food to spare.

Hybrid corn has proved to be a catalyst affecting the entire agricultural economy wherever it has touched it. Even the most skeptical farmers, once they have proved to their own satisfaction the superiority of hybrid corn, turn to the experiment stations for other innovations growing out of agricultural research. The higher cost of hybrid seed is an inducement to strive for maximum yields, and in the U. S. this has led to the adoption of improved agricultural practices, including the use of fertilizers, crop rotations and the growing of soil-improving crops of soybeans and other leguminous plants that gather soil-enriching nitrogen from the atmosphere. The result of all this is that the increases in corn yields obtained by American farmers on their own farms have been much larger than in experiment stations. Whereas hybrid corn grown in controlled experiments usually yields about 20 to 30 per cent more than the original open-pollinated corn from which it derives, the average farm yield of corn per acre in the U. S. has increased by about 50 per cent: from about 22 bushels in the early 1930s, when hybrid corn first began to be used commercially, to approximately 33 bushels in the late 1940s, when it occupied some 75 per cent of the total corn acreage. Under favorable conditions, yields of 100 bushels per acre for hybrid corn are common, and yields exceeding 200 bushels are regularly reported. This substantial increase can be attributed to the use of fertilizers and other soil-improvement practices as well as hybrid corn.

The success of hybrid corn in the U. S. promises to be repeated in other parts of the world where corn is an important plant. One of the first countries to benefit is Italy, which fortunately has been able to use hybrids developed in the U. S. Corn hybrids are usually so well "tailored" to a particular environment that it is seldom possible to move them successfully from one country, or even from one region, to another. Italy has proved to be an exception to this rule and is now importing hybrid seed corn from the U. S. on a substantial scale—enough to plant approximately a million acres in 1950.

In the countries of Latin America, in many of which corn is a basic food plant, new hybrids especially adapted to local conditions are being developed. Corn-breeding programs aimed at this objective are in progress in Mexico, Guatemala, El Salvador, Costa Rica, Cuba, Colombia, Venezuela, Brazil, Uruguay, Argentina, Peru and Chile. The corn-breeding program in Mexico, a cooperative project of the Mexican Government and the Rockefeller Foundation, has been particularly successful. Begun in 1943, it has already made itself felt in the Mexican economy; in 1948, for the first time since the Revolution of 1911, Mexico produced enough corn to feed her own population.

To Mexico hybrid corn is perhaps even more important than to the U. S. In the U. S. three fourths of all corn is fed to livestock and is transformed into meat, milk, eggs and other animal products before reaching the ultimate consumer. In Mexico corn is used directly; it is literally the staff of life of millions of people—the daily bread, which, eaten 365 days a year, fuels most of the human metabolism. Corn has an almost sacred significance to the Mexican farmer, as it had to his ancestors for centuries past. It turns out, however, that the Mexican farmer, for all of his inherent conservatism, is, like his American counterpart, willing to try new kinds of corn.

What has been done in corn to utilize the phenomenon of hybrid vigor can be done in any crop plant that lends itself to mass hybridization. Plants of the gourd family are especially easy to hybridize. Like corn, they bear male and female flowers separately on the same plant. They are therefore easily self-pollinated to produce inbred strains and readily emasculated to effect crossing. Hybrid forms of cucumbers, squashes and watermelons are now grown. Like hybrid corn, they are characterized by vigor, productiveness and uniformity.

Plants in which both the male and female elements occur in the same flower present greater difficulties. In some, like the tomato, whose flower parts are relatively large and whose fruit contains a large number of seeds, hand pollinations to produce hybrid seed are feasible. In other species, such as onions and sugar beets, whose flowers are much too small and delicate to permit emasculation on a commercial scale, forms of cytoplasmic pollen sterility, similar in their effect to that described above for corn, have been used for some years. Since onions and sugar beets are grown for their vegetative parts, the problem of restoring fertility in the final hybrid is not involved. Other crop plants in which hybrid vigor is either being used or tested are alfalfa, barley, rye and sorghum.

Hybridized Animals

Work on the development of hybrid vigor has also been extended to domestic animals. The production of hybrid chickens has already become an enterprise second in importance only to the hybrid seed-corn industry. Hybrid pigs are coming into common use, and hybrid sheep and cattle are well along in the experimental stage. In farm animals the problem of crossing is simple, because the animals are bisexual and can reproduce only by cross-fertilization. But the problem of producing inbred strains is more difficult than in plants. Inbreeding by matings between brothers and sisters—the most intensive form possible in bisexual animals—is only one third as effective as self-pollinations in plants. Since individual animals are more valuable than individual plants, inbreeding on the vast scale on which it is practiced in plants is not yet feasible. The results so far obtained, however, have been very promising. Hybrid chickens grow faster and lay more eggs. Hybrid pigs make more pork with less feed. Hybrid cattle produce more beef in less time. The animal breeder, like the corn breeder, has found hybrid vigor a powerful force to be harnessed in raising the physiological efficiency of organisms.

The time is rapidly approaching when the majority of our cultivated plants and domestic animals will be hybrid forms. Hybrid corn has shown the way. Man has only begun to exploit the rich "gifts of hybridity."

FERTILE TASSEL FIELD in Connecticut has had tassels removed from most of its rows. The tasseled rows appear in center and at left and right.

STERILE TASSEL FIELD in Connecticut has tassels on every row. Plants bearing fertile tassels are planted only in the rows where they are needed.

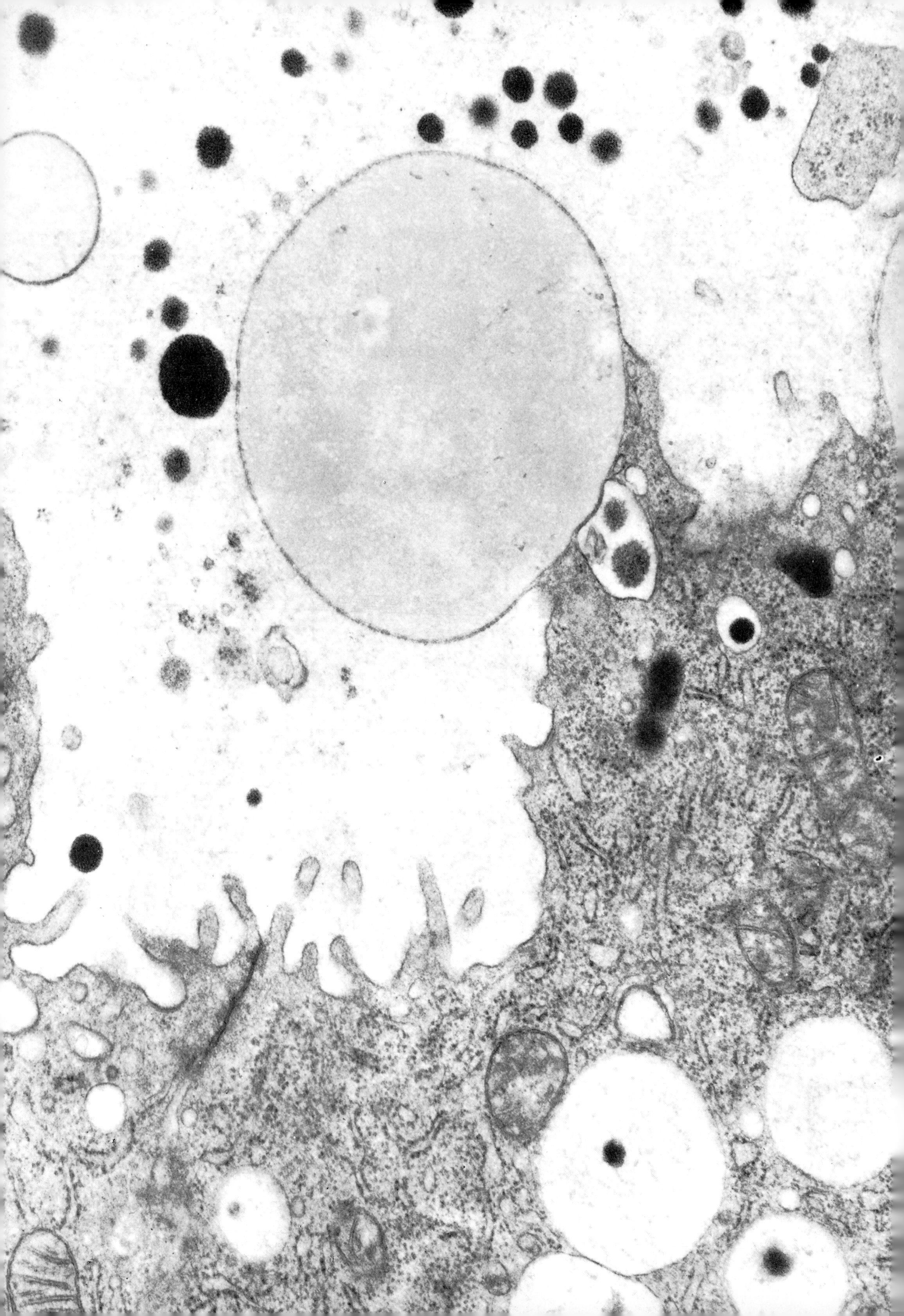

14

MILK

STUART PATTON
July 1969

The fluid made by the mammary gland is a remarkable blend of complex biological molecules. How the gland does its work is the subject of active investigation

According to the census of manufactures taken in 1967 the production, distribution and sale of dairy products constituted the seventh largest industry in the U.S., exceeded in value of shipments only by the motor vehicle, steel, aircraft, meat, petroleum and industrial-chemical industries. The basic product of the dairy industry is of course milk, which in the year of the census was produced in the amount of 118,769,000,000 pounds by 15,198,000 cows. As one might expect, the basic product has been studied intensively: nearly every state university has a program of dairy research, and the industry itself maintains a substantial research program. Notwithstanding these activities, much remains to be learned about milk. One reason is that milk is a remarkably complex substance; another is that the cellular processes whereby it is produced in the mammary tissue are highly intricate.

Milk's role, as a nearly complete food, in sustaining life processes is well known. Of equal importance is its role as a product of life processes. Milk is a record of the exquisite functioning of a cell, a fascinating cell that might be described as a factory, but a factory with the unusual property of becoming, to a certain extent, a product. Indeed, the lactating mammary cell ranks second in importance only to the photosynthesizing cell as a factor in sustaining life. For these reasons I shall focus here on the biology of milk, dealing to a lesser extent with its physical and chemical properties.

One's senses readily ascertain that cow's milk is a white, opaque liquid with characteristics of odor and flavor that are normally quite faint; a taste shows that it is slightly sweet and just perceptibly salty. One might go a step further and reason that rather large particles or molecules must be suspended in milk, because if all the constituents were fairly small dissolved molecules, milk would be as clear a solution as water is. Milk does have large components in suspension; they are mainly globules of fat and particles of protein.

Constituents of Milk

These observations indicate the gross composition of cow's milk: it is about 3.8 percent fat, 3.2 percent protein, 4.8 percent carbohydrate, .7 percent minerals and 87.5 percent water. Such an analysis, however, greatly oversimplifies cow's milk. For example, milk contains a large number of trace organic substances, some that pass through the mammary gland directly from the blood and others that result from the synthesis of milk in the mammary tissue. Moreover, the fat globules contain thousands of different molecules and are enclosed by a complex membrane acquired at the time of secretion. Milk protein was originally thought to have three components: casein, albumin and globulin. It is now known that there are four caseins, each with a number of genetic variants, and that albumin and globulin are actually a complex group of proteins known as the whey proteins. The number of proteins eventually discovered in this group probably will be limited only by the patience of the investigators and the sensitivity of the methods they apply. Only lactose, the sugar of milk, seems to be a pure and relatively simple compound.

The statements that can be made about cow's milk do not apply uniformly to the milk of other mammals, because there are large variations in the composition of milk. For example, the pinnipeds (the group of aquatic mammals including seals, sea lions and walruses) have milk that is often like heavy cream, containing 40 to 50 percent fat. In addition, depending on the species, pinniped milk contains little or no lactose. These variations can be explained in terms of their value in assisting the survival of the young of the species. A young pinniped is in special need of fat (in the form of blubber) as insulation against its cold environment, as an aid to buoyancy, as a source of energy and as a source of metabolic water in a salty environment.

A Closer Look

With the request that the reader keep in mind the important fact that milk differs substantially among mammalian species, I shall now be discussing milk in terms of cow's milk. Because of its commercial importance as a food and a raw material for foods, more is known about it than about the milk of other mammals. Moreover, the mechanisms of the synthesis of milk by the cow have been investigated closely because of the cow's importance as a unit of agriculture.

In addition to the major constituents already described, milk contains a large number of substances that occur in small amounts, ranging from .1 percent or so down to parts per billion. Among them

LACTATING CELL secretes a droplet of milk fat in the electron micrograph on the opposite page. The fat droplet is the large circular object at top center. The dark region from which it is emerging is the cell; the light region the droplet is entering is the lumen, or hollow portion, of an alveolus, one of the many pear-shaped structures that are basic units in lactation. The small dark circles visible in several places are granules of protein. The electron micrograph, which is of mammary tissue of a mouse, was made by S. R. Wellings of the University of Oregon Medical School; the enlargement is about 48,000 diameters.

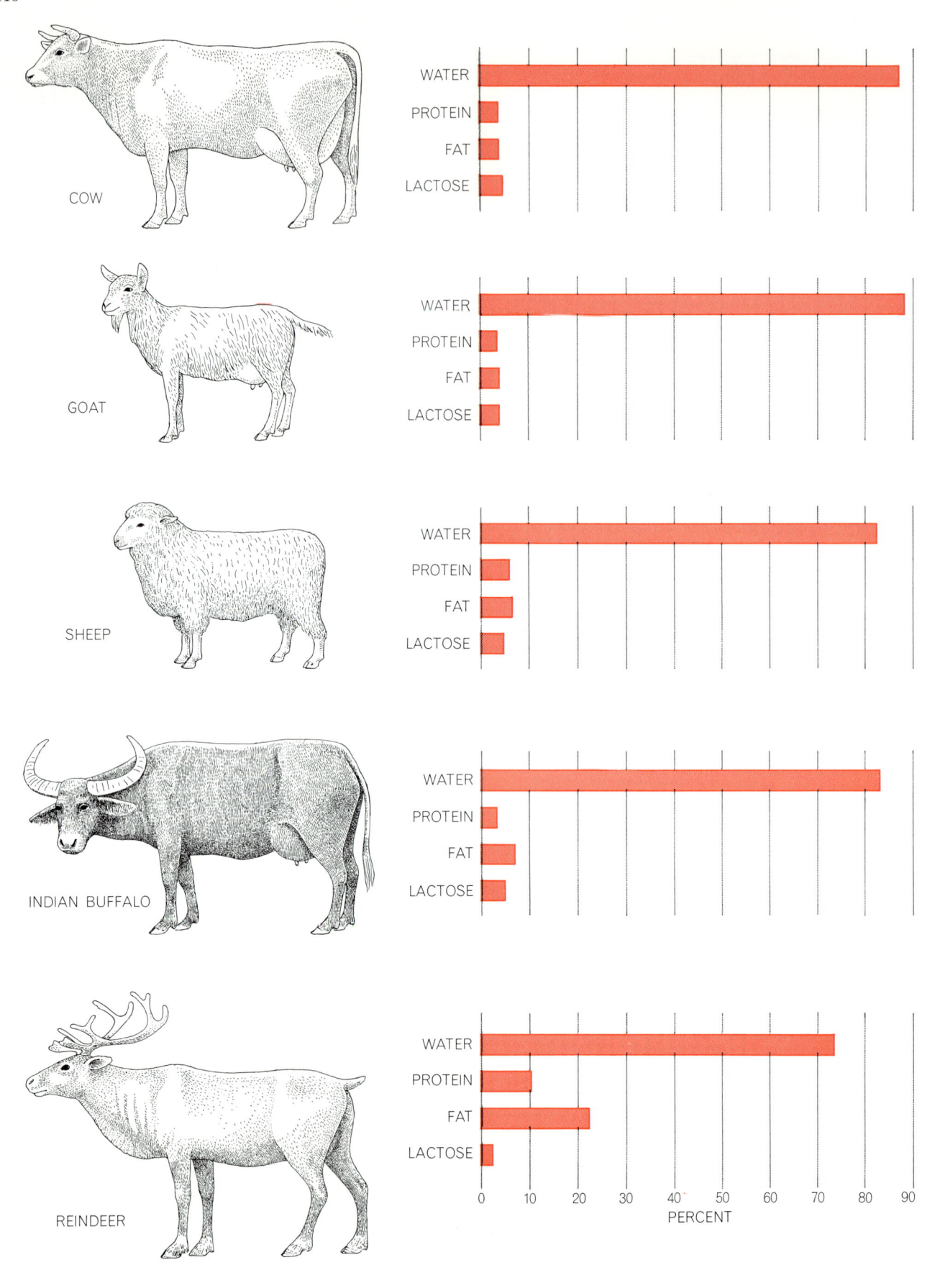

COMPOSITION OF MILK yielded by five kinds of animal is compared. In a few species the variation is even more marked; for example, the pinniped group, which includes seals and walruses, has milk that is about 50 percent fat and contains little or no lactose.

are fatty acids, amino acids, sugars and sugar phosphates, proteoses, peptones, nitrogenous bases, gases and other volatiles. Many of these substances, such as the vitamins and minerals, play a key role in nutrition. Nonetheless, the most important components of milk are the lipids (fats), the proteins and the carbohydrate (lactose). A more precise description of them will lay a foundation for considering the remarkable processes of their synthesis and secretion by the cells of the mammary gland.

The term lipid specifies a broad group of fatty (greasy, waxy or oily) substances found in biological systems, including those used for food. The term fat is often used interchangeably with lipid, but in fact fat refers more narrowly to edible oils or the characteristically fatty tissue of the animal body. The lipids in milk are sometimes called its butterfat content; they exist as minute droplets or globules that under proper conditions will rise to form a layer of cream. The process known as homogenization reduces the globules in size and stabilizes their suspension, so that they no longer form a layer of cream. Agitation, in the form of churning, causes the globules to aggregate into granules that can be gathered and worked into butter. Butter is about 80 percent fat, and the part that is not fat is mainly water. If butter is melted, clarified and dried, it yields a product that is almost 100 percent fat and is known as butter oil; it is used commercially in the making of candy and baked goods.

The fat droplets in milk have an average diameter of three to four microns (about .00014 inch). A droplet consists of a membranous coat about .02 micron thick and a core that is virtually pure glyceride material. A glyceride is the ester, or product, resulting from the combination of glycerol with fatty acid. Because a molecule of glycerol has three reactive sites, it is possible to have monoglycerides, diglycerides or triglycerides, depending on how many molecules of fatty acid react with each molecule of glycerol. The lipids of milk are mostly triglycerides.

The fatty acids that are esterified with glycerol to form glycerides can vary in many ways. At least 150 different fatty acids can be found in the glycerides of milk, but only 10 of them occur consistently in amounts larger than 1 percent of the total. The principal ones are oleic acid, palmitic acid and stearic acid, which are also common in the glycerides of many other natural fats. The fat of cow's milk is unusual in that it contains the short-chain fatty acids, including butyric acid and caproic acid. Short-chain fatty acids are also found in the milk fat of other ruminants, such as the sheep and the goat. As I shall describe more fully below, the rumen, or first stomach, in these animals has a profound effect on their metabolism and on the composition of their milk fat. Another point to note in passing is that the short-chain fatty acids are highly odorous, and when they are released from the glycerides by the enzymes known as lipases, they contribute significantly to the flavor of many kinds of cheese.

The membrane that forms the surface of the milk-fat droplet is derived from the outer membrane of the lactating mammary cell at the time of secretion. It also appears to include materials that were at the surface of the droplet while it was still in the cell. The structure and composition of the membrane are the subject of intensive study. It is known that the portion of lipids not accounted for in the triglyceride fraction is involved in the membrane. The membrane lipids include part of the milk's cholesterol, phospholipids and glycolipids and most if not all of the vitamin A and carotene (a yellow pigment). The membrane also comprises unique proteins and enzymes, and its structure seems to be an aggregate of lipoprotein subunits. All in all, the milk-fat globule—a droplet of fat wrapped in a membrane—is a remarkable biological package.

Proteins of Milk

As with proteins in general, the proteins of milk are fundamentally chains of amino acid units. Since there are 18 common amino acids, the number of protein chains that could be formed is very large indeed. About 80 percent of the protein in milk, however, is casein. No other natural protein is quite like it. One aspect of its uniqueness is that it contains phosphorus; it is known as a phosphoprotein. In milk the molecules of casein are marshaled in aggregates called micelles, which are roughly spherical in shape and average about 100 millimicrons in diameter.

Casein occurs in four distinct types called alpha, beta, gamma and kappa, respectively representing about 50, 30, 5 and 15 percent of this protein. The four types differ in molecular weight and in a number of other characteristics. Kappa casein is unique in that it contains a carbohydrate, sialic acid. Little is known about the internal organization of the casein micelle and its subunits. It is assumed, however, that each subunit contains each of the four caseins.

The alpha, beta and gamma caseins can be made to aggregate by calcium ions, but kappa casein is highly resistant to such aggregation. Hence kappa casein serves as a protective colloid that keeps the casein micelles themselves from aggregating, which would give milk a curd-like consistency. In the making of cheese the enzyme rennin is added to milk to promote the formation of curds; the enzyme splits from kappa casein a peptide containing sialic acid, thereby destabilizing the casein micelles and giving rise to the formation of curds. After the resulting whey, or watery portion, has been drawn off, the curd can be used to make cheese.

Another protein unique to milk is beta-lactoglobulin, which accounts for about .4 percent of milk and is found in two common forms, A and B, and two uncommon ones, C and D. Beta-lactoglobulin contains a comparatively high proportion of the amino acid cysteine, which bears a reduced sulfur group ($-SH$). When milk is heated, these groups (starting at a temperature of about 70 degrees Celsius) are released from the protein as hydrogen sulfide; this is the source of the cooked flavor in heated milk.

Beta-lactoglobulin has much practical importance for the processing properties of milk proteins. If it is denatured beforehand, evaporated milk is stabilized against coagulating during sterilization by heat. On the other hand, if milk for cottage cheese is overheated so that the beta-lactoglobulin is denatured, an unsatisfactory soft curd is formed. Presumably the denatured protein is adsorbed on the surface of the casein micelles, thus hindering the action of rennin and the coalescence of the casein into a curd.

Enzymes are of course proteins too, and freshly secreted milk contains a great abundance of them. Robert D. McCarthy, working with radioactively labeled substances in our laboratory at Pennsylvania State University, has shown that enzymes in milk can incorporate fatty acids into glycerides and phospholipids and can convert stearic acid into oleic acid. It is also known that milk can synthesize lactose from added glucose. Such activities make it appropriate to describe milk as an unstructured tissue, in many ways resembling the enzymatically active solid tissues of the body.

The Carbohydrate of Milk

The substance responsible for the slightly sweet taste of milk is lactose, a

CONSTITUENTS OF COW'S MILK, exclusive of water and minerals, are portrayed with diagrams of basic chemical structure of its fat, protein and lactose. Casein is the major protein, and lactose the carbohydrate, of milk. Milk has many other fats and proteins.

carbohydrate with about a fifth the sweetness of ordinary sugar. Like casein, lactose is found only in milk. Lactose is composed of a molecule of galactose combined with a molecule of glucose, the simple sugar of the blood.

Since lactose is found only in milk, and only in the milk of certain species, one wonders why it is there. Indeed, it is reasonable to ask why milk contains carbohydrate of any kind, inasmuch as the most obvious role of lactose—providing a source of energy for the newborn—is filled by fat in milk from species such as the pinnipeds. The synthesis of lactose in the mammary gland does lock up molecules of glucose drawn from the blood, and since glucose is a highly active metabolite that might otherwise go elsewhere in the body or be metabolized in a different way, it may be that the synthesis of lactose provides a means of ensuring that glucose remains in the lactating cell and so becomes a part of the milk. Another possible role for lactose arises from its solubility; soluble molecules are important to the osmotic relations of cells, and lactose, which accounts for approximately 5 percent of milk, probably affects the osmotic relations of the lactating cell. Lactose may also be the carbohydrate of milk because it encourages certain desirable bacteria, which form lactic acid, to thrive in the intestine. Lactic acid is thought to promote the absorption of the calcium and phosphorus the young animal needs for the formation of bone. In any event, it would appear that the net effect of lactose from an evolutionary point of view was to promote the survival of the young, and so its synthesis was favored by natural selection.

A factor in the synthesis of lactose is the enzyme lactose synthetase, which is composed of two proteins. One of them, the B protein, was identified by Urs Brodbeck and Kurt E. Ebner of Oklahoma State University as alpha-lactalbumin. Thus for the first time a metabolic function for one of the principal milk proteins was identified. Then it was shown by a group at Duke University that the A protein is an enzyme that normally incorporates galactose into glycoproteins. In the presence of alpha-lactalbumin the enzyme has its specificity changed to the promotion of the reaction of galactose with glucose to form lactose. This seems to be the only case known where such a protein modifies the specificity of an enzyme. In subsequent work led by Roger W. Turkington the Duke group showed that organ cultures of mouse mammary gland, when pretreated with the hormones insulin and hydrocortisone, would produce both A and B proteins after treatment with the hormone prolactin. These three hormones are known to be necessary for the synthesis of milk in the mouse to begin.

In sum, the synthesis of lactose depends on enzymes, and the synthesis of the enzymes depends in turn on several hormones, which ultimately are also regulating the synthesis of the other components of milk. It is particularly interesting that lactose synthetase not only figures in the synthesis of lactose but also is present in the milk. This is evidence for my earlier observation that in milk production the factory becomes to a certain extent the product.

The Lactating State

In considering the synthesis of milk it is necessary to recognize that the process is related to all the other processes going on within the animal. It is an integral part of the animal's total metabolism. A case in point is the relation of milk fat to the other fats in the animal. Milk fat is immediately derived from two main sources: lipids circulating in the blood and synthesis from simple metabolites in the mammary gland. The origin of the simple metabolites traces back to the blood, to various sites in the body and ultimately to the food. The lipids circulating in the blood arise from all the many locations of lipid synthesis, transformation and storage in the body [*see top illustration on page 119*].

It is also necessary to consider metabolic activity at the cellular level. Clearly the lactating mammary cell, which is continuously turning out fat, protein, carbohydrate and many other substances, is not a resting cell—a cell that is simply maintaining itself. It is a busy place, with substances constantly moving in through the basal parts of the cell and out through the secreting parts. Some of the substances are used to maintain the cell and others are merely transported through the cell, but most of them are used by the lactating cell in the synthesis of the major constituents of milk.

Another consideration in the cow is the rumen, which is in effect a large fermentation tank ranging in capacity from 30 to 60 gallons depending on the size of the animal. Plant materials eaten by the cow are broken down in the rumen by a large and highly diverse population of bacteria and protozoa. The changes in the food are of major importance. Cellulose, which man cannot digest, is readily broken down in the rumen, and the products—acetate, propionate and butyrate—are prime metabolites in the bovine metabolic economy. Another significant change taking place in the rumen involves lipids. The lipids of plants are highly unsaturated, meaning that they have many free bonding sites where they can add more hydrogen molecules or form new chemical compounds. In the rumen the fatty acids are released enzymatically from such feed lipids and are then hydrogenated, so that they are converted into saturated fatty acids (mainly palmitic acid and stearic acid). These acids are subsequently absorbed and become part of the lipids of both meat and milk, which is why meat, milk and milk products of the ruminant animal contain saturated fats. In contrast, the milk fat of animals with a single stomach (such as human beings) will readily reflect dietary unsaturated fatty acids.

Another interesting fact about the rumen is that the microorganisms involved in fermentation become part of the milk as a result of subsequent digestion. Mark Keeney of the University of Maryland has estimated that at least 10 percent of the fatty acids of bovine milk are derived from the bacteria and protozoa in the rumen. Similarly, the amino acids used in the synthesis of milk proteins originate partly with microbes in the rumen.

Lactogenesis, the process that sets in motion the synthesis and secretion of milk, depends on the action of hormones. Hormonal changes in the female following conception lead to proliferation and differentiation of certain mammary cells. The organelles of the cell increase in size and quantity. Enzymes required to synthesize the various milk constituents appear in the cells, some gradually and some rather suddenly at about the time the animal gives birth. It is probably conservative to say that 100 enzymes are newly formed or greatly intensified in activity during the lactogenic transformation of tissue.

The mode of action of a hormone at the molecular level has not been established with certainty. As a result of work by Yale J. Topper and his colleagues at the National Institutes of Health, however, considerable progress has been made in determining what hormones are involved in lactogenesis and what effects they have at the cellular level. Working in vitro with mammary tissue from virgin mice, Topper's group has shown that the hormones insulin, hydrocortisone and prolactin, acting synergistically, are required to stimulate the synthesis of milk by the mammary tissue.

The hormone progesterone has an inhibitory effect on the differentiation of

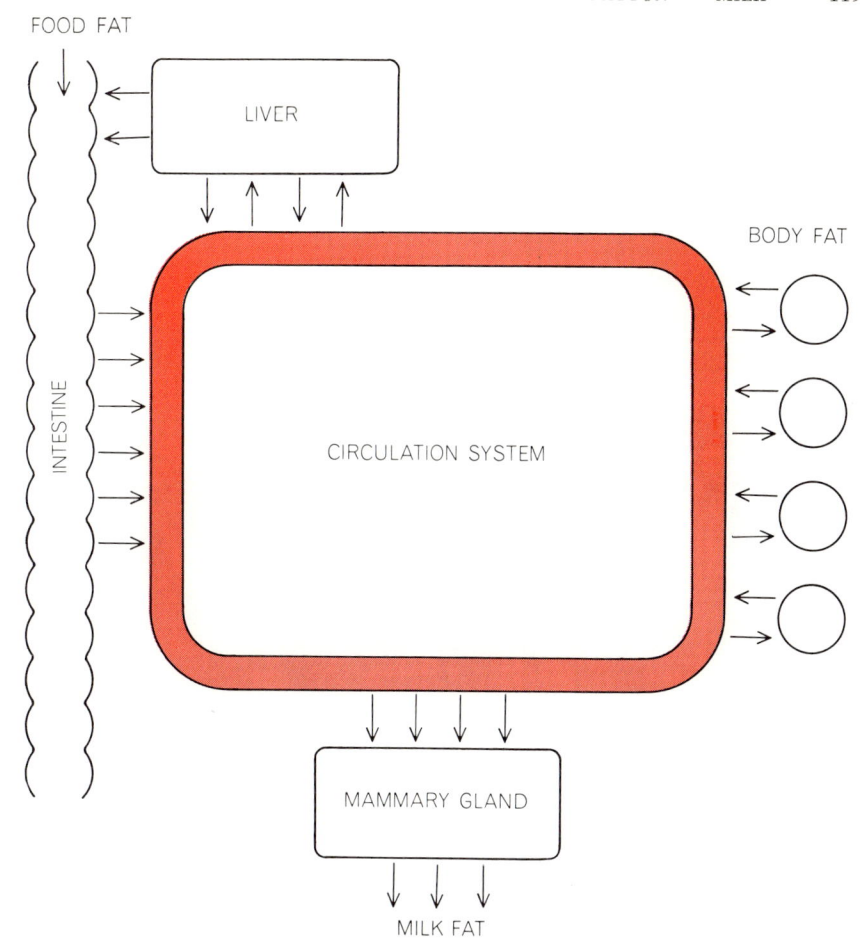

PATHWAYS OF FAT in the body indicate the sources of the fat in milk and thereby the mechanisms by which milk is synthesized. Fat from food enters the bloodstream through the intestines and also from the body's reserves of fat and from the liver. The mammary gland draws on these sources of raw material for the synthesis of the droplets of fat in milk.

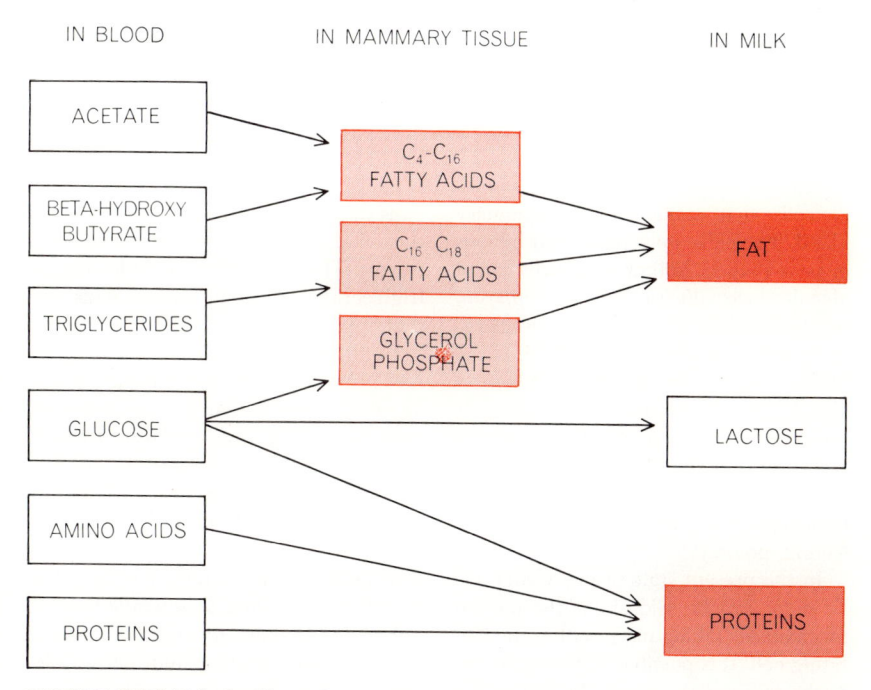

RAW MATERIALS of milk are depicted in a scheme showing the materials from the blood that are used by the mammary tissue in the synthesis of milk. Information on the materials going into the synthesis is obtained with radioactive tracers and by measuring changes in concentration of a substance between arterial and venous blood in mammary gland.

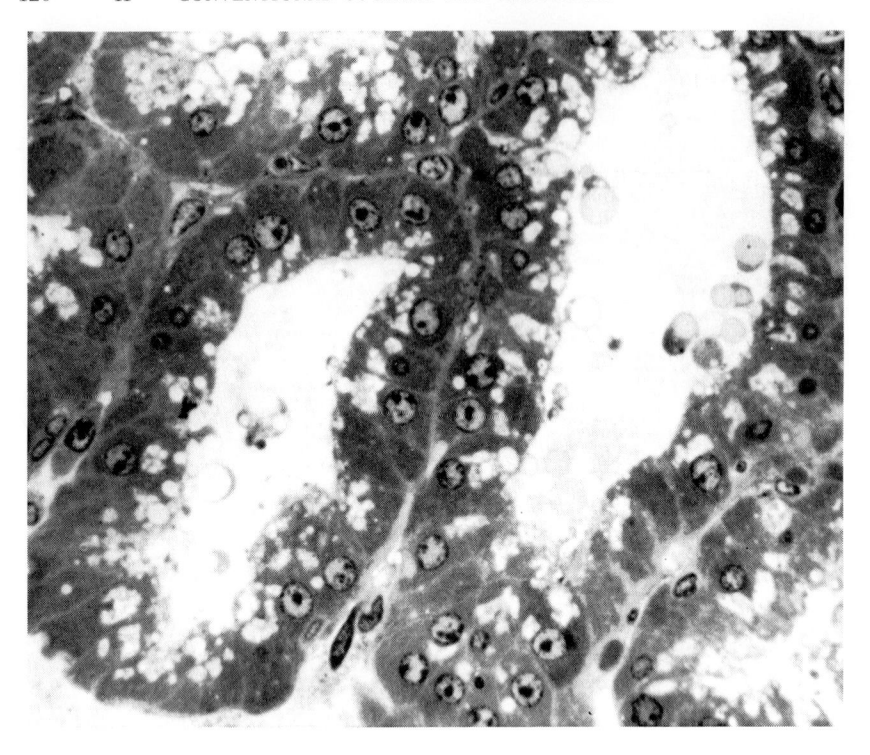

TWO ALVEOLI in the mammary gland of a lactating rat appear in a photomicrograph made by C. W. Heald in the laboratory of R. G. Saacke at the College of Agriculture of the Virginia Polytechnic Institute. The light areas are the lumens, which are surrounded by lactating cells. Between the two alveoli is a capillary. The enlargement is 2,500 diameters.

mammary tissue and the secretion of milk. Thus lactogenesis results in part from suppression of the activity of progesterone. Another important regulator of milk synthesis and secretion is the removal of milk from the mammary gland. Unless the milk is removed regularly, synthesis stops.

The Synthesis of Milk

Milk is produced by the vast number of cells that make up the mammary gland. The cells are formed into billions of pear-shaped, hollow structures called alveoli [see illustration on opposite page]. Each cell in an alveolus discharges its milk into the lumen, which is the hollow part of the structure. When an alveolus is full, its outer cells contract under the influence of the hormone oxytocin, causing the alveolus to discharge its milk into a duct system that carries it to the cistern, or sac, that is the main collecting point.

In the present state of knowledge little more can be said about the precise mechanisms taking place within the lactating cell. It is possible, however, to describe to a certain extent the raw materials the cell draws from the blood and how they get from the blood into the cell. Much of the knowledge about the raw materials or metabolites comes from painstaking experiments by John M. Barry of the University of Oxford and J. L. Linzell and E. F. Annison of the British Agricultural Research Council's Institute of Animal Physiology. The principle of their work has been that any compounds being used by the mammary gland will show a drop in concentration between the entering arterial blood and the departing venous blood. The British workers have measured such arteriovenous differences and also have amplified their findings through use of radioactive tracers. The metabolites include acetate, triglycerides, glucose, amino acids and proteins.

In order to reach the cell the metabolites must move through the walls of the blood-carrying capillaries, across the endothelium lining the capillaries, through intercellular spaces and into the alveolar epithelium where the milk is synthesized. For the transport of small ions from the blood there is a selective system, as is shown by the fact that compared with the blood serum milk is much reduced in sodium and chloride ions and much elevated in potassium ions. Molecules such as the amino acids, glucose and acetate could in principle simply diffuse through the system. In the light of the rapid, selective and continuing uptake of these substances, however, it seems likely that here too there are special transport systems. The same is true for certain large molecules of protein that appear to pass unchanged from the blood into the milk. They include serum albumin and the immune globulins. Unless there are extremely large discontinuities in the cellular structure all the way from the blood to the milk, one is almost obliged to invoke special transport mechanisms for these large molecules. (Most of the milk proteins are made within the cell by the usual method of transcription by ribonucleic acid on the ribosomes of the cell.)

This question of how large particles can migrate through cell membranes without destroying the integrity of the cells arises for the exports of the lactating cells as well as for its imports. Indeed, the fat droplets steadily secreted by the cell are at times nearly as large as the cell itself. The first evidence of the remarkable biophysical mechanisms required for this task was supplied in 1959 by electron microscopy done in Germany by Wolfgang L. Bargmann and his coworkers at the University of Kiel. From their micrographs of mouse and hamster mammary tissue it was deduced that the fat droplets are secreted as a result of being progressively engaged in and enveloped by the limiting membrane at the apex of the cell [see illustration on page 114]. When a fat droplet is completely surrounded by the membrane in this way, it is effectively displaced from inside the cell out into the lumen of the alveolus. All that remains for completion of its secretion is for the slender membrane bridge to be pinched off. From our calculation of the sizable forces (as much as 100 atmospheres) involved in the attraction of the membrane to the surface of the droplet it is possible that once the droplet makes a close approach to the membrane it is quickly and forcefully snapped through.

Bargmann and his colleagues reported that their electron micrographs suggested the existence of milk-protein granules inside cell vacuoles that arise from the Golgi apparatus [see illustration on opposite page]. According to the German workers the contents of the vacuoles were secreted by being emptied through the cell membrane. Our group believes the membrane processes in the two mechanisms of secretion (for fat droplets and protein granules) are related. The membrane around the Golgi vacuole carrying protein granules becomes continuous with the cell membrane at the time the vacuole empties its contents into the

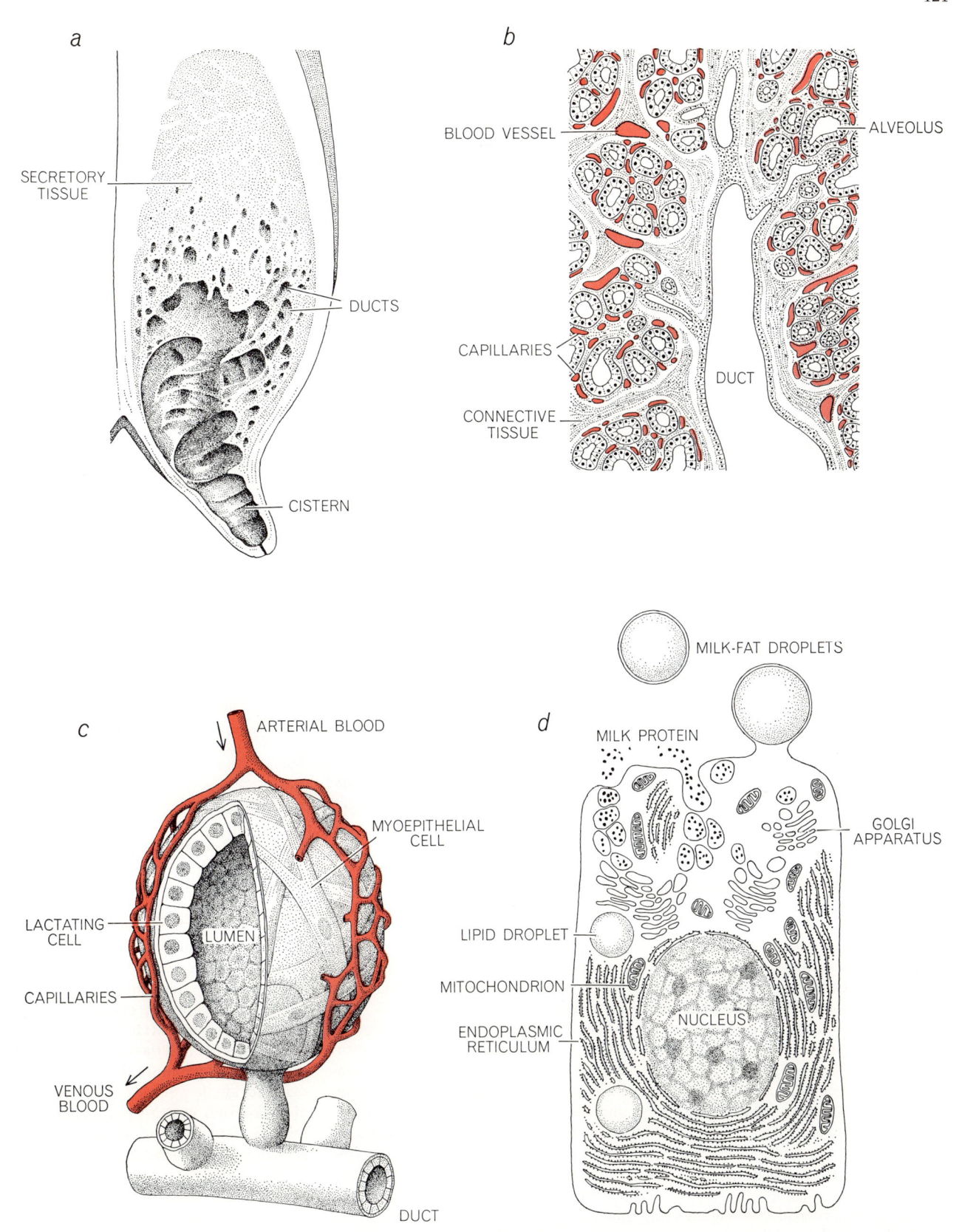

MILK-PRODUCING TISSUE of a cow is shown at progressively larger scale. At (*a*) is a longitudinal section of one of the four quarters of the mammary gland. The boxed area is reproduced at (*b*), where the arrangement of the alveoli and the duct system that drains them is apparent. A single alveolus (*c*) consists of an elliptical arrangement of lactating cells surrounding the lumen, which is linked to the duct system of the mammary gland. A lactating cell (*d*), similar to the one in the electron micrograph on page 114, is shown as it discharges a droplet of fat into the lumen. Part of the cell membrane apparently becomes the membranous covering of the fat droplet. Dark circular bodies in the vacuoles of Golgi apparatus are granules of protein, which are discharged into the lumen.

STORAGE TANKS in a milk and ice cream plant of the Borden Company in West Allis, Wis., hold 48,000 quarts each. Raw milk delivered to the plant from dairy farms is stored in the tanks at a temperature of about 37 degrees Fahrenheit until it is processed. The five slender pipes at bottom are used in loading and unloading the tanks. An inspection port and a gauge are at top of each tank.

lumen. The cell membrane then is engaged by the milk-fat droplet and becomes the membrane around the secreted milk-fat globule. Evidence from both electron microscopy and biochemical studies is tending to substantiate these mechanisms of secretion for the lipids and proteins of milk, but many questions of both a gross and a refined nature remain to be answered.

Further Questions

The basal portion of the lactating cell, as distinguished from its apical, or secreting, end, contains extensive membranous processes known as the endoplasmic reticulum. The evidence is convincing that these membranes are the sites of synthesis for the major constituents of milk: triglycerides, proteins and lactose. The means whereby the components are gathered for secretion is not known. For example, it is not understood how all the triglyceride molecules are gathered into a droplet.

The precise operation of the Golgi apparatus is not established. The apparatus is defined as an organelle that accomplishes the differentiation of membranes and the "packaging" of materials for secretion, but just how it does these things in the lactating cell is unclear. It is now a reasonable assumption that alpha-lactalbumin, the B protein of lactose synthetase, joins the A protein in the Golgi apparatus, thus allowing the synthesis of lactose at that site. The lactose, milk protein and other constituents of milk serum are then packaged into Golgi vacuoles for secretion. One wonders, however, if the Golgi vacuoles are the vehicle of secretion for all the milk proteins. Electron micrographs show clearly that the granules the vacuoles contain have the appearance of casein micelles. Perhaps the other proteins are also present in the vacuoles but are not evident because they are transparent to electrons. We have suggested that these vacuoles, since they must carry some of the fluid of milk, may provide the vehicle for the secretion of milk-serum constituents such as lactose. Investigations of these questions and inferences are needed.

In sum, the lactating mammary cell, like all cells, is an almost incredible unit of organization and action. We are beginning to gain an understanding of this cell, which is so important to mammalian life, but the detailed revelation of its elegant mechanisms is still to come. The findings may lead to more and better food products. At the very least they will mean a deeper understanding of cellular processes and of life itself.

CATTLE

RALPH W. PHILLIPS
June 1958

They can convert otherwise useless vegetation into milk and meat. Physiology and genetics are now showing how they can be made to do so more efficiently in widely varying environments

Cattle stand first among the animals serving man. They are outnumbered, it is true, by sheep, and they are outranked in man's esteem by the horse and the dog, but no other domestic animal renders such a variety of important services to human well-being. To the American or European consumer, cattle represent beef, veal, milk, butter, cheese and leather; behind the scenes in the packing house they yield in addition hormones and vitamin extracts, bone meal for feed and fertilizer and high-protein concentrates for livestock feeding. This does not exhaust the catalogue of their utility. More than a third of the world's 800 million cattle are engaged primarily in the generation of brute energy for the tasks of plowing, hauling and milling.

Considered as machines for converting vegetable matter into human food, cattle are not particularly efficient. The best such machine is the pig, which converts about a fifth of what it eats into food for human consumption. A dairy cow converts less than a sixth, a beef steer no more than a twentieth. Even these figures refer to animals bred for food production and raised by up-to-date techniques; the cattle of Asia and Africa, bred mainly for work, are less efficient. Cattle, however, convert foodstuffs which are otherwise useless to man. The efficient pig must subsist almost entirely on concentrated carbohydrates and proteins; its food could, at least in theory, be consumed directly by human beings. But cattle, though they need more food than pigs to yield the same number of calories, feed in part on cellulose, which they digest with the help of certain microorganisms in their enormous stomachs. By using cattle as intermediaries we can process the vegetation of semi-arid grasslands which cannot be farmed in any other way. Recent studies suggest that some day we may even use cattle to produce food from sawdust [see "The Metabolism of Ruminants," by Terence A. Rogers; SCIENTIFIC AMERICAN, February].

But if the world's food problem is to be solved, we must find ways to improve

IMPORTANCE OF CATTLE early in human history is shown by their recurrence in wall paintings and sculptures such as this Sumerian frieze. In early civilizations cattle were used not for food but mainly for work, as in most of Africa and Asia today.

the efficiency with which cattle convert fodder, of whatever sort, into meat and milk. Selective breeding of cattle to this end has been going on for several centuries in western Europe. There, and more recently in America, cattle breeders have achieved remarkably good results considering the empirical methods they have relied upon. Only during the past 20 or 30 years have scientific physiology and genetics come into play. Though many important questions remain unanswered, scientists have already done much to help cattlemen improve existing breeds and develop new breeds which can produce efficiently in unfavorable environments.

Breeds

We do not know when or where cattle were first domesticated. Cave paintings and bits of charred bone tell us that primitive man in Europe and Asia hunted wild cattle of various species, and our domestic cattle must be descended from one or more of these. In Europe the wild species are all extinct, though one of them, the aurochs, survived in remote parts of eastern Europe as late as the 17th century. Similar wild species still roam the forests and savannas of southeast Asia. The Americas have no native cattle, nor does Australia. Our best guess is that cattle were domesticated at least 10,000 years ago somewhere in central or southern Asia by nomadic tribesmen who raised them for meat and milk. As agricultural and urban societies developed, cattle came to be used primarily as draft animals. So great was their economic importance in this role that the Egyptians, Assyrians and other ancient peoples worshipped them as gods. Indeed, until the coming of steam they were man's main source of power other than his own muscles; the heavy draft horse is a relatively recent development.

Even in ancient times herdsmen seem to have practiced some sort of selective breeding. The Mosaic law specifically provides that "thou shalt not let thy cattle gender with a diverse kind." Jacob, under his shrewdly drawn contract with Laban, succeeded in making his fortune by judicious cattle breeding. As the 30th chapter of Genesis records, he relied in part on superstition, but he also employed the perfectly sound genetic principle that like tends to produce like. His "speckled and spotted" cattle produced calves of like coloring.

Thousands of years of domestication have produced dozens of more or less distinct breeds of cattle [see drawings on page 126 to 129]. Almost all of them, however, seem to stem from two species: European cattle (*Bos taurus*) and Indian or zebu cattle (*Bos indicus*).

From the original European species breeders in western Europe and especially in the British Isles developed all but one or two of the popular milk and beef breeds in the world today. Their distribution on the world map [see below] follows that of the European settlers who took them along to the Temperate Zones of the Americas, New Zealand and Australia. In addition some minor breeds are found in northern and eastern Asia.

The beef breeds, including the white-faced Herefords and the black Aberdeen Angus of our midwestern and plains states, are typically low-set and blocky in appearance, with a relatively small percentage of bone and a good deal of fat. Dairy cattle, by contrast, are lean and angular, bred to turn every possible bit of feed into milk. Their udders are, of course, much larger than those of the beef breeds, and their swollen mid-sections bespeak a digestive tract capable of handling large quantities of grass.

The most important dairy breeds are the Holstein, the Jersey and the Guernsey. The Holstein, largest of the three, is also the most copious producer, but the other two give richer milk and are favored by dairymen who specialize in butter production and farmers who keep a few "family cows" to produce butter and cream as well as milk. The Ayrshire, perhaps the original "friendly cow, all

1. AYRSHIRE
2. WEST HIGHLAND
3. ANGUS
4. SHORTHORN
5. HEREFORD
6. JERSEY
7. HOLSTEIN
8. CHAROLAIS
9. BROWN SWISS
10. CHIANINI
11. BLANCO OREJINEGRO
12. WEST AFRICAN SHORTHORN
13. KANKREJ
13a. BRAHMAN
14. ONGOLE
15. SAHIWAL
16. KANGAYAM
17. BORAN
18. MADAGASCAR
19. AFRICANDER
20. SANTA GERTRUDIS
21. EGYPTIAN
22. ANKOLE
23. CHINESE "YELLOW COW"

CATTLE OF EUROPEAN TYPE

NATIVE ZEBU CATTLE

CATTLE OF INTERMEDIATE TYPE

INTRODUCED ZEBU CATTLE

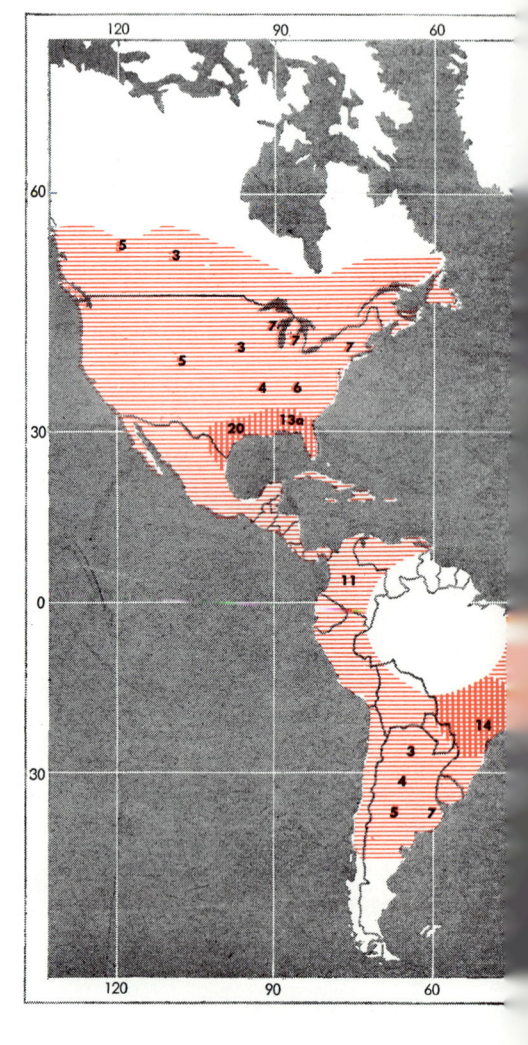

WORLD DISTRIBUTION of the two main species of cattle indicates their adaptation to different climates. European cattle (*Bos taurus*) are found in most temperate regions; they

red and white," is less well known, though it is a good milk producer.

A number of European breeds are dual- or triple-purpose animals, used for milk and meat or for milk, meat and work. The Shorthorn is generally considered a dual-purpose breed, though different strains have been selected primarily for meat or for milk production. The Brown Swiss and the Simmenthal, also a Swiss breed, are triple-purpose animals in their native country. Many other European countries have developed their own dual- and triple-purpose breeds, but few of these have spread to other lands.

The Zebu

The zebu, the other great species of domestic cattle, probably originated in India but long ago spread, or was brought by man, into Africa and parts of southeast Asia. Thousands of years of natural selection have inured it to tropical conditions. In recent decades it has been successfully introduced into Brazil, the U. S. Gulf Coast and other tropical and semitropical regions.

The zebu differs from European cattle most obviously in having a large hump on its shoulders and a heavy dewlap. The biological function of these organs is uncertain. Until recently it was believed that by increasing the animal's surface area they helped to dissipate heat. But recent experiments indicate that even when these parts of its anatomy are surgically removed the zebu remains heat-tolerant. The hump apparently does not provide any important food reserve for the animal, as the camel's does; the zebu's hump does not shrink much when the animal has to get along on sparse food rations. Zebus are generally more alert and more active than European cattle. They do not moo or bellow but emit a kind of coughing grunt.

The zebus of the Indian peninsula have evolved into many breeds, most of which inhabit fairly limited areas. The great majority are work animals, but several rather similar breeds found in Pakistan and India are known for their milking qualities. The best of these milking breeds, the Sahiwal, has been introduced into Jamaica; another, the Gir, is used extensively in Brazil. Experiments with the Sindhi breed are being carried on in the U. S. The "Brahman" cattle of our Gulf States are a mixture of several Indian working breeds, chiefly the Kankrej; their beef qualities have

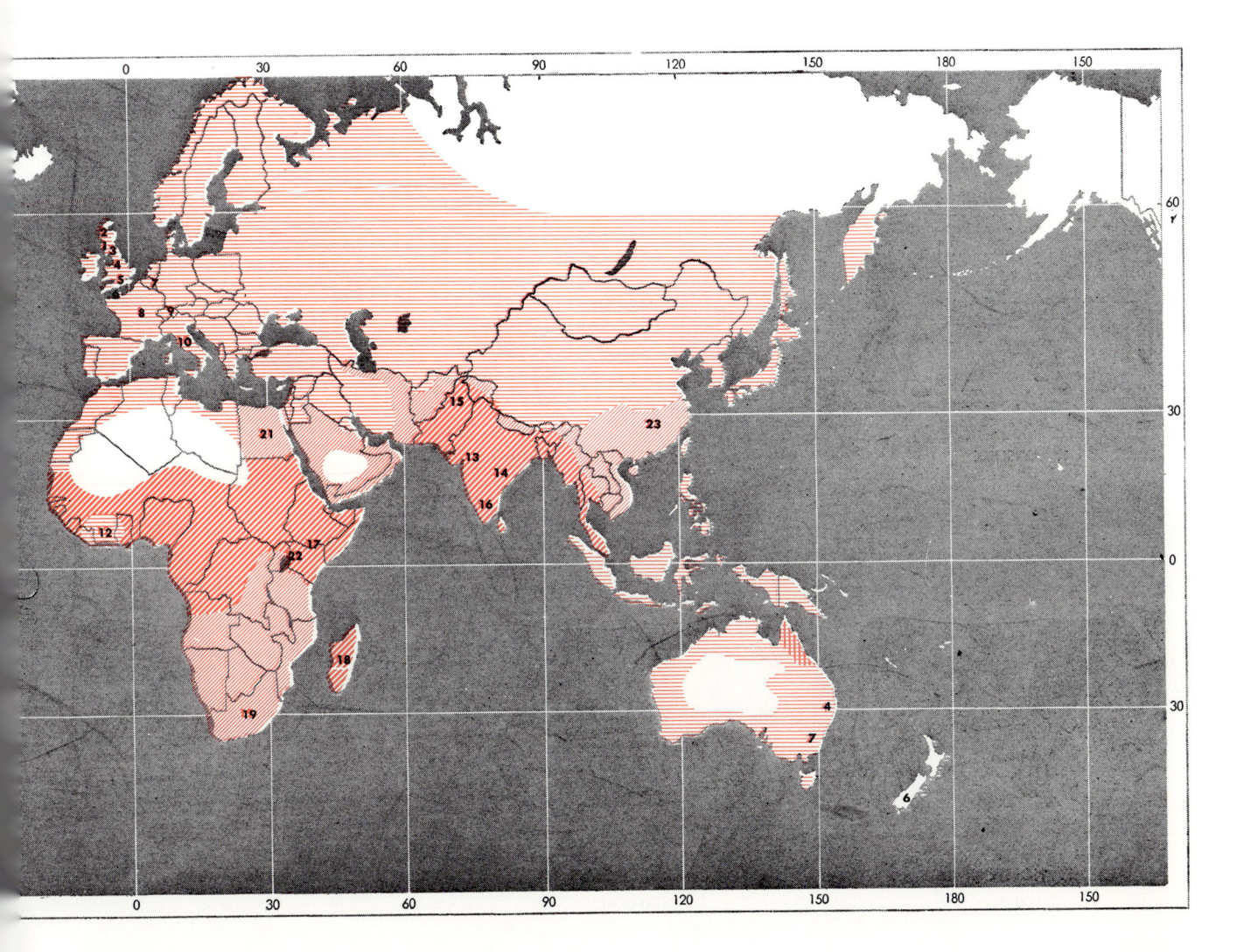

seldom do well in the tropics. Zebu cattle (*Bos indicus*) originated in India and have spread or been introduced into other hot regions. Numbers suggest the distribution of some important breeds, which are depicted in drawings on the next four pages.

been considerably improved by selection.

In addition to the more or less improved breeds, the zebu cattle of India and Pakistan include large numbers of small and relatively unproductive "village cattle" and "hill cattle"; the latter sometimes are only about the size of a large dog.

As one might expect, zebus have been crossbred with European cattle where the two species have come in contact. Cattle breeds in southern China, the Near East and some along the northeast shore of the Mediterranean as far west as Italy show evidences of zebu ancestry. In Africa centuries of tribal migrations have so mixed the two species as to make classification difficult. Some African breeds, such as the Ankole, differ from European and zebu cattle in possessing enormous, bulbous horns. Broadly speaking, the cattle of northwest Africa stem from the European species or some similar humpless type; zebus inhabit a wide belt across Madagascar and central Africa; elsewhere the two species have mingled to produce bewildering variety. European cattle, zebus, and their intermixtures account for almost all the cattle in the world. The only significant additions are two close relatives, the bantin of Java and the gayal of Assam and upper Burma, which have been domesticated on a small scale.

We should not, however, overlook a distant cousin which has great economic importance in some parts of the world—the water buffalo. India, with some 140 million cattle, also has more than 40 million buffaloes; Thailand actually has more buffaloes than cattle. In some countries, such as China, buffaloes are used primarily for work; elsewhere, as in India and Egypt, they are kept mainly for milk. Surplus animals are slaughtered for meat almost everywhere, though the meat is of poor quality by our standards. Buffaloes are particularly useful in the tropics because they seem to be better able than cattle to digest the crude fiber that forms a large part of much tropical vegetation. Curiously, however, they resist heat less well than even European cattle. Buffaloes apparently have no sweat glands, except in their muzzles. For this reason and possibly others, their heat-regulating mechanism is inadequate, and in hot weather they must be drenched with water periodically or allowed to wallow in water or mud if their working or milk-producing capacity is to be maintained.

It stands to reason that cattle bred for work will be inefficient producers of food. In the underdeveloped countries of the world, where the food problem is most acute, the usefulness of cattle is still further reduced by primitive slaughtering methods. The hides, too, are often damaged by knife-cuts or are poorly tanned. In India, of course, Hindu religious taboos generally forbid the slaughtering of cattle. A similar situation prevails among the tribal cultures of

1. AYRSHIRE 
2. WEST HIGHLAND 
3. ANGUS

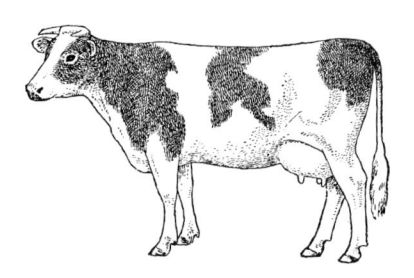

7. HOLSTEIN
8. CHAROLAIS 
9. BROWN SWISS 

EUROPEAN CATTLE include almost all the specialized dairy (1, 6, 7) and beef (3, 5, 8) breeds. Shorthorns are used for both purposes; the Brown Swiss, a dairy breed in the U. S., is used for milk, meat and work in Switzerland. The Chianini, though unspe-

Africa and the Near East, where cattle, along with other livestock, are a kind of currency. (Our own word "pecuniary" comes from the Latin word *pecus*, meaning cattle.) Where a man's wealth is measured by the size of his herds, and the price of a wife is stated in cows, the tribesman will be concerned with the numbers rather than with the quality of his cattle. Some tribes have developed bizarre ways of getting food from cattle without killing them. The Masai of East Africa, for example, bleed their cattle periodically and drink the fresh blood or combine it with other foods.

Cattle Breeding

Systematic efforts to improve the productivity of cattle began in Great Britain during the 18th century with the work of Robert Bakewell, the great pioneer in animal husbandry. Bakewell and his successors in Britain and western Europe produced almost all of the dairy and beef breeds we know today. These early breeders, of course, knew nothing of scientific genetics. Their success in developing so many productive breeds testifies that they had a good grasp of the empirical principles and a certain amount of good luck.

Breeders have been most successful with dairy cattle, because the productivity of a milker is easily measured in pounds of milk and percentage of butterfat content. The best milkers could be chosen as breeding animals, and even bulls could be selected by the productivity of their daughters.

The productivity of beef cattle is more difficult to measure. How quickly they put on weight, which determines how quickly the cattleman can turn over his capital, can be measured fairly easily. But it takes an elaborate analysis of each carcass to judge qualities such as the ratio of meat to bone and the extent to which meat is "marbled" with fat. Lacking any simple measure of quality, breeders have tended to estimate animals by their appearance, selecting breeds with deep, wide bodies, well-developed loins and hindquarters (which contain the more expensive cuts) and a blocky, smooth exterior. Such visual criteria put emphasis on a thick layer of fat under the skin. Breeders have a saying: "Fat is a pretty color." Much of this pretty fat, however, is trimmed away on the butcher's block to please the American taste. Moreover, the amount of fat on the outside of the carcass seems to have little bearing on the fat inside, which makes for tender and juicy meat, or on the proportion of lean meat to bone.

A number of scientists have been working on better methods of evaluating beef cattle on the hoof. In one promising method certain harmless chemicals which are absorbed much more rapidly by fat than by muscle are injected into the animal's bloodstream. By taking blood samples at intervals one can

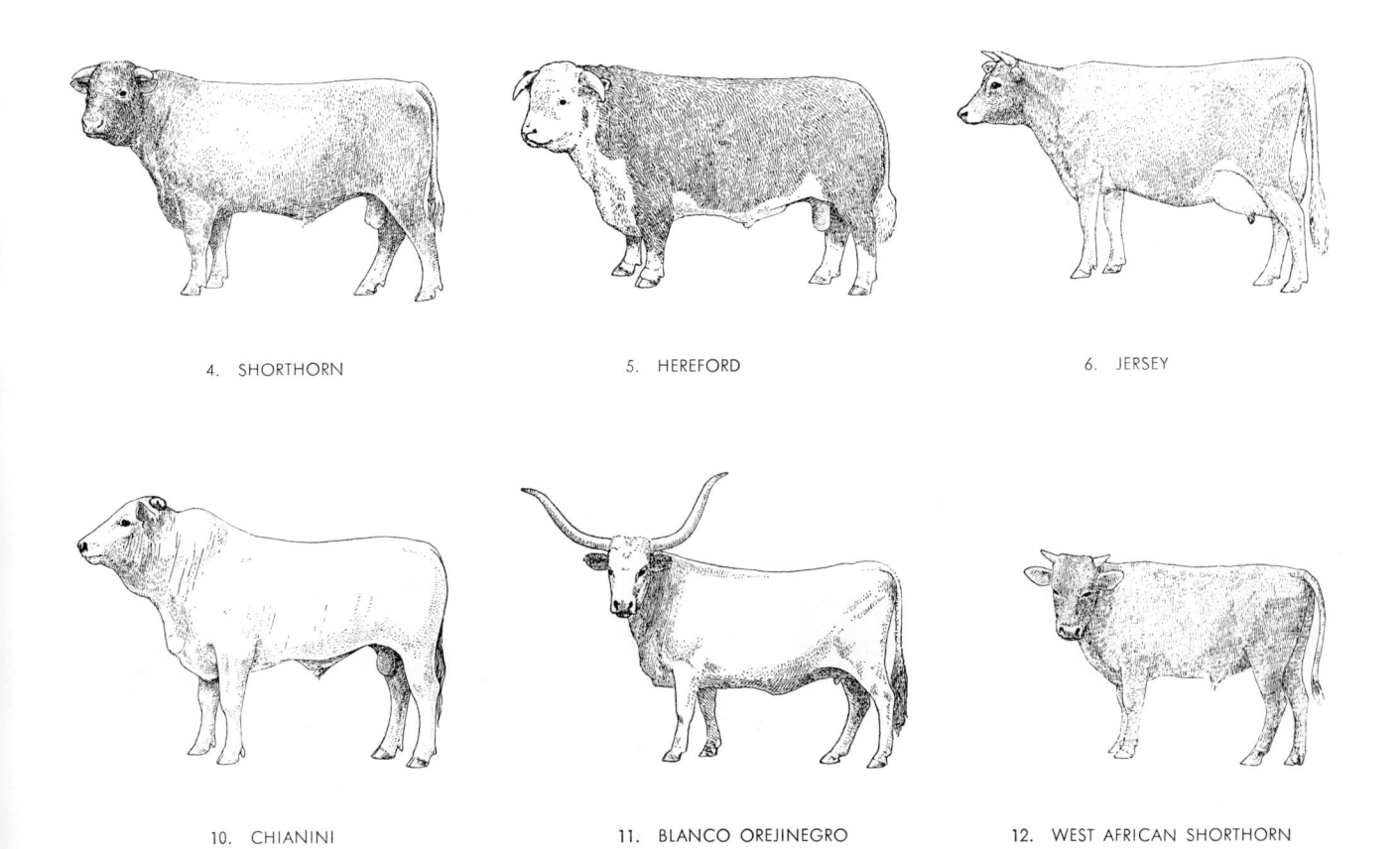

4. SHORTHORN

5. HEREFORD

6. JERSEY

10. CHIANINI

11. BLANCO OREJINEGRO

12. WEST AFRICAN SHORTHORN

cialized, is the best beef producer among Italian breeds. The West Highland is adapted to a cold, damp climate; the Blanco Orejinegro and West African Shorthorn (no relation to the Shorthorn) are among the few breeds of European type which thrive in the tropics.

measure the rate at which the chemicals are absorbed and thus estimate the amount of fat inside the carcass.

The most promising work in cattle improvement, however, is drawing upon the science of genetics. Although this is a new undertaking, it has moved ahead rapidly and is already showing results.

Genetic Traits

A few traits in cattle are known to be inherited by simple Mendelian principles. The black coat and hornlessness of the Aberdeen Angus and the white face of the Hereford are Mendelian dominants, controlled by single pairs of genes. These traits, however, are not of major economic importance. The more significant qualities of milk production, percentage of butterfat, rate of growth and efficiency of feed utilization involve many pairs of genes and are also powerfully influenced by environment. Nonetheless geneticists have made progress in estimating the relative weight of the genetic and environmental factors that determine these traits. By studying the extent to which related animals, such as half-brothers or half-sisters, are more alike than randomly selected animals reared under the same conditions, it is possible to estimate the degree to which a particular trait can be inherited and thus to predict how effective selection for that trait is likely to be.

In dairy cows, for example, butterfat production is about 30 per cent inheritable. That is, if we select a group of heifers whose butterfat production averages 100 pounds a year more than the herd-average and breed them to bulls of similar superior stock, the offspring will produce about 30 pounds a year above the average. According to studies by the U. S. Range Experiment Station at Miles City, Mont., the indications are that the birth weight of beef cattle is 53 per cent inheritable and the weight at 15 months (just before slaughtering) is 86 per cent inheritable. The grade of the carcass is estimated to be 33 per cent inheritable.

In the early 1940s the Miles City workers began to select cattle for rapid growth, and they have developed some superior strains. These results have been accomplished by selecting on the basis of performance tests rather than appearance. That looks can be deceiving was illustrated some time ago when a distinguished foreign visitor to the station, after being shown some very good performers, spied a herd of fat, blocky steers just as he was leaving. "Why didn't you show me these before?" he exclaimed. He was startled to learn that these seemingly superior cattle were in fact the poorest producers on the station!

With more experimental work of this sort breeders may soon be able to provide bulls which transmit to their offspring high feeding efficiency, optimum proportions of bone, muscle and fat, a rapid growth rate and perhaps even tenderer meat. For the general public

13. KANKREJ

13a. BRAHMAN

14. ONGOLE

18. MADAGASCAR

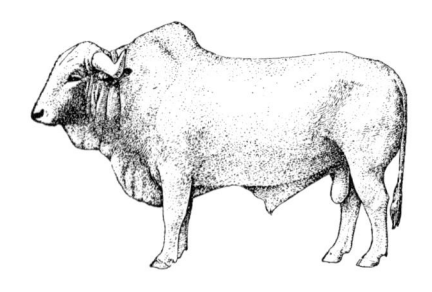

19. AFRICANDER

20. SANTA GERTRUDIS

ZEBU CATTLE (13-18) are mostly used for work; the few dairy breeds, such as the Sahiwal, produce far less than European milk cattle. The Brahman is a mixture of several Indian zebu breeds, mainly the Kankrej. Interbreeding between zebus and European

this will mean cheaper and better steaks and roasts.

Backward Areas

Work of this kind has been carried on so far in the Temperate Zone countries where levels of production are already high. Little or nothing has been done to improve the cattle in more needful regions of the world, even by empirical methods. Effective selection implies a sizable herd to select from, but the average farmer in these regions has only one or two cattle, and often these are work oxen which cannot breed. The farmers owning larger herds can seldom afford to purchase superior breeding stock, nor can the near-subsistence economies of these countries spare much money for large-scale breeding experiments.

Moreover, the attempts that have been made to improve the productivity of zebus have not been very fruitful so far, partly because too little is yet known about the genetic potential of the various strains and partly because in many areas the feeding and management of the cattle are not efficient enough to bring out their full possibilities. The best zebu performances have been far below those of European breeds. In India a few well-handled Sahiwal cows have produced somewhat more than 10,000 pounds of milk in a year. In the U. S., Holsteins have produced as much as 40,000 pounds. The high productivity of European cattle is the result of several centuries of selective breeding. Even assuming that the economic difficulties can be overcome, it would take a long time to raise the best zebu breeds, such as the Sahiwal, to similar levels.

Nor has much attention been given to improving the zebu as a work animal. Some agricultural leaders in the underdeveloped countries hold that such research is a waste of money, believing that draft cattle will soon be replaced by tractors. I myself am not so sure. Small fields, a low economic level, the need for manure and, in rice-growing areas, the water-covered ground are all likely to delay the substitution of tractors for cattle.

It may be that the most rapid improvement of cattle in the underdeveloped areas of the world will be gained by crossing the European and zebu animals. The pure European breeds do not do well in these regions. Their digestive systems are not adapted to the coarse and often scanty grasses; parasites and disease are additional hazards. Worst of all is the heat. In hot climates European cattle suffer from the bovine equivalent of heat exhaustion. They eat poorly and do not seek food actively (as cattle must where pastures are sparse). Their fertility is lowered by poor nutrition and still further reduced by high body temperatures.

The zebu, of course, thrives in the tropics. Its skin, thicker than that of European cattle, can better resist ticks

15. SAHIWAL

16. KANGAYAM

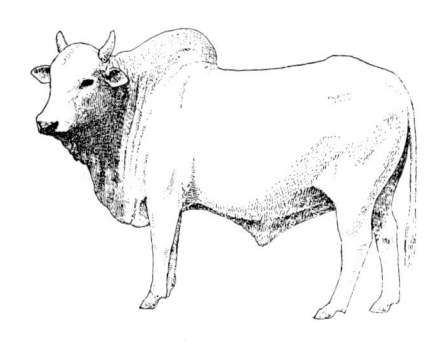

17. BORAN

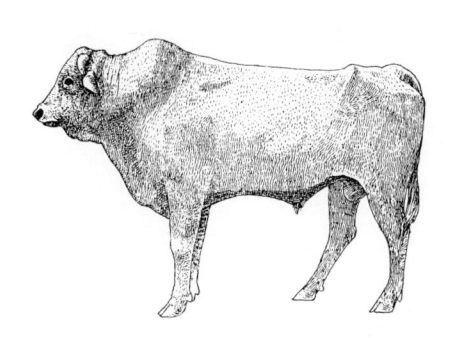

21. EGYPTIAN

22. ANKOLE

23. CHINESE "YELLOW COW"

cattle in many parts of the world has produced mixtures of quite varied appearances (19-23). The Santa Gertrudis, a recently developed breed based on a Brahman-Shorthorn cross, has in recent years become an important beef producer in the Gulf states.

and stinging flies. It can digest crude fodder, though not so well as the buffalo. And it keeps cool. For one thing, its coat is thinner than those of the European breeds; for another, most zebus are light-colored and absorb less sunlight. There are indications that the zebu may have more, or more effective, sweat glands than European cattle. Apparently the principal reason the zebu keeps cool is that it produces less body heat, even though it is typically more active than European cattle. How it manages this metabolic trick is a mystery which investigators are currently trying to unravel.

Efforts to combine the zebu's resistance to heat and the European breeds' high productivity have already achieved considerable success. An outstanding example is the Santa Gertrudis, a breed developed from a Brahman-Shorthorn cross, which during the past 20 years has become an important producer in our Gulf States. Crosses between Jerseys and various milking breeds of zebus also are yielding good results. The Jamaica Hope, a Jersey-Sahiwal cross, already approaches the U. S. average in milk production.

A less urgent but equally challenging objective is the development of breeds adapted to the cold climates of northern Canada and Siberia. The Mongolians and Tibetans have long crossed cattle with the yak to produce an animal combining some of the yak's hardiness with the cow's milking capacity. Unfortunately only the females of these crosses are fertile. The Canadian government has crossed cattle with bison to produce the "catalo," and has even bred a cattle-bison-yak, but neither of these combinations has yet shown any particular economic advantages.

Not very much is known about the cattle breeds in the underdeveloped areas of the world. It may well be that combinations of these types with the better-known breeds would produce more productive breeds of cattle for specific conditions. One obstacle to such experimentation is that infections such as the hoof-and-mouth disease and rinderpest are prevalent among cattle in many underdeveloped regions, and it is dangerous to import breeding animals or even semen from such areas. But we can hope that the obstacles will be overcome, so that better cattle and better raising methods will become available to meet the growing world population's need for protein food and to add more meat to the diet of the many peoples in underdeveloped countries who now get very little.

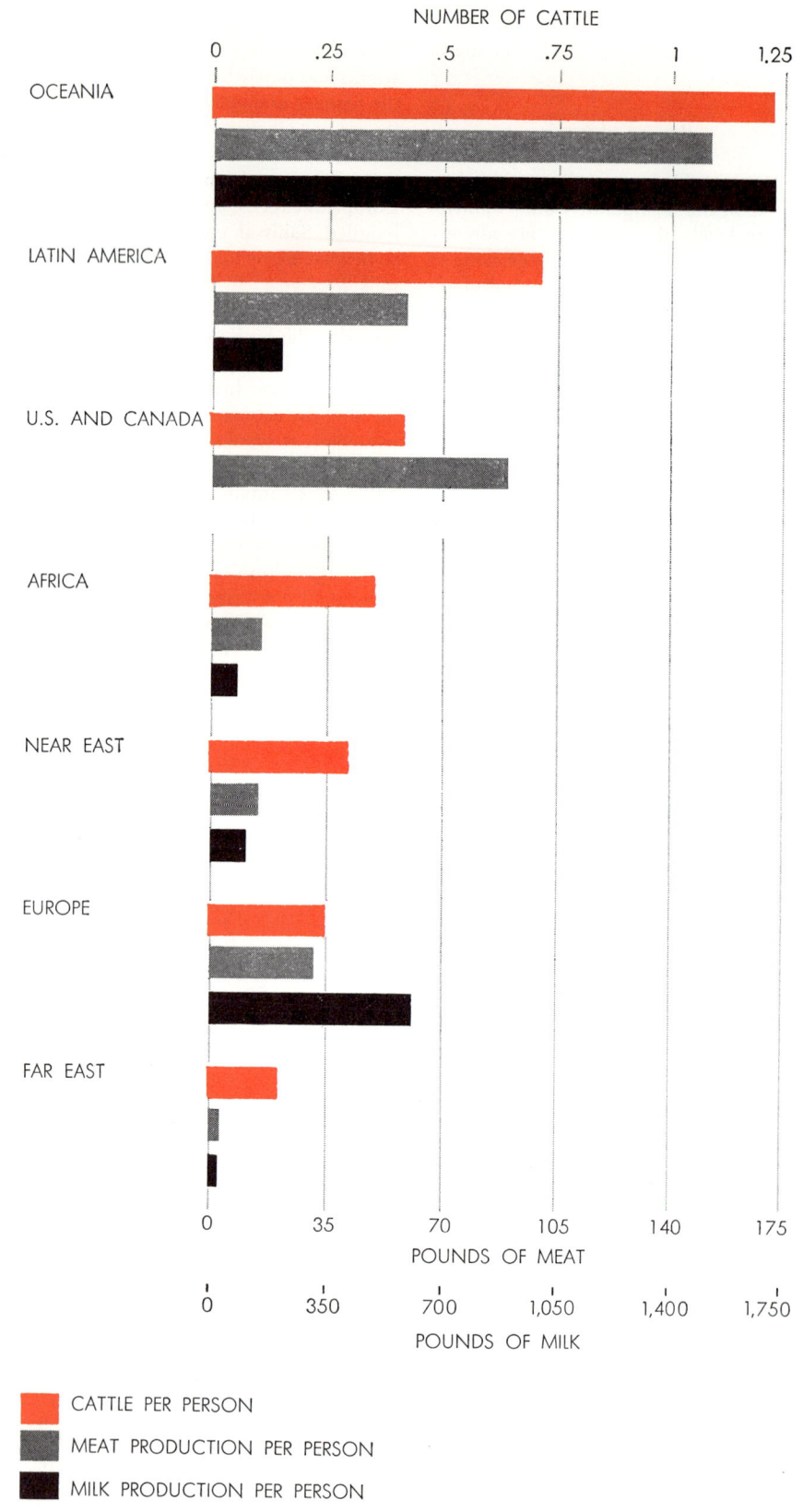

NUMBERS AND PRODUCTIVITY of cattle in proportion to population vary in different regions. High figures for Oceania reflect large cattle industries and low population of Australia and New Zealand. In Latin America dairying is much less important; cattle in most areas are of poor quality. U. S., Canada and Europe have fewer but more productive cattle. In Africa, Near East and Far East cattle are used mainly for work and produce little food.

POULTRY PRODUCTION

WILBOR O. WILSON
July 1966

The per capita consumption of poultry in the U.S. has more than doubled during the past 30 years. To meet the demand, automatic factories today convert tons of feed into tons of meat and eggs

The term "chicken feed" used to be a synonym for insignificance. Biologically and agriculturally the domestic fowl were not a major factor in American life. Over the past 30 years, however, their status has changed remarkably. Today the production of poultry is no longer a trivial or small-scale business. A few figures will illustrate the dimensions of the change. In 1935 the annual consumption of poultry in the U.S. amounted to 13.1 pounds of chicken and 1.5 pounds of turkey per capita; in 1965 the consumption per person had risen to 33.3 pounds of chicken and 7.4 pounds of turkey. Thirty years ago comparatively few commercial egg farmers kept more than 2,500 hens; nowadays ranches consisting of 30,000 laying hens are not uncommon, and the average annual production of eggs has been increased from 121 per hen in 1930 to 217 per hen today.

Paradoxically, although the poultry industry has grown greatly in size, it has almost disappeared from sight on the American scene. A generation ago nine out of 10 farms in the U.S. kept chickens or other poultry; today in much of the countryside the chicken yard is becoming a rarity. Poultry production is now conducted mainly in establishments that are best described as factories. A technological revolution has transformed this field of agriculture, and in so doing it has raised poultry to a position of new importance in man's economy.

Origins of Poultry Production

The cultivation of poultry as a food source is actually a rather recent development. Chickens were domesticated early in man's history (witness the cock's crow mentioned in the Bible and the painting of a cock on a potsherd found in the Egyptian tomb of Tutankhamen), but it appears that these animals at first were used primarily for the sport of cockfighting. Until the 20th century the chicken was prized more as a showpiece than as an item for the table. Beautiful breeds of chickens were raised for exhibition, and more than 200 varieties of them, bearing names such as the Golden Laced Wyandotte and the Speckled Sussex, were measured by a "Standard of Perfection" in appearance that was established by the American Poultry Association in 1874. It was not until about 1910 that the raising of hens for egg-laying became a more important enterprise in the U.S. than the breeding of fancy poultry for exhibition.

Nonetheless, the domestic fowl have historically contributed to man's material welfare and his culture in a multitude of ways. The Declaration of Independence was written with a quill pen made from a goose feather. Painters since early times have used egg yolk as a durable vehicle for pigments. In California today geese are employed to weed the cotton fields: they eat the grassy weeds and leave the cotton plants alone. Another useful fowl, developed in our laboratory at the University of California at Davis, is the Japanese quail: requiring very little cage space and laying more than 300 eggs a year, this bird has proved to be an excellent subject for the testing of antifertility drugs.

Our debt to the chicken in science and medicine is profound. It was the ill effects of a diet of polished rice on a flock of chickens, first investigated by the Dutch physician Christiaan Eijkman in 1896, that led to the discovery of vitamins and their dietary importance. The chicken was one of the chief early instruments for studies of the sex hormones, because of its conspicuous manifestations of their effects, particularly on the cock's comb. Louis Pasteur's development of the first vaccine for a bacterial disease (anthrax of cattle) originated from his investigation of fowl cholera. Later the chick embryo—that is, the fertilized chick egg—was found to be an ideal medium for culturing microorganisms, including viruses, and this led to the conquest of many infectious diseases. Today a stubborn disease of poultry—fowl leukosis—serves as one of the most useful experimental tools in the investigation of cancer.

Modern Poultry Production

This article is concerned with the production of poultry as food. In the U.S. this essentially means the production of chickens and turkeys. Other birds—guinea fowl, ducks, geese, swans, pigeons, peafowl and quail—are important contributors to the food supply elsewhere in the world and may become so in the U.S. in the future, but they are not a large factor here at the present time. The chicken, of course, is universal. The turkey is indigenous to America and was raised by the Indians long before the Europeans arrived; according to the archaeological evidence, Indians in New Mexico domesticated the bird thousands of years ago.

Until recent years the practicable size of poultry flocks was rigorously limited by technical difficulties. Diseases and other factors that attacked the birds under crowded conditions made it impossible to handle and sustain large flocks economically. Elaborate forms of management were tried but all failed. In the 1930's, however, intensive research promoted by the Poultry Science Association and carried out by investigators at agricultural experiment stations in the U.S. began to yield solutions to the problems. The advances fall under four headings: improved breeding, improved feeding, control of disease and improved management, including mechanization.

The breeding of chickens has gone through an evolution of drastic change in objectives. Originally and up to fairly recent times the breeders selected chickens primarily for their fighting ability. Then, in the exhibition era, the animals were bred for fancy feathers, combs, colors and shapes. Today the breeders' objectives are utilitarian and twofold: maximum meat production and maximum egg production.

As it happens, these goals are difficult to attain in one bird. Large birds tend to have low egg production, and good egg-layers tend to be small—about half the size of the meat breeds. Chickens such as the Plymouth Rock, the Wyandotte and the Rhode Island Red were developed in the latter half of the 19th century as a compromise. Produced by crossbreeding between the two types, they are of fairly good size and give fairly good egg production. In the present system of poultry production, however, specialization is the rule. Poultry farmers raise their birds either for meat or for egg production, and they select their breeds for high performance in one or the other.

The pioneer of modern fowl breeding was the British biologist William Bateson, who even before Gregor Mendel's genetic experiments with plants were generally known had discovered the same basic principles of inheritance in experiments with chickens. These principles, involving the action of single genes, apply with particular fidelity to feather color and comb type. Rate of growth—the ability to gain weight rapidly in the first few weeks of life—is under the control of a number of genes that act additively. This too is a highly heritable characteristic.

One instance of selection concerns the work of British breeders. They developed a tightly feathered, well-muscled chicken called the Cornish. It laid few eggs and had low fertility, and for many years it was used only for exhibition. The Cornish, however, eventually was found to be an excellent stock for meat birds, and most of the modern strains of fryers or broilers are descended from that stock on one side of the family tree.

Breeding for egg production turned

POULTRY STRAINS that lead in popularity today often have some distant European and Asiatic ancestors in common, but they are fundamentally the product of selective breeding programs in which many new varieties and strains have been developed during the past 20 years. A strain-cross involving two strains of the single-comb White Leghorn variety (*a*) yields a superior producer of white eggs. A variety-cross of the Rhode Island Red with the

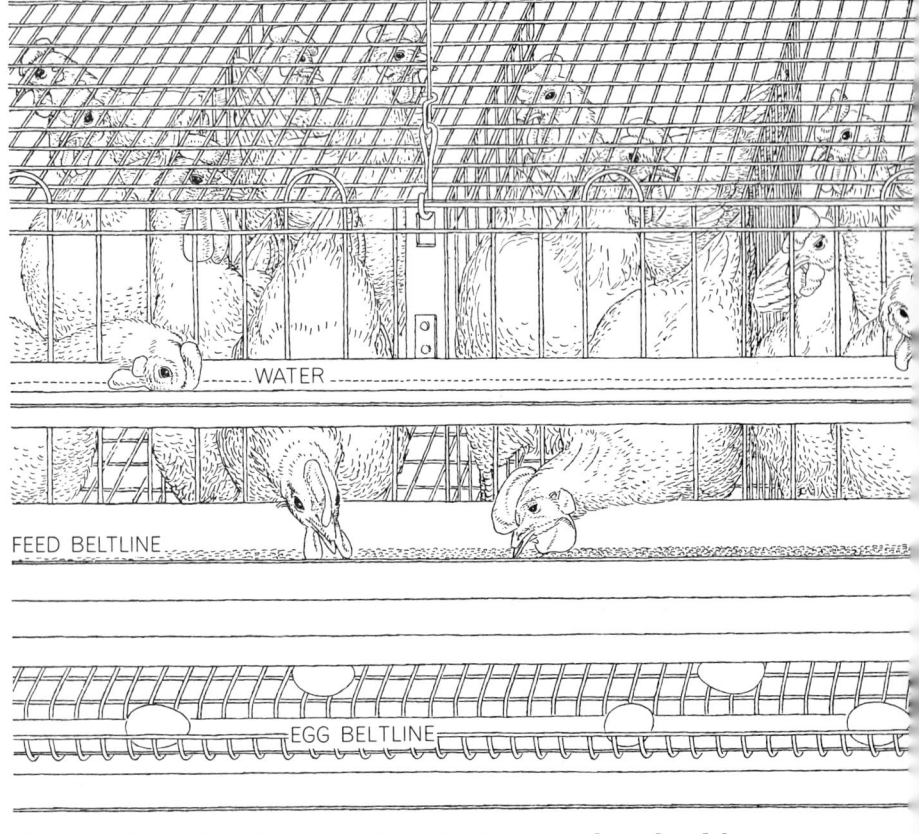

MODERN EGG FACTORY automatically handles the nutrient demands and the egg output of large numbers of virtually immobilized laying hens. Feed reaches the birds on a moving

Barred Plymouth Rock (*b*) yields chicks with a sex-linked gene affecting feather color. The cockerels are readily culled 24 hours after hatching; the hens are superior producers of brown eggs. The meat fowl are larger than egg fowl and often have Cornish blood in their ancestry. One such rooster (*c*) and a White Plymouth Rock hen, when crossed, yield a hen whose offspring are prime broiler fowl. Because dark pinfeathers are objectionable, the Broad-Breasted Bronze turkey (*d*) is not often raised for market. Instead the Bronzes have been bred with white-feathered turkeys, such as the White Holland, to produce birds with the best features of both.

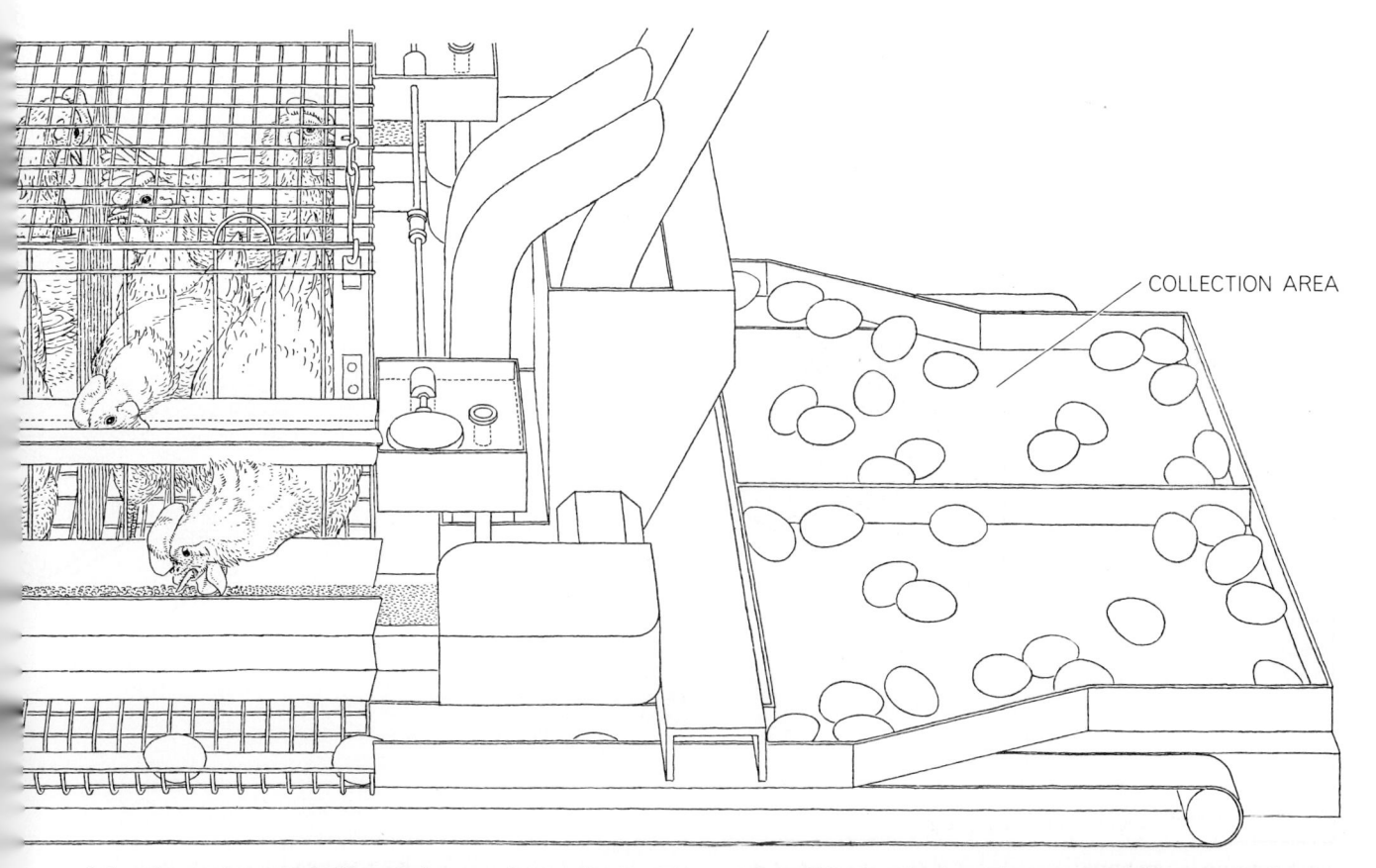

belt and water in a trough. The cage bottoms slope so that, as soon as a hen lays an egg, it rolls away to a moving belt and is carried to a collection area. A single factory building may house more than 50,000 hens, which produce an average 3,000 dozen eggs a day.

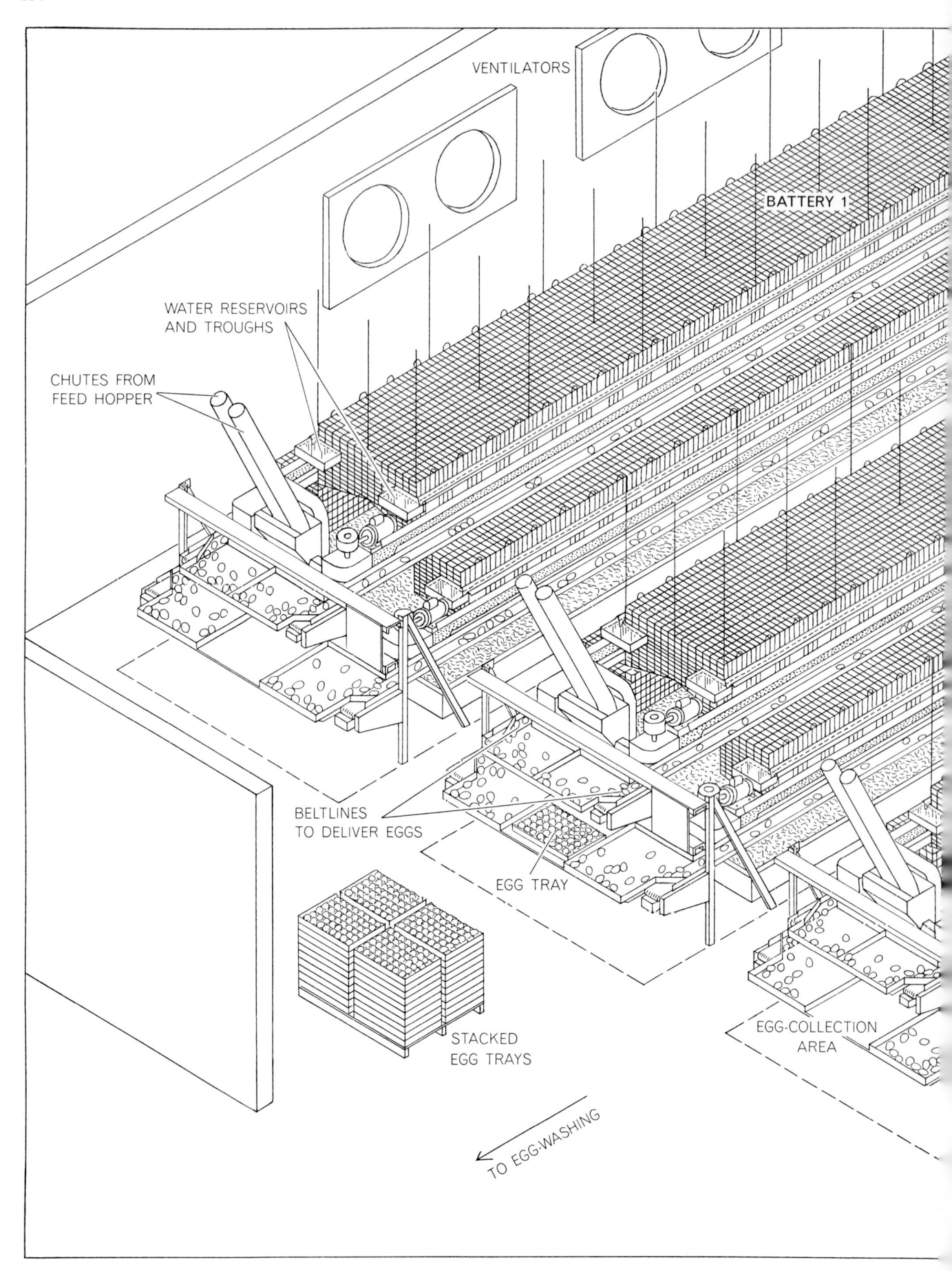

TWO-TIERED BATTERIES are suspended from the roof of the egg-production unit illustrated. In cross section the four rows of cages in each battery form two "stairsteps" back to back. Each cage contains two or three hens. Suspension from above facilitates me-

out to be more difficult. This capacity seems to be less accurately controlled by a bird's genes than body weight or feather color is. Moreover, egg production is greatly influenced by diet and by environmental circumstances, making it difficult to assess the fowl's inherent laying capacity. Finally, an egg farmer is interested not only in the number of eggs a hen produces but also in the size, color and quality of the eggs, and these properties are not under a single genetic control. Scientific testing in recent years has shown, however, that heredity is an important factor in the improvement of laying breeds. Different strains of hens, reared under basically the same conditions, have been found to vary in production by as many as 45 eggs a year.

A bird, unlike a plant, is not altogether at the mercy of its environment. It maintains its own internal stability (homeostasis) and thus can tolerate considerable variation in the weather. Furthermore, in poultry husbandry today conditions such as temperature and light are carefully controlled; diet can be accurately suited to the bird; resistance to disease can be supplied by vaccination. All of this helps to simplify the breeding of chickens and turkeys for productive capacity; the breeder does not need to be so concerned, as in plant-crop breeding, with genetic adaptation to local climates or specific diseases. Indeed, today's breeders have developed birds that are raised the world around.

Since 1932 the Poultry Husbandry Department of the University of California at Berkeley has been breeding a population of hens for improvement in egg production. The feeding, housing and management of the birds have been kept more or less uniform; no outside genetic material has been introduced since 1941, and the only important variable has been the progressive selection of the best layers in the flock for reproduction. The experiment has produced a steady rise in the annual production of eggs per hen [see bottom illustration on page 136], even though inbreeding, such as this flock has experienced, usually reduces egg-laying capacity. Hybridization by the crossing of inbred strains could have increased the gain, and the use of hybrid chickens is now common practice in commercial husbandry.

Of the nearly 200 varieties of chickens that used to be raised in the U.S., only four or five are commercially important today. The meat breeds, as I have mentioned, can all trace their ancestry in part to the Cornish breed. Practically all the important egg-laying strains are derived from the Leghorn breed. The popular present strains of turkeys (featuring white feathers and a plump breast) can also be traced back to a single superior stock: a breed called the Broad-Breasted Bronze that was developed in England and introduced in the U.S. in the 1930's.

Chicken Feed

Turning now to the feeding of poultry, we must observe that the modern fowl thrives on a diet almost totally foreign to any food it ever found in nature. Its feed is a product of the laboratory. The nutrition of the chicken has been investigated more thoroughly than that of most other animals, including man. It was by experiments on chickens that investigators determined the needs of animals for vitamin D (the sunshine, or cod-liver-oil, vitamin), the antihemorrhagic vitamin K, the vitamin-B complex, vitamin G (riboflavin) and various essential minerals. Fowl are primarily grain eaters, but research has established that they cannot live by grain alone. Their requirements of protein, minerals, vitamins and energy-suppliers have been established in much detail, and ways have been found to enhance the efficiency of their diet by artificial supplements such as antibiotics. Since cost is a prime factor in successful poultry husbandry, the computer has been enlisted to calculate the correct proportions of various available ingredients that differ in price in order to achieve a ration of fixed dietary value at minimum expense.

The barnyard fowl used to live on scraps from the farmer's table and what insects and grain it could find in the field. Later it was promoted to a standard feed consisting of a mixture of four grains and meat and bone scraps, supplemented with milk and greens. In the present poultry factories the ration is one omnibus mixture containing all the necessary ingredients, presented in the form of a mash or in pellets. The ration varies, of course, with the bird: a growing pullet, for example, needs more vitamins and protein than a mature, laying hen does.

The efficiency of a fowl's conversion of feed into meat or eggs, under favorable conditions, is impressive. In a 1964 egg-laying test in California the average production of the hens entered was better than a pound of eggs for each three pounds of feed consumed by the bird. Young fryers marketed at the age of eight weeks weigh about four pounds and generally yield about a pound of

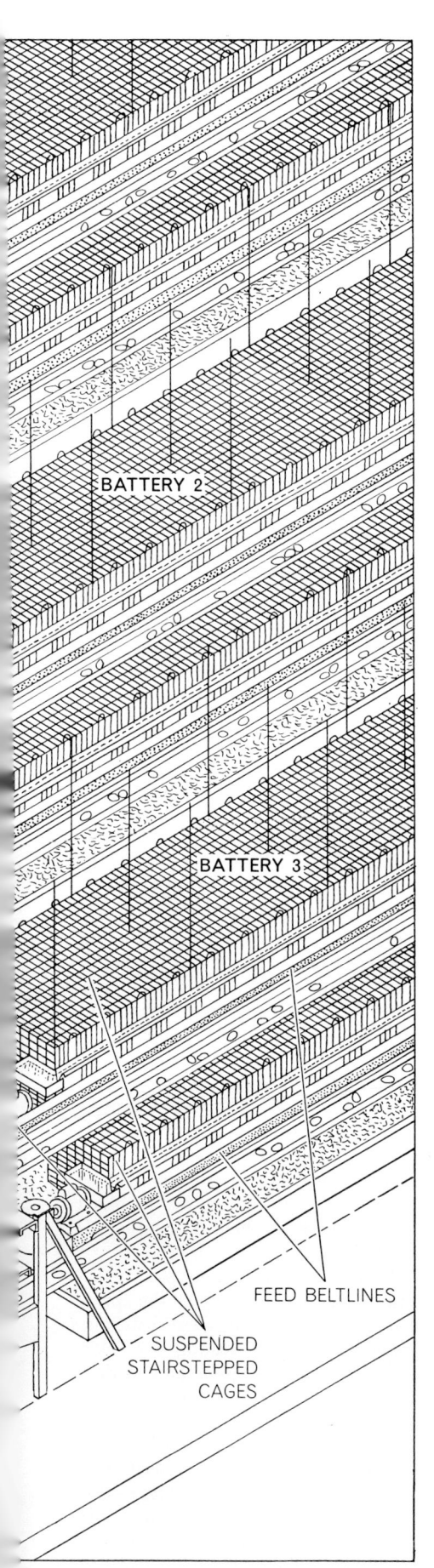

chanical cleaning; a 20,000-bird flock produces more than a ton of droppings a day.

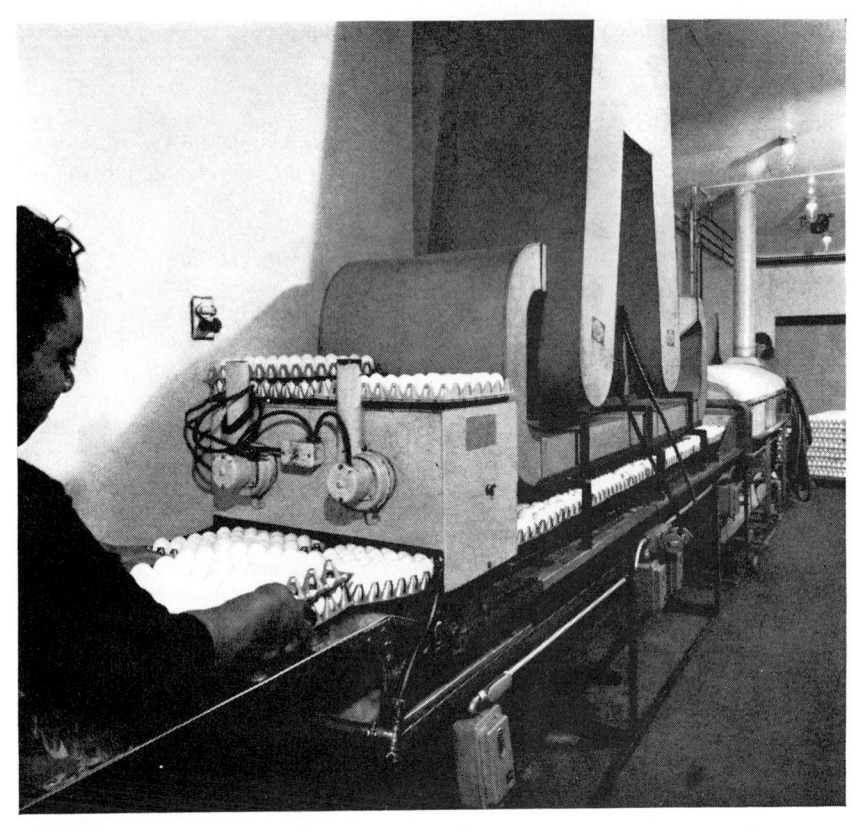

WASHING EGGS is one of the final steps en route to market. After leaving the washing machine eggs often receive light coating of oil to reduce evaporation before consumption.

CANDLING MACHINE moves 30 dozen eggs a minute past two inspectors who keep watch not only for eggs that are not clean or have cracked shells but also for any internal defects.

body weight for each two pounds of feed they have eaten. The turkey does even better: up to the age of six weeks it converts each pound of food into nearly a pound of tissue. From the sixth to the 26th week turkeys gain weight at the rate of more than a pound a week. As chickens and turkeys grow larger and older, the efficiency of their conversion of feed into meat declines.

Along with the advances in nutrition, considerable progress has been made in the control of poultry diseases. By improved sanitary practices, the use of medicated feeds and vaccination poultrymen in the U.S. have eradicated fowl plague and greatly reduced the toll from formerly catastrophic diseases such as coccidiosis, pullorum disease, bronchitis, laryngotracheitis, Newcastle disease (a viral invasion of the nervous system), fowl pox, fowl cholera and fowl typhoid. In spite of these gains, however, the overall disease mortality among chickens has been reduced only moderately: from about 20 percent 25 years ago to 15 percent today. The chief reason for the persisting high rate is leukosis, the cancer-like disease of the blood. In chickens and turkeys, as in man, this leukemic disorder still frustrates the search for prevention or cure.

Mechanization

Undoubtedly the most striking change that has taken place in the poultry industry is in the scale of its operations and the standardization, or mechanization, of nearly all its processes. Once the hen has delivered its offspring in the form of eggs, the hatching and rearing of the young can be taken over entirely by artificial devices. In present practice the procedure is so highly mechanized that from the hatching of the egg to the delivery of the final product in the supermarket (a dozen boxed eggs or a neatly packaged fryer) almost no human handling is involved.

There are highly efficient poultry factories today that integrate all the operations under one management: hatching, production of feed, rearing both egg-layers and meat chickens and marketing the products. For the most part, however, poultrymen still obtain their raw materials from special processors: chicks from hatcheries and feed from dealers in that commodity. The feed is delivered not in the cotton sacks that once provided material for the farmer's wife's dresses but by the ton in bulk. In the egg-producing branch of the industry there are specialists who rear the

AUTOMATIC FEEDING of turkeys is accomplished by a weekly filling of hoppers that hold 500 pounds of feed at the Ephrata Turkey Farm in Ephrata, Pa. Up to the age of six weeks turkeys eat only a little more than a pound of feed for each pound that they gain.

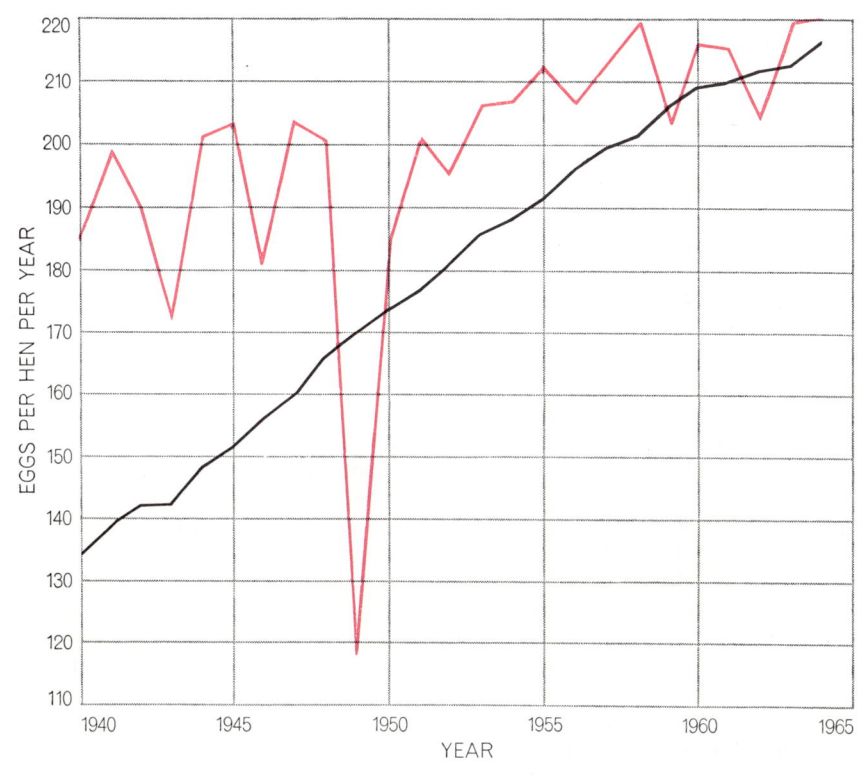

NUMBER OF EGGS produced in a year by the average hen in the U.S. has risen more than 40 percent in the past 25 years (*black curve*). Although part of the gain is due to improved feeding and shelter, selective breeding has been the predominant factor. One example is the 15 percent increase within a genetically closed flock at the University of California at Berkeley (*colored curve*); each generation's best layers mothered the next generation. The large production dip in 1949 reflects an outbreak of Newcastle disease during that year. The chart is based on the work of Hans Abplanalp and I. M. Lerner of the University of California.

chicks through the pullet stage and then deliver them to the egg rancher. The pullet rancher receives only female chicks; the crowing of the chanticleer is never heard on his ranch. The supplying hatchery determines the sex of its chicks when they are a day old. The supplier then kills the males and ships the females.

The term "ranch" in this industry is now in a sense a misnomer, as the "ranches" consist of roofed buildings. In the comparatively mild climate of California these are generally open to the air. Many modern poultry houses, however, are entirely enclosed (some even have no windows) so that the light, temperature, humidity and ventilation can be controlled with precision. It has been found that the control of light during the rearing of pullets can increase their later egg production as laying hens and even influence the size of their eggs; it can also improve the growth of meat chickens and turkeys and reduce cannibalism and other vices of poultry. Control of temperature and humidity is also important, particularly during the early weeks of growth. After the first few weeks of brooding, during which the young fowl must be kept warm, the control is designed to maintain a cool, even temperature: poultry produce best at a temperature between 50 and 70 degrees Fahrenheit.

The chicken's or turkey's home today is generally a small cage, whose dimensions have been reduced as mechanization has proceeded. The laying hen used to be allowed an individual cage about 16 inches high, 12 inches wide and 18 inches deep—affording a total floor space of 1.5 square feet. Many poultrymen now keep three hens in a cage of this size, and it has been found feasible to maintain two hens in a cage only eight inches wide. The feeding of caged poultry has been thoroughly mechanized. Commonly the feed is sluiced mechanically into a trough outside the wire front of the cage, and the food delivery is regulated by a time clock. Other systems employ an electrically driven feed hopper or a large hopper in which the birds receive bulk rations that last for several days. "Chicken feed" today is measured in tons: for a flock of 60,000 hens, although each bird eats only about a quarter of a pound a day, the daily ration amounts to seven and a half tons.

The cleaning of the poultry house, the most unpleasant chore of the old-fashioned chicken farm, is now handled by skip-loading tractors or small powered cleaners of various types. The gathering of eggs, formerly the most pleasant aspect of keeping chickens, also is now fully mechanized. The hen's cage or nest is usually designed with a sloping floor so that the egg rolls gently out of the cage as soon as it is laid. (As far as can be determined, the disappearance of the egg does not make the hen neurotic.) A moving belt catches and carries off the eggs to a collection area, where they are picked up and packed by pneumatic "fingers." Before they are packed they are washed, dried and sometimes sprayed lightly with oil to protect them against evaporation and loss in quality on the way to the consumer.

The Turkey

Turkeys are raised by mass-production methods similar to those used for chickens destined for the meat market. In the turkey's case, however, the breeding of the birds for large size has markedly reduced their fertility. Consequently a large proportion of the turkeys produced today (about 90 percent of those in California) are bred by artificial insemination.

The composite result of the improvements in poultry-raising technology is a spectacular increase in the birds' health and productivity. Turkeys are marketed at 18 weeks (for females) or 22 weeks (for males) instead of at 30 to 35 weeks, and the amount of feed required to raise them to market weight has been nearly halved.

Similar improvements have been achieved with chickens. Twenty years ago it took 14 weeks and 12 pounds of feed to produce a three-pound fryer chicken; today it takes only six to seven weeks and five or six pounds of feed. Hens in well-run egg factories now produce considerably more than 240 eggs a year (the minimum required for commercial success in a modern establishment).

The mechanization of the industry naturally has reduced drastically the amount of human labor required. Studies by the University of California Agricultural Extension Service over the years show that, whereas in 1935 the labor requirement on a commercial egg farm averaged two man-hours per hen per year, in 1964 it averaged only three-tenths of a man-hour per year. The present price of eggs (and of chicken and turkey) of course reflects the improvements in production and the savings in labor. The real price of eggs, allowing for the depreciated dollar, is lower today than it was before World War II, and the price of poultry meat is considerably lower. The year-round availability of eggs and poultry has also been improved. The laying season, formerly concentrated in the months of February, March, April and May, has been extended over the entire year, and it is now uncommon to find cold-storage eggs in the market. Freshly killed turkeys, once marketed only at Thanksgiving and Christmas, are now available throughout the year. The same is true of fryer chickens, which used to be known as "spring" chickens.

Economics

The new poultry technology has radically altered both the economics of the industry and the position its products occupy in the American diet. It has made poultry production a large-scale business and yet in a sense a shrinking enterprise from the standpoint of the number of people engaged in it. As in other branches of agriculture, the pressures of price competition and advancing technology in the poultry industry compel an ever increasing enlargement of the unit of production. The small poultry farm cannot compete in efficiency with a modern mechanized ranch. Moreover, this field of agriculture receives no governmental protection in the form of price supports or production quotas. The result has been a rapid decimation of the number of poultry farmers. Even the specialized units, while growing in size, have been reduced in number. The number of chick hatcheries in California, for example, decreased from 371 in 1947 to 81 in 1964, and the number of hatcheries for turkeys from 142 to 74—this in spite of the great increase in consumption of poultry during that period. Of course, the shrinkage in the number of producing units has been more than made up for by the expansion of the size of the surviving establishments. The poultry industry today requires large capital, high technical skill, business acumen and fewer and fewer workers.

The new role of poultry in the U.S. diet represents no less pronounced a change than the position of poultry in agriculture. Turkey or chicken was once a special item reserved for Sunday dinner or holiday feasts; today it is an everyday staple. Poultry has become competitive in price with red meat and fish and is offered in inviting new forms. The aged, noble hen that used to require several hours of boiling to be made edible has been relegated to canned dog food and is replaced in the market by young fryers or broilers or by the chicken "TV dinner" and turkey roll that need only warming up. Chickens and turkeys now come with a stamp of guaranteed quality; about 85 percent of the dressed poultry sold in the U.S. is Government-inspected.

As we have noted, the annual consumption of poultry meat in the U.S. has more than doubled in the past 30 years—from 14.6 pounds per capita to 40.7 pounds. This is still considerably less than the 167 pounds of red meat the average American ate in 1965, but it seems likely that poultry will continue to gain a larger share of the meat diet.

Eggs too have been gaining steadily in favor. An egg contains only about 70 to 75 calories (thereby qualifying as a friend of the dieter), yet it is a rich source of vitamins, unsaturated fats, protein and other essential nutrients. Indeed, it would be a completely balanced food if one ate the shell! The shell's contribution (calcium) can easily be obtained from a supplement such as milk or a vegetable. Other aspects that promise a bright future for the egg as food are the extreme simplicity with which it can be prepared (notably as the boiled breakfast food) and its versatility. The egg's culinary possibilities, still only partly explored, cover a wide range, from the conversion of egg white into meringue and candies to the use of the yolk's emulsifying property to make mayonnaise or its yellow color to lend attractiveness to other dishes.

Research, particularly in the land-grant colleges and universities of the U.S., has been primarily responsible for the extraordinary development of the efficient new poultry technology and its products as a growing contribution to the U.S. food supply. It seems fair to say that continuation of the research will yield increasing benefits as time goes on.

17

THE FOOD RESOURCES OF THE OCEAN

S. J. HOLT
September 1969

The present harvest of the oceans is roughly 55 million tons a year half of which is consumed directly and half converted into fish meal. A well-managed world fishery could yield more than 200 million tons

I suppose we shall never know what was man's first use of the ocean. It may have been as a medium of transport or as a source of food. It is certain, however, that from early times up to the present the most important human uses of the ocean have been these same two: shipping and fishing. Today, when so much is being said and written about our new interests in the ocean, it is particularly important to retain our perspective. The annual income to the world's fishermen from marine catches is now roughly $8 billion. The world ocean-freight bill is nearly twice that. In contrast, the wellhead value of oil and gas from the seabed is barely half the value of the fish catch, and all the other ocean mineral production adds little more than another $250 million.

Of course, the present pattern is likely to change, although how rapidly or dramatically we do not know. What is certain is that we shall use the ocean more intensively and in a greater variety of ways. Our greatest need is to use it wisely. This necessarily means that we use it in a regulated way, so that each ocean resource, according to its nature, is efficiently exploited but also conserved. Such regulation must be in large measure of an international kind, particularly insofar as living resources are concerned. This will be so whatever may be the eventual legal regime of the high seas and the underlying bed. The obvious fact about most of the ocean's living resources is their mobility. For the most part they are lively animals, caring nothing about the lines we draw on charts.

The general goal of ecological research, to which marine biology makes an important contribution, is to achieve an understanding of and to turn to our advantage all the biological processes that give our planet its special character. Marine biology is focused on the problems of biological production, which are closely related to the problems of production in the economic sense. Our most compelling interest is narrower. It lies in ocean life as a renewable resource: primarily of protein-rich foods and food supplements for ourselves and our domestic animals, and secondarily of materials and drugs. I hope to show how in this field science, industry and government need each other now and will do so even more in the future. First, however, let me establish some facts about present fishing industries, the state of the art governing them and the state of the relevant science.

The present ocean harvest is about 55 million metric tons per year. More than 90 percent of this harvest is finfish; the rest consists of whales, crustaceans and mollusks and some other invertebrates. Although significant catches are reported by virtually all coastal countries, three-quarters of the total harvest is taken by only 14 countries, each of which produces more than a million tons annually and some much more. In the century from 1850 to 1950 the world catch increased tenfold—an average rate of about 25 percent per decade. In the next decade it nearly doubled, and this rapid growth is continuing [*see illustration on page 144*]. It is now a commonplace that fish is one of the few major foodstuffs showing an increase in global production that continues to exceed the growth rate of the human population.

This increase has been accompanied by a changing pattern of use. Although some products of high unit value as luxury foods, such as shellfish, have maintained or even enhanced their relative economic importance, the trend has been for less of the catch to be used directly as human food and for more to be reduced to meal for animal feed. Just before World War II less than 10 percent of the world catch was turned into meal; by 1967 half of it was so used. Over the same period the proportion of the catch preserved by drying or smoking declined from 28 to 13 percent and the proportion sold fresh from 53 to 31 percent. The relative consumption of canned fish has hardly changed but that of frozen fish has grown from practically nothing to 12 percent.

While we are comparing the prewar or immediate postwar situation with the present, we might take a look at the composition of the catch by groups of species. In 1948 the clupeoid fishes (herrings, pilchards, anchovies and so on), which live mainly in the upper levels of the ocean, already dominated the scene (33 percent of the total by weight) and provided most of the material for fish meal. Today they bulk even larger (45 percent) in spite of the decline of several great stocks of them (in the North Sea and off California, for example). The next most important group, the gadoid fishes (cod, haddock, hake and so on), which live mainly on or near the bottom, comprised a quarter of the total in 1948. Although the catch of these fishes has continued to increase absolutely, the proportion is now reduced to 15 percent. The flounders and other flatfishes, the rosefish and other sea perches and the mullets and jacks have collectively stayed at about 15 percent; the tunas and mackerels, at 7 percent. Nearly a fifth of the total catch continues to be recorded in statistics as "Unsorted and other"—a vast number of species and groups, each contributing a small amount to a considerable whole.

The rise of shrimp and fish meal production together account for another major trend in the pattern of fisheries development. A fifth of the 1957 catch was sold in foreign markets; by 1967, two-

140 II · CONVENTIONAL SOURCES AND RESOURCES

fifths were entering international trade and export values totaled $2.5 billion. Furthermore, during this same period the participation of the less developed countries in the export trade grew from a sixth to well over 25 percent. Most of these shipments were destined for markets in the richer countries, particularly shrimp for North America and fish meal for North America, Europe and Japan. More recently several of the less developed countries have also become importers of fish meal, for example Mexico and Venezuela, South Korea and the Republic of China.

The U.S. catch has stayed for many years in the region of two million tons, a low figure considering the size of the country, the length of the coastline and the ready accessibility of large resources on the Atlantic, Gulf and Pacific seaboards. The high level of consumption in the U.S. (about 70 pounds per capita) has been achieved through a steady growth in imports of fish and fish meal: from 25 percent of the total in 1950 to more than 70 percent in 1967. In North America 6 percent of the world's human population uses 12 percent of the world's catch, yet fishermen other than Americans take nearly twice the amount of fish that Americans take from the waters most readily accessible to the U.S.

There has not been a marked change in the broad geography of fishing [*see illustration on these two pages*]. The Pacific Ocean provides the biggest share (53 percent) but the Atlantic (40 percent, to which we may add 2 percent for the Mediterranean) is yielding considerably more per unit area. The Indian Ocean is still the source of less than 5 percent of the catch, and since it is not a biologically poor ocean it is an obvious target for future development. Within the major ocean areas, however, there have been significant changes. In the Pacific particular areas such as the waters off Peru and Chile and the Gulf of Thailand have rapidly acquired importance. The central and southern parts of the Atlantic, both east and west, are of growing interest to more nations. Al-

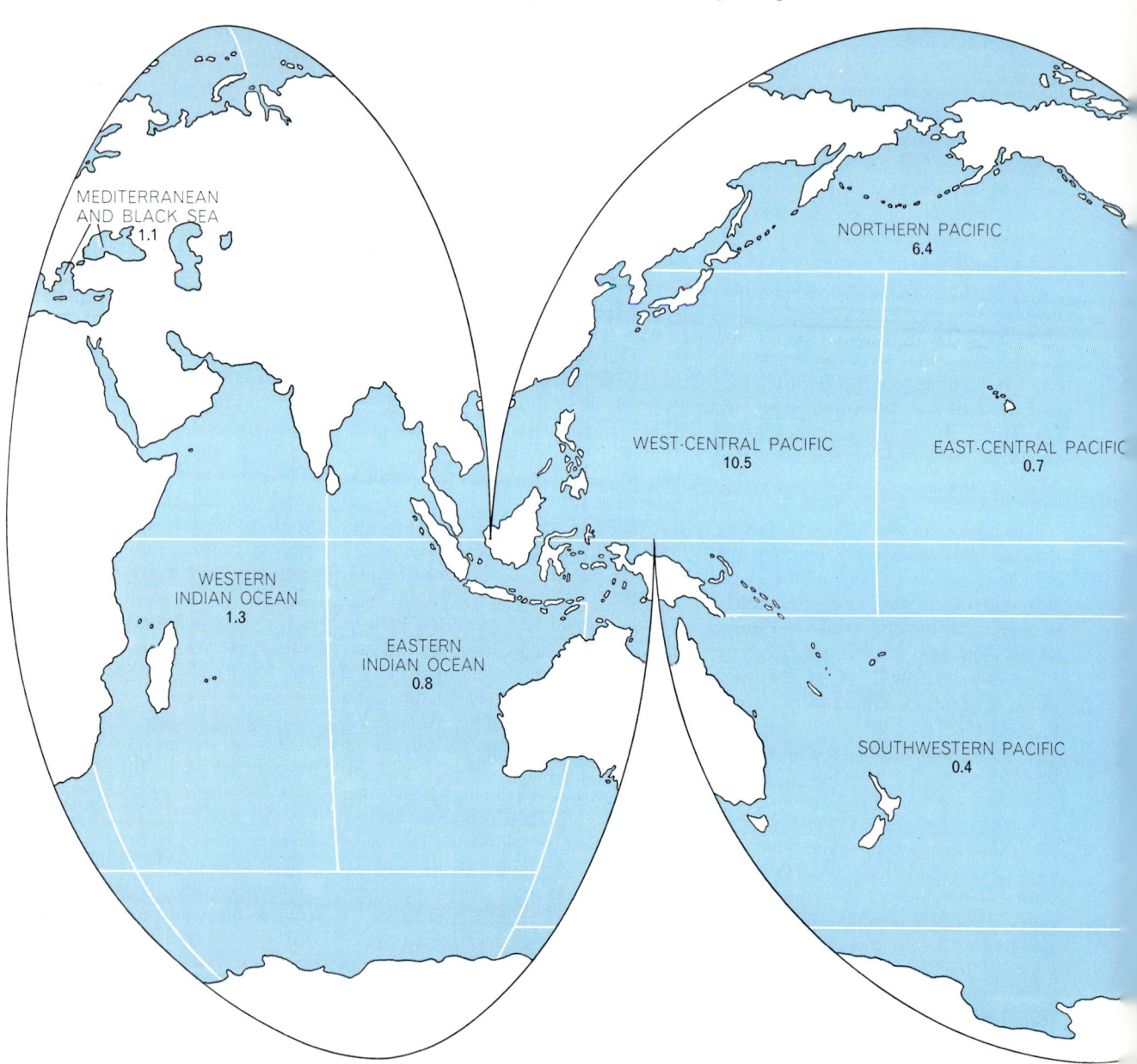

MAJOR MARINE FISHERY AREAS are 14 in number: two in the Indian Ocean (*left*), five in the Pacific Ocean (*center*) and six in the Atlantic (*right*). Due to the phenomenal expansion of the Peru fishery, the total Pacific yield is now a third larger than the Atlantic total. The bulk of Atlantic and Pacific catches, however, is still taken well north of the Equator. The Indian Ocean, with a

though, with certain exceptions, the traditional fisheries in the colder waters of the Northern Hemisphere still dominate the statistics, the emergence of some of the less developed countries as modern fishing nations and the introduction of long-range fleets mean that tropical and subtropical waters are beginning to contribute significantly to world production.

Finally, in this brief review of the trends of the past decade or so we must mention the changing importance of countries as fishing powers. Peru has become the leading country in terms of sheer magnitude of catch (although not of value or diversity) through the development of the world's greatest one-species fishery: 10 million tons of anchovies per year, almost all of which is reduced to meal [see illustration on page 146]. The U.S.S.R. has also emerged as a fishing power of global dimension, fishing for a large variety of products throughout the oceans of the world, particularly with large factory ships and freezer-trawlers.

At this point it is time to inquire about the future expectations of the ocean as a major source of protein. In spite of the growth I have described, fisheries still contribute only a tenth of the animal protein in our diet, although this proportion varies considerably from one part of the world to another. Before such an inquiry can be pursued, however, it is necessary to say something about the problem of overfishing.

A stock of fish is, generally speaking, at its most abundant when it is not being exploited; in that virgin state it will include a relatively high proportion of the larger and older individuals of the species. Every year a number of young recruits enter the stock, and all the fish—but particularly the younger ones—put on weight. This overall growth is balanced by the natural death of fish of all ages from disease, predation and perhaps senility. When fishing begins, the large stock yields large catches to each fishing vessel, but because the pioneering vessels are few, the total catch is small.

Increased fishing tends to reduce the level of abundance of the stock progressively. At these reduced levels the losses accountable to "natural" death will be less than the gains accountable to recruitment and individual growth. If, then, the catch is less than the difference between natural gains and losses, the stock will tend to increase again; if the catch is more, the stock will decrease. When the stock neither decreases nor increases, we achieve a sustained yield. This sustained yield is small when the stock is large and also when the stock is small; it is at its greatest when the stock is at an intermediate level—somewhere between two-thirds and one-third of the virgin abundance. In this intermediate stage the average size of the individuals will be smaller and the age will be younger than in the unfished condition, and individual growth will be highest in relation to the natural mortality.

The largest catch that on the average can be taken year after year without causing a shift in abundance, either up or down, is called the maximum sustainable yield. It can best be obtained by leaving the younger fish alone and fishing the older ones heavily, but we can also get near to it by fishing moderately, taking fish of all sizes and ages. This phenomenon—catches that first increase and then decrease as the intensity of fishing increases—does not depend on any correlation between the number of parent fish and the number of recruits they produce for the following generation. In fact, many kinds of fish lay so many eggs, and the factors governing survival of the eggs to the recruit stage are so many and so complex, that it is not easy to observe any dependence of the number of recruits on the number of their parents over a wide range of stock levels.

Only when fishing is intense, and the stock is accordingly reduced to a small

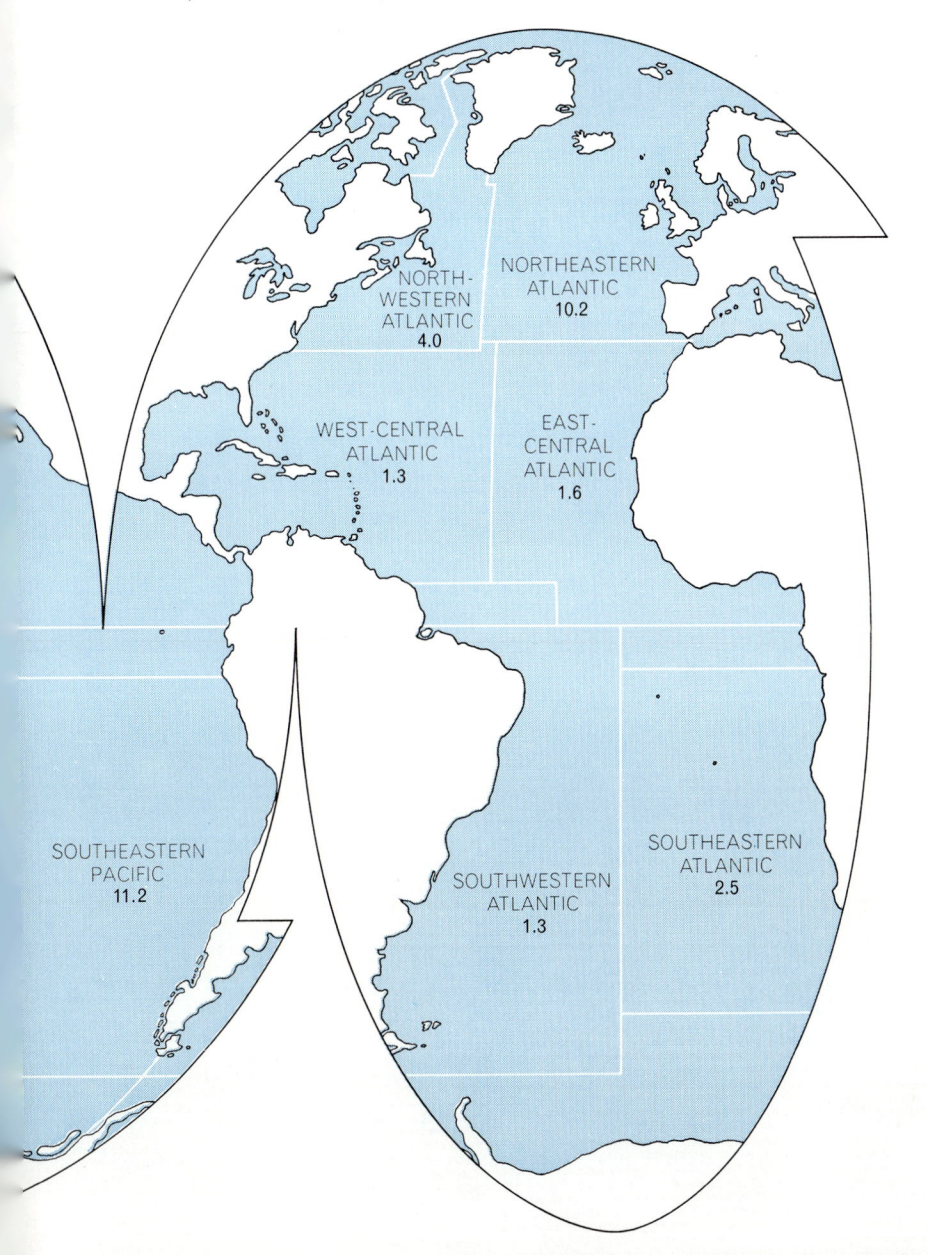

total catch of little more than two million metric tons, live weight, is the world's major underexploited region. The number below each area name shows the millions of metric tons landed during 1967, as reported by the UN Food and Agriculture Organization.

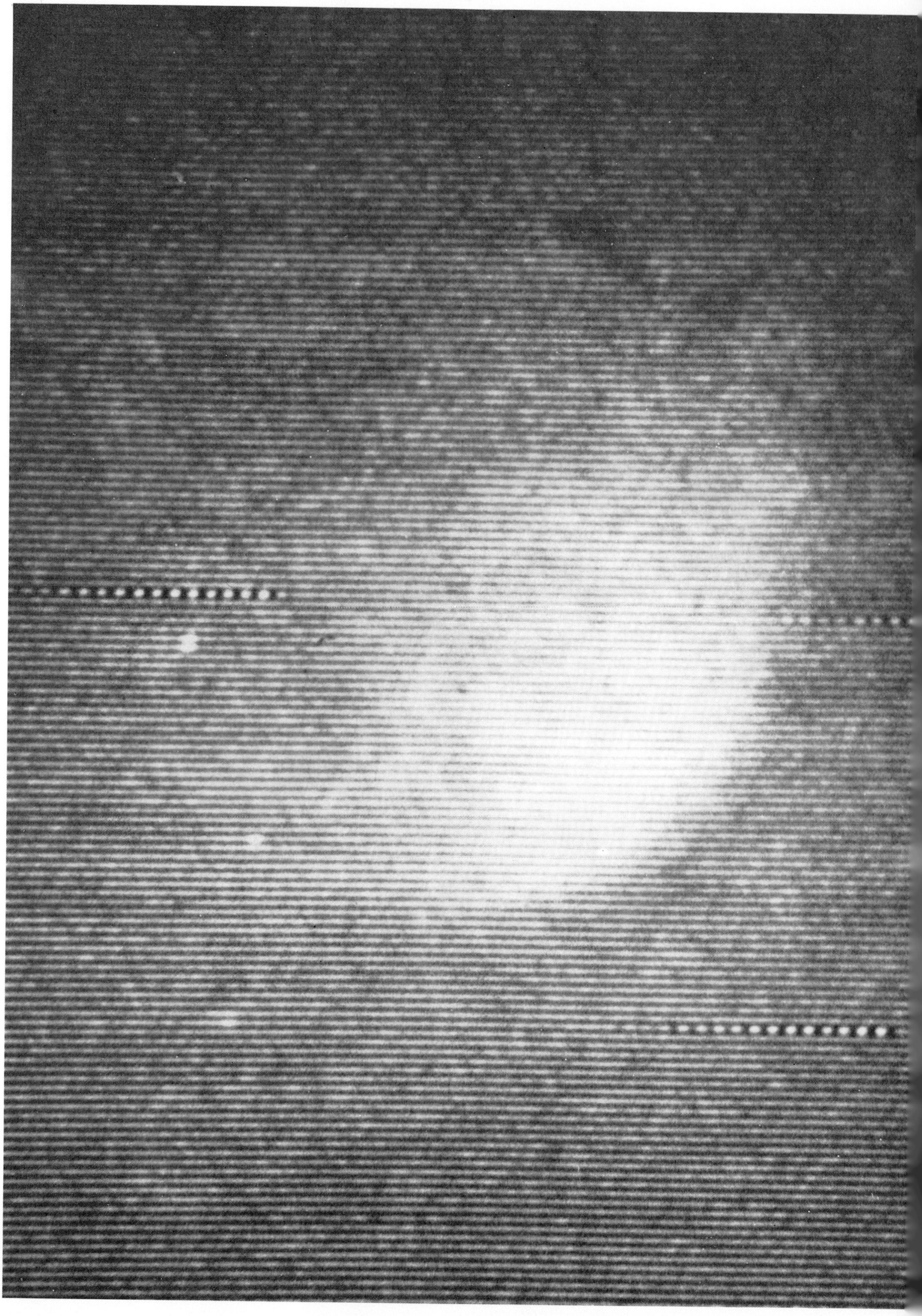

SCHOOL OF FISH is spotted from the air at night by detecting the bioluminescent glow caused by the school's movement through the water. As the survey aircraft flew over the Gulf of Mexico at an altitude of 3,500 feet, the faint illumination in the water was amplified some 55,000 times by an image intensifier before appearing on the television screen seen in the photograph on the opposite page. The fish are Atlantic thread herring. Detection of fish from the air is one of several means of increasing fishery efficiency being tested at the Pascagoula, Miss., research base of the U.S. Bureau of Commercial Fisheries.

fraction of its virgin size, do we see a decline in the number of recruits coming in each year. Even then there is often a wide annual fluctuation in this number. Indeed, such fluctuation, which causes the stock as a whole to vary greatly in abundance from year to year, is one of the most significant characteristics of living marine resources. Fluctuation in number, together with the considerable variation in "availability" (the change in the geographic location of the fish with respect to the normal fishing area), largely account for the notorious riskiness of fishing as an industry.

For some species the characteristics of growth, natural mortality and recruit-

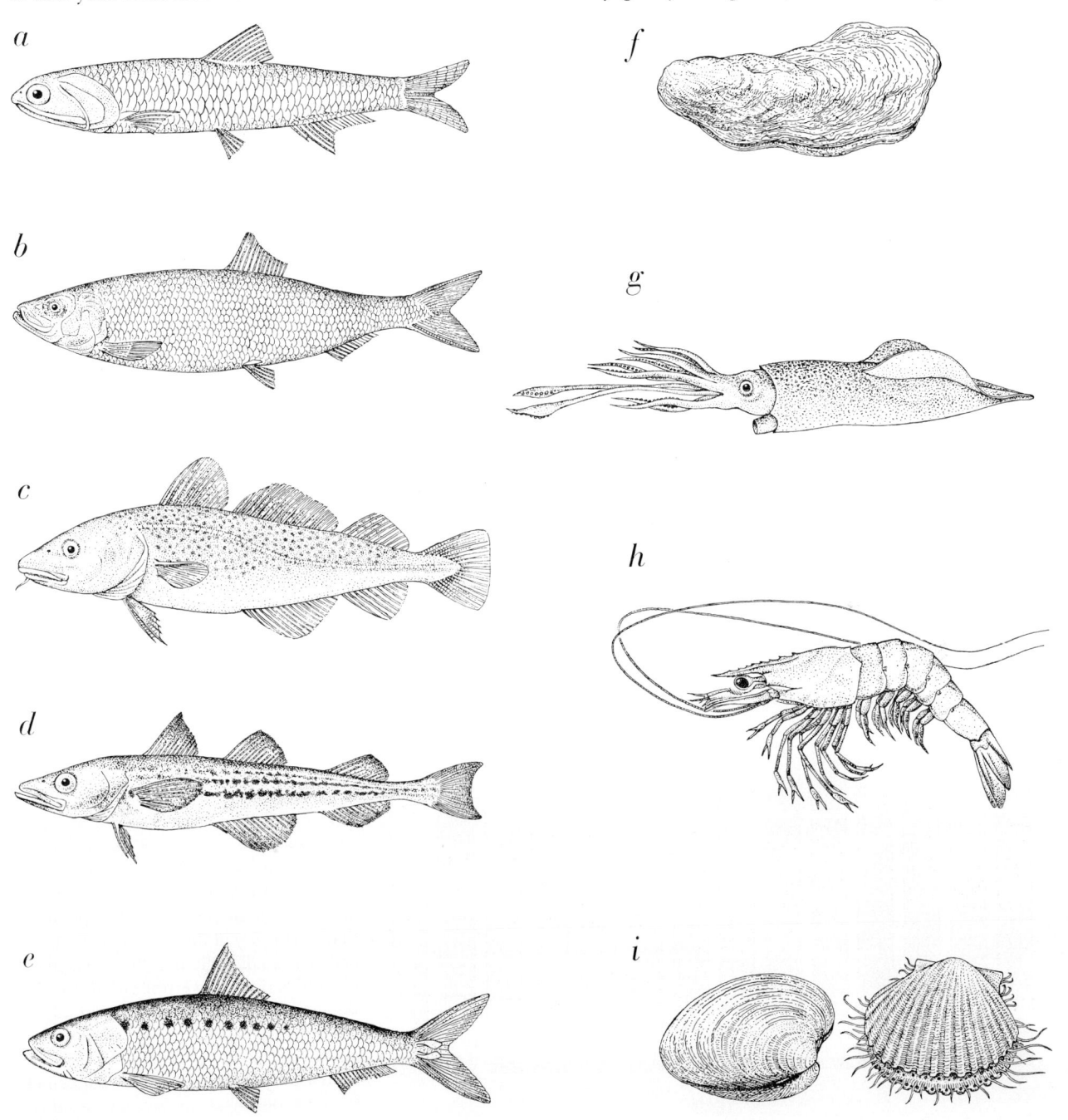

LARGEST CATCHES of individual fish species include the five fishes shown here (left). They are, according to the most recent detailed FAO fishery statistics (1967), the Peruvian anchoveta (a), with a catch of more than 10.5 million metric tons; the Atlantic herring (b), with a catch of more than 3.8 million tons; the Atlantic cod (c), with a catch of 3.1 million tons; the Alaska walleye pollack (d), with a catch of 1.7 million metric tons, and the South African pilchard (e), with a catch of 1.1 million tons. No single invertebrate species (right) is harvested in similar quantities. Taken as a group, however, various oyster species (f) totaled .83 million tons in 1967; squids (g), .75 million tons; shrimps and prawns (h), .69 million tons; clams and cockles (i), .48 million tons.

ment are such that the maximum sustainable yield is sharply defined. The catch will decline quite steeply with a change in the amount of fishing (measured in terms of the number of vessels, the tonnage of the fleet, the days spent at sea or other appropriate index) to either below or above an optimum. In other species the maximum is not so sharply defined; as fishing intensifies above an optimum level the sustained catch will not significantly decline, but it will not rise much either.

Such differences in the dynamics of different types of fish stock contribute to the differences in the historical development of various fisheries. If it is unregulated, however, each fishery tends to expand beyond its optimum point unless something such as inadequate demand hinders its expansion. The reason is painfully simple. It will usually still be profitable for an individual fisherman or ship to continue fishing after the *total* catch from the stock is no longer increasing or is declining, and even though his own rate of catch may also be declining. By the same token, it may continue to be profitable for the individual fisherman to use a small-meshed net and thereby catch young as well as older fish, but in doing so he will reduce both his own possible catch and that of others in future years. Naturally if the total catch is declining, or not increasing much, as the amount of fishing continues to increase, the net economic yield from the fishery—that is, the difference between the total costs of fishing and the value of the entire catch—will be well past its maximum. The well-known case of the decline of the Antarctic baleen whales provides a dramatic example of overfishing and, one would hope, a strong incentive for the more rational conduct of ocean fisheries in the future.

There is, then, a limit to the amount that can be taken year after year from each natural stock of fish. The extent to which we can expect to increase our fish catches in the future will depend on three considerations. First, how many as yet unfished stocks await exploitation, and how big are they in terms of potential sustainable yield? Second, how many of the stocks on which the existing fisheries are based are already reaching or have passed their limit of yield? Third, how successful will we be in managing our fisheries to ensure maximum sustainable yields from the stocks?

The first major conference to examine the state of marine fish stocks on a global basis was the United Nations Scientific Conference on the Conservation and Utilization of Resources, held in 1949 at Lake Success, N.Y. The small group of fishery scientists gathered there concluded that the only overfished stocks at that time were those of a few high-priced species in the North Atlantic and North Pacific, particularly plaice, halibut and salmon. They produced a map showing 30 other known major stocks they believed to be underfished. The situation was reexamined in 1968. Fishing on half of those 30 stocks is now close to or beyond that required for maximum yield. The fully fished or overfished stocks include some tunas in most ocean areas, the herring, the cod and ocean perch in the North Atlantic and the anchovy in the southeastern Pacific. The point is that the history of development of a fishery from small beginnings to the stage of full utilization or overutilization can, in the modern world, be compressed into a very few years. This happened with the anchovy off Peru, as a result of a massive local fishery growth, and it has happened to some demersal, or bottom-dwelling, fishes elsewhere through the large-scale redeployment of long-distance trawlers from one ocean area to another.

It is clear that the classical process of fleets moving from an overfished area to another area, usually more distant and less fished, cannot continue indefinitely. It is true that since the Lake Success

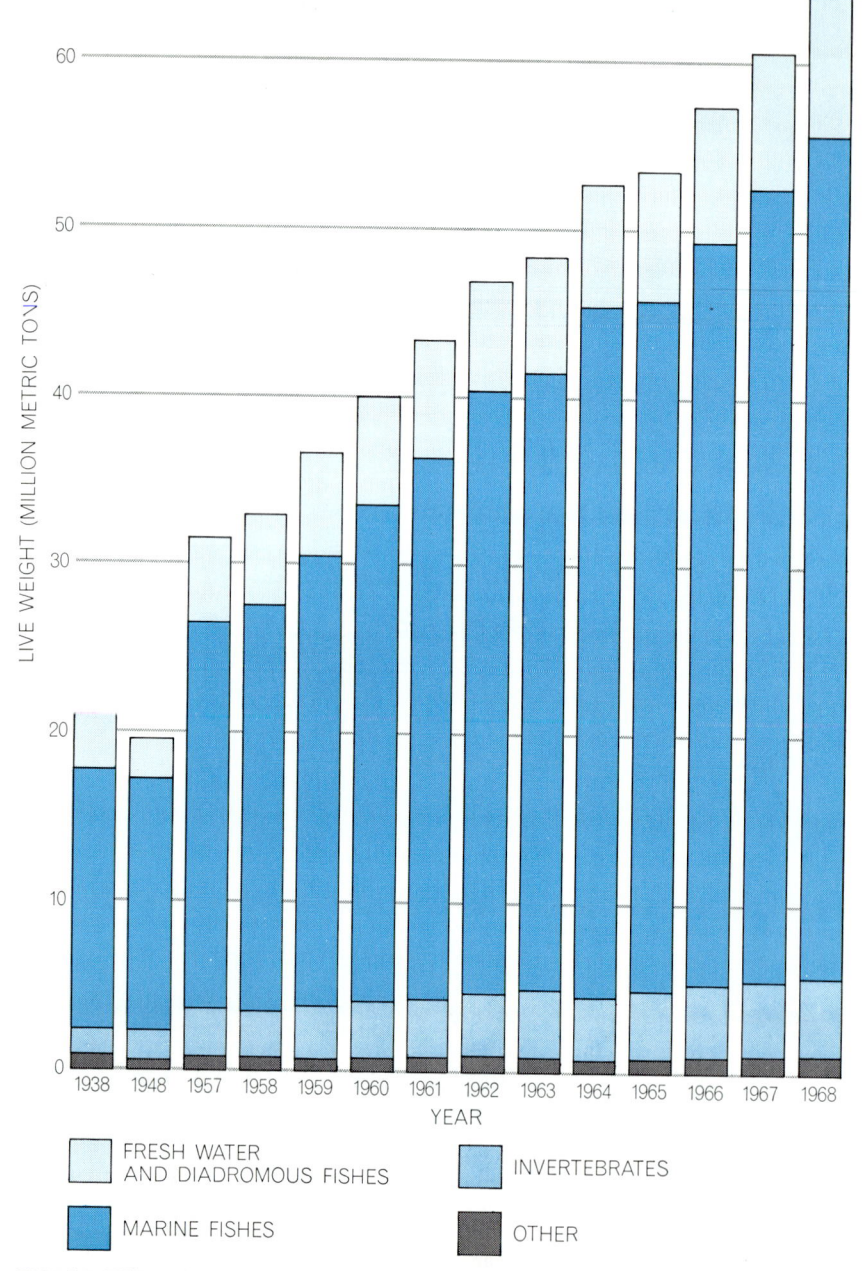

WORLD FISH CATCH has more than tripled in the three decades since 1938; the FAO estimate of the 1968 total is 64 million metric tons. The largest part consists of marine fishes. Humans directly consume only half of the catch; the rest becomes livestock feed.

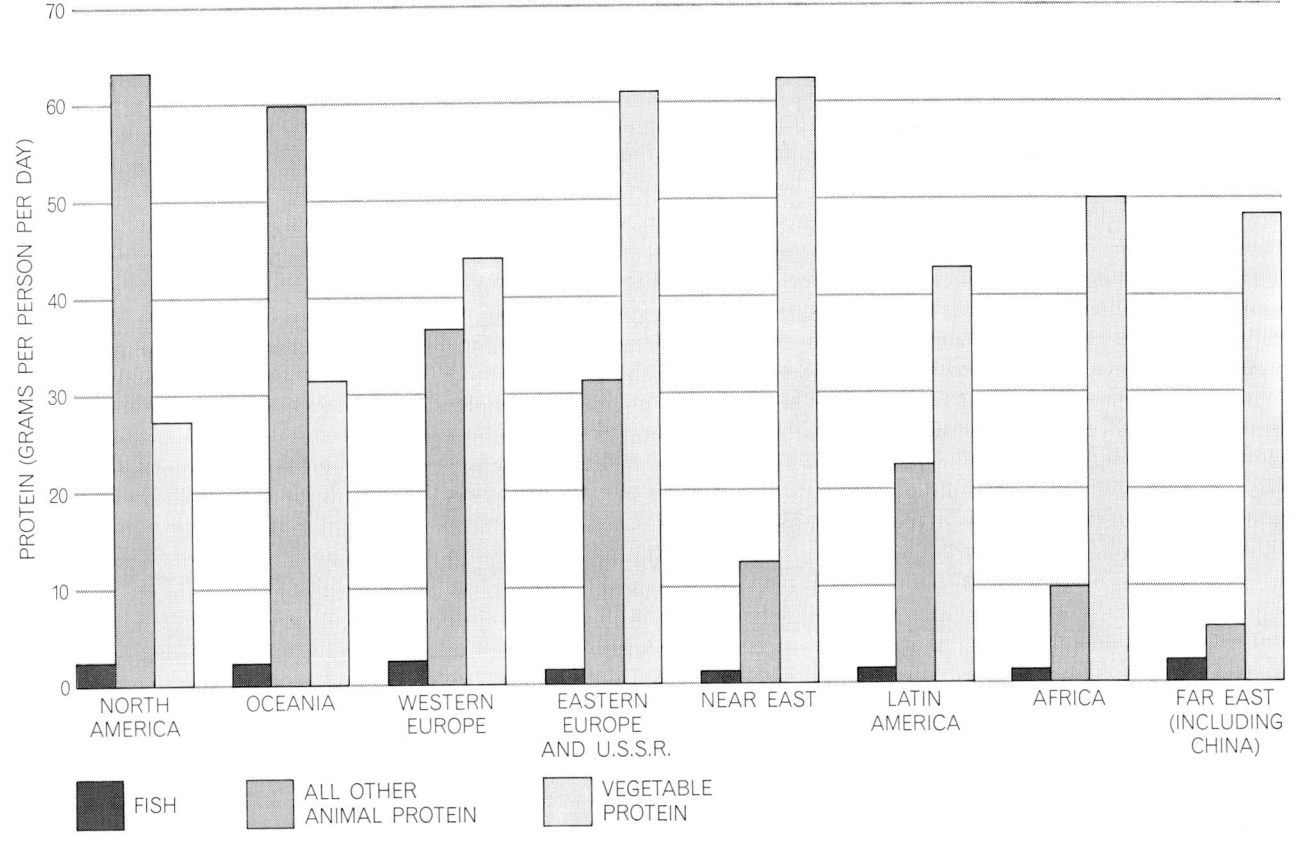

RELATIVELY MINOR ROLE played by fish in the world's total consumption of protein is apparent when the grams of fish eaten per person per day in various parts of the world (*left column in each group*) is compared with the consumption of other animal protein (*middle column*) and vegetable protein (*right column*). The supply is nonetheless growing more rapidly than world population.

meeting several other large resources have been discovered, mostly in the Indian Ocean and the eastern Pacific, and additional stocks have been utilized in fishing areas with a long history of intensive fishing, such as the North Sea. In another 20 years, however, very few substantial stocks of fish of the kinds and sizes of commercial interest and accessible to the fishing methods we know now will remain underexploited.

The Food and Agriculture Organization of the UN is now in the later stages of preparing what is known as its Indicative World Plan (IWP) for agricultural development. Under this plan an attempt is being made to forecast the production of foodstuffs in the years 1975 and 1985. For fisheries this involves appraising resource potential, envisioning technological changes and their consequences, and predicting demand. The latter predictions are not yet available, but the resource appraisals are well advanced. With the cooperation of a large number of scientists and organizations estimates are being prepared in great detail on an area basis. They deal with the potential of known stocks, both those fished actively at present and those exploited little or not at all. Some of these estimates are reliable; others are naturally little more than reasonable guesses. One fact is abundantly clear: We still have very scrappy knowledge, in quantitative terms, of the living resources of the ocean. We can, however, check orders of magnitude by comparing the results of different methods of appraisal. Thus where there is good information on the growth and mortality rates of fishes and measures of their numbers in absolute terms, quite good projections can be made. Most types of fish can now in fact virtually be counted individually by the use of specially calibrated echo sounders for area surveys, although this technique is not yet widely applied. The size of fish populations can also be deduced from catch statistics, from measurements of age based on growth rings in fish scales or bands in fish ear stones, and from tagging experiments. Counts and maps of the distribution of fish eggs in the plankton can in some cases give us a fair idea of fish abundance in relative terms. We can try to predict the future catch in an area little fished at present by comparing the present catch with the catch in another area that has similar oceanographic characteristics and basic biological productivity and that is already yielding near its maximum. Finally, we have estimates of the food supply available to the fish in a particular area, or of the primary production there, and from what we know about metabolic and ecological efficiency we can try to deduce fish production.

So far as the data permit these methods are being applied to major groups of fishes area by area. Although individual area and group predictions will not all be reliable, the global totals and subtotals may be. The best figure seems to be that the potential catch is about three times the present one; it might be as little as twice or as much as four times. A similar range has been given in estimates of the potential yield from waters adjacent to the U.S.: 20 million tons compared with the present catch of rather less than six million tons. This is more than enough to meet the U.S. demand, which is expected to reach 10 million tons by 1975 and 12 million by 1985.

Judging from the rate of fishery development in the recent past, it would be entirely reasonable to suppose that the maximum sustainable world catch of between 100 and 200 million tons could be reached by the second IWP target date, 1985, or at least by the end of the century. The real question is whether or not this will be economically worth the effort. Here any forecast is, in my view, on soft ground. First, to double the catch we have to more than double the amount of fishing, because the stocks decline in abundance as they are exploited. Moreover, as we approach the global maximum more of the stocks that are lightly fished at present will be brought down to intermediate levels. Second, fishing will become even more competitive and costly if the nations fail to agree, and agree soon, on regulations to cure overfishing situations. Third, it is quite uncertain what will happen in the long run to the costs of production and the price of protein of marine origin in relation to other protein sources, particularly from mineral or vegetable bases.

In putting forward these arguments I am not trying to damp enthusiasm for the sea as a major source of food for coming generations; quite the contrary. I do insist, however, that it would be dangerous for those of us who are interested in such development to assume that past growth will be maintained along familiar lines. We need to rationalize present types of fishing while preparing ourselves actively for a "great leap forward." Fishing as we now know it will need to be made even more efficient; we shall need to consider the direct use of the smaller organisms in the ocean that mostly constitute the diet of the fish we now catch; we shall need to try harder to improve on nature by breeding, rearing and husbanding useful marine animals and cultivating their pasture. To achieve this will require a much larger scale and range of scientific research, wedded to engineering progress; expansion by perhaps an order of magnitude in investment and in the employment of highly skilled labor, and a modified legal regime for the ocean and its bed not only to protect the investments but also to ensure orderly development and provide for the safety of men and their installations.

To many people the improvement of present fishing activities will mean increasing the efficiency of fishing gear and ships. There is surely much that could be done to this end. We are only just beginning to understand how trawls, traps, lines and seines really work. For example, every few years someone tries a new design or rigging for a deep-sea trawl, often based on sound engineering and hydrodynamic studies. Rarely do these "improved" rigs catch more than the old ones; sometimes they catch much less. The error has been in thinking that the trawl is simply a bag, collecting more or less passive fish, or at least predictably active ones. This is not so at all. We really have to deal with a complex, dynamic relation between the lively animals and their environment, which includes in addition to the physical and biological environment the fishing gear itself. We can expect success in understanding and exploiting this relation now that we can telemeter the fishing gear, study its hydrodynamics at full scale as well as with models in towing tanks, monitor it (and the fish) by means of underwater television, acoustic equipment and divers, and observe and experiment with fish behavior both in the sea and in large tanks. We also probably have something to learn from studying, before they become extinct, some kinds of traditional "primitive" fishing gear still used in Asia, South America and elsewhere—mainly traps that take advantage of subtleties of fish behavior observed over many centuries.

Successful fishing depends not so much on the size of fish stocks as on their concentration in space and time. All fishermen use knowledge of such concentrations; they catch fish where they have gathered to feed or to reproduce, or where they are on the move in streams or schools. Future fishing methods will surely involve a more active role for the fishermen in causing the fish to congregate. In many parts of the world lights or sound are already used to attract fish. We can expect more sophistication in the employment of these and other stimuli, alone and in combination.

Fishing operations as a whole also depend on locating areas of concentration and on the efficient prediction, or at least the prompt observation, of changes in these areas. The large stocks of pelagic, or open-sea, fishes are produced mainly in areas of "divergencies," where water is rising from deeper levels toward the surface and hence where surface waters are flowing outward. Many such areas are the "upwellings" off the western coasts of continental masses, for example off western and southwestern Africa, western India and western South America. Here seasonal winds, currents and continental configurations combine to cause a periodic enrichment of the surface waters.

Divergencies are also associated with

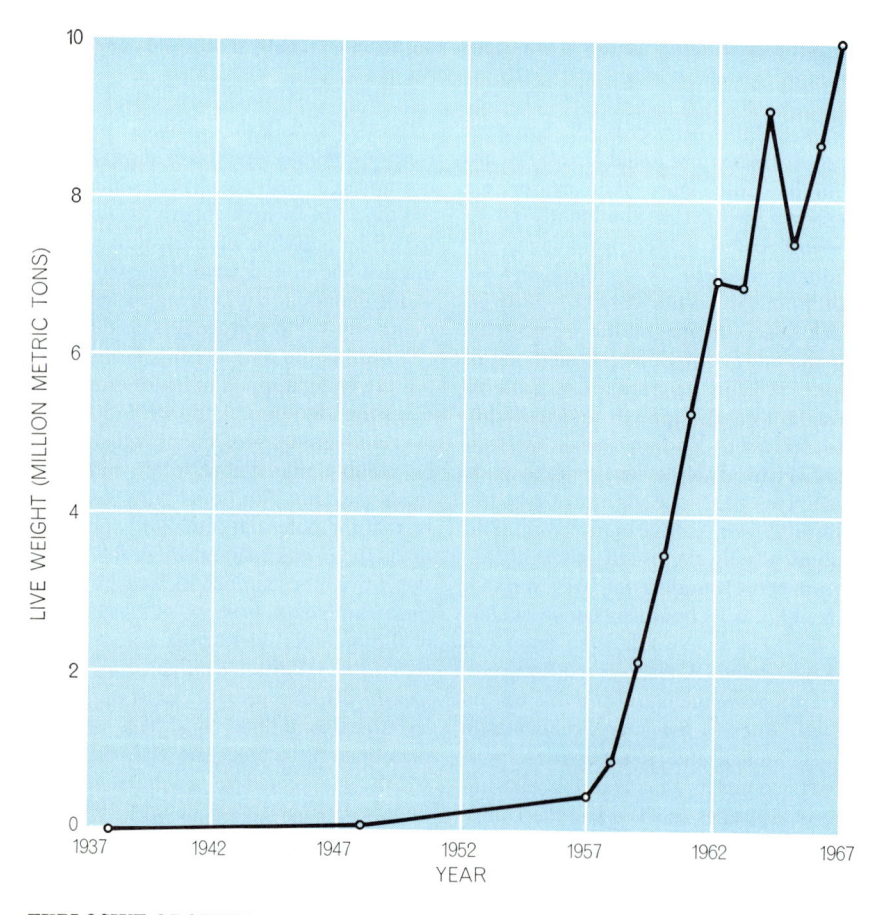

EXPLOSIVE GROWTH of the Peruvian anchoveta fishery is seen in rising number of fish taken between 1938 and 1967. Until 1958 the catch remained below half a million tons. By 1967, with more than 10.5 million tons taken, the fishery sorely needed management.

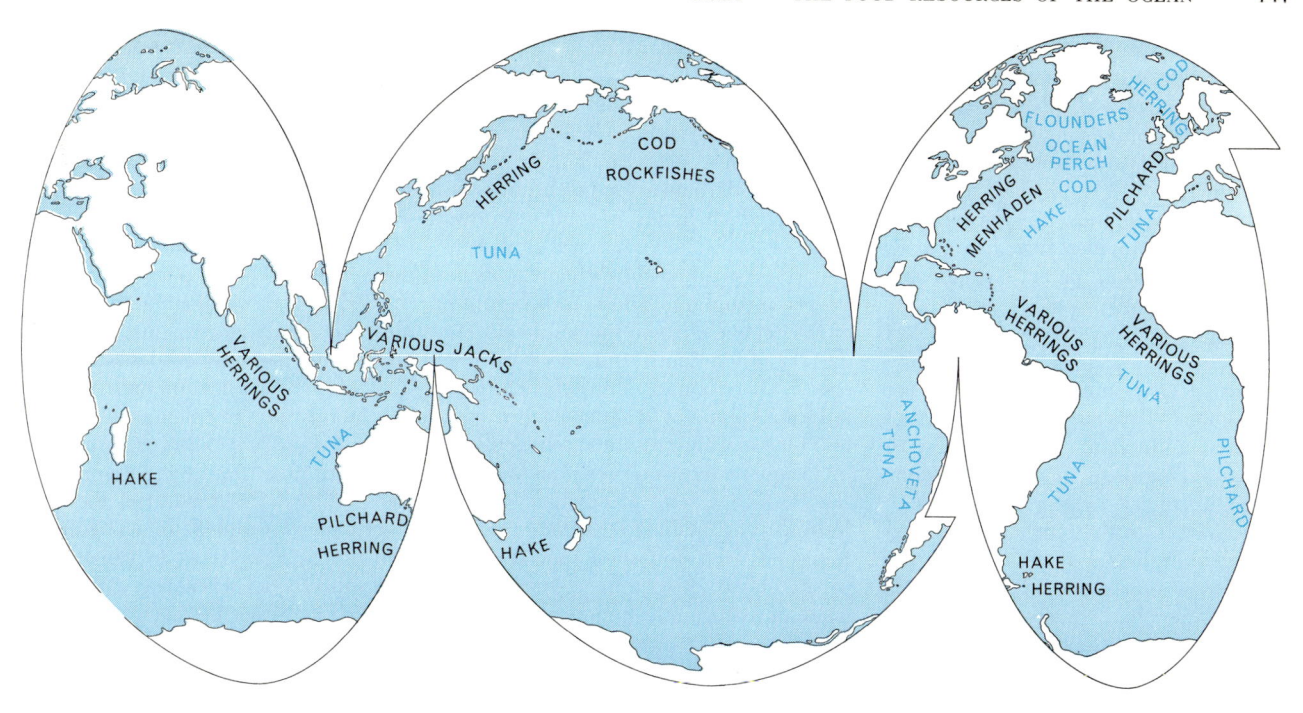

EXPLOITATION OF FISHERIES during the past 20 years is evident from this map, which locates 30 major fish stocks that were thought to be underfished in 1949. Today 14 of the stocks (*color*) are probably fully exploited or in danger of being overfished.

certain current systems in the open sea. The classical notion is that biological production is high in such areas because nutrient salts, needed for plant growth and in limited supply, are thereby renewed in the surface layers of the water. On the other hand, there is a view that the blooming of the phytoplankton is associated more with the fact that the water coming to the surface is cooler than it is associated with its richness in nutrients. A cool-water regime is characterized by seasonal peaks of primary production; the phytoplankton blooms are followed, after a time lag, by an abundance of herbivorous zooplankton that provides concentrations of food for large schools of fish. Fish, like fishermen, thrive best not so much where their prey are abundant as where they are most aggregated. In any event, the times and places of aggregation vary from year to year. The size of the herbivore crop also varies according to the success of synchronization with the primary production cycle.

There would be great practical advantage to our being able to predict these variations. Since the weather regime plays such a large part in creating the physical conditions for high biological production, the World Weather Watch, under the auspices of the World Meteorological Organization, should contribute much to fishery operations through both long-range forecasting and better short-term forecasting. Of course our interest is not merely in atmospheric forecasts, nor in the state of the sea surface, but in the deeper interaction of atmosphere and ocean. Thus, from the point of view of fisheries, an equal and complementary partner in the World Weather Watch will be the Integrated Global Ocean Station System (IGOSS) now being developed by the Intergovernmental Oceanographic Commission. The IGOSS will give us the physical data, from networks of satellite-interrogated automatic buoys and other advanced ocean data acquisition systems (collectively called ODAS), by which the ocean circulation can be observed in "real time" and the parameters relevant to fisheries forecast. A last and much more difficult link will be the observation and prediction of the basic biological processes.

So far we have been considering mainly the stocks of pelagic fishes in the upper layers of the open ocean and the shallower waters over the continental shelves. There are also large aggregations of pelagic animals that live farther down and are associated particularly with the "deep scattering layer," the sound-reflecting stratum observed in all oceans. The more widespread use of submersible research vessels will tell us more about the layer's biological nature, but the exploitation of deep pelagic resources awaits the development of suitable fishing apparatus for this purpose.

Important advances have been made in recent years in the design of pelagic trawls and in means of guiding them in three dimensions and "locking" them onto fish concentrations. We shall perhaps have such gear not only for fishing much more deeply than at present but also for automatically homing on deep-dwelling concentrations of fishes, squids and so on, using acoustic links for the purpose. The Indian Ocean might become the part of the world where such methods are first deployed on a large scale; certainly there is evidence of a great but scarcely utilized pelagic resource in that ocean, and around its edge are human populations sorely in need of protein. The Gulf of Guinea is another place where oceanographic knowledge and new fishing methods should make accessible more of the large sardine stock that is now effectively exploited only during the short season of upwelling off Ghana and nearby countries, when the schools come near the surface and can be taken by purse seines.

The bottom-living fishes and the shellfishes (both mollusks and crustaceans) are already more fully utilized than the smaller pelagic fishes. On the whole they are the species to which man attaches a particularly high value, but they cannot have as high a global abundance as the pelagic fishes. The reason is that they are living at the end of a longer food chain. All the rest of ocean life depends on an annual primary production of 150 billion tons of phytoplankton in the 2 to 3 percent of the water mass into which light penetrates and photosynthesis can occur. Below this "photic" zone dead and dying organisms sink as a continual rain of organic matter and are eaten or decompose. Out in the deep ocean little, if any, of this organic matter reaches the bottom, but nearer land a substantial quantity does; it nourishes an entire community of marine life, the benthos, which itself provides food for animals such as cod, ocean perch, flounder and shrimp that dwell or visit there.

Thus virtually everywhere on the bed of the continental shelf there is a thriving demersal resource, but it does not end there. Where the shelf is narrow but primary production above is high, as in the upwelling areas, or where the zone of high primary production stretches well away from the coast, we may find considerable demersal resources on the continental slopes beyond the shelf, far deeper than the 200 meters that is the average limiting depth of the shelf itself. Present bottom-trawling methods will work down to 1,000 meters or more, and it seems that, at least on some slopes, useful resources of shrimps and bottom-dwelling fishes will be found even down to 1,500 meters. We still know very little about the nature and abundance of these resources, and current techniques of acoustic surveying are not of much use in evaluating them. The total area of the continental slope from, say, 200 to 1,500 meters is roughly the same as that of the entire continental shelf, so that when we have extended our preliminary surveys there we might need to revise our IWP ceiling upward somewhat.

Another problem is posed for us by the way that, as fishing is intensified throughout the world, it becomes at the same time less selective. This may not apply to a particular type of fishing operation, which may be highly selective with regard to the species captured. Partly as a result of the developments in processing and trade, and partly because of the decline of some species, however, we are using more and more of the species that abound. This holds particularly for species in warmer waters, and also for some species previously neglected in cool waters, such as the sand eel in the North Sea. This means that it is no longer so reasonable to calculate the potential of each important species stock separately, as we used to do. Instead we need new theoretical models for that part of the marine ecosystem which consists of animals in the wide range of sizes we now utilize: from an inch or so up to several feet. As we move toward fuller utilization of all these animals we shall need to take proper account of the interactions among them. This will mean devising quantitative methods for evaluating the competition among them for a common food supply and also examining the dynamic relations between the predators and the prey among them.

These changes in the degree and quality of exploitation will add one more dimension to the problems we already face in creating an effective international system of management of fishing activities, particularly on the high seas. This system consists at present of a large number—more than 20—of regional or specialized intergovernmental organizations established under bilateral or multilateral treaties, or under the constitution of the FAO. The purpose of each is to conduct and coordinate research leading to resource assessments, or to promulgate regulations for the better conduct of the fisheries, or both. The organizations are supplemented by the 1958 Geneva Convention on Fishing and Conservation of the Living Resources of the High Seas. The oldest of them, the International Council for the Exploration of the Sea, based in Copenhagen and concerned particularly with fishery research in the northeastern Atlantic and the Arctic, has had more than half a century of activity. The youngest is the International Commission for the Conservation of Atlantic Tunas; the convention that establishes it comes into force this year.

For the past two decades many have hoped that such treaty bodies would ensure a smooth and reasonably rapid approach to an international regime for ocean fisheries. Indeed, a few of the organizations have fair successes to their credit. The fact is, however, that the fisheries have been changing faster than the international machinery to deal with them. National fishery research budgets and organizational arrangements for guiding research, collecting proper statistics and so on have been largely inadequate to the task of assessing resources. Nations have given, and continue to give, ludicrously low-level support to the bodies of which they are members, and the bodies themselves do not have the powers they need properly to manage the fisheries and conserve the resources. Add to this the trend to high mobility and range of today's fishing fleets, the problems of species interaction and the growing number of nations at various stages of economic development participating in international fisheries, and the regional bodies are indeed in trouble! There is some awareness of this, yet the FAO, having for years been unable to give adequate financial support to the fishery bodies it set up years ago in the Indo-Pacific area, the Mediterranean and the southwestern Atlantic, has been pushed, mainly through the enthusiasm of its new intergovernmental Committee on Fisheries, to establish still other bodies (in the Indian Ocean and in the east-central and southeastern Atlantic) that will be no better supported than the ex-

RUSSIAN FACTORY SHIP *Polar Star* lies hove to in the Barents Sea in June, 1968, as two vessels from its fleet of trawlers unload their catch for processing. The worldwide activities of the Russian fishing fleet have made the U.S.S.R. the third-largest fishing nation.

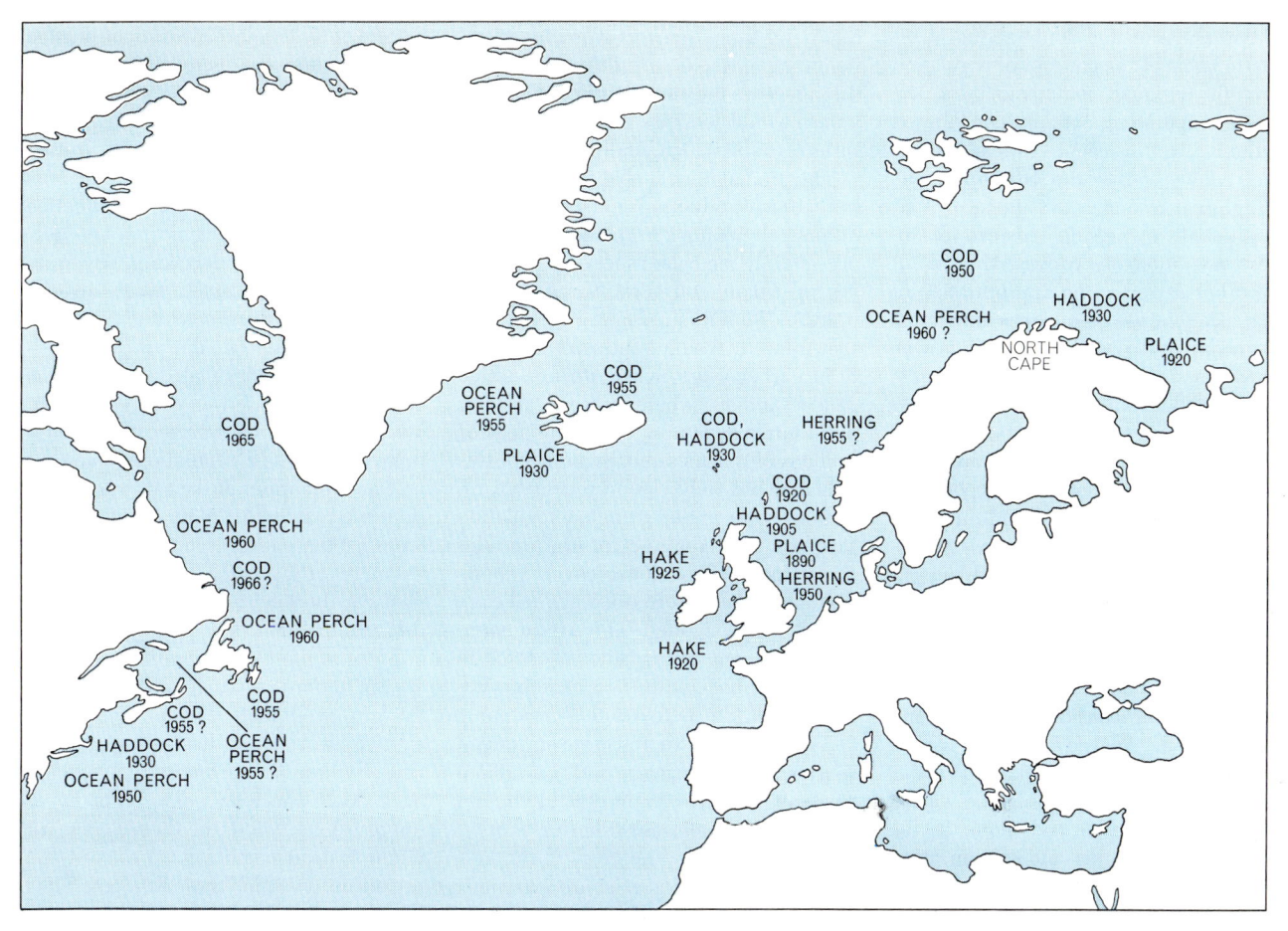

OVERFISHING in the North Atlantic and adjacent waters began some 80 years ago in the North Sea, when further increases in fishing the plaice stock no longer produced an increase in the catch of that fish. By 1950 the same was true of North Sea cod, haddock and herring, of cod, haddock and plaice off the North Cape and in the Barents Sea, of plaice, haddock and cod south and east of Iceland and of the ocean perch and haddock in the Gulf of Maine. In the period between 1956 and 1966 the same became true of ocean perch off Newfoundland and off Labrador and of cod west of Greenland. It may also be true of North Cape ocean perch and Labrador cod.

isting ones. A grand plan to double the finance and staff of the FAO's Department of Fisheries (including the secretariats and working budgets of the associated regional fishery bodies) over the six-year period 1966–1971, which member nations endorsed in principle in 1965, will be barely half-fulfilled in that time, and the various nations concerned are meanwhile being equally parsimonious in financing the other international fishery bodies.

Several of these bodies are now facing a crucial, and essentially political, problem: How are sustainable yields to be shared equitably among participating nations? It is now quite evident that there is really no escape from the paramount need, if high yields are to be sustained; this is to limit the fishing effort deployed in the intensive fisheries. This could be achieved by setting total quotas for each species in each type of fishery, but this only leads to an unseemly scramble by each nation for as large a share as possible of the quota. This can only be avoided by agreement on national allocations of the quotas. On what basis can such agreement be reached? On the historical trends of national participation? If so, over what period: the past two years, the past five, the past 20? On the need for protein, on the size or wealth of the population or on the proximity of coasts to fishing grounds? Might we try to devise a system for maximizing economic efficiency in securing an optimum net economic yield? How can this be measured in an international fishery? Would some form of license auction be equitable, or inevitably loaded in favor of wealthy nations? The total number or tonnage of fishing vessels might be fixed, as the United Kingdom suggested in 1946 should be done in the North Sea, but what flags should the ships fly and in what proportion? Might we even consider "internationalizing" the resources, granting fishing concessions and using at least a part of the economic yield from the concessions to finance marine research, develop fish-farming, police the seas and aid the participation of less developed nations?

Some of my scientific colleagues are optimistic about the outcome of current negotiations on these questions, and indeed when the countries participating are a handful of nations at a similar stage of economic and technical development, as was the case for Antarctic whaling, agreement can sometimes be reached by hard bargaining. What happens, however, when the participating countries are numerous, widely varying in their interests and ranging from the most powerful nations on earth to states most newly emerged to independence? I must confess that many of us were optimistic when 20 years ago we began proposing quite reasonable net-mesh regulations to conserve the young of certain fish stocks. Then we saw these simple—I suppose oversimple—ideas bog down in consideration of precisely how to measure a mesh of a particular kind of twine, and how to take account of the innumerable special situations that countries pleaded for, so that fishery research sometimes seemed to be becoming perverted from its earlier clarity and broad perspective.

Apprehension and doubt about the ultimate value of the concept of regulation through regional commissions of the present type have, I think, contributed to the interest in recent years in alternative regimes: either the "appropriation" of high-seas resources to some form of international "ownership" instead of today's condition of no ownership or, at the other extreme, the appropriation of increasingly wide ocean areas to national ownership by coastal states. As is well known, a similar dialectic is in progress in connection with the seabed and its mineral resources. Either solution would have both advantages and disadvantages, depending on one's viewpoint, on the time scale considered and on political philosophy. I do not propose to discuss these matters here, although personally I am increasingly firm in the conclusion that mankind has much more to gain in the long run from the "international" solution, with both seabed and fishery resources being considered as our common heritage. We now at least have a fair idea of what is economically at stake.

Here are some examples. The wasted effort in capture of cod alone in the northeastern Atlantic and salmon alone in the northern Pacific could, if rationally deployed elsewhere, increase the total world catch by 5 percent. The present catch of cod, valued at $350 million per year, could be taken with only half the effort currently expended, and the annual saving in fishing effort would amount to $150 million or more. The cost of harvesting salmon off the West Coast of North America could be reduced by three-quarters if management policy permitted use of the most efficient fishing gear; the introduction of such a policy would increase net economic returns by $750,000 annually.

The annual benefit that would accrue from the introduction and enforcement of mesh regulations in the demersal fishery—mainly the hake fishery—in the east-central Atlantic off West Africa is of the order of $1 million. Failure to regulate the Antarctic whaling industry effectively in earlier years, when stocks of blue whales and fin whales were near their optimum size, is now costing us tens of millions of dollars annually in loss of this valuable but only slowly renewable resource. Even under stringent regulation this loss will continue for the decades these stocks will need to recover. Yellowfin tuna in the eastern tropical Pacific are almost fully exploited. There is an annual catch quota, but it is not allocated to nations or ships, with the classic inevitable results: an increase in the catching capacity of fleets, their use in shorter and shorter "open" seasons and an annual waste of perhaps 30 percent of the net value of this important fishery.

Such regulations as exist are extremely difficult to enforce (or to be seen to be enforced, which is almost as important). The tighter the squeeze on the natural resources, the greater the suspicion of fishermen that "the others" are not abiding by the regulations, and the greater the incentive to flout the regulations oneself. There has been occasional provision in treaties, or in *ad hoc* arrangements, to place neutral inspectors or internationally accredited observers aboard fishing vessels and mother ships (as in Antarctic whaling, where arrangements were completed but never implemented!). Such arrangements are exceptional. In point of fact the effective supervision of a fishing fleet is an enormously difficult undertaking. Even to know where the vessels are going, let alone what they are catching, is quite a problem. Perhaps one day artificial satellites will monitor sealed transmitters compulsorily carried on each vessel. But how to ensure compliance with minimum landing-size regulations when increasing quantities of the catch are being processed at sea? With factory ships roaming the entire ocean, even the statistics reporting catches by species and area can become more rather than less difficult to obtain.

Some of these considerations and pessimism about their early solution have, I think, played their part in stimulating other approaches to harvesting the sea. One of these is the theory of "working back down the food chain." For every ton of fish we catch, the theory goes, we might instead catch say 10 tons of the organisms on which those fish feed. Thus by harvesting the smaller organisms we could move away from the fish ceiling of 100 million or 200 million tons and closer to the 150 billion tons of primary production. The snag is the question of concentration. The billion tons or so of "fish food" is neither in a form of direct interest to man nor is it so concentrated in space as the animals it nourishes. In fact, the 10-to-one ratio of fish food to fish represents a use of energy—perhaps a rather efficient use—by which biomass is concentrated; if the fish did not expend this energy in feeding, man might have to expend a similar amount of energy—in fuel, for example—in order to collect the dispersed fish food. I am sure the technological problems of our using fish food will be solved, but only careful analysis will reveal whether or not it is better to turn fish food, by way of fish meal, into chickens or rainbow trout than to harvest the marine fish instead.

There are a few situations, however, where the concentration, abundance and homogeneity of fish food are sufficient to be of interest in the near future. The best-known of these is the euphausiid "krill" in Antarctic waters: small shrimp-like crustaceans that form the main food of the baleen whales. Russian investigators and some others are seriously charting krill distribution and production, relating them to the oceanographic features of the Southern Ocean, experiment-

JAPANESE MARICULTURE includes the raising of several kinds of marine algae. This array of posts and netting in the Inland Sea supports a crop of an edible seaweed, *Porphyra*.

ing with special gear for catching the krill (something between a mid-water trawl and a magnified plankton net) and developing methods for turning them into meal and acceptable pastes. The krill alone could produce a weight of yield, although surely not a value, at least as great as the present world fish catch, but we might have to forgo the whales. Similarly, the deep scattering layers in other oceans might provide very large quantities of smaller marine animals in harvestable concentration.

An approach opposite to working down the food chain is to look to the improvement of the natural fish resources, and particularly to the cultivation of highly valued species. Schemes for transplanting young fish to good high-seas feeding areas, or for increasing recruitment by rearing young fish to viable size, are hampered by the problem of protecting what would need to be quite large investments. What farmer would bother to breed domestic animals if he were not assured by the law of the land that others would not come and take them as soon as they were nicely fattened? Thus mariculture in the open sea awaits a regime of law there, and effective management as well as more research.

Meanwhile attention is increasingly given to the possibilities of raising more fish and shellfish in coastal waters, where the effort would at least have the protection of national law. Old traditions of shellfish culture are being reexamined, and one can be confident that scientific bases for further growth will be found. All such activities depend ultimately on what I call "productivity traps": the utilization of natural or artificially modified features of the marine environment to trap biological production originating in a wider area, and by such a biological route that more of the production is embodied in organisms of direct interest to man. In this way we open the immense possibilities of using mangrove swamps and productive estuarine areas, building artificial reefs, breeding even more efficient homing species such as the salmon, enhancing natural production with nutrients or warm water from coastal power stations, controlling predators and competitors, shortening food chains and so on. Progress in such endeavors will require a better predictive ecology than we now have, and also many pilot experiments with corresponding risks of failure as well as chances of success.

The greatest threat to mariculture is perhaps the growing pollution of the sea. This is becoming a real problem for fisheries generally, particularly coastal ones, and mariculture would thrive best in just those regions that are most threatened by pollution, namely the ones near large coastal populations and technological centers. We should not expect, I think, that the ocean would not be used at all as a receptacle for waste—it is in some ways so good for such a purpose: its large volume, its deep holes, the hydrolyzing, corrosive and biologically degrading properties of seawater and the microbes in it. We should expect, however, that this use will not be an indiscriminate one, that this use of the ocean would be internationally registered, controlled and monitored, and that there would be strict regulation of any dumping of noxious substances (obsolete weapons of chemical and biological warfare, for example), including the injection of such substances by pipelines extending from the coast. There are signs that nations are becoming ready to accept such responsibilities, and to act in concert to overcome the problems. Let us hope that progress in this respect will be faster than it has been in arranging for the management of some fisheries, or in a few decades there may be few coastal fisheries left worth managing.

I have stressed the need for scientific research to ensure the future use of the sea as a source of food. This need seems to me self-evident, but it is undervalued by many persons and organizations concerned with economic development. It is relatively easy to secure a million dollars of international development funds for the worthy purpose of assisting a country to participate in an international fishery or to set up a training school for its fishermen and explore the country's continental shelf for fish or shrimps. It is more difficult to justify a similar or lesser expenditure on the scientific assessment of the new fishery's resources and the investigation of its ocean environment. It is much more difficult to secure even quite limited support for international measures that might ensure the continued profitability of the new fishery for all participants.

Looking back a decade instead of forward, we recall that Lionel A. Walford of the U.S. Fish and Wildlife Service wrote, in a study he made for the Conservation Foundation: "The sea is a mysterious wilderness, full of secrets. It is inhabited only by wild animals and, with the exception of a few special situations, is uncultivated. Most of what we know about it we have had to learn indirectly with mechanical contrivances to probe, feel, sample, fish." There are presumably fewer wild animals now than there were then—at least fewer useful ones— but there seems to be a good chance that by the turn of the century the sea will be less a wilderness and more cultivated. Much remains for us and our children to do to make sure that by then it is not a contaminated wilderness or a battlefield for ever sharper clashes between nations and between the different users of its resources.

AUSTRALIAN MARICULTURE includes the production of some 60 million oysters per year in the brackish estuaries of New South Wales. The long racks in the photograph have been exposed by low tide; they support thousands of sticks covered with maturing oysters.

18

FOOD ADDITIVES

G. O. KERMODE
March 1972

Perhaps as many as 2,500 substances are currently being added to foods for flavoring, coloring, preservation and other purposes. How are the necessity and safety of these substances determined?

Men have added nonfood substances to their food throughout recorded history, but in recent decades they have become concerned about such practices because of the large number of substances and motivations that have become involved. The questions at issue for any food additive are whether or not it is necessary and, if so, whether or not it is safe. For many years the United Nations (through the Food and Agriculture Organization and the World Health Organization) and many governments have kept watch on additives with these questions in view. The questions must be faced whenever a new additive is proposed; sometimes, as the recent case of cyclamate additives in the U.S. showed, they must be reconsidered when new evidence puts the safety of an old additive in doubt.

The distinction between food ingredients and food additives is somewhat imprecise. Sugar, being a natural product, is usually regarded as an ingredient, whereas saccharin, being an artificial sweetener, is likely to come under the heading of an additive. Perhaps the best method of classification is by function. Additives are employed for such purposes as enhancing flavor, improving color, extending shelf life and protecting the nutritional value of a food. They are, in short, valuable but not always essential items in the manufacture of food products.

Whatever one's views on additives may be, it is true that without additives many food products could not be offered for sale in their present form. This is exemplified in particular by the many convenience foods that have become popular in North America and in western Europe. Moreover, if food production is to increase enough to keep pace with population growth and the effort to improve nutrition generally in undernourished areas, chemicals that are not normally part of food will inevitably play an increasingly important role.

From the earliest times foods were preserved with incidental additives that resulted from cooking. Food was also preserved extensively in ancient times by heating, drying, salting, pickling, fermenting and smoking. Food colors were used in ancient Egypt. In China kerosene was burned to ripen bananas and peas; the reason the method succeeded, although the Chinese did not know it, was that the combustion produced the ripening agents ethylene and propylene. Flavoring and seasoning were arts in many ancient civilizations, with the result that spices and condiments were important items in commerce.

Additives have not invariably been employed with beneficial aims. The adulteration of food, in order to pass an inferior product off as a good one, is as old as trade. Expensive items such as tea, coffee, sugar, spices and essential oils were often adulterated. Common adulterants included coloring substances and burned or roasted vegetable material, which was mixed with flour. Bread, beer, and wine were widely adulterated.

Eventually such practices led the authorities of the time and place to try to suppress them. The earliest food laws were often designed to control the more obvious forms of adulteration and fraud. In addition to these efforts the merchant guilds tried to protect the genuineness and the reputation of their products. The means at hand for testing foods were limited; checking the appearance, taste and smell of a food was about all one could do. The basis of knowledge making possible the national food laws that are common today was not established until about the middle of the 19th century. In the latter part of the century pure-food laws were enacted in country after country to control the composition of food and regulate the use of additives.

These developments coincided with a number of discoveries, mainly in organic chemistry, that led to the production of several of the important food additives now in use. For example, discoveries that resulted in the development of aniline and the coal-tar dyes led eventually to many of the synthetic colors now added to food. The active principles of odor and flavor were isolated from vegetables and other organic materials, leading first to alcoholic solutions of those materials as flavors and later to synthetic flavors, some of which did not appear to be present in natural edible aromatic substances used to flavor foods and some of which proved to have more flavoring

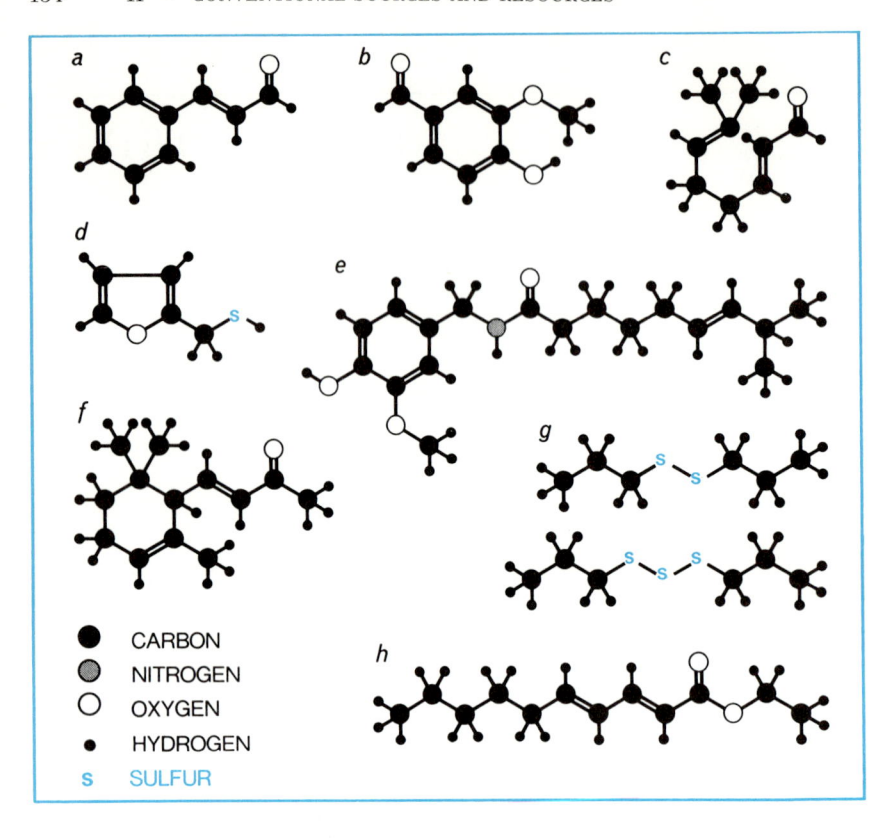

TYPICAL FLAVORING COMPOUNDS have chemical structures shown here. Cinnamaldehyde (*a*) supplies a cinnamon flavor; vanillin (*b*), a vanilla flavor; citral (*c*), lemon; furfuryl mercaptan (*d*), coffee; capsaicin (*e*), the pungent ingredient of red pepper; alpha-ionone (*f*), a principal component of strawberry and raspberry flavors; propyl disulfide (*g*), onion, and ethyl *trans*-2,*cis*-4-decadienoate (*h*), pear. Some 1,400 flavorings are in use.

power than the analogous natural flavors. By 1900 the flavorings in use were nearly all artificial and, except for vanilla, lemon, orange, peppermint and wintergreen, were being made with synthetic substances.

More than 40 functions now served by food additives can be listed. In this discussion, however, I shall group additives broadly in five categories: flavors, colors, preservatives, texture agents and a miscellaneous group.

Flavors constitute the largest class of food additives; estimates of the number of natural and synthetic flavors available range from 1,100 to 1,400. It is probably fair to say that flavors pose the largest regulatory task, not only because there are so many of them but also because of insufficient toxicological data, rapid changes in the field and many other factors. In general little is known about the toxicological aspects of flavors. Part of the problem is that many natural flavors have been used for centuries, and fully evaluating them all for safety would be an immense task. It is often argued that doing so would divert a large part of the effort that is needed to investigate the safety of more important and potentially more dangerous additives.

Over the past 30 years the use of flavorings has grown tremendously, paralleling the expansion in new types of food, new food-processing techniques and new methods of distribution. Governments have approached the question of controlling flavors from various directions. Some publish lists of permitted and prohibited flavors; some have a short list of prohibited flavors, many of which are natural, and others allow flavorings (both natural and synthetic) that are found only in the aromatic oils of edible plants.

Related to flavors are the additives known as flavor-enhancers. The commonest of them is monosodium glutamate (MSG), which is the monosodium salt of glutamic acid, one of the amino acids. A good deal of research is under way to find other flavor-enhancers, particularly in the group of substances known as the 5'-nucleotides. Similar work is being done on enhancers for fruit flavors. In recent years the use of maltol, which can intensify or modify the flavor of preserves, desserts, fruit, soft drinks and foods generally high in carbohydrates, has expanded greatly.

Manufacturers are also doing considerable research to find flavors that are cheaper or more effective than existing flavoring agents and flavor-enhancers. It is probably in this field that the greatest need for new additives will arise in the future, particularly for additives that can be put in simulated food products to imitate the complex flavor properties of traditional foods. At present the most widely sold simulated products are meat substitutes made from spun soybean proteins or proteins from other vegetables. With the addition of flavors, colors, vitamins, emulsifiers, acidifying agents and preservatives these proteins are sold as "vegetable steaks," "soya chicken breast" and "vegetable bacon" or are included in compounded products that normally have meat as a major ingredient. Other simulated foods are substitutes for dairy products. Flavored drinks, made so as to simulate the properties of genuine fruit juices, are also on the list. Because additive flavorings are expected to play such an expanding role in these products, they represent the field where ways of protecting the consumer's interest will need close attention, particularly with regard to designation and labeling of simulated foods.

Colors are put in food mainly to give it an appetizing appearance, on the tested assumption that the way food looks has an effect on its palatability. Foods are also colored to enhance the appreciation of flavor. Many people have become accustomed to the standardized color of a food product and would not accept the product if the color were substantially changed, even though nothing else had been done to the food. One need think only of blue or red butter to recognize the importance of accepted colors.

Much research has gone into food coloring. The colors most used in the food industry are synthetic dyestuffs. They are notably pure. Since they also have strong coloring power, little coloring is needed to achieve the desired result in a food product.

The manufacturer needs a color that not only produces the desired appearance but also will remain stable under certain conditions of manufacture, storage and cooking. Color put into candy, cakes and biscuits must be stable both to high temperature and to the action of carbon dioxide. Other colors must be able to withstand high processing temperatures and the action of acids.

Color regulation, like flavor regulation, varies from country to country. Many countries have fairly short lists of permitted food colors. The regulations specify purity and identity for the permitted colors and also restrict the number of foods to which color can be added. Since most of the lists are based on the toxicological evaluation of the dyes, one might expect a reasonable degree of uniformity among the lists. It is not so, however, and therefore one of the most troublesome problems facing a food manufacturer who wants to export his products is the need to vary the color according to the different regulations of the importing countries.

The World Health Organization has evaluated more than 140 kinds of coloring matter, declaring a number to be unsafe and publishing a fairly short list of colors deemed to be safe. In some countries the food industry manages quite well with a choice of no more than a dozen dyes. Other countries allow more dyes. The difference is illustrated by a

CERTAIN COLORS employed as food additives are portrayed according to their chemical structure. The colors have both numerical and descriptive names: (a) red 2, amaranth; (b) red 3, erythrosine; (c) yellow 5, tartrazine; (d) yellow 6, sunset yellow; (e) green 3, fast green; (f) violet 1, benzylviolet, and (g) blue 2, indigotine. The characteristic ring structure evident in the seven diagrams is more likely than an aliphatic, or open-chain, structure to produce color because of the way it absorbs and reflects light.

a *b* *c*

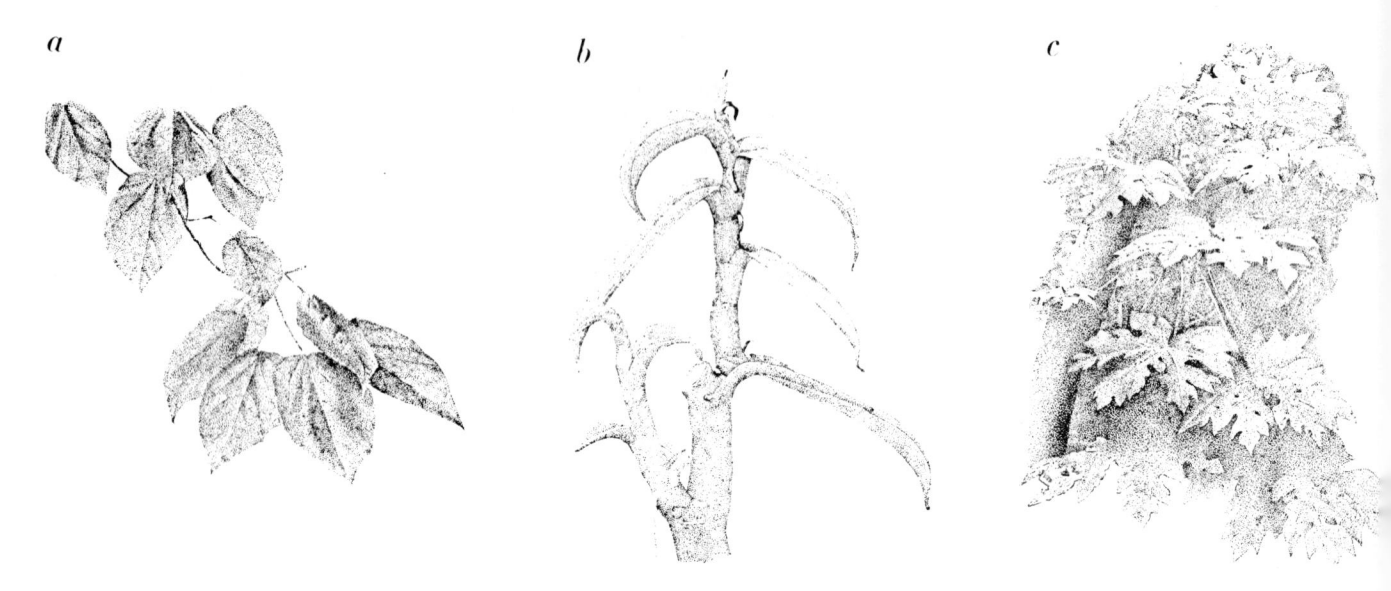

BOTANICAL SOURCES of four natural additives are depicted. The annatto (*a*) is a tropical tree, *Bixa orellana*, that produces a yellowish-red coloring agent made from the pulp around the seeds. Natural vanilla extract comes from the pods of several species of orchid, chiefly *Vanilla planifolia* (*b*). Sap from the papaya tree (*c*), *Carica papaya*, is the source of the enzyme papain, which is

problem that the British will face when their country becomes a member of the European Economic Community: kippers will no longer be golden and sausages will no longer be "nicely pink" unless the Community's list of permitted colors is extended.

Preservative additives are one means of deterring food spoilage caused by microorganisms. The seriousness of spoilage is shown by the World Health Organization's estimate that about 20 percent of the world's food supply is lost in this way. Indeed, shortages of food in many parts of the world could be alleviated with the wider use of preservatives.

Spoilage can be prevented or retarded not only with additives but also with physical and biological processes such as heating, refrigeration, drying, freezing, souring, fermenting and curing. Some of these processes, however, achieve only partial preservation. Additives therefore have a role in prolonging a food's keeping qualities.

A number of different types of preservative have to be employed, depending on the kind of food, the method of manufacture, the way the food is packaged and stored and the nature of the microorganisms involved. Baked goods, for example, go stale rapidly. Once made, they are often exposed to mold spores that become active in warm weather or high humidity. In bread the spores produce a condition called "rope." Sodium diacetate, acetic acid, lactic acid, monocalcium phosphate, sodium propionate and calcium propionate are all effective in preventing rope. Sorbic acid and its salts have many uses, such as preventing mold in cheese, syrup and confections containing fruit or sugar. Benzoic acid and sodium benzoate serve as preservatives in margarine, fruit-juice concentrates, juices and pickled vegetables. Sulfur dioxide is widely used to inhibit mold and discoloration in wine, fruit pulps, fruit-juice concentrates, fruit drinks requiring dilution and dried fruits and vegetables.

Sulfur dioxide is giving rise to concern in a number of countries where the average wine consumption is so high that the people who drink a good deal of wine are in danger of exceeding the acceptable average daily intake of sulfur dioxide. The acceptable daily level is 1.5 milligrams per kilogram of body weight, which means about 100 milligrams a day or a half-liter of wine containing 200 parts per million of sulfur dioxide. Studies on sulfite in the rat found that .1 percent in the diet inhibited the growth rate, probably because sulfite destroys vitamin B_1. The significance of this finding in man, whose diet does not consist exclusively of sulfited food as in the experiments with rats, is questionable; nonetheless, more work is needed to dispel the uncertainty about the toxicity of sulfur dioxide and sulfites.

As a result of such uncertainties serious attempts to find alternatives to preserving foods with chemicals are under way. Among the recent advances is the development of antibiotics as antimicrobial additives. Antibiotics commonly have a more transitory effect than the traditional preservatives and are more selective. These advantages are significant when antibiotics are directed against known food pathogens and when their action is required only during the manufacturing stage. Antibiotics can be said to have a major disadvantage, however, in that by changing the normal spoilage pattern of certain foods they may result in unfamiliar forms of spoilage that consumers cannot recognize.

A number of countries have permitted such antibiotics as tetracyclines, nystatin, nisin and pimaricin as direct or indirect additives to chilled or raw fish, meat, poultry, cheese and bananas. The applications are strictly limited. Many other countries, although they recognize the efficacy of antibiotic additives, have taken the view that it would be unwise to approve them widely for food, since the antibiotics are important in medicine and their liberal use in food might produce resistant strains of pathogens that could affect humans.

Another development that has attracted interest as an alternative way of protecting food is the experimental work wherein ionizing radiation is employed to destroy the microorganisms and insects that cause food spoilage. An advantage of irradiation is that it produces little or no rise in the temperature of the food during treatment. A disadvantage at present is the possibility that irradiation will have an effect on the food and leave residues. For example, it is possible for the extranuclear structure of atoms to be excited under the influence of ionizing radiation. If the atoms are constituents of a molecule, the molecule as a whole may be excited, which may lead to rupture of one or more chemical

employed as a meat tenderizer. One source of wintergreen flavor is the leaves of the evergreen plant *Gaultheria procumbens* (*d*).

bonds, giving rise to free radicals. The free radicals may be capable of starting chemical chain reactions.

Nonetheless, work with irradiation has advanced to a point where in a small number of countries the sale of certain irradiated foodstuffs is now allowed. Irradiation raises the possibility that perishable foodstuffs could be more widely distributed in a fresh or nearly fresh condition. It is likely to take several years, however, for the irradiation of food to become a widespread practice because of the effort that must still be devoted to developing procedures for testing irradiated foods. The International Atomic Energy Agency, in conjunction with the Food and Agriculture Organization and the World Health Organization, has indicated a number of possible treatments by ionizing radiation to achieve long-term preservation, without refrigeration or chemical preservatives, of perishable foods and also to prevent food poisoning by destroying microorganisms such as salmonella.

Many traditional preservatives—notably salt, vinegar and sugar—still play an important role in homes and factories. It can be argued that recent improvements in food processing, coupled with improved standards of hygiene, should reduce the need for chemical preservatives. On the other hand, developments in making ready-to-use foods and the widespread resort to prepackaging have tended to increase the need for preservatives.

Related to preservatives are antioxidants, which are added to fatty foods primarily to prevent rancidity. Typical products containing these additives are margarine, cooking oils, biscuits, potato chips, cereals, salted nuts, soup mixes and precooked meals containing fish, poultry or meat. Certain foods, such as virgin olive oil, contain their own natural antioxidants in the form of tocopherols and therefore do not need the addition of antioxidants. If such foods are heated in a manufacturing process, however, they tend to lose their natural antioxidants, which should be restored if the product is to have a reasonable shelf life.

The most widely added antioxidants are butylated hydroxyanisole, butylated hydroxytoluene, propyl, octyl and dodecyl gallates and natural or synthetic tocopherols singly or in combination. Certain acids (ascorbic, citric and phosphoric) combined with antioxidants increase the antioxidant effect.

Preventing rancidity is not the only problem with a number of foods. The growing practice of using transparent wrapping for food presents its own problems by exposing the product to light and increasing the likelihood of discoloration. Ascorbic and isoascorbic acid have proved effective in preventing discoloration in certain fruit juices, soft drinks, canned vegetables, frozen fruits and cooked cured meat such as ham.

Often more than one antioxidant is put into a food, producing a synergistic action that allows more effective control of the product. Many countries authorize several antioxidants as food additives, but a number of others will allow only the so-called natural antioxidants, such as ascorbic acid (vitamin C) and the tocopherols (vitamin E). Much research is in progress to find compounds that are more potent than the present antioxidants. The search is particularly keen for antioxidants that are less likely than the present ones to impart odor, flavor or color to foods. Another quest is for antioxidants with a required solubility in both water and oil. With the development of simulated foods the search for antioxidants that are more effective in extending shelf life will gain further impetus.

In the class of texture agents I have included emulsifiers, stabilizers and thickening agents. In terms of quantity consumed they probably constitute the largest class of additives, being employed extensively in preparing bread, pastry, ice cream, frozen desserts, whipped products, margarine, candy and certain soft drinks and milk products. Many of the newer convenience foods have only become practicable as a result of the development of new and improved emulsifiers and stabilizers. Among other things, the texture agents permit oil to be dispersed in water, produce a smooth and even texture and supply the desired body and consistency of many food products.

The first emulsifiers were few in number and were either natural substances such as gums, alginates and soaps or synthetic substances of fairly simple composition. Their action was often variable. Progress in chemical synthesis has now made available a large number of new texture agents with characteristics suitable for almost any requirement. Among the most common emulsifiers and stabilizers, aside from the natural ones, are stearyl tartrate, complete glycerol esters, partial glycerol esters, partial polyglycerol esters, propylene glycol esters, monostearin sodium sulfoacetate, sorbitan esters of fatty acids and their polyoxyethylene derivatives, cellulose ethers and sodium carboxymethyl cellulose. Thickeners include natural products such as agar, alginates, celluloses, starches, vegetable gums, dextrins and pectin; modified celluloses such as methyl cellulose, and starches modified by bleaching, oxidizing and phosphating.

The miscellaneous group of additives is so numerous that I can only indicate a few of the functions they serve. Acids, alkalis, buffers and neutralizing agents are added to many processed foods where the degree of acidity or alkalinity is important; manufacturers of baked goods, soft drinks, chocolate and processed cheese employ these additives extensively. The baking industry also makes heavy use of bleaching and maturing agents, which render flour whiter and bring it to maturity sooner. Sequestrants are added to food to bind trace metals and thus prevent any oxidative activity the metals in an ionized state might have on the food; in shortening, for example, unsequestered metals could catalyze processes leading to rancidity. Humectants, which are hygroscopic, offset changes in the humidity of the environment to which food is exposed, so that a desired level of moisture can be maintained in a food product such as shredded coconut. Anticaking agents keep many salts and powders free-flowing. Glazing agents make certain food surfaces shiny and in some cases protect the product from spoiling. Firming and crisping agents prevent flaccidity in processed fruits and vegetables and also aid the coagulation of certain cheeses. Release agents help food to separate from surfaces it touches during manufacture or transport. Foaming agents coupled with propellants make whipped

ANTICAKING AGENTS
Aluminum calcium silicate
Calcium silicate
Magnesium silicate
Sodium aluminosilicate
Sodium calcium aluminosilicate
Tricalcium silicate

CHEMICAL PRESERVATIVES
Ascorbic acid
Ascorbyl palmitate
Benzoic acid
Butylated hydroxyanisole
Butylated hydroxytoluene
Calcium ascorbate
Calcium propionate
Calcium sorbate
Caprylic acid
Dilauryl thiodipropionate
Erythorbic acid
Gum guaiac
Methylparaben
Potassium bisulfite
Potassium metabisulfite
Potassium sorbate
Propionic acid
Propyl gallate
Propylparaben
Sodium ascorbate
Sodium benzoate
Sodium bisulfite
Sodium metabisulfite
Sodium propionate
Sodium sorbate
Sodium sulfite
Sorbic acid
Stannous chloride
Sulfur dioxide
Thiodipropionic acid
Tocopherols

EMULSIFYING AGENTS
Cholic acid
Desoxycholic acid
Diacetyl tartaric acid esters of mono- and diglycerides
Glycocholic acid
Mono- and diglycerides
Monosodium phosphate derivatives of above
Propylene glycol
Ox bile extract
Taurocholic acid

NUTRIENTS AND DIETARY SUPPLEMENTS
Alanine
Arginine
Ascorbic acid
Aspartic acid
Biotin
Calcium carbonate
Calcium citrate
Calcium glycerophosphate
Calcium oxide
Calcium pantothenate
Calcium phosphate
Calcium pyrophosphate
Calcium sulfate
Carotene
Choline bitartrate
Choline chloride
Copper gluconate
Cuprous iodide
Cysteine
Cystine
Ferric phosphate
Ferric pyrophosphate
Ferric sodium pyrophosphate
Ferrous gluconate
Ferrous lactate
Ferrous sulfate
Glycine
Histidine
Inositol
Iron, reduced
Isoleucine
Leucine
Linoleic acid
Lysine
Magnesium oxide
Magnesium phosphate
Magnesium sulfate
Manganese chloride
Manganese citrate
Manganese gluconate
Manganese glycerophosphate
Manganese hypophosphite
Manganese sulfate
Manganous oxide
Mannitol
Methionine
Methionine hydroxy analogue
Niacin
Niacinamide
D-pantothenyl alcohol
Phenylalanine
Potassium chloride
Potassium glycerophosphate
Potassium iodide
Proline
Pyridoxine hydrochloride
Riboflavin
Riboflavin-5-phosphate
Serine
Sodium pantothenate
Sodium phosphate
Sorbitol
Thiamine hydrochloride
Thiamine mononitrate
Threonine
Tocopherols
Tocopherol acetate
Tryptophane
Tyrosine
Valine
Vitamin A
Vitamin A acetate
Vitamin A palmitate
Vitamin B_{12}
Vitamin D_2
Vitamin D_3
Zinc sulfate
Zinc gluconate
Zinc chloride
Zinc oxide
Zinc stearate

SEQUESTRANTS
Calcium acetate
Calcium chloride
Calcium citrate
Calcium diacetate
Calcium gluconate
Calcium hexametaphosphate
Calcium phosphate, monobasic
Calcium phytate
Citric acid
Dipotassium phosphate
Disodium phosphate
Isopropyl citrate
Monoisopropyl citrate
Potassium citrate
Sodium acid phosphate
Sodium citrate
Sodium diacetate
Sodium gluconate
Sodium hexametaphosphate
Sodium metaphosphate
Sodium phosphate
Sodium potassium tartrate
Sodium pyrophosphate
Sodium pyrophosphate, tetra
Sodium tartrate
Sodium thiosulfate
Sodium tripolyphosphate
Stearyl citrate
Tartaric acid

STABILIZERS
Acacia (gum arabic)
Agar-agar
Ammonium alginate
Calcium alginate
Carob bean gum
Chondrus extract
Ghatti gum
Guar gum
Potassium alginate
Sodium alginate
Sterculia (or karaya) gum
Tragacanth

MISCELLANEOUS ADDITIVES
Acetic acid
Adipic acid
Aluminum ammonium sulfate
Aluminum potassium sulfate
Aluminum sodium sulfate
Aluminum sulfate
Ammonium bicarbonate
Ammonium carbonate
Ammonium hydroxide
Ammonium phosphate
Ammonium sulfate
Beeswax
Bentonite
Butane
Caffeine
Calcium carbonate
Calcium chloride
Calcium citrate
Calcium gluconate
Calcium hydroxide
Calcium lactate
Calcium oxide
Calcium phosphate
Caramel
Carbon dioxide
Carnauba wax
Citric acid
Dextrans
Ethyl formate
Glutamic acid
Glutamic acid hydrochloride
Glycerin
Glyceryl monostearate
Helium
Hydrochloric acid
Hydrogen peroxide
Lactic acid
Lecithin
Magnesium carbonate
Magnesium hydroxide
Magnesium oxide
Magnesium stearate
Malic acid
Methylcellulose
Monoammonium glutamate
Monopotassium glutamate
Nitrogen
Nitrous oxide
Papain
Phosphoric acid
Potassium acid tartrate
Potassium bicarbonate
Potassium carbonate
Potassium citrate
Potassium hydroxide
Potassium sulfate
Propane
Propylene glycol
Rennet
Silica aerogel
Sodium acetate
Sodium acid pyrophosphate
Sodium aluminum phosphate
Sodium bicarbonate
Sodium carbonate
Sodium citrate
Sodium carboxymethylcellulose
Sodium caseinate
Sodium citrate
Sodium hydroxide
Sodium pectinate
Sodium phosphate
Sodium potassium tartrate
Sodium sesquicarbonate
Sodium tripolyphosphate
Succinic acid
Sulfuric acid
Tartaric acid
Triacetin
Triethyl citrate

SYNTHETIC FLAVORING SUBSTANCES
Acetaldehyde
Acetoin
Aconitic acid
Anethole
Benzaldehyde
N-butyric acid
d- or *l*-carvone
Cinnamaldehyde
Citral
Decanal
Diacetyl
Ethyl acetate
Ethyl butyrate
Ethyl vanillin
Eugenol
Geraniol
Geranyl acetate
Glycerol tributyrate
Limonene
Linalool
Linalyl acetate
1-malic acid
Methyl anthranilate
3-Methyl-3-phenyl glycidic acid ethyl ester
Piperonal
Vanillin

GROUP OF ADDITIVES included in the U.S. Food and Drug Administration's list of additives "generally recognized as safe" is given, except for large groups of natural flavors and oils. To be on this list an additive must have been in use before 1958 and have met certain specifications of safety. Additives brought into use since 1958 must be approved individually. Occasionally substances are removed from the list by the FDA in the light of new evidence; recent examples include the cyclamate sweeteners and saccharin.

toppings come out of their containers as a foam, whereas foam inhibitors have an opposite role, where a tendency to foam, as with pineapple juice, makes filling a container difficult. Clarifying agents remove small particles of minerals from liquids such as vinegar, which might otherwise turn cloudy. Solvents serve as carriers for flavors, colors and other additives, and solvent extraction is the method whereby oil is obtained from oilseeds, coffee is decaffeinated and a number of instant beverages are prepared.

Additives have become a public issue because of recurrent episodes bringing into question the safety of certain additives that have been used for some time. Cyclamates were tested extensively in the U.S. before they were put on the market as artificial sweeteners, but in 1969 it was reported that large doses had caused bladder cancer in rats. The U.S. Government ordered cyclamates off the market. Subsequently it was reported that rats fed with cyclamate and saccharin at a sixth of the dose that led to the original ban also developed bladder cancer. As a result saccharin is now being critically reviewed in the U.S. and other countries. Sodium nitrite, which fixes a red color in frankfurters, sausages and hams, is currently under review in many countries because of the possibility that it may form a cancer-producing agent during digestion and storage. Laboratory evidence has linked monosodium glutamate with the "Chinese restaurant syndrome" (more precisely Kwok's disease), a tightening of the muscles of the face and neck, occasionally accompanied by headache, nausea and giddiness, experienced by some people who have eaten in restaurants where monosodium glutamate has been used in large amounts. Many countries have therefore restricted the use of monosodium glutamate or required its presence in food to be prominently stated on the label.

Food additives, unlike the chemicals put in pesticide preparations, are not designed to be toxic, and most of them would have to be ingested in large single doses to produce acute toxic symptoms. Many additives by nature are of extremely low potential toxicity. It is therefore difficult to determine their possible hazards to man, even after exhaustive testing. It is probably true to say that there will always be an area of doubt concerning the possible effects of ingesting small amounts of additives over the course of a lifetime. One cannot be fully sure of the safety of an additive until it has been consumed by people of all ages in specified amounts over a long period of time and has been shown conclusively, by careful toxicological examination, to have no harmful effects.

Since humans cannot be used for testing by exposing them to unknown chemicals for a substantial period of time, tests are made on rats and other animals such as mice and dogs. Test animals are fed quantities of the additive that far exceed the amount likely to be found in food. Tests are made both for short periods and over the animal's lifetime and are often continued into succeeding generations. Any change in growth, body function, tissue and reproduction is reported, as is the incidence of tumors.

The largest dose that appears to produce no effects in animals is taken, and a safety factor reducing that dose by about 100 is applied in most countries in order to arrive at an acceptable dose for humans. The "acceptable daily intake" thus calculated is the daily intake that for an entire lifetime appears to be without appreciable risk on the basis of all known facts at the time. It is expressed in terms of milligrams of the additive per kilogram of body weight. One must then calculate how much of the additive a person might be expected to ingest in a day from all dietary sources and compare this figure with the acceptable daily intake in order to decide whether the applications of the additive should be permitted and whether the specific tolerances or maximum limits required for it by good manufacturing practices in individual foods are safe to the health of the consumer.

Many national authorities publish information on the tests they require for proposed additives. International guidelines have been published by the Joint Expert Committee on Food Additives of the Food and Agriculture Organization and the World Health Organization. They require a comprehensive series of tests on laboratory animals, including short- and long-term studies covering acute toxicity, metabolism of the additive and carcinogenic effects, among others.

Assessing safety on the basis of toxicological tests calls for expert judgment of all the evidence available. The judgment may have to be modified in the light of further experiments and experience with the additive in food for humans. The tests required to obtain approval of an additive can cost upward of $100,000.

It is therefore the hope of the government and the food industry in many countries that the work of such international bodies as the Codex Alimentarius Commission of the Food and Agriculture Organization and the World Health Organization will lead to a greater exchange of toxicological data and to the evaluation of the safety of more additives as soon as possible. The commission has published a list of six general principles on the use of food additives. The first is that the use of an additive is justified only when it has the purpose of maintaining a food's nutritional quality, enhancing its keeping quality or stability, making the food attractive, providing aid in processing, packing, transporting or storing food or providing essential components for foods for special diets, and that an additive is not justified if the proposed level of use constitutes a hazard to the consumer's health, if the additive causes a substantial reduction in the nutritive value of a food, if it disguises faulty quality or the use of processing and handling techniques that are not allowed, if it deceives the customer or if the desired effect can be obtained by other manufacturing processes that are economically and technologically satisfactory.

The second principle is that the amount of additive should not exceed the level reasonably required to achieve the desired effect under good manufacturing practice. The third principle calls for additives to conform with an approved standard of purity; the fourth holds that all additives, in use or proposed, should be subjected to adequate toxicological evaluation and that permitted additives should be kept under observation for possible deleterious effects; the fifth states that approval of an additive should be limited to specific foods for specific purposes and under specific conditions, and the sixth relates to the use of additives in foods consumed mainly by special groups in the community. In this case the intake of the food by the group should be taken into account before authorizing the use of the additive.

Food additives have become part of everyday life and undoubtedly will play an increasing role with advances in food technology. The prospect is not necessarily bad, because properly used additives can bring the consumer significant benefits. Moreover, provided that in each case sound justification for the additive is demonstrated, that government and manufacturers exercise the utmost care to ensure that the additive entails no appreciable risks to health and that clear labeling informs the consumer of the nature and composition of the product he is buying, consumers should be reasonably assured as to the safety of officially authorized food additives.

19

BEER

ANTHONY H. ROSE
June 1959

Man has made this exquisite beverage for 6,000 years, but it is only in the past century that he has begun to understand the subtle enzyme chemistry and microbiology of the process

Any solution of the sugary substances of grains, if permitted to stand, will soon become infected by microorganisms. With a little care, the fermentation process that follows can be made to yield a potable, mildly alcoholic beverage. Men have made this discovery wherever they have cultivated grains. Archaeological evidence shows that brewing had developed into a serious art as long as 6,000 years ago in the valley of the Nile. The peoples of the Orient long ago learned to brew sake and related beverages from rice. In the New World, in 1502, Columbus was presented with "a sort of wine made from maize, resembling English beer."

What we call beer—the brew of barley malt flavored with the bitter essences of the hop flower—has been the folk beverage of northern Europe from earliest times. In the monasteries of medieval Europe brewing was as widely practiced as baking. The monastic imprint is seen today in the symbols of quality XX and XXX; in Bavaria one nunnery still has a sister brewmistress! But beer was also one of the first commodities to be industrialized. By the middle of the 17th century such great brewing centers as Oxford, Burton-on-Trent and Munich were already establishing their reputations. It fell to Charles I of England to recognize beer as a source of tax revenue; he imposed the first beer duty in 1643. Brewed and consumed in increasing quantity throughout the 18th and 19th centuries, beer became a major source of nourishment, refreshment and solace to the peoples of Western civilization. In the words of A. E. Housman, "Malt does more than Milton can,/To justify God's ways to man." Today the Belgians, consuming 31 gallons per capita per year, lead the beer drinkers of the world; the U. S. ranks about sixth.

While brewing has not lacked for esthetic appreciation throughout its long history, it is only recently that we have begun to understand what a remarkable art it really is. Now that we know a little microbiology and biochemistry we can see that the brewmaster, by trial and error, has been manipulating some of the subtlest processes of life. To scientific studies we owe many improvements in brewing technology, especially under the heading of quality control. But in some ways the debt runs more heavily the other way. A study of the diseases of beer led Louis Pasteur to discover that yeasts bring about the desired fermentation to alcohol, and that "sickness" in beer is caused by bacteria that yield lactic acid, acetic acid or other unwanted end-products. This discovery not only laid the foundations of the scientific approach to brewing but also helped to open up the whole field of microbiology. The problems of brewing technology played a similar role in the birth of biochemistry. When the German brothers Eduard and Hans Buchner showed in 1897 that cell-free extracts of yeast could cause fermentation of sugar, they exploded once and for all the cherished notions of "vitalism." Their discovery opened the way for all subsequent work on the chemistry of life. As a result of two generations of scientific investigation, the ancient lore of brewing is now enriched by knowledge that has relevance to the enjoyment as well as to the brewing of beer.

The Barley Corn

The key step in the brewing process is of course the addition of yeast to the brew; the yeast ferments or breaks down certain of the grain sugars to alcohol and carbon dioxide, producing "young" or "green" beer. This step, however, comes only as the climax to a whole series of operations that play a decisive part in determining the ultimate taste, aroma and appearance of beer. Of the first importance is the character of the grain from which beer is made. The word "beer" comes from the Saxon word for barley: *baere*. Barley was one of the most important cereals in the early civilizations. Even when barley was displaced by wheat as a raw material for baking, it retained its pre-eminence in brewing.

The barley corn or seed is a spindle-shaped structure. If we remove the protective husk of the corn, we see the tiny embryo of the plant and the relatively large mass of endosperm tissue, which consists mainly of food reserves that support the germination of the embryo. It is the food reserves, in particular the polysaccharide constituents, that are important to the brewer. These polysaccharides are large molecules made up of smaller sugar units such as glucose and maltose.

Now if brewer's yeast is merely added to a suspension of ground raw barley corns in water, no fermentation occurs. The yeast cannot convert the barley polysaccharides directly into alcohol and carbon dioxide; it can only act upon the simple sugars from which the polysaccharides are formed. The polysaccharides must therefore be hydrolyzed (broken down with the addition of water) to their component sugars. This could be accomplished quite simply by cooking the grain with a dilute mineral acid, but since the object is to produce a palatable beverage, such a procedure is far too drastic. The brewer employs a much gentler process.

It happens that the polysaccharides must be broken down in the process of germination in order to supply the sprouting embryo with the simpler sugar units it requires for growth. This breakdown is brought about by the action of certain enzymes that are manufactured inside the grain, several different enzyme systems taking part in the breakdown of various endosperm constituents. The most important of these are the amylases, which hydrolyze the polysaccharides. But barley also contains proteins, and these large molecules are also broken down into their component peptides and amino acids. The brewers of old learned to prepare the grain for fermentation by utilizing this elegant built-in enzymic apparatus, even though they could hardly have suspected how it works.

The first step in brewing, then, is to germinate the barley. In this "malting" process the grain is steeped in water and then transferred to aerated chambers or slowly revolving drums in which careful control of temperature, moisture and oxygen promotes uniform germination. When the desired stage of growth has been reached, gentle heating brings germination to a halt, with temperature again carefully controlled to minimize the damage to heat-sensitive enzymes Prolonged heating produces a darker grain, sometimes employed in the brewing of darker beers. At this point, however, only a small proportion of the endosperm polysaccharides has been broken down. The object in malting is not to get the hydrolysis well under way, but simply to allow the grain to manufacture all of the necessary enzymes. Malting is predominantly a mobilizing or "tooling-up" process. Nowadays, in fact, malting is not strictly a part of the brewer's operations; it is carried out by maltsters, who then deliver prepared malt to the brewery.

The Mashing Process

The brewing process proper begins with "mashing": Ground malt is mixed with hot water, and permitted to stand for a short time. Now the malt enzymes go to work, and the breakdown of the polysaccharides begins. Since the enzymic capacity of the malt far exceeds that required to break down all of the endosperm starch, other starchy materials are added to the mash. These "adjuncts" increase the volume of fermentable sugars but contribute little if anything to the taste and aroma of the beer. As the enzymes digest the starch and proteins of the malt, the breakdown products—sugars, peptides and amino acids—dissolve and diffuse into the water to make sweet malt "wort," the liquor that the yeast is later to ferment.

Generations of brewmasters learned empirically to subject the mashing process to precise control by the regulation of temperature, the temperature cycle being designed in each case to yield the sugar content and other qualities in the wort called for by the type of beer being brewed. Usually the malt is first mixed with water at a temperature of 105 degrees Fahrenheit, and is kept at this temperature for an initial "resting" period of 30 minutes. Meanwhile, in a separate mash tub, the cereal adjuncts are infused with water at the same temperature and brought gradually to a boil. When the contents of this tub have been cooked to a gelatinous texture, they are added to the malt mash, resulting in a final mixing temperature of some 157 degrees F. After being maintained at about this temperature for another half hour, the mixture is "mashed off" or stabilized by heating it up to 175 degrees, a temperature that destroys most of the enzymes.

Today we can explain the importance of temperature control during mashing because we have made the acquaintance of the principal enzymic actors in the process. Each of these enzymes functions best in a characteristic range of temperature. During the resting period, when the temperature is held at 105 degrees, the protein-decomposing enzymes find the environment most congenial. The peptides and amino acids produced by the breakdown of proteins do not contribute directly to the production of alcohol; however, they provide essential food substances for the yeast and give the beer body as well as head-retaining properties. Thus it is important that just the right amount of protein should be broken down in the mashing process.

As the mash is heated up by the addi-

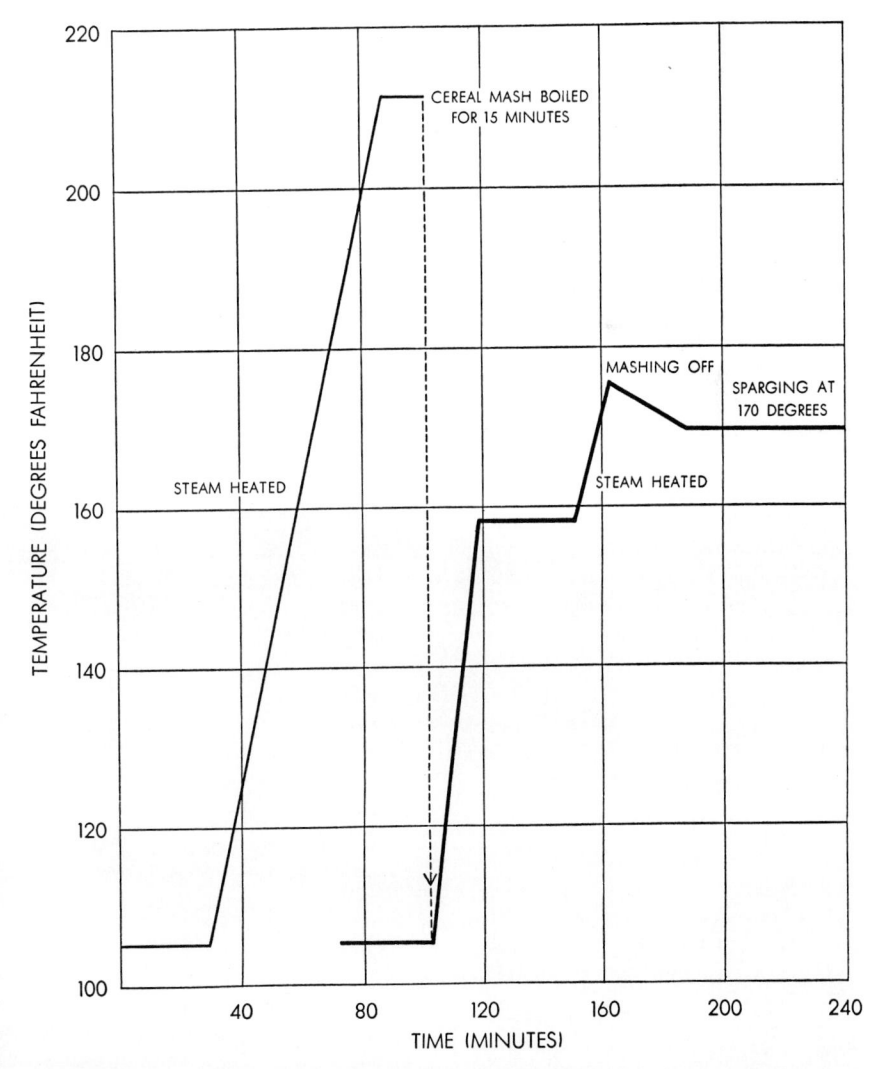

TEMPERATURE of cereal-mash adjuncts (*curve at left*) and malt (*curve at right*) is plotted against time. The malt is heated largely by the addition (*broken line*) of the adjuncts.

BREW KETTLE in a New York brewery is filled with malt wort produced by allowing the enzymes of barley corns to digest the protein and starch of the barley and of "adjuncts." Here the wort is boiled to destroy the enzymes. Hops are added by the man at bottom.

SETTLING TANK is where the wort cools and solids settle out of it after it has left the brew kettle. The wort is now further cooled and sent to the fermenting tanks (*see illustration at top of next page*). The entire process is outlined on pages 164 and 165.

OPEN FERMENTING TANK is where yeast is added to the wort, which has been filtered of its hops and cooled. The yeast enzymes now ferment the wort sugars to alcohol. Here the yeast sinks to the bottom of the tank; on the top is a foam caused by fermentation.

LAGER TANKS are where the "green" beer is aged for several weeks at 32 degrees F. The beer is then filtered to remove traces of yeast and a suspension of protein that is precipitated by chilling. Finally the beer is carbonated and bottled, canned or barreled.

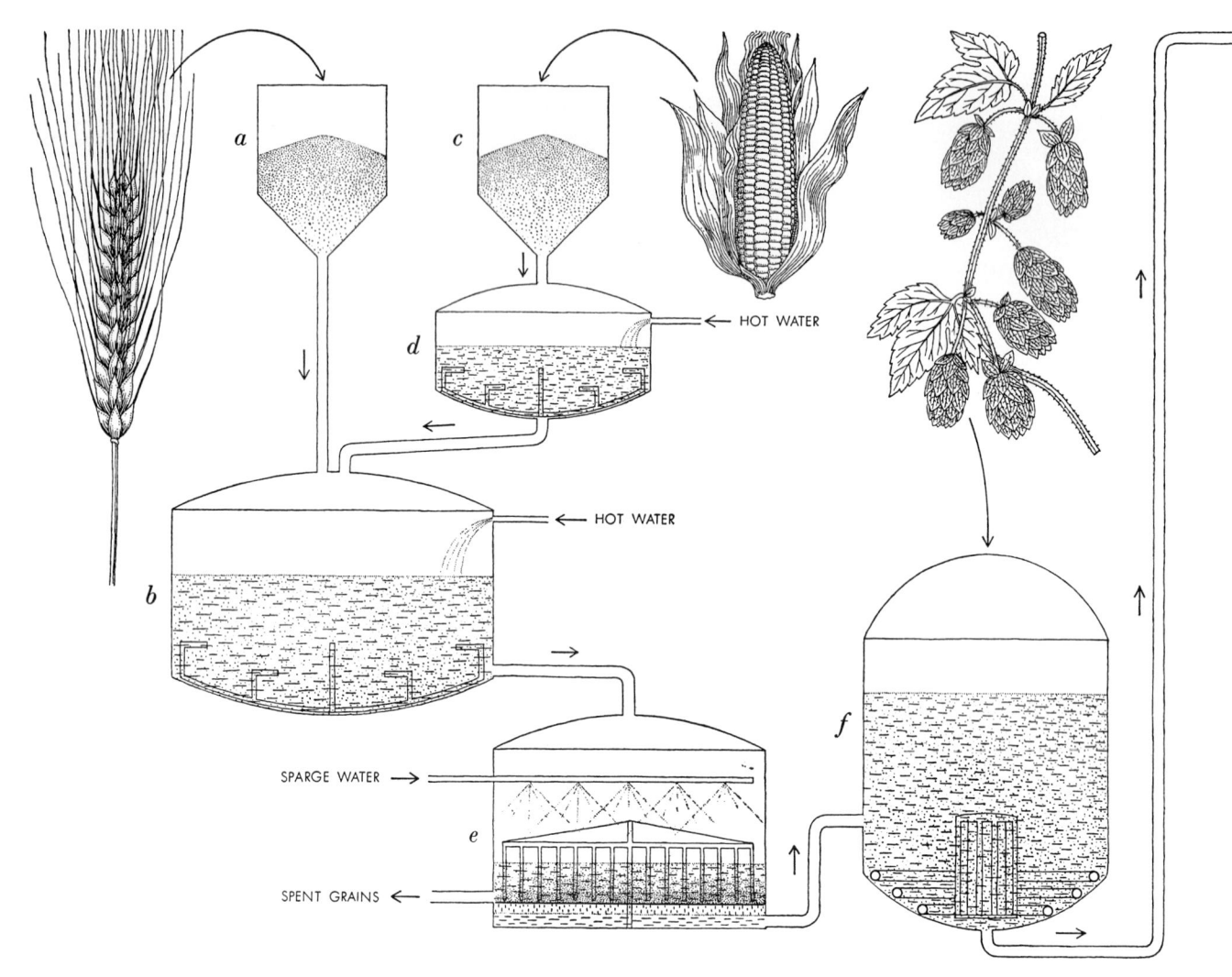

ENTIRE BREWING PROCESS is outlined in this flow chart. The barley corns are ground and placed in the malt hopper (*a*); from thence they go to the mash tub (*b*). Corn (or other adjuncts) is placed in the adjunct hopper (*c*), boiled in the adjunct cooker (*d*) and added to the mash. The malt wort is then filtered in the lauter tub (*e*). The clear wort goes to the brew kettle (*f*), where hops

tion of the adjunct mixture, the starch-digesting enzymes—the amylases—come into play. Starch is not a simple polysaccharide, but consists of a mixture of two glucose polymers: amylose, made up of straight chains of glucose units, and amylopectin, made up of branched chains. Moreover, there are at least two distinct starch-hydrolyzing enzymes in malt: alpha- and beta-amylase. The unbranched amylose chains are broken down by beta-amylase, which chops off the glucose units two at a time to give the disaccharide maltose. Theoretically beta-amylase can break down the amylose completely; in practice the reaction is inhibited by the accumulation of breakdown products. But beta-amylase cannot completely break down the amylopectin molecule, because its action is halted at points where the chain branches. The other enzyme, alpha-amylase, makes up for this deficiency; it is able to split the branched chains into smaller fragments and thus provide additional straight chains that can be nibbled away by the beta-amylase. The beta enzyme prefers temperatures in the region of 140 degrees F., while the alpha enzyme acts most efficiently at the slightly higher temperature of 150 to 170 degrees. Thus the relative proportions of alpha- and beta-amylase activity can be controlled by the temperature of the mash and by the profile of the curve on which the temperature is shifted.

Higher temperatures will tend to promote alpha action and discourage beta, and will thus result in a smaller proportion of fermentable sugars. Worts of this type have a correspondingly higher proportion of dextrins (short units, both branched and unbranched), which cannot be fermented by brewer's yeast but which contribute to the character and body of the beer and help to maintain a stable foam. Brewers use worts of this type to brew beers with a low content of alcohol. Thus careful control of temperature during mashing has always given the brewmaster an opportunity to exercise his skill. Only recently have we come to realize that he is in fact the choreographer of an enzymic ballet.

After mashing off, the contents of the tub are transferred to the "lauter" tub (*lauter* in German means "clear"). This is a cylindrical tank having a false bottom of slotted plates, through which the clear malt wort is run off, the cereal husks forming an ideal filter bed. The husks are further "sparged," or leached with hot water to augment the volume of wort extracted. At this point the brewing process yields a valuable by-product in the form of the spent grains, which make excellent cattle feed.

The Addition of Hops

The clear malt wort is now run into a steam-heated copper or stainless-steel brew kettle, in which it is boiled for 30 to 60 minutes. In the process any remaining enzymes are destroyed, and the

are added. The hops are removed by the hop strainer (g); other substances, by a settling tank (h). The wort is now cooled (i) and sent to open (j) and closed (k) fermenting tanks. In the closed tank carbon dioxide is collected and later used to carbonate the beer. After fermentation the green beer goes to lagering tanks (l, n and p). As it passes from one tank to next it is filtered (m and o).

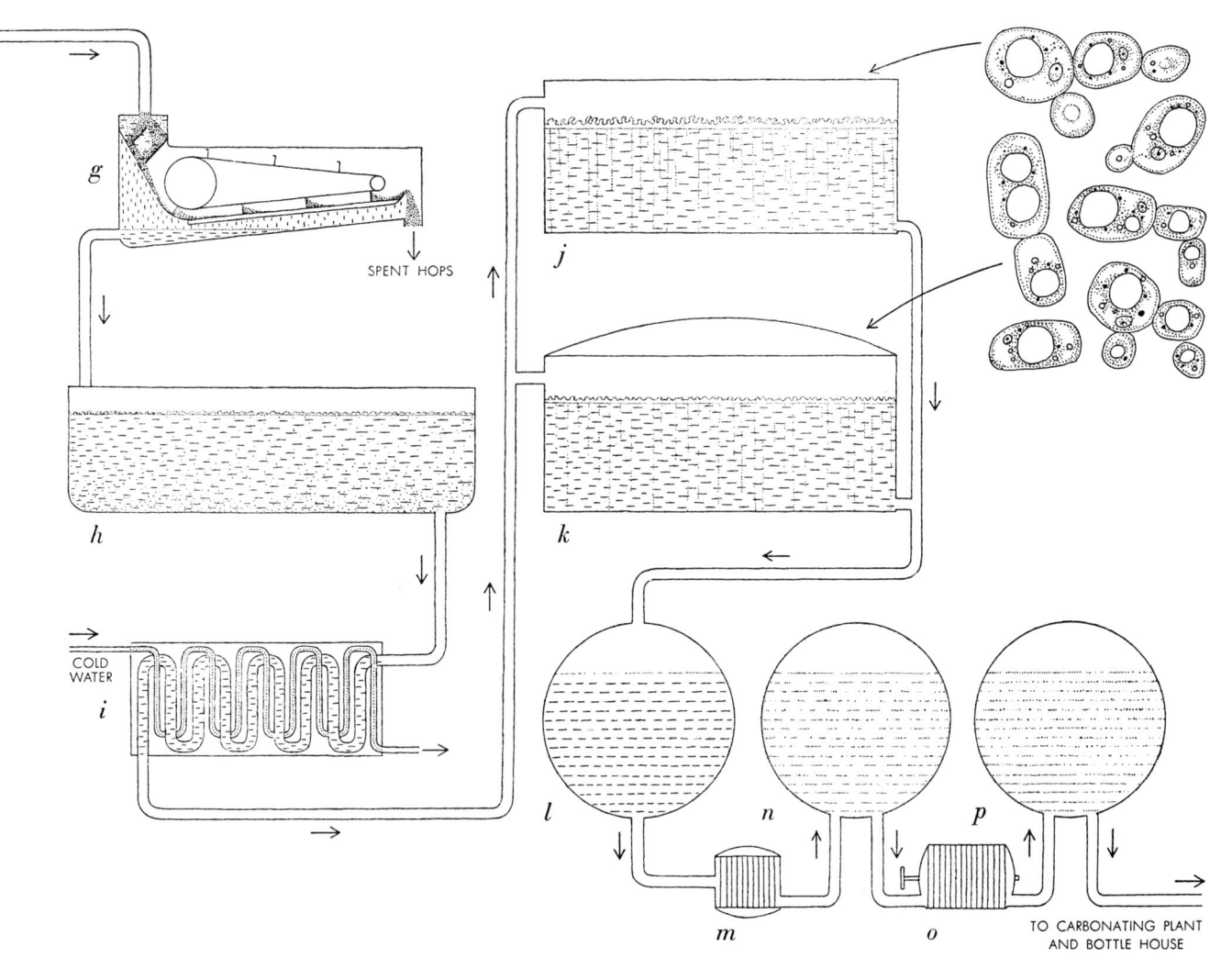

wort is sterilized and somewhat concentrated. More important, dried hops are added to the boiling wort in amounts and at intervals that vary with the type of beer. German beers and the U. S. beers that are modeled on them are usually hopped at the rate of about half a pound for each barrel, but for the English ales the rate is much higher, in some cases as high as a pound and a half per barrel. Hops are added primarily to impart the characteristic aroma and pleasant bitterness of beer. Although hops are now universally used for this purpose, it is interesting to note that prior to the 17th century mixtures of various herbs were commonly employed to flavor beer. Thus in Thomas Tryon's *A New Art of Brewing Beer, Ale and Other Sorts of Liquors*, published in 1691, we read: "Here give me leave to tell you that there are a great number of brave Herbs and Vegitations that will do the business in brewing as well as Hops. . . . Penny Royal and Balsam . . . are of excellent use in Beer and Ale: the like is to be understood of Mint, Tansie, Wormwood, Betony . . . and good Hay." The hops of brewing are the cone-shaped flowers of the female hop plant, each cone consisting of a spindle with between 50 and 100 petals. The hop flowers are picked when ripe, and are dried and pressed before being shipped to the brewery. A century ago most of the hops in the U. S. came from New York and Vermont; the principal hop-producing areas are now along the Pacific coast and in Idaho.

Boiling in the brew kettle extracts from the hops a variety of substances. These include oils and complex bittering substances such as humulone, cohumulone and adhumulone, all of which contribute to the flavor and aroma of beer. Antiseptic substances are also extracted; these help to prevent microbial spoilage in the finished beer. In addition, the hops contribute tannins. These are of special importance in the brewing process, for they combine with the protein in wort to form an insoluble sludge that settles to the bottom of the brew kettle. If the protein is allowed to remain in the wort, it tends to precipitate later as a haze in the beer, a considerable hazard to consumer acceptance.

After boiling, the hops are strained off and the wort is cooled to 45 or 50 degrees F. Cooling throws down a further deposit of protein-tannin sludge, which is filtered off. Just before the cool wort is transferred to the fermentation tank, it is aerated with sterile air to make it more hospitable to the yeast that is to be planted in it.

Top- and Bottom-Fermentation

Here we come to one of the major differences between British and Continental practice. It is this difference that occasions so much confusion among U. S. consumers, who enjoy the privilege of choice between the products of both types of brewing. The distinction arises

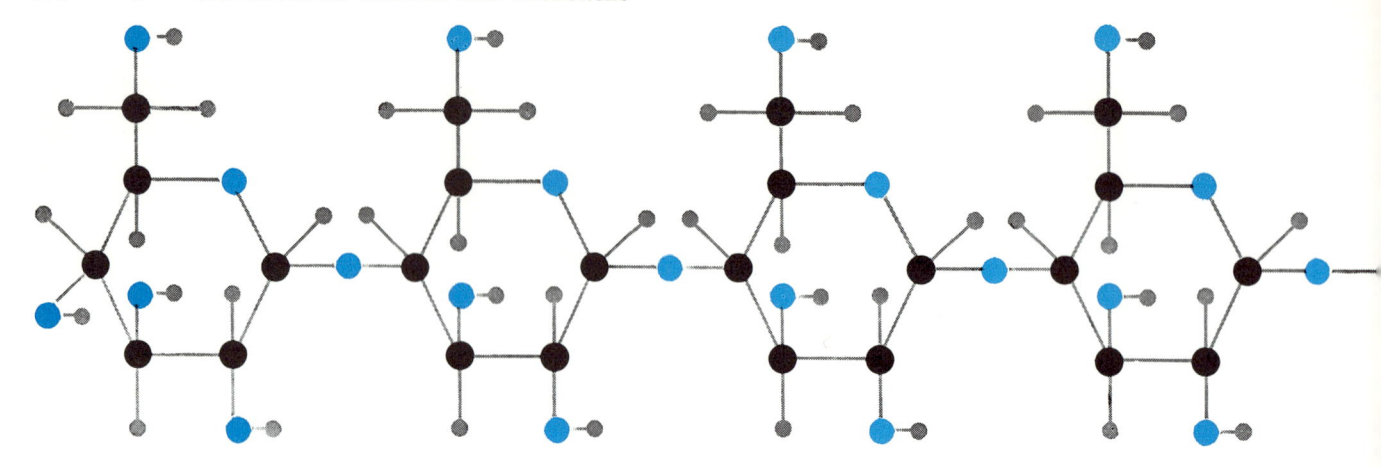

STARCH of malt is a polymer of glucose, that is, a repeating chain of glucose units. A single glucose unit is shown to the right of the broken line, which indicates that the chain is repeated. The black balls represent carbon atoms; the gray balls, hydrogen atoms; the colored balls, oxygen atoms. Starch is actually a mixture of two glucose polymers: amylose, consisting of a straight chain of

from the behavior of the yeast during fermentation. In Britain brewers still employ types of yeast that rise to the surface during fermentation. The "top-fermentation" beers come in many varieties, from relatively pale ales to porter (a dark, heavy ale popular in Ireland) and stout (also dark and heavy, but with a higher alcoholic content). In the U. S. top-fermentation and a taste for ales arrived on the *Mayflower*. The Pilgrims recorded that they landed at Plymouth with misgivings and were forced to settle on that forbidding shore because they had drunk all their beer. But they had brought their yeast balm, and ales are still preferred in New England.

Elsewhere in the U. S. the brewing industry derives its traditions from the brewmasters who came from Germany in the 19th century to set up large commercial breweries. The Germans brought the new technique of "bottom-fermentation," which, as the term indicates, employs a yeast that settles to the bottom during fermentation. The German "lager" beers are usually paler than ales, and are rather more mellow in flavor. There are three main types: Münchner, Dortmunder and Pilsener, named after the towns in which they were first brewed and here listed in order of their color from dark to pale. Under the pressures of standardization arising from mass distribution U. S. beers have tended to become increasingly pale and thus to resemble the Pilsener beer; they have less hop flavor, however, and are much more highly carbonated. A seasonal exception to this trend is bock beer, the dark, full-flavored beer that certain U. S. brewers still put on the market in the spring. Originally brewed in Bavaria during the Easter celebrations, bock beer gets its name from the German word for goat, which animal is the zodiacal sign for the month of March.

Whether top- or bottom-fermentation is used, about one pound of yeast slurry is "pitched" into the tank for each barrel of beer. Malt wort furnishes an ideal diet for yeast; during the fermentation period of six to nine days the organisms not only multiply about threefold but also break down a large proportion of the sugars in the wort to alcohol and carbon dioxide. The concentration of alcohol at the end of the process is about 4 per cent in lager beers and somewhat higher in ales. Thanks to investigations founded by the Buchner brothers, we now know of the dozen or so enzyme reactions involved in the fermentation of sugar to alcohol. Some of the energy that is produced is utilized for growth, but by far the greater part of it escapes as heat. To keep the fermenting brew at the optimum temperature (55 degrees F. for lager beers and 60 to 65 degrees for British ales) the fermentation tank must be refrigerated. Before the advent of mechanical refrigeration, beer was commonly fermented in caves or underground cellars; the fermentation section of a brewery is still quite often referred to as the "cellar." In addition to fermenting the sugar, yeast also brings about a host of other changes in the chemical composition of the wort; very little is known, however, of the nature of many of these changes.

The Yeast Organism

Most of the bottom-fermentation yeasts used in the U. S. and in Europe today are strains of *Saccharomyces carlsbergensis*, which takes its name from the great Carlsberg brewery in Copenhagen, or of *Saccharomyces cerevisiae*. Top-fermentation yeasts are all strains of *Saccharomyces cerevisiae*. Our familiarity with these microorganisms goes back only to Pasteur. But even before the mid-19th century brewing yeasts were selected by spontaneous fermentation and by long-continued and repeated transfers from one brew to another. At least one archaeologist has claimed that traces of yeast found in urns dating back to 1440 B.C. were decidedly superior to those in vessels of 3400 B.C. The Danish botanist Emil Christian Hansen was one of the first to develop techniques for isolating yeasts in pure culture, and he introduced these yeasts into breweries. Today many brewers employ pure strains of yeast that are especially suited to brewing. The cultures are renewed at intervals varying from a few months to several years; by careful control the yeast may be kept reasonably free from contaminating microorganisms.

At the end of fermentation the yeast has settled to the bottom of the vessel. The green beer is now pumped into large lager tanks, where it is kept at about 32 degrees F. for several weeks. The yeast, separated from the beer, can be used again. Lagering permits the beer to mature, with the result that both taste and aroma become decidedly mellower. We are, however, almost completely ignorant of the nature of these maturation changes. In all probability they are largely attributable to the production of minute amounts of unidentified alcohols and esters by the traces of yeast that remain in the beer. After lagering, further filtration through diatomaceous earth removes these traces of yeast and also a fine suspension of protein that is precipitated by chilling. The beer is then carbonated, usually by the injection of carbon dioxide but occasionally by a secondary fermentation under pressure, known as "krausening." When the product is bottled or canned, it must be pas-

glucose units, and amylopectin, consisting of branched chains. The straight chain of amylose may consist of as many as 300 units.

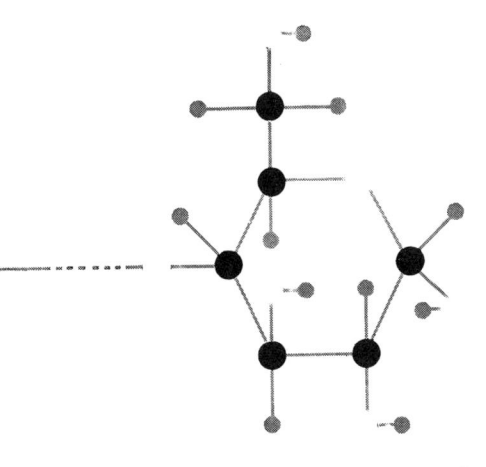

teurized by heating it to a temperature of about 140 degrees F. for 15 to 20 minutes, a treatment that is sufficient to kill most of the microorganisms capable of growing in beer. The beer marketed in aluminum or stainless-steel kegs to the restaurant and bar trades is not pasteurized, and so is kept under refrigeration until it is consumed.

The sequence of operations for converting barley and hops into beer that we have reviewed here is the result of centuries of empirical development. Though the knowledge gained in the past 50 years has disclosed the solid scientific foundations upon which the art has rested, it has so far improved upon it only in detail. However, with the deeper understanding provided by the biochemist, the brewmaster is better equipped to deal with problems that continue to arise even after 6,000 years.

The Problem of Haze

Probably the most pressing brewing research problem arises from the new habit of drinking beer from cans and bottles that have been kept in storage and are then decanted into clear glasses. For centuries beer was dispensed from kegs and drunk out of mugs and tankards; it was then judged solely by taste and smell. But in the recent past the locus of beer drinking has shifted to the home. It has now become necessary to produce beers that can be shipped long distances and kept on the shelf for unpredictable periods of time in a variety of temperatures, and will still be crystal-clear when they are poured into a glass. Unfortunately beers that have been so treated often tend to develop a haze, and consumer demand requires that this be eliminated.

One type of haze is caused by infec-

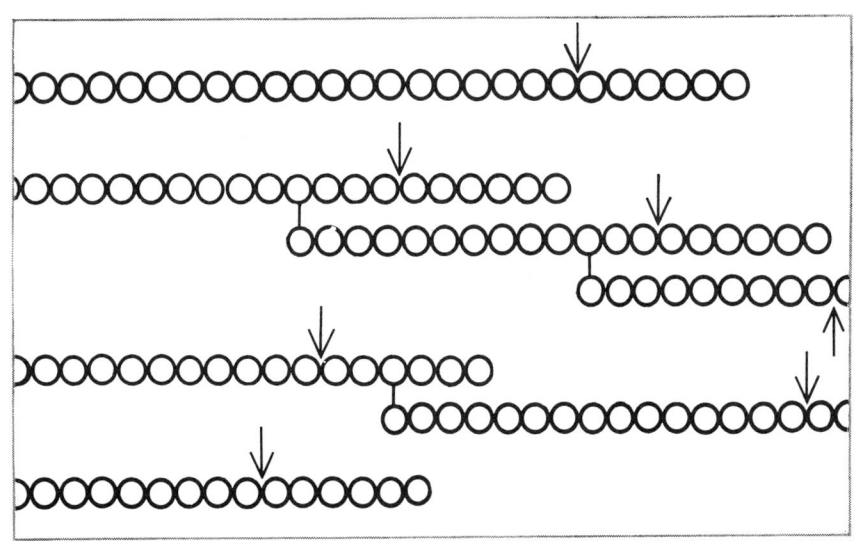

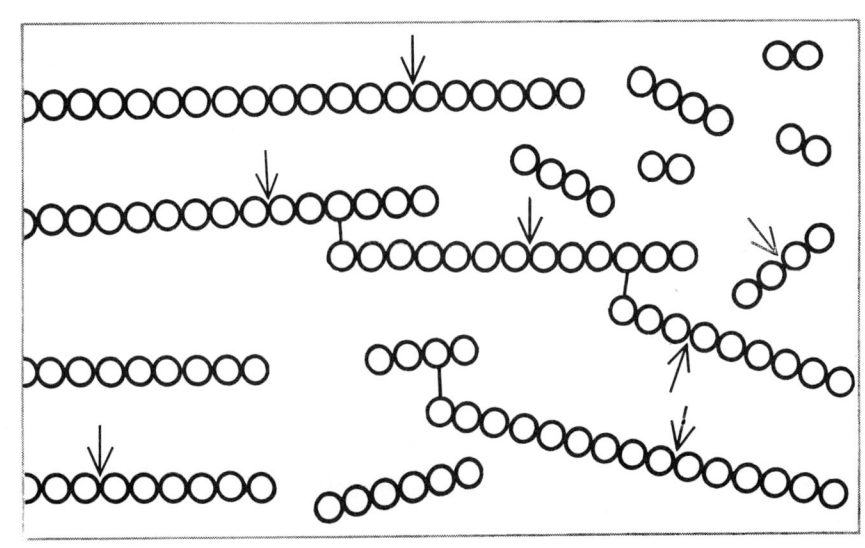

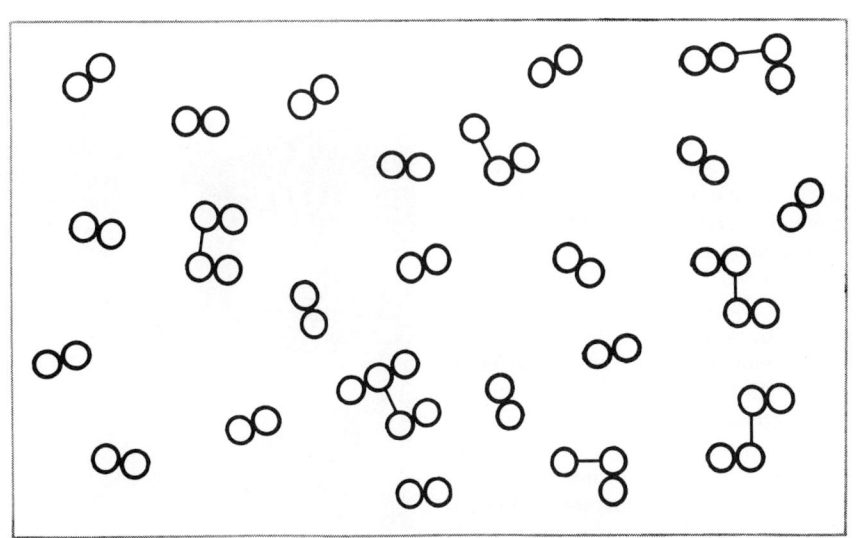

STARCH IS BROKEN DOWN by the enzymes alpha-amylase (*black arrows*) and beta-amylase (*colored arrows*). In the top drawing each glucose unit is represented by a small circle. At the top and bottom of this drawing are straight chains; in the middle are branched chains. In the middle drawing the beta-amylase splits off two glucoses at a time; the alpha-amylase splits off a larger number of glucoses, which are in turn broken down by beta-amylase. In the bottom drawing is the mixture of maltose (a two-glucose sugar) and dextrins (short, branched chains of glucose) that ultimately results from the process.

tion. Even after fermentation the finished beer contains sufficient food substances to support growth of a large number of microorganisms. Infection can occur in spite of pasteurization and the additional protection afforded by hop antiseptics in the beer. Fortunately the acidity of beer precludes the possibility of infection by microorganisms that cause disease in humans. The offending microorganisms are either bacteria (*e.g.*, species of *Pediococcus, Lactobacillus* and *Acetobacter*) or so-called wild yeasts, microorganisms closely related to the yeast used in fermentation. Beers infected by these microorganisms become hazy, and develop undesirable flavors. Although such spoilage can be troublesome, it can usually be prevented by strict attention to cleanliness in the brewhouse.

Far more serious are the nonbiological hazes. Here the turbidity is the result of the precipitation of fine particles of organic matter, predominantly protein. As we have seen, most of the protein is removed from wort when it is boiled and infused with hops, the tannins in the hops (and some from the malt husk) combining with the proteins to form an insoluble sludge. However, this protein-tannin complex continues to precipitate slowly from the beer even after packaging, so that after a period of storage the beer may well develop a pronounced haze. One cure for the condition is to add protein-digesting enzymes to the finished beer. This "chill-proofing" is not entirely satisfactory because too much enzyme may break down those peptides that give the beer its head-retaining properties. Another approach is based upon the fact that oxygen is conducive to haze formation. Thus various antioxidants, including ascorbic acid (vitamin C), have been added to beer to improve its stability. In recent years, however, a more fundamental attack on the problem has been launched; this work aims at identifying the haze components, tracking down their origin and then removing them from the scene of action. Unfortunately the chemistry of the proteins and tannins that make up hazes is extremely complex. Recent work at the Brewing Industry Research Foundation in England suggests, however, that we may be on the right track. Chemical analysis has shown that the trouble is often caused by one particular group of tannin substances known as anthocyanogens; they are commonly found in association with the proteins in hazes. It happens that these anthocyanogens can be removed from beers by adsorption on a polyamide resin such as nylon. Experimental brews treated in this way have shown a considerably extended shelf-life.

The Intrusion of Science

Since he deals in such evanescent commodities as taste and aroma, the brewer is understandably cautious in his approach to innovation in the brewing process. He has nonetheless been encouraged by the success of the scientific techniques so far employed and has begun to take a more critical view of the time-honored methods of his craft. The biochemist and microbiologist are now well established in brewing research laboratories; soon they will be joined by representatives of other disciplines. Brewers are looking to geneticists, for example, to improve the strains of yeast. Perhaps chemical engineers will bring about the most revolutionary changes in brewing during the next decade or so. For example, techniques for replacing the traditional batch-method of brewing by a continuous process are already in the pilot-plant stage. Clearly the intrusion of science into the art of brewing promises to bring great changes in the procedures that have served so well for six millennia.

BREWING IN ANCIENT EGYPT is depicted by this relief in the Rijksmuseum of Leiden. At left in the third row a brewer pours water into a vat; at right the beer is poured into jars.

WINE

MAYNARD A. AMERINE
August 1964

This happy invention of man is a solution of hundreds of subtly interacting substances. Modern understanding of the wine-making process cannot explain a great wine but guarantees a good one

Wine is a chemical symphony composed of ethyl alcohol, several other alcohols, sugars, other carbohydrates, polyphenols, aldehydes, ketones, enzymes, pigments, at least half a dozen vitamins, 15 to 20 minerals, more than 22 organic acids and other grace notes that have not yet been identified. The number of possible permutations and combinations of these ingredients is enormous, and so, of course, are the varieties and qualities of wines. Considering the complexity of the subject, it is not surprising that perhaps more nonsense has been written about the making, uses and appreciation of wine than about any other product of man or nature.

Nevertheless, it can be said that in the 20th century wine making has become a reasonably well-understood art. The chemical processes involved are now sufficiently known so that the production of a sound wine is no longer an accident (although the production of a great wine may still be). For this we are indebted primarily to Louis Pasteur, who founded the modern technology of wine making along with several branches of chemistry, microbiology and medicine. Pasteur put the making of wine (and of beer as well) on a rational basis by explaining fermentation, which for thousands of years had been an unsolved mystery.

It seems likely that man's discovery of wine came later than that of beer (a fermentation product of grain) or of mead (a fermentation product of honey), because grapes grow only in certain climates and environments. By Neolithic times, however, the peoples of the Middle East were well acquainted with the fermented juice of the grape, and one of the oldest inscriptions in Egypt (on the tomb of Ptahhotep, who lived about 2500 B.C.) depicts the making of wine. The "blood of the grape" attracted ancient man not only as a beverage but also as a medicine and a symbolic offering to the gods.

The grape is its own wine maker. One simply pressed out the juice, let it stand, and its sugars turned into alcohol. Not until the 19th century did chemists begin to unravel the nature of this process. In 1810 Joseph Louis Gay-Lussac made the first crucial contribution toward solution of the mystery by discovering the general chemical formula of the breakdown of sugar into alcohol and carbon dioxide: $C_6H_{12}O_6 \rightarrow 2\ C_2H_5OH + 2\ CO_2$. Plainly this change did not take place spontaneously. What caused the sugar to break down? Gay-Lussac conjectured from his experiments that the process was stimulated somehow by oxygen. The German chemist Justus von Liebig put forward another hypothesis: that the fermentation arose from the "vibrations" of a decomposing "albuminoid" substance. Liebig's authority was so powerful that his view was not seriously challenged until the young Pasteur embarked on his studies of fermentation in the 1850's.

The Role of Yeast

"How account," Pasteur asked, "for the working of the vintage in the vat?" With his gift for designing experiments that went to the heart of the matter, Pasteur soon demonstrated that the working was produced by the microscopic organisms known as yeast. "Fermentation," he concluded, "is correlative with life." He showed that an infusion of yeast would convert even a simple sugar solution into alcohol, and he went on to identify some of the factors, such as acidity or alkalinity, that controlled the metabolic activities of the yeast organisms and thus determined the properties of a wine. Pasteur announced his main discoveries in two historic papers: *Mémoire sur la fermentation appelée lactique* (published in 1857) and *Études sur le vin* (1866).

How does the grape acquire its yeast? As every gardener knows, the skin of growing grapes is covered with a delicate natural bloom. It consists of a waxy film that collects cells of molds and wild yeasts, which are deposited on the grape by agencies such as the wind and insects. The skin of a single grape may bear as many as 10 million yeast cells. Of these, 100,000 or more are cells of the varieties called wine yeasts, of which the principal one is *Saccharomyces cerevisiae* var. *ellipsoideus*. It is the enzymes of the wine yeasts that are responsible for the fermentation of the grape's sugars to alcohol and for the creation of the numerous by-products that partially account for the flavor and other properties of the wine. The nature of the activity of the yeasts importantly affects the wine's quality, consequently it is one of the factors modern wineries are careful to control. In some old European vineyards the grapes and yeasts seem to have established over the centuries a natural harmony that brings out the grapes' best qualities in the wine. But most wineries, even in Europe, now improve on nature by adding pure cultures of desirable yeasts and using chemicals to suppress the growth of undesirable yeasts present on the grape skins.

The Effect of Climate

The making of a wine starts long before the grapes reach the winery—indeed, long before the grapes are har-

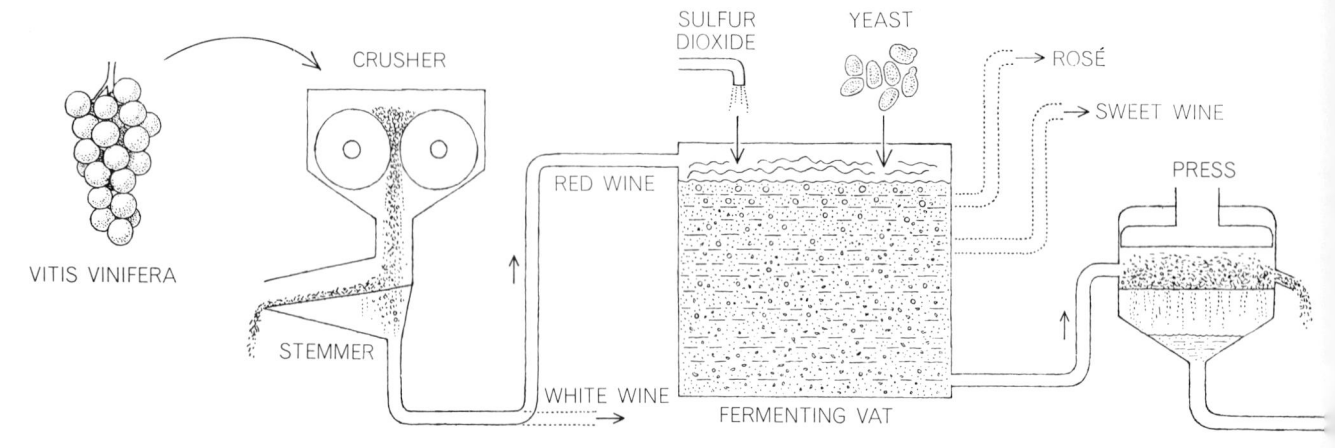

WESTERN U.S. METHOD of producing red wine duplicates the European process. The grapes are crushed between rollers (*left*), forming an intermediate product known as "must." The must is piped to a fermenting vat where yeasts speed the transformation

vested from the vine. The grape is a complex product of soil, water, sun and temperature. Of these factors, the most significant single one is temperature. Grapes will grow only within the belts of the Northern and Southern hemispheres where the average annual temperature is between 50 and 68 degrees Fahrenheit [*see lower illustration on page 178*]. Even in these regions the European grape *Vitis vinifera* does not survive in areas marked by certain unfavorable conditions: summer temperatures not warm enough to ripen the fruit (as in most of Britain), high summer humidity that excessively exposes it to mold diseases or insect predators (as in the southeastern U.S.) or late spring frosts (as in the northwestern U.S.).

The ideal climate for wine grapes is one that is warm but not too warm, cool but not too cool. On the one hand, a long growing season is required so that the grapes will produce a high content of sugar for conversion into alcohol. On the other hand, comparatively cool temperatures are desirable because they produce grapes with high acidity, an important contributor to the quality of wine, particularly the dry table wines. Both of these climatic conditions are well fulfilled in areas such as the Bordeaux district of France, northern Spain, central and northern Italy, Yugoslavia and northern California—and those areas produce fine red table wines. In areas with cooler or shorter growing seasons, such as Germany, Switzerland, Austria, the eastern U.S. and even the Burgundy district of France, the grapes in some years do not develop enough sugar, and sugar must be added when they are brought to the winery. This addition cannot, however, replace flavor components that are missing when the grapes have not ripened fully. The variability of the summer climate in Europe is the main reason for the fluctuation in the quality of its wines from year to year and for the emphasis on vintage years.

Although a warm climate (such as that of southern Spain, Sicily, Cyprus and southern California) produces grapes with a high sugar content, they have the handicap of comparatively low acidity. These grapes are suitable for the sweet dessert wines, but they lack the subtle flavors and color of grapes grown in cooler areas. Moreover, they are sometimes overripe when they come to the fermenting vats, with sad effects on quality if one attempts to produce a table wine from them.

The Grape

No less important than the characteristics of the climate are the characteristics of the grape. One of the benign aspects of the grape plant—which holds much promise for future wines—is its great variability. One species alone, *Vitis vinifera*, has some 5,000 known varieties, and even the less popular species are available in about 2,000 varieties. Grape breeders

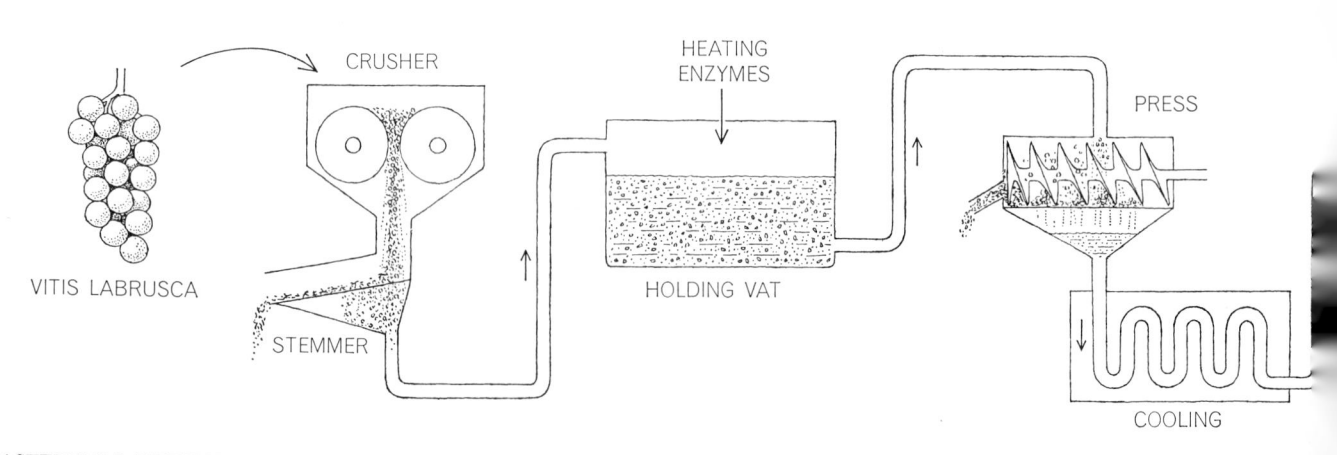

EASTERN U.S. METHOD of producing red wine begins with the crushing (*left*) of *Vitis labrusca* grape, a species low in sugar. Must is piped into a holding vat, where enzymes are added to break down mucilaginous substances in and around the pulp. The desired color

of sugars into alcohol, and then to a press where skin and seeds are separated out. The juice proceeds through two settling vats, wherein the "fining" process removes impurities. It is filtered, sometimes heated and cooled, and aged in casks prior to bottling.

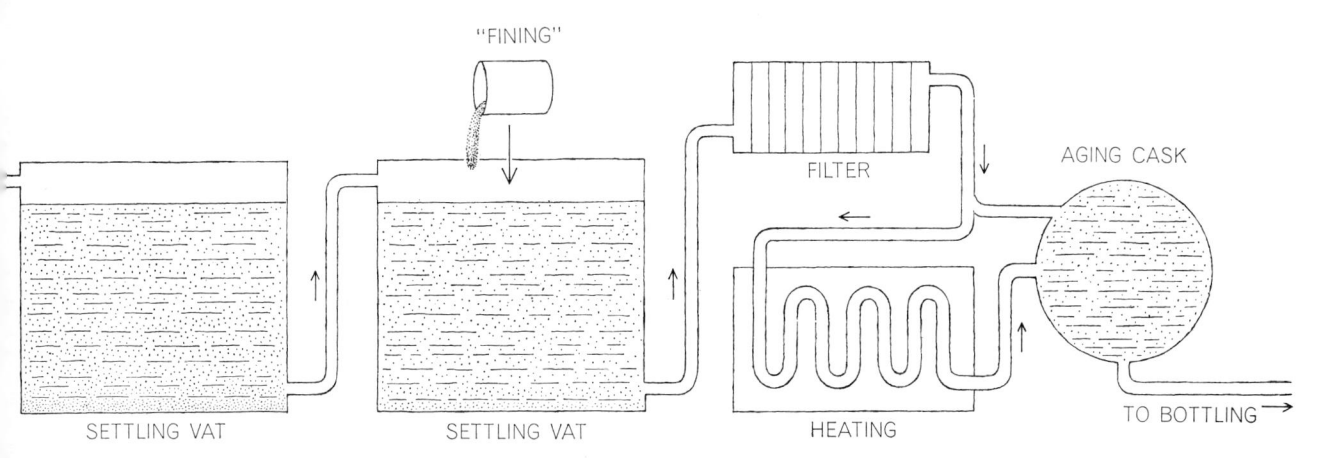

have also produced many hybrids between the species. The grape varieties differ in color (white, green, pink, red or purple), in the size of the grape clusters, in the texture of the grape (firm and pulpy or soft and liquid), in sugar content, in acidity, in earliness or lateness of ripening and in susceptibility to insects and diseases. With this variability in the material, plant geneticists look forward to breeding new varieties of grapes that will be tailored to specific climates, to the types of wine and to new heights of taste, aroma and bouquet. (As wine experts define the terms, aroma refers to the fragrance of the grape; bouquet, to the fragrance imparted by fermentation and aging.)

Vitis vinifera is by far the preponderant species of wine grape grown in vineyards throughout the world. The plant is believed to have originated near the shores of the Caspian Sea in what is now the southern U.S.S.R. From there early travelers and traders spread it around the Mediterranean, then to northern Europe and eventually explorers transported it to continents overseas. (More than 81 percent of the world's vineyard acreage and wine production are still concentrated, however, in Europe and North Africa, with France the leader.) In the U.S. the *vinifera* species has found a hospitable home in California, and some 100 varieties of this species are cultivated commercially there. *Vinifera* is vulnerable to the diseases and insects that thrive in a hot and humid summer climate; for this reason many vineyards in the eastern U.S., Canada, Brazil and certain areas in Europe cultivate other species, such as *Vitis labrusca* or *Vitis rotundifolia*.

Now let us examine the wine-making process. To follow it in detail we shall consider the typical procedure in a modern California winery.

The Wine-making Process

To begin, let us analyze the raw material. In a mature grape about 10 to 20 percent of the material by weight is accounted for by the skin, stem and seeds, and the remaining 80 to 90 percent is pulp and juice. The pulp and juice, when piped into the fermenting vat, is called "must." Chemically the grape must is mostly water, but between 18 and 25 percent by weight is sugar (the amount varying with the variety and ripeness of the grape). The sugar consists mainly of dextrose (that is, glucose that rotates polarized light to the right) and levulose (or fructose, which rotates polarized light to the left). The grapes from which table wines are made usually contain dextrose and levulose in about equal amounts; for sweet wines vintners would prefer grapes with a higher proportion of levulose, because it is nearly twice as sweet as dextrose. In addition to these two principal sugars, grapes also contain small quantities of other carbohydrates, such as sucrose, pentoses and pentosans.

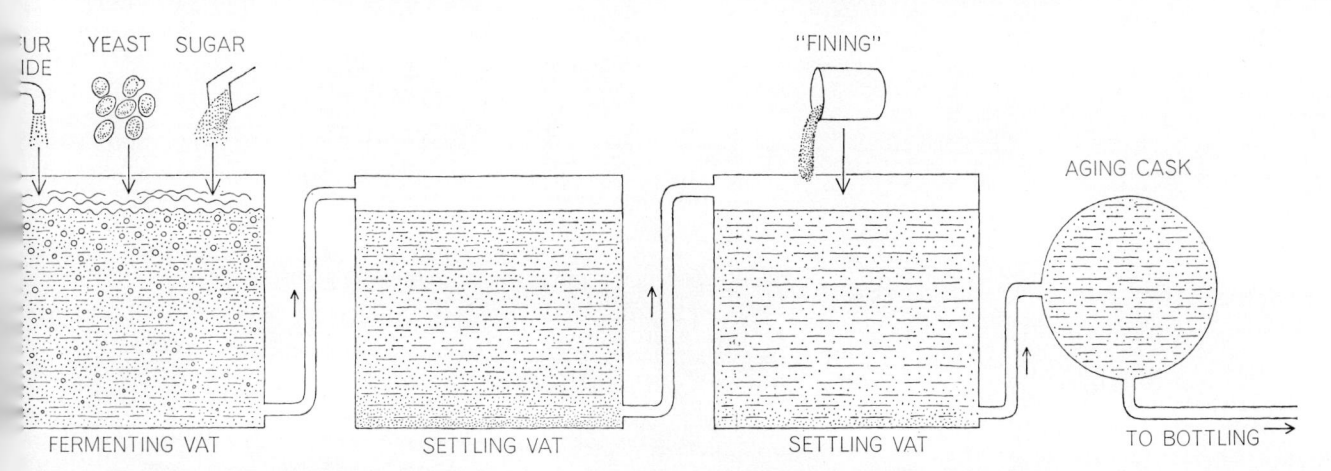

is attained by heating. Must proceeds to a fermenting vat where sugar as well as yeast and sulfur dioxide are added. Removal of impurities by fining takes place in settling vats, and the wine is then aged. Some Eastern wines are pasteurized before bottling.

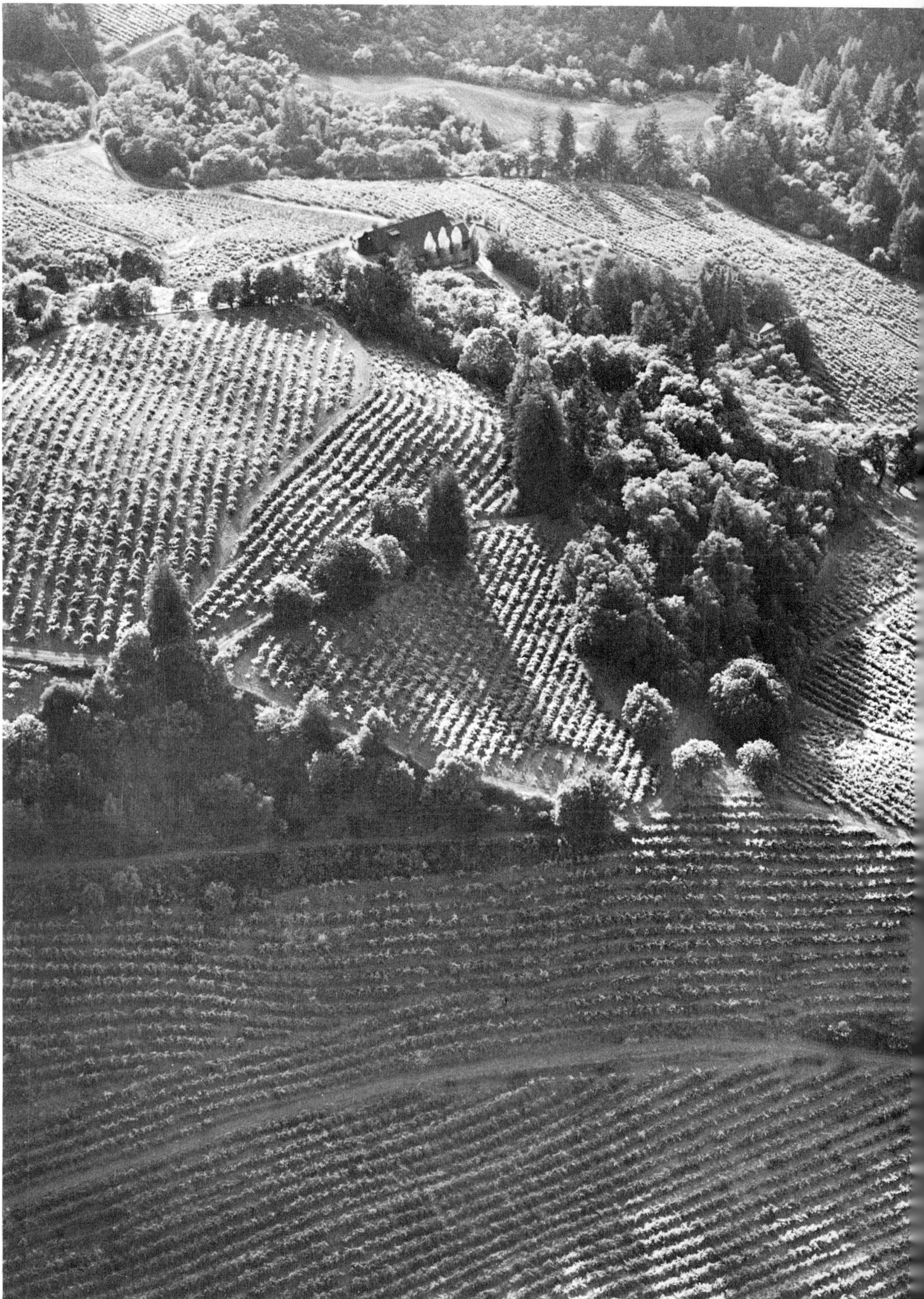

CALIFORNIA VINEYARDS cover the hills surrounding the Napa Valley. Varieties of *Vitis vinifera*, the species of grape from which most European wines are made, adapt readily to the warm California environment.

Acids make up between .3 and 1.5 percent of the grape must by weight. The two principal acids again are optically opposite forms: dextrorotatory tartaric acid and levorotatory malic acid. There are also small amounts of other acids: citric, oxalic, glucuronic, gluconic and phosphoric. The *p*H, or active acidity, of mature *Vitis vinifera* grapes in California runs between 3.1 and 3.9.

Among the many other substances that have been identified in analyses of grape must are 20 amino acids (found in the free state as well as in proteins), 13 anthocyanins (the pigments of many colored flowers), other pigments, tannins, odoriferous compounds and the various vitamins, enzymes, minerals and other ingredients already mentioned. Obviously many of these substances contribute to the making of wine by providing nutrient for the fermenting yeasts. The contributions of individual ingredients to the quality of wine, however, are imperfectly understood; presumably no one will ever be able to write a formula for a perfect wine, because personal taste is an indispensable part of the equation.

The fermentation process is enormously complicated [*see illustration on page 176*]. The breakdown of glucose alone involves no fewer than 22 enzymes, six or more coenzymes and magnesium and potassium ions. A number of other sequences, including the well-known Krebs cycle, participate in the process. From these many reactions emerges a mixed collection of other products in addition to alcohol, among them acetaldehyde, glycerol, succinic acid, esters and other aromatic compounds. The problem of the wine maker is to control the production and accumulation of this multitude of diverse products. In a modern winery this is done by various chemical and physical means.

Grapes have to be taken from the vine to the winery as quickly and carefully as possible in order to minimize their loss of water and sugar after picking and to prevent spoilage. At the winery they are immediately put in a crusher, which crushes the skins, freeing the pulp and juice (without breaking the seeds), and removes the stems. In the case of a white wine the juice is pressed out at this point and sent alone to the fermenting vat. For the making of red wine the entire contents of the crusher—juice, pulp, skins and seeds—go into the fermentation process. The red wine will take its color from the pigment in the skins and its strong flavor and astringency from tannins and other substances in the skin and seeds. (The rosé wines that have become more popular in recent years are made by starting the fermentation with the skin and pulp present, then, after about 24 hours, pressing out the juice and letting it complete the process alone.)

Wine in the Vat

In the fermenting vat (in California it is usually constructed either of red-

DELICATE BLOOM of grape skin consists of a waxy film that collects molds and yeasts. A single grape may accumulate 100,000 yeast cells with enzymes responsible for fermentation. Where the waxy film has been brushed off several grapes (*center*) a bright shine results.

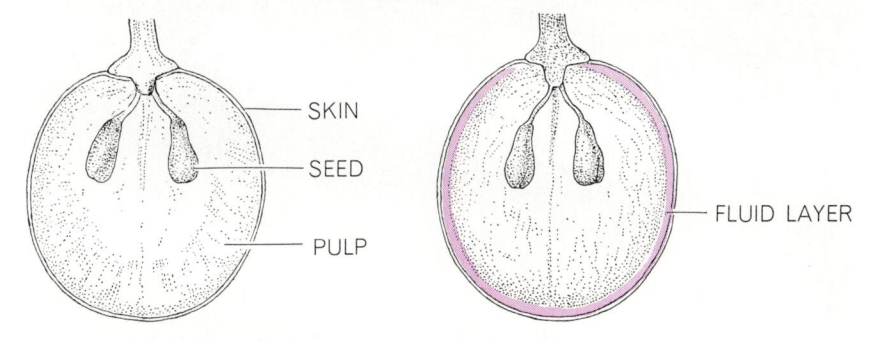

CABERNET FRANC, shown here in cross section, is an Old World grape of relatively low acidity that flourishes in California.

CONCORD GRAPE of the northeastern U.S. has a mucilaginous layer separating skin and pulp, hence its "slip skin" classification.

RECEIVING TANKS at left transfer must from a crusher on the floor above to the holding vats at right, enabling the winery to process the harvest of two types of grape. This photograph and the one below were made at the Taylor Winery in Hammondsport, N.Y.

PRESSES receive crushed grapes from holding vats on the floor above through pipes (*top*). The black rubber bag visible inside the press in the foreground will be inflated with air, forcing residual skins and seeds to cling to the sides of the stainless steel cylinder.

wood or of concrete) the first step is treatment of the must with liquefied sulfur dioxide or a sulfurous acid or salt. The main function of this chemical is to inhibit the growth of the wild yeasts on the grape skins. They are replaced by the addition of pure cultures of yeasts that will produce a better wine. Besides suppressing the deleterious yeasts the sulfur dioxide reduces oxidation (which may have a baneful effect, particularly on the quality of white wines) and also helps to acidify and clarify the wine. Sulfur dioxide is a dangerous tool—an excess of it will ruin the wine—but all in all its use has been a major 20th-century benefit to wine making, contributing in various ways to better regulation of the fermentation, a higher yield of alcohol from the sugar and a more flavorful product. When sulfur dioxide is used, the natural yeast flora from the grape are largely inhibited and an actively fermenting culture of yeast must be added.

Another recent innovation is careful control of temperature in the fermenting vat. Cooling systems are used to carry off the heat produced by fermentation so that the temperature in the vat is kept below 85 degrees F. (for red table wines) or below 60 degrees (for white wines). The slow fermentation at low temperatures produces more esters and other aromatic compounds, a higher yield of alcohol and a wine that is easier to clear and that is less susceptible to bacterial infection. In the opinion of most enologists it results in a better bouquet and aroma. The duration of the fermentation in a modern winery varies from a few days to a few weeks, depending on the temperature, the type of yeast used, the sugar content of the grapes and the kind of wine to be produced.

All wine is divided into two general classes, defined by the alcohol content. The table wines (also called "dinner," "dry" or "light" wines) contain not more than 14 percent of alcohol by volume. The "aperitif" and "dessert" wines (sherry, port, muscatel and the like) have a higher content, usually about 20 percent. They are given this high alcohol content by the addition of brandy distilled from wine. Added during the fermentation, the brandy stops the action of the yeast, and the wine is then left with some of its sugar unconverted to alcohol. In the making of muscatel, for example, the brandy is added and the fermentation halted when the juice still contains 10 to 15 percent of grape

"STORMY" STAGE of fermentation is under way in this vat at the United Vintners winery in Asti, Calif. Approximately 36 hours after yeast is added the temperature of the juice rises as high as 85 degrees and carbon dioxide bubbles violently to the surface.

FERMENTING TANKS shown here can hold 100,000 gallons. They are made of concrete with a glass lining. The thin pipes between the tanks exchange heat to maintain a uniform temperature.

REDWOOD VATS house the aging wine and facilitate mellowing by admitting oxygen through redwood planks. These vats, photographed at the Taylor Winery, have a capacity of 63,000 gallons.

sugars by weight; the result is a very sweet wine. For port the fermentation is stopped a little later (at a sugar level of 9 to 14 percent) and for a dry sherry it may be allowed to proceed until the sugar content is 2.5 percent or less.

For the sake of simplicity let us proceed with the more typical case of a red table wine. When part of its sugar has been converted to alcohol and adequate color has been extracted from the skins, the partially fermented juice is separated from the pulp. At this time the skins are mainly free and floating on top; the liquid is drained off as "free run" and is considered to make the best wine. The rest of the juice is pressed out of the pulp by the familiar wine press (which most people confuse with the machine used to crush the grapes before they are put in the fermenting vat). The press used in many modern wineries still looks much as it has always looked—a hardwood container with a plunger—but nowadays a hydraulic ram replaces the old screw contrivance turned by hand. Recently developed cylindrical presses and roller presses are also in use.

The juice now proceeds to the completion of its fermentation and to the clearing and aging stages. Not to be guilty of omitting entirely from this account the important category of sparkling wines, I shall merely mention here that they are made from dry table wines by means of a secondary fermentation in a closed container, involving the addition of a calculated amount of sugar and 1 percent of a pure yeast culture. This fermentation produces the extra carbon dioxide—amounting to an internal pressure of four or five atmospheres in the bottle—that accounts for the fizz of champagne.

For clarification of the wine the fermented juice goes to settling vats. There the suspended yeast cells, cream of tartar and small particles of skin and pulp rapidly settle out of the liquid. Various chemical processes and a form of fermentation still continue, however. Wine, it has been said, is a living thing, and indeed in a sense it does go on growing and maturing—in the settling vats and later in its aging periods in cask and bottle. In the vats the yeast cells, as they break down, particularly in a wine juice of high acidity, stimulate the growth of *Lactobacillus* bacteria. Enzymes from these bacteria decarboxylate the wine's malic acid (that is, remove COOH groups) and convert it to lactic acid. This malo-lactic "fermentation," replacing a strong acid with

FERMENTATION entails the breakdown of the six-carbon sugar, glucose (*top left*) and the consequent production of alcohol. The splitting of the carbon backbone occurs when the intermediate product, fructose (*top right*), gives way to two molecules of glyceraldehyde phosphate. The major intermediate products are shown from top to bottom. The enzymes and coenzymes needed to power the process are represented by ATP and ADP, and DPN and DPNH. The reversible steps in the process are indicated by two-way arrows.

a weak one, mellows the high-acid wine. Without it the high-quality wines of northern Europe could not be made.

As soon as possible the clearing wine is racked, or drawn off, from the settling lees to prevent excessive working and protect its flavor. The racking is repeated again and again, leaving behind lees at each step. During these off-pourings the wine also sheds the carbon dioxide with which it was charged in the fermentation process and absorbs oxygen from the air, which will help in its aging. To assist the clearing of the wine when racking alone does not suffice, wineries commonly inject "fining" substances (such as bentonite clay, gelatin, isinglass or egg white) that clump and precipitate the tiny particles in the wine; they may also apply pressure filtration, heat or chilling as aids to clearing.

Wine in Cask and Bottle

The aging of the wine begins in an oak cask. It is an extremely complex process of oxidation, reduction and esterification. The new wine gradually loses its yeasty flavor and harshness, declines in acidity and acquires a complex, delicate bouquet. As its pigments and tannin are oxidized, red wine turns a tawny color and white wine develops an amber hue. The amount of oxidation of its ingredients, by means of oxygen absorbed through the pores of the cask, is crucial to the eventual quality of the wine: the length of time it is left in the cask may make the difference between allowing a great wine to attain its potential and turning it into an ordinary one. If wine is bottled too soon, it may spoil or mature too slowly; if it is bottled too late, it will be vapid and off-color. The decision as to when to bottle is one of the most important in the wine maker's art. In present practice fine red table wines are kept in wooden cooperage for at least two years; white wines, from a few months to two years. Lesser-quality wines are stored in redwood, concrete or lined iron tanks.

After bottling, wine does not cease to "work." Aging in the bottle serves to eliminate the aerated odor the wine acquired at the time of bottling, reduce the wine's content of free sulfur dioxide and improve its bouquet. It is a mistake, however, to suppose the older the wine, the better, or that a bottle encrusted with the grime of many years is likely to contain a wine of rare distinction. The contents may, in fact, have become worthless long ago. Only a few

FILTERING UNIT shown at right in this photograph removes sediment from the wine in settling tanks (*left center*). Below the filter is a trough into which residue is dumped.

NEW BOTTLES containing domestic U.S. champagne are stacked on a "riddling" shelf of ash, counterpart of the French A-frame. Sediment accumulates in the neck and can be discarded by briefly uncorking the bottle. Both photographs were made at the Taylor Wineries.

very fine red wines benefit from prolonged aging. As a general rule, for a good red wine five to 10 years in the bottle is long enough, and a white wine will have reached its peak after two to five years. Wines of lesser quality require less time.

To summarize, the modern technology of wine making began with Pasteur's discovery that fermentation was produced by yeasts and that the process was far more complicated, with many more by-products, than Gay-Lussac's simple formula for the conversion of sugar to alcohol had suggested. The major modern developments have been the use of selected pure yeasts, the breeding and cultivation of superior varieties of grapes, the control of fermentation by certain chemicals and physical conditions (such as sulfur dioxide and cooling) and a gradual accumulation of more exact knowledge about the chemistry of the fermentation and aging processes. For all these advances, a truly great wine is still more or less a happy accident arising from time to time out of a particularly fortunate blend of the weather, the grape and the vintner's intuitive art. Much of the guesswork has been eliminated, however, from commercial wine making, and the quality of wines is a great deal more uniform than it used to be.

Even a brief account of wine making, which can touch only on the highlights, cannot pass over the fascinating subject of the consumption of the product. The wine maker and the wine consumer are themselves partners in a peculiarly intimate symbiosis; indeed, historically they used to be one and the same person! Modern enology sheds interesting light on some of the folklore of wine drinking.

The matching of wines to food (red wine with red meat, white wine with fish) cannot be defended, objectively speaking, as much more than a superstition. It is true that red wine shares with meat a complexity of taste and texture, and that the high acidity of white wine may add spice to the blandness of fresh fish and, in earlier times

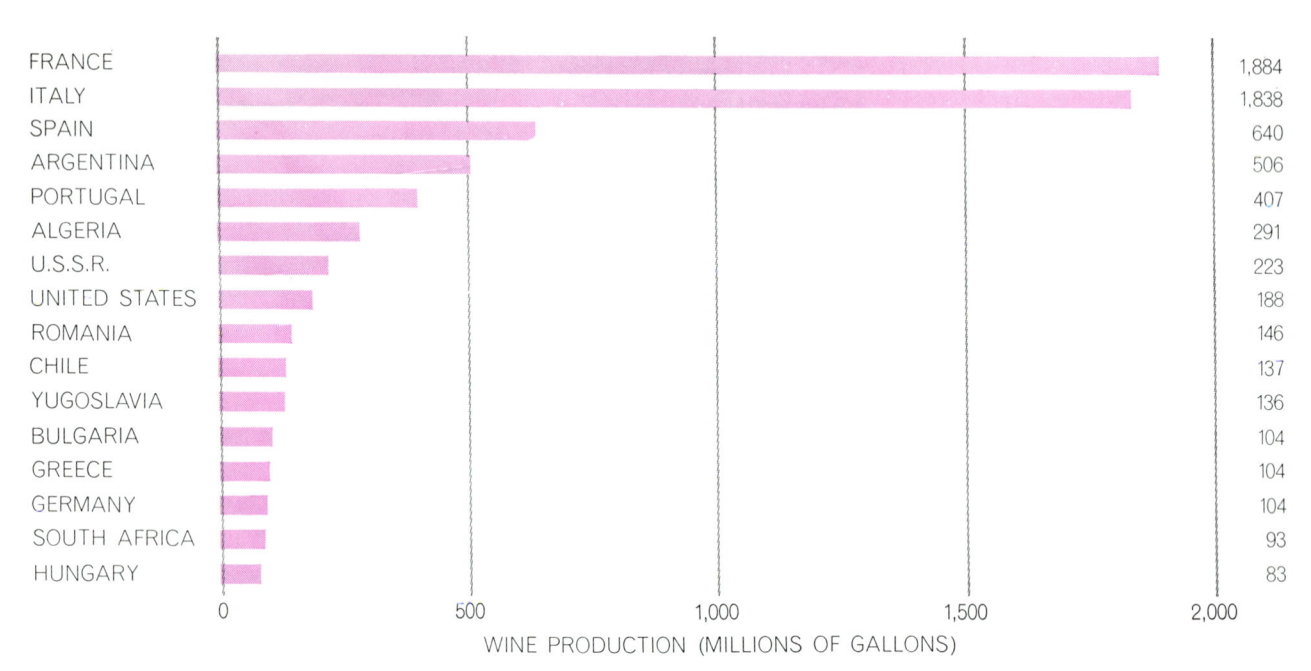

Country	Wine Production (millions of gallons)
FRANCE	1,884
ITALY	1,838
SPAIN	640
ARGENTINA	506
PORTUGAL	407
ALGERIA	291
U.S.S.R.	223
UNITED STATES	188
ROMANIA	146
CHILE	137
YUGOSLAVIA	136
BULGARIA	104
GREECE	104
GERMANY	104
SOUTH AFRICA	93
HUNGARY	83

LEADING PRODUCERS of wine are listed according to 1962 output in millions of gallons. The figures for Algeria, the U.S.S.R. and Chile are estimates. No statistics are available for China. France and Italy together produced about half of the world supply.

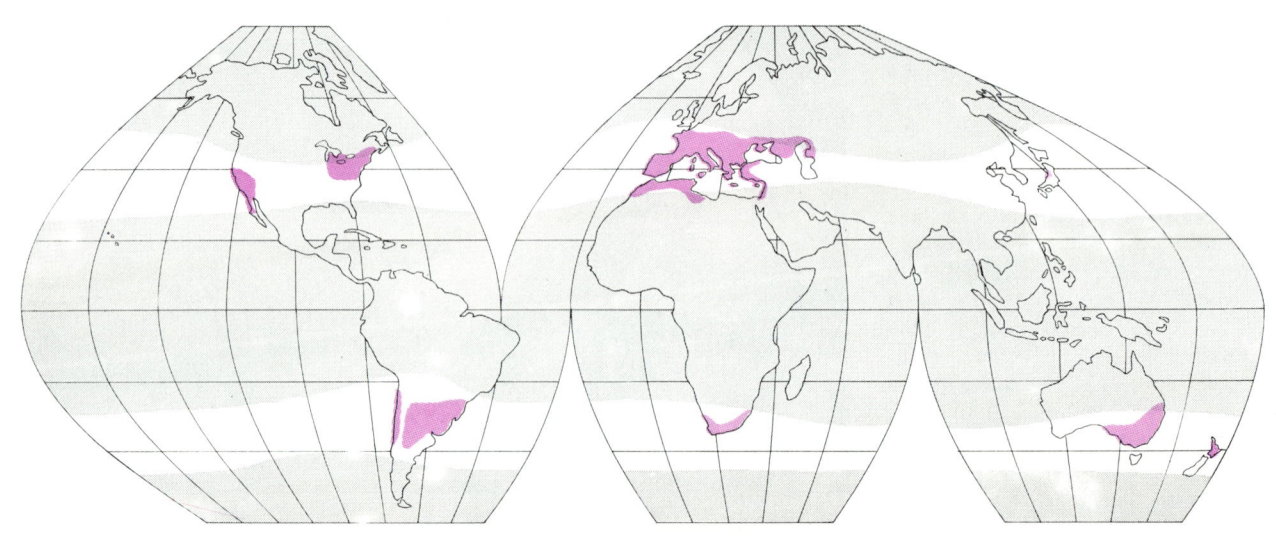

WINE-GROWING REGIONS of the world lie within belts where average annual temperature is between 50 and 68 degrees Fahrenheit. The hot summer of the southwestern U.S. and the humidity in the Southeast preclude the cultivation of *Vitis vinifera* grapes.

of nonrefrigeration, may have helped to mask the odor and taste of decaying fish. Most likely, however, the traditional ideas about food-wine pairing grew originally out of the simple geographical fact that a particular type of wine happened to be grown in a region that favored a particular food; that is, the coupling developed from agricultural rather than epicurean considerations.

The use of wine as medicine is another and much more interesting story. The medical historian Salvatore P. Lucia, of the University of California Medical School in San Francisco, asserts in his *A History of Wine as Therapy* that it is "the oldest of medicines." Salves made with wine were used in Sumer as early as the third millennium B.C., according to a clay tablet found in the ruins of Nippur. Virtually every culture has employed wine for medicinal purposes, either directly or as a solvent. It used to be listed in the U.S. *Pharmacopeia,* but it was dropped during prohibition (which all but killed the appreciation of wine in the U.S.) and has not been reinstated since. Many physicians, however, have resumed prescribing it for various ailments.

Wine is considered a specific for certain disorders because its alcohol is absorbed from the digestive tract into the bloodstream slowly (as opposed to the rapid absorption of pure ethyl alcohol) and because some of its ingredients may be metabolically helpful to the body. The physicians who believe in its therapeutic powers recommend it variously as an analgesic for minor pain, as a tranquilizer or sedative, as a vasodilator for hypertensive patients, as a diuretic, as a nutritional supplement for diabetics and as an aid to the absorption of fat by the intestines after an operation for ulcers or stomach cancer. The noted medical teacher William Dock, professor of medicine at the Downstate Medical Center of the State University of New York, has remarked: "It is useful to think what would happen if alcohol should be discovered all over again.... The sales for all other sedatives and tranquilizers would go down; there would be four-page spreads with color in all the medical journals... and the stock of the patent licensees would go right through the ceiling on Wall Street. The lucky discoverers would get every possible honor, as did the men who discovered insulin."

III

THE FUTURE: FEAST OR FAMINE?

III

THE FUTURE: FEAST OR FAMINE?

INTRODUCTION

Optimism pervades the story of man. From a backward look, things generally seem to have been constantly improving, at least to those who write history. The necessities of life, including food, come with less effort than before, life span lengthens, and as a final proof, population increases. Many of our problems (from polio to lumpy oatmeal) seem to be solved by advances in technology. And if man can escape from his planet and return, this surely suggests that a solution to unpleasant problems can be found if "someone" will set his mind to it. If happiness and contentment have seemed elusive to the contemplative, who equate them with the "simplicity" of days past, nevertheless few people, given the opportunity, return to simple ways for long. Even natives of unspoiled Pacific paradises quickly adapt to and soon demand outboard motors, canned food, and transistor radios.

However, a generation of prognosticators have found great uncertainties in the future course of mankind. They argue persuasively that our planet is finite, that population is increasing at a rate faster than food supply, and that if it is true that life is better for more people today than ever before, it is equally true that it is also more squalid for more people than ever before.

The problem of adequately feeding the population of the world has never been solved. It has been argued that the problem is one of mere distribution — caused by the lack of incentive for farmers in productive areas to raise enough for the food-deficit areas, or, by the lack of purchasing power of hungry peoples. While food shortages due to crop failure create famine or near-famine conditions in one area, gluts and low prices threaten the equanimity of producers in others. This was the situation in the 1950's, with India representing one extreme and the United States the other. An Asian catastrophe was averted because under the aegis of political goodwill and international development, food was exported from the United States as a gift. No doubt much of the world's present food problem is a distribution problem, and proposals for solving it have been made the basis of political ideologies that are supported passionately and often violently.

A look into the next century brings into focus the emergence of a crisis situation (even assuming perfect distribution of resources) because of expanding world population. At the present rate of increase (2.0 percent per year), the world population doubles in only 35 years. With a present population of about 4.0 billion (1973), this extrapolates to a population of 32 billion by 2073. For a population of this size to be fed at even the same inadequate level as that of today will require a corresponding eightfold increase in food production. The essays in this final section address themselves to this situation.

In "The Human Population," Edward S. Deevey, Jr., reviews the earth's human numbers from a broad historical point of view. The first surge in population (1,000,000 to 10,000 years ago) is viewed as a response to advances in tool making. From 10,000 to 300 years ago there occurred a steady, relatively slow increase in numbers from an estimated 5 million to 500 million, or an average of 50,000 per year. This boost in the rate of increase is attributed to technological advances in food production. In the past 300 years population has increased to about 4,000 million (4 billion) or an average increase of 10 million per year. (The present rate is 80 million per year!) This exponential population increase is viewed as a consequence of the scientific-industrial revolution. Population, the residue between births and deaths, has been increasing because of a sharply declining death rate in all parts of the world, and is balanced off only by a declining birth rate in the developed parts of the world. The resultant increases in world population have become menacing. Even natural disasters have but a minimal impact upon population increase; for example, the 300,000 people killed in 1971 by a typhoon in Bangladesh represent less than 100 days of population increase in that country! And after almost 20 years of war in Vietnam, with casualties in the millions, the population (both North and South) has increased by two million each.

In his provocative but quietly written essay, Deevey defines the population problem as a function of the earth's food resources. He frames the problem in terms of land, energy, and productivity on the one hand and dynamic human population on the other. The suggestion is made that the answers to population must be one of self-imposed restraint: *"And if the human method of adjusting numbers to resources fails to work in the next 1,000 years as it has in the last million, subhuman methods are ready to take over."*

In his article "Food," Nevin S. Scrimshaw analyzes the problem of supplying sufficient food for increasing world populations in terms of poor nations (underdeveloped or developing nations, if you wish) and rich nations (developed nations). In contrast to rich nations, poor nations have the triple burden of insufficiency of food, inefficient agriculture, and rapidly increasing population. Scrimshaw suggests that the solution lies in increasing the efficiency and scope of traditional agriculture of poor countries. This improvement can come about through expansion of present technology, such as chemicals (fertilizers, pest control), improvements in crop breeding and animal feeding, food preservation, mechanization (improving efficiency through optimum timing of cultural operations, but, more important, releasing land devoted to raising feed for draft animals), and other innovations such as nutrient enrichment of food (iodized salt, vitamin supplemented flour). But perhaps the greatest need is a change in attitude. It is currently more difficult to improve a nation's agriculture than to develop a steel industry because advances in agriculture involve alterations in the structure of a society. A complete change in attitude is needed to turn agriculture from an extractive feudal operation into a modern business enterprise. The consequences are that poor countries still find it more convenient to buy food than to modernize their agriculture.

Another side of the problem is shown in Lester R. Brown's warning that expanded food-production technology must not be considered out of its biologic context. His article, "Human Food Production as a Process in the Biosphere," is concerned with the environmental consequences of greatly expanding the human food supply. Mechanization may be increased if stored energy (fossil fuels) is available, but expanding agriculture to unsuitable locations leads to dustbowls and periodic crop failure. The consequences can be disastrous, as was the experience in the southwestern United States in the 1930's, and as is the present Soviet experience of expanding grain production into the virgin lands of Kazakstan. Irrigation, too, can have detrimental effects on water tables and salinization, whereas dam construction results in new problems due to silting and, in the tropics, to shistosomiasis (snail fever). Expansion in the use of agricultural chemicals increases problems of pollution and eutrophication; environmentalists in food surplus areas have already brought about the banning of DDT. The improvement of diets increases the stress on the ecosystem. North Americans have four times the demand on agricultural resources (because they consume animal products) as compared with residents in poor countries who subsist primarily on plant foods. But the consequence of rising aspirations and increasing populations means that production at present levels should have to be doubled or tripled in the next decade.

A blueprint designed to take advantage of present agricultural technology is outlined by Addeke H. Boerma of the FAO in "A World Agricultural Plan." The straightforward aim is to overcome the rising food gap anticipated by extrapolating the world population from 1970 to 1985 with present increases in food productivity. The plan is based on increased production of cereals. The rate of production growth (2.6 percent per year) will have to be increased to 3.6 percent. This seemingly modest goal, however, represents a 50 percent increase in the improvement rate averaged over the world!

The success of the short-stemmed wheats and rice, those "miracle" grains that spawned the Green Revolution, have given rise to cautious optimism that a reprieve has been obtained. Further progress in meeting 1985 goals may be met by expansion to new lands. Although movement into new areas will be modest, because man has already filled to overflowing all of the most productive areas, increases in the intensity of production mechanization and double cropping are promising. Finally, greater production of fertilizers seems assured.

Analysis of the future world food needs leads to the conclusion that the food problem is more clearly stated by emphasis on protein. The impending world food crisis is in reality a protein shortage. Notwithstanding his optimism, Boerma admits that new technology is required to ameliorate the protein deficiency, because a switch to animal agriculture is self-defeating in countries that already have a caloric shortage.

There are more direct methods of attacking the world protein shortage than by increasing the efficiency of conventional agriculture. In "Orthodox and Unorthodox Methods of Meeting World Food Needs," N. W. Pirie warns against rejecting alternative means because of mere cynicism or skepticism. "Unorthodox" methods of increasing protein production include search for new herbivores, especially aquatic types (here skeptics do have a field day: the capybora, a giant South American rodent seems too lovable to eat, and manatees, when used for aquatic weed control in Florida, were found to have a predilection for pneumonia); wider use of fish protein; increased use of vegetable protein, especially legumes (primitive oil-extraction procedures render much of the protein-rich presscake inedible, a most extravagant waste); direct protein extraction from leaves; new crops (including algae); microbial protein from petroleum fermentation; and amino acid supplements. It has been considered realistic to ignore nonconventional solutions because many have proved impractical under limited testing (algae culture, for example). But Pirie points out that until accepted, novelty remains novel. Pirie makes a plea for research in this area and outlines a program for adoption. The facts are that protein availability is a bottleneck to better nutrition.

In "Marine Farming," Gifford B. Pinchot suggests a "new method for increasing protein that is in reality an expansion of an ancient technology. The raising of fish in ponds and the culture of oysters date back thousands of years; fish ponds have always contributed an important fraction of the food supply in Asia. Freshwater fish farming is still a long way from reaching its potential, but is a likely means of augmenting protein supplies in subtropical and tropical regions, where the greatest need exists. Pond culture offers exciting possibilities in the developed countries as well; catfish farming is a recent success story in the southern part of the United States, but here it relies on the availability of concentrated feed additives. The raising of fish in developing countries should be based on growing aquatic plants to develop a managed food chain. The basic nutrients can be (and often have been) provided by sewage wastes, but there is evidence that inorganic fertilization of ponds may be efficient. A distinct advantage of the system is that, properly executed, it is pollution-free.

Pinchot makes the further interesting but probably impractical suggestion that the naturally fertile deep ocean waters could be used as another source of nutrients. Cold water is heavy and becomes a sink of unusable nutrients except where upwelling currents make it available, as in some of the world's great fishing areas. Artificial upwelling caused by the pumping of deep water into lagoons could provide nutrient-rich water as well as cold water that could be transferred for use in industrial cooling or condensed to fresh water.

The upgrading of plant protein is still another approach to the problem. This can be accomplished in at least three ways. The first is the complementation of various foods, each of which is by itself deficient in a particular amino acid. An example of this is the combination of maize and beans (*tortillas y frijoles*), a dietary staple in Mexican and Central American diets. Not only do these complement each other fairly well in the diet, but so do the crop plants in the field: under primitive agricultural systems, the beans provide nitrogen from nodule-forming bacteria, and the corn stalks support the twining bean plants in their search for the sun. Beans are more expensive than maize, and, when times are hard, skimping leads to protein-starvation in children. A further example of plant-source complementation is the modern development of superior rations for animal feeding. Protein-rich "supplements," particularly soybean and cottonseed meal, are combined with various other energy sources (from maize to pineapple bran), depending on local circumstances and economics.

The second method, the direct enrichment with the limiting amino acid as well as other deficient nutrients through fortification, is especially promising for infant foods. The method is sound in principle, but actual experience so far is discouraging, probably because basic eating patterns need to be changed. Finally, factory-made supplements are often costly compared to those produced by traditional agriculture.

The third approach is the genetic improvement of the protein quality of individual plant sources. An example is the 1963 discovery of Oliver Nelson and Edwin Mertz that a gene mutant in maize with opaque kernels increases lysine by 70 percent. Because lysine is the limiting amino acid in maize for monogastric (single stomach) animals, such as man, pig, chicken, maize with increased lysine could greatly aid in alleviating protein deficiency where maize is the major crop. This would work in two ways: directly when maize is consumed by man, and indirectly through increased efficiency in pork and chicken production. In the United States, where protein supplement is readily available and maize is not an important human food, the value is marginal. Its effect on pork production, for example, will depend on the relative price of supplement vis-a-vis the yield response of high-lysine maize.

The improvement of protein quality in maize by the transference of the high-lysine character and its relation to human and animal nutrition is the subject of Dale D. Harpstead's "High-Lysine Corn." At present, yields of opaque hybrids are still inferior to but are approaching normal maize hybrids. Breeding programs are underway in Brazil, and new high-lysine hybrids are being well received because the increased feeding value in pigs is dramatic and obvious to farmers who do not ordinarily use supplements. However, a premature release of a nonadapted type by the Brazilian government was a failure. The combination of increased yields, increased total protein, and high lysine could be a tremendous breakthrough in those tropical regions where corn is already well adapted. The similar improvement of other cereals and beans (deficient in the sulfur-containing amino acids cysteine and methionine) is also under study, but so far no comparable mutants have been found.

Microorganisms have long been used in the food industries for their action in producing subtle changes in flavor (cheesemaking), in preservation (pickling), and, of course, in fermentation (alcoholic beverages). The work of microorganisms is expanded upon by Alfred Champagnat in "Protein from Petroleum." The observation that certain molds and bacteria grow on petroleum products has led to large-scale feasibility studies of the use of petroleum as a source of protein. The idea, fantastic at first hearing, has advantages to the oil industry, because a relatively useless fraction, treated as a waste product, can be used. At present a number of industrial plants are in operation, and results suggest that the process is useful in producing feeds. It will not provide the panacea we seek for man because of low palatability and the low protein quality, but it does give an indication of the possibilities of new foods and new techniques, providing needed time for man to determine his destiny and his numbers.

ROMAN TOMBSTONE from the first century A.D. records the death of Cominia Tyche, aged 27 years, 11 months, 28 days. Tombstones are a source of information on life expectancy in the ancient world. Stone is in the Metropolitan Museum of Art in New York.

21

THE HUMAN POPULATION

EDWARD S. DEEVEY, JR.
September 1960

In the short span of his existence man has come to consume more food than all other land animals put together. This raises the question of how many men the earth can support

Almost until the present turn in human affairs an expanding population has been equated with progress. "Increase and multiply" is the Scriptural injunction. The number of surviving offspring is the measure of fitness in natural selection. If number is the criterion, the human species is making great progress. The population, now passing 2.7 billion, is doubling itself every 50 years or so. To some horrified observers, however, the population increase has become a "population explosion." The present rate of increase, they point out, is itself increasing. At 1 per cent per year it is double that of the past few centuries. By A.D. 2000, even according to the "medium" estimate of the careful demographers of the United Nations, the rate of increase will have accelerated to 3 per cent per year, and the total population will have reached 6.267 billion. If Thomas Malthus's assumption of a uniform rate of doubling is naive, because it so quickly leads to impossible numbers, how long can an accelerating annual increase, say from 1 to 3 per cent in 40 years, be maintained? The demographers confronted with this question lower their eyes: "It would be absurd," they say, "to carry detailed calculations forward into a more remote future. It is most debatable whether the trends in mortality and fertility can continue much longer. Other factors may eventually bring population growth to a halt."

So they may, and must. It comes to this: Explosions are not made by force alone, but by force that exceeds restraint. Before accepting the implications of the population explosion, it is well to set the present in the context of the record of earlier human populations. As will be seen, the population curve has moved upward stepwise in response to the three major revolutions that have marked the evolution of culture [*see bottom illustration on page 192*]. The tool-using and toolmaking revolution that started the growth of the human stem from the primate line gave the food-gatherer and hunter access to the widest range of environments. Nowhere was the population large, but over the earth as a whole it reached the not insignificant total of five million, an average of .04 person per square kilometer (.1 person per square mile) of land. With the agricultural revolution the population moved up two orders of magnitude to a new plateau, multiplying 100 times in the short span of 8,000 years, to an average of one person per square kilometer. The increase over the last 300 years, a multiplication by five, plainly reflects the first repercussions of the scientific-industrial revolution. There are now 16.4 persons per square kilometer of the earth's land area. It is thus the release of restraint that the curve portrays at three epochal points in cultural history.

But the evolution of the population size also indicates the approach to equilibrium in the two interrevolutionary periods of the past. At what level will the present surge of numbers reach equilibrium? That is again a question of restraint, whether it is to be imposed by the limitations of man's new command over his environment or by his command over his own nature.

The human generative force is neither new nor metabiological, nor is it especially strong in man as compared to other animals. Under conditions of maximal increase in a suitable environment empty of competitors, with births at maximum and deaths negligible, rats can multiply their numbers 25 times in an average generation-time of 31 weeks. For the water flea *Daphnia*, beloved by ecologists for the speedy answers it gives, the figures are 221 times in a generation of 6.8 days. Mankind's best efforts seem puny by contrast: multiplication by about 1.4 times in a generation of 28 years. Yet neither in human nor in experimental populations do such rates continue unchecked. Sooner or later the births slow down and the deaths increase, until—in experiments, at any rate—the growth tapers off, and the population effectively saturates its space. Ecologists define this state (of zero rate of change) as equilibrium, without denying the possibility of oscillations that average out to zero, and without forgetting the continuous input of energy (food, for instance) that is needed to maintain the system.

Two kinds of check, then, operate to limit the size of a population, or of any living thing that grows. Obviously the environment (amount of space, food or other needed resources) sets the upper limit; sometimes this is manipulatable, even by the population itself, as when it exploits a new kind of food in the same old space, and reaches a new, higher limit. More subtly, populations can be said to limit their own rates of increase. As the numbers rise, female fruit-flies, for example, lay fewer eggs when jostled by their sisters; some microorganisms battle each other with antibiotics; flour beetles accidentally eat their own defenseless eggs and pupae; infectious diseases spread faster, or become more virulent, as their hosts become more numerous. For human populations pestilence and warfare, Malthus's "natural restraints," belong among these devices for self-limitation. So, too, does his "moral restraint," or voluntary birth control. Nowadays a good deal of attention is being given, not only to voluntary methods,

YEARS AGO	CULTURAL STAGE	AREA POPULATED	ASSUMED DENSITY PER SQUARE KILOMETER	TOTAL POPULATION (MILLIONS)
1,000,000	LOWER PALEOLITHIC		.00425	.125
300,000	MIDDLE PALEOLITHIC		.012	1
25,000	UPPER PALEOLITHIC		.04	3.34
10,000	MESOLITHIC		.04	5.32
6,000	VILLAGE FARMING AND EARLY URBAN		1.0 / .04	86.5
2,000	VILLAGE FARMING AND URBAN		1.0	133
310	FARMING AND INDUSTRIAL		3.7	545
210	FARMING AND INDUSTRIAL		4.9	728
160	FARMING AND INDUSTRIAL		6.2	906
60	FARMING AND INDUSTRIAL		11.0	1,610
10	FARMING AND INDUSTRIAL		16.4	2,400
A.D. 2000	FARMING AND INDUSTRIAL		46.0	6,270

but also to a fascinating new possibility: mental stress.

Population control by means of personality derangement is probably a vertebrate patent; at least it seems a luxury beyond the reach of a water flea. The general idea, as current among students of small mammals, is that of hormonal imbalance (or stress, as defined by Hans Selye of the University of Montreal); psychic tension, resulting from overcrowding, disturbs the pituitary-adrenal system and diverts or suppresses the hormones governing sexuality and parental care. Most of the evidence comes from somewhat artificial experiments with caged rodents. It is possible, though the case is far from proved, that the lemming's famous mechanism for restoring equilibrium is the product of stress; in experimental populations of rats and mice, at least, anxiety has been observed to increase the death rate through fighting or merely from shock.

From this viewpoint there emerges an interesting distinction between crowding and overcrowding among vertebrates; overcrowding is what is perceived as such by members of the population. Since the human rate of increase is holding its own and even accelerating, however, it is plain that the mass of men, although increasingly afflicted with mental discomfort, do not yet see themselves as overcrowded. What will happen in the future brings other questions. For the present it may be noted that some kind of check has always operated, up to now, to prevent populations from exceeding the space that contains them. Of course space may be non-Euclidean, and man may be exempt from this law.

The commonly accepted picture of the growth of the population out of the long past takes the form of the top graph on the next page. Two things are wrong with this picture. In the first place the basis of estimates, back of about A.D. 1650, is rarely stated. One suspects that writers have been copying each other's guesses. The second defect is that the scales of the graph have been chosen so as to make the first defect seem unimportant. The missile has left the pad and is heading out of sight—so it is said; who cares whether there were a million or a hundred million people around when Babylon was founded? The difference is nearly lost in the thickness of the draftsman's line.

I cannot think it unimportant that (as I calculate) there were 36 billion Paleolithic hunters and gatherers, including the first tool-using hominids. One begins to see why stone tools are among the commonest Pleistocene fossils. Another 30 billion may have walked the earth before the invention of agriculture. A cumulative total of about 110 billion individuals seem to have passed their days, and left their bones, if not their marks, on this crowded planet. Neither for our understanding of culture nor in terms of man's impact upon the land is it a negligible consideration that the patch of ground allotted to every person now alive may have been the lifetime habitat of 40 predecessors.

These calculations exaggerate the truth in a different way: by condensing into single sums the enormous length of prehistoric time. To arrive at the total of 36 billion Paleolithic hunters and gatherers I have assumed mean standing populations of half a million for the Lower Paleolithic, and two million for the Middle and Upper Paleolithic to 25,000 years ago. For Paleolithic times there are no archeological records worth considering in such calculations. I have used some figures for modern hunting tribes, quoted by Robert J. Braidwood and Charles A. Reed, though they are not guilty of my extrapolations. The assumed densities per square kilometer range from a tenth to a third of those estimated for eastern North America before Columbus came, when an observer would hardly have described the woods as full of Indians. (Of course I have excluded any New World population from my estimates prior to the Mesolithic climax of the food-gathering and hunting phase of cultural evolution.) It is only because average generations of 25 years succeeded each other 39,000 times that the total looms so large.

For my estimates as of the opening of the agricultural revolution, I have also depended upon Braidwood and Reed. In their work in Mesopotamia they have counted the number of rooms in buried houses, allowing for the areas of town sites and of cultivated land, and have compared the populations so computed with modern counterparts. For early village-farmers, like those at Jarmo, and for the urban citizens of Sumer, about 2500 B.C., their estimates (9.7 and 15.4 persons per square kilometer) are probably fairly close. They are intended to apply to large tracts of inhabited country, not to pavement-bound clusters of artisans and priests. Nevertheless, in extending these estimates to continent-wide areas, I have divided the lower figure by 10, making it one per square kilometer. So much of Asia is unirrigated and nonurban even today that the figure may still be too high. But the Maya, at about the same level of culture (3,000 or 4,000 years later), provide a useful standard of comparison. The present population of their classic homeland averages .6 per square kilometer, but the land can support a population about a hundred times as large, and probably did at the time of the classic climax. The rest of the New World, outside Middle America, was (and is) more thinly settled, but a world-wide average of one per square kilometer seems reasonable for agricultural, pre-industrial society.

For modern populations, from A.D. 1650 on, I have taken the estimates of economic historians, given in such books as the treatise *World Population and Production*, by Wladimir S. and Emma S. Woytinsky. All these estimates are included in the bottom graph on the next page. Logarithmic scales are used in order to compress so many people and millennia onto a single page. Foreshortening time in this way is convenient, if not particularly logical, and back of 50,000 years ago the time-scale is pretty arbitrary anyway. No attempt is made to show the oscillations that probably occurred, in glacial and interglacial ages, for example.

The stepwise evolution of population size, entirely concealed in graphs with arithmetic scales, is the most noticeable feature of this diagram. For most of the million-year period the number of hominids, including man, was about what would be expected of any large Pleistocene mammal—scarcer than

---

POPULATION GROWTH, from inception of the hominid line one million years ago through the different stages of cultural evolution to A.D. 2000, is shown in the chart on the opposite page. In Lower Paleolithic stage, population was restricted to Africa (*colored area on world map in third column*), with a density of only .00425 person per square kilometer (*fourth column*) and a total population of only 125,000 (*column at right*). By the Mesolithic stage, 10,000 years ago, hunting and food gathering techniques had spread the population over most of the earth and brought the total to 5,320,000. In the village farming and early urban stage, population increased to a total of 86,500,000 and a density of one person per square kilometer in the Old World and .04 per square kilometer in the New World. Today the population density exceeds 16 persons per square kilometer, and pioneering of the antarctic continent has begun.

III • THE FUTURE: FEAST OR FAMINE?

horses, say, but commoner than elephants. Intellectual superiority was simply a successful adaptation, like longer legs; essential to stay in the running, of course, but making man at best the first among equals. Then the food-gatherers and hunters became plowmen and herdsmen, and the population was boosted by about 16 times, between 10,000 and 6,000 years ago. The scientific-industrial revolution, beginning some 300 years ago, has spread its effects much faster, but it has not yet taken the number as far above the earlier base line.

The long-term population equilibrium implied by such base lines suggests something else. Some kind of restraint kept the number fairly stable. "Food supply" offers a quick answer, but not, I think, the correct one. At any rate, a forest is full of game for an expert mouse-hunter, and a Paleolithic man who stuck to business should have found enough food on two square kilometers, instead of 20 or 200. Social forces were probably more powerful than mere starvation in causing men to huddle in small bands. Besides, the number was presumably adjusted to conditions in the poorest years, and not to average environments.

The main point is that there were adjustments. They can only have come about because the average female bore two children who survived to reproduce. If the average life span is 25 years, the "number of children ever born" is about four (because about 50 per cent die before breeding), whereas a population that is really trying can average close to eight. Looking back on former times, then, from our modern point of view, we might say that about two births out of four were surplus, though they were needed to counterbalance the juvenile death toll. But what about the other four, which evidently did not occur? Unless the life expectancy was very much less

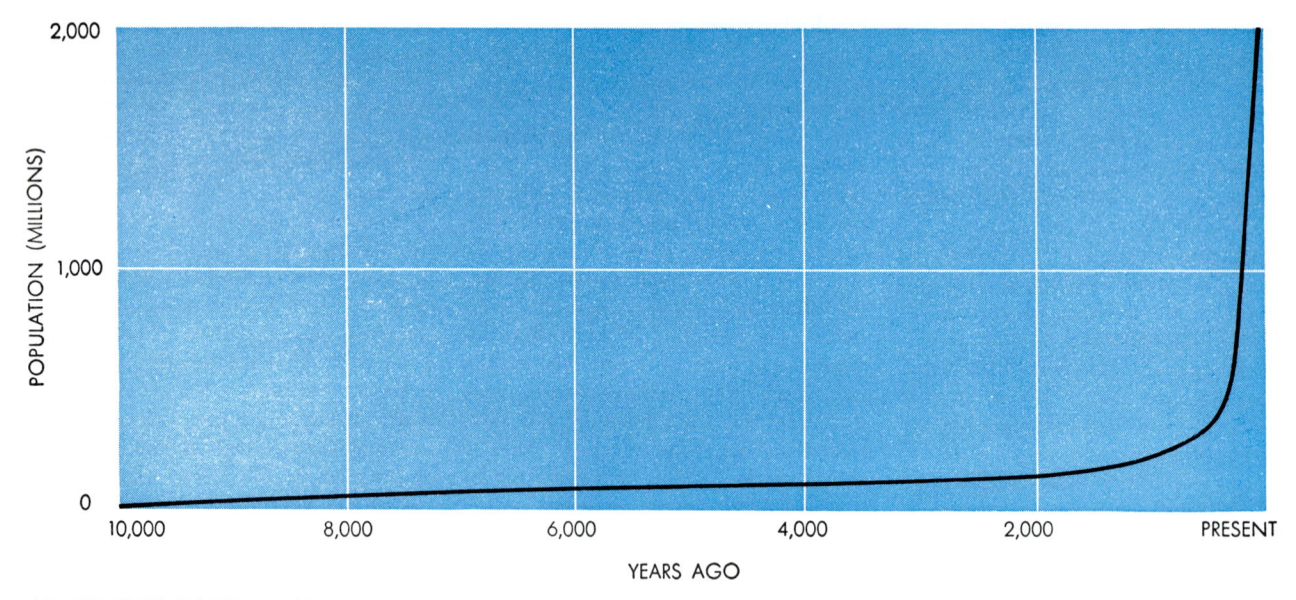

ARITHMETIC POPULATION CURVE plots the growth of human population from 10,000 years ago to the present. Such a curve suggests that the population figure remained close to the base line for an indefinite period from the remote past to about 500 years ago, and that it has surged abruptly during the last 500 years as a result of the scientific-industrial revolution.

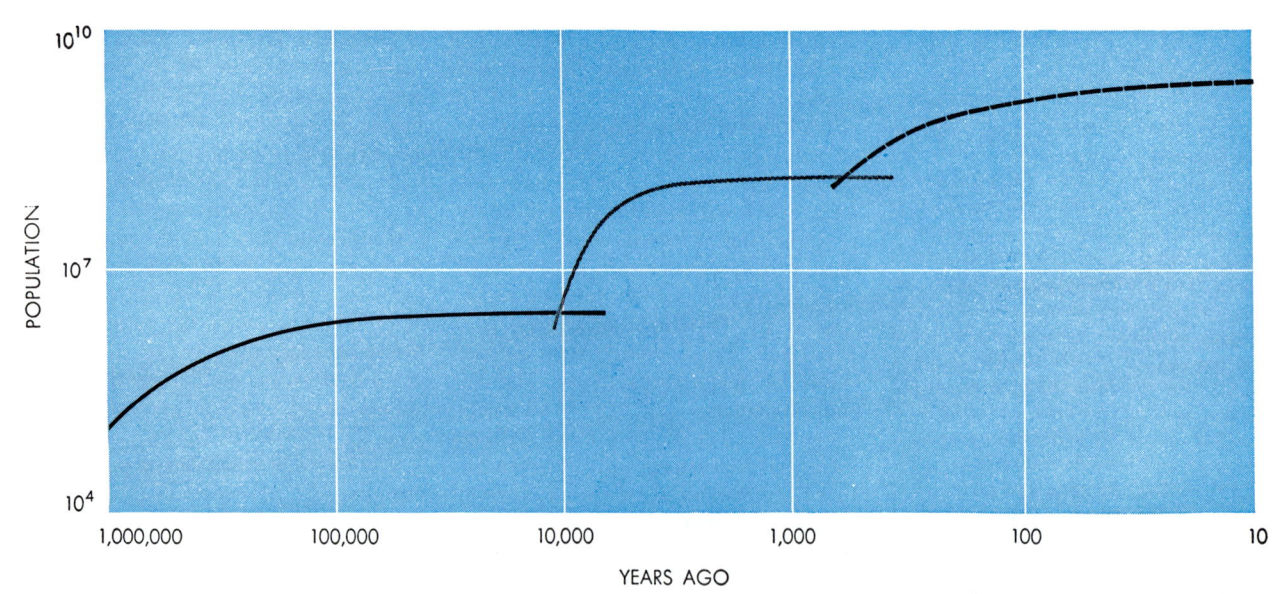

LOGARITHMIC POPULATION CURVE makes it possible to plot, in a small space, the growth of population over a longer period of time and over a wider range (from 10^4, or 10,000, to 10^{10}, or 10 billion, persons). Curve, based on assumptions concerning relationship of technology and population as shown in chart on page 4, reveals three population surges reflecting toolmaking or cultural revolution (*solid line*), agricultural revolution (*gray line*) and scientific-industrial revolution (*broken line*).

than I have assumed (and will presently justify), some degree of voluntary birth control has always prevailed.

Our 40 predecessors on earth make an impressive total, but somehow it sounds different to say that nearly 3 per cent of the people who have ever lived are still around. When we realize that they are living twice as long as their parents did, we are less inclined to discount the revolution in which we are living. One of its effects has just begun to be felt: The mean age of the population is increasing all over the world. Among the more forgivable results of Western culture, when introduced into simpler societies, is a steep drop in the death rate. Public-health authorities are fond of citing Ceylon in this connection. In a period of a year during 1946 and 1947 a campaign against malaria reduced the death rate there from 20 to 14 per 1,000. Eventually the birth rate falls too, but not so fast, nor has it yet fallen so far as a bare replacement value. The natural outcome of this imbalance is that acceleration of annual increase which so bemuses demographers. In the long run it must prove to be temporary, unless the birth rate accelerates, for the deaths that are being systematically prevented are premature ones. That is, the infants who now survive diphtheria and measles are certain to die of something else later on, and while the mean lifespan is approaching the maximum, for the first time in history, there is no reason to think that the maximum itself has been stretched. Meanwhile the expectation of life at birth is rising daily in most countries, so that it has already surpassed 70 years in some, including the U. S., and probably averages between 40 and 50.

It is hard to be certain of any such world-wide figure. The countries where mortality is heaviest are those with the least accurate records. In principle, however, mean age at death is easier to find out than the number of children born, the frequency or mean age at marriage, or any other component of a birth rate. The dead bones, the court and parish records and the tombstones that archeology deals with have something to say about death, of populations as well as of people. Their testimony confirms the impression that threescore years and ten, if taken as an average and not as a maximum lifetime, is something decidedly new. Of course the possibilities of bias in such evidence are almost endless. For instance, military cemeteries tend to be full of young adult males. The hardest bias to allow for is the deficiency of infants and children; juvenile bones are less durable than those of adults, and are often treated less respectfully. Probably we shall never know the true expectation of life at birth for any ancient people. Bypassing this difficulty, we can look at the mean age at death among the fraction surviving to adolescence.

The "nasty, brutish and short" lives of Neanderthal people have been rather elaborately guessed at 29.4 years. The record, beyond them, is not one of steady improvement. For example, Neolithic farmers in Anatolia and Bronze Age Austrians averaged 38 years, and even the Mesolithic savages managed more than 30. But in the golden ages of Greece and Rome the life span was 35 years or less. During the Middle Ages the chances of long life were probably no better. The important thing about these averages is not the differences among them, but their similarity. Remembering the crudeness of the estimates, and the fact that juvenile mortality is omitted, it is fair to guess that human life-expectancy at birth has never been far from 25 years— 25 plus or minus five, say—from Neanderthal times up to the present century. It follows, as I have said, that about half

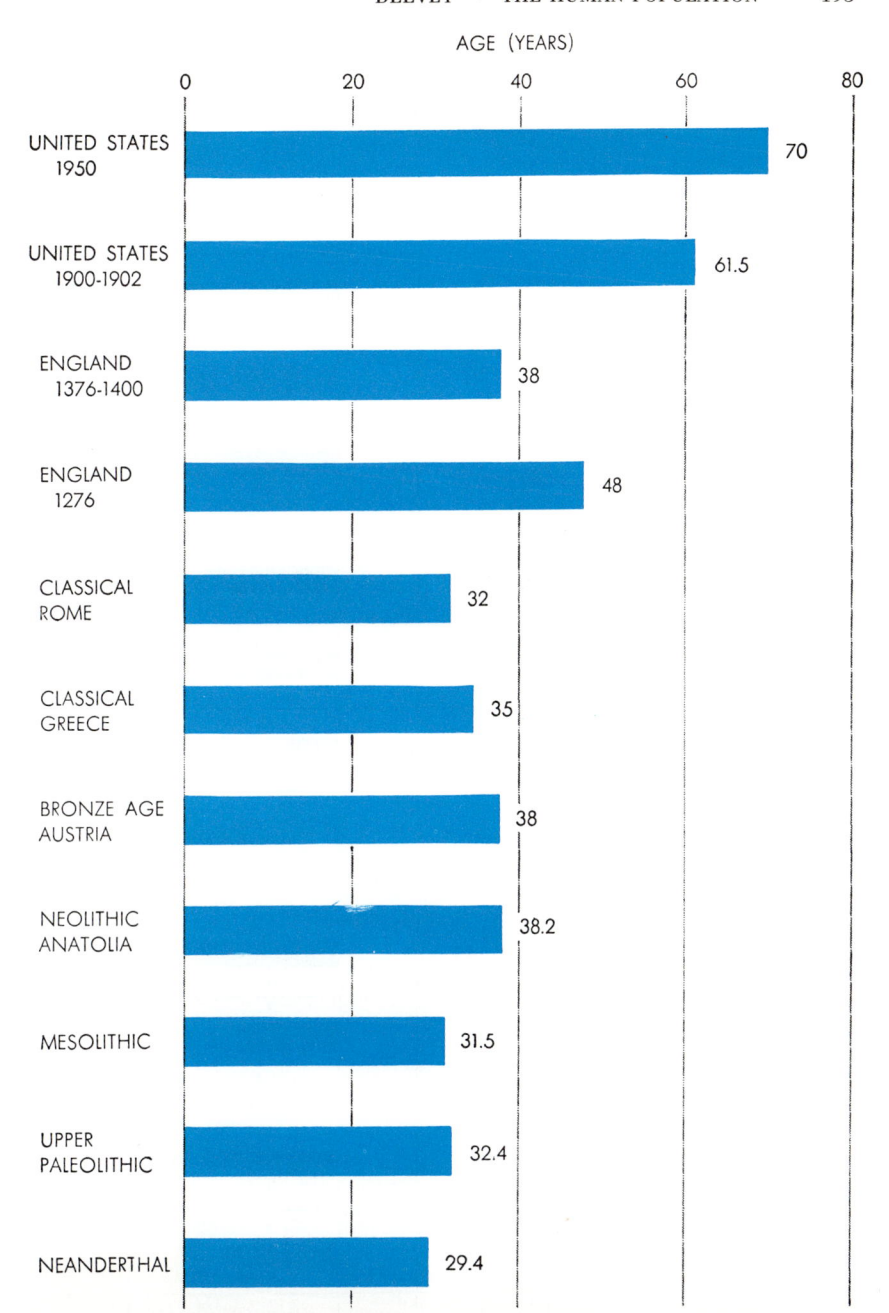

LONGEVITY in ancient and modern times is charted. From time of Neanderthal man to 14th century A.D., life span appears to have hovered around 35 years. An exception is 13th-century England. Increase in longevity partly responsible for current population increase has come in modern era. In U.S. longevity increased about 10 years in last half-century.

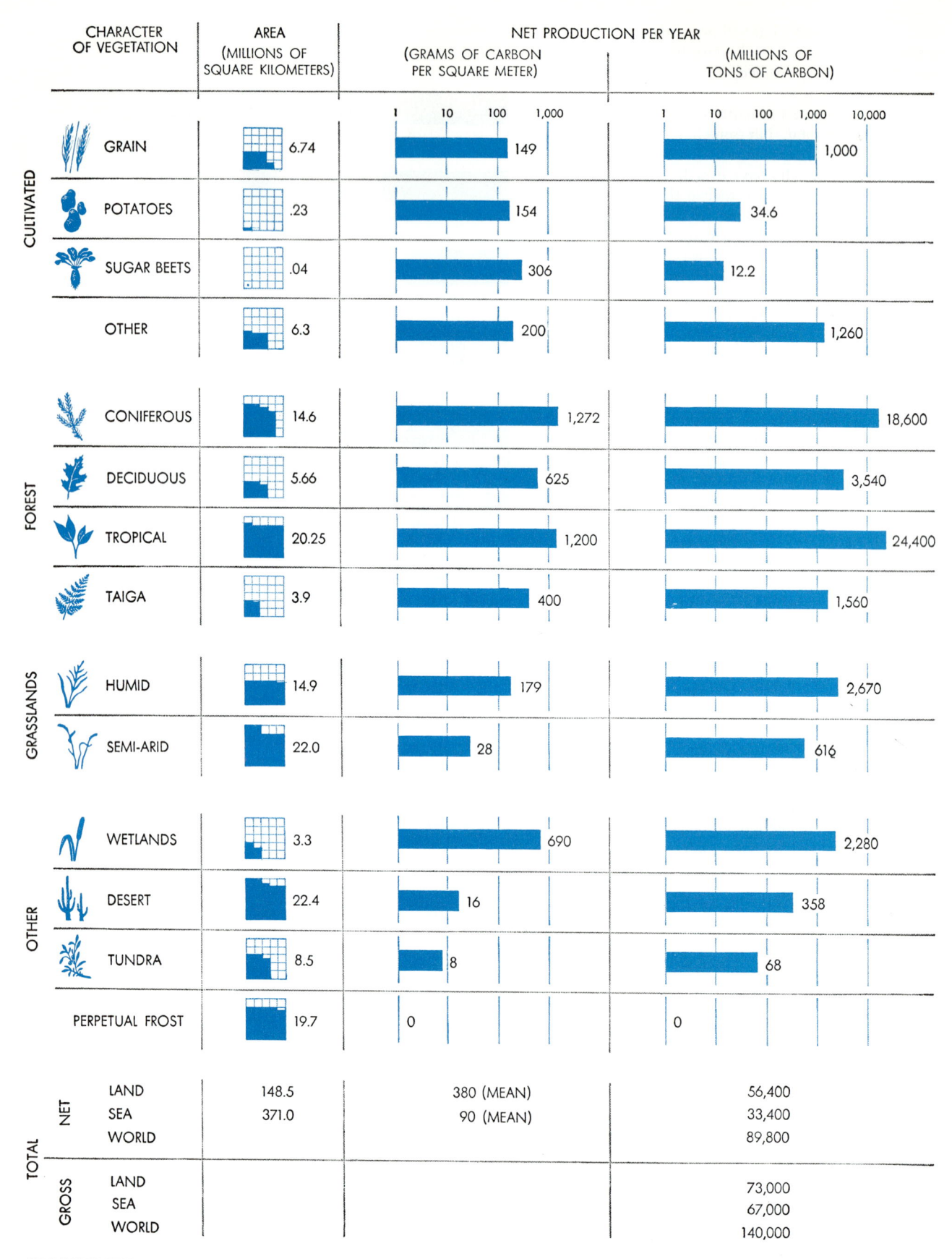

CHARACTER OF VEGETATION		AREA (MILLIONS OF SQUARE KILOMETERS)	NET PRODUCTION PER YEAR (GRAMS OF CARBON PER SQUARE METER)	NET PRODUCTION PER YEAR (MILLIONS OF TONS OF CARBON)
CULTIVATED	GRAIN	6.74	149	1,000
	POTATOES	.23	154	34.6
	SUGAR BEETS	.04	306	12.2
	OTHER	6.3	200	1,260
FOREST	CONIFEROUS	14.6	1,272	18,600
	DECIDUOUS	5.66	625	3,540
	TROPICAL	20.25	1,200	24,400
	TAIGA	3.9	400	1,560
GRASSLANDS	HUMID	14.9	179	2,670
	SEMI-ARID	22.0	28	616
OTHER	WETLANDS	3.3	690	2,280
	DESERT	22.4	16	358
	TUNDRA	8.5	8	68
	PERPETUAL FROST	19.7	0	0
TOTAL NET	LAND	148.5	380 (MEAN)	56,400
	SEA	371.0	90 (MEAN)	33,400
	WORLD			89,800
TOTAL GROSS	LAND			73,000
	SEA			67,000
	WORLD			140,000

PRODUCTION OF ORGANIC MATTER per year by the land vegetation of the world—and thus its ultimate food-producing capacity—is charted in terms of the amount of carbon incorporated in organic compounds. Cultivated vegetation (*top left*) is less efficient than forest and wetlands vegetation, as indicated by the uptake of carbon per square meter (*third column*), and it yields a smaller over-all output than forest, humid grasslands and wetlands vegetation (*fourth column*). The scales at top of third and fourth columns are logarithmic. Land vegetation leads sea vegetation in efficiency and in net and gross tonnage (*bottom*). The difference between the net production and gross production is accounted for by the consumption of carbon in plant respiration.

the children ever born have lived to become sexually mature. It is not hard to see why an average family size of four or more, or twice the minimum replacement rate, has come to seem part of a God-given scheme of things.

The 25-fold upsurge in the number of men between 10,000 and 2,000 years ago was sparked by a genuine increase in the means of subsistence. A shift from animal to plant food, even without agricultural labor and ingenuity, would practically guarantee a 10-fold increase, for a given area can usually produce about 10 times as much plant as animal substance. The scientific-industrial revolution has increased the efficiency of growing these foods, but hardly, as yet, beyond the point needed to support another 10 times as many people, fewer of whom are farmers. At the present rate of multiplication, without acceleration, another 10-fold rise is due within 230 years. Disregarding the fact that developed societies spend 30 to 60 times as much energy for other purposes as they need for food, one is made a little nervous by the thought of so many hungry mouths. Can the increase of efficiency keep pace? Can some of the apparently ample energy be converted to food as needed, perhaps at the cost of reducing the size of Sunday newspapers? Or is man now pressing so hard on his food supply that another 10-fold increase of numbers is impossible?

The answers to these questions are not easy to find, and students with different viewpoints disagree about them. Richard L. Meier of the University of Michigan estimates that a total of 50 billion people (a 20-fold increase, that is) can be supported on earth, and the geochemist Harrison Brown of the California Institute of Technology will allow (reluctantly) twice or four times as many. Some economists are even more optimistic; Arnold C. Harberger of the University of Chicago presents the interesting notion that a larger crop of people will contain more geniuses, whose intellects will find a solution to the problem of feeding *still* more people. And the British economist Colin Clark points out that competition for resources will sharpen everyone's wits, as it always has, even if the level of innate intelligence is not raised.

An ecologist's answer is bound to be cast in terms of solar energy, chlorophyll and the amount of land on which the two can interact to produce organic carbon. Sources of energy other than the sun are either too expensive, or nonrenewable or both. Land areas will continue for a very long time to be the places where food is grown, for the sea is not so productive as the land, on the average. One reason, sometimes forgotten, is that the plants of the sea are microscopic algae, which, being smaller than land plants, respire away a larger fraction of the carbon they fix. The culture of the fresh-water alga *Chlorella* has undeniable promise as a source of human food. But the high efficiencies quoted for its photosynthesis, as compared with agricultural plants, are not sustained outdoors under field conditions. Even if Chlorella (or another exceptionally efficient producer, such as the water hyacinth) is the food plant of the future, flat areas exposed to sunlight will be needed. The 148.5 million square kilometers of land will have to be used with thoughtful care if the human population is to increase 20-fold. With a population of 400 per square kilometer (50 billion total) it would seem that men's bodies, if not their artifacts, will stand in the way of vital sunshine.

Plants capture the solar energy impinging on a given area with an efficiency of about .1 per cent. (Higher values often quoted are based on some fraction of the total radiation, such as visible light.) Herbivores capture about a 10th of the plants' energy, and carnivores convert about 10 per cent of the energy captured by herbivores (or other carnivores). This means, of course, that carnivores, feeding on plants at second hand, can scarcely do so with better than 1 per cent efficiency ($1/10 \times 1/10$ equals $1/100$). Eugene I. Rabinowitch of the University of Illinois has calculated that the current crop of men represents an ultimate conversion of about 1 per cent of the energy trapped by land vegetation. Recently, however, I have re-examined the base figure—the efficiency of the land-plant production—and believe it should be raised by a factor of three or four. The old value came from estimates made in 1919 and in 1937. A good deal has been learned since those days. The biggest surprise is the high productivity of forests, especially the forests of the Temperate Zone.

If my new figures are correct, the population could theoretically increase by 30 or 40 times. But man would have to displace all other herbivores and utilize all the vegetation with the 10 per cent efficiency established by the ecological rule of tithes. No land that now supports greenery could be spared for nonagricultural purposes; the populace would have to reside in the polar regions, or on artificial "green isles in the sea, love"—scummed over, of course, by 10 inches of Chlorella culture.

The picture is doubtless overdrawn. There is plenty of room for improvement in present farming practice. More land could be brought under cultivation if a better distribution of water could be arranged. More efficient basic crops can be grown and used less wastefully. Other sources of energy, notably atomic energy, can be fed back into food production to supplement the sun's rays. None of these measures is more than palliative, however; none promises so much as a 10-fold increase in efficiency; worse, none is likely to be achieved at a pace equivalent to the present rate of doubling of the world's population. A 10-fold, even a 20-fold, increase can be tolerated, perhaps, but the standard of living seems certain to be lower than today's. What happens then, when men perceive themselves to be overcrowded?

The idea of population equilibrium will take some getting used to. A population that is kept stable by emigration, like that of the Western Islands of Scotland, is widely regarded as sick—a shining example of a self-fulfilling diagnosis. Since the fall of the death rate is temporary, it is those two or more extra births per female that demand attention. The experiments with crowded rodents point to one way they might be corrected, through the effect of anxiety in suppressing ovulation and spermatogenesis and inducing fetal resorption. Some of the most dramatic results are delayed until after birth: litters are carelessly nursed, deserted or even eaten. Since fetuses, too, have endocrine glands, the specter of maternal transmission of anxiety now looms: W. R. Thompson of Wesleyan University has shown that the offspring of frustrated mother mice are more "emotional" throughout their own lives, and my student Kim Keeley has confirmed this.

Considered abstractly, these devices for self-regulation compel admiration for their elegance. But there is a neater device that men can use: rational, voluntary control over numbers. In mentioning the dire effects of psychic stress I am not implying that the population explosion will be contained by cannibalism or fetal resorption, or any power so naked. I simply suggest that vertebrates have that power, whether they want it or not, as part of the benefit—and the price —of being vertebrates. And if the human method of adjusting numbers to resources fails to work in the next 1,000 years as it has in the last million, subhuman methods are ready to take over.

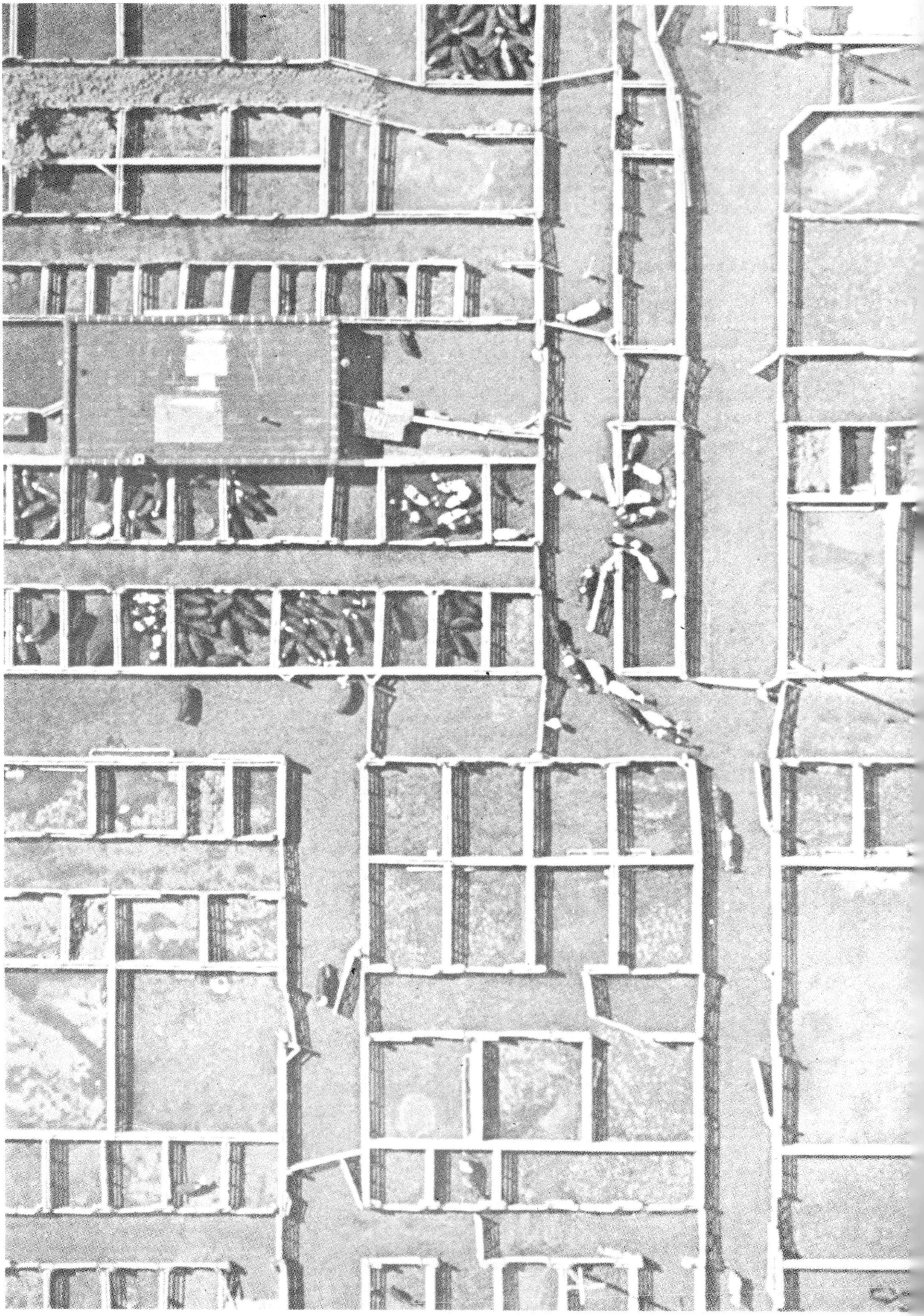

22

FOOD

NEVIN S. SCRIMSHAW
September 1963

The first task of a poor country is to improve both the quantity and the quality of its nutrition. Basically this calls for education, not only in agriculture but also in food economics and technology

Nearly half the world's population is underfed or otherwise malnourished. The lives of the people in the underdeveloped areas are dominated by the scramble for food to stay alive. Such people are perpetually tired, weak and vulnerable to disease—prisoners of a vicious circle that keeps their productivity far below par and so defeats their efforts to feed their families adequately. Because their undernourishment begins soon after birth, it produces permanently depressing and irremediable effects on the population as a whole. Malnutrition and disease kill a high proportion of the children by the age of four; the death rates for these young children are 20 to 60 times higher than in the U.S. and western Europe. Among those who survive, few escape physical or mental retardation or both.

Obviously the first necessity, if the underdeveloped countries are to develop, is more and better food. Much has been said about the need for industrialization of these countries as the quickest and most effective way to raise their incomes and level of living. But they cannot industrialize successfully without a substantial improvement in their nourishment and human efficiency. This must depend primarily on improvement of their agriculture and utilization of food. In these countries from 60 to 80 per cent of the people are engaged in farming, but their productivity is so low that it falls far short of feeding the population. That stands as a roadblock against their advance. Unless they improve their food-producing efficiency, any diversion of their working force to industry will only make their food problem more desperate.

Moreover, during the coming decades their food requirements will rise astronomically, both because of their rapid population growth and because of the demand for a better scale of living that comes with industrialization. The Food and Agriculture Organization of the United Nations has estimated that to provide a decent level of nutrition for the world's peoples the production of food will have to be doubled by 1980 and tripled by 2000.

Can the developing nations make the grade? Is our planet capable of feeding the hungry half of the world and supporting its vast, growing population? This is a complex question that involves many issues other than the volume of food production. Just as important are the conservation of food, the kinds of foods produced and the ways in which food is used. Food supply is not merely a matter of the number of bushels of grain the farmer harvests or the number of chickens he raises. Other vital elements in the equation are the selection, handling, processing, storage, transportation and marketing of the food crops. Each factor allows opportunities for improvement of efficiency that can greatly enhance the food supply.

Let us consider what science and technology have to contribute to the food problem.

The simplest way to increase food production, one might suppose, is to bring more land under cultivation and put more people to work on it. The U.S.S.R. and some of the underdeveloped countries have resorted to this straightforward approach, without notable success. It contains several fallacies. For one thing, it usually means moving into marginal land where the soil and climatic conditions give a poor return. Cultivation may quickly deplete this soil, ruining it for pasture or forest growth. It is often possible, of course, to turn such lands into useful farms by agricultural know-how; for instance, a sophisticated knowledge of how to use the available water through an irrigation system may reclaim semiarid grasslands for crop-growing. But the cultivation of marginal lands is in any case unsuccessful unless it is carried out by farmers with a centuries-old tradition of experience or by modern experts with a detailed knowledge of the local conditions and the varieties of crops that are suitable for those conditions. Such knowledge is conspicuously absent in the underdeveloped countries.

Furthermore, we know that the highly developed countries have not increased the number of acres under cultivation but on the contrary have abandoned their marginal lands and steadily reduced the proportion of the population engaged in farming. Efficient farming calls for concentration on the most efficient lands, and it also results in greater production with fewer people. The U.S., for example, produces a huge surplus of food with only about 10 per cent of its people working on the farms.

The problem of the underdeveloped countries, then, is to increase the productivity of their farms and farmers. This would allow them to industrialize and to feed their people more adequately. It is not easy to accomplish, however. The peasant farmers are conservative and resistant to change in their methods of cultivation. The entire population

---

CHICAGO STOCKYARDS are a focal point in the distribution of protein in the U.S., handling more than three million head of cattle, hogs and sheep a year. Only a few of its hundreds of pens appear in the aerial photograph on the opposite page. When this picture was taken, the pens contained Hereford, black Angus and Holstein cattle.

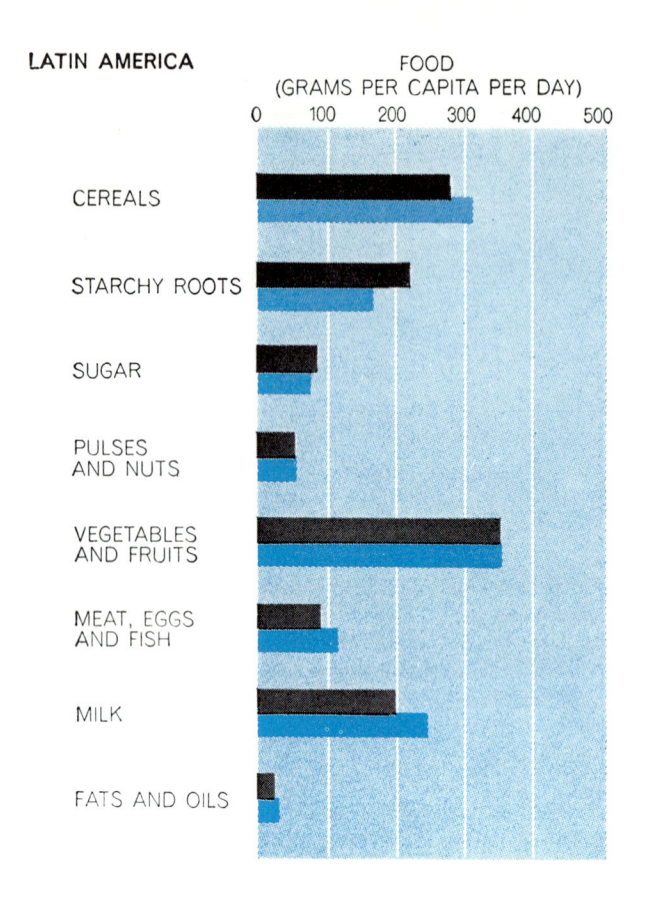

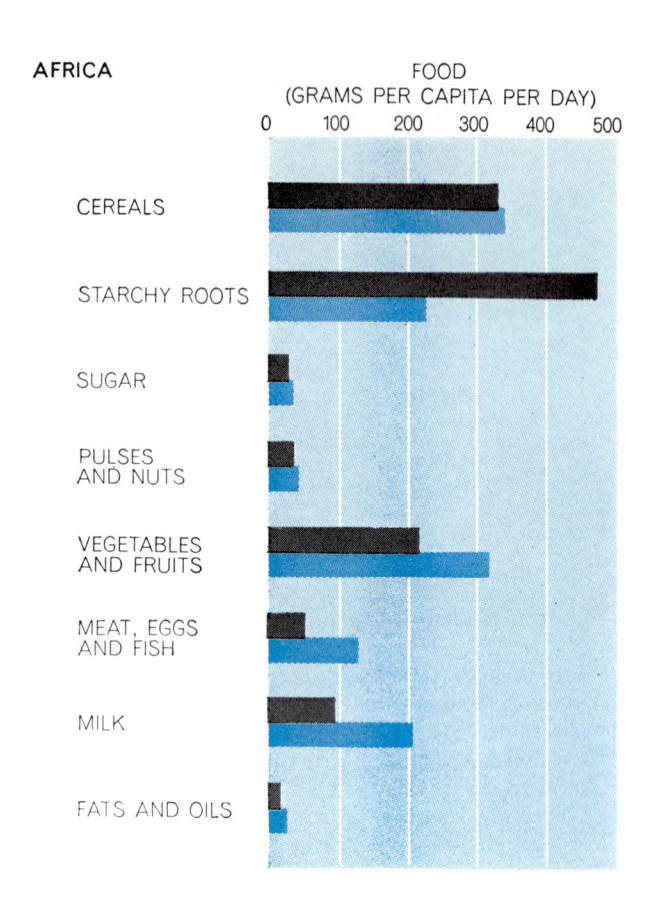

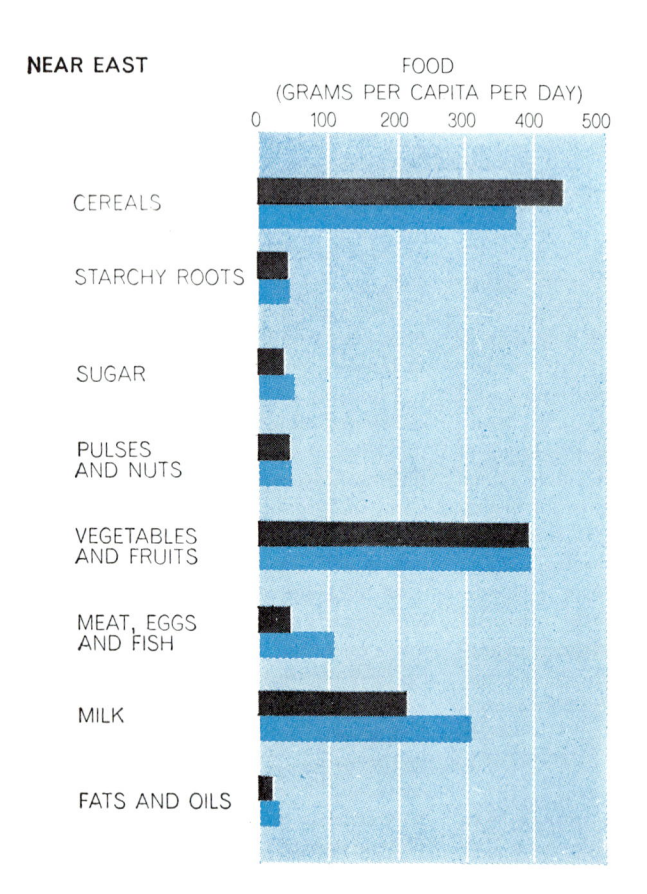

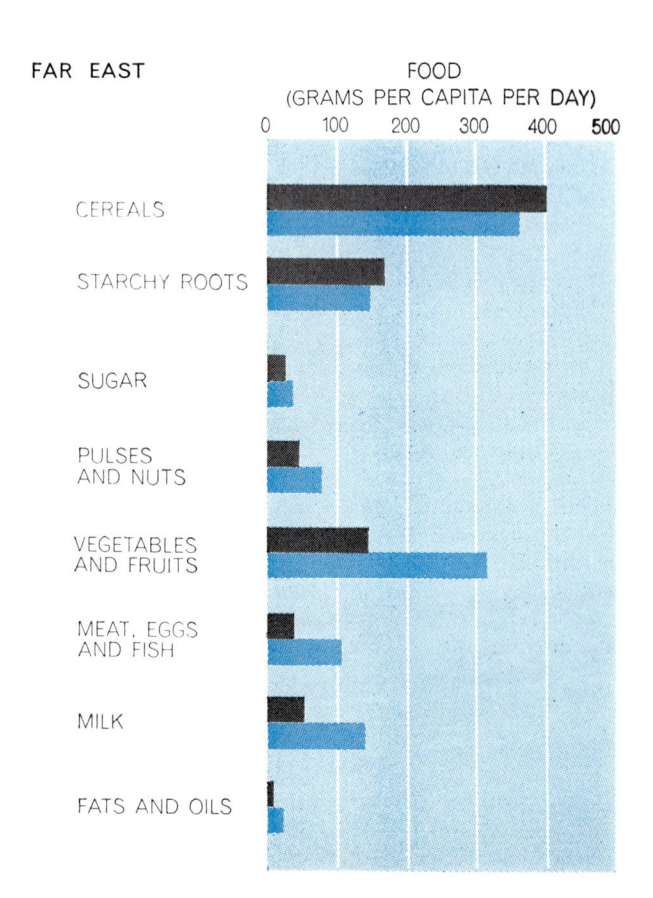

FOOD SUPPLIES available (*gray bars*) and needed (*colored bars*) vary widely in four underdeveloped regions, according to studies by the Food and Agriculture Organization (FAO). All the regions suffer from both shortages of food and badly unbalanced diets. The lack of proteins is particularly acute and plays an important role in malnutrition. Pulses include leguminous crops such as peas and beans. The relatively well-fed countries of Paraguay, Uruguay and Argentina are omitted from the Latin America chart.

needs to be indoctrinated in the possibilities offered by scientific agriculture, including the officials who must provide the necessary funds, planning, legislation, training and research programs. The underdeveloped countries are greatly in need of studies and experiments to help them to adapt modern agricultural methods to their own conditions.

During the past two decades some of these countries have increased their food production, but their populations have in the meantime grown faster; therefore they are farther behind than before. Furthermore, the food increase has been gained at the expense of using up marginal lands. In productivity per acre or per man they have not gained at all.

Meanwhile the efficiency of farming in the developed countries has progressed phenomenally. In the U.S. the productivity per farm worker has tripled since 1940 [see illustration on page 204]. With a 7 per cent reduction in the total acreage under cultivation, U.S. production of cereal grains has jumped 50 per cent; the increase in the corn output, thanks to hybrid corn, has been even greater.

The "secret" of these improvements can be summed up in a few words: chemicals, mechanization, breeding and feeding.

Fertilizers are an old story to farmers, even in backward countries, but the practitioners of modern farming have raised the use of chemical fertilizers to a high art. To these they have added a pharmacopoeia of chemicals for special purposes: poisons to kill insects, fungi and other pests; plant-growth regulators to control weeds, force early sprouting, stimulate ripening and prevent premature dropping of fruit; soil-conditioners to improve the physical characteristics of the soil. Most of these techniques and materials could easily be introduced on the farms of the underdeveloped areas. They require capital investment, but they would pay for themselves many times over in higher yields.

The mechanization of farming has become so familiar in Western countries that we have forgotten the many changes it has brought about. It has released for human food a great deal of land formerly devoted to growing feed for draft animals. Feeding fuel to a machine is cheaper than feeding a horse, and the machine needs less care and maintenance. The machine not only plows and cultivates but also digs ditches and postholes, loads and handles heavy materials, harvests, threshes, chops forage, cleans vegetables and does many other things the intelligent horse could never do. It does all these things swiftly and virtually at a moment's notice, so that the farmer no longer has to worry about whether or not he can get a job done before threatening weather ruins his planting or his harvest.

The machine has also facilitated the building and development of irrigation systems. It makes easy work of the construction of dams, the digging of water channels and the pumping of water. In the U.S. irrigation has made it possible to increase the crop yield of Western lands by 50 to 100 per cent. In the arid zones of India and the Middle East, which for centuries have been entirely dependent on irrigation for their farming, extension of their systems with machinery would be a great boon. In some areas where enough water could be furnished by irrigation, two or three crops a year could be produced and the crops could be diversified.

Finally, a combination of selective breeding and efficient feeding has generated astonishing bounties in both plant and animal production. For most of the major plant crops, thanks to modern genetics, we have seen the development of new varieties that give a higher yield and are more resistant to disease. The same is true of the animals that supply our meat, milk and eggs. "Hybrid vigor" has become a magic phrase in the U.S. farm belt. Furthermore, the farmer today can buy selected seeds he knows will do certain specific things with high reliability: produce plants that mature faster or are adapted to a wide range of conditions or grow to a uniform height and all ripen at the same time so that they can be harvested by machine.

We now have wilt-resisting peas and cabbages, mosaic-resisting snap beans, virus-resisting potatoes, mildew-resisting cucumbers and lima beans, anthracnose-resisting watermelons and leaf-spot-resisting strawberries. We have new cereal grains rich in high-quality protein, special squash rich in vitamin A, cottonseed from which the toxic pigment called gossypol has been bred out. We have cows that give richer milk, hogs that grow exceptionally fast on less feed, hogs with more lean meat and less fat, poultry with a high ratio of lean meat.

To improvement of the animal breeds the advanced countries have coupled scientific husbandry: finely calculated diets and rations, synthetic hormones, pesticides and sanitary stalls, drugs and vaccines to control disease and many other measures that have heightened the efficiency of production. The results are most strikingly shown in poultry raising. There are now breeds of hens that lay more than 200 eggs a year and broilers that grow to a three-pound market size within 10 weeks. Diseases, waste motion and costs have been sharply reduced. Raised in individual cages arrayed in batteries of hundreds or thousands, the chickens minimize the expenditure of energy by themselves and their caretakers and facilitate record-keeping, so that the less productive birds can easily be eliminated.

In general it would not be difficult to apply most of the agricultural improvements to the countries that need them so urgently. The main biological problem would be to select the right plants and animals for transfer to those countries. For instance, Temperate Zone varieties of corn and soybeans do not grow well in hotter areas; prize pigs from mild climates are often unable to nurse their young in the Tropics; plants and animals that are successful in one region may quickly succumb to diseases in another. But analysis of the ecological conditions and testing can resolve these problems. It is known, for example, that certain plants can readily be transplanted from areas in the U.S. to areas in Japan because the climatic conditions are much the same. The identification and classification of such ecological analogues on a world-wide scale would greatly facilitate the transfer of agricultural techniques to the underdeveloped regions.

Aside from more efficient methods, however, those countries need a sounder over-all policy, which is to say, in most cases, more diversification of crops. Many of the underdeveloped nations are enslaved by a single cash crop, such as rubber, hemp, cotton, coffee, tea, sugar or olive oil, with deadly effects on their basic food supply. It is true that the export of the single crop provides cash with which to buy food, but it places the country at the mercy of crop failure and price fluctuations in the world market. There have been periods when it has meant mass starvation for a whole region.

Without giving up its profitable crop, each country should be able to expand its own food production and achieve a better-balanced agricultural economy. In some cases it could improve its food supply immediately without radical changes. For example, the cotton-raising countries usually export the cottonseed-oil meal along with the fiber;

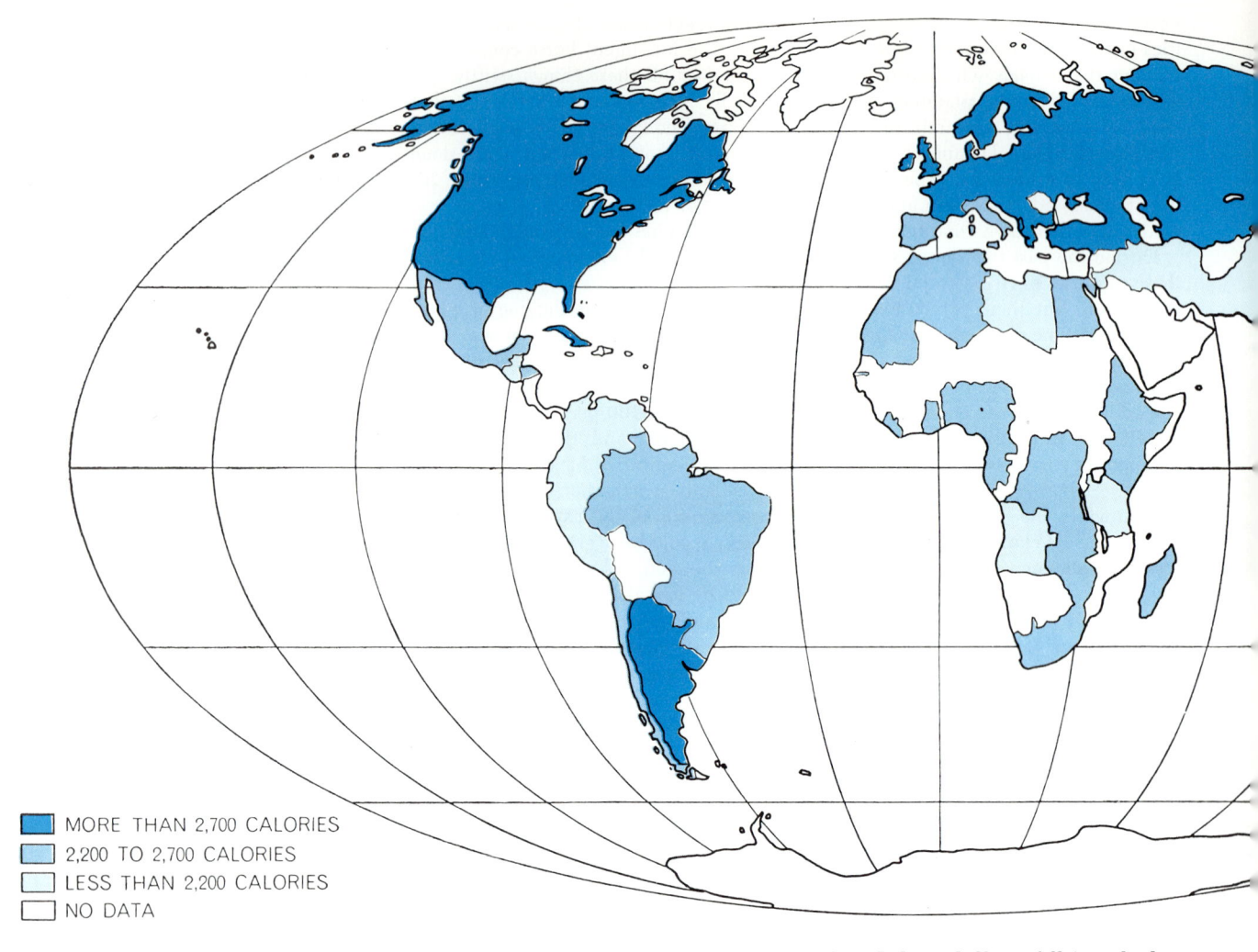

■ MORE THAN 2,700 CALORIES
■ 2,200 TO 2,700 CALORIES
□ LESS THAN 2,200 CALORIES
□ NO DATA

NUMBER OF CALORIES per person per day as estimated by the FAO in 1962 is plotted on a map of the world. Several heavily populated countries, such as India and China, fall into the lowest classification, which means that a large part of the world's

instead they could keep the meal and use it for animal feed and even as human food.

Thus in their campaign against hunger the developing countries need first of all to increase their food production. The second way in which they could make great strides is by better food conservation or preservation. In this field the advanced countries have achieved improvements fully as spectacular as in production.

For food-raising *Homo sapiens* the perishability of foodstuffs has always been a major problem. Gradually he learned that his food supply would go further if he kept it edible longer by smoking, drying or salting it, or by keeping it cool in caves, wells, snow or ice from ponds. With limited effectiveness, these devices have served man for many centuries. But general food conservation on a large scale did not begin until the 19th century, with the arrival of the insulated refrigerator.

Within the past two decades we have seen freezing become a major means of preserving food in the U.S. Still newer is the recent development of freeze-drying—a system of vacuum dehydration of frozen food that makes it possible to store many foods without refrigeration and still retain their fresh flavor and characteristic properties. This method is ideal for keeping food in tropical areas, but it is still comparatively expensive. Vacuum-drying without freezing, however, is less costly and can preserve certain foods with little change in their flavor or texture. Also cheaper than freeze-drying is the new process of foam-mat drying, which is particularly good for fruit juices and purées.

Sterilization of food by ionizing radiation, which once seemed very promising, now looks impractical, because it damages the flavor and nutritional value. But irradiation with smaller doses, in the pasteurization range, may help to prolong the storage life of foods, although they will have to be refrigerated. Bacon preserved by this process has recently been approved for sale in the U.S. Another new technique is dipping the food in an antibiotic bath; this works well for fresh fish and meat. Of course there are also the chemical preservatives and other additives that have been used in food for some time, such as propionates to inhibit molds in bread, antioxidants to slow down the process by which fats become rancid, emulsifying agents, bleaching agents and so on.

In many other ways, some obvious and some subtle, modern food industries have contrived to reduce the attrition of food between its harvesting in the field and its delivery to the consumer. These include scientific storage at the right temperature and humidity with protection from rodents and insects, protective packaging (for which polyethylene and other synthetic wrappings have been particularly useful) and rapid transportation in refrigerated ships, cars and airplanes. Today there is virtually no food that cannot be delivered fresh and

population is undernourished. While production is rising, so is the number of people.

with only minor losses to consumers everywhere.

Better food production and better food conservation are the prime requirements of the ill-fed countries. There is a third modern development that could also help them tremendously—artificial enrichment of their food with vitamins and other substances.

Everyone knows the story of the dramatic conquest of goiter in the U.S. and elsewhere by the simple device of adding iodine to the salt. Iodized salt in the 1920's practically eliminated goiter in the U.S. Middle West and Switzerland, where iodine is missing from the normal inland diet. In recent years Guatemala by the iodization of salt has abruptly reduced the incidence of goiter to less than 10 per cent in areas where it was formerly 30 to 60 per cent, and Colombia has achieved similar results. Salt iodization is now an officially sponsored practice in a number of underdeveloped countries.

Other deficiency diseases, such as pellagra and beriberi, can be eliminated by the simple addition of vitamins to wheat flour and polished rice. Here it is usually a case of restoring valuable food elements that are lost in the processing of the whole grain into the "refined" food. Since 1941 the enrichment of wheat flour with thiamine, riboflavin and niacin has been a general practice in the U.S. and Canada, and it is required by law in Puerto Rico and the Central American countries. Such legislation should be adopted by all countries depending on refined wheat flour as a basic food. The same goes for polished rice. In a test on a large scale in the Philippines from 1948 to 1950 it was shown that enrichment of polished rice with vitamins was very effective in combating beriberi in this rice-eating population. Corn meal also needs to be enriched; a diet consisting mainly of corn may produce pellagra, the disease resulting from a deficiency of the vitamin niacin combined with a diet low in the amino acid tryptophan.

Enrichment of a nation's wheat, corn and rice with the vitamins thiamine, riboflavin and niacin, plus calcium and iron, costs only a few cents per person per year. It would produce significant improvements in the health of most ill-fed populations, and it is strongly recommended by international health organizations.

A great part of the hungry half of the world suffers primarily from a deficiency of protein. In most vegetables and other plant foods the protein content is low in quantity and poor in quality—meaning that it is only partly metabolized by the body. High-quality protein is hard to come by. In many of the underdeveloped countries it would require the relatively wasteful allocation of land to pasture for animals, whereas it is often more efficient at present to devote the land to the direct growing of food for human beings.

Fortunately, however, low-protein foods can be enriched economically by adding a source of the missing amino acids that are essential to the synthesis of proteins by the body. The nutritive value of corn meal, for example, can be greatly improved by adding to it a supplement of 3 per cent fish flour, 3 per cent egg powder, 3 per cent food yeast, 5 per cent skim milk, 8 per cent soybean flour or 8 per cent cottonseed flour. Any of these supplements will supply material for protein synthesis and also improve the efficiency of utilization of the protein in the corn meal.

A most promising development is the progress that is being made in the artificial synthesis of amino acids themselves. Synthetic methionine is already being fed to animals in the U.S. on a considerable scale. The addition of lysine to wheat flour or bread can raise the proportion of the wheat's usable protein from about a half to two-thirds, and the amino acid threonine could make grain protein almost as fully usable as the proteins of meat and milk. The main problem so far is the cost of the synthetic amino acids. As more of them are synthesized and the price is brought down, these products of laboratory chemistry will make it possible to turn grain into meat for the meatless regions of the world.

Already nutritionists, using only natural sources, have concocted mixtures that can make a purely vegetarian diet richer in protein. The basic ingredients are a cereal grain, such as corn, rice or wheat, and an oilseed meal. This meal, or flour, is made from the cakes that are left when the oil is pressed out of the seed. It is consequently less expensive than comparable animal protein because it is a dividend remaining after sale of the oil. It generally contains about 50 per cent protein. Good sources of oilseed meal are cottonseed, soybean seeds, sesame seeds, sunflower seeds and peanuts.

When a properly processed oilseed meal is mixed with a grain in the ratio of one part meal to two parts grain, the combination contains about 25 per cent protein of meatlike quality. With the addition of a small amount of yeast and vitamin A it makes a highly nutritious food. In tropical and subtropical areas it could serve as a complete basic food lacking only vitamin C (which is supplied in abundance by tropical fruits and vegetables) and sufficient calories. The latter are obtained readily from sugar, starchy vegetables and such fruits as bananas and plantains.

Low-cost mixtures of this kind have been developed by the Institute of Nutrition of Central America and Panama. Under the generic name of Incaparina, they are already being manufactured and sold as basic foods in Guatemala, El Salvador, Mexico and Colombia and will soon be available in other Latin-American countries. Incaparina has been found to be almost as good a protein source for young children as milk, and it has proved to be effective in preventing or curing protein malnutrition in children. Almost every region of the world either has already or can grow the raw materials for this food. The basic formula is about

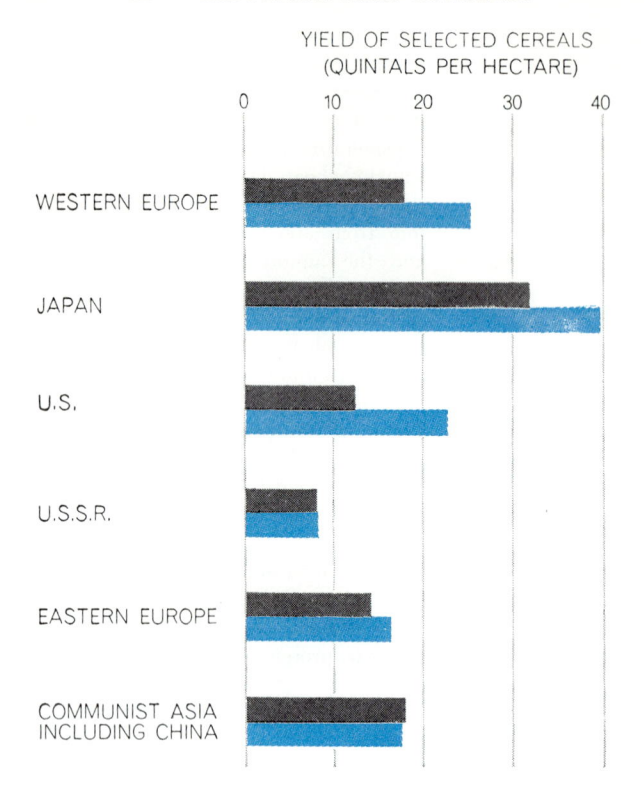

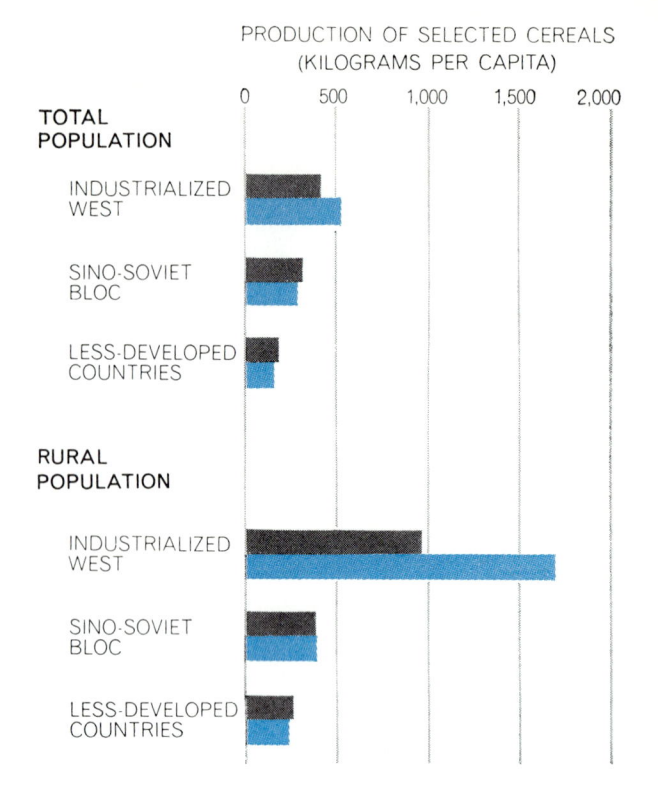

EFFICIENCY OF AGRICULTURAL PRODUCTION has grown in industrialized areas but has remained static or even declined elsewhere. Gray bars represent years 1935–1939, colored bars the year 1959. Chart at left shows yields of selected cereals. A quintal is 100,000 grams, or about 220 pounds. A hectare is 2.47 acres. Charts at right show production of selected cereals per capita of total population (*top*) and of rural population (*bottom*). The latter includes people living in both rural areas and small villages.

55 per cent grain (corn, sorghum, rice, wheat or whatever other cereal is available locally), 38 per cent oilseed meal, 3 per cent torula yeast, 3 per cent leaf meal (as a source of vitamin A) and 1 per cent calcium carbonate.

Many other schemes for getting more protein from plants have been studied. One on which a great deal of work has been done is the growing in liquid culture of the single-celled alga *Chlorella*. Efforts have also been made to concentrate or extract protein from grass, vegetables, cereals and other plant materials. But so far all these investigations have been disappointing in one way or another: the food produced is either too expensive, unpalatable or low in nutritive value.

Then there is the sea, whose tremendous population of fish and other edibles continues to excite the imagination of those concerned with the world's food problem. The main obstacle here is the cost of storing the catch of fish; such storage requires mechanical refrigeration, not generally available in the underdeveloped countries. The grinding of fish to make a protein-rich flour looks like a promising answer to this problem, but it calls for technical skill and costs more than providing protein in the form of surplus dried skim milk or oilseed meal. Moreover, large quantities of fish flour are not attractive in a basic daily diet. All in all, it must be said that sea food offers possibilities one should not neglect but that it cannot be regarded as a panacea for prompt solution of the world's food problems.

Finally, there is the dream of manufacturing completely synthetic foods at a cost low enough to end all food worries. After all, the essential nutrients man requires are basically chemicals whose formulas are well known. Most of them can be synthesized in the laboratory, either by direct chemical manipulation or with the help of microorganisms. We already have synthetic vitamins, synthetic amino acids, hydrogenated fats, artificial flavoring and coloring agents and so on. From a concentrate of soybean protein the skill of the food chemist can prepare a meat-like product that with proper flavoring, coloring and molding can pass for pressed ham or chicken.

The cost of such creations is still exorbitant. But the progress of chemistry is steadily reducing the cost, and almost certainly we shall eventually have synthetic foods that will compete in cost, palatability and nutritive value with the products of the farm. Although that day is too far away to promise relief of the present food crisis in the underdeveloped regions, it may help to forestall the crises threatened for the future by the growth of the world's population.

Along with modern food technology go modern dangers. As man takes a more active hand in shaping and extending his food supply he introduces new hazards in what he eats—mainly potentially dangerous new food additives. Thus the safety of our food has become a paramount issue in the industrial age.

Indeed, it has always been something of an issue. We tend to overlook the fact that there are toxic substances in most of the plants we use for food, even the common ones. Fortunately they are usually eliminated or reduced to harmless proportions by cooking or other processing.

Many legumes (notably soybeans) contain an inhibitor that interferes with the action of the protein-digesting enzyme trypsin. Some also have substances that clump the red blood cells. Cabbages and several other common vegetables contain materials that deny iodine to the thyroid gland and so tend to produce goiter. Certain vegetables and cereals have high concentrations of oxalates and phytates, which bind iron and calcium and prevent the use of these minerals by the body. There are also common plants that harbor some of the deadliest poisons known to man. The cassava root contains cyanides; lima beans, the common vetch and the broad bean have a glucoside that gives rise to cyanides; the broad bean also contains a compound that causes hemolytic anemia; the chick-pea contains an unknown substance that produces the disease lathyrism (spastic paralysis of the legs). Consequently man has always had to be careful, and still needs to be, in his choice and processing of natural foods.

The new dangers arise from the increasing and necessary use of chemicals at all stages in the production and handling of food, from the planting of the seed to the packaging of the final product. The hazard begins with the pesticides and other poisons used to protect and promote the growth of the plant. (One may hope that another contaminant—radioactive fallout from nuclear tests—will now effectively be eliminated.) After harvesting, grain and legumes become subject to poisoning by molds unless they are properly stored. Then there is the potential toxicity of residues of the hormones and antibiotics that have become a standard part of the feeding of meat animals. Next come the chemicals added to foods during the processing for flavor, color and preservative purposes. Along the way the food may pick up traces of toxic detergents that have been used to clean the tanks or containers in which it is processed. Finally, the wrappings in which the food is packaged may inadvertently add some toxic contamination.

The whole sequence is imperfectly known; no one can be quite sure just where all the dangers lurk. Gradually the advanced countries have awakened to the need for vigilance in all stages of the handling of food. With respect to the chemical treatment of foods, U.S. legislation and the policy of the Food and Drug Administration are now based on the principle that "there are no harmless substances; there are only harmless ways of using them."

If the technically developed countries are concerned about the safety of their food supplies, obviously the less developed ones must be even more so as they attempt a rapid modernization of their food-producing and food-processing methods. The control of food contamination has become a world-wide problem, and the World Health Organization and the Food and Agriculture Organization of the United Nations have initiated conferences, committees and periodic reports on control regulations in the various countries. International research and standards will be helpful, but each country must take the responsibility for guarding the safety of its own food supply.

What can be done to help the hungry half of the world pull itself up from its undernourished state and speed up the developments that would enable it to feed itself decently?

Even pessimists must note, first of all, that the prospects of the impoverished peoples are brightened by a most remarkable turn in human history. Whereas in the past men have been concerned only with feeding their own families and have fought long and bitter wars for food, we see today a new and remarkable world-wide concern for feeding the hungry wherever they are. Whether this arises out of advanced humanitarianism, the fears of the well-fed or the contest between the West and Communism is less important than the fact that the wealthy countries are taking an interest in the peoples of the poor countries.

During the past nine years the U.S. has sent more than $12 billion worth of its surplus food to these countries. The Food and Agriculture Organization, at the suggestion of Canada and the U.S., has launched an international effort for the same purpose with a $100 million fund as a starter, and it is now conducting a five-year Freedom from Hunger campaign.

This emergency help is not to be underestimated, and one hopes that it will be continued and even enlarged, preferably under international auspices.

A second way in which the developed countries are helping substantially is by example and by technical advice and assistance to the developing areas. The example, again, is important. The U.S. Department of Agriculture has estimated

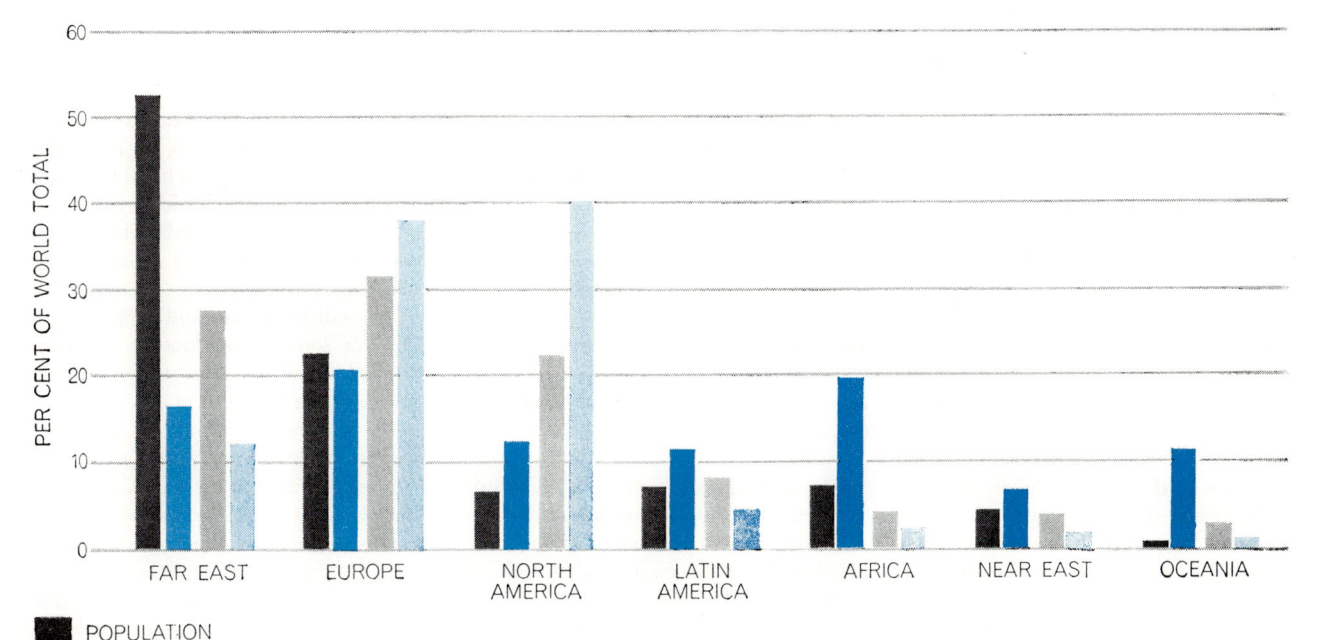

UNEQUAL DISTRIBUTION of world's income, agricultural land and agricultural production in relation to population shows up plainly on chart. Far East, with more than half the world's population, has less than 15 per cent of the income. Figures come from a study by the FAO in 1956. The category of Oceania embraces only Australia and New Zealand.

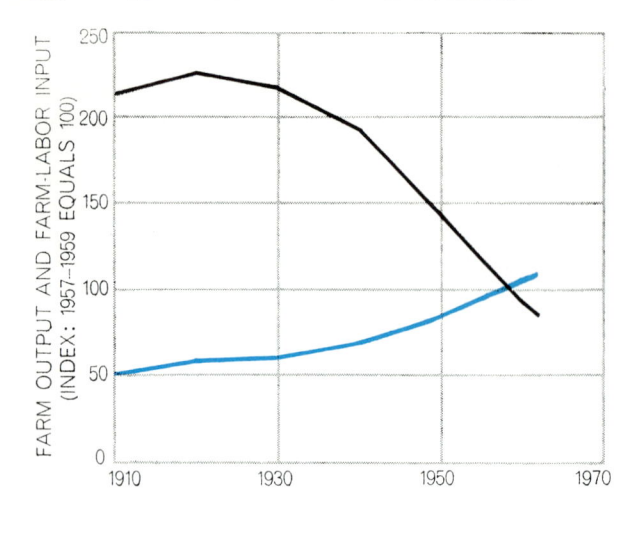

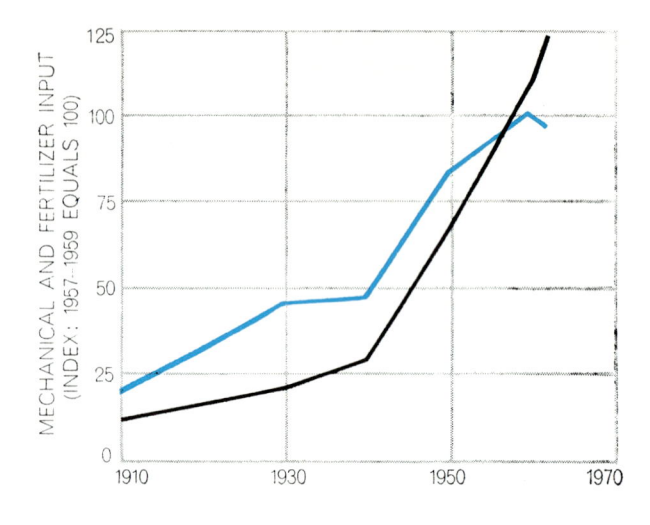

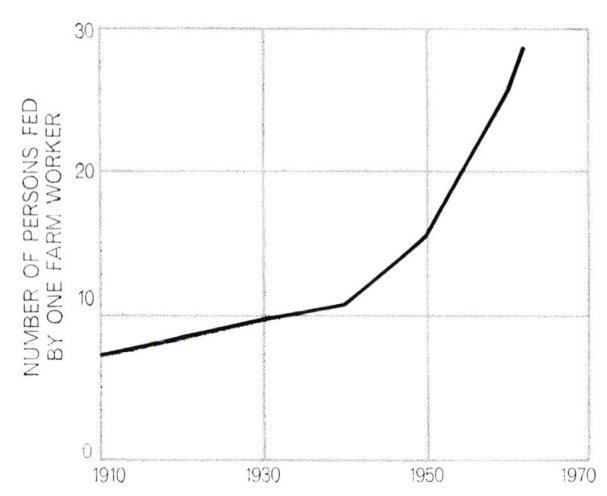

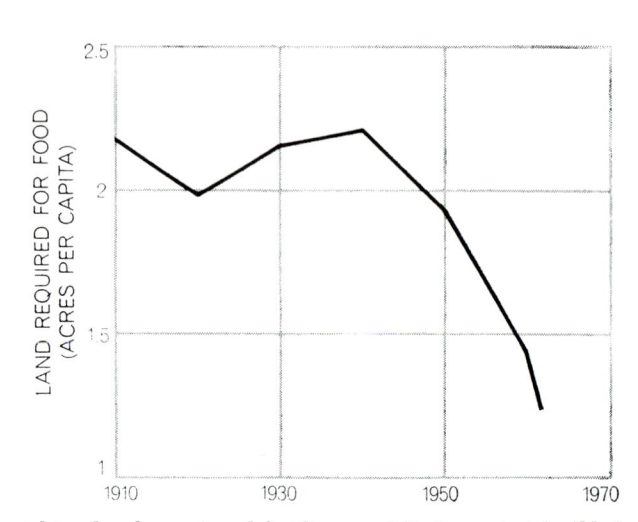

VAST IMPROVEMENT of agricultural production in U.S. demonstrates value of modern techniques. At top left, index of farm-labor input (*black curve*) declined from 212 in 1910 to 85 in 1962, while the farm output index (*colored curve*) rose from 51 to 108. The change was due in great part to increased use of machinery (*top right, colored curve*) and fertilizers and liming materials (*black curve*). The number of persons supplied by one farm worker in 1820 was 4.12. By 1910 it had risen to 7.07 (*bottom left*) and in 1962 it had jumped to 28.57. The number of acres needed to feed one person declined from 2.17 in 1910 to 1.23 in 1962 (*bottom right*).

that at the present rate of progress in agricultural productivity the developed countries will be able to produce almost twice as much food as they need by the year 2000. Such an advance cannot fail to infect and stimulate the backward countries.

Yet when all is said and done, these countries must themselves generate the means for their emancipation from hunger. To do so they will have to change long-established habits and attitudes. Neither well-meant exhortations nor government decrees are likely to persuade them—certainly not in a hurry. Concrete steps may, however, speed reforms by quickly convincing the people of their value.

It is easy to list effective projects that the governments of these countries might undertake. Make available to the farmers the seeds and stocks of improved plant varieties and animal breeds. Build chemical-fertilizer plants. Supply agricultural chemicals for pest control and other special purposes. Provide new implements and machinery suitable for the local types of farming. Extend credit to the farmers for their new seeds and equipment. Pay them subsidies to start urgently needed new crops. And above all, establish training programs that will show them how to handle their new materials and equipment and to farm more efficiently.

Education must receive the first priority for the advancement of these countries. The development of each one of the Western countries has been founded on the literacy and knowledge of its population. This applies to their progress in agriculture as well as to their achievements in industrial technology and professional services. To raise itself the underdeveloped country requires a population that understands modern agriculture and nutrition, is equipped with teachers and experts in all the fields of food technology and is led by political and administrative officials who appreciate the possibilities of science and technology.

This will be a long and difficult program for some of the poorly educated and ill-fed nations. But investment in education is a far more practical and effective program for them than investment in big buildings, dams, roads and factories that are put up mainly as visible symbols of progress. Just as the strength of the so-called developed countries lies in their educational systems and their culture, so the great hope and promise of the future for the underdeveloped countries resides in the fact that they too will come to share in the full wealth of mankind's knowledge and contribute to it themselves.

HUMAN FOOD PRODUCTION AS A PROCESS IN THE BIOSPHERE

LESTER R. BROWN
September 1970

Human population growth is mainly the result of increases in food production. This relation raises the question: How many people can the biosphere support without impairment of its overall operation?

Throughout most of man's existence his numbers have been limited by the supply of food. For the first two million years or so he lived as a predator, a herbivore and a scavenger. Under such circumstances the biosphere could not support a human population of more than 10 million, a population smaller than that of London or Afghanistan today. Then, with his domestication of plants and animals some 10,000 years ago, man began to shape the biosphere to his own ends.

As primitive techniques of crop production and animal husbandry became more efficient the earth's food-producing capacity expanded, permitting increases in man's numbers. Population growth in turn exerted pressure on food supply, compelling man to further alter the biosphere in order to meet his food needs. Population growth and advances in food production have thus tended to be mutually reinforcing.

It took two million years for the human population to reach the one-billion mark, but the fourth billion now being added will require only 15 years: from 1960 to 1975. The enormous increase in the demand for food that is generated by this expansion in man's numbers, together with rising incomes, is beginning to have disturbing consequences. New signs of stress on the biosphere are reported almost daily. The continuing expansion of land under the plow and the evolution of a chemically oriented modern agriculture are producing ominous alterations in the biosphere not just on a local scale but, for the first time in history, on a global scale as well. The natural cycles of energy and the chemical elements are clearly being affected by man's efforts to expand his food supply.

Given the steadily advancing demand for food, further intervention in the biosphere for the expansion of the food supply is inevitable. Such intervention, however, can no longer be undertaken by an individual or a nation without consideration of the impact on the biosphere as a whole. The decision by a government to dam a river, by a farmer to use DDT on his crops or by a married couple to have another child, thereby increasing the demand for food, has repercussions for all mankind.

The revolutionary change in man's role from hunter and gatherer to tiller and herdsman took place in circumstances that are not well known, but some of the earliest evidence of agriculture is found in the hills and grassy plains of the Fertile Crescent in western Asia. The cultivation of food plants and the domestication of animals were aided there by the presence of wild wheat, barley, sheep, goats, pigs, cattle and horses. From the beginnings of agriculture man naturally favored above all other species those plants and animals that had been most useful to him in the wild. As a result of this favoritism he has altered the composition of the earth's plant and animal populations. Today his crops, replacing the original cover of grass or forest, occupy some three billion acres. This amounts to about 10 percent of the earth's total land surface and a considerably larger fraction of the land capable of supporting vegetation, that is, the area excluding deserts, polar regions and higher elevations. Two-thirds of the cultivated cropland is planted to cereals. The area planted to wheat alone is 600 million acres—nearly a million square miles, or an area equivalent to the U.S. east of the Mississippi. As for the influence of animal husbandry on the earth's animal populations, Hereford and Black Angus cattle roam the Great Plains, once the home of an estimated 30 to 40 million buffalo; in Australia the kangaroo has given way to European cattle; in Asia the domesticated water buffalo has multiplied in the major river valleys.

Clearly the food-producing enterprise has altered not only the relative abundance of plant and animal species but also their global distribution. The linkage of the Old and the New World in the 15th century set in motion an exchange of crops among various parts of the world that continues today. This exchange greatly increased the earth's capacity to sustain human populations, partly because some of the crops transported elsewhere turned out to be better suited there than to their area of origin. Perhaps the classic example is the introduction of the potato from South America into northern Europe, where it greatly augmented the food supply, permitting marked increases in population. This was most clearly apparent in Ireland, where the population increased rapidly for several decades on the strength of the food supply represented by the potato. Only when the potato-blight organism (*Phytophthora infestans*) devastated the potato crop was population growth checked in Ireland.

The soybean, now the leading source of vegetable oil and principal farm export of the U.S., was introduced from China several decades ago. Grain sorghum, the second-ranking feed grain in the U.S. (after corn), came from Africa as a food store in the early slave ships. In the U.S.S.R. today the principal source of vegetable oil is the sunflower, a plant that originated on the southern Great Plains of the U.S. Corn, unknown in the Old World before Columbus, is now grown on every continent. On the other hand, North America is indebted to the Old World for all its livestock and poultry species with the exception of the turkey.

To man's accomplishments in exploiting the plants and animals that natural evolution has provided, and in improving them through selective breeding over the millenniums, he has added in this century the creation of remarkably productive new breeds, thanks to the discoveries of genetics. Genetics has made possible the development of cereals and other plant species that are more tolerant to cold, more resistant to drought, less susceptible to disease, more responsive to fertilizer, higher in yield and richer in protein. The story of hybrid corn is only one of many spectacular examples. The breeding of short-season corn varieties has extended the northern limit of this crop some 500 miles.

Plant breeders recently achieved a historic breakthrough in the development of new high-yielding varieties of wheat and rice for tropical and subtropical regions. These wheats and rices, bred by Rockefeller Foundation and Ford Foundation scientists in Mexico and the Philippines, are distinguished by several characteristics. Most important, they are short-statured and stiff-strawed, and are highly responsive to chemical fertilizer. They also mature earlier. The first of the high-yielding rices, IR-8, matures in 120 days as against 150 to 180 days for other varieties.

Another significant advance incorporated into the new strains is the reduced sensitivity of their seed to photoperiod (length of day). This is partly the result of their cosmopolitan ancestry: they were developed from seed collections all over the world. The biological clocks of traditional varieties of cereals were keyed to specific seasonal cycles, and these cereals could be planted only at a certain time of the year, in the case of rice say at the onset of the monsoon season. The new wheats, which are quite flexible in terms of both seasonal and latitudinal variations in length of day, are now being grown in developing countries as far north as Turkey and as far south as Paraguay.

The combination of earlier maturity and reduced sensitivity to day length creates new opportunities for multiple cropping in tropical and subtropical regions where water supplies are adequate, enabling farmers to harvest two, three and occasionally even four crops per year. Workers at the International Rice Research Institute in the Philippines regularly harvest three crops of rice per year. Each acre they plant yields six tons annually, roughly three times the average yield of corn, the highest-yielding cereal in the U.S. Thousands of farmers in northern India are now alternating a crop of early-maturing winter wheat with a summer crop of rice, greatly increasing the productivity of their land. These new opportunities for farming land more intensively lessen the pressure for bringing marginal land under cultivation, thus helping to conserve precious topsoil. At the same time they increase the use of agricultural chemicals, creating environmental stresses more akin to those in the advanced countries.

The new dwarf wheats and rices are far more efficient than the traditional varieties in their use of land, water, fertilizer and labor. The new opportunities for multiple cropping permit conversion of far more of the available solar energy into food. The new strains are not the solution to the food problem, but they are removing the threat of massive famine in the short run. They are buying time for the stabilization of population, which is ultimately the only solution to the food crisis. This "green revolution" may affect the well-being of more people in a shorter period of time than any technological advance in history.

The progress of man's expansion of food production is reflected in the way crop yields have traditionally been calculated. Today the output of cereals is expressed in yield per acre, but in early civilizations it was calculated as a ratio of the grain produced to that required for seed. On this basis the current ratio is perhaps highest in the U.S. corn belt, where farmers realize a four-hundred-fold return on the hybrid corn seed they plant. The ratio for rice is also quite high, but the ratio for wheat, the third of the principal cereals, is much lower, possibly 30 to one on a global basis.

The results of man's efforts to increase the productivity of domestic animals are equally impressive. When the ancestors of our present chickens were domesticated, they laid a clutch of about 15

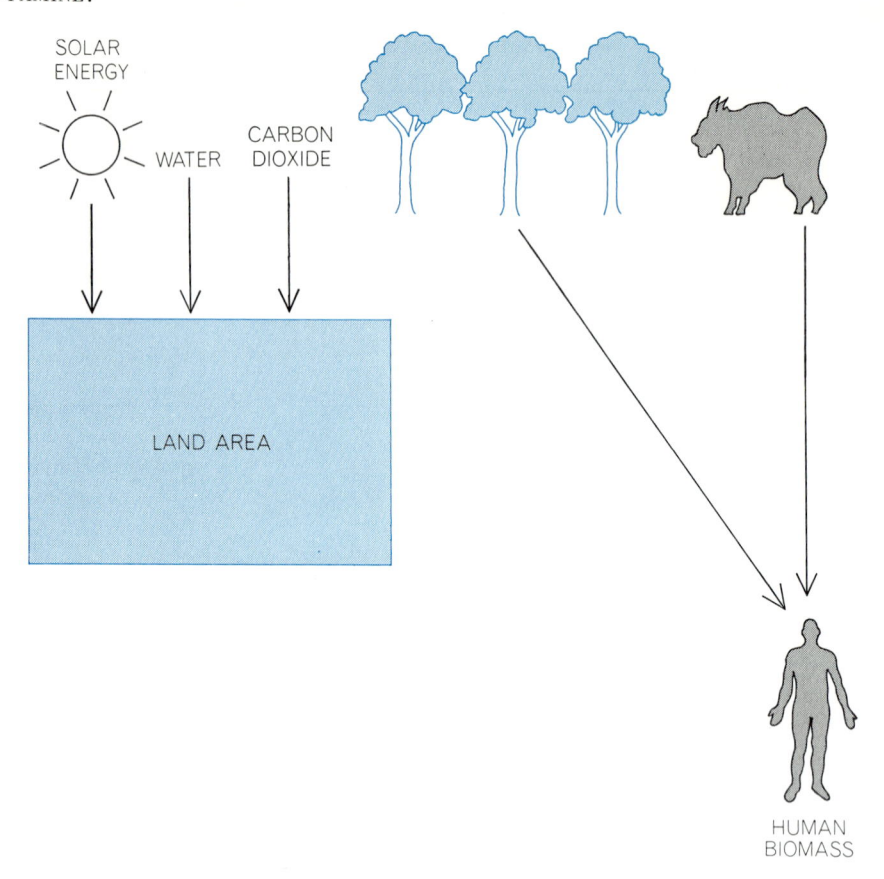

IMPACT OF THE AGRICULTURAL REVOLUTION on the human population is outlined in these two diagrams. The diagram at left shows the state of affairs before the invention of agriculture: the plants and animals supported by photosynthesis on the total land area could support a human population of only about 10 million. The diagram at right shows the state of affairs after the invention of agriculture. The 10 percent of the land now under the plow, watered and fertilized by man, is the primary support for a human population of 3.5 billion. Some of the agricultural produce is consumed directly by man; some is consumed indirectly by first being fed to domestic animals. Some of the food for domestic animals, however, comes from land not under the plow (*curved arrow at bottom left*). Man also obtains some food from sources other than agriculture, such as fishing.

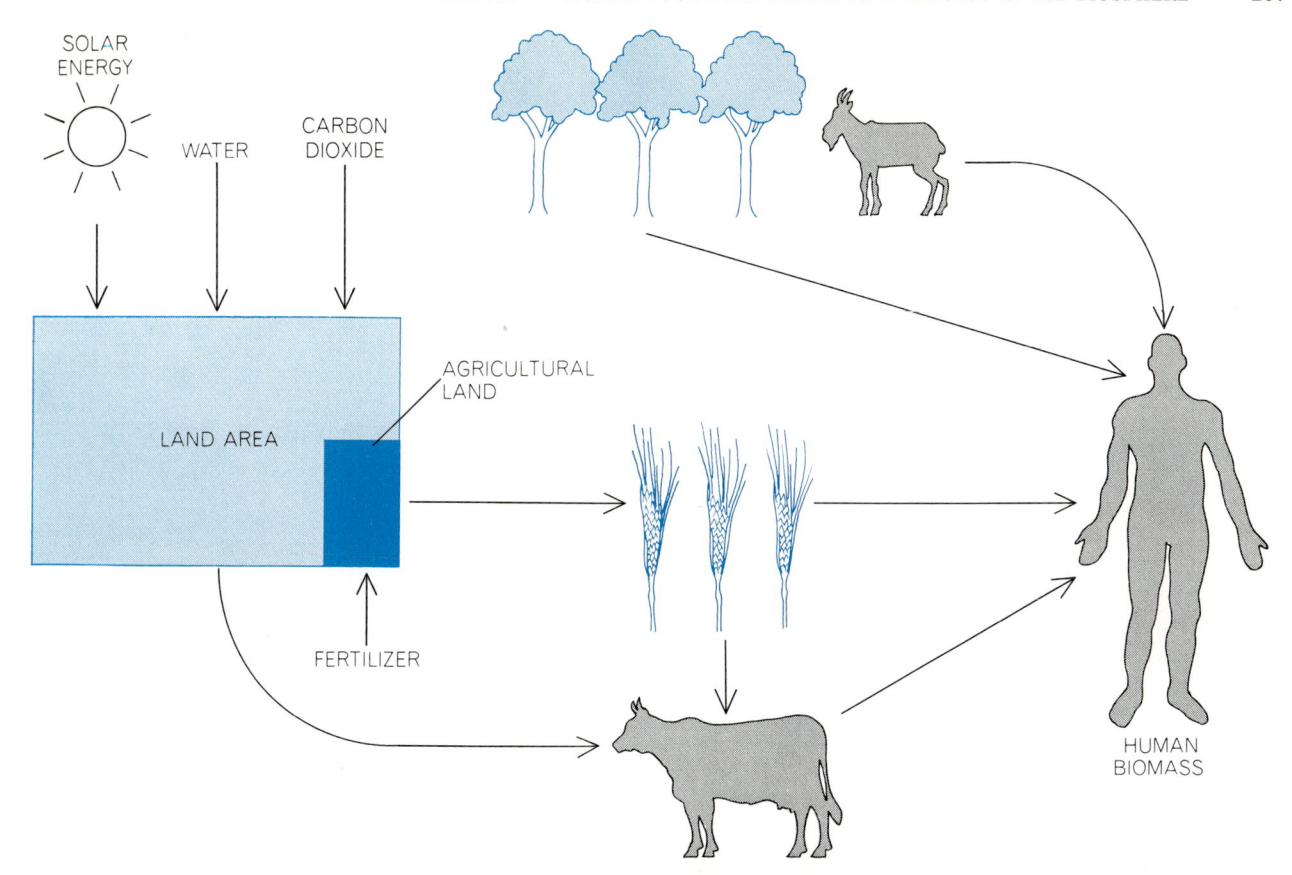

eggs once a year. Hens in the U.S. today average 220 eggs per year, and the figure is rising steadily as a result of continuing advances in breeding and feeding. When cattle were originally domesticated, they probably did not produce more than 600 pounds of milk per year, barely enough for a calf. (It is roughly the average amount produced by cows in India today.) The 13 million dairy cows in the U.S. today average 9,000 pounds of milk yearly, outproducing their ancestors 15 to one.

Most such advances in the productivity of plant and animal species are recent. Throughout most of history man's efforts to meet his food needs have been directed primarily toward bringing more land under cultivation, spreading agriculture from valley to valley and continent to continent. He has also, however, invented techniques to raise the productivity of land already under cultivation, particularly in this century, when the decreasing availability of new lands for expansion has compelled him to turn to a more intensive agriculture. These techniques involve altering the biosphere's cycles of energy, water, nitrogen and minerals.

Modern agriculture depends heavily on four technologies: mechanization, irrigation, fertilization and the chemical control of weeds and insects. Each of these technologies has made an important contribution to the earth's increased capacity for sustaining human populations, and each has perturbed the cycles of the biosphere.

At least as early as 3000 B.C. the farmers of the Middle East learned to harness draft animals to help them till the soil. Harnessing animals much stronger than himself enabled man to greatly augment his own limited muscle power. It also enabled him to convert roughage (indigestible by humans) into a usable form of energy and thus to free some of his energy for pursuits other than the quest for food. The invention of the internal-combustion engine and the tractor 5,000 years later provided a much greater breakthrough. It now became possible to substitute petroleum (the product of the photosynthesis of aeons ago) for oats, corn and hay grown as feed for draft animals. The replacement of horses by the tractor not only provided the farmer with several times as much power but also released 70 million acres in the U.S. that had been devoted to raising feed for horses.

In the highly mechanized agriculture of today the expenditure of fossil fuel energy per acre is often substantially greater than the energy yield embodied in the food produced. This deficit in the output is of no immediate consequence, because the system is drawing on energy in the bank. When fossil fuels become scarcer, man will have to turn to some other source of motive energy for agriculture: perhaps nuclear energy or some means, other than photosynthesis, of harnessing solar energy. For the present and for the purposes of agriculture the energy budget of the biosphere is still favorable: the supply of solar energy—both the energy stored in fossil fuels and that taken up daily and converted into food energy by crops—enables an advanced nation to be fed with only 5 percent of the population directly employed in agriculture.

The combination of draft animals and mechanical power has given man an enormous capacity for altering the earth's surface by bringing additional land under the plow (not all of it suited for cultivation). In addition, in the poor-

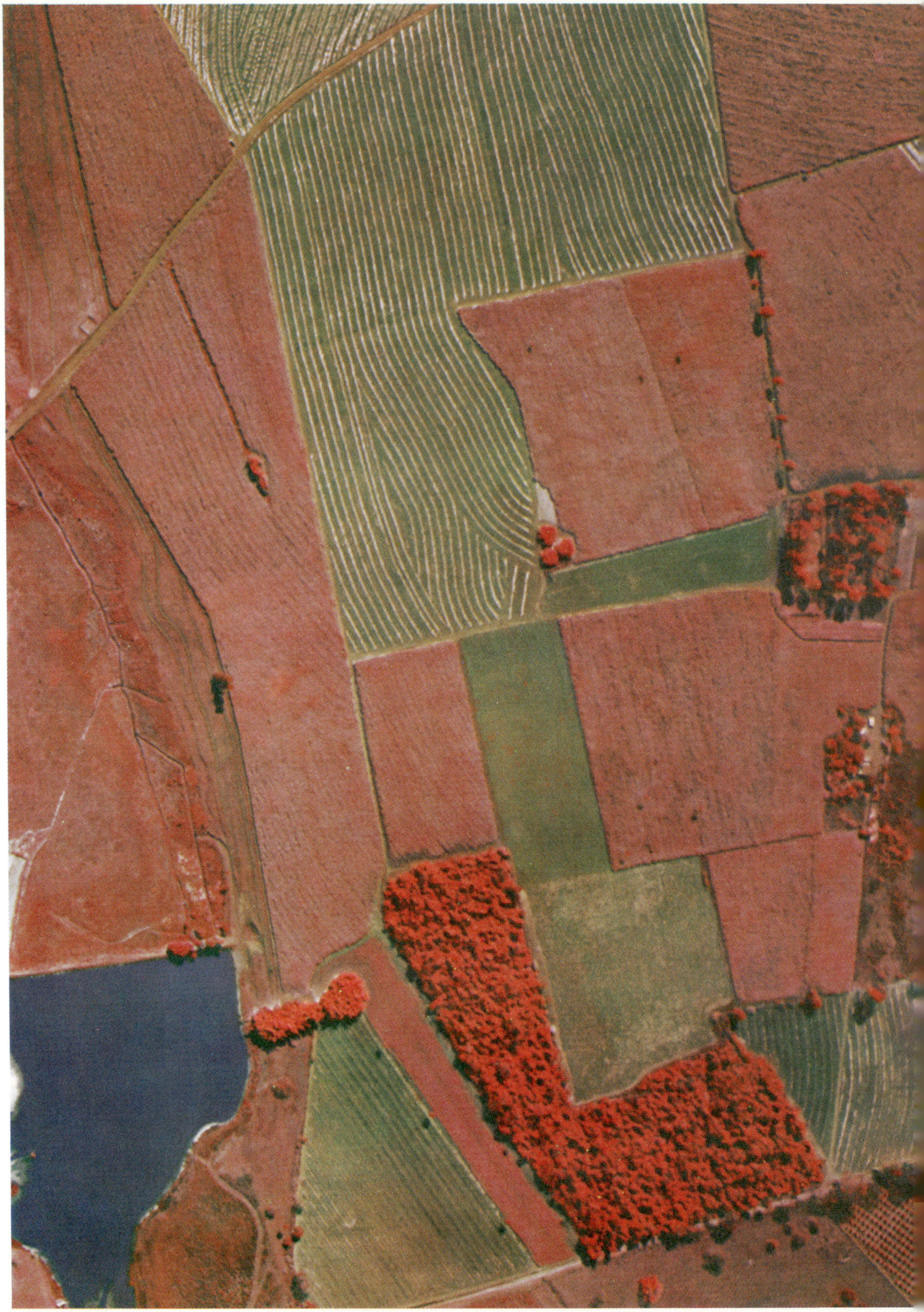

EXPERIMENTAL FARM in Brazil, one of thousands around the world where improvements in agricultural technology are pioneered, is seen as an image on an infrared-sensitive film in the aerial photograph on the opposite page. The reflectance of vegetation at near-infrared wavelengths of .7 to .9 micron registers on the film in false shades of red that are proportional to the intensity of the energy. The most reflective, and reddest, areas (*bottom*) are land still uncleared of forest cover. Most of the tilled fields, although irregular in shape, are contour-plowed. Regular patterns (*left and bottom right*) are citrus-orchard rows. The photograph was taken by a National Aeronautics and Space Administration mission in cooperation with the Brazilian government in a joint study of the assessment of agricultural resources by remote sensing. The farm is some 80 miles northwest of São Paulo.

er countries his expanding need for fuel has forced him to cut forests far in excess of their ability to renew themselves. The areas largely stripped of forest include mainland China and the subcontinent of India and Pakistan, where much of the population must now use cow dung for fuel. Although statistics are not available, the proportion of mankind using cow dung as fuel to prepare meals may far exceed the proportion using natural gas. Livestock populations providing draft power, food and fuel tend to increase along with human populations, and in many poor countries the needs of livestock for forage far exceed its self-renewal, gradually denuding the countryside of grass cover.

As population pressure builds, not only is more land brought under the plow but also the land remaining is less suited to cultivation. Once valleys are filled, farmers begin to move up hillsides, creating serious soil-erosion problems. As the natural cover that retards runoff is reduced and soil structure deteriorates, floods and droughts become more severe.

Over most of the earth the thin layer of topsoil producing most of man's food is measured in inches. Denuding the land of its year-round natural cover of grass or forest exposes the thin mantle of life-sustaining soil to rapid erosion by wind and water. Much of the soil ultimately washes into the sea, and some of it is lifted into the atmosphere. Man's actions are causing the topsoil to be removed faster than it is formed. This unstable relationship between man and the land from which he derives his subsistence obviously cannot continue indefinitely.

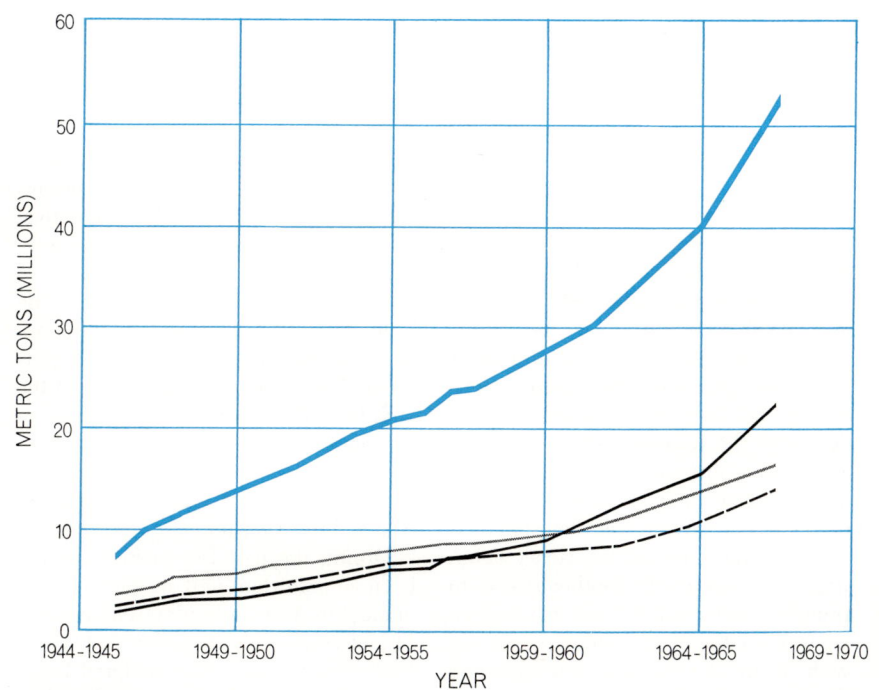

Robert R. Brooks of Williams College, an economist who spent several years in India, gives a wry description of the process occurring in the state of Rajasthan, where tens of thousands of acres of rural land are being abandoned yearly because of the loss of topsoil: "Overgrazing by goats destroys the desert plants which might otherwise hold the soil in place. Goatherds equipped with sickles attached to 20-foot poles strip the leaves of trees to float downward into the waiting mouths of famished goats and sheep. The trees die and the soil blows away 200 miles to New Delhi, where it comes to rest in the lungs of its inhabitants and on the shiny cars of foreign diplomats."

Soil erosion not only results in a loss of soil but also impairs irrigation systems. This is illustrated in the Mangla irrigation reservoir, recently built in the foothills of the Himalayas in West Pakistan as part of the Indus River irrigation system. On the basis of feasibility studies indicating that the reservoir could be expected to have a lifetime of at least 100 years, $600 million was invested in the construction of the reservoir. Denuding and erosion of the soil in the watershed, however, accompanying a rapid growth of population in the area, has already washed so much soil into the reservoir that it is now expected to be completely filled with silt within 50 years.

A historic example of the effects of man's abuse of the soil is all too plainly visible in North Africa, which once was the fertile granary of the Roman Empire and now is largely a desert or near-desert whose people are fed with the aid of food imports from the U.S. In the U.S. itself the "dust bowl" experience of the 1930's remains a vivid lesson on the folly of overplowing. More recently the U.S.S.R. repeated this error, bringing 100 million acres of virgin soil under the plow only to discover that the region's rainfall was too scanty to sustain continuous cultivation. Once moisture reserves in the soil were depleted the soil began to blow.

Soil erosion is one of the most pressing and most difficult problems threatening the future of the biosphere. Each year it is forcing the abandonment of millions of acres of cropland in Asia, the Middle East, North Africa and Central America. Nature's geological cycle continuously produces topsoil, but its pace is far too slow to be useful to man. Someone once defined soil as rock on its way to the sea. Soil is produced by the weathering of rock and the process takes several centuries to form an inch of topsoil. Man is managing to destroy the topsoil

FERTILIZER CONSUMPTION has increased more than fivefold since the end of World War II. The top line in the graph (*color*) shows the tonnage of all kinds of fertilizers combined. The lines below show the tonnages of the three major types: nitrogen (*black*), now the leader, phosphate (*gray*) and potash (*broken line*). Figures, from the most recent report by the UN Food and Agriculture Organization, omit fertilizer consumption in China.

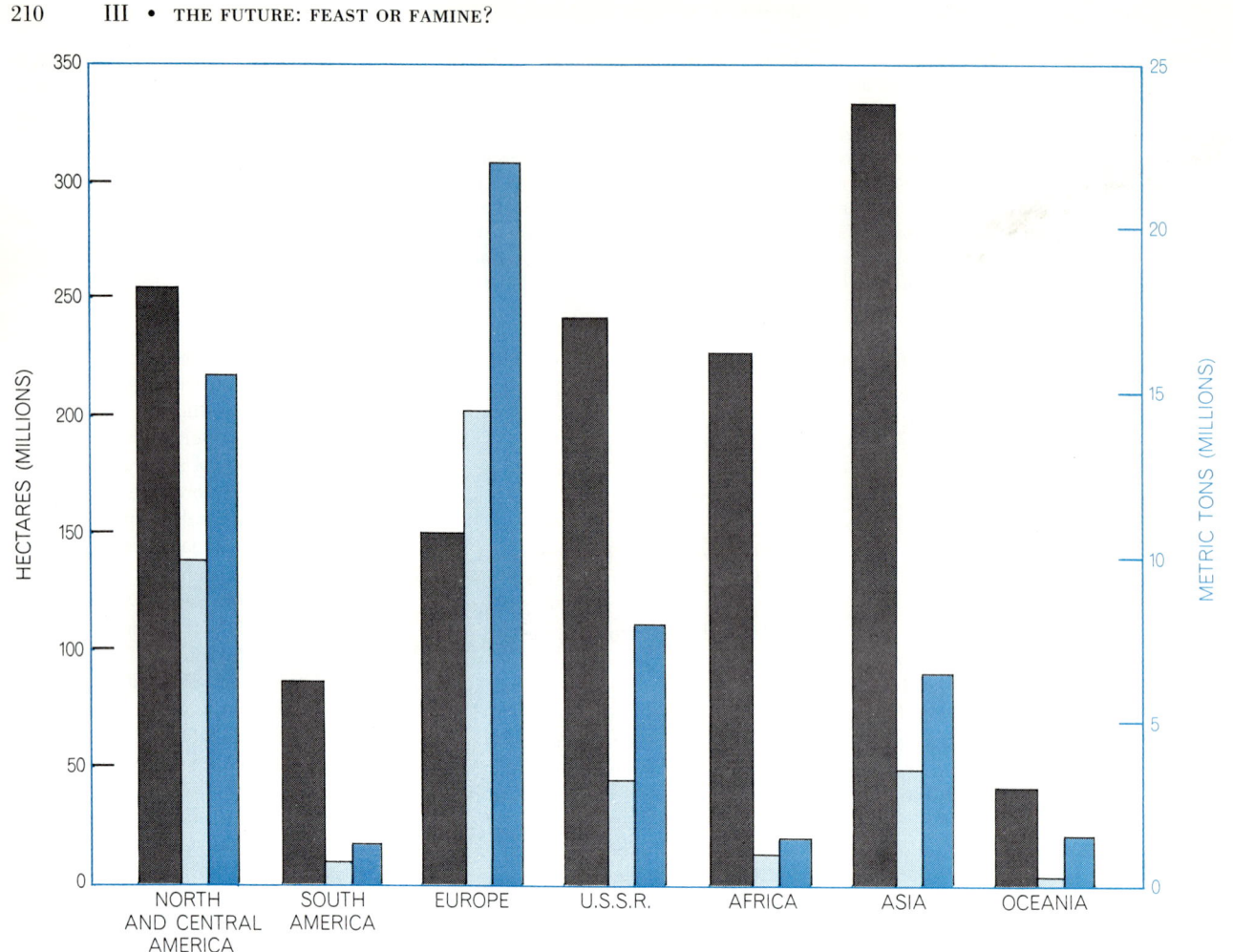

TONS OF FERTILIZER used in seven world areas are compared with the amount of agricultural land in each area. Two tonnages are shown in each instance: the amount used in 1962–1963 (*light color*) and the amount used in 1967–1968 (*solid color*). The greatest use of fertilizer occurs in Europe, the least fertilized area is Africa and the greatest percentage increase in the period was in Australia and New Zealand. Figures, from the Food and Agriculture Organization, omit China, North Korea and North Vietnam.

in some areas of the world in a fraction of this time. The only possible remedy is to find ways to conserve the topsoil more effectively.

The dust-bowl era in the U.S. ended with the widespread adoption of conservation practices by farmers. Twenty million acres were fallowed to accumulate moisture and thousands of miles of windbreaks were planted across the Great Plains. Fallow land was alternated with strips of wheat ("strip-cropping") to reduce the blowing of soil while the land was idle. The densely populated countries of Asia, however, are in no position to adopt such tactics. Their food needs are so pressing that they cannot afford to take large areas out of cultivation; moreover, they do not yet have the financial resources or the technical skills for the immense projects in reforestation, controlled grazing of cattle, terracing, contour farming and systematic management of watersheds that would be required to preserve their soil.

The significance of wind erosion goes far beyond the mere loss of topsoil. As other authors in this issue have observed, a continuing increase in particulate matter in the atmosphere could affect the earth's climate by reducing the amount of incoming solar energy. This particulate matter comes not only from the technological activities of the richer countries but also from wind erosion in the poorer countries. The poorer countries do not have the resources for undertaking the necessary effort to arrest and reverse this trend. Should it be established that an increasing amount of particulate matter in the atmosphere is changing the climate, the richer countries would have still another reason to provide massive capital and technical assistance to the poor countries, joining with them to confront this common threat to mankind.

Irrigation, which agricultural man began to practice at least as early as 6,000 years ago, even earlier than he harnessed animal power, has played its great role in increasing food production by bringing into profitable cultivation vast areas that would otherwise be unusable or only marginally productive. Most of the world's irrigated land is in Asia, where it is devoted primarily to the production of rice. In Africa the Volta River of Ghana and the Nile are dammed for irrigation and power purposes. The Colorado River system of the U.S. is used extensively for irrigation in the Southwest, as are scores of rivers elsewhere. Still to be exploited for irrigation are the Mekong of southeastern Asia and the Amazon.

During the past few years there has been an important new irrigation development in Asia: the widespread installation of small-scale irrigation systems on individual farms. In Pakistan and India, where in many places the water table is close to the surface, hundreds of thousands of tube wells with pumps have been installed in recent years. Interestingly, this development came about partly as an answer to a problem that had been presented by irrigation itself.

Like many of man's other interventions in the biosphere, his reshaping of the hydrologic cycle has had unwanted side effects. One of them is the raising of the water table by the diversion of river water onto the land. Over a period of time the percolation of irrigation water downward and the accumulation of this water underground may gradually raise the water table until it is within a few feet or even a few inches of the surface. This not only inhibits the growth of plant roots by waterlogging but also results in the surface soil's becoming salty as water evaporates through it, leaving a concentrated deposit of salts in the upper few inches. Such a situation developed in West Pakistan after its fertile plain had been irrigated with water from the Indus for a century. During a visit by President Ayub to Washington in 1961 he appealed to President Kennedy for help: West Pakistan was losing 60,000 acres of fertile cropland per year because of waterlogging and salinity as its population was expanding 2.5 percent yearly.

This same sequence, the diversion of river water into land for irrigation, followed eventually by waterlogging and salinity and the abandonment of land, had been repeated many times throughout history. The result was invariably the decline, and sometimes the disappearance, of the civilizations thus intervening in the hydrologic cycle. The remains of civilizations buried in the deserts of the Middle East attest to early experiences similar to those of contemporary Pakistan. These civilizations, however, had no one to turn to for foreign aid. An interdisciplinary U.S. team led by Roger Revelle, then Science Adviser to the Secretary of the Interior, studied the problem and proposed among other things a system of tube wells that would lower the water table by tapping the ground water for intensive irrigation. Discharging this water on the surface, the wells would also wash the soil's salt downward. The stratagem worked, and the salty, waterlogged land of Pakistan is steadily being reclaimed.

Other side effects of river irrigation are not so easily remedied. Such irrigation has brought about a great increase in the incidence of schistosomiasis, a disease that is particularly prevalent in the river valleys of Africa and Asia. The disease is produced by the parasitic larva of a blood fluke, which is harbored by aquatic snails and burrows into the flesh of people standing in water or in water-soaked fields. The Chinese call schistosomiasis "snail fever"; it might also be called the poor man's emphysema, because, like emphysema, this extremely debilitating disease is environmentally induced through conditions created by man. The snails and the fluke thrive in perennial irrigation systems, where they are in close proximity to large human populations. The incidence of the disease is rising rapidly as the world's large rivers are harnessed for irrigation, and today schistosomiasis is estimated to afflict 250 million people. It now surpasses malaria, the incidence of which is declining, as the world's most prevalent infectious disease.

As a necessity for food production water is of course becoming an increasingly crucial commodity. The projected increases in population and in food requirements will call for more and more water, forcing man to consider still more massive and complex interventions in the biosphere. The desalting of seawater for irrigation purposes is only one major departure from traditional practices. Another is a Russian plan to reverse the flow of four rivers currently flowing northward and emptying into the Arctic Ocean. These rivers would be diverted southward into the semiarid lands of southern Russia, greatly enlarging the irrigated area of the U.S.S.R. Some climatologists are concerned, however, that the shutting off of the flow of relatively warm water from these four rivers would have far-reaching implications for not only the climate of the Arctic but also the climatic system of the entire earth.

The growing competition for scarce water supplies among states and among various uses in the western U.S. is also forcing consideration of heroic plans. For example, a detailed engineering proposal exists for the diversion of the Yukon River in Alaska southward across Canada into the western U.S. to meet the growing need for water for both agricultural and industrial purposes. The effort would cost an estimated $100 billion.

Representing an even greater intervention in the biosphere is the prospect that man may one day consciously alter the earth's climatic patterns, shifting some of the rain now falling on the oceans to the land. Among the steps needed for the realization of such a scheme are the construction of a comprehensive model of the earth's climatic system and the development of a computational facility capable of simulating

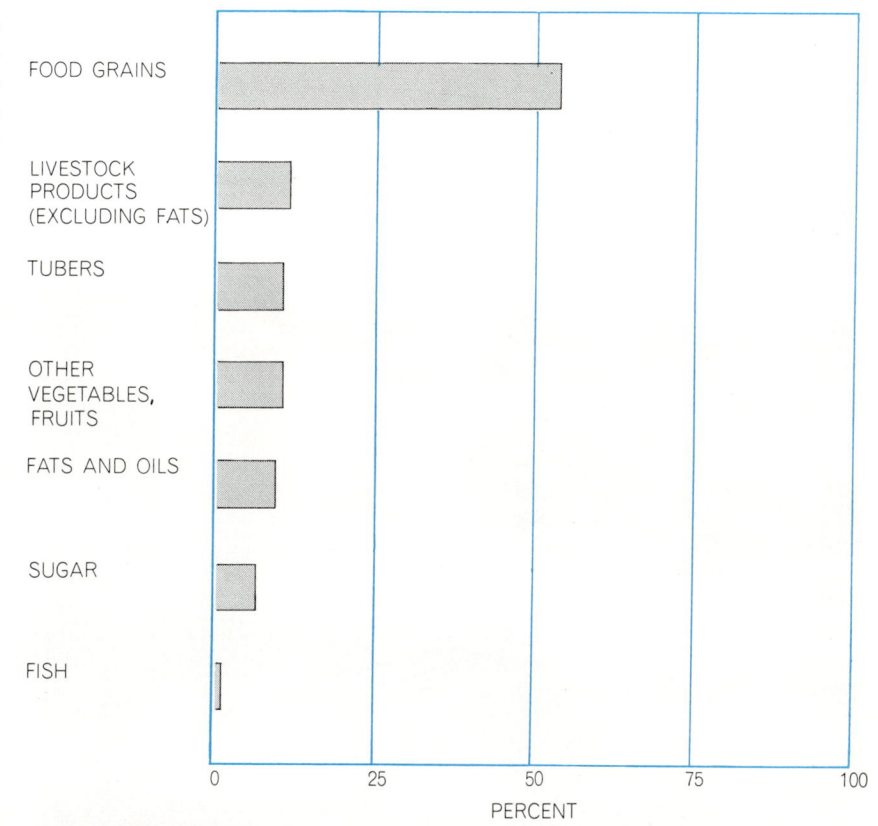

WORLDWIDE FOOD ENERGY comes in different amounts from different products. Cereals outstrip other foodstuffs; wheat and rice each supply a fifth of mankind's food energy.

and manipulating the model. The required information includes data on temperatures, humidity, precipitation, the movement of air masses, ocean currents and many other factors that enter into the weather. Earth-orbiting satellites will doubtless be able to collect much of this information, and the present generation of advanced computers appears to be capable of carrying out the necessary experiments on the model. For the implementation of the findings, that is, for the useful control of rainfall, there will of course be a further requirement: the project will have to be managed by a global and supranational agency if it is not to lead to weather wars among nations working at cross purposes. Some commercial firms are already in the business of rainmaking, and they are operating on an international basis.

The third great technology that man has introduced to increase food production is the use of chemical fertilizers. We owe the foundation for this development to Justus von Liebig of Germany, who early in the 19th century determined the specific requirements of nitrogen, phosphorus, potassium and other nutrients for plant growth. Chemical fertilizers did not come into widespread use, however, until this century, when the pressure of population and the disappearance of new frontiers compelled farmers to substitute fertilizer for the expansion of cropland to meet growing food needs. One of the first countries to intensify its agriculture, largely by the use of fertilizers, was Japan, whose output of food per acre has steadily risen (except for wartime interruptions) since the turn of the century. The output per acre of a few other countries, including the Netherlands, Denmark and Sweden, began to rise at about the same time. The U.S., richly endowed with vast farmlands, did not turn to the heavy use of fertilizer and other intensive measures until about 1940. Since then its yields per acre, assisted by new varieties of grain highly responsive to fertilizer, have also shown remarkable gains. Yields of corn, the production of which exceeds that of all other cereals combined in the U.S., have nearly tripled over the past three decades.

Experience has demonstrated that in areas of high rainfall the application of chemical fertilizers in conjunction with other inputs and practices can double, triple or even quadruple the productivity of intensively farmed soils. Such levels of productivity are achieved in Japan and the Netherlands, where farmers apply up to 300 pounds of plant nutrients per acre per year. The use of chemical fertilizers is estimated to account for at least a fourth of man's total food supply. The world's farmers are currently applying 60 million metric tons of plant nutrients per year, an average of nearly 45 pounds per acre for the three billion acres of cropland. Such application, however, is unevenly distributed. Some poor countries do not yet benefit from the use of fertilizer in any significant amounts. If global projections of population and income growth materialize, the production of fertilizer over the remaining three decades of this century must almost triple to satisfy food demands.

Can the projected demand for fertilizer be met? The key ingredient is nitrogen, and fortunately man has learned how to speed up the fixation phase of the nitrogen cycle [see "The Nitrogen Cycle," by C. C. Delwiche; SCIENTIFIC AMERICAN Offprint 1194]. In nature the nitrogen of the air is fixed in the soil by certain microorganisms, such as those present in the root nodules of leguminous plants. Chemists have now devised various ways of incorporating nitrogen from the air into inorganic compounds and making it available in the form of nitrogen fertilizers. These chemical processes produce the fertilizer much more rapidly and economically than the growing of leguminous-plant sources such as clover, alfalfa or soybeans. More than 25 million tons of nitrogen fertilizer is now being synthesized and added to the earth's soil annually.

The other principal ingredients of chemical fertilizer are the minerals potassium and phosphorus. Unlike nitrogen, these elements are not replenished by comparatively fast natural cycles. Potassium presents no immediate problem; the rich potash fields of Canada alone are estimated to contain enough potassium to supply mankind's needs for centuries to come. The reserves of phosphorus, however, are not nearly so plentiful as those of potassium. Every year 3.5 million tons of phosphorus washes into the sea, where it remains as sediment on the ocean floor. Eventually it will be thrust above the ocean surface again by geologic uplift, but man cannot wait that long. Phosphorus may be one of the first necessities that will prompt man to begin to mine the ocean bed.

The great expansion of the use of fertilizers in this century has benefited mankind enormously, but the benefits are not unalloyed. The runoff of chemical fertilizers into rivers, lakes and underground waters creates two important hazards. One is the chemical pollution

EXPERIMENTAL PLANTINGS at the International Rice Research Institute in the Philippine Republic are seen in an aerial photograph. IR-8, a high-yield rice, was bred here.

RUINED FARM in the "dust bowl" area of the U.S. in the 1930's is seen in an aerial photograph. The farm is near Union in Terry County, Tex. The wind has eroded the powdery, drought-parched topsoil and formed drifts among the buildings and across the fields.

of drinking water. In certain areas in Illinois and California the nitrate content of well water has risen to a toxic level. Excessive nitrate can cause the physiological disorder methemoglobinemia, which reduces the blood's oxygen-carrying capacity and can be particularly dangerous to children under five. This hazard is of only local dimensions and can be countered by finding alternative sources of drinking water. A much more extensive hazard, profound in its effects on the biosphere, is the now well-known phenomenon called eutrophication.

Inorganic nitrates and phosphates discharged into lakes and other bodies of fresh water provide a rich medium for the growth of algae; the massive growth of the algae in turn depletes the water of oxygen and thus kills off the fish life. In the end the eutrophication, or overfertilization, of the lake slowly brings about its death as a body of fresh water, converting it into a swamp. Lake Erie is a prime example of this process now under way.

How much of the now widespread eutrophication of fresh waters is attributable to agricultural fertilization and how much to other causes remains an open question. Undoubtedly the runoff of nitrates and phosphates from farmlands plays a large part. There are also other important contributors, however. Considerable amounts of phosphate, coming mainly from detergents, are discharged into rivers and lakes from sewers carrying municipal and industrial wastes. And there is reason to believe that in some rivers and lakes most of the nitrate may come not from fertilizers but from the internal-combustion engine. It is estimated that in the state of New Jersey, which has heavy automobile traffic, nitrous oxide products of gasoline combustion, picked up and deposited by rainfall, contribute as much as 20 pounds of nitrogen per acre per year to the land. Some of this nitrogen washes into the many rivers and lakes of New Jersey and its adjoining states. A way must be found to deal with the eutrophication problem because even in the short run it can have damaging effects, affecting as it does the supply of potable water, the cycles of aquatic life and consequently man's food supply.

Recent findings have presented us with a related problem in connection with the fourth technology supporting man's present high level of food production: the chemical control of diseases, insects and weeds. It is now clear that the use of DDT and other chlorinated hydrocarbons as pesticides and herbicides is beginning to threaten many species of animal life, possibly including man. DDT today is found in the tissues of animals over a global range of life forms and geography from penguins in Antarctica to children in the villages of Thailand. There is strong evidence that it is actually on the way to extinguishing some animal species, notably predatory birds such as the bald eagle and the peregrine falcon, whose capacity for using calcium is so impaired by DDT that the shells of their eggs are too thin to avoid breakage in the nest before the fledglings hatch. Carnivores are particularly likely to concentrate DDT in their tissues because they feed on herbivores that have already concentrated it from large quantities of vegetation. Concentrations of DDT in mothers' milk in the U.S. now exceed the tolerance levels established for foodstuffs by the Food and Drug Administration.

It is ironic that less than a generation after 1948, when Paul Hermann Müller of Switzerland received a Nobel prize for the discovery of DDT, the use of the insecticide is being banned by law in many countries. This illustrates how little man knows about the effects of his intervening in the biosphere. Up to now he has been using the biosphere as a laboratory, sometimes with unhappy results.

Several new approaches to the problem of controlling pests are now being explored. Chemists are searching for pesticides that will be degradable, instead of long-lasting, after being deposited on vegetation or in the soil, and that will be aimed at specific pests rather than acting as broad-spectrum poisons for many forms of life. Much hope is placed in techniques of biological control, such as are exemplified in the mass sterilization (by irradiation) of male screwworm flies, a pest of cattle that used to cost U.S. livestock producers $100 million per year. The release of 125 million irradiated male screwworm flies weekly in the U.S. and in adjoining areas of Mexico (in a cooperative effort with the Mexican government) is holding the fly population to a negligible level. Efforts are now under way to get rid of the Mexican fruit fly and the pink cotton bollworm in California by the same method.

Successes are also being achieved in breeding resistance to insect pests in various crops. A strain of wheat has been developed that is resistant to the Hessian fly; resistance to the corn borer and the corn earworm has been bred into strains of corn, and work is in progress on a strain of alfalfa that resists aphids and leafhoppers. Another promising approach, which already has a considerable history, is the development of insect parasites, ranging from bacteria and viruses to wasps that lay their eggs in other insects. The fact remains, however, that the biological control of pests is still in its infancy.

I have here briefly reviewed the major agricultural technologies evolved to meet man's increasing food needs, the problems arising from them and some possible solutions. What is the present balance sheet on the satisfaction of human food needs? Although man's food supply has expanded several hundredfold since the invention of agriculture, two-thirds of mankind is still hungry and malnourished much of the time. On the credit side a third of mankind, living largely in North America, Europe, Australia and Japan, has achieved an adequate food supply, and for the remaining two-thirds the threat of large-scale famine has recently been removed, at least for the immediate future. In spite of rapid population growth in the developing countries since World War II, their peoples have been spared from massive famine (except in Biafra in 1969–1970) by huge exports of food from the developed countries. As a result of two consecutive monsoon failures in India, a fifth of the total U.S. wheat crop was shipped to India in both 1966 and 1967, feeding 60 million Indians for two years.

Although the threat of outright famine has been more or less eliminated for the time being, human nutrition on the global scale is still in a sorry state. Malnutrition, particularly protein deficiency, exacts an enormous toll from the physical and mental development of the young in the poorer countries. This was dramatically illustrated when India held tryouts in 1968 to select a team to represent it in the Olympic games that year. Not a single Indian athlete, male or female, met the minimum standards for qualifying to compete in any of the 36 track and field events in Mexico City. No doubt this was partly due to the lack of support for athletics in India, but poor nutrition was certainly also a large factor. The young people of Japan today are visible examples of what a change can be brought about by improvement in nutrition. Well-nourished from infancy, Japanese teen-agers are on the average some two inches taller than their elders.

Protein is as crucial for children's mental development as for their physical development. This was strikingly shown in a recent study extending over several years in Mexico: children who had been severely undernourished before the age of five were found to average 13 points lower in I.Q. than a carefully selected control group. Unfortunately no amount of feeding or education in later life can repair the setbacks to development caused by undernourishment in the early years. Protein shortages in the poor countries today are depreciating human resources for at least a generation to come.

Protein constitutes the main key to human health and vigor, and the key to the protein diet at present is held by grain consumed either directly or indirectly (in the form of meat, milk and eggs). Cereals, occupying more than 70 percent of the world's cropland, provide 52 percent of man's direct energy intake. Eleven percent is supplied by livestock products such as meat, milk and eggs, 10 percent by potatoes and other tubers, 10 percent by fruits and vegetables, 9 percent by animal fats and vegetable oils, 7 percent by sugar and 1 percent by fish. As in the case of the total quantity of the individual diet, however, the composition of the diet varies greatly around the world. The difference is most marked in the per capita use of grain consumed directly and indirectly.

The two billion people living in the poor countries consume an average of about 360 pounds of grain per year, or about a pound per day. With only one pound per day, nearly all must be consumed directly to meet minimal energy requirements; little remains for feeding to livestock, which may convert only a tenth of their feed intake into meat or other edible human food. The average American, in contrast, consumes more than 1,600 pounds of grain per year. He eats only about 150 pounds of this directly in the form of bread, breakfast cereal and so on; the rest is consumed indirectly in the form of meat, milk and eggs. In short, he enjoys the luxury of the highly inefficient animal conversion of grain into tastier and somewhat more nutritious proteins.

Thus the average North American currently makes about four times as great a demand on the earth's agricultural ecosystem as someone living in one of the poor countries. As the income levels in these countries rise, so will their demand for a richer diet of animal products. For the increasing world population at the end of the century, which is expected to be twice the 3.5 billion of today, the world production of grain would have to be doubled merely to maintain present consumption levels. This increase, combined with the projected improvement in diet associated with gains in income over the next three decades, could nearly triple the demand for grain, requiring that the food supply increase more over the next three decades than it has in the 10,000 years since agriculture began.

There are ways in which this pressure can be eased somewhat. One is the breeding of higher protein content in grains and other crops, making them nutritionally more acceptable as alternatives to livestock products. Another is the development of vegetable substitutes for animal products, such as are already available in the form of oleomargarine, soybean oil, imitation meats and other replacements (about 65 percent of the whipped toppings and 35 percent of the coffee whiteners now sold in U.S. supermarkets are nondairy products). Pressures on the agricultural ecosystem would thus drive high-income man one step down in the food chain to a level of more efficient consumption of what could be produced by agriculture.

What is clearly needed today is a cooperative effort—more specifically, a world environmental agency—to monitor, investigate and regulate man's interventions in the environment, including those made in his quest for more food. Since many of his efforts to enlarge his food supply have a global impact, they can only be dealt with in the context of a global institution. The health of the biosphere can no longer be separated from our modes of political organization. Whatever measures are taken, there is growing doubt that the agricultural ecosystem will be able to accommodate both the anticipated increase of the human population to seven billion by the end of the century and the universal desire of the world's hungry for a better diet. The central question is no longer "Can we produce enough food?" but "What are the environmental consequences of attempting to do so?"

24

A WORLD AGRICULTURAL PLAN

ADDEKE H. BOERMA
August 1970

The Food and Agriculture Organization of the United Nations has developed an integrated program to close the gap between the curves for food production and population growth by 1985

There have been frequent prophecies of famine on a global scale since Thomas Malthus published his essay on population in 1798. So far demographers and scientists echoing Malthus' forebodings have always been proved wrong, but by the beginning of the second half of this century there were ominous signs of a steadily widening gap between supply and demand for food in the developing countries. At that time many of these countries had only recently been freed from colonial rule, and some of them lacked adequate financial and technical resources to immediately become self-supporting. The gap was reflected in rapidly rising imports of staple cereals, particularly in the Near East and Asia, and by mounting requests for food aid through such channels as the program of U.S. Public Law 480, the World Food Program and charitable foundations.

History of the Plan

It was against this background that the first World Food Congress was convened in Washington in 1963 under the Freedom from Hunger Campaign, a private group that raises funds and provides other support for the Food and Agriculture Organization of the United Nations (FAO). It was decided that the FAO should be asked to prepare a survey of the world food situation in relation to population and overall economic development, together with a plan for action that would indicate the long-term prospects for closing the food gap. It soon became apparent that even a study undertaken within such broad terms of reference would be inadequate. The scope of the proposed survey was therefore widened and deepened still further by the FAO's governing conference of member states. The conference decided that the study should become a "world plan for agricultural production, trade and development," highlighting the national and international actions needed to redress the alarming imbalance between food and population currently afflicting the world.

The mandate was fulfilled through four years of interdisciplinary work. Regional studies were conducted in Africa south of the Sahara, in Asia, in Latin America and in the Near East. An overall world study summed up the regional work and highlighted its conclusions. These findings, projections and policy recommendations, which became known as the Indicative World Plan for Agricultural Development, were submitted in provisional form to the FAO's Fifteenth Conference in November, 1969.

The plan, encompassing 23 years from a base year of 1962 to horizons of 1975 and 1985, is intended to provide a framework within which national and regional programs can be developed. It is hoped that governments will be able to use the plan to create and implement agricultural policies, and that it may also form a useful standard of reference for the resolution of conflicts of production and trade policies between nations. Moreover, it should serve as a guide to both donors and recipients of international aid. In this respect the plan is also intended to focus the activities of the FAO itself on the major operational priorities of world agriculture.

The plan aroused enormous interest among member nations participating in the FAO's Fifteenth Conference. Although it became apparent from the discussions that some countries hoped for a more complete blueprint for development from the plan, which had perhaps been oversold when it was first conceived, reaction was largely favorable. Few speakers disagreed with its main goals and recommendations, the chief critics being the South American countries, which objected not to the overall concepts of the world study but to the growth rates considered feasible in the provisional study for their region. These rates the South Americans believed to be too low to meet national aspirations. Nevertheless, the South Americans made plain their interest in maintaining global planning by proposing a resolution, approved by the conference, that called for the continuation and strengthening of such work in close collaboration with regional and national planners. The representatives hoped that this intensified effort would fill any gaps in the plan, and that it would provide a more balanced long-term view of the problems facing agriculture in both developing and developed countries.

It can be fairly concluded that the Indicative World Plan has succeeded in achieving its main objective: to provide a broad framework of guidelines for the planning of future world agricultural development, based on a reasoned analysis of the main issues likely to arise in the 1970's and the early 1980's. Since the plan was the focal point for the Second World Food Congress held at The Hague in June, and is also the main source of agricultural policy for UN strategy for the Second Development Decade (1970–1980), this seems a particularly good time to examine its main conclusions and recommendations.

The World Food Problem

The Indicative World Plan is both an attempt to look into the future and an effort to influence the future by proposing specific objectives for the agricultural sector together with recommendations for their attainment. Achieving these goals will clearly be difficult and challenging. First and foremost is of course the problem represented by the race between food and population. In 1965 there were 1.5 billion people living in the developing or less developed countries, which the UN classifies as Zone C countries. This excludes mainland China, whose population was then estimated at between 700 and 800 million. By 1985, assuming that the "medium" UN population-growth projection of 2.6 percent is accurate and that there is no world cataclysm, the population of Zone C will have risen by a billion to 2.5 billion. Neither present efforts in family planning nor rising income in developing countries is likely to affect this rate of growth significantly. Since population in the economically advanced countries increases much more slowly, 85 out of every 100 additional persons between 1965 and 1985 will be in the poor countries, including China, many of which are already overburdened by the size of their population.

This growth of population alone would require an 80 percent increase in food supplies by 1985 compared with 1962, without any improvement in quantity or quality of individual diets. Success in raising income levels along the lines of the most optimistic projections of the plan's economic model, and consequent improvements in purchasing power, would increase the demand for food by 142 percent above the 1962 level, an average geometric rate of increase of 3.9 percent per year. The trend in food production over the decade 1956–1966 for the developing countries as a whole was only 2.7 percent per year.

An unchecked continuation of this trend would result in a gap between demand and supply that, if it had to be filled by imports from other parts of the world, would by 1985 cost the developing countries $43 billion per year (assuming constant 1962 prices). Shortages of staple cereals and animal protein would be particularly acute. For Asia, the Near East and northwestern Africa cereal imports would theoretically be required exceeding 90 million metric tons (nine times those in 1962); otherwise 100 million hectares would have to be diverted from other crops and livestock. Only a quarter of the extra animal protein required by 1985 could be produced domestically if livestock production continued to grow at current slow rates and could not be tripled by policy changes over the plan period.

Import requirements of this magnitude are unlikely since the developing countries had considerable difficulty finding even $3 billion for food imports in 1962. Scarcity would drive food prices up, economic growth would slacken and demand would fall. Not only would real incomes fail to grow as desired but also the rise in food prices would cause severe hardship in the poorer sections of the community.

Of the one billion additional people perhaps 400 million would be employed in agriculture. They would have to seek work in a sector where unemployment and underemployment are already serious, and where pressures of population on scarce resources of arable land in Asia, the Near East and northwestern Africa are already critical. If additional jobs are not created in both agriculture and related industries, many will be unable to find productive work, per capita incomes will fall, economic growth will slow down, social problems will multiply and discontent will grow more intense.

The most immediate and urgent problem may appear to be acceleration of food production in order to prevent widespread famine and starvation, but a sober analysis of the potentials for ex-

FIELDWORKER bearing a gasoline-powered knapsack sprayer applies weed killer to a rice crop growing in a paddy on an experimental station in the Indian state of Hyderabad. Such stations have been established to develop, test and demonstrate new technology.

panding food output and for providing work for a rapidly increasing number of young people in the developing countries suggests that the latter may prove the more intractable problem. The crucial dilemma may lie in the fact that the very measures that might raise productivity and economic growth most rapidly both in agriculture and in many industries could lead as well to a reduction rather than an increase in requirements for human labor. The creation of jobs does not have the emotional appeal of the face of a hungry child, but unless the problem of employment is given priority equal to that of food supplies the end result could be disastrous.

In view of the alarming trends in supply and demand for food the Organization for Economic Cooperation and Development (OECD) was asked to examine the possibility that the developed countries could produce enough surplus food to meet the major needs of the rest of the world, at least in the short run. The OECD study suggests that a sufficient surplus could in fact be generated, mainly from North America and Oceania, given appropriate measures to bring unutilized land into use. There are, however, important flaws in such a solution. The food would have to be provided at highly subsidized prices if it were to be within the purchasing power of the developing countries. This kind of aid would do nothing to provide employment in the developing regions, and might even tend to discourage efforts to increase agricultural production.

It is obvious that the developing countries must achieve both economic growth and a satisfactory level of income and employment for themselves. They must also plan their population growth instead of letting it happen. The underdeveloped countries are not able, however, to carry out this task unaided, and a heavy burden rests with developed countries to provide adequate and well-coordinated assistance. For high-income countries it is not a question of charity, of duty or of the "white man's burden" but of helping to secure a stable and just society for their own children as much as for those of the developing countries. The plan attempts to show that the providing of aid can be mutually beneficial. An example is the immense market for manufactured products, including those related to agriculture, that expansion of the economy of the developing countries could provide.

A major challenge of the development problem is how to export a greater volume of agricultural products from developing countries to developed ones. The FAO commodity projections indicate that at constant prices exports of agricultural products from developing countries could be expected to grow at only 1.8 percent per year over the period 1962–1975, and probably even less rapidly during the second decade covered by the Indicative World Plan. This would make it extremely difficult for many of these countries to finance imports of machinery, seed, fertilizer, pesticides and other requisites for economic expansion, let alone massive food imports. The overall economic frame within which the agricultural objectives of the plan have been set would require an annual increase of 3.4 percent in exports, compared with around 2.5 percent over the period 1955–1967. Agricultural imports could be allowed to increase at only 2.8 percent, compared with a past growth of about 5 percent.

This analysis implies that trends toward increased self-sufficiency among the developed countries in many agricultural products must be reversed, and that some of these countries (including those with centrally planned economies) must relax protectionist policies. Here again the Indicative World Plan stresses that this is a question not of benevolence on the part of the developed countries but of economic rationality in terms of an optimum international division of labor. At the same time it must be recognized that bringing about the necessary structural changes in agriculture and industry in those countries may be a long and in some cases painful process. The effort calls for understanding on the part of the developing countries. All nations, both developed and developing, must recognize that there would be no international trade at all if the world were composed entirely of exporters!

On each of these points the Indicative World Plan shows that if present trends continued or were adjusted only through force of circumstances, the results would be quite incompatible with the achievement of the goals that the developing countries have set themselves and that are being embodied in the plans of the UN for the Second Development Decade. The most important purpose of the plan has therefore been to identify the critical sectors and major objectives in agricultural development, and to indicate deliberate policies that would permit more rapid progress toward achieving those objectives.

The Indicative World Plan contains many recommendations designed to achieve the expansion of agriculture needed to provide a firm foundation for accelerated economic growth in the developing world. The objectives considered to be of greatest importance in the light of the problems outlined above are (1) securing staple food supplies, mainly through a faster increase in cereal production, (2) diversifying and improving the quality of the diet, (3) earning and/or saving the foreign exchange crucial to overall development, (4) providing additional employment in agriculture and related industries and (5) increasing productivity through more intensive use of physical resources and modern agricultural technology.

Cereals

Since cereals dominate the cropping pattern of most developing countries and are the main staple for both calories and protein, they have an overwhelming psychological, nutritional and economic importance for farmers and governments. For these reasons planners have devoted a large proportion of technical and financial resources to trying to improve performance in cereal production, with adverse repercussions on technical progress in other food crops and in the livestock sector. Nonetheless, a faster growth rate of cereal production, particularly where population pressure on land is heavy, could eventually free resources to promote other key crops. Faster growth in cereal production, particularly in the second decade of the Indicative World Plan, would then allow a balance to be maintained between supply and the changing pattern of demand. Higher cereal yields are also essential to the massive increase of 80 million tons in concentrate feeds required to meet the plan's livestock objectives. Assurance of the basic cereal supplies must be regarded as the basis for development of other sectors of the economy.

Accordingly the plan calls for a growth of cereal production over the 23 years 1962–1985 of 3.6 percent, compared with around 2.6 percent in the decade 1955–1965. Although this may not appear too formidable a task, it should be noted that the growth of food production, particularly the production of cereals, in Zone C countries fell in all regions except Latin America in the first five years of the 1960's compared with the last five years of the preceding decade. In absolute terms cereal output in the developing countries will have to rise from about 230 million metric tons in 1962 to nearly 520 million tons by 1985 in order to meet the predicted demand for both human consumption and livestock feed.

Until recently a major obstacle to a faster rate of growth of cereal output was the absence of varieties that would give an economic response to the use of modern technology. Determined national and international cooperation, however, has finally resulted in the development of the new high-yield cereal varieties. These varieties are more responsive to irrigation and fertilizers and have a much higher yield ceiling than the varieties formerly available when they are used in combination with pesticides, weed control and other proper farming methods.

These new varieties mature quickly and (in the case of rice) are not strongly season-bound. Two or three harvests can be reaped in a year where the water supply is adequate and there is no serious frost hazard. It is thus technically possible for cereal growers to reduce unit costs by doubling or tripling yields and to obtain the benefits more than once a year. Although the new varieties have been introduced in significant quantities only recently, it is difficult to assess the rate at which their apparently high potential will be reflected in rapidly increasing national average yields. There is nonetheless a sufficient weight of evidence to strongly suggest that a genuine technical breakthrough has been made. For this reason the Indicative World Plan recommends that wider adoption of the new varieties be the driving force of development in the medium term.

It is estimated that these new varieties could be grown on a third of the cereal area in the developing countries by 1985, compared with about 5 percent in 1968. Such widespread planting would, however, require a correspondingly rapid advance in supplies of good seed, fertilizer and pesticides, and in the development of irrigation facilities, better institutions and supporting services and a greatly strengthened research effort. I shall return to these points below.

Protein

The problem of changing the structure and improving the composition of the diet to meet future demand appears to lie essentially with protein supplies rather than with sugars, tubers, fruits and vegetables, a large bulk of which can be produced from a relatively small area of land. Although the Indicative World Plan stresses the need for special measures to produce these crops on a more systematic basis for urban areas, the supply seems comparatively elastic.

This is not the case for meat and milk from ruminants such as cattle and sheep, which at present provide the bulk of protein of animal origin, and which have a slow potential for expansion because of their long reproductive cycle. Animal

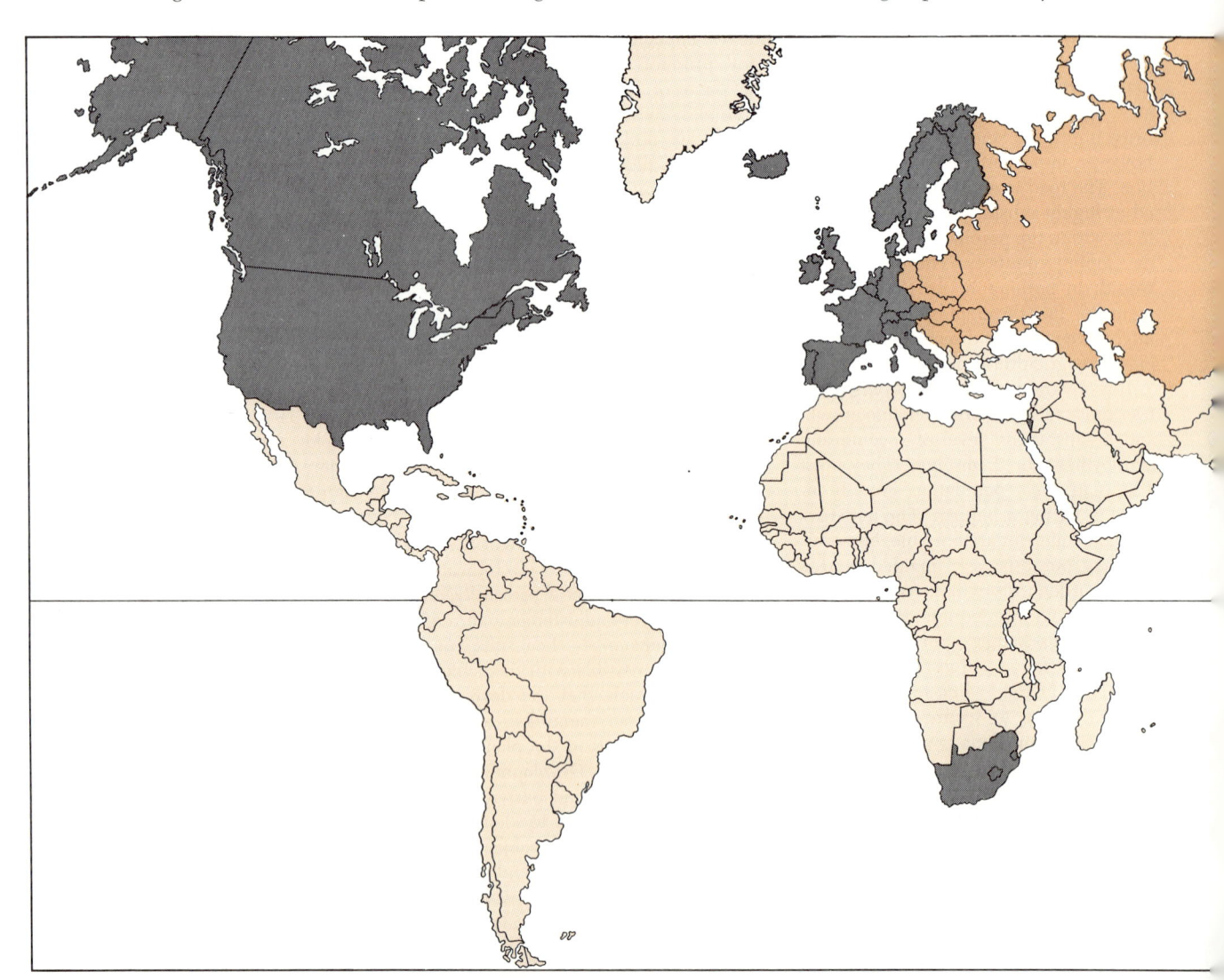

UNITED NATIONS CLASSIFICATION divides nations into three zones. Zone A consists of market-economy countries such as those of western Europe and North America (*gray*). Zone B countries such as the U.S.S.R. and other nations of eastern Europe have

production would, in fact, have to advance during the decade 1975–1985 more than twice as fast as in the recent past to reach parity with demand. The alternatives would be either a drastic decrease in per capita intake of animal protein (for example from 14.4 grams per day in the Near East in 1962 to only 9.6 grams per day by 1985) or a massive rise in import requirements.

The oceans have often been regarded as a virtually boundless protein resource. Until some means can be found of utilizing marine plankton and other plants and animals that are not yet exploited, however, such a harvest must be regarded as illusory. The world average increase in the fish catch for 1958–1965 was 7 percent, but a detailed study of the potential of conventional fisheries suggests that only a modest annual increase of 4.7 percent from the 1967 catch level of 60.5 million tons would exhaust the estimated potential of 140 million tons from combined oceanic and inland fisheries by 1985. It is clear that, long before the point of exhaustion was reached, marginal costs would rise sharply to a point where it would no longer be profitable to continue to expand fishing. The sharp drop in the growth of the world fish catch from 8.1 percent per year between 1958 and 1962 to 5.7 percent between 1962 and 1965 may indicate that this point is being reached. The estimated potential of 140 million tons, however, excludes consideration of expanded production from marine culture as well as expanding inland areas under fish culture. The long-run possibilities in these fields are considerable, but the contribution they will be able to make to the total world fish production by 1985 is difficult to predict quantitatively.

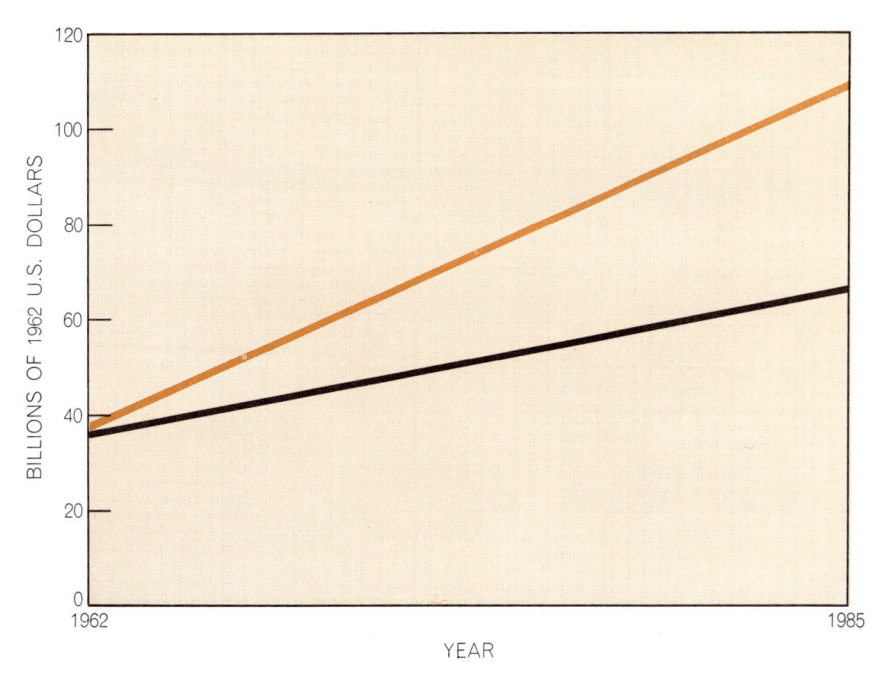

Although the Indicative World Plan contains proposals that could improve the fishery prospects toward the end of the plan period, one of the main effects of these recommendations in developed countries would be to reduce costs rather than to increase the catch. At the same time even the implementation of the policies recommended for developing regions, although leading to an increased catch, would not fully satisfy projected food demands in any of the four regions considered. It also seems unlikely that fishes now used for the production of fish meal could fill the protein gap. There are marketing difficulties, including the fact that the areas of greatest fish abundance are often distant from the areas of greatest potential shortage, and problems of consumer preference and taste as well.

Nor could the protein gap be filled, at least on the basis of present technology, solely from vegetable sources. Pulses such as peas, beans and lentils, which are the main sources of high-quality vegetable protein, generally have a very low yield. To suggest that arable land should be used for producing vegetable rather than animal protein in countries with a serious protein deficit ignores both this point and human psychological and dietary preferences.

Because of the inability of any individual sector to meet the full domestic demand for protein by 1985, except in a few countries with a high potential for a special type of product, special priority is given in the Indicative World Plan to a broad-based program to increase protein supplies from all sources more rapidly than has been done in the past. For the immediate future the emphasis is on filling the gap in meat supplies through a rapid expansion of pig and poultry production. This effort should be supplemented by measures to increase the output of vegetable protein through the introduction of leguminous crops in rotation and through improved agricultural practices. Children and other population

FOOD GAP is caused by demand (*top curve*), measured in 1962 U.S. dollars, which is rising faster than supply (*lower curve*). Unless developing countries increase food production more rapidly than they have, demand for food will exceed supply by about $43 billion in 1985.

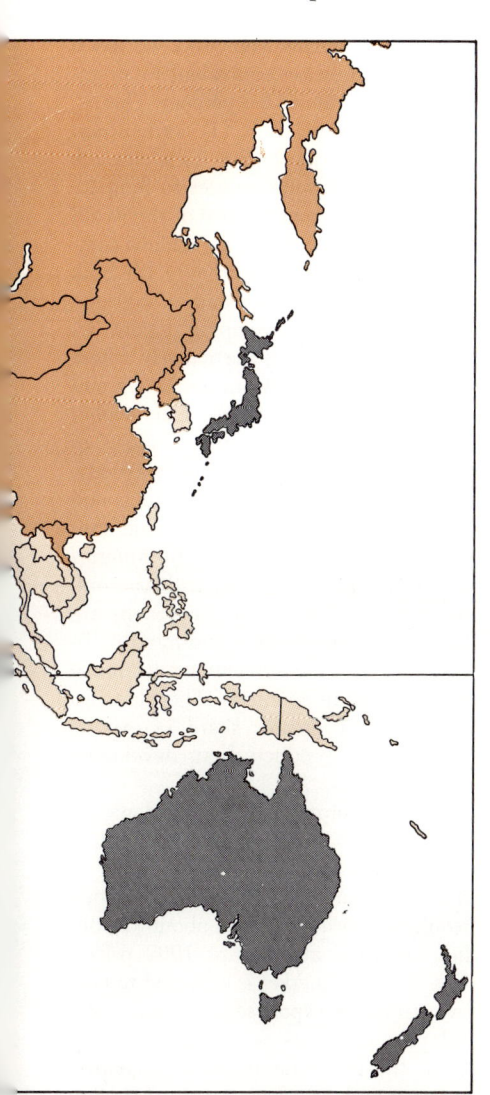

centrally planned economies (*dark color*). Zone C is developing nations (*light color*).

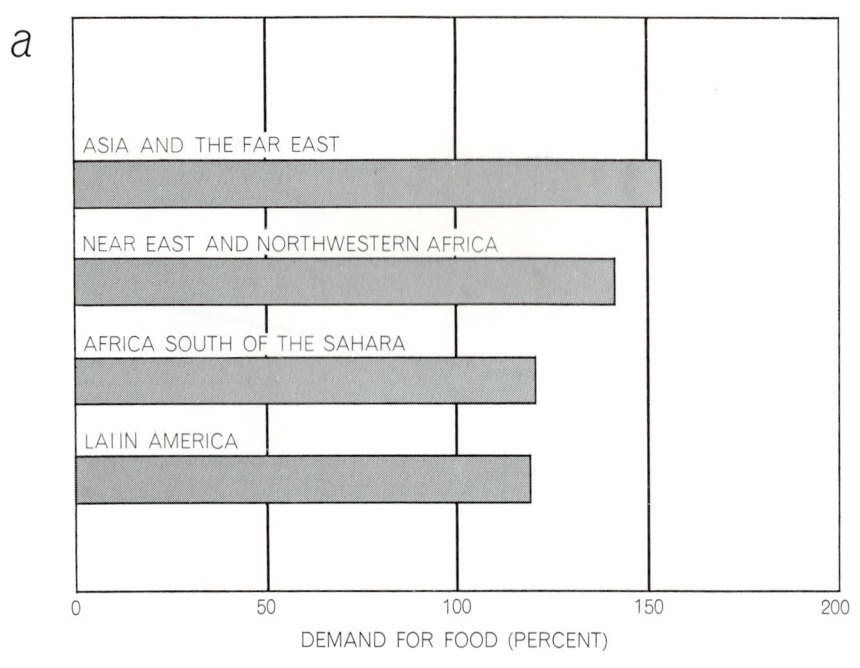

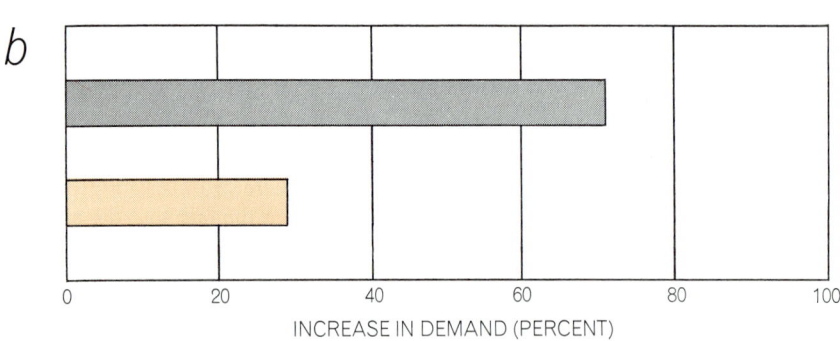

INCREASED DEMAND FOR FOOD is shown in *a*. By 1985 demand in Asia and Far East will be 154 percent of 1962 level (*top bar*). Demand in Near East and northwestern Africa will exceed 1962 levels by 143 percent (*second from top*). Demand in Africa south of the Sahara will increase by 122 percent (*third*). The demand in Latin America will increase by 120 percent (*fourth*). In *b* top bar represents 71 percent of the total increase caused by population growth; bottom bar represents 29 percent caused by growth in family income.

groups highly vulnerable to protein malnutrition should be protected by the development of formulated protein-rich foods and the distribution of these carefully designed items and processed milk products. In the more distant future a more varied supply of protein should be provided by the development of higher-yielding varieties of pulses, the buildup of ruminant-livestock inventories, the improvement of ocean-fishing practices and increases in output from inland fisheries. This would meet the projected demand by 1985 except in the case of milk. An average growth of pig and poultry production of between 5 and 10 percent over the entire period of the plan would, however, have to be attained. This formidable goal would have to be achieved largely by industrial methods, in which a key factor would be availability of concentrate feeds at economic prices.

Research will be of vital significance to the success of the entire effort to increase protein supplies. Cereals at present provide some 70 percent of the total available protein, but their content of certain essential amino acids is inadequate for a healthy diet. The development of varieties that would provide a high yield of better-quality protein would be a major breakthrough, as would the production of higher-yielding varieties of protein-rich crops such as peanuts, soya and pulses. Once such improved varieties were developed special efforts would be needed to multiply the seed and distribute it to farmers.

Finally, the Indicative World Plan examines the prospects for bridging the protein gap by the commercial development of new and potentially important protein-manufacturing processes now in the experimental or pilot-project stage. It concludes that such techniques offer exciting long-range possibilities for human nutrition once the problems of translating experimental techniques into large-scale manufacturing processes and overcoming consumer resistance have been solved. In the near future, however, synthetic proteins may prove most useful as components of animal feed, as is now the case with synthetic amino acids. Work on these processes can best be done in the developed countries; meanwhile real and substantial progress in increasing supplies can still be made in the developing countries by more conventional methods.

Financing Agricultural Development

On the basis of the Indicative World Plan proposals, net agricultural exports (valued at constant 1961–1963 average prices) would rise from $6.2 to $14.6 billion, an increase equivalent to an annual growth rate of 3.8 percent. This assumes, however, that (1) agricultural exports from developing countries are allowed better opportunities to compete with products from the rest of the world to the extent that they can achieve comparative economic advantage; (2) both production and processing of agricultural products in developing regions become more efficient, particularly where there is competition from synthetics, and (3) developing countries can exploit opportunities for expanding exports of commodities of high-income elasticity, particularly tropical-forest products and beef. Beef exports of four million tons might be envisioned in South America alone by 1985, compared with one million tons in 1962, if positive steps are taken to eliminate foot-and-mouth disease and suitable agreements are made with importing countries. The plan also argues for a greater share in exports of processed products from developing countries.

A major effort to substitute domestic products for imports at competitive prices is also proposed. Achievement of the cereal and livestock targets alone would save imports worth about $15 billion by 1985 at constant 1962 prices. The domestic market is expected to take over from the export sector in many developing countries as the main driving force toward modernization, increased income and employment in farming. Two factors will generate this trend. One is the growing percentage of the population living in cities; the other is the tremendous growth in food production that is anticipated.

Because of the inadequate data on unemployment and underemployment in agriculture it did not prove possible to propose specific employment targets. The Indicative World Plan has therefore concentrated on an approach to its production objectives that would add to the total man-hours required in agriculture and related occupations. In addition to measures that could add directly to labor requirements within agriculture itself the plan proposes programs to conserve natural resources and to build irrigation structures, roads, rural community centers and other facilities that would help to develop the entire infrastructure basic to economic and social progress. Such programs (which might be supported by food or other aid from developed countries) would thus be aimed at the creation of additional productive capacity and not merely at providing work.

The plan also proposes that agriculture be positively linked to industry. More agricultural products could be processed, and other industries could supply seed, fertilizers, pesticides, machinery, machinery servicing and other necessities.

Population

The Indicative World Plan argues for both a faster growth in urban employment and a slower growth of population. No specific measures for family planning are proposed, however; this technology lies outside the sphere of the FAO's activities. It is emphasized that the process of transforming traditional agriculture and increasing employment requires considerable capital expenditure on irrigation, mechanization and other investments, and in addition a massive increase in credit for the purchase of annual cash inputs. More and better-trained technicians for research and other services are also needed. These demands are unlikely to be satisfied in an economic situation where capital accumulation is frustrated by high rates of population growth. Even countries that have large underdeveloped and underpopulated areas must generate most of their capital from within their economy. If an increasing proportion of national resources has to be used to provide the minimum essential infrastructure for an escalating population in settled areas, such capital accumulation will be frustrated. An increasing world population would make it difficult, if not impossible, to solve the problems of agricultural production and employment, not only because there would be more mouths to feed and more jobs to find but also because the mobilization of resources needed for increasing output and labor input through more intensive use of capital resources would become more difficult.

The current low productivity of agriculture in developing regions is reflected in two principal ways. As a result of traditional methods of husbandry, yields per unit of cultivated land are low and so are cropping intensities. Even on irrigated land only one crop may be taken every other year, and in many parts of Africa and Latin America the intervals may be still longer. The traditional farming methods that produce this pattern tend to be associated with the heavy utilization of labor and low utilization of capital resources. Until recently, however, the majority of developing countries have managed to maintain production in line with national requirements by increasing the net area cultivated at the expense of nonarable land (usually pasture and forest). This policy has sometimes led to the permanent destruction of valuable resources for a relatively short-run gain in agricultural output in areas that have proved to be marginal for crops.

An analysis of growth trends in the output of 12 major crops in developed and developing regions makes the point most clearly. In developed countries the cultivated area remained virtually static between 1948 and 1959 and decreased slightly between 1959 and 1966, but the yield per hectare rose by 19 percent in the first period and 18 percent in the second. In contrast the cultivated area in developing regions rose by 21 percent and by 11 percent but yields increased by only 9 percent and 10 percent.

The Indicative World Plan empha-

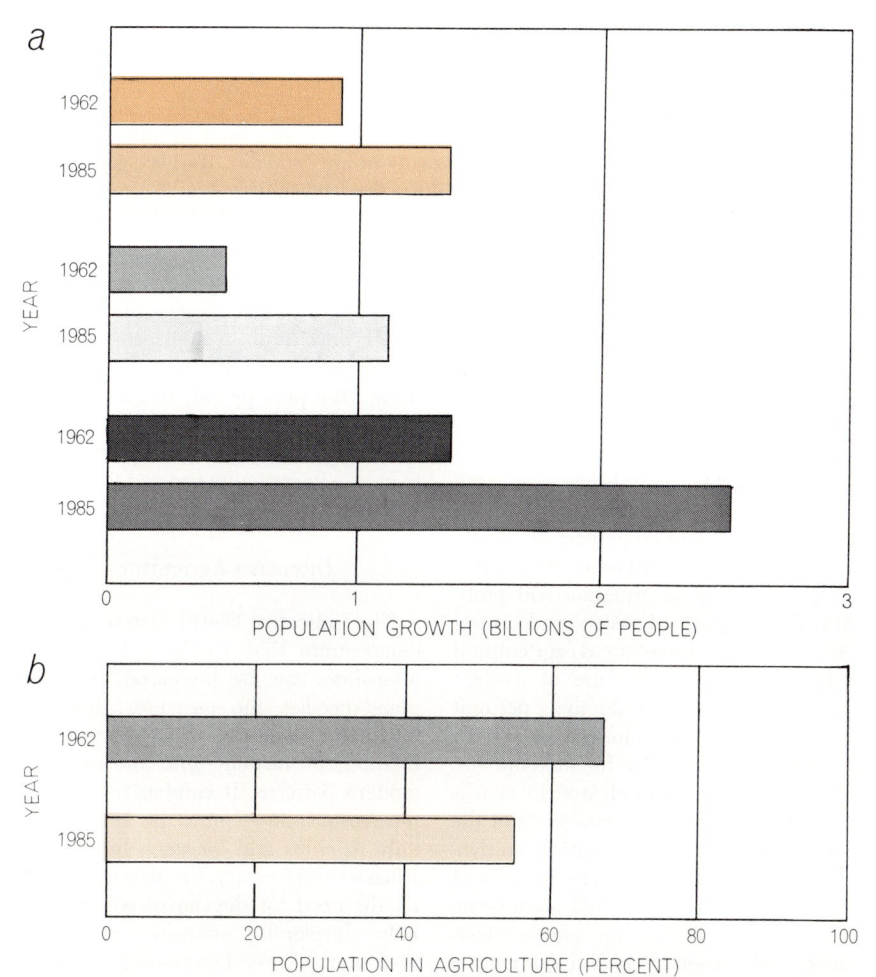

POPULATION GROWTH in the agricultural sector of undeveloped countries (excluding mainland China), represented by the two bars at the top, will be comparatively modest: from 935 million in 1962 (*dark color*) to almost 1.4 billion by 1985 (*light color*). The two bars in middle show that the nonagricultural population will increase from 460 million in 1962 (*dark gray*) to 1.1 billion by 1985 (*light gray*). The two bars at the bottom show total population of these regions: 1.4 billion in 1962 (*dark gray*) and a projected 2.5 billion by 1985 (*light gray*). In *b* bar at top shows that in 1962, 67 percent of population in these countries was agricultural. Bottom bar shows that by 1985, 55 percent will be agricultural.

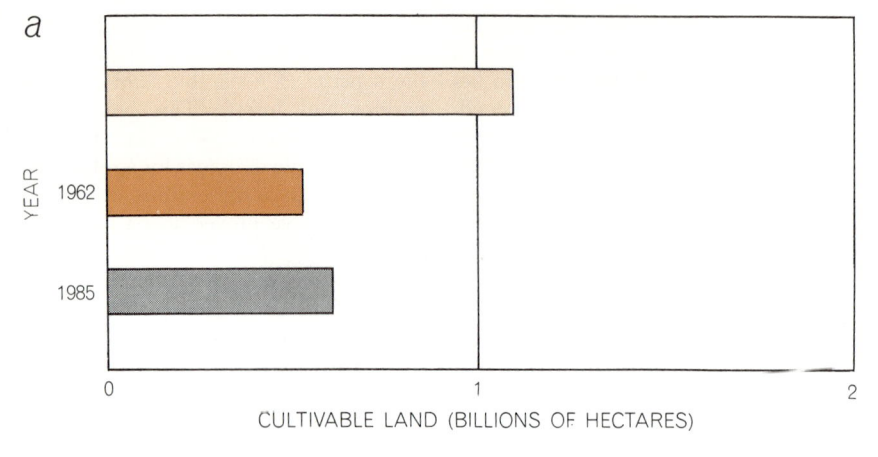

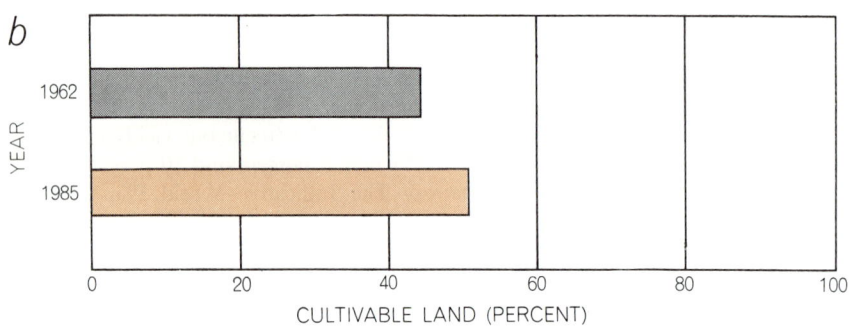

TOTAL CULTIVABLE LAND on the earth, shown in *a*, has an area of 1.1 billion hectares (*top*). In 1962, 512 million hectares were actually in use (*middle*). By 1985, 600 million hectares will be in use (*bottom*). In *b* top bar shows that land cultivated in 1962 is 45 percent of potential. Bottom bar shows that 53 percent of potential area may be in use by 1985.

sizes that throughout the developing regions good cultivable land is becoming steadily scarcer. Practically the entire potential arable area in South Asia and northwestern Africa will be under the plow by 1985, and a number of countries in the Near East will also be very close to utilizing their full potential. In Central America about 80 percent of the potential arable land will be under cultivation, and a similar situation will probably exist in parts of eastern and central Africa. In all these areas agricultural intensification and the use of modern technology to raise productivity per unit of cultivated land must therefore be regarded as imperative for survival.

Although the ratio of land to man is higher in the rest of Africa south of the Sahara and in South America, cultivation of the apparently large reserves of land in those regions would often mean massive expenditure on jungle clearance, soil conservation and the control of malaria and the tsetse fly. These areas would also have to be populated through migration, and encouraging people to move is a notoriously difficult human problem. The Indicative World Plan has therefore taken the view that better utilization of existing arable land is likely to prove more immediately rewarding in those regions than large-scale opening up of new land. New land would of course still be brought under cultivation during the plan period, but at a slower rate than in the past, and its development would be more carefully scheduled to ensure its optimum use and to prevent waste of resources.

Intensive Agriculture

The Indicative World Plan sets out to demonstrate that yields and cropping intensities can be increased, and the plan specifies the measures that will have to be taken to transform traditional methods of farming into the essential modern patterns. It emphasizes that intensive techniques must be applied not only to crops and livestock but also to fisheries and forestry. Emphasis is placed on the need for developed countries to help developing countries modernize their agriculture. Developing countries can also help one another the way Malaysia has helped other countries to improve methods for processing natural rubber.

In spite of some depressing past experiences in attempts to raise yields by introducing the use of modern farming techniques to peasant farmers in developing countries, the plan presents optimistic views concerning the future of cereals and industrial crops. The new cereal varieties and the related technology have been taken up by farmers in much of Asia at an unprecedented rate even if fertilizer and other materials are still not applied in large enough quantities. Farmers have shown themselves willing to respond to price and other incentives provided by governments and are able to utilize the new methods once they are convinced of the benefits. Similar trends are becoming evident around the Mediterranean basin, in Iran and Afghanistan and in parts of Africa. New high-yielding varieties of export crops such as tea, cocoa, rubber, coconut and oil palm have been developed and are being planted in an increasingly large area each year.

In the long run the possibility of increasing cropping intensities may be even more exciting than that of increasing yields. In much of North Africa and the Near East more than half of the arable area lies fallow every year. This situation exists in spite of the fact that ruminant livestock are seriously underfed, that natural grazing lands are under increasingly heavy pressure and that consequently wind and water erode the cropped land and even have damaging repercussions on urban areas. It is proposed that this fallow land be planted with pulses or leguminous fodder crops in areas where the rainfall exceeds 400 millimeters per year. There is strong experimental evidence that the approach is technically feasible and that it could increase income and employment through the introduction of a second crop. Cereal yields would increase and the traditional dichotomy between crop production and livestock production would be mitigated. Pasture yields can also be increased through the use of fertilizers and herbicides and the introduction of improved annual and perennial species of grasses and legumes, both in tropical and in temperate latitudes. Particular weight has been given to these techniques in Latin America.

Multiple-cropping systems can also be introduced in irrigated and tropical areas where moisture and temperature are suitable. Recent research in Asia suggests that this method may be the most potent yet devised for this region of producing maximum output per hectare and of diversifying the crop pattern. These experimental efforts have produced as much as 20 tons of food per hectare per year. In Hong Kong, where multiple cropping is linked to small livestock production, nearly 2,000 man-days per hectare can be absorbed to produce a net cash income of $2,000, a high return by developing-country standards. This system offers particular advantages for increasing the production of crops for urban marketing and processing, and thus for the greater market and industrial orientation of production that is an important objective of the plan.

The Indicative World Plan places great weight on expanding the area watered by modern irrigation systems and on investment in flood control and drainage. An assured and controlled water supply allows wider use of high-yielding varieties of annual crops, makes multiple cropping possible and permits the introduction of crops of higher unit value for processing. Particular stress has therefore been laid on irrigation in the main food-deficit regions of Asia, the Near East and northwestern Africa. Between 25 and 30 percent of all the arable area would be irrigated in the first two regions by 1985, and the irrigated harvested area in all the developing countries would almost double over the plan period. Experience has shown that high levels of production depend not merely on efficient irrigation and drainage systems but on an entire "package" of complementary inputs, including of course responsive varieties of crops and breeds of livestock.

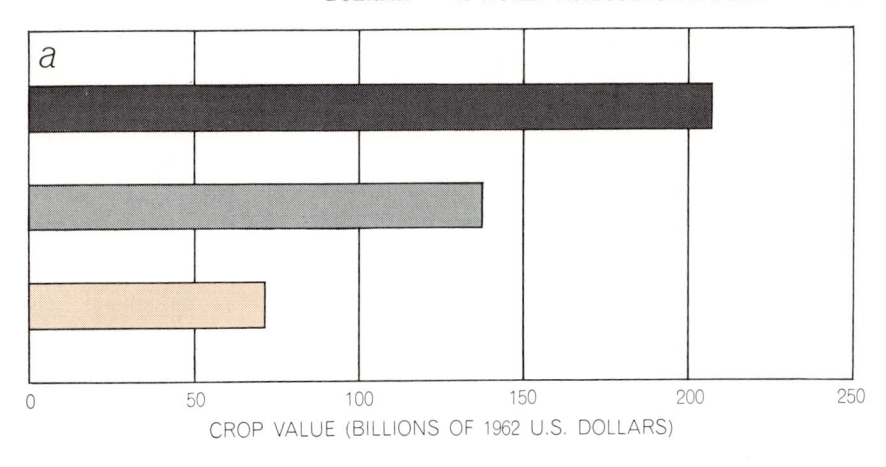

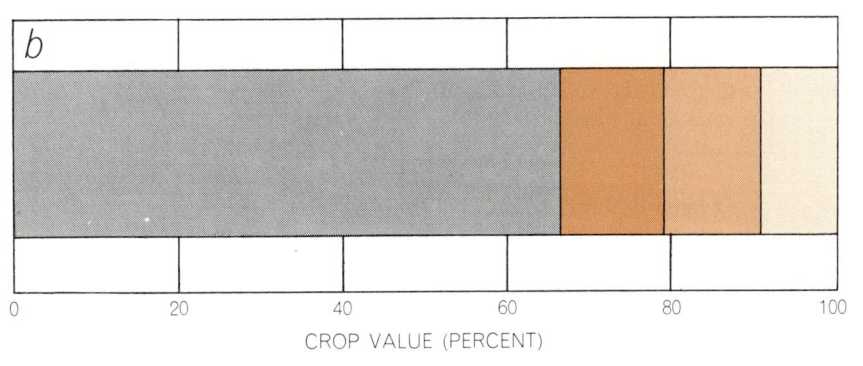

POTENTIAL VALUE of the world's crop production for a typical current year is indicated in *a* by bar at top as being equal to $207 billion. Bar in middle shows that the value of actual harvest is $137 billion. The bar at the bottom shows that difference between actual harvest and potential is $70 billion. In *b* harvest (*gray*) is 66 percent of potential crop. The loss is caused by pests (*dark color*), diseases (*lighter color*) and weeds (*lightest color*).

Fertilizer

The elimination of weaknesses in research and production services for high-yielding seeds has been given high priority, but the importance of fertilizer has also been stressed. Fertilizer should be used most heavily in the regions where the main irrigation developments are foreseen, such as Asia, the Near East, northwestern Africa and (to a lesser extent) Latin America. An increase in fertilizer production to 28.6 million nutrient tons is envisioned by 1985, compared with an estimated consumption of 2.6 million tons in 1962. This would raise the average fertilizer consumption per hectare harvested for the 64 countries studied from 6.7 kilograms in 1962 to 60 kilograms by 1985.

These various considerations hold the key to initial success in improving yields, but experience in developing countries with relatively high yields and intensive crop rotations suggests that as productivity rises and cropping systems become more complicated a vital component of the production package becomes the protection of crops against losses in the field and in storage. The proposed annual expenditure of $2 billion for crop protection by 1985 is therefore regarded as cheap insurance against losses that were estimated even in 1965 to be $50 billion, an amount roughly equal to the value of the entire proposed increase in crop output required to meet the 1985 targets.

Mechanization also grows increasingly significant over the plan period. Although it is not contended that mechanization is essential to higher crop yields, the more precise cultivation requirements of the new high-yielding cereal varieties, the importance of timely sowing, the elimination of fallow in rain-fed areas and the narrower interval between harvests in more intensive crop rotations argue strongly in its favor. Increased mechanization is not necessarily at variance with a policy of developing labor-intensive agriculture, since the plan proposes a selective strategy that would apply machinery to tasks that could not be done effectively by other means, or that would raise yields or facilitate more intensive land use. The fact is that farming in the developing world is critically underpowered. In 1967 the Science Advisory Committee of the President of the U.S. estimated that the horsepower per capita available from all sources (men, animals and machines) was .05 in Africa, .19 in Asia and .27 in Latin America, compared with a minimum requirement of .5 horsepower for achieving the full agricultural yield potential. In North America about one horsepower is available per capita.

Although the growth rates proposed for mechanization, fertilizers and pesticides are high and would require a major sustained effort, particularly in Africa and Asia, expansion in many developing countries has recently been fast. Fertilizer use has grown with particular rapidity, increasing at a rate of 12 percent per year over the past decade. This trend, together with the possibility of increases in yields and cropping intensities to be attained through advanced technology within the next two decades, gives ground for optimism well beyond the period covered by the plan.

There are, however, no grounds for complacency. If the investments in land and water development are to be recovered and plowed back into the economy, if the costs of the cash inputs essential to modern agriculture are to be recouped by farmers, if the foreign-exchange component of these capital and recurrent costs is to be replaced, and if debt-servicing of foreign financial aid is not to be an insuperable burden, a wide range of supporting actions will have to be initiated in economic, social and institutional fields. Marketing, credit and extension services must be strengthened or even created, manpower must be trained and other institutions must be built. In credit alone a fivefold increase in annual operational lending (from about $8 billion in 1962 to nearly $40 billion by 1985) would be required. Cumulative credit needs for medium- and long-term development are estimated at $86 billion by 1985. In many countries there are no adequate mechanisms either for disbursing and recovering credit at equitable rates or for mobilizing rural savings.

Land Reform

Land reform is likely to be required in all regions, but it has been given special emphasis in many Latin American countries, where much of the land is locked up in underutilized latifundia: large estates descended from the past. Provided that land reform is linked to measures to raise productivity and is not just an abstract slogan, it can not only contribute to a better utilization of resources but also create fresh markets for domestic production through income redistribution and increased purchasing power for the rural population.

Land reform is thus of crucial importance to the Indicative World Plan since the modernization of agricultural techniques and land use is inevitably bound up with the gradual spread of the monetary economy into rural areas. Whereas overall production would rather more than double over the plan period, marketed output is expected to increase between three and four times. The providing of government services therefore needs to be attuned progressively to the rate and direction of the spread of commercialization. The need for government guidance is particularly acute in Africa south of the Sahara, where subsistence production, which is outside the monetary economy, represents a larger share of the total economy than it does in other regions.

Among the many proposals aimed at mobilizing human resources to improve the life of rural populations in the developing countries, the need for providing trained manpower is stressed. Unless action is taken, such manpower may not exist when the need for it is greatest. An acute shortage is foreseen in the supply of intermediate or technical-level personnel for the agricultural services—the people who do the fieldwork. In contrast to this possibility, a potential surplus of university graduates is noted in many countries.

Remedies for these deficiencies will require important decisions at the national level affecting both the future staffing structure of government agricultural services and the related pattern of the agricultural education and training system. Unfortunately it is clear from the regional studies that, whereas almost all countries are actively engaged in agricultural and overall planning, it is comparatively rare for these plans to be related adequately to the trained manpower required to implement them. At a minimum something like 70,000 graduates and 35,000 field-staff people will be needed by 1975 in the countries studied, and 130,000 graduates and 640,000 field-workers will be needed by 1985, if lack of trained personnel is not to act as a serious constraint on development.

These estimated manpower require-

OLD WAY of harvesting a crop of wheat is practiced on an experimental farm at Kanganwal in the Punjab. Agricultural worker wearing turban, canvas shoes and light cotton tunic squats so that he can bunch stalks together and then cut them off at the base.

ments may seem high, but they would, on the basis used, amount to only about a quarter of a percent of the predicted agricultural labor force by 1975 and to less than half a percent by 1985. In contrast to these percentages, the proportion of professional and technical workers in the total labor force in most highly developed economies is 5 percent; in the developing countries the technical work force does not exceed 2 percent of the total labor force.

It can be concluded that there is an obvious need for well-thought-out and coordinated manpower and educational strategies in "donor" countries and international agencies as well as in the developing countries if the need for manpower is to be met. Here lies a challenge that the qualified young men and women of the developed countries might welcome provided that they had some assurance their talents could be put to good use within an organized program.

It is perhaps necessary to stress that the Indicative World Plan provides no panacea and proposes no miraculous solutions. It prescribes better planning and a multidisciplinary scientific approach to technical problems, supported by sound institutions and administrative services attuned to the needs of farmers. Even if it contains no startling revelations, the plan has by its very comprehensiveness been able to outline clearly the crucial problems facing world agriculture. By drawing on the wide expertise of a world organization it has also been able to propose fresh solutions and approaches to these problems, and to indicate (often ahead of other contemporary thinking) where and when changes in international or national policies may be required.

The Future

Assuming that the main recommendations contained in the plan could be incorporated into national plans in accordance with local needs and priorities, an average annual increase of about 3.7 percent per year in gross value of agricultural production appears feasible over the next two decades. This would represent a significant improvement over the past decade or so, when production has only just kept up with population growth. It will nevertheless be a difficult task, since the growth rates in both production and trade in the elapsed period of the plan have been rather lower than was anticipated, although there are now encouraging signs of an upward trend in production, particularly in Asia. It is also expected that the growth of the sector will accelerate, from 3.6 percent for the 1962–1975 planning period to 3.9 percent between 1975 and 1985, as constraints on the slower-growing branches of crop and livestock production are reduced by research and as agricultural institutions and services are improved.

The growth rates proposed are to be sustained over a long period and would be difficult to exceed. It follows that for many countries an increase in the gross domestic product of more than 6 percent throughout the period would hardly be feasible, although a faster growth might be possible after 1975. Further work by the FAO in conjunction with other UN agencies in connection with the UN Sec-

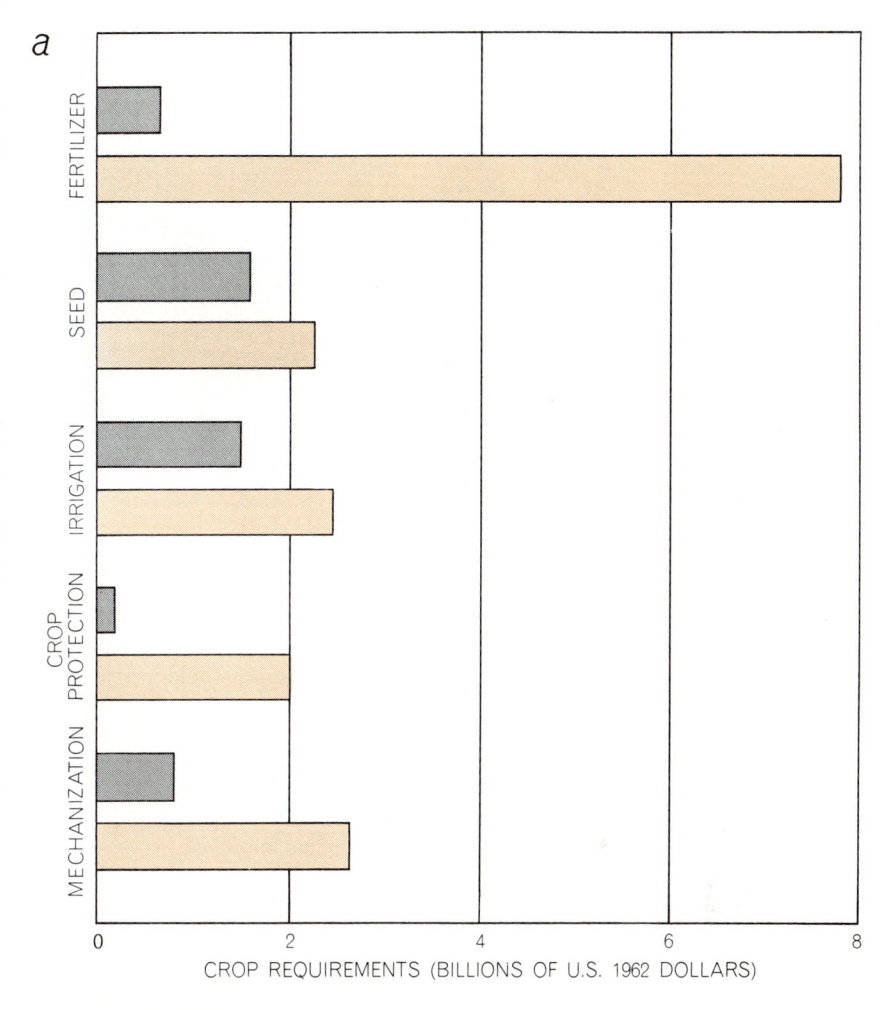

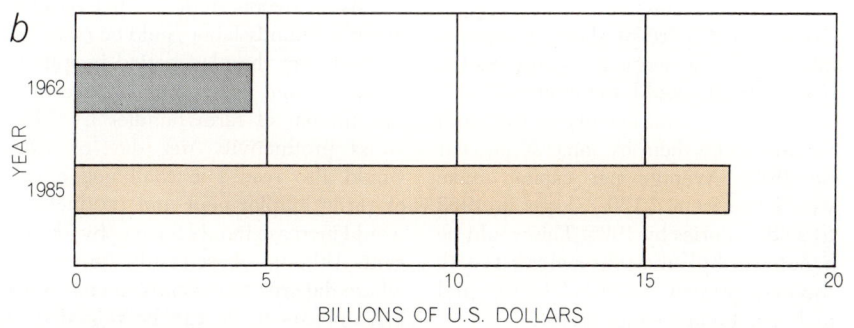

CROP INPUTS are represented by pairs of bars. The bar at top indicates that $664 million was spent on fertilizers in 1962 (*gray*). Next bar shows that if the crop-production goals of Indicative World Plan are to be met this expenditure must increase to $7.8 billion by 1985 (*color*). The bars second from top show that expenditure on seed must increase from $1.6 billion (*gray*) to $2.2 billion (*color*). Bars third from top show that expenditure on irrigation must increase from almost $1.5 billion (*gray*) to $2.4 billion (*color*). Bars fourth from top show that expenditures on crop protection must increase from $180 million (*gray*) to $2 billion (*color*). Last pair of bars shows that expenditure on mechanization must increase from $797 million to $2.6 billion. In *b* top bar (*gray*) represents total spent on crop inputs in 1962. Bottom bar shows spending on inputs that will be needed by 1985.

NEW WAY to harvest wheat is practiced on same farm as is shown in picture on page 224. Ox-drawn reaper fells crop with mowing bar while driver pushes cut wheat straws to the side with a pitchfork. The bundles at left are made by workers following the reaper.

ond Development Decade will test the validity of this conclusion. A sustained 6 percent rate of economic growth would, however, be no mean achievement in any country.

In terms of food supply the "high" alternative proposed in the world study, based on accelerated pig and poultry production, would amount to an increase in net food production retained for domestic consumption of about 3.8 percent per year, compared with only 2.7 percent in the decade prior to 1966. From the nutritional viewpoint calorie supplies (which fell 6 percent short of requirements in the developing countries in the base period) would therefore approximately equal requirements by 1975 and would exceed them by some 10 percent by 1985. Average per capita intake would rise from 2,130 calories in 1962 to 2,480 calories by 1985. This would be a noteworthy advance compared with the ever present specter of famine and malnutrition in the recent past.

A small proportion of the population would nevertheless still be underfed by 1985 as a result of inequalities of income. In the less developed countries protein would be the part of the diet most likely to be scarce. In those areas the staple food tends to provide the bulk of the supply, and the supplementary sources required to improve the quality of the protein in the diet are likely to be relatively expensive. Thus, although the total protein supply would increase from 93.2 to 105.6 percent of nutritional requirements between 1962 and 1985, the situation of low-income groups could even deteriorate if inequalities of distribution are not mitigated and protein sources are not improved.

The best solution to the problem of distribution is employment, and the provisions of the Indicative World Plan should generate many new jobs. A study of the absorptive capacity for labor of the Asian region suggests that requirements for family labor could be raised 15 percent over the plan period in spite of an anticipated increase of 55 percent in the number of farm families by 1985. Gross productivity per day of work would also rise. The combined effects of rising employment and productivity would increase family income by 58 percent. Although these results for an area where the crux of the employment problem appears to lie can be regarded as encouraging, it must be emphasized that they represent only a very preliminary approach by the plan to a problem of vital importance to the future stability of the entire world.

In many respects the conclusions of the Indicative World Plan are optimistic. They show that, given the adoption of the technical, institutional and economic measures proposed, the main problems of hunger and malnutrition could be overcome, trade flows could be improved and a substantial contribution could be made toward providing additional employment. At the same time it must be faced that even if, through the technological measures proposed in the plan, two blades of grass were to be grown where only one grew before, the costs would not be low. Cumulative investments in crops, livestock, forestry and fisheries would total an estimated $112 billion between 1962 and 1985 (of which 42 percent would be for land and water development), plus a further $3 billion for providing the trained workers who would help to implement the proposals. Recurrent annual costs of seed, fertilizer, pesticides and machinery operation—the vital package of inputs—plus the cost of animal-feed supplies would total $26 billion by 1985, more than three times the 1962 level.

The financing of development is therefore likely to be one of the crucial problems of the next two decades. Such financing will largely determine the success or failure of the efforts of the developing countries to achieve self-sustaining growth. Sufficient capital cannot be formed unless a number of conditions prevail. The value of trade in developing countries must grow more rapidly. The private commercial sector must become more deeply involved in the development process, and the internal savings accumulated by the more prosperous farmers must be mobilized. Yet the rapid rise envisioned in inputs and investments, and the comparatively slow expansion of foreign-exchange earnings, imply that the need for financial assistance to developing countries will also rise. Even allowing for the substantial expansion proposed in domestic manufacturing capacity, the annual foreign disbursements on agricultural needs might be of the order of $7 billion by 1985. The developed countries could do much to ease this burden. They could supply these needs on easy terms, provide technical assistance in the establishment of local industries and make other loans for the purchase of plant and equipment. The inclusion of a package of agricultural necessities in aid-financed projects is a further possibility, and this would help in obtaining a more rapid return on capital investments. A number of delegations to the FAO conference, particularly those from the developing countries, considered that higher priority in future planning should be given to this kind of aid and to manufacturing expertise.

In qualitative terms the plan envisions some important changes of emphasis in aid requirements. Food aid, for example, would shift from massive supplies of staple cereals toward high-protein foods (particularly milk products), although "fire brigade" action to supply grains to meet specific emergencies would still be required, and grains would probably form a continuing component of aid in relation to works projects. In determining priorities for such projects the plan stresses the need to develop those that will yield large gains over a short period during the early years in order to achieve the rapid increase in basic food supplies required by 1975.

The need for research is frequently stressed, and it is believed foreign aid could often operate most usefully in assisting the establishment of multidisciplinary research stations to tackle key problems affecting several countries, leaving adaptive research to be undertaken at the national level. There are three research priorities on which international assistance might profitably be focused. The demand is rising more rapidly for such crops as oilseeds, pulses, vegetables and fodders and for ruminant livestock than it is for cereals. Yet the research base from which expansion must come is exceedingly weak, particularly in tropical areas.

Research may also help to increase farm income and employment in areas of lower agricultural yield. A potentially dangerous gap is appearing in several countries between the prosperity in areas where high-yielding varieties can be grown and large responses to inputs can be obtained and the continuing stagnation in poorer regions that are often unirrigated and arid or at high elevations. The Indicative World Plan does not advocate holding back progress in the better areas while solutions are found to this problem (which might in part lie outside agriculture), but it does argue that an additional research effort should be devoted to these poorer regions, possibly supported by social programs to provide work and alleviate distress.

The relatively unsophisticated farmers in the developing countries must be provided with safe, effective and economic pesticides that neither present high short-term toxic hazards nor pollute the environment by accumulating over many years. In many respects the adoption of the plan's proposals would contribute greatly to the conservation of natural resources, but it would also result in a greatly increased use of agricultural chemicals. In view of the widespread alarm over DDT in the U.S. and some other developed countries, it is necessary to put the matter into perspective by emphasizing that even if the plan's recommendations were adopted in full, levels of use per hectare cultivated in the developing countries would by 1985 still be well below the 1965 levels in much of the developed world. To put a brake on technical progress and risk widespread famine cannot be contemplated. A calculated short-run risk must be taken on the continued use of existing chemicals in developing countries at the relatively low levels proposed, while research is redoubled in the developed countries to provide suitable alternatives. The potential size of the commercial market should in itself provide an adequate incentive for such research.

With respect both to research and to extension services the emphasis would be increasingly on training trainers so as to enable technical assistance in such fields to be tapered off gradually. Technical assistance will be completed, however, only when training and research institutions in the developing world are self-supporting. In view of the large increases in trained personnel proposed in the plan this goal is clearly still a long way off. Generally it is recommended that aid should be given more on a team basis and less on an individual basis, with effort spread more evenly between the technology and the economics of production. Nevertheless, there will still be certain fields such as processing (including seed technology) and storage in tropical areas where expertise is limited and individual advice could make a valuable contribution.

The task of national and international planning would be considerably easier if statistics were better, if more evidence could be gathered on levels of nutrition as a result of food-consumption surveys

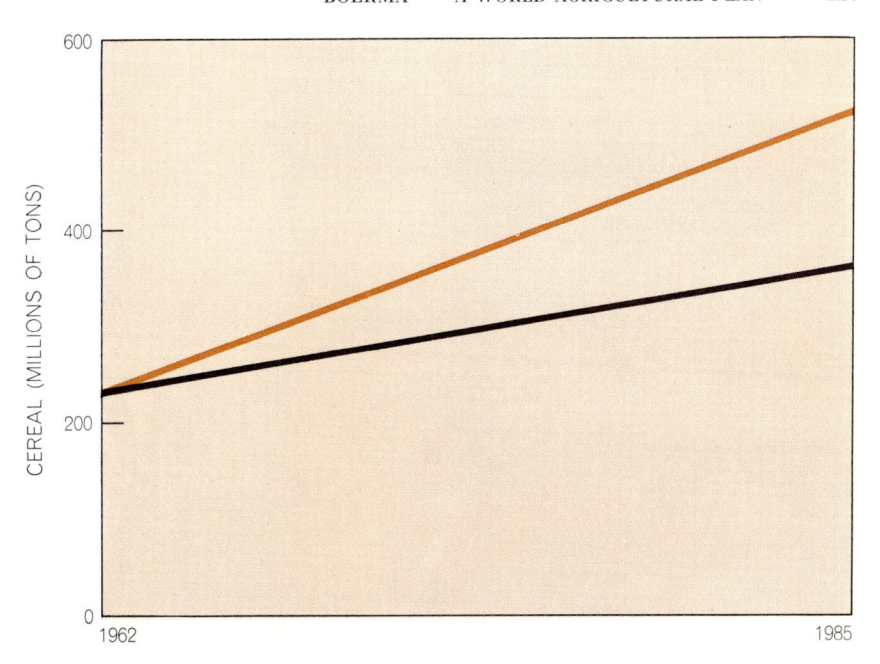

CEREAL PRODUCTION currently increases at a rate of 2.6 percent per year (*lower curve*). At this rate annual production by 1985 should equal 360 million metric tons. Rate of increase must be raised (*upper curve*) so production by 1985 equals 520 million tons.

GUARD armed with rifle protects stand of high-yield wheat on an experimental station in India. Without protection the plot might be raided by farmers who want new seed. High-yielding seed has also appeared in black-market trading in some developing nations.

and if physical resources and their potential could be more accurately assessed. Additional technical assistance would be fruitful in all these fields as an essential basis for planning and policy-making.

In the wider sense international assistance could help developing countries to establish agricultural services that would cater more adequately to such needs, and that might eventually lead to a more uniform approach to both short-term and long-term planning. This could be beneficial both to national planners and to continuing work on global-perspective planning by international agencies. It would also facilitate the continuous evaluation of world-agricultural progress that would permit the establishment of "early warning" systems to alert the world to threatened crises in the fields of production, aid and trade. Clearly such matters require a close and continuing discussion among international, regional and national planners. My own hope is that the FAO's Indicative World Plan will act as a catalyst in this respect.

FETISH was set up to protect two acres of IR-8 high-yield rice growing on a farm in Coimbatore in southern India. An extension worker, at right in dark pants, discusses care of the crop with two field hands, while farmer, dressed in white cotton, looks on.

ORTHODOX AND UNORTHODOX METHODS OF MEETING WORLD FOOD NEEDS

N. W. PIRIE
February 1967

The orthodox methods must be pressed, but it seems they cannot solve the problem without the aid of the unorthodox ones. And the adoption of unorthodox methods calls for basic changes in cultural attitudes

The world has been familiar with famine throughout recorded history. Until the present century some people have been hungry all the time and all the people have been hungry some of the time. Now a few industrialized countries have managed, by a mixture of luck, skill and cunning, to break loose from the traditional pattern and establish systems in which most of the population can expect to go through life without knowing hunger. Instead their food problems are overnutrition (about which much is now being written) and malnutrition. Malnutrition appears when the food eaten is supplying enough energy, or even too much, but is deficient in some components of a satisfactory diet. Its presence continually and on a large scale is a technical triumph of which primitive man was incapable because he lacked the skill to process the food he gathered in a manner that would remove some of the essential components but leave it palatable and pleasing in appearance. Furthermore, until the development of agriculture few foods contained the excess carbohydrate that characterizes much of the world's food today. The right policy in technically skilled countries, however, is not to try to "go back to nature" and eat crude foods. Processing does good as well as harm. What we now need is widespread knowledge of the principles of nutrition and enough good sense to use our technical skill prudently.

It is salutary to remember how recently this pattern was established. There was some hunger in Britain 50 years ago and much hunger 50 years before that. Still earlier many settlements in now well-fed regions of Australia and the U.S. had to be abandoned because of starvation. It is said that scurvy killed about 10,000 "forty-niners," and California was the scene of some of the classic descriptions of the disease. One has to learn how to live and farm in each new region; it cannot be assumed that methods that are successful in one country will work elsewhere. It is therefore probable that methods will be found for making the currently ill-fed regions productive and self-sufficient. The search for them should be started immediately and should be conducted without too much regard for traditional methods and preconceptions.

The problem can be simply stated: How can human affairs be managed so that the whole world can enjoy the degree of freedom from hunger that the industrialized countries now have?

It is well known that in many parts of the world not only is there a food shortage but also the population is increasing rapidly. Some of the reasons for this situation are fairly easy to establish. When the conditions of life change slowly, compensating changes can keep pace with them. In Europe during the 16th century half of the children probably never reached the age of five. There are no general statistics for this period, but in the 17th century 22 out of the 32 British royal children (from James I to Anne) died before they were 21, and it is unlikely that the poor fared better than royalty. The establishment of our present standards of infant mortality had little to do with medical knowledge. Until this century the farther away one could keep from doctors, except for the treatment of physical injury, the better. It was increasing technical skill in bringing in clean water and getting rid of sewage that made communities healthy, and this skill was applied by people who had never heard of germs or, like Florence Nightingale, disbelieved what they were told. But the change came slowly enough for families to adjust the birthrate to suit the new conditions. Moreover, there was incompletely filled land to be used. What René Dubos calls the "population avalanche" is on us because it is now possible to undertake public health measures on a larger scale and finish them quicker than heretofore.

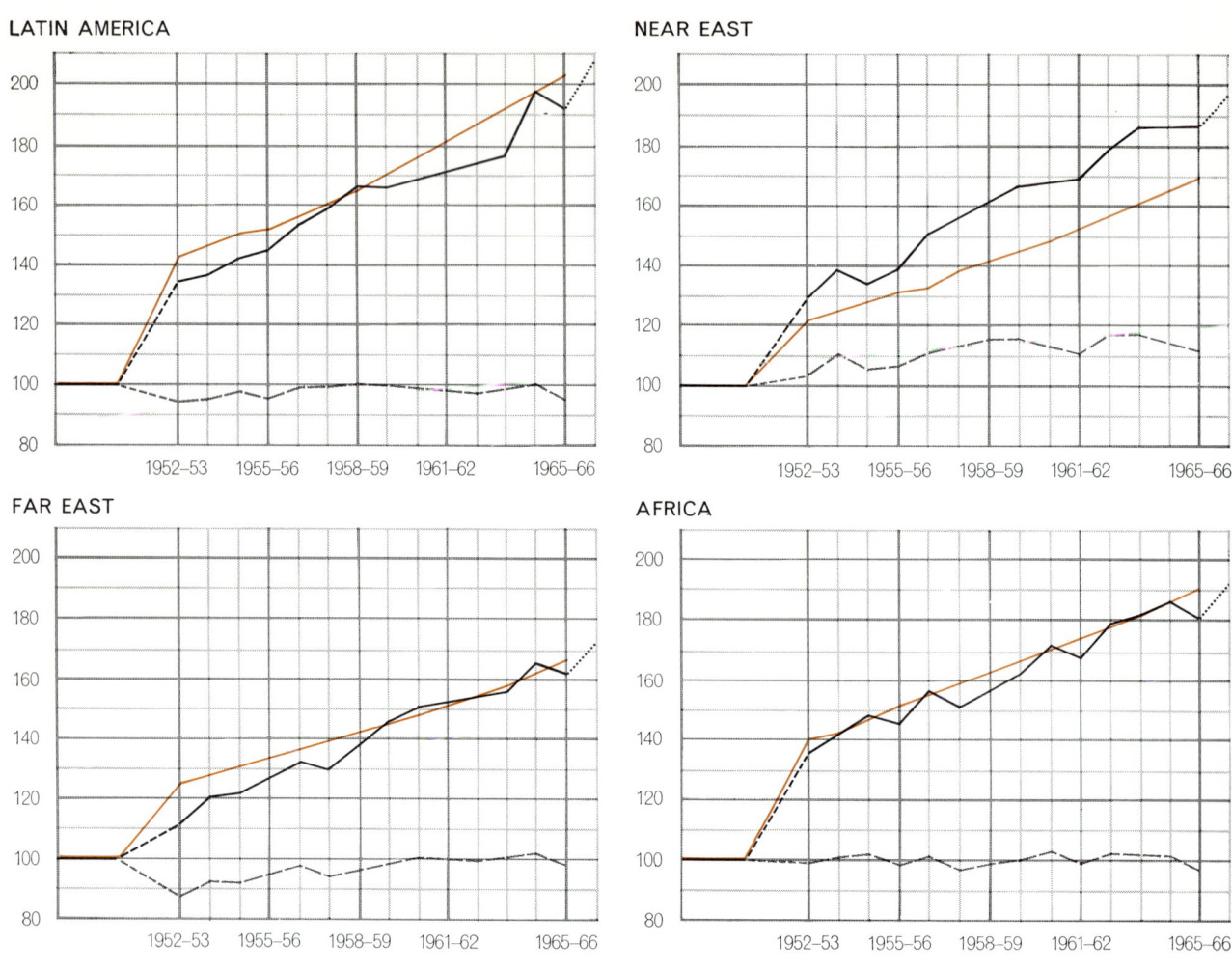

POPULATION AND FOOD PRODUCTION are compared for four developing regions in these charts prepared by the Food and Agriculture Organization of the United Nations. The colored curve is population; the solid black curve, food production; the broken gray curve, food production per caput. The figures for population are in millions; those for food production are given according to an index of 100 for the prewar average. The food production figures for 1965–1966 (July 15, 1965, to July 15, 1966) show the effects of adverse weather in many parts of the world. In that period world food production per caput fell 2 percent. The dots at end of food production curve show increase required to regain per caput level of 1964–1965. Mainland China is not represented in Far East figures.

Once the principles are understood the hygiene of an area can be improved quickly by a few people, and the population as a whole gets the advantage of improved health without having to take any very active steps to achieve it. Even where methods for improving conventional agriculture are known their application is of necessity slower, because it depends on a change in the outlook of most of the people in a farming community rather than in the outlook of the few who control water and sewage. Furthermore, fecundity is potentially unlimited but food production is not. Clearly, therefore, the "avalanche" will have to be stopped. It is important to remember, however, that it cannot be stopped in any noncoercive way without the cooperation of the people; that means more education, which means more hygiene and so, at least for a time, a still greater increase in the population. The first result of an effective campaign for contraception will be an increase in population rather than a diminution. More effort should be put into the encouragement of contraception. And more research is needed on improved methods, leading to the ideal: that people should have to do something positive to reverse a normal state of infertility, so that no conception would be inadvertent. This, however, is a complement to, and not a substitute for, work on the production of more food. Strained as existing supplies are, it seems inevitable that they will be strained still further during the next half-century. After that the entire world may have established the population equilibrium that now exists in some industrialized countries.

The normal humane reaction in the presence of misery is pity, and this reaction is followed, where appropriate, by charity. Hence the immense effort that is now being put into shipping the food surpluses, accumulated in some parts of the world, to areas of need. This is commendable and spiritually satisfying to the donor, but for two reasons it has little effect on the real problem. The amount of surplus food is not large enough to make much of a dent in the world's present need. The surplus could be increased, but the logistic problem of shipping still greater quantities of food would be formidable. The more serious objection to charity, except during temporary periods of crisis, is that it discourages the recipient. A century ago the philanthropist Edward Denison remarked: "Every shilling I give away does fourpence worth of good by keeping the recipients' miserable bodies alive and eightpence worth of harm by helping to destroy their miserable souls." Nearly 1,000 years ago Maimonides categorized the forms of charity and concluded that the most commendable form was to act in such a way that charity would become unnecessary.

Trade is the obvious alternative to charity. Unfortunately the developing countries are in a poor bargaining position. Since 1957 the prices paid for their primary products declined so much that the industrialized countries made a saving of $7,000 million and an extra profit of $3,000 million because of the increased cost of manufactured goods. The developing countries thus lost $10,000 million—about the same as the total "aid" they received from commercial, private and international sources. (The figures are from the *Financial Times* of London for July 19, 1965.) With the market rigged against them in this way it is not likely that they will soon be able to buy their food as countries such as Britain do. At present the industrialized countries are exporting about 30 million tons of grain a year, largely against credit. It is unlikely that this state of affairs can last; half of the world cannot permanently feed the other half.

The idea that the developing parts of the world should be fed by either charity or trade depends on the assumption that they are in some way unsuited for adequate food production. This idea is baseless. Once the methods have been devised, food can be produced in most places where there is sunlight and water; for political stability food must be produced where the mouths are. Any country dependent on imports for its main foodstuffs is to some extent controlled by others.

The problem can be more narrowly stated: How to produce enough food in the more populous parts of the world?

Food production can and will be increased in many orthodox ways. There is still some uncultivated but cultivable land, irrigation and drainage can be improved and extended, fertilizers can be used on a much greater scale and the general level of farming technique can be improved. If all the farmers in a region were as skilled as the best 10 percent of them, there would probably be enough food for everyone today. These improvements could be achieved by vigorous government action and without further research.

In the Temperate Zone plant breeders have greatly increased cereal yields during the past 20 years, and these improved varieties could be used more widely. There have been no comparable developments with food crops in the Tropical Zone, but there is no reason to think that progress there could not be equally spectacular. This research should not be limited to cereals. In many parts of the wet Tropics yams (*Dioscoria* and *Colocasia*) are staple foods but the varieties used contain little protein. There is, however, some evidence that the protein content of yams varies; a New Guinea variety called Wundunggul contains 2.5 percent nitrogen. If this nitrogen is all in protein, the yam contains 15 percent protein and is worthy of serious study.

It is generally agreed that pests and diseases rob us of as much as a third of our crops. When the improvements outlined above have been made, the proportional loss as well as the absolute one could become greater, since well-nourished crops, growing uniformly in large fields, are particularly susceptible. The cost of treatment may be only a tenth of the value of the crop saved; the methods are well publicized by firms making pesticides. There is no need to labor this aspect of the problem here. More attention should, however, be given to losses during storage; the need for

SYNTHETIC FOOD is represented by Incaparina, made of maize, sorghum and cottonseed by the Quaker Oats Company. The product has been skillfully promoted by Quaker Oats in Central America. The Spanish words at the top of this 500-gram package mean: "For 25 glasses or portions." Those below "Incaparina" mean: "It is very nourishing and costs little."

satisfactory storage techniques for use in primitive conditions is especially acute. So much mystical nonsense has been written by believers in the merits of "natural" foods that most scientists show understandable impatience at the idea that pesticide residues may be harmful to the ultimate consumer of the protected crop. Furthermore, a food shortage may well do more harm to a community than sensibly applied pesticides can do. There is, nevertheless, great scope here for research on improved techniques.

There are such good prospects that productivity can be increased by each, or even all, of these methods if they are assiduously developed that it seems to many experts that there is no immediate need for any more radical approach to the problem of world feeding. This is the attitude of the United Nations Food and Agriculture Organization (F.A.O.). One cannot praise too highly its work in compiling statistics and persistently calling attention to the need for agricultural improvements. On the other hand, while recognizing that the F.A.O. is not a research organization, one can deplore its equally persistent tendency to denigrate every unorthodox approach to the problem. History may partly excuse this attitude. Ever since the time of Malthus prophets have been making our flesh creep with warnings of impending famine. Conditions have remained much the same—or have improved. These prophecies remain unfulfilled because 400 years of exploration enabled new land to be cultivated, 200 years of biological research laid the foundation for scientific agriculture, and 50 years of rational chemistry made it possible to produce fertilizers by fixing the nitrogen of the air. The cautious prophet should therefore not say that hunger is inevitable but that it is probable unless the relevant research is done on an adequate scale. The time to do it is now, before the need has become more acute.

The main product of agriculture is carbohydrate. The foods that make up the world's diet—the cereals, potatoes, yams, cassava and so on—are from 1 to 12 percent protein on the basis of dry weight. An adult man needs 14 percent protein in his food; children and pregnant or lactating women need from 16 to 20 percent. However great an increase there may be in the consumption of conventional bulk foods, there will be a protein deficit. Moreover, it will be exacerbated if food is made palatable by the addition of fats and sugar, which give energy but contain no protein. Too much stress cannot be laid on the fact that the percentage of protein in a diet is the vital thing; increased consumption of low-protein food makes the consumer fat but as malnourished as before.

Recognition of the importance of protein sources, and their deficiency in most of the world's diet, has come slowly. It is nonetheless gathering momentum. Fifteen years ago little attention was paid to protein sources by international agencies and gatherings such as the International Nutrition Congress. Now protein is one of the main themes. Audiences at these gatherings are a step ahead of the management. At the International Congress of Food Science and Technology last year, for example, the session "Novel Protein Sources" proved more popular than those who had allocated the rooms had foreseen; that session was more uncomfortably overcrowded than any other. The remainder of this article will be exclusively concerned with protein. All the components of a diet are needed, but the need for protein will be the most difficult to meet.

Animal products—meat, milk, cheese, eggs, fish—are widely esteemed and are used as protein concentrates to improve diets that are otherwise mainly carbohydrate. About a third of the world's cattle population is in Africa and India; most of these animals are relatively unproductive and are maintained largely for reasons of prestige and religion. It is easy to sidestep the main problem and argue that the protein shortage in these countries could be ameliorated, even if it could not be abolished, if herds were culled and the remainder made fully productive. The more thoughtful Africans and Indians realize this, and the situation will doubtless change. But every community tends to devote an amount of effort to nonproductive activity that seems to outsiders unreasonable. In the Middle Ages cathedrals were built by people who lived in hovels, and we now spend more on space research than on research in agriculture and medicine. Change is inevitable, and contemporary forms of religious observance and prestige are certain to be modified; the transition will not be hastened by nagging from outside.

According to most forecasters, the need to grow crops on land now used to maintain animals will lead to a decline in meat consumption in industrial countries, and the essential disappearance of meat is sometimes predicted. Although the decline is probable, the disappearance is not. There is much land that is suitable for grazing but not for tillage. Furthermore, there will always be a great deal of plant residue that (perhaps after supplementation with urea) can be more conveniently used as animal feed than in any other way. It is by no means certain, however, that we will always use the ideal herbivore. There is good reason to think that several species of now wild herbivore, running together, give a greater return of human food in many areas of tropical bush or savanna than domesticated species [see "Wildlife Hus-

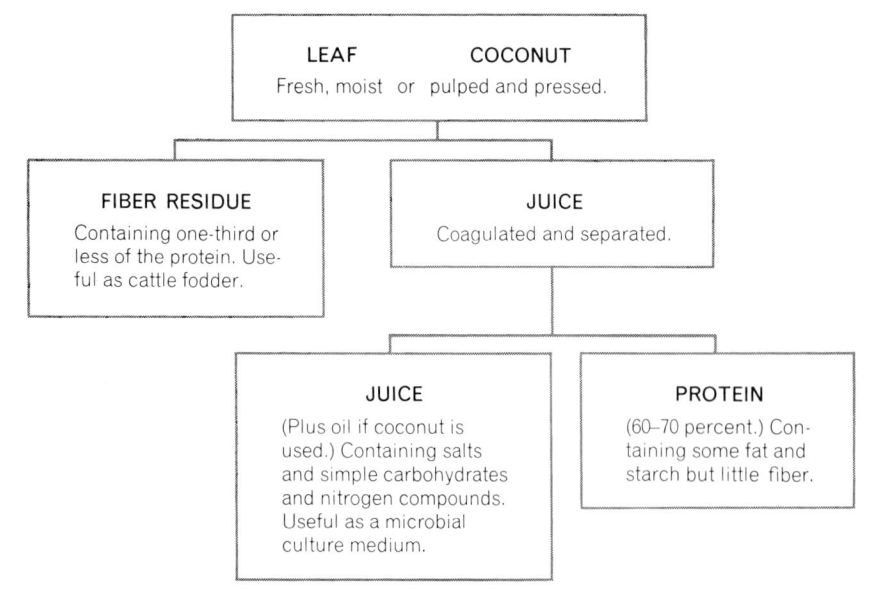

LEAVES AND COCONUT are a source of protein if fiber and juice are removed from them. This chart shows the steps of the process and also indicates the uses of by-products.

bandry in Africa," by F. Fraser Darling; SCIENTIFIC AMERICAN, November, 1960]. In addition, wild herbivores generally yield more protein per pound "on the hoof" than domestic species. These are matters that are being investigated by the International Biological Program. Even better results may be achieved after a few years of skilled breeding. Ruminants such as the antelope and the water buffalo are not the only species worthy of attention, and land is not the only site available for grazing. The capybara, a large rodent, is well adapted to South America and is palatable. Water weeds, and plants growing in swamps and on lake margins, contribute hardly anything to human nutrition. They could be collected and fed to land animals, but it would seem to be more efficient to domesticate the *Sirenia* (the freshwater manatee and the marine dugong) and use them as sources of meat. These herbivores are wholly aquatic and so, unlike semiaquatic species such as tapirs and hippopotamuses, do not compete for food with more familiar animals.

It is usual in articles such as this one to stress the importance of fish. This is admirable, but stress should not be allowed to drift into obsession. The more cautious forecasters estimate that the fish catch could be increased only two- or threefold without depleting stocks. Moreover, much of the world's population lives far from large bodies of water, and since fishing has an accident rate twice as high as coal mining it is likely to remain a relatively unattractive occupation. In the past decade the wet weight of fish caught annually increased from 29 million tons to 52 million, but the proportion used as human food decreased from 83 percent to 63. The remainder was used as fodder, mainly in the already well-fed countries. When still more fish are caught, the temptation to use a still larger proportion as fodder will be greater because much of the extra catch will consist of unfamiliar species. By grinding and solvent extraction these unfamiliar fishes can be turned into an edible product containing 80 percent protein. This process has suffered from every form of misfortune: the use of unsuitable solvents, commercial overstatement, excessive hygienic caution and political intrigue. It is nevertheless sound in principle and will do much to increase the amount of food protein made on an industrial scale and distributed through international channels.

One also hears of "fish farming." Activity that could properly be given this

MANATEE, an aquatic mammal, is an example of an unorthodox source of meat. It can also control aquatic weeds, which it eats. An adult manatee is between nine and 15 feet long.

CAPYBARA, a large rodent that lives in South America, has also been suggested as a source of meat. Like the manatee, it feeds on aquatic weeds. An adult is about four feet long.

ELAND, a large African antelope, is an accepted meat animal. Its importance as a food source is that it is adapted to grazing on marginal lands that are not suited to agriculture.

title is possible in lagoons but unlikely in the oceans because fish move too freely, and fertilizer, intended to encourage the growth of their food, spreads too easily into the useless unlit depths. With mollusks and crustaceans, farming becomes much more promising and deserves more scientific attention than it gets. Food for such marine invertebrates does not seem to be the limiting factor; many of them can use the world's largest biological resource, the million million tons of organic matter in suspension in the sea. Sedentary mollusks are limited by predators and attachment sites. The predators could be controlled and the sites, with modern materials, could be increased.

Animals that live on something that we could not use as food—forage growing in rough country, straws and other residues, phytoplankton and other forms of marine organic matter—cannot properly be said to have a "conversion efficiency." We either use an animal converter or these materials are wasted. Efficiency has a real meaning when we consider animals that live either on crops that people could eat or on crops grown on land that could have grown food. The inefficiency of animal conversion, expressed as pounds of protein the animal must eat to make a pound of protein in the animal product that people eat, is much greater than is generally realized. This unawareness probably arises from the tendency among animal feeders to present their results as the ratio of the dry food eaten to the wet weight (including all inedible parts) of the carcass produced. Furthermore, the figures generally relate only to one phase of the animal's life, without allowance for unproductive periods. It is unlikely that the true efficiency of protein conversion is often greater than one pound of food protein for every seven pounds of fodder protein; it is generally less. Although animal products are highly esteemed in most countries, their production is an extravagance when it depends on land or fodder that could have been used to feed people. The extravagance may be tolerated in well-fed countries but not in those that are short of food.

As I have indicated, the world's main food crops need to be supplemented with protein. Peas and beans, which are 25 to 40 percent protein, are traditionally used. Green vegetables and immature flowers are gaining recognition. They can yield 400 pounds of edible protein per acre in a three-to-four-month growing period, but because they contain fiber and other indigestible components a person cannot get more than two or three grams of protein from them in a day. This amount, however, is much more than is normally consumed, and such plants offer a rewarding field for research. The varieties cultivated in industrialized countries are often ill-adapted to other climatic conditions. The work of vegetable improvement that was done in Europe in the 18th and 19th centuries should now be replicated in the wet Tropics. Biochemical control would be needed to ensure that what is being produced is not only nontoxic but also nutritionally valuable. This would be an excellent project for the International Biological Program; the raw materials have worldwide distribution and the need is also worldwide.

The residue that is left when oil is expressed from soya, groundnut, cottonseed and sunflower is now for the most part used as animal feed or fertilizer or is simply discarded. It contains about 20 million tons of protein, that is, twice the world's present estimated deficit. Because its potential value is not yet widely realized, most of this material is at present so contaminated, or damaged by overheating during the expressing of the oil, that it is useless as a source of human food. But methods are being devised, notably in the Indian state of Mysore and in Guatemala, for processing the oilseeds more carefully in order to produce an acceptable food containing 40 to 50 percent protein. The avoidance of damage during processing is not the only problem that arises with oilseeds; each species contains, or may contain, harmful components, for example gossypol in cottonseed, enzyme inhibitors in soya and aflatoxin in peanuts. Gossypol can be extracted or low-gossypol strains of cotton can be used (it is said, however, that these are particularly attractive to insect pests); enzyme inhibitors can be destroyed, and the infestation that produces aflatoxin can be prevented by proper harvesting and storage. The alternative of extracting a purified protein concentrate from the residues is often advocated. This approach seems mistaken; it increases the cost of the protein fivefold. In addition, the process is in the main simply the removal of starch or some other digestible carbohydrate, and carbohydrate has to be added to the protein concentrate again during cooking.

The residue left after expressing oil from an oilseed can be used because it contains little fiber. Coconuts and the leaves from many species of plants are also potential protein sources, but they contain so much fiber that it is essential to separate the protein if more than two or three grams is being eaten each day. The process of separation, although simple, is still in its infancy, and many improvements remain to be made. Units for effecting it are working in Mysore, at the Rothamsted Experimental Station and elsewhere. In wet tropical regions the conventional seed-bearing plants often do not ripen, but coconuts thrive and leaves grow exuberantly. It is in these

TANKS ARE FILLED WITH LITTLE FISH from a truck (*left*) at a fish meal plant in the Peruvian port of Callao. The fish are anchovetas, a variety of anchovy. By grinding and solvent extraction they are converted into a product that contains 80 percent protein.

BAGS OF FISH MEAL are piled in the yard of the same plant. Fish meal is currently used primarily as a supplement to feed for domestic animals. In 1965 Peru harvested 7.46 million metric tons of fish, a catch that makes it the world's leading fishing nation.

regions that protein separation has its greatest potentiality.

The protein sources discussed in the last two paragraphs would be opened up by handling conventional agricultural products in unusual ways. Attention is also being given to completely novel forms of production based on photosynthesis by unicellular algae and other microorganisms. The early work was uncritical and, considering the small increases in the rate of fixation of carbon dioxide given by these methods compared with conventional agriculture, the necessary expenditure on equipment was out of proportion. It is an illusion to think that algae have any special photosynthetic capacity. Their merit is that it is much easier to spread an algal suspension, rather than a set of slowly expanding seedlings, uniformly over a sunlit surface so as to make optimal use of the light. Recently more realistic methods, using open tanks and the roofs of greenhouses in which other plants can be grown during the winter, have been tried in Japan and Czechoslovakia. The product resembles leaf protein in many ways but contains more indigestible matter because the algal cell walls are not removed; it may prove possible either to separate the protein from the cell walls or to digest the walls with enzymes.

All the processes discussed so far depend on what might be called current photosynthesis. Microorganisms that do not themselves photosynthesize can produce foodstuffs from the products of photosynthesis in the immediate past (straw, sawdust or the by-product liquor from leaf-protein production) or in the remote past (petroleum, coal or methane). The former substrates would have to be collected over a wide area, whereas the latter are concentrated in a few places and so lend themselves to convenient large-scale industrial processing. At first sight this seems advantageous, and in fact it would be so were we merely concerned with increasing the amount of food in the world. That will be the problem later; now the important thing is, as I have said, to make food where the mouths are, and elaborate and sophisticated techniques are not well adapted to this end. The most valuable aspect of the research now being done in many countries on microbial growth on fossil substrates such as petroleum is that it will familiarize people with the idea of microbial food and so will hasten its acceptance when it is produced from local materials.

Finally, there is synthetic food. Plants make fats and carbohydrates so economically that it is unlikely synthesis could be cheaper. Many of the abundant plant proteins do not have an amino acid composition ideally suited to human needs. These proteins are sometimes complementary, so that the deficiencies of each can be made good by judicious mixing. When this is not possible, the deficient amino acids can be synthesized or made by fermentation and then added to the food. Production of amino acids for this purpose will probably be possible only in industrialized countries; their use may therefore seem to violate the principle that food must be where the mouths are. The quantities needed, however, are small. It is obviously better to upgrade an abundant local protein by adding .5 percent of methionine to it rather than import a whole protein to make up this one deficiency.

The food that is now needed or that will soon be needed in the underprivileged parts of the world might be supplied by charity, by the extension of existing methods of agriculture or by novel processes. I have argued that the first cannot be satisfactory and that it would be dangerous to assume that the second will suffice. Without wishing in any way to minimize the importance of what is being done in these two directions, it seems necessary to take novelties seriously. By definition a novelty is novel. That is to say, it may have an unfamiliar appearance, texture or flavor. In commenting on any of the proposals made—the use of strange animals, oilseed residues or leaf and microbial protein—it is irrelevant to say that they are unfamiliar. If the world is to be properly fed, products such as these will probably have to be used. Our problem is to make them acceptable.

Socrates, when one of his companions said he had learned little by foreign travel, replied: "That is not surprising. You were accompanied by yourself." Similarly, food technologists, accustomed to the dietary prejudices of Europe and the U.S., are apt to project their prejudices onto other communities. They have two opposite obsessions: to fabricate a "chewy" texture in their product and to produce a bland stable powder with an indefinite shelf life. Neither quality is universal in the familiar foods of most of the world. The former may have merits, although these probably do not outweigh the extra difficulties involved. It is odd that, at a time when people in industrialized countries are beginning to revolt against uniform and prepacked foods, we should be bent on foisting the latter quality off on others. Instead, novelties should be introduced into regions where they will most smoothly conform with local culinary habits. Novel forms of fish and mollusks are probably well adapted to Southeast Asia, where fermented fish is popular. Leaf, oilseed or microbial protein would fit smoothly into a culture accustomed to porridge, gruel and curry. It is important to remember the irrational diversity of our tastes. Even in Europe and the U.S. a flavor and appearance unacceptable in an egg is acceptable in cheese, a smell unacceptable in chicken is acceptable in pheasant or partridge, and a flavor unacceptable in wine is acceptable in grapefruit juice. These things are a matter of habit, and habits, although they will not change in a day or even a month, can readily be changed by suitable example and persuasion. The essential first step is to find out what is meant by the word "suitable."

Enough experience is now accumulating for us to define the parameters of success. The four most important are:

First, research on the novelty should be done privately and completely, so that when popularization starts there can be no rationally based doubts about the merits of the product.

Second, the novelty should manifestly be eaten by the innovators themselves. It is folly to ask people to practice what we only preach—we must practice it ourselves.

Third, example is the main factor leading to a change in habits; it is therefore essential to get the support of influential local people—from film stars to political leaders. Care should be taken that the first users are not underprivileged groups (prisoners, refugees and so on), because the stigma will not easily be removed.

Last, an adequate and regular supply of the product should be assured before there is any publicity, because it is hard to reawaken interest that has waned because the product is not obtainable.

All these proposals, except that of the simplest form of agricultural extension, call for research. It is worth considering who should do it and what form opposition is likely to take. Opposition to innovation is an interesting and underinvestigated part of psychopathology. It takes three main forms: total, quasi-logical and "instant."

Total opposition is the denial of the problem. Even today there are those who, in the course of condemning some specific proposal, sometimes deny that a protein shortage exists or is impending. This is a point that should be settled at the very beginning: "Do we have a problem or not?" Fortunately for research, and for humanity, the international agencies are in agreement that we do.

Quasi-logical opposition comes from economists. They may accept the problem but argue that some proposed solutions will be too expensive. There are two relevant questions: "Compared with what?" and "How do you know when it has not been tried?" When there are several equally feasible methods for getting the extra food that is needed in a region, a comparison of their probable costs is obviously worthwhile. But when all costs are, for various reasons, unknown, the exercise becomes futile because assumptions play a larger part in it than rigid economic argument, and scientists are better qualified than economists to make the assumptions; they know more of the facts, are aware of more possibilities and are less subject to romantic illusion.

"Instant opposition" arises because innovators are apt to irritate right-minded people, and enthusiasm invites skepticism. The innovator must therefore expect to run into trouble. When someone made the old comment that genius was an infinite capacity for taking trouble,

MUSSELS ARE GROWN in this floating "park" in Vigo Bay on the northwestern coast of Spain. Suspended from each of the large anchored raftlike structures are ropes on which the mussels are seeded and grow to maturity (*see photograph on opposite page*).

Samuel Butler replied: "It isn't. It is an infinite capacity for getting into trouble and for staying in trouble for as long as the genius lasts." In an attenuated form the principle applies even when genius is not involved. There are many different ways of getting into trouble, and it is as naïve and illogical to assume that an idea must be correct because it is meeting opposition as it is to take "instant opposition" seriously.

The governments of countries with a food shortage know that, for a decade at least, more people will be better fed if money is spent on importing food rather than on setting up a research project on means to make more food from local products for local consumption. The more farsighted statesmen realize that ultimately the research will have to be done, but it is hard to resist political pressure, and resistance is hampered by the high cost of primitive agriculture. In a market in New Guinea local sweet potatoes cost three times as much per calorie as imported wheat, and fresh fish cost twice as much per gram of protein as canned fish. So poor countries are hardly likely to mount research projects.

At the other extreme are the giants of private enterprise. They already do very well selling soft drinks and patent foods in underdeveloped countries, and their skill in creating a market, regardless of the real merits of their product, is unrivaled. Thus baby foods, which few experts regard as superior to mother's milk, were used in Uganda by 42 percent of the families in 1959, whereas only 14 percent had used them in 1950. Undoubtedly there are efficient firms that operate with strict integrity, and a few of them have ventured into the production of low-cost protein-rich foods. After the necessary research and preliminary publicity had been done with money from international sources, the Quaker Oats Company has done a masterly job in making, distributing and popularizing Incaparina (maize, sorghum and cottonseed) in Central America. And skilled advertising increased the sales of Pronutro (soya, peanuts and fish) tenfold in two years. Other attempts have failed because the possible profit, when one is selling to poor people without misleading them with meretricious advertising, is too small to cover the costs of the preliminary educational campaign. That, as I have suggested, can be managed only with the cooperation of governments and the local leaders of opinion.

Large-scale private enterprise will probably not find this activity lucrative, and from some points of view the methods of production that would be used may not be desirable. Already more than a third of the world's city population (12 percent of the total population) live in shantytowns on the fringes of cities, and rural depopulation is accelerating. This, together with transport difficulties, makes it at least arguable that research attention should be focused on simple techniques adapted for use in a large village or small town, rather than on fully industrialized techniques. The latter have their place, but they should not become our exclusive concern.

If neither the governments of needy countries nor private enterprise is likely to undertake the necessary research and development, it remains for the governments of industrialized countries, the international agencies and the foundations. So far these groups have been reluctant to admit that any radical changes in research policy will be needed, but times are changing. The novelties are now at least mentioned by the F.A.O. even if only to be gently damned with a few misstatements. On the Barnum principle, "I don't care what people say about me so long as they talk about me," this is a step forward. The governments of wealthy countries supply most of the support for the international agencies, they support other forms of aid, and much knowledge that is of use in poorer countries is an international by-product of their more parochial research. They may feel that they are already doing their share. Our best hope must therefore lie with the foundations. Several institutes of food technology are needed to undertake fundamental and applied research on the production of food from local products for local consumption. At least one of the institutes should be in the wet Tropics and all should give particular attention to protein sources. Using locally available material, each institute should study all the types of raw material discussed here. This will ensure that similar criteria are applied to all of them and that the assessment of their merits is made objectively and is not colored by interinstitutional rivalry. These institutes should also be responsible for work on the presentation and popularization of the products made. It may be that an extension of normal agriculture will meet the world's food needs for a few more years, but ultimately more radical research will be needed. It would be prudent to start it before the need is even more pressing than it is at present.

ROPE COVERED WITH MUSSELS is lifted from the water after mussels are mature.

MARINE FARMING

GIFFORD B. PINCHOT
December 1970

Man gets food from the sea essentially by hunting and gathering. Yet the farming of fish and shellfish has been pursued for some 2,000 years, and its potentialities are far from being exhausted

A major concern of modern man is the possibility that the earth will not be able to produce enough food to nourish its expanding population. A particularly controversial issue is the question of how much food can ultimately be obtained from the sea. It is argued on the one hand that, on the basis of area, the oceans receive more than twice as much solar energy—the prime source of all biological productivity—as the land. This suggests that the oceans' potential productivity should greatly exceed the land's. On the other hand, most of the sea is biologically a desert. Its fertile areas are found where runoff from the land or the upwelling of nutrient-rich deep water fertilizes the surface water and stimulates the growth of marine plants, the photosynthetic organisms on which all other marine life depends. Even at today's high level of exploitation the fisheries of the world provide only a small fraction of human food needs, and there is some danger that they may supply even less in the future because of overfishing.

Does this mean that there is no hope of increasing our yield of food from the sea? I do not think so. It does mean, however, that instead of concentrating exclusively on more efficient means of fishing we must also learn to develop the potential of the oceans by farming them, just as early man learned that farming rather than hunting was the more effective method of feeding a human population. The purpose of this article is to examine briefly the contribution marine farming now makes to our food supply, and to consider some possibilities for its future role.

Marine farming has a long history. The earliest type of farming was the raising of oysters. Laws concerning oyster-raising in Japan go back to well before the time of Christ. Aristotle discusses the cultivation of oysters in Greece, and Pliny gives details of Roman oyster-farming in the early decades of the Christian Era. By the 18th century the natural oyster beds in France were beginning to be overexploited and were saved only by extensive developments in rearing practices.

Carp (*Cyprinus carpio*) were commonly raised in European freshwater ponds in both Roman and medieval times. Records concerning the regulation of salt or brackish ponds for raising milkfish (*Chanos chanos*) in Java date back to the 15th century. Carp and milkfish are both herbivores that thrive on a diet of aquatic plants. Oysters, as filter-feeders, can also be loosely classified as herbivores.

Oysters are particularly appropriate for marine farming because their spawn can be collected and used for "seeding" new areas of cultivation. An oyster produces more than 100 million eggs at a single spawning. The egg soon develops into a free-swimming larval form, known as a veliger, which settles to the bottom after two or three weeks. Veligers attach themselves to any clean surface and develop into miniature adult oysters, called "spat" because oystermen once believed the adult oysters spat them out. At this point the oyster farmer enters the picture. He distributes a supply of "cultch": clean material with a smooth, hard surface, such as old oystershell or ceramic tile. The cultch receives a "set" of spat and is then used to seed new oyster beds.

The bottom is prepared for seeding by removing as many natural enemies of the oyster as possible. In the eastern U.S. this is usually done by dragging a rope mat along the bottom to sweep the area clear of starfish, one of the major predators. In France, where more intensive labor is employed, the spat are usually planted on the exposed bottom of an estuary at low tide. The predators are removed by hand and the oyster bed is fenced to prevent their return. The oysters are moved after a few years to *claires*, special fattening areas where the water is rich in diatoms. This produces oysters of improved taste and color. When the oysters have reached marketable size, they are moved again to shallower water, where they must stay closed for longer periods at low tide. The French oystermen believe this treatment prepares the oysters for their trip to the market.

A significant advance in oyster-farming is the use of suspension cultures. This method, pioneered in Japan, is now spreading to the rest of the world. The spat are collected on shells that are strung in long bundles and immersed in tidal water. The strings, which do not touch the bottom, are sometimes attached to stakes but more generally are attached to rafts. The suspension method has a number of advantages over growth on the bottom. The oysters are protected from predators and from silting, and they feed on the suspended food in the entire column of water rather than being limited to what reaches the bottom. The result is faster growth, rounder shape and superior flavor.

In small areas of Japan's Inland Sea suspension cultures of oysters annually yield 46,000 pounds of shucked meats per acre of cultivated area. This does not mean that one can multiply the total acreage of the Inland Sea by this figure to estimate the potential productivity of the area. Tidal flow allows the anchored oysters to filter much larger volumes of water than surround them at any given time. In addition, inshore waters are generally more productive than those farther from land. The figure does illustrate, however, the production of meat that is possible with our present farming practices in inshore waters.

Luther Blount of Warren, R.I., has tested oyster suspension cultures in Rhode Island waters over the past several years, using spat set on scallop shells. Blount spaces seven scallop shells well apart on each suspension string. At the end of seven months' growth he harvested one group of suspended oysters from 3,200 square feet of float area. The oysters weighed nearly 40,000 pounds and yielded 2,500 pounds of oyster meat. His experience suggests that the coastal waters of the eastern U.S. might yield more than 16,000 tons of meat per square mile of float per year.

Although the farming of oysters in suspension cultures is a comparatively recent development, the same technique has long been used in Europe to raise mussels. The Bay of Vigo is one of the many Spanish ports where acres of mussel floats are a common sight. French and Italian mussel growers are less inclined to use rafts. Their mussel strings are usually suspended from stakes set in the estuary bottom.

John H. Ryther and G. C. Matthiessen of the Woods Hole Oceanographic Institution have studied the yields obtained by the mussel farmers of Vigo. The annual harvest produces an average of 240,000 pounds of mussel meat per acre. This is equivalent to 70,000 tons of meat per square mile of float, or better than four times the yield of oysters in suspension cultures in the U.S. and Japan.

The farming of fish is more difficult than the farming of bivalves for at least two reasons. First, the fish, being motile, must be held in ponds. Second, the saltwater species that are most commonly farmed—milkfish and mullet (*Mugil*)—breed only at sea. This means that the fry have to be caught where and when they occur naturally, and in some years the supply is not adequate. Furthermore, unwanted species and predators have to be sorted out by hand, with the inevitable result that some of both are introduced into the ponds along with the desired species.

In spite of such handicaps pond farm-

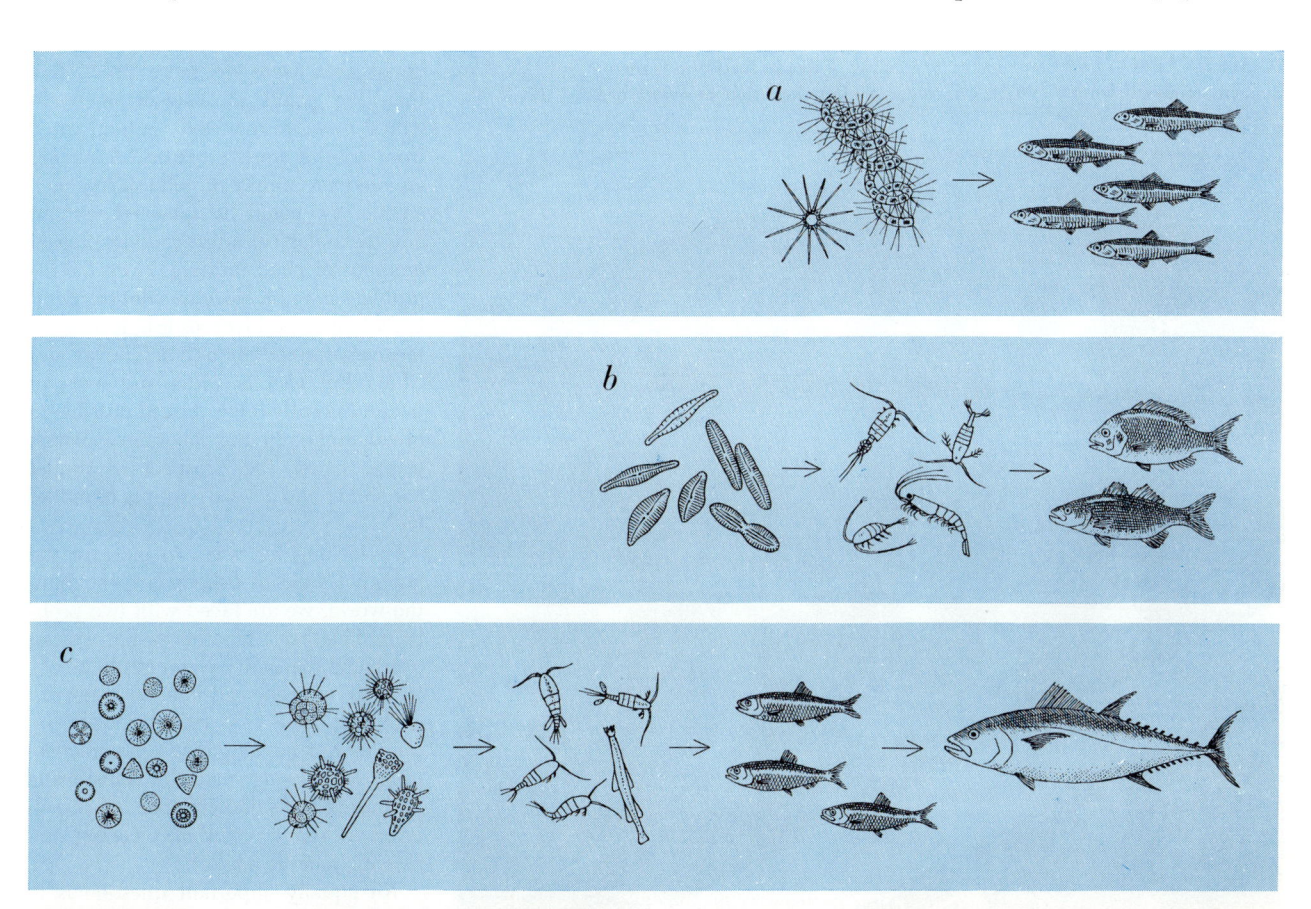

HIGH PRODUCTIVITY of upwelling areas and coastal waters, in contrast to the low productivity of the open sea, is not due only to greater mineral enrichment. In upwelling areas (*a*) the phytoplankton at the bottom of the food chain are usually aggregates of colonial diatoms that are large enough to feed fish of exploitable size. As a result the food chain is very short, with an average of 1.5 steps. The food chain in coastal water (*b*) is longer, averaging 3.5 steps. In the open sea (*c*), where phytoplankton at the bottom of the chain are widely scattered, single-celled diatoms, five steps are needed to produce exploitable fish and the energy transfer at each step is low in efficiency. The length of the chains was calculated by John H. Ryther of the Woods Hole Oceanographic Institution.

OYSTER FARM at Port Stephens in New South Wales in Australia is seen at low tide. The rack-and-stick cultivation system was adopted after depletion of oyster beds in the 1870's.

SUSPENSION CULTURE of young oysters dangles from a float in a Rhode Island oyster pond. Each string supports a series of scallop shells set with oyster spat, a product used commercially for seeding conventional oyster beds. Luther Blount, who is farming the oyster suspension cultures experimentally, has recorded four-year weight gains of 1,000 percent.

ing is remarkably productive. In the Philippine Republic, for example, the annual milkfish harvest is estimated at some 21,000 tons and the productivity of the ponds averages 78 tons per square mile. A comparable estimate for the annual productivity of free-swimming fish in coastal waters, as calculated by Ryther and Matthiessen, falls between six and 17 tons per square mile. In the Philippines, moreover, it is not customary to enrich the pond waters artificially, a process that accelerates the growth of the fishes' plant food. In Taiwan, where milkfish ponds are fertilized, the average annual yield is 520 tons per square mile, and in Indonesia, where sewage is diverted into the ponds in place of commercial fertilizer, the annual yield reaches 1,300 tons per square mile.

Fish farming in Asia is still a long way from reaching its maximum potential. The United Nations Food and Agriculture Organization has calculated that more than 140,000 square miles of land in southern and eastern Asia could be added to the area already devoted to milkfish husbandry. Even if this additional area were no more productive than the ponds of Taiwan, its yield would be more than today's total catch from all the world's oceans. Assuming an adequate supply of milkfish fry, such an increase could be achieved without any technological advance over present methods of pond farming. Even the fry problem may be close to solution. Mullet, a largely herbivorous fish, is now extensively farmed not only in Hawaii and China but also in India and even in Israel. Recently it has proved possible to breed mullet in the laboratory, which brings closer the prospect of mullet hatcheries and a steady supply of mullet fry.

In looking for ways to increase the potential yield of fishponds throughout the world, we are faced with two problems. The first is whether or not we can overcome the sanitary and aesthetic objections to using sewage as a growth stimulant. This is a complex question, but it is worth noting that some practical progress is being made by transferring shellfish from polluted areas to unpolluted ones for a period of "cleaning" before shipment to market.

An equally important question is to what degree commercial fertilizer could increase productivity. Oysters or mussels suspended from rafts in small ponds should provide a simple test organism for such experiments, and they are particularly appropriate because of their high natural yields.

The effect of adding commercial fertilizer to Long Island Sound water has been studied by Victor L. Loosanoff of the U.S. Fish and Wildlife Service. He wanted to produce large amounts of marine plants as food for experiments in rearing oysters and clams. He found marked stimulation of plant growth, but the zooplankton—the marine animals in the water—also grew and ate the plants, thus competing with the shellfish for food. After trying various methods of inhibiting the zooplankton's growth, Loosanoff finally came to the use of pure cultures of the plants, but this would be a very expensive practice on a commercial scale.

The growing of both marine plants and marine animals in a pond could be rewarding, and the zooplankton could be converted from a pest to an asset by adding an organism that feeds on them. Rainbow trout might fill this requirement: they are carnivorous, adapt readily to salt water and are said to grow faster and have a better flavor than when they live in fresh water. In addition they are readily available from hatcheries and have a good market value. To dispose of the inevitable organic debris sinking to the bottom of the pond one might add clams and a few lobsters, since both are in demand and their young are being reared in hatcheries and could be obtained.

It seems to me of the utmost importance that we follow the principles of ecology in our efforts to develop marine farming, by working with nature to establish balanced, stable communities rather than by supporting large single crops artificially, as we do on land, with what are now becoming recognized as disastrous side effects. Perhaps the single most exciting challenge we have in marine farming is this opportunity to make a new start in the production of food, utilizing the ecological knowledge now available.

If the results of the pond experiments are satisfactory, it is technically feasible to consider applying fertilizer to estuaries or even to the open ocean. The mechanical problem here is that the applied fertilizer sinks to the bottom in estuaries and tends to become absorbed by mud, and in the open ocean it simply sinks below the zone where the marine plant life grows. A solution for this problem would be to combine the fertilizer with some floating material that would disintegrate and liberate it slowly. The political and legal problems of controlling the harvest of the crop seem more difficult than the technical one of developing floating fertilizer.

Beyond the continental shelf in the open ocean the surface water is normally poor in nutrients and as barren as any desert on land. As irrigation projects have frequently shown, the addition of water makes the desert bloom. Adding nutrients to the ocean has much the same effect. There is, however, a significant difference between the two measures. The availability of fresh water may ultimately limit our agricultural output on land, but the deep ocean holds an immense supply of nutrients that is constantly being renewed.

The concentration of nitrogen and phosphorus compounds in the ocean reaches its maximum value at depths of from 2,000 to 3,000 feet below the surface. That is well below the region penetrated by sunlight, making the nutrients unavailable for plant growth. What then

ARTIFICIAL PONDS are widely used in Asia to raise fish fry, netted at sea, until they reach edible size. The ponds seen here are in Indonesia, where the use of sewage as fertilizer for pond algae brings a harvest that is equal to 1,300 tons of fish per square mile.

is the practical possibility of bringing these nutrients to the surface? If we were able to do it, would the number of fish increase? The answer to the second question can be found in nature. The upwelling of nutrient-rich deep water occurs naturally in some parts of the ocean, and the world's most productive fisheries are found in these areas. One of the best-known of these is the Peru Current on the west coast of South America. Along the shores of Chile and Peru the southeast trade winds blow the surface water away from the land, with the result that it is replaced by deeper water containing the nutrients needed for plant growth. In 1968, 10.5 million tons of fish—mostly anchovies—were harvested in an area 800 miles long and 30 miles wide along this coast. That is a yield of 440 tons per square mile of ocean surface. If, as seems likely, an equal quantity of fish was taken by predators, it means that this area of natural upwelling approaches the productivity of the heavily fertilized Asiatic fishponds. Incidentally, it far surpasses the production of protein by the raising of cattle on pastureland, which Ryther and Matthiessen give as between 1.5 and 80 tons per square mile.

The Peru Current demonstrates that bringing nutrient-rich water to the surface leads to an enormous increase in fish growth. In fact, the areas of natural upwelling, which comprise only .1 percent of the oceans' surface, supply almost half of the total fish catch, whereas the open oceans, where upwelling does not occur, account for 90 percent of the surface and yield only about 1 percent of the catch. In other words, natural upwelling increases the productivity of the open ocean almost 50,000-fold in terms of fish actually landed.

It would obviously be worthwhile to stimulate upwelling artificially, not only because of the probability of high fish yields but also because the stable ecological communities that inhabit the natural areas of ocean upwelling are models of efficient food production for man, with none of the drawbacks—such as herbicides, pesticides, pollution and excessive human intervention—that such highly productive systems usually entail ashore.

To achieve artificial upwelling we need first some kind of container. Deep water is cold and therefore dense, and without a container it would sink again, taking its nutrients with it. We also need to surround the fish we hope to grow, not only to protect them from predators and to simplify harvesting, but even more important to keep them from being caught by fishermen who have not paid for the upwelling. We also need a land area where the pumping and processing activities can be located and of course a supply of deep water nearby.

There are hundreds of coral atolls in the Pacific and the Indian Ocean that meet these specifications. Rings of coral reef surrounding shallow lagoons, atolls vary in area from less than a square mile to more than 800 square miles. Low islands are often found on the encircling reef, and since atolls are the remains of sunken volcanic peaks topped with coral they are steepsided, with deep water generally less than a mile from the reef itself. The trade winds blow over many of these islands and carry energy enough to bring deep water to the surface; that, after all, is the mechanism in many natural upwelling areas. There is even a built-in stirring system: the trade winds produce a downwind current on the lagoon surface that is matched by a return current near the bottom of the lagoon.

FRESHWATER FISH, the herbivorous carp, has been reared in ponds around the world for more than two millenniums. The carp in the photograph are from a pond in Burma. The 1968 crop of carp and carplike fishes in neighboring China totaled 1.5 million tons.

Given an atoll lagoon filled with nutrient-rich water from the deeps, what kinds of marine plants and animals should be grown in it? Perhaps the simplest procedure would be to leave the passages between lagoon and ocean open and allow nature to take its course in introducing new species. A balanced and stable community such as the one found in the Peru Current might establish itself. If it did not, colonies of plants and fishes from the Peru Current could be introduced in the hope that they could establish themselves in the new location.

Perhaps a crop of suitably large zooplankton such as krill—the shrimplike animals that are the principal food of the baleen whales in the Antarctic—could be raised in a fertilized lagoon. In that case another particularly interesting experiment might be possible. This would be to determine whether or not baleen whales, particularly the now almost vanished blue whales, could adapt to such a restricted environment. A school of blue whales raised in captivity could be regularly culled for a significant yield in meat and edible oil, and at the same time its existence would protect the species from what now seems to be certain extinction.

We know that blue whales migrate into the tropical Pacific to bear their young. The migrants could be followed by attaching radio transmitters to them in Antarctica. Techniques for capturing, transporting and keeping smaller whales have already been worked out. Humpback whales, which are about half the length of blue whales, have been captured at sea by investigators at the Sea Life Park in Hawaii by dropping a net over the whale's head. There is a real possibility that whale farms could be started by capturing pregnant female blue whales and confining them in fertilized atolls.

Artificial upwelling, on a small scale at least, has already been achieved by Oswald A. Roels, Robert D. Gerard and J. Lamar Worzel of the Lamont-Doherty Geological Observatory of Columbia University. They have installed on St. Croix in the Virgin Islands a 3½-inch plastic pipe that extends nearly a mile into the Caribbean, enabling them to pump deep water with a temperature of 40 degrees Fahrenheit into small ponds on shore. They find that selected plant life from the seawater off St. Croix grows 27 times faster in water from the pipe than in water from the surface. They are now exploring the possibilities of feeding a variety of marine herbivores on these artificial blooms.

The Lamont-Doherty group has also

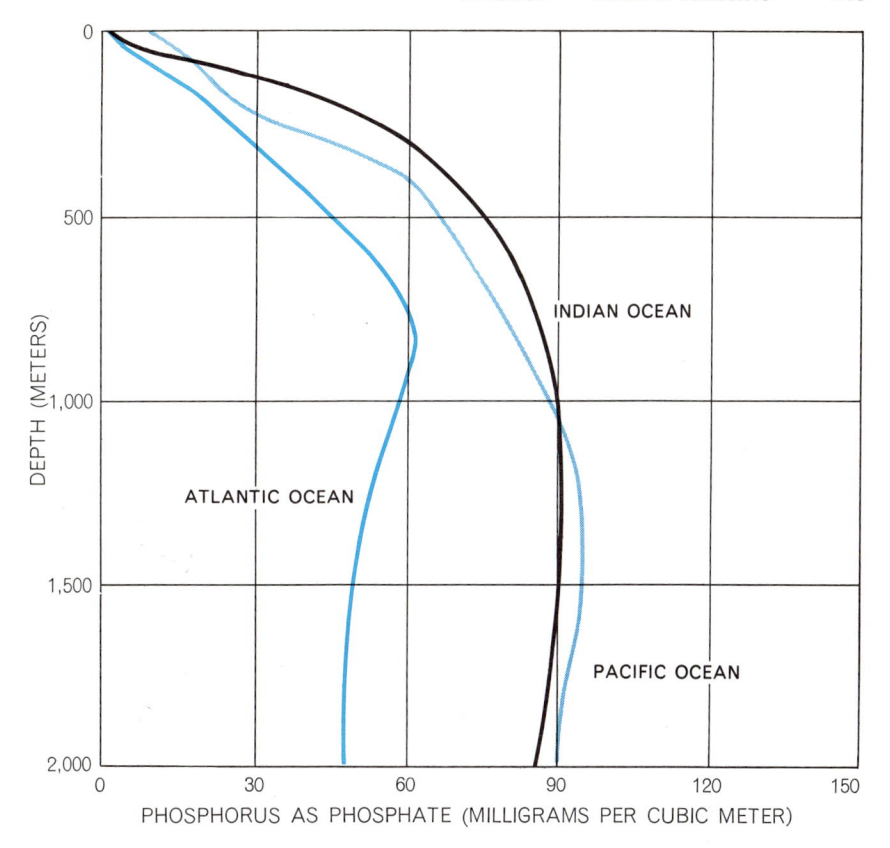

PHOSPHATE IN SEAWATER, present only in small amounts at the surface, increases in the deeper zones and reaches a near-maximum concentration of 90 milligrams per cubic meter in the Pacific and Indian Ocean and about 60 milligrams in the Atlantic at a depth of 1,000 meters. Data are from a study by Lela M. Jeffrey of the University of Nottingham.

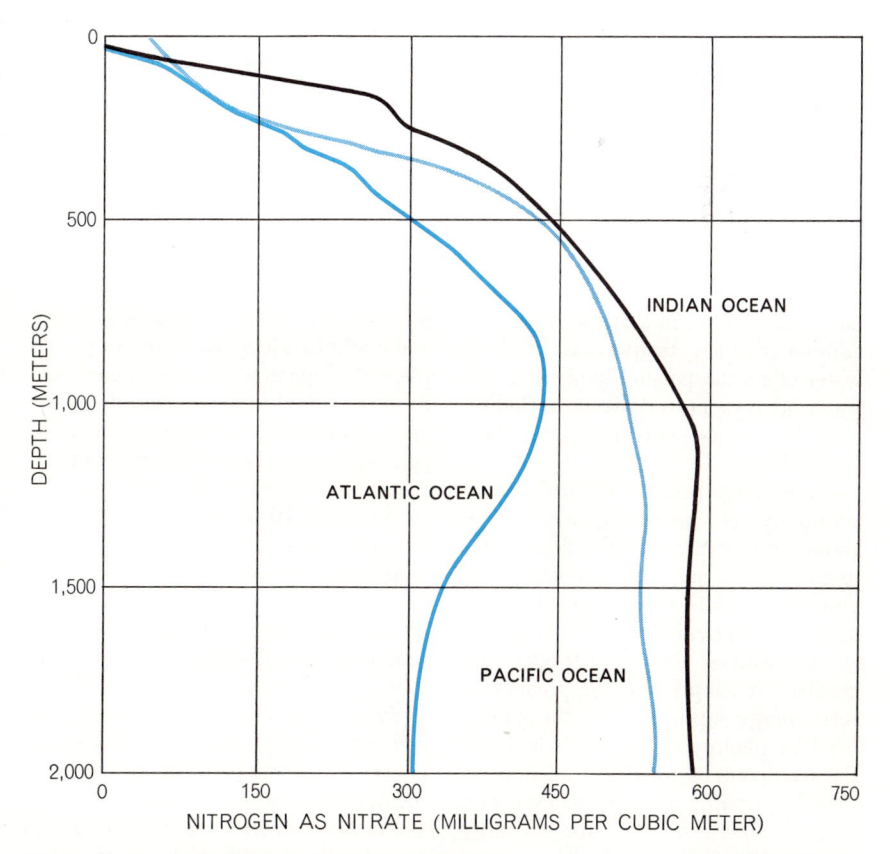

NITRATE IN SEAWATER is also scarce at the surface but approaches its maximum concentration at 1,000 meters. Again the Atlantic has the least; data are from Miss Jeffrey.

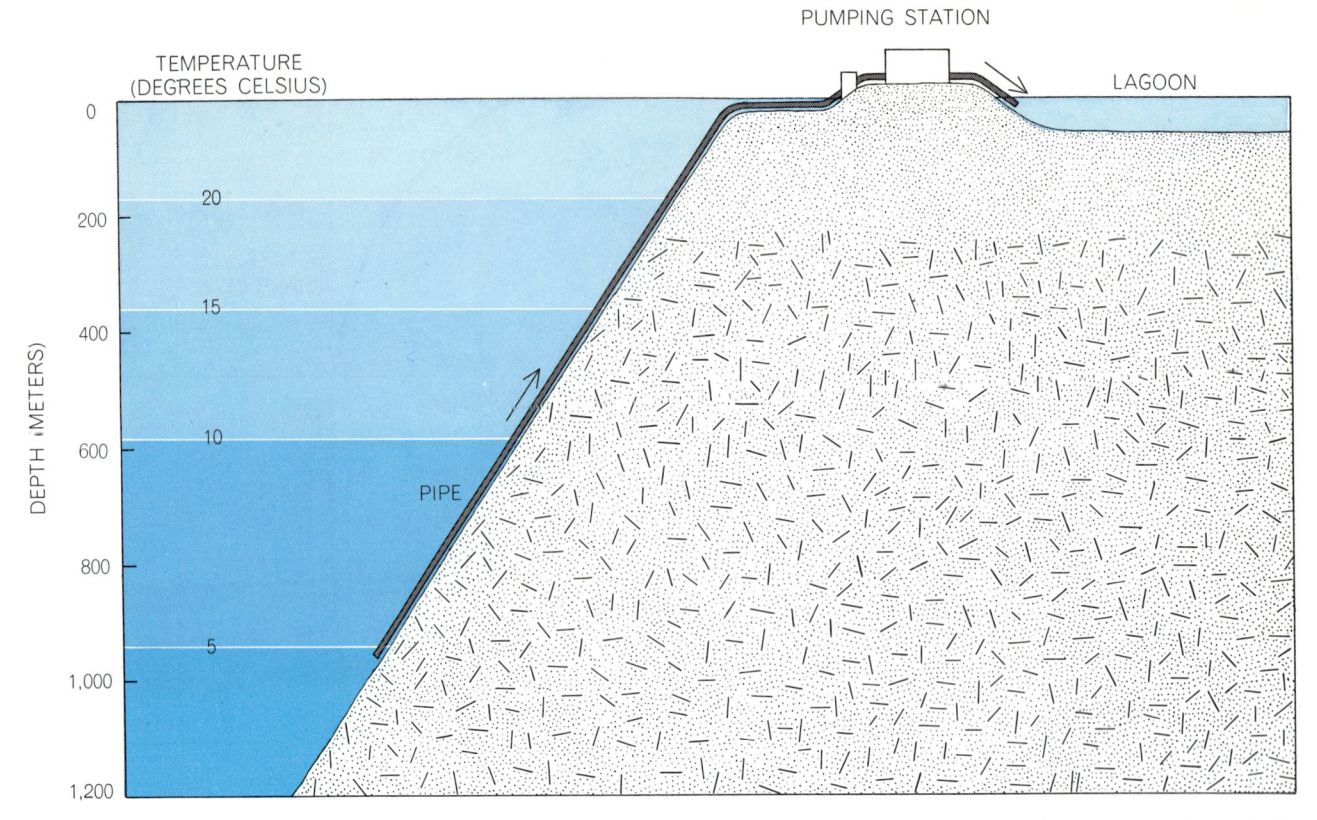

ARTIFICIAL UPWELLING of deep water might be contrived in an atoll setting, as this diagram suggests. The atoll's steep drop to seaward means that the wanted water would be pumped the least possible distance. The central lagoon would provide a catchment basin for the pumped water, retaining its nutrients at or near the surface. The difference in temperature between the surface and the deep water might be used to generate more power than is required for the pumps. A pilot version of this experiment is being conducted by workers in the Virgin Islands, who are pumping deep-sea water ashore and accelerating the growth of phytoplankton in ponds.

pointed out in a recent report that the energy represented by the nearly 40-degree difference in temperature between deep water and surface water can be used for air conditioning, the generation of power and the condensation of fresh water from the atmosphere. (The last idea emerged after observation of the condensation of atmospheric moisture on a Martini glass in a St. Croix bar.) In addition the low temperature of deep water offers the possibility of using the water to cool power plants, including nuclear reactors, without causing thermal pollution.

These fringe benefits, particularly the possibility of producing more than enough power to pump the deep water to the surface, may at first seem to suggest the dream of getting something for nothing. No physical laws would be violated, however; the water-temperature gradient is simply another product of solar-energy input, just as the energy fixed by photosynthetic plants is. From the standpoint of practical economics artificial upwelling may be too expensive to be feasible exclusively for fish farming at the present time. The system seems entirely practical, however, if its cost can be shared with some additional service such as air conditioning or the cooling of power plants.

A less elegant but much cheaper means of enriching the lagoons of atolls would be the addition of commercial fertilizer. To bring an atoll one square mile in area and 30 feet deep to a level of phosphate concentration equal to the level of nutrient-rich deep water would require only about 10 tons of fertilizer and might cost less than $500. In principle, if the lagoon were entirely enclosed, fertilizer would be removed only as the end product of the farming operation. In actual practice, of course, there would be other losses. Even assuming that one recovered only 10 percent of the fertilizer in marketable fish, however, the cost would be only half a cent per pound of fish produced. From the economic point of view this would seem to be a highly practical experiment.

Advances in technology frequently generate further threats to the quality of our already overburdened environment. It is encouraging to realize that the use of deep water from the sea both to stimulate food production and to obtain power or fresh water is a pollution-free process. The deep water returns to the sea at the same temperature and with about the same nutrient concentration as the waters that receive it, without having an adverse effect on either the atmosphere or the ocean. The same is true of the use of commercial fertilizer in atoll lagoons, since the fertilizer is almost wholly consumed in the process. Yet at the same time animal-protein production could be stimulated to a level not yet approached by conventional agriculture. Large areas of our planet could be developed into highly productive marine farms. The time seems ripe for applying the fundamental knowledge we already possess to the practical problems of developing them.

27

HIGH-LYSINE CORN

DALE D. HARPSTEAD
August 1971

As a source of protein for men and other nonruminant animals corn is deficient in the amino acid lysine. This deficiency is now being remedied by the breeding of high-lysine strains

Mankind depends on grain crops for 70 percent of its consumption of protein, the most essential food. For the vast populations of the developing countries, unable to afford the luxury of animal protein, cereal grain is practically the only important source of protein in the daily diet. One of these dietary mainstays is corn; in total world production it is outranked only by rice and wheat, and it is the principal staple in many countries, particularly in the Tropics and sub-Tropics. Advanced countries, notably the U.S., also rely heavily on corn, as it is the main feed used for the production of animal protein in the form of meat, milk and eggs.

Yet corn is a poor source of protein for a single-stomach animal (including animals such as the pig and the chicken as well as man). The protein of corn is not

KERNELS OF HIGH-LYSINE CORN (*left*) are compared with those of a normal tropical flint corn (*right*). The endosperm within the kernels of the high-lysine ear is opaque and floury, whereas the endosperm in kernels of the normal ear is translucent and darker.

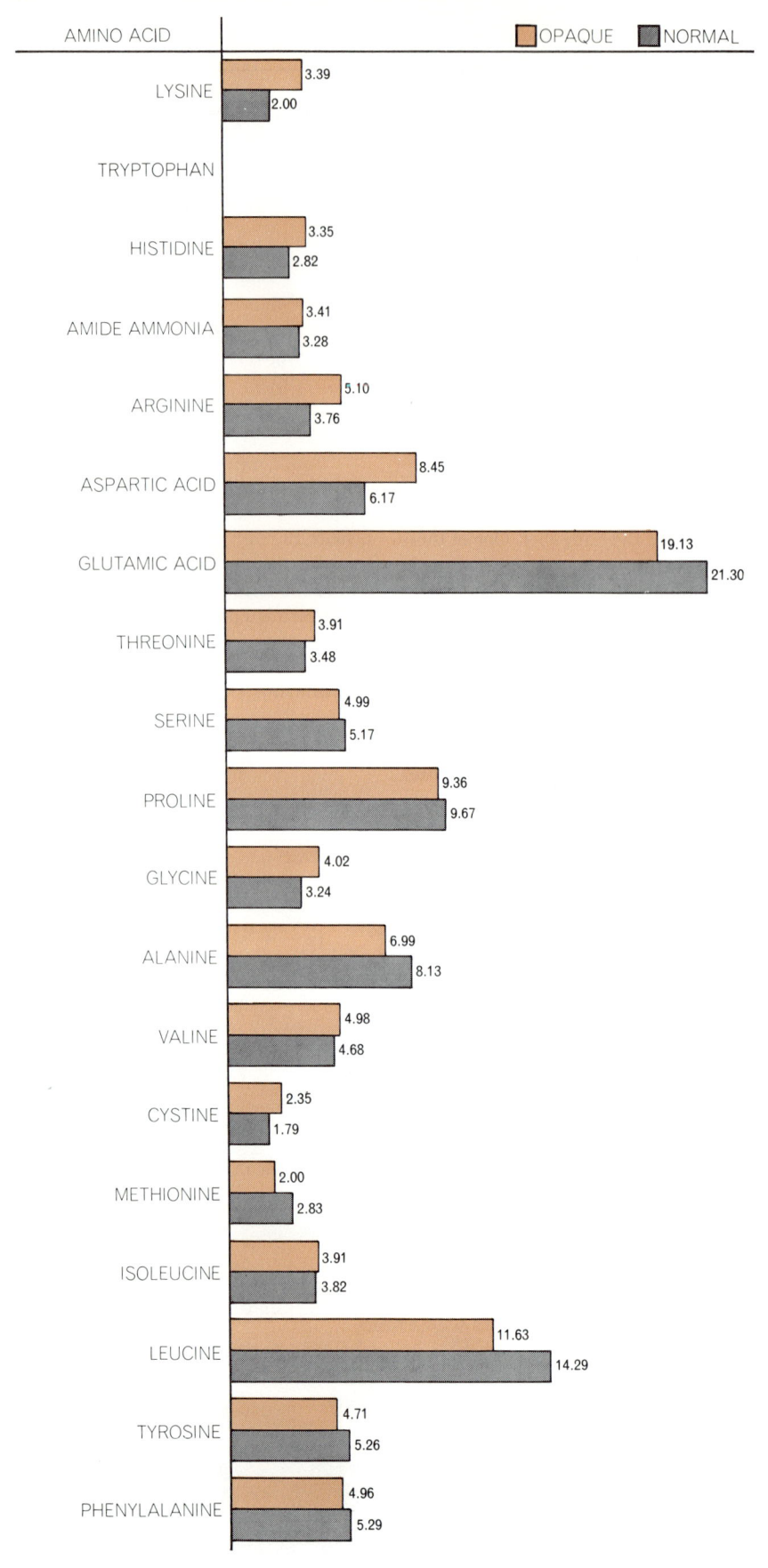

Amino Acid	Opaque	Normal
LYSINE	3.39	2.00
TRYPTOPHAN	—	—
HISTIDINE	3.35	2.82
AMIDE AMMONIA	3.41	3.28
ARGININE	5.10	3.76
ASPARTIC ACID	8.45	6.17
GLUTAMIC ACID	19.13	21.30
THREONINE	3.91	3.48
SERINE	4.99	5.17
PROLINE	9.36	9.67
GLYCINE	4.02	3.24
ALANINE	6.99	8.13
VALINE	4.98	4.68
CYSTINE	2.35	1.79
METHIONINE	2.00	2.83
ISOLEUCINE	3.91	3.82
LEUCINE	11.63	14.29
TYROSINE	4.71	5.26
PHENYLALANINE	4.96	5.29

AMINO ACID CONTENT of endosperm from opaque and normal kernels is tabulated. The units are grams of amino acid per 100 grams of protein. No figures are given for tryptophan because it is destroyed by the hydrolyzing agents used to break protein down into its amino acid units. The measurements were made by Edwin T. Mertz and his colleagues.

only low in quantity (about 10 percent); it is also low in quality as food. About 50 percent of the protein in corn is zein, which cannot be digested by a nonruminant (single-stomach) animal. Corn's most serious deficiency in terms of nutritive value is its low content of lysine, an essential amino acid that man and other nonruminant animals do not synthesize and must obtain from their food.

Many years ago Thomas Burr Osborne and his associates at the Connecticut Agricultural Experiment Station found in experiments with rats that a diet containing corn as the sole source of protein produced obvious signs of malnutrition. They were able to correct the deficiency by supplementing the corn diet with small amounts of lysine and tryptophan, another amino acid that is present in corn only in meager amounts. At the human level the inadequacy of corn as a protein source is shown strikingly by children in countries where corn is the principal food; among these children there exists a high frequency of the protein-deficiency syndrome called kwashiorkor.

Over the decades since Osborne's discoveries plant geneticists have been working to breed varieties of corn with higher protein quality. It has been widely recognized that success in this effort would be a major breakthrough in the worldwide food problem [see the article "A World Agricultural Plan," by Addeke H. Boerma, beginning on page 215]. Up to a few years ago all the breeding efforts met with failure. A high-lysine corn has at last been produced, however, and the breakthrough now seems well under way.

In the 1950's Edwin T. Mertz and Ricardo Bressani of Purdue University began to search for corn variants that might be exceptionally rich in protein. Working with varieties of corn from Central America, they found no significant leads. Oliver E. Nelson, who had been studying starchy mutants of corn, joined the team as a second attempt at protein modification was being planned; the group then turned to certain soft-kernel mutants known as the "opaque" and the "floury" types. The "opaque" mutants were named for the fact that, in contrast to the translucence of kernels in normal corn, the endosperm of these mutants does not transmit light; the "floury" mutants were named for their soft, fine-textured kernels (a property that is also present in the opaque type). The properties are governed by the presence of a recessive gene or genes. In both of these groups of mutants when the homozygous recessive situation prevails (only the recessive form of the gene being present), the endosperm lacks the hard, vitreous body characteristic of ordinary corn, and the kernels look dull and faded in color. These distinctive properties are highly convenient as markers for tracing the gene in breeding experiments.

The Purdue investigators soon turned up a rich find in a gene called "opaque-2" (because it was the second mutant to be discovered in the opaque group, which had been identified and catalogued many years before). Mertz's team found that this gene, when introduced into an ordinary strain of corn, could increase the kernels' lysine content by as much as 69 percent. Shortly afterward they discovered that a gene in the floury series, called "floury-2," also had a similar capability.

The nutritional proteins in corn kernels are classified in four categories according to solubility: (1) albumins, soluble in water; (2) globulins, soluble in saline solutions; (3) prolamines, soluble in moderately strong alcohol, and (4) glutelins, soluble in dilute alkaline solutions. Of these four fractions the dominant ones in "normal" corn are prolamine, which includes zein, accounting for 40 to 55 percent of the protein total, and glutelin, which accounts for about 30 to 35 percent of the protein total and carries all or almost all the endosperm's lysine. By biochemical analysis the Purdue investigators and others established that in kernels modified by the opaque-2 or floury-2 gene the zein fraction was substantially reduced and the glutelin fraction was correspondingly increased. Thus the lysine content of the endosperm was raised from the ratio in ordinary corn (two grams per 100 grams of protein) to a ratio of 3.39 grams per 100 of protein [see illustration on opposite page]. There were also noteworthy increases in tryptophan and several other amino acids.

The Mertz group's discovery of a means of producing high-lysine corn, published in 1964, came as a breath of fresh air to plant breeders and nutritionists. It stirred the imagination of many people who were concerned with the worldwide problem of protein need. The possibility that corn might become an agent for relief of the world hunger for protein appeared to be as important a find as the historic discovery that pellagra could be prevented by niacin.

The new corn was soon put to the test of its actual value in nutrition. Preliminary tests with laboratory rats and pigs, made as soon as supplies of the modified corn seed became available, showed that

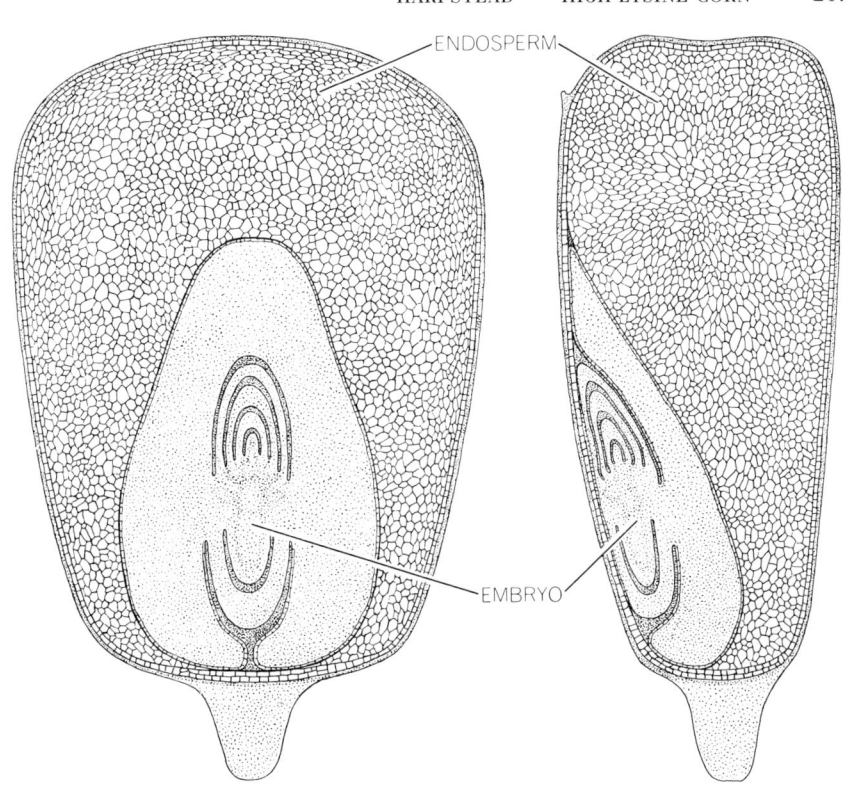

ENDOSPERM OF HIGH-LYSINE KERNEL is shown in longitudinal section (*left*) and transverse section (*right*). The endosperm of the normal kernel is dense at the sides.

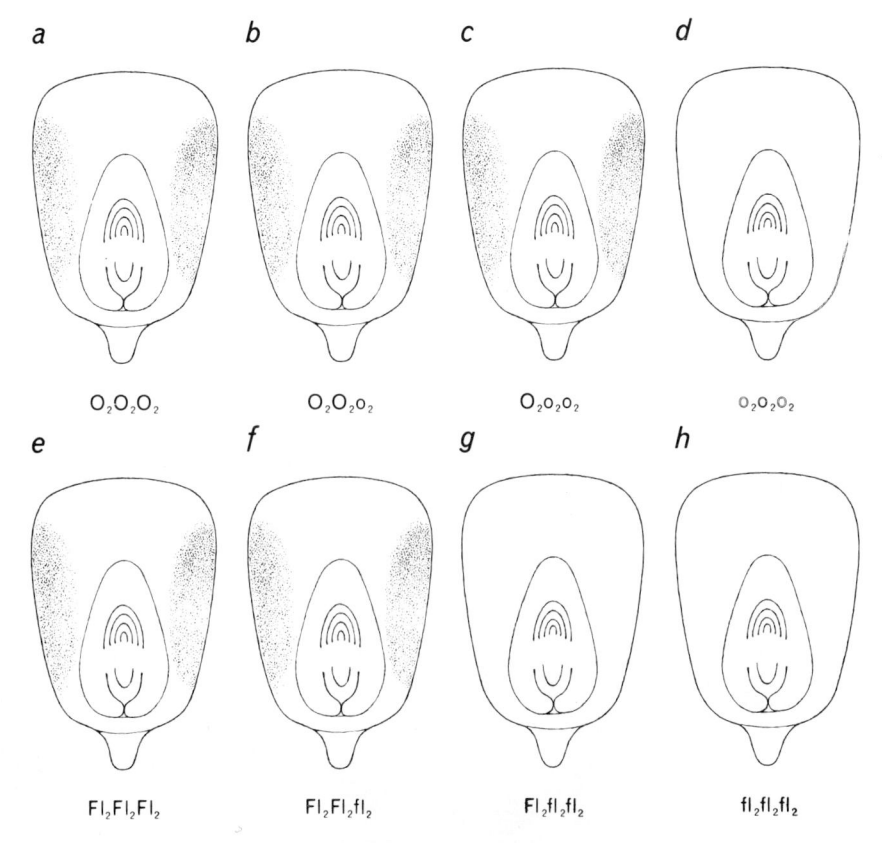

GENES FOR HIGH LYSINE CONTENT are the recessive "opaque" gene (o) and the recessive "floury" gene (fl). The dominant genes at the same loci on the chromosome (O and Fl) are associated with normal endosperm. It takes three doses of the recessive opaque gene to give rise to a high-lysine kernel (*d*) but only two doses of the recessive floury gene (*g and h*). Three genes are involved because endosperm of corn results from what is called double fertilization, so that cell nuclei contain three sets of chromosomes instead of usual two.

the high-lysine corn was indeed a dramatic improvement over ordinary corn as a food. It could be assumed that not all the new corn's improvement in nutritive value was attributable to its increase in lysine content. No doubt the increase in tryptophan also made a significant contribution, and so might some of the other amino acids whose ratio was enhanced. At all events, the change of the protein pattern in opaque-2 and floury-2 corn and the nutritive effects demonstrated that the laboratory discovery had in fact yielded a new product quite unlike "normal" corn.

It was my privilege to be working in Colombia as "quarterback" of a team of investigators—plant breeders, animal nutritionists, physicians, grain millers, government officials—that was seeking to improve the protein yield from plants. We had an ideal situation for exploring the potentialities of the new corn. The Colombian government was greatly interested in the protein problem and was willing to support a bold program for solving it. Our team of diverse talents was able to make full use of the available materials and technology for development of the new discovery. And Colombia's tropical climate and year-round growing season allowed rapid progress in the plant-breeding work.

The first requirement was to breed the new genes into normal corn stocks that were suitable for commercial production, so that large-scale tests could be made of the new product's growth potential and value. The introduction of the genes will itself be a demanding enterprise. Corn is not a monolithic plant; it has many varieties, each adapted genetically to its own locality and the use for which it has been bred. Hence in each case the high-lysine gene will have to be introduced into a stock that fits the locality and desired use. For hybrid corn it will be necessary to insert the high-lysine gene in each of the inbred lines that make up the parent stock [see the article "Hybrid Corn," by Paul C. Mangelsdorf, beginning on page 105].

Using as stocks the locally adapted varieties of hybrid corn in Colombia, we proceeded to transfer the opaque-2 or floury-2 gene into the inbred lines by the standard technique of backcrossing. By cross-pollination, selection of the daughter plants found to be carrying the desired gene and repeated crossing back onto the original stock one finally obtains, usually after five or six generations, a seed that carries the new gene and in other respects nearly duplicates the characteristics of the original line. In the case of the high-lysine genes one has the great advantage of detecting the presence of the gene at each passage just by

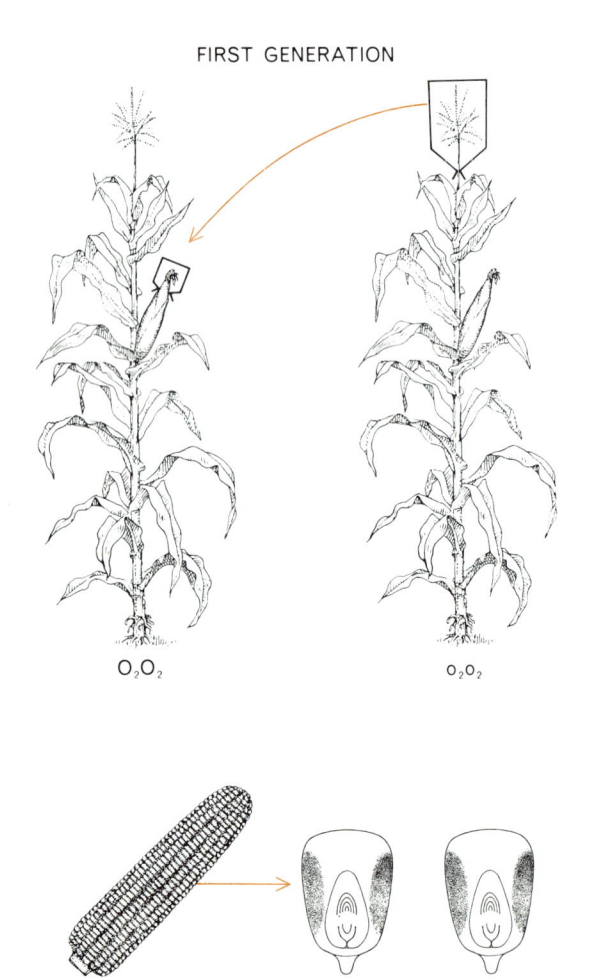

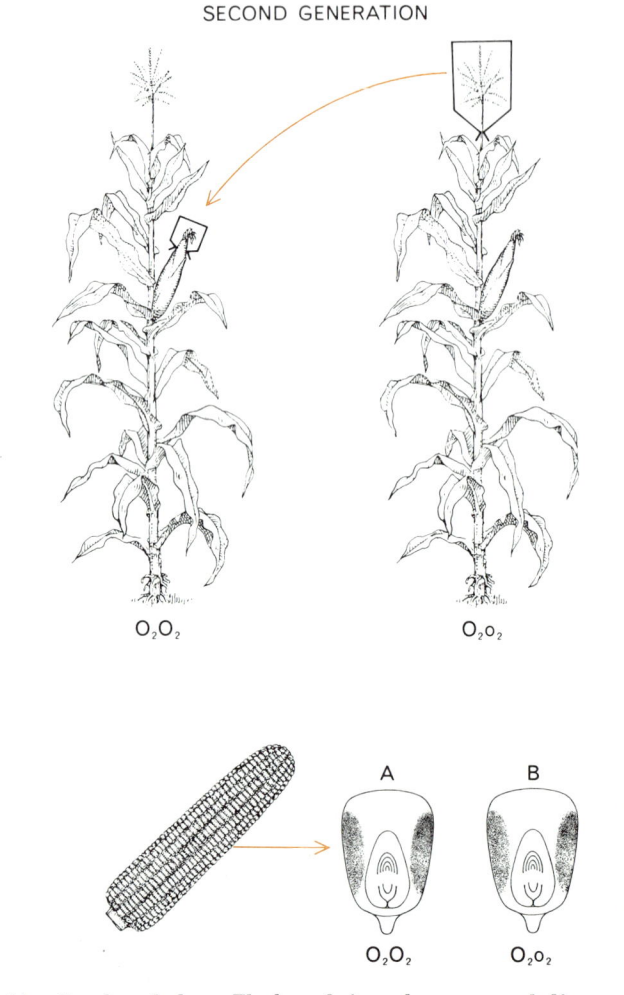

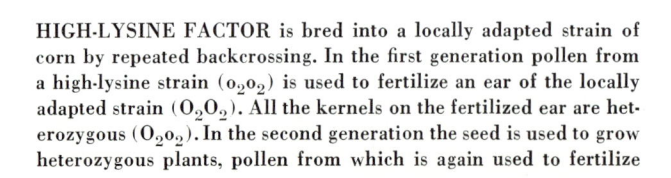

HIGH-LYSINE FACTOR is bred into a locally adapted strain of corn by repeated backcrossing. In the first generation pollen from a high-lysine strain (o_2o_2) is used to fertilize an ear of the locally adapted strain (O_2O_2). All the kernels on the fertilized ear are heterozygous (O_2o_2). In the second generation the seed is used to grow heterozygous plants, pollen from which is again used to fertilize ears of locally adapted plants. The kernels from these ears are half homozygous for the local strain (O_2O_2) and half heterozygous (O_2o_2), but there is no difference in appearance between them. In the third generation the homozygous seed (A) and the heterozygous (B) are used to grow new plants. When pollen from one of these plants is used to fertilize one of its own ears, the appearance of the

visual examination, since it shows its presence by producing soft, floury kernels. With this marker present, one knows that the kernels carry the improved protein without having to make a chemical analysis or biological assay. A technique involving both cross-pollination and self-pollination of the male parent makes it easy to identify plants that will transmit the recessive gene [*see illustration below*].

By January, 1967, we had enough high-lysine corn to start large-scale trials of its nutritional effects. For tests in animals the pig is a most useful subject: its digestive system is very similar to man's, its feeding requirements are well known, and these requirements are themselves a matter of great interest because the development of a low-cost, high-quality feed for hogs would have considerable economic importance. The complex mixed feeds used for hog-raising are costly.

The effect of a given feed on the pig can be measured rather quickly and precisely, as there are well-established standards. A pig raised on an adequate, balanced diet will reach a weight of 200 pounds (90 kilograms) in 156 days. Its growth is defined in two stages: rapid early body-building, up to a weight of 110 pounds (50 kilograms), and the "finishing" stage of fattening to 200 pounds. Richard A. Pickett of Purdue had already found in preliminary tests of the new corn that piglets grew three and a half times faster on high-lysine corn than on normal corn as the sole protein source. The ratio of units of feed required per unit of weight gain was only 3.3 to one for the high-lysine corn as against seven to one for normal corn. And young pigs did about as well on high-lysine corn as on a mixed feed of normal corn and soybean meal supplying the same amount of nitrogen. The Purdue investigators went on to test high-lysine corn as a finishing feed and got essentially the same comparative results. During this stage, when the pig's growth rate is not quite as rapid, the pigs on high-lysine corn grew 50 percent faster than those on normal corn without a supplement.

In Colombia, Jerome Maner of our team in collaboration with members of the Colombian animal husbandry institute set out on a systematic study of the comparative effectiveness of high-lysine corn as measured against normal corn with various amounts of protein supplement. They tested the experimental diets with weanling pigs 35 days old and weighing 20 pounds. After 130 days it was found that the pigs on high-lysine corn had gained 73.2 pounds (an average of 256 grams per day) whereas the

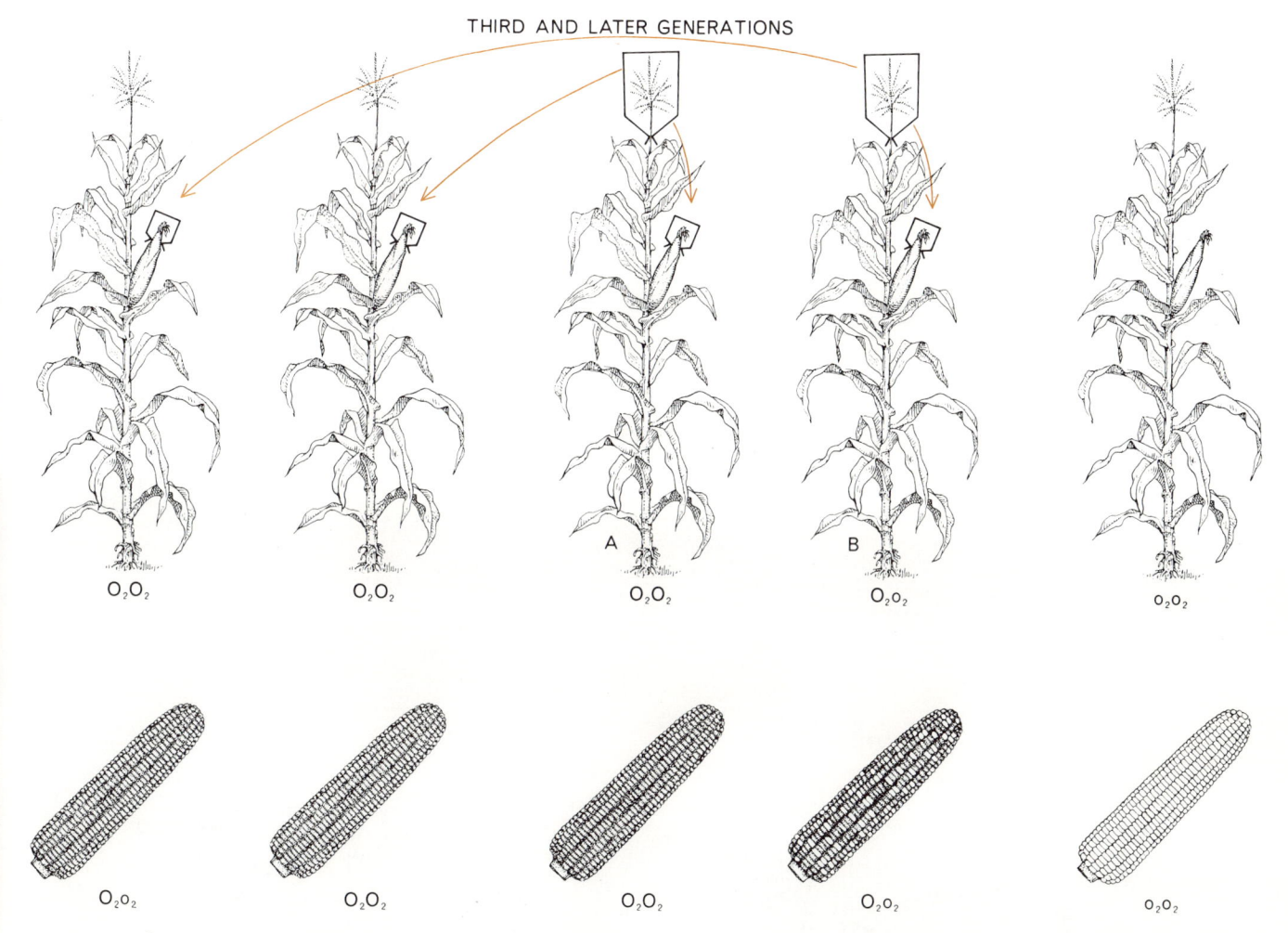

THIRD AND LATER GENERATIONS

ear now indicates whether it is homozygous or heterozygous. The kernels of the homozygous ear all look the same, and the ear is discarded. Moreover, now that it is known that the plant is homozygous, the ears from backcrossing of the same plant and the homozygous locally adapted plants can also be discarded. The kernels on the ear of the self-fertilized heterozygous plant, however, segregate into normal kernels and the opaque high-lysine kernels; the ratio of segregation is three normal kernels to one opaque kernel. After five or six generations of backcrossing, which is necessary to ensure that most of the other genes are those of the locally adapted strain of corn, opaque seed from the segregated ears can be used to grow plants that are homozygous for the high-lysine factor (*far right*).

weight gain of pigs on unsupplemented normal corn was only 6.6 pounds (21 grams per day). Even the high-lysine corn supplies substantially less protein than an optimal diet for pigs. Nevertheless, the pigs fed the new corn were healthy, were normal in general bodily appearance and were inferior to optimally fed animals only in a slight lack of development in some internal tissues. On the other hand, the pigs on the diet of normal corn without supplement showed atrophy of essential organelles within the cells, stunting of the skeletal system and fatty degeneration of the liver tissues. These defects in the pigs were similar to those found in human beings who have suffered severe and prolonged protein deficiency.

The series of tests conducted by Maner and his associates demonstrated that the weight gain achieved with high-lysine corn fell substantially short of that produced by an optimal feed of corn and soybean meal supplying a balance of essential nutrients and protein at the 16 percent level (including nonusable as well as usable protein). There is practical wisdom, however, in a Spanish proverb that says, "The best is an enemy of the better"—meaning that reaching for the unattainable may sometimes thwart improvement. In most of the developing countries to discuss optimal diets for man or animal is in fact utopian, as far as large segments of the population are concerned. In Colombia, for example, the availability of fish meal or soybean meal as a corn supplement is limited and cannot be counted on. Enriched feeds for pigs are beyond the economic reach of the small farmer. Therefore our research has focused on the objective of using high-lysine corn to obtain a high yield of

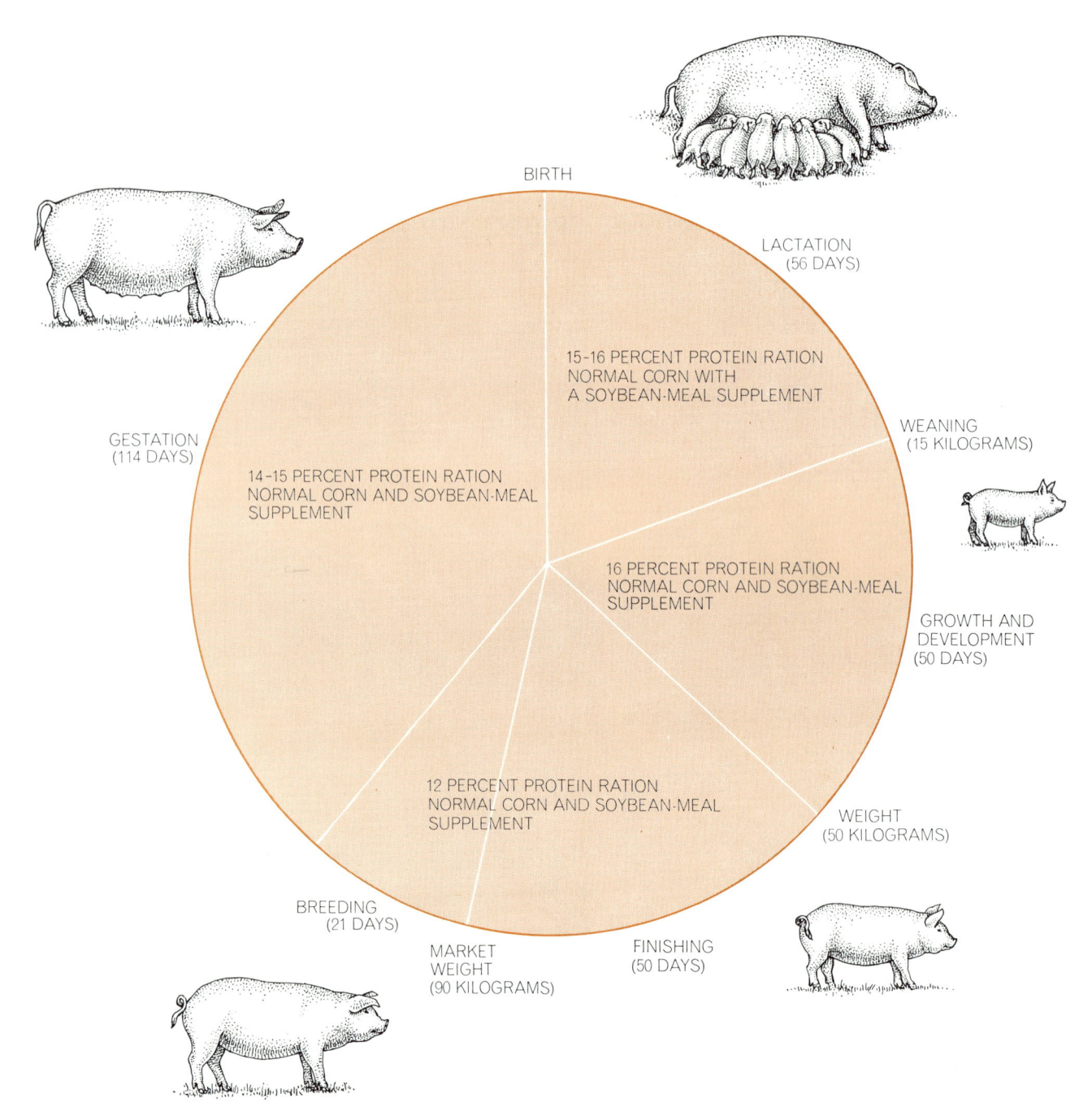

SIMPLIFIED SYSTEM OF PORK PRODUCTION based on high-lysine corn has been developed at the International Center of Tropical Nutrition in Colombia and at several major universities in the U.S. At left is the system based on normal corn; a suitable pro-

meat production with a minimum of supplementation of the corn by imported or costly products. A system using only a small supplement of soybean meal during the growth period and no supplement at all during finishing has worked well, yielding the standard weight achieved by well-fed pigs after 156 days [*see illustration below*]. Similar results have been demonstrated at experiment stations and farms in the U.S.; the economic savings are less striking there, however, because of the ready availability of soybean meal.

Even before the nutrition studies with animals were completed, Alberto G. Pradilla of Colombia recognized the significance of an improved corn protein and began investigations of its characteristics. His work has paralleled the research on the use of high-lysine corn for farm animals, and it has included highly rewarding studies of the value of high-lysine corn as a food for man. The team of physicians working under Pradilla at the University of Valle began in 1967 a series of trials of the new corn for the treatment of malnourished children. They used a diet, previously tested in laboratory animals, that was made up mainly of high-lysine corn with a small supplement of proteins from milk or vegetables. Their first patients were two children, aged five and six, who were suffering from third-degree malnutrition and were under intensive care in the university hospital. The youngsters had been so severely undernourished that their anthropometric development was less than that of a 24-month-old child. On the corn diet they rapidly recovered vital functions, and within 90 days they were showing excellent absorption and retention of nitrogen.

Encouraged by this success, the physi-

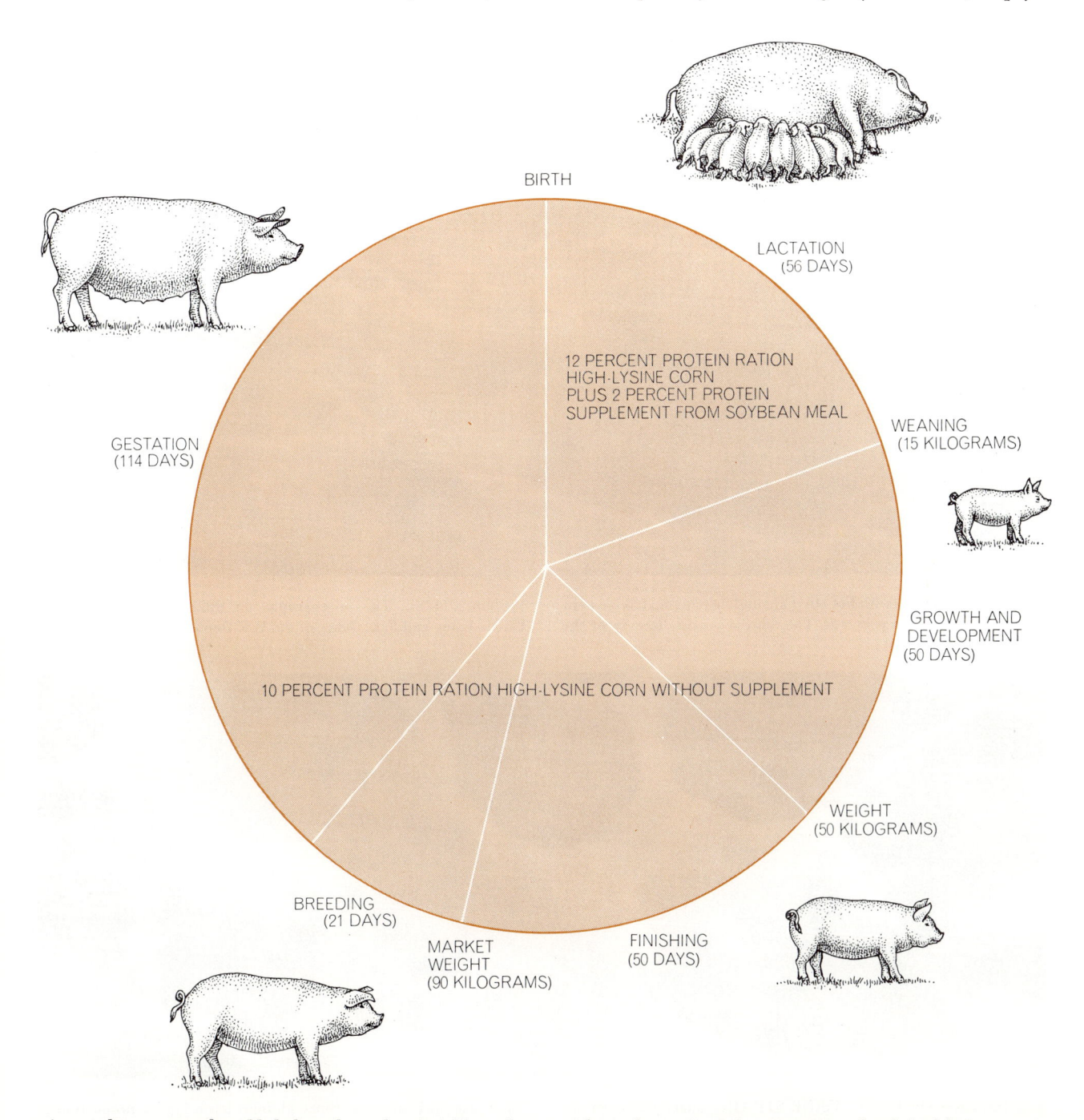

tein supplement must be added throughout the pigs' life cycle. At right is the system based on high-lysine corn; high-lysine corn with supplement is used at one stage and only high-lysine corn is required at all the other stages in the life cycle of the animals.

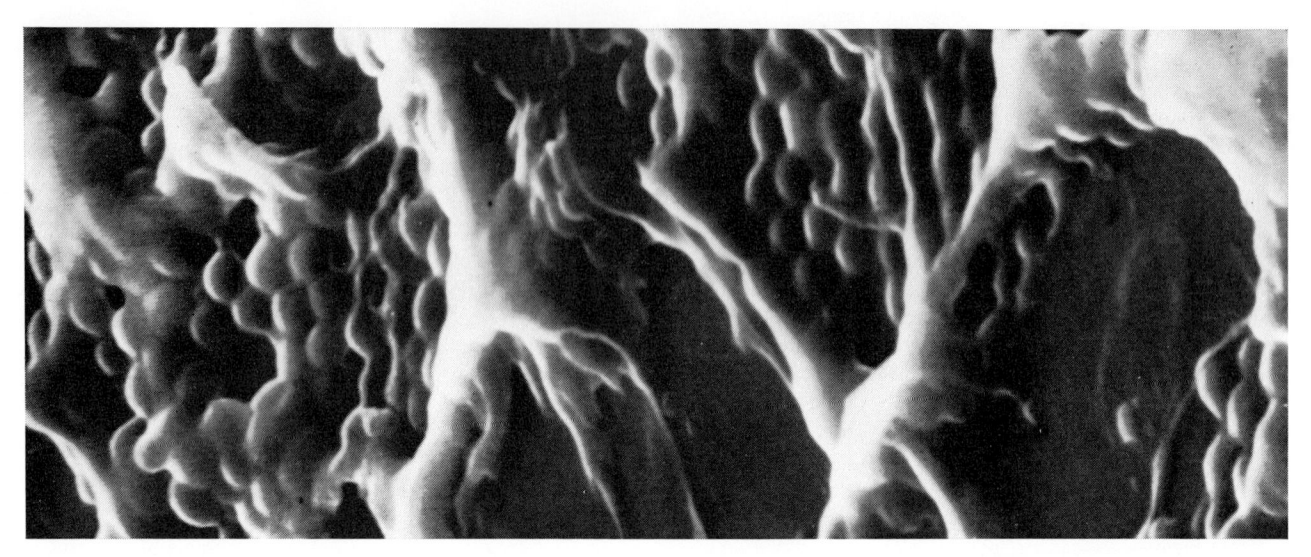

ENDOSPERM OF NORMAL CORN is enlarged 2,750 diameters in scanning electron micrograph. Starch has been dissolved with enzyme amylase, leaving two protein components: zein (*round bodies*) and matrix proteins. Zein is deficient in lysine and tryptophan.

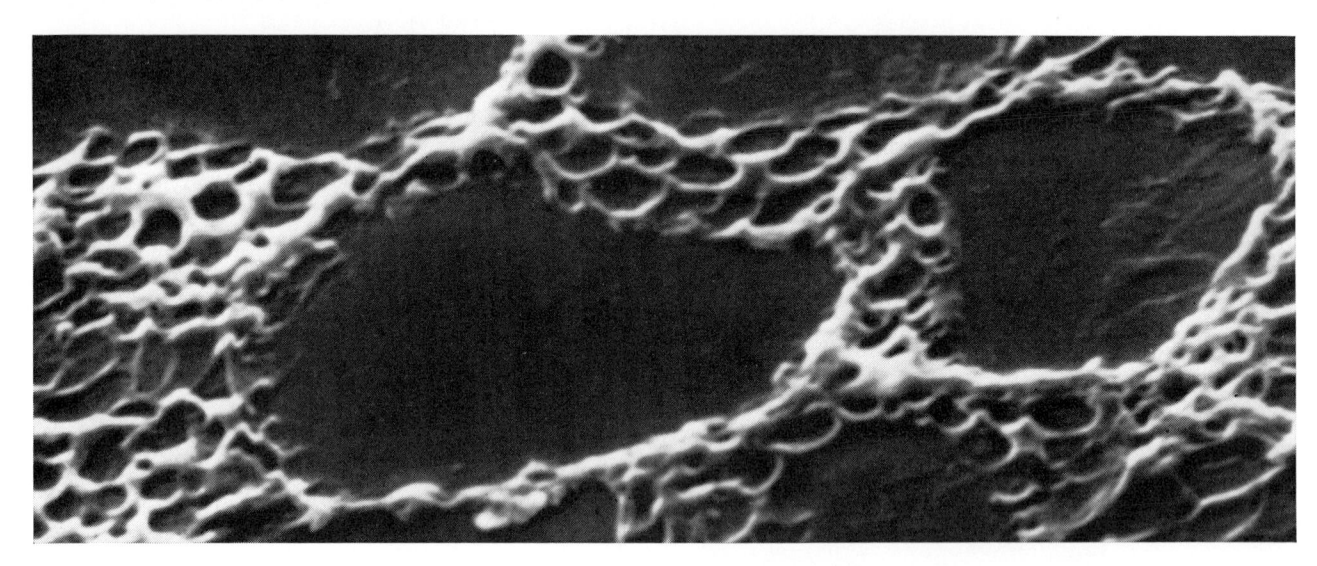

ZEIN IS REMOVED with hot ethyl alcohol, leaving matrix protein with holes where the zein was. The matrix consists largely of the protein glutelin. The micrographs on this page were made by Uheng Khoo and F. L. Baker of the U.S. Department of Agriculture.

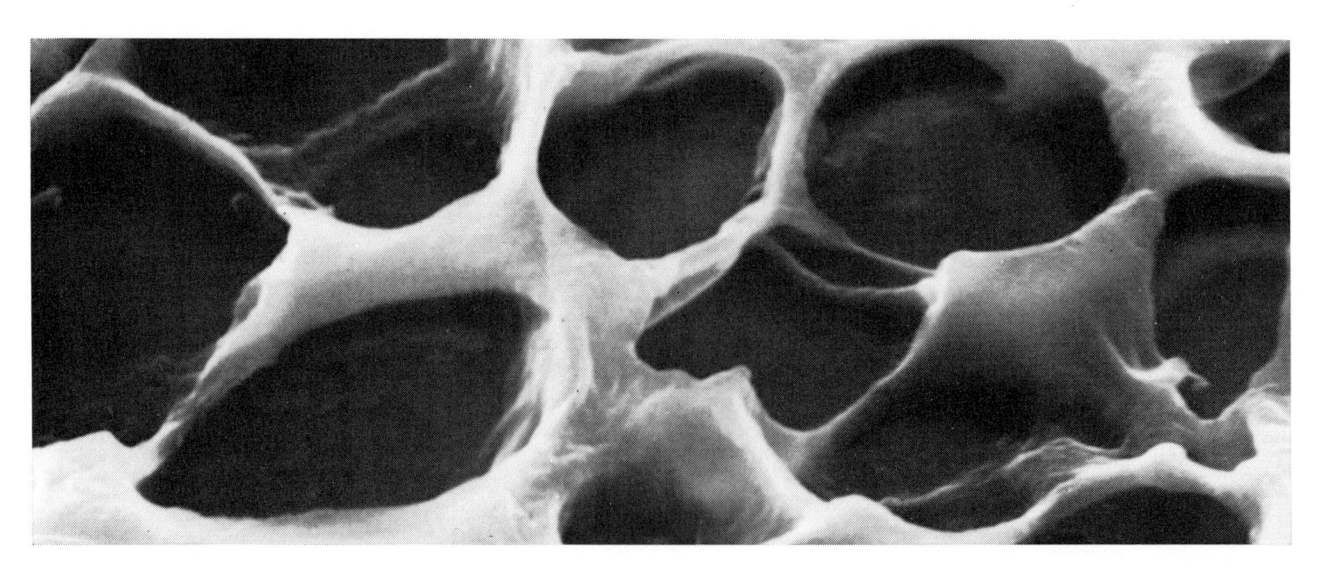

ENDOSPERM OF HIGH-LYSINE STRAIN "opaque-2" is shown with starch dissolved away. Zein component is absent, so that principal protein is glutelin. Since glutelin has a higher proportion of essential amino acids than zein, so does endosperm as a whole.

cians went on to treat children hospitalized for malnutrition with high-lysine corn as the sole source of protein. One of the most remarkable cases of recovery was that of a nine-year-old orphaned girl who had been brought to the hospital by a desperate relative. She was too weak to walk, unresponsive to food, afflicted with severe diarrhea and weighed less than 46 pounds. After a few days of liquid feeding she was able to begin eating high-lysine corn as a solid food. Her response to this diet was so receptive that after 100 days she was discharged from the hospital in good health, with a gain of 11 pounds.

In a country where corn is a familiar and accustomed food, the high-lysine variety is an ideal "prescription" carrying therapeutic values that go beyond its enriched content of protein. The children accepted it readily, without the psychological or physiological resistance that might be offered to a strange diet or "medication." More than 20 malnourished children were treated in the hospital in the series of tests by the university physicians, and they found it to be a very flexible diet, thanks to its acceptability, its superior digestibility over common corn and its essential amino acids. High-lysine corn is now being used successfully for children's diets that, if they were based on normal corn, would be considered well below an optimal level for proper nourishment.

The demonstration of the new corn's ability to "cure" children ill of undernourishment has of course excited considerable interest in its worth as a food among the general population. A food producer in Colombia, the Maizena Company, soon began to market products made from high-lysine corn, notably a precooked baby food offered at relatively low cost. A number of other prepared foods, utilizing high-lysine corn in mixtures or as a precooked corn flour, are being developed. The new corn is still in an exploratory phase as a general food; it has not yet reached the stage where the mass of the population is buying high-lysine corn in the market or growing it for family consumption.

Like most radical innovations in the development phase, high-lysine corn still has certain flaws, mostly due to the softness and floury texture of the kernels. It grinds to a fine flour forming a dough that will require new methods of preparation to arrive at the familiar products baked from corn. For industrial processing the only method available to reduce the grain to flour is dry milling. In the field the soft kernel of the growing corn is vulnerable to attack by insects. And the yield by weight is 6 to 10 percent smaller than in normal corn varieties because of the lower density of the kernels. In the present state of the art the user who is least likely to find fault with the new corn is the farmer operating an integrated corn-pig enterprise.

The shortcomings can be corrected. The historic wonders wrought in the breeding of corn have proved it to be such a supple plant that any permutation seems possible. Already there are indications that we can have high-lysine corn with hard, corneous kernels. The breeding work hitherto has focused on the soft-kernel mutants because the distinctive kernel provides a ready, visible marker to indicate the presence of the improved protein. Recently, however, a number of investigators have discovered that hard endosperm not unlike that in common corn occasionally crops up in kernels known to be carrying the opaque-2 gene. These genetic varieties have now been isolated and are being used in efforts to breed high-lysine corn with kernels of normal texture.

Longer-term projects based on the opaque-2 gene are also in view. They call for increasing the total protein content of corn, now averaging about 10 percent, to 12 to 15 percent and for maintaining production yields at the high level characteristic of hybrid corn. If these goals are attained, corn will truly become a "supergrain" carrying an economical answer to the protein needs of peoples in many parts of the world.

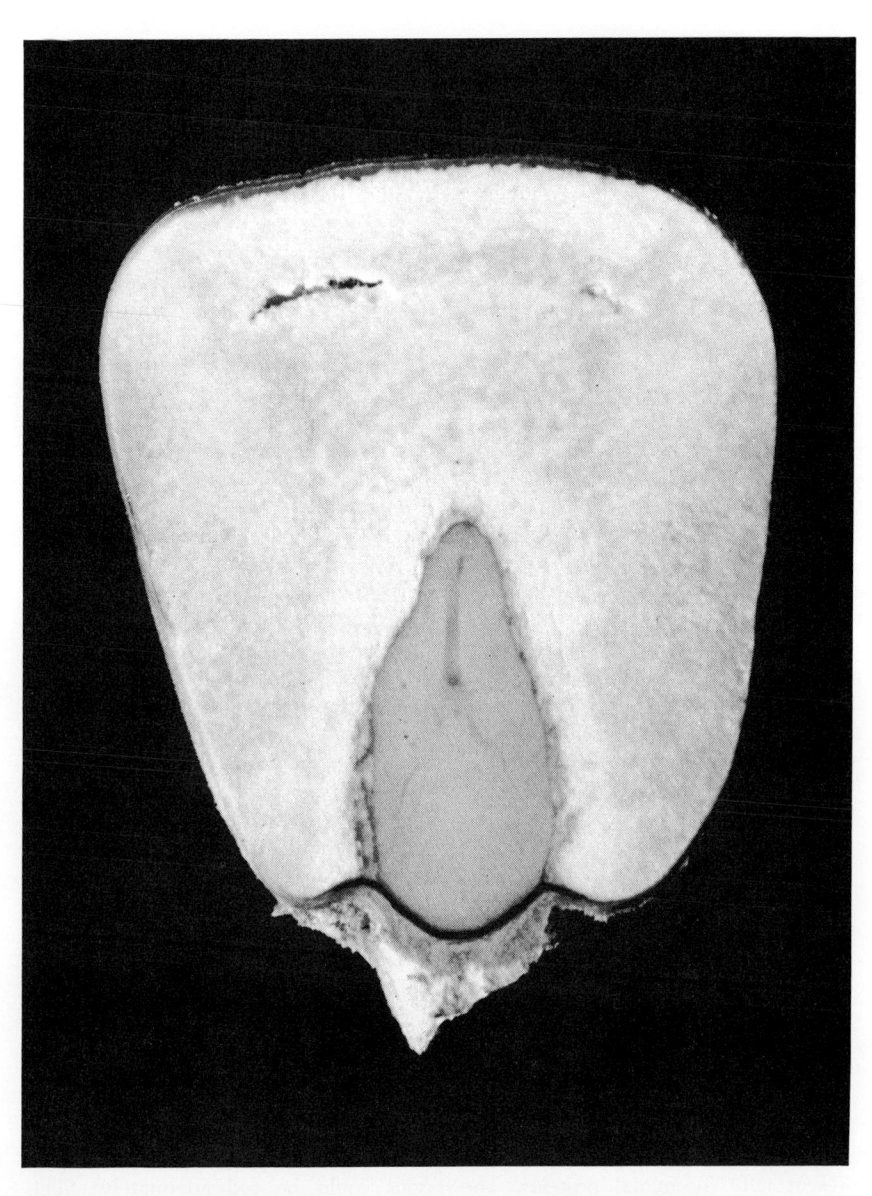

SOFT, FLOURY ENDOSPERM of an opaque-2 kernel is clearly visible in this section. High-lysine corn grinds to a fine flour that calls for new methods of preparation for baking.

28

PROTEIN FROM PETROLEUM

ALFRED CHAMPAGNAT
October 1965

Certain microorganisms thrive on hydrocarbons. In growing they synthesize proteins rich in amino acids that plant foods lack. Protein from petroleum may help solve the world's food problem

The title of this article may suggest science fiction, but it is a statement of fact. In a pilot plant at Lavera in France substantial amounts of high-grade protein are being produced by microorganisms growing on a diet consisting mainly of petroleum hydrocarbons. This unusual concept, tested by a research team of the Société Française des Pétroles BP, has proved so successful that there is good reason to believe petroleum will become an important food resource for the earth's growing population.

Why turn to petroleum to solve the food problem? After all, the store of petroleum in the earth is limited, and at the rate it is being burned for fuel it will be used up before many more decades have passed. Before considering the ways and means of producing food from petroleum, it is well to survey the rationale of such a program and see if it would be worthwhile.

To begin with, it is now quite clear that the world nutrition problem is essentially a question of proteins. At present roughly half of the people in the world have a poorly balanced diet that retards normal growth. The main lack in their diet is animal protein; they live principally on grains and tubers, which may supply enough calories but which contain inferior proteins lacking certain essential amino acids that are present only in animal proteins. The peoples of Europe and North America, with a favorable climate and the development of animal husbandry, have usually been able to enjoy a diet based largely on meat and fish. Not so the inhabitants of the earth's tropical regions. As the undernourished countries grow in population, the inadequacy of their diet, and particularly the protein deficiency, is becoming more pronounced. Kwashiorkor, the protein-deficiency disease, is on the increase among the children of these countries. In general, it can be said that protein poverty is one of the principal factors holding back the underdeveloped areas.

By the year 2000 the present world population of three billion is expected to have more than doubled, to above six billion. The protein problem then will be worldwide. In 1958 the total world production of animal proteins was about 20 million tons, of which 14 million were consumed by the less than one billion population of the advanced countries and six million by the two billion inhabitants of the underdeveloped countries. In the year 2000, to feed properly the expected world population of some 6.3 billion the production of high-quality protein should be trebled, to at least 60 million tons per year.

How is this to be done? The British economist Colin G. Clark has estimated that with intensive cultivation of all the earth's arable land 10 billion persons could be fed adequately. Such a program would call, however, for prodigies of effort, investment and political discipline that seem unrealistic to expect in the short time that remains before the world food problem will become desperate.

Let us examine our present conventional sources of protein. The primary source is plant life, which by utilizing the carbon in the carbon dioxide of the air manufactures organic substances, including proteins. Now, a nonruminant mammal such as man can assimilate proteins directly from plants by eating grains and certain roots and tubers. The proteins of the most common vegetable foods, however, lack some of the essential amino acids. The cereal grains, for example, generally lack the amino acid lysine, and frequently they are poor in methionine and tryptophan. It is the missing amino acids that make most vegetable proteins inferior in quality from the standpoint of human nutrition. Of the 20-odd amino acids required by the human body, man must get 11 in his food because his body does not synthesize them. There are, of course, plant products that contain well-balanced proteins with most of the essential amino acids; among these are soybeans, chick-peas and meal made from the oilseeds of certain plants. These are important potential staples for protein nutrition, but they have not yet been developed into major foods.

The meat of ruminant animals, which with the help of intestinal bacteria convert vegetable food into proteins containing a full stock of amino acids, is man's main present means of maintaining a balanced diet. As the human population multiplies, however, there is a growing recognition that raising animals is a highly expensive way of producing food: pound for pound it is much less efficient than raising plant crops. It takes seven calories of plant carbohydrate to produce one calorie of beef protein, and even in the more efficient procedure of chicken raising the yield is one calorie of chicken protein from 3.5 calories of feed. In the Tropics the problem of producing meat protein is compounded by tropical insects and diseases. At best, even in favorable climates, the production of protein through agriculture must be accounted costly when one considers the required investment of labor, machinery and fertilizers and the uncertainties of weather, soil and water supply.

Some of the same considerations apply when we contemplate increasing our harvest of protein from the ocean. The rich fishing grounds of the cold seas could be exploited more fully than they have been, but the fish life is not unlimited. In the warm seas of the Tropics, where phosphorus, nitrogen and plankton are less abundant, the fish life is sparser. Some authors have proposed harvesting the protein-rich plankton of the oceans for human food, but it must be remembered that if the plankton is removed on a large scale, the fish population will decline. The cultivation of fish in freshwater lakes and ponds, providing the fish with food rations in much the same way that land is enriched with fertilizer, is a promising method of producing more protein in the Tropics, but it certainly could not completely fill the gap for the populations of these regions.

In the long run man will have to organize all the earth's land and sea resources for the most efficient production of living organic matter, because that is the only way he can assure himself of a continuing, expanding food supply. It will take a great deal of time and progress in technology and social wisdom, however, for mankind to establish any such comprehensive control on a worldwide basis. In the meantime, what about the immediate future —the next 35 years, during which the world population seems bound to double? It seems as if the human race must find some quick means of multiplying its supply of protein. This is the necessary and sufficient reason for giving serious thought to the possibilities in petroleum—the large store of organic material that mankind has, so to speak, in the bank.

The production of protein by microorganisms from carbon-containing compounds is not, of course, a new idea. For many years the growing of yeast for animal food and even human foods has been an appreciable, although small, industry. The yeast fungi are grown on carbohydrates (most commonly molasses), and they produce vitamins and pro-

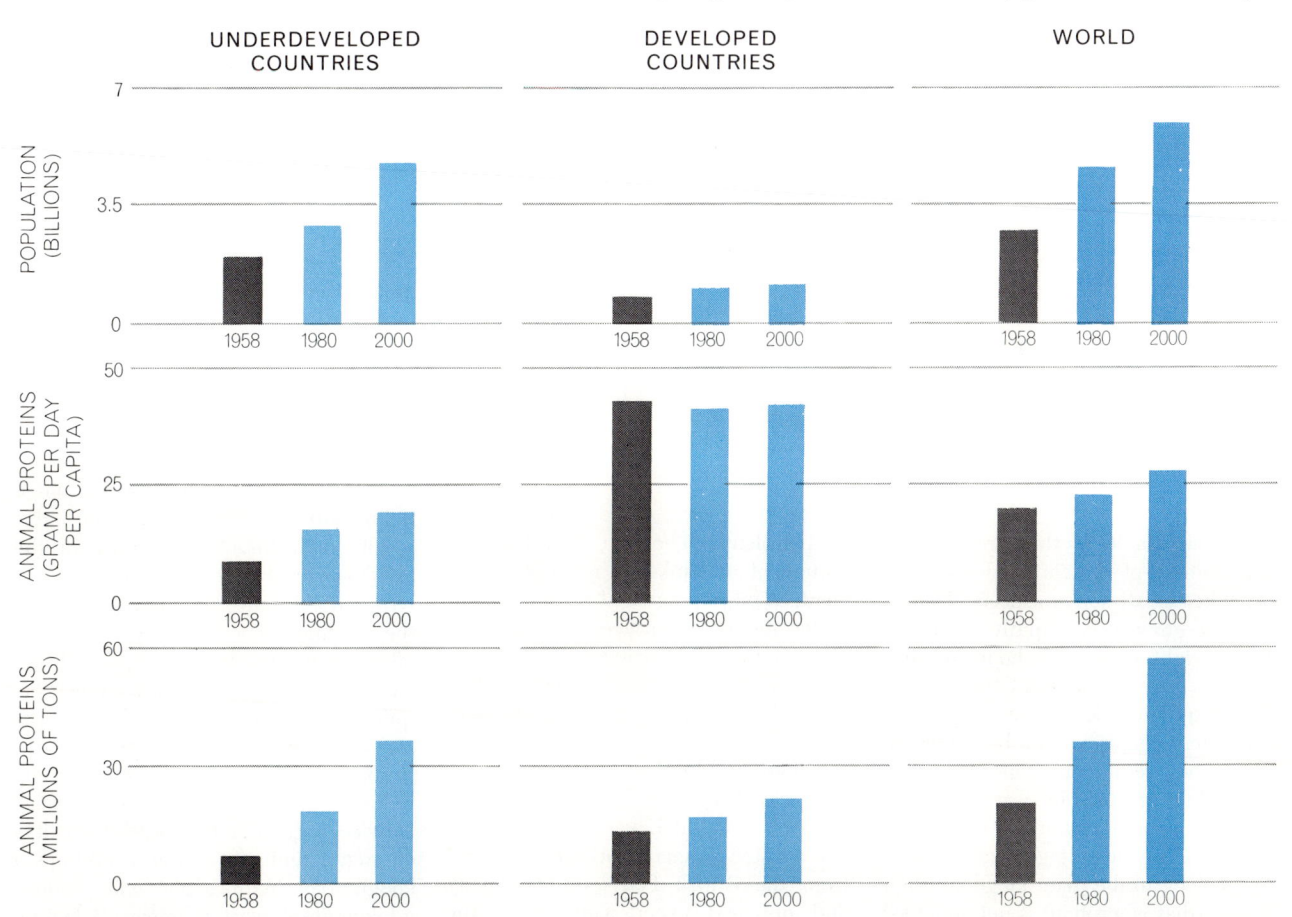

WORLD NUTRITION PROBLEM is essentially a question of proteins. The top row of charts shows the trend of the world's population. The next row shows the amount of animal protein available per capita in 1958 and the goals considered desirable for 1980 and 2000. The bottom row shows the supply of animal protein required to meet these goals for the increasing population. The underdeveloped countries include those in the Far East, Near East, Africa and Latin America (excluding the countries in the Río de la Plata region). The developed countries include those in Europe, North America, Oceania (Australia and New Zealand) and the Río de la Plata region. Data for the graphs were drawn from the report "The World's Hunger and Future Needs in Food Supplies," prepared in 1961 by P. V. Sukhatme for the Food and Agriculture Organization (FAO) of the United Nations.

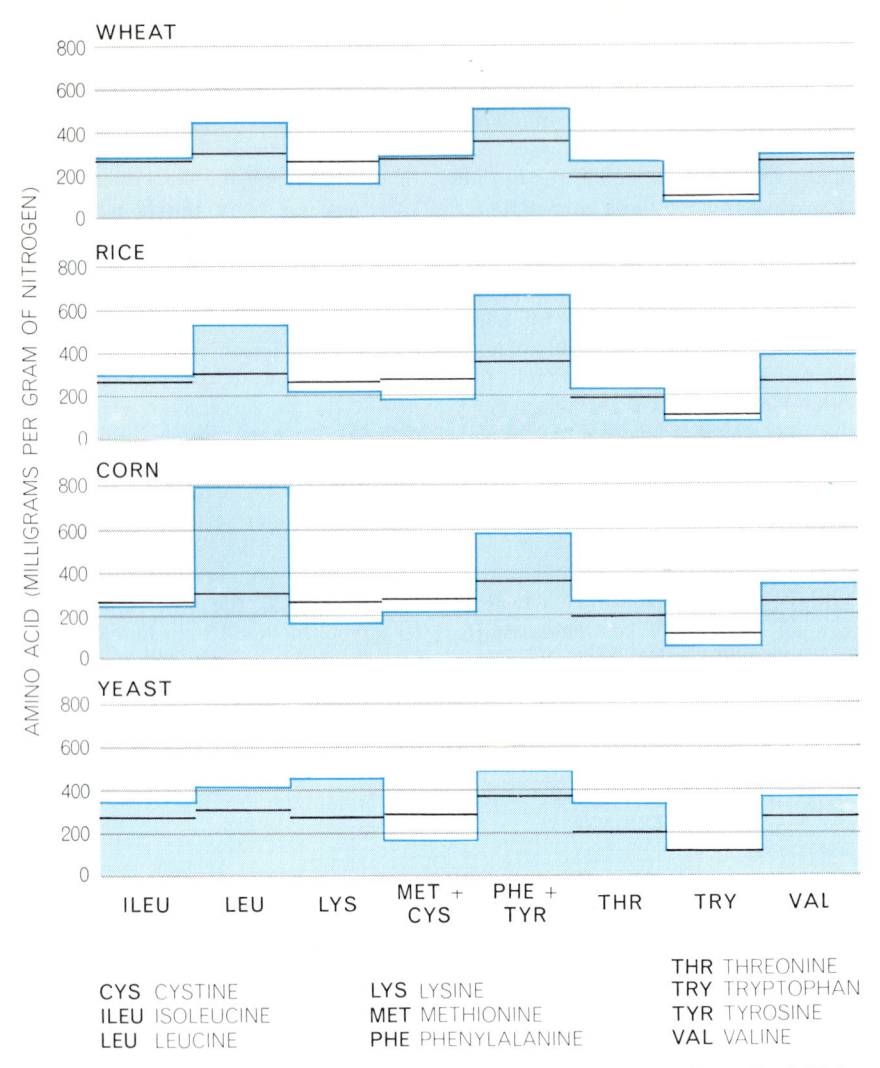

PROTEIN-DEFICIENT GRAINS make up a large part of the diet of roughly half the people in the world. The grains supply enough calories but contain inferior proteins that lack certain essential amino acids present only in animal proteins. The three cereal grains shown here, for example, generally lack the amino acid lysine, and frequently they are poor in methionine and tryptophan as well. In each case the daily amino acid requirement of an average human (formulated by the FAO Committee on Protein Requirement) is indicated by the black line. The amino acid content of a typical yeast is shown at bottom.

teins comparable to those of animals. This method of protein production has a number of attractive aspects. The organisms grow very rapidly, doubling their weight every five hours or less, which is several thousand times faster than farm animals synthesize protein. The microorganisms can be grown in tanks: they require no soil or sunlight or rainfall or assistance from human labor. The fungi also afford the special but important advantage that, because they belong to the plant kingdom, their "meat" (that is, protein) is not outlawed by religious or traditional taboos anywhere in the world.

A question arose: Could hydrocarbons, instead of carbohydrates, serve as the basic medium for the growth of microorganisms? It has been known for a long time that molds commonly grow on petroleum. They are found in the bottom of oil tanks, in refinery equipment, in oil-impregnated soils and even under the tarry surfaces of roads. In 1952 a German biologist, Felix Just, reported that in the laboratory he had succeeded in growing yeast on pure hydrocarbons of the paraffinic family (distinguished by their waxy content).

It was this report that launched our research group at Lavera on its project. We enlisted financial and other support from the British Petroleum Company and obtained expert counsel on the fundamental microbiological problems from the bacteriologist Jacques Senez of the Centre National de Recherche Scientifique. We set out to explore the techniques that would be necessary for the large-scale cultivation of yeasts on petroleum fractions.

Let us consider first the basic mechanics of the process. When yeast is grown on sugar, the medium for the fermentation usually consists of the carbohydrate in a water solution, soluble mineral and organic compounds containing nitrogen, phosphorus and potassium and additions of certain trace elements and growth vitamins. A flow of air is bubbled through the liquid to provide oxygen and maintain a good mixture of the materials throughout the fermentation vessel. The temperature and acidity also are carefully controlled for maximal reproduction of the yeast cells. Eventually the cells are harvested by centrifuging or filtering them out of the medium. The cells are then washed and dried and thus become available in solid form as a food stock containing about 50 percent protein. With flavoring added, this stock has been used as a basis for a variety of prepared foods, from soups to ice cream.

The growing of yeasts on petroleum instead of sugar introduces certain complications. One is the insolubility of hydrocarbons in water. The oily hydrocarbons can be mixed in the watery medium only in suspension, and to keep the oil droplets well dispersed throughout the medium it must be stirred strongly. This is relatively easy to do in a laboratory apparatus but presents formidable difficulties on a large scale.

A second major difficulty is the greater need for oxygen. Whereas sugar molecules contain about 50 percent oxygen, hydrocarbon molecules have no oxygen. Consequently the oxygen supply delivered to the organisms by the bubbling of air through the medium must be at least three times greater on a hydrocarbon substrate than on a sugary substrate. Moreover, because this results in a threefold increase in the cells' output of heat, a cooling system is required to control the temperature of the medium. These disadvantages are offset, however, by an important advantage. Because all of the oxygen required by the cells is supplied by the air, their consumption of the carbon-supplying substrate is correspondingly reduced. The rate of production of yeast is twice as great on hydrocarbons as it is on sugar: under favorable conditions a kilogram of hydrocarbon will produce a kilogram of yeast, whereas a kilogram of sugar yields only half a kilogram of yeast.

Along with studies of adaptations of the culture process that had to be made to grow yeasts on petroleum went a search for the most suitable raw materials. The Lavera laboratory set out to determine if microorganisms could be grown efficiently on fractions from crude petroleum rather than on the pure, synthesized hydrocarbons that Just had used. It was known that some aromatic hydrocarbons were hostile to the growth of microorganisms; hence a mixture containing the various classes of hydrocarbons (paraffins, isoparaffins, naphthenes and aromatics) was ruled out. As had been expected, the most productive fractions proved to be paraffinic ones, which include kerosene and certain gas oils. At present the favored fraction on which the yeasts are being grown is a gas oil, a fraction between kerosene and lubricating oil.

This particular food for microorganisms yields an important dividend beyond protein. The organisms feed mainly on the wax in the paraffinic oil; thus they deparaffinize the oil. With the wax removed, the oil is more fluid and becomes usable as No. 2 fuel oil, suitable for diesel engines and domestic heating. This by-product would be especially significant in Europe, where No. 2 fuel oil is in great demand for these uses. (In the U.S. most of the heavily paraffinic gas oil is converted into gasoline.)

In addition to the selection of the best food for the organisms there is the matter of selection of the organisms themselves. As in wine making, some yeasts are better than others when it comes to the making of proteins. No doubt it will be found that for each petroleum fraction there is a species of microorganism most efficient in turning it into protein. The species of organisms also differ in the kinds of proteins they produce. By selection and genetic breeding of the organisms it will be possible to make proteins to order. Our laboratory has studied only a few species of organisms so far, but it is already clear that the range of possibilities for creating proteins is wide—much wider than through agriculture or animal husbandry. For further inspiration there is the example of what has been achieved within the past decade by research on the abilities of microorganisms to produce antibiotics and other drugs in almost endless variety.

On a sizable pilot scale the development center at Lavera is now producing protein from petroleum around the clock, improving the process as the work proceeds. The medium is similar to that for the growing of yeasts on sugar, except that oil is substituted for the sugar. Nitrogen is added to the medium in the form of ammonia salts; phosphorus and potassium are supplied in the form of general fertilizers; trace elements and growth vitamins are added. The product of the organisms feeding on this medium is more than 50 percent protein.

The proteins produced by the fermentation of petroleum differ in no essential respect from those made by any other natural process—whether by beef cattle, poultry, fishes, plants or yeasts growing on sugar. They are rich in B vitamins and in a well-balanced variety of amino acids; in particular, they have a high content of lysine, which makes them a useful complement to the lysine-poor cereals. In experiments on rats it has been found that they have a digestibility of 85 to 90 percent. There is no reason to believe there is anything bizarre about the biological matter that has been grown on petroleum. Because of the strangeness of the source, however, a long and costly program of tests is being carried out on experimental animals to determine the nutritional value of the petroleum-based protein and its freedom from toxicity. Once it has passed these tests, we plan to incorporate it in food products designed for commercial production and to submit these products to international organizations for them to test.

When the yeasts grown on petroleum have been dried and purified, the concentrate is in the form of a powder or whitish flakes with no pronounced odor or taste; it has less odor than yeast grown on sugar. Like concentrated protein from meat, fish, yeast or soybeans, the protein from petroleum can be transformed into many different foods. Its first use is likely to be in feeds for livestock. We have prepared a number of sophisticated versions of the food, ranging from tasty meat concentrates to fermented fish sauces of strong aroma that are highly esteemed in Asia. We have also considered ways of packaging it as a pure, concentrated protein, like powdered skim milk.

The British Petroleum Company, which operates in several countries, has now thrown its full weight behind the development of petroleum fermentation as a food resource. In addition to the semi-industrial development center at Lavera it is supporting a laboratory for fundamental research in the Paris area and a research and development center at Grangemouth in Scotland. The company has also acquired land in Nigeria for an experimental farm where it hopes to examine, under tropical field condi-

DRIED YEAST CELLS are shown emerging from the laboratory drum dryer at the Lavera refinery of the Société Française des Pétroles BP in France. The yeasts were grown on petroleum and have been dried and purified; the concentrate, in the form of pale flakes with no pronounced odor or taste, contains more than 50 percent high-quality protein.

tions, the effects of rearing animals on diets consisting primarily of locally grown feed supplemented by protein from petroleum. British Petroleum is not alone; large organizations in several other countries are now taking up the same field of research.

It is easy to illustrate the potential importance of this movement with a few figures. We have calculated that with an outlay of some 40 million tons of petroleum (a small fraction of the 1.25 billion tons of crude oil produced in 1962) 20 million tons of pure protein could be produced per year. This alone would double the present total annual production of protein. For comparison with other possible sources, consider sea fishing, which also might produce a quick increase in yield. At present it brings in some 40 million tons of fish a year, representing about six million tons of pure protein. By tremendous efforts the catch might be increased to a maximum of 100 million tons of fish a year (any larger take would endanger the reproduction of fish), which amounts to 15 million tons of protein. This does not come up to the potential yield from petroleum, and it would be a more difficult effort.

Petroleum is relatively cheap and stable in price. It can easily be transported anywhere in the world by tankers. There are more than 700 refineries, distributed in almost all countries, that could set up units that would produce protein and at the same time deparaffinize crude oil. The oil industry is highly organized and flexible, as it has shown in turning quickly to the manufacture of a great variety of chemical products from petroleum. The production of protein would widen the diversification of the industry and thus further strengthen its foundations. The industry therefore has strong reason to take an active interest in this new development.

One must recognize that this fossil liquid petroleum will not last forever. Yet food is certainly as important to man as fuel. To burn all or nearly all of the petroleum and fail to allot even a small portion of it to producing food, if that proves practicable, would be a serious mistake. Protein from petroleum, although not a total or permanent solution to the world food problem, nevertheless deserves our most serious efforts because of its high promise and the great needs of the near future. It will require a large investment of research and money, but the studies so far indicate that it would pay high returns to mankind in health and peace.

LARGE PILOT PLANT at the Lavera refinery is now producing protein from petroleum on a scale permitting engineering studies. With an outlay of some 40 million tons of petroleum the world's refineries could produce 20 million tons of pure protein per year.

BIBLIOGRAPHIES

I NUTRITION AND MALNUTRITION

1. Smell and Taste

THE CHEMICAL SENSES. R. W. Moncrieff. 3rd edition. L. Hill, 1967.

PRINCIPLES OF SENSORY EVALUATION OF FOOD. Maynard A. Amerine, Rose Marie Pangborn and Edward B. Roessler. Academic Press, 1965.

ON THE THEORY OF ODORS. G. B. Kistiakowsky in *Science*, Vol. 112, No. 2909, pages 154–155; August 4, 1950.

THE PHYSIOLOGY OF SENSE ORGANS. DeForest Mellon Jr., W. H. Freeman and Company, 1968.

FLAVOR RESEARCH: PRINCIPLES AND TECHNIQUES. Roy Teranishi, Irwin Hornstein, Phillip Issenberg and Emily L. Wick. Marcel Dekker, Inc., 1971.

2. The Sources of Muscular Energy

THE REVOLUTION IN MUSCLE PHYSIOLOGY. A. V. Hill in *Physiological Reviews*, Vol. 12, No. 1, pages 56–67; January, 1932.

KINETICS AND MECHANISM OF OXYGEN DEBT CONTRACTION IN MAN. R. Margaria, P. Cerretelli, P. E. diPrampero, C. Massari and G. Torelli in *Journal of Applied Physiology*, Vol. 18, No. 2, pages 371–377; March, 1963.

EXERCISE AT ALTITUDE. R. Margaria. Excerpta Medica Foundation, 1967.

ENERGETICS OF MUSCULAR CONTRACTION. W. F. H. M. Mommaerts in *Physiological Reviews*, Vol. 49, No. 3, pages 427–508; July, 1969.

3. Appetite and Obesity

THE PHYSIOLOGICAL BASIS OF OBESITY AND LEANNESS. Jean Mayer in *Nutrition Abstracts and Reviews*, Vol. 25, No. 3, pages 597–611; July, 1955; Vol. 25, No. 4, pages 871–883; October, 1955.

OBESITY AND EATING. Stanley Schachter in *Science*, Vol. 161, No. 3843, pages 751–756; August, 1968.

OVERWEIGHT: CAUSES, COST, AND CONTROL. Jean Mayer. Prentice-Hall, Inc., 1968.

4. Proteins

PROTEINS AND LIFE. M. V Tracey. The Pilot Press, Ltd., 1948.

THE STRUCTURE AND ACTION OF PROTEINS. Richard E. Dickerson and Irving Geis. Harper & Row, Publishers, 1969.

5. Lactose and Lactase

A RACIAL DIFFERENCE IN INCIDENCE OF LACTASE DEFICIENCY. Theodore M. Bayless and Norton S. Rosensweig in *The Journal of the American Medical Association*, Vol. 197, No. 12, pages 968–972; September 19, 1966.

MILK. Stuart Patton in *Scientific American*, Vol. 221, No. 1, pages 58–68; July, 1969.

PRIMARY ADULT LACTOSE INTOLERANCE AND THE MILKING HABIT: A PROBLEM IN BIOLOGIC AND CULTURAL INTERRELATIONS. II. A CULTURAL HISTORICAL HYPOTHESIS. Frederick J. Simoons in *The American Journal of Digestive Diseases*, Vol. 15, No. 8, pages 695–710; August, 1970.

LACTASE DEFICIENCY: AN EXAMPLE OF DIETARY EVOLUTION. R. D. McCracken in *Current Anthropology*, Vol. 12, No. 4–5, pages 479–517; October–December, 1971.

MEMORIAL LECTURE: LACTOSE AND LACTASE—A HISTORICAL PERSPECTIVE. Norman Kretchmer in *Gastroenterology*, Vol. 61, No. 6, pages 805–813; December, 1971.

6. The Physiology of Starvation

THE BIOLOGY OF HUMAN STARVATION. Ancel Keys, Josef Brožek, Austin Henschel, Olaf Mickelsen and Henry Longstreet Taylor. The University of Minnesota Press, 1950.

PROTEIN MALNUTRITION IN YOUNG CHILDREN. Nevin S. Scrimshaw and Moisés Béhar in *Science*, Vol. 133, No. 3470, pages 2039–2047; June 30, 1961.
MAN UNDER CALORIC DEFIENCY. Francisco Grande in *Handbook of Physiology, Section 4: Adaptation to the Environment*. American Physiological Society, 1964.
STARVATION IN MAN. George F. Cahill, Jr., in *The New England Journal of Medicine*, Vol. 282, No. 12, pages 668–675; March 19, 1970.

7. Kwashiorkor

KWASHIORKOR. H. C. Trowell and R. F. A. Dean in *British Encyclopedia of Medical Practice*, Interim Supplement 113. Butterworth & Co., Ltd., 1952.
A NUTRITIONAL DISEASE OF CHILDREN ASSOCIATED WITH A MAIZE DIET. Cicely D. Williams in *Archives of Disease in Childhood*, Vol. 8, No. 48, pages 423–433; December, 1933.
PROBLEMS RAISED BY KWASHIORKOR. H. C. Trowell in *Nutrition Reviews*, Vol. 8, No. 6, pages 161–163; June, 1950.
INTERNATIONAL ACTION TO AVERT THE IMPENDING PROTEIN CRISIS. Advisory Committee on the Application of Science and Technology to Development. United Nations, 1968.
THE EFFECTS OF SEVERE PROTEIN DEFICIENCY ON THE HUMAN INFANT. J. S. Garrow in *Protein Metabolism and Biological Function*, edited by C. Paul Bianchi and Russell Hilf. Rutgers University Press, 1970.

8. Biotin

BIOTIN AND BACTERIAL GROWTH. I: RELATION TO ASPARTATE, OLEATE AND GROWTH. Harry P. Broquist and Esmond E. Snell, *Journal of Biological Chemistry*, Vol. 188, No. 1, pages 431–444, January 1951.
THE CHEMISTRY OF BIOTIN. Donald B. Melville in *Vitamins and Hormones*, Vol. 2, pages 29–60, Academic Press, 1944.
EVIDENCE FOR THE PARTICIPATION OF BIOTIN IN THE ENZYMIC SYNTHESIS OF FATTY ACIDS. Salih J. Wakil, Edward B. Titchener and David M. Gibson in *Biochimica et Biophysica Acta*, Vol. 29, No. 1, pages 225–226, July, 1958.
POSSIBLE BIOCHEMICAL IMPLICATIONS OF THE CRYSTAL STRUCTURE OF BIOTIN. W. Traub in *Science*, Vol. 129, No. 3343, page 210, January, 1959.

GENERAL BIOCHEMISTRY. Second edition. Joseph S. Fruton and Sofia Simmonds. John Wiley & Sons, Inc., 1958.

9. Endemic Goiter

ETIOLOGY AND PREVENTION OF SIMPLE GOITER. David Marine in *Medicine*, Vol. 3, No. 4, pages 453–479; November, 1924.
THYROXINE. Edward C. Kendall. The Chemical Catalog Company, Inc., 1929.
ENDEMIC GOITRE. World Health Organization Monograph Series No. 44. World Health Organization, 1960.
THE THYROID GLAND. Rulon W. Rawson in *Clinical Symposia, Ciba Pharmaceutical Company*, Vol. 17, No. 2, pages 35–63; April-May-June, 1965.

10. Toxic Substances and Ecological Cycles

ENVIRONMENTAL RADIOACTIVITY. Merril Eisenbud. McGraw-Hill Book Company, Inc., 1963.
PESTICIDES AND THE LIVING LANDSCAPE. Robert L. Rudd. University of Wisconsin Press, 1964.
REPORT OF THE UNITED NATIONS SCIENTIFIC COMMITTEE ON THE EFFECTS OF ATOMIC RADIATION. Official Records of the General Assembly, 13th Session, Supplement No. 17, 1958; 17th Session, Supplement No. 16, 1962; 19th Session, Supplement No. 14, 1964.
POPULATION, RESOURCES, ENVIRONMENT: ISSUES IN HUMAN ECOLOGY. Second edition. Paul R. Ehrlich and Anne H. Ehrlich. W. H. Freeman and Company, 1972.

11. Mercury in the Environment

THE GENERAL PHARMACOLOGY OF THE HEAVY METALS. H. Passow, A. Rothstein and T. W. Clarkson in *Pharmacological Reviews*, Vol. 13, No. 2, pages 185–224; June, 1961.
ABSORPTION AND EXCRETION OF MERCURY IN MAN: I-XIV. Leonard J. Goldwater et al. Papers published in *Archives of Environmental Health*, 1962–1968.
CHEMICAL FALLOUT: CURRENT RESEARCH ON PERSISTENT PESTICIDES. Edited by Morton W. Miller and George C. Berg. Charles C Thomas, Publisher, 1969.
MERCURY IN THE ENVIRONMENT. Geological Survey Professional Paper 713. United States Government Printing Office, 1970.

II CONVENTIONAL SOURCES AND RESOURCES

12. Wheat

THE ORIGIN, VARIATION, IMMUNITY AND BREEDING OF CULTIVATED PLANTS. Nikolai I. Vavilov. Chronica Botanica, 1951.

THE WHEAT PLANT. John Percival. Duckworth and Company, 1921.
WHEAT AND WHEAT IMPROVEMENT. K. S. Quisenberry

(editor). American Society of Agronomy. Madison, Wisconsin, 1967.

WHEAT, BOTANY, CULTIVATION AND UTILIZATION. R. F. Peterson. Interscience, 1965.

13. Hybrid Corn

CORN AND CORN IMPROVEMENT. Edited by George F. Sprague. Academic Press, 1955.

A PROFESSOR'S STORY OF HYBRID CORN. Herbert K. Hayes. Burgess Publishing Company, 1963.

14. Milk

PRINCIPLES OF DAIRY CHEMISTRY. Robert Jenness and Stuart Patton. John Wiley & Sons, Inc., 1959.

MILK: THE MAMMARY GLAND AND ITS SECRETION. Edited by S. K. Kon and A. T. Cowie. Academic Press, 1961.

MILK PROTEINS. H. A. McKenzie in *Advances in Protein Chemistry*, edited by C. B. Anfinsen, Jr., M. L. Anson, John T. Edsall and Frederic M. Richards, Vol. 22, pages 55–234; 1967.

THE ROLE OF THE PLASMA MEMBRANE IN THE SECRETION OF MILK FAT. Stuart Patton and Frederick M. Fowkes in *Journal of Theoretical Biology*, Vol. 15, No. 3, pages 274–281; June, 1967.

15. Cattle

BREEDING LIVESTOCK ADAPTED TO UNFAVORABLE ENVIRONMENT. Ralph W. Phillips. FAO Agricultural Studies, No. 1, 1948.

THE CATTLE OF INDIA. Ralph W. Phillips in *Journal of Heredity*, Vol. 35, No. 9, pages 273–288, September, 1944.

CROSSBREEDING BEEF CATTLE. Edited by T. J. Cunha, M. Koger and A. C. Warnick. University of Florida Press, 1963.

INTRODUCTION TO LIVESTOCK PRODUCTION. Edited by H. H. Cole. Second edition. W. H. Freeman and Company, 1966.

BEEF CATTLE. A. L. Neumann and Roscoe R. Snapp. John Wiley & Sons, Inc., 1969.

16. Poultry Production

THE AMERICAN STANDARD OF PERFECTION. American Poultry Association, Inc., 1966.

A HISTORY OF DOMESTICATED ANIMALS. F. E. Zerner. Hutchinson of London, 1963.

THE SIGNIFICANT ADVANCES OF THE PAST FIFTY YEARS IN POULTRY NUTRITION. L. C. Nottis in *Poultry Science*, Vol. 37, No. 2, pages 256–274, March, 1958.

POULTRY PRODUCTION. Tenth edition. Leslie E. Card and Malden C. Nesheim. Lea and Febiger, Philadelphia, 1966.

17. The Food Resources of the Ocean

LIVING RESOURCES OF THE SEA: OPPORTUNITIES FOR RESEARCH AND EXPANSION. Lionel A. Walford. The Ronald Press Company, 1958.

FISHERIES BIOLOGY: A STUDY IN POPULATION DYNAMICS. D. H. Cushing. University of Wisconsin Press, 1968.

MARINE SCIENCE AND TECHNOLOGY: SURVEY AND PROPOSALS. REPORT OF THE SECRETARY-GENERAL. United Nations Economic and Social Council, E/4487, 1968.

THE STATE OF WORLD FISHERIES. World Food Problems No. 7. Food and Agriculture Organization of the United Nations, 1968.

WORK OF FAO AND RELATED ORGANIZATIONS CONCERNING MARINE SCIENCE AND ITS APPLICATIONS. FAO Fisheries Technical Paper No. 74. Food and Agriculture Organization of the United Nations, September, 1968.

18. Food Additives

FOOD STANDARDS COMMITTEE REPORTS. Great Britain Ministry of Agriculture, Fisheries and Food. Her Majesty's Stationary Office, London.

REPORTS OF THE CODEX COMMITTEE ON FOOD ADDITIVES. Food and Agriculture Organization of the United Nations, Rome.

REPORTS OF THE JOINT FAO/IAEA/WHO EXPERT COMMITTEE ON FOOD IRRADIATION. Food and Agriculture Organization of the United Nations, Rome.

REPORT OF THE JOINT FAO/WHO EXPERT COMMITTEE ON FOOD ADDITIVES. Food and Agriculture Organization of the United Nations, Rome.

HANDBOOK OF FOOD ADDITIVES. Edited by Thomas E. Furia. The Chemical Rubber Co., 1968.

19. Beer

THE ART AND SCIENCE OF BREWING. C. A. Kloss. Stuart and Richards, 1949.

BEER HAS A HISTORY. Frank A. King. Hutchinson's Scientific and Technical Publications, 1947.

THE BIOCHEMISTRY OF BREWING. I. A. Preece. Oliver & Boyd, 1954.

BREWING: SCIENCE AND PRACTICE. H. Lloyd Hind. Chapman & Hall, Ltd., 1938.

MICROBIAL TECHNOLOGY. Edited by Henry J. Peppler. Reinhold, 1967.

20. Wine

AMERICAN WINES AND WINE-MAKING. Philip M. Wagner. Alfred A. Knopf, 1956.

GENERAL VITICULTURE. A. J. Winkler. University of California Press, 1962.

THE NOBLE GRAPES AND THE GREAT WINES OF FRANCE. A. L. Simon. McGraw-Hill Book Company, Inc., 1957.

THE TECHNOLOGY OF WINE MAKING. (3rd ed.), M. A.

Amerine, H. W. Berg, and W. V. Cruess. The Avi Publishing Company, Inc., 1972.

WINES OF FRANCE. Alexis Lichine. Alfred A. Knopf, 1965.

WINES OF GERMANY. Frank Schoonmaker. Hastings House, Publishers, Inc., 1956.

DESSERT WINES. Maynard A. Joslyn and M. A. Amerine. University of California, Division of Agricultural Sciences, 1962.

TABLE WINES: THE TECHNOLOGY OF THEIR PRODUCTION. Maynard A. Amerine and Maynard A. Joslyn. University of California Press, 1969.

III THE FUTURE: FEAST OR FAMINE?

21. The Human Population

THE NEXT HUNDRED YEARS: MAN'S NATURAL AND TECHNICAL RESOURCES. Harrison Brown, James Bonner and John Weir. Viking Press, Inc., 1957.

POPULATION AHEAD. Roy Gustaf Francis. University of Minnesota Press, 1958.

THE POPULATION CRISIS AND THE USE OF WORLD RESOURCES. Edited by Stuart Mudd. World Academy of Art and Science. Indiana University Press, 1964.

SCIENCE AND ECONOMIC DEVELOPMENT: NEW PATTERNS OF LIVING. Richard L. Meier. John Wiley & Sons, Inc., 1956.

WORLD POPULATION AND PRODUCTION: TRENDS AND OUTLOOK. W. S. Woytinsky and E. S. Woytinsky. Twentieth Century Fund, 1953.

22. Food

SCIENCE, TECHNOLOGY, AND DEVELOPMENT, VOLUME III: AGRICULTURE. United States Papers Prepared for the United Nations Conference on the Application of Science and Technology for the Benefit of the Less Developed Areas. U.S. Government Printing Office, 1962.

SCIENCE, TECHNOLOGY, AND DEVELOPMENT, VOLUME VI: HEALTH AND NUTRITION. United States Papers Prepared for the United Nations Conference on the Application of Science and Technology for the Benefit of the Less Developed Areas. U.S. Government Printing Office, 1963.

PROSPECTS OF THE WORLD FOOD SUPPLY: PROCEEDINGS OF A SYMPOSIUM. National Academy of Sciences, 1966.

THE WORLD FOOD PROBLEM: A REPORT, VOLS. I, II, III. The President's Science Advisory Committee. U.S. Government Printing Office, 1967.

FAMINE — 1975! AMERICA'S DECISION: WHO WILL SURVIVE? William and Paul Paddock. Little, Brown and Company, 1967.

23. Human Food Production as a Process in the Biosphere

MALNUTRITION AND NATIONAL DEVELOPMENT. Alan D. Berg in *Foreign Affairs*, Vol. 46, No. 1, pages 126–136; October, 1967.

ON THE SHRED OF A CLOUD. Rolf Edberg. Translated by Sven Ahmån. The University of Alabama Press, 1969.

POLITICS AND ENVIRONMENT: A READER IN ECOLOGICAL CRISIS. Edited by Walt Anderson. Goodyear Publishing Company, Inc., 1970.

POPULATION, RESOURCES, ENVIRONMENT: ISSUES IN HUMAN ECOLOGY. Paul R. Ehrlich and Anne H. Ehrlich. W. H. Freeman and Company, 1970.

SEEDS OF CHANGE: THE GREEN REVOLUTION AND DEVELOPMENT IN THE 1970's. Lester R. Brown. Praeger Publishers, 1970.

24. A World Agricultural Plan

A STRATEGY FOR THE CONQUEST OF HUNGER: PROCEEDINGS OF A SYMPOSIUM CONVENED BY THE ROCKEFELLER FOUNDATION. Rockefeller Foundation, 1968.

CREATING A PROGRESSIVE RURAL STRUCTURE. A. T. Mosher. The Agricultural Development Council, 1969.

PROVISIONAL INDICATIVE WORLD PLAN FOR AGRICULTURAL DEVELOPMENT, VOLS. I AND II: A SYNTHESIS AND ANALYSIS OF FACTORS RELEVANT TO WORLD, REGIONAL AND NATIONAL AGRICULTURAL DEVELOPMENT. Food and Agriculture Organization of the United Nations. FAO, Rome, 1970.

PROVISIONAL INDICATIVE WORLD PLAN FOR AGRICULTURAL DEVELOPMENT: SUMMARY AND MAIN CONCLUSIONS. Food and Agriculture Organization of the United Nations. FAO, Rome, 1970.

25. Orthodox and Unorthodox Methods in Meeting World Food Needs

INTERNATIONAL ACTION TO AVERT THE IMPENDING PROTEIN CRISIS. Advisory Committee on the Application of Science and Technology to Development. United Nations, 1968.

LEAF PROTEIN AS A HUMAN FOOD. N. W. Pirie in *Science*, Vol. 152, No. 3730, pages 1701–1705; June 24, 1966.

THE PRODUCTION AND USE OF LEAF PROTEIN. N. W. Pirie in *Proceedings of the Nutrition Society*, Vol. 28, page 85; 1969.

COMPLEMENTARY WAYS OF MEETING THE WORLD'S PROTEIN NEED. N. W. Pirie in *Proceedings of the Nutrition Society*, Vol. 28, page 255; 1969.

FOOD RESOURCES: CONVENTIONAL AND NOVEL. N. W. Pirie. Penguin Books Inc., 1969.

THE FOOD RESOURCES OF THE OCEANS. S. J. Holt in *Scientific American*, Vol. 221, No. 3, pages 178–194; September 1969.

26. Marine Farming

THE OYSTERS OF LOCMARIAQUER. Eleanor Clark. Pantheon Books, 1964.

WHALE CULTURE—A PROPOSAL. Gifford B. Pinchot in *Perspectives in Biology and Medicine*, Vol. 10, No. 1, pages 33–43; Autumn, 1966.

AQUACULTURE, ITS STATUS AND POTENTIAL. J. H. Ryther and G. C. Matthiessen in *Oceanus*, Vol. 14, No. 4, pages 2–14; February, 1969.

THE FOOD RESOURCES OF THE OCEAN. S. J. Holt in *Scientific American*, Vol. 221, No. 3, pages 178–194; September, 1969.

PHOTOSYNTHESIS AND FISH PRODUCTION IN THE SEA. John H. Ryther in *Science*, Vol. 166, No. 3901, pages 72–76; October 3, 1969.

27. High-lysine Corn

PROCEEDINGS OF THE HIGH LYSINE CORN CONFERENCE. Edited by Edwin T. Mertz and Oliver E. Nelson. Corn Refiners Association, Washington, D.C., 1966.

WORLD PROTEIN RESOURCES: ADVANCES IN CHEMISTRY SERIES, 57. American Chemical Society, 1966.

GENETIC MODIFICATION OF PROTEIN QUALITY IN PLANTS. Oliver E. Nelson in *Advances in Agronomy*, Vol. 21, pages 171–194; 1969.

28. Protein from Petroleum

CONSIDERATIONS SUR L'EVENTUALITE DE LA PRODUCTION DE PROTEINES PAR L'INDUSTRIE DU PETROLE. Alfred Champagnat in *Bulletin de l'Academie Nationale de Medecine*, Vol. 147, No. 9–10, pages 182–186; March 5, 1963.

PROTEINS FROM PETROLEUM FERMENTATION—A NEW SOURCE OF FOOD. Alfred Champagnat in *Impact of Science on Society*, Vol. 14, No. 2, pages 119–133; 1964.

THE WORLD'S HUNGER AND FUTURE NEEDS IN FOOD SUPPLIES. P. V. Sukhatme in *Journal of the Royal Statistical Society*, Series A, Vol. 124, Part IV, pages 463–525; 1961.

SINGLE-CELL PROTEIN. R. I. Mateles and S. R. Tannebaum. *Economic Botany*, Vol. 22, pages 42–50; 1968.

INDEX

Acidosis, 19
ACTH, 26
Adenosine diphosphate (ADP)
 in fermentation, 176
 in muscle, 13
Adenosine triphosphate (ATP)
 in fermentation, 176
 in muscle, 13
 in peptide bond synthesis, 33
 synthesis, 48, 50
Adulteration of food, 153
Agricultural revolution, 192, 206–207
Agriculture
 arable land, 205, 222
 development, 205–207
 and fossil fuel energy, 207
 land, production and income
  distribution, 203
 mercury, use in, 83
 productivity, 199, 202
 in undeveloped countries, 216–228
 world plan, 215–228
Alanine, 47, 50
Albumin
 in milk, 47, 122
 in blood serum, 120
Alexander, J., 11
Alexander, Lyle T., 74
Algae, 213, 235
Allison, Franklin, 57
Amerine, Maynard A., article by, 169–179
Amino acids
 cysteine, 29, 117
 glutamic acid, 29, 154
 level in blood, 47, 49
 lysine, 29, 245, 246, 248
 nutritional lack, 49, 254
 tryptophan, 29, 247, 248
 zein, 246, 247, 252
Anchovies, 252
Animal husbandry, 205
Animal products, vegetable substitutes
 for, 214
Antibiotics as food preservatives, 156
Antioxidants, 157
Appetite and obesity, 21–26
Avidin, 59

Bakewell, Robert, 127
Barger, George, 65
Barley, 160, 161
Bateman, G., 57
Baumann, Eugen 65
Bayless, Theodore, 37
Beal, William, 105
Beer, 95, 160–168
 bitterness, 165

brewing process, 164–168
diseases, 160
Egyptian recipe, 95
fermentation, 163–167
haze, 165, 167, 168
history, 160
hops, 164, 165
infections, 168
mashing, 161, 164
microorganisms, 168
pasteurization, 167
turbidity, 168
types, 166
Benedict, F. G., 44
Benzoic acid, 156
Bergmann, Max, 29, 30
Berzelius, Jöns Jacob, 27
Biological control of pests, 213, 214
Biological systems
 pathways of pollutants, 74
 toxic substances in, 74–79
Biosphere, stress by population, 205
Biotin, 57–62
 biochemical roles, 61
 body requirements, 57
 in carbon dioxide transfer, 59
 as co-enzyme, 61
 deficiency by avidin, 59
 deficiency symptoms, 60
 in liver, 58, 59
 microbiological assay, 62
 in purine synthesis, 60–61
 synthesis, 59, 60
 in tissue, 59
Bjälfe, G., 57
Blackhull, 101
Bleaching agents in flour, 157
Blood, in mammary gland, 120, 121
Blood sugar levels, 22
Bloom, Walter Lyon, 45
Body fat, 46
Boerma, Addeke H., article by, 215–228
Borlaug, Norman, 103
Bos taurus, 124–127
Braconnot, Henri, 28
Braidwood, Robert, 94
Brain
 consumption of glucose, 45, 46
 ketone bodies in, 48
Brand, Erwin, 29
Brassica. See Goiter
Bread, 100
 "rope" in, 156
 stale, 156
Breeding
 cattle, 127, 129–131
 high-lysine corn, 246–249

hybrid corn, 105–109
grape, 171
hog, 219
poultry, 132–138
wheat, 100–103. *See also* Genetics
Bressani, Ricardo, 246
Brewing. *See* Beer
British Petroleum Company, 256
Brooks, Robert R., 209
Brown, Harrison, 195
Brown, Lester R., article by, 205–214
Buchanan, John M., 61
Burnham, Charles R., 110
Burström, D., 57
Butter, 117
Butyric acid, 117

Cahill, George F., Jr., 46, 49, 50
Calcium, 117, 118
Calories, 198–199, 226
Camphor, 10
Cannon, Walter B., 22
Caproic acid, 117
Carbohydrates
 in barley, structure, 164–167
 in diet, 232
 galactose, 35, 118
 glucose, 45, 49, 118
 glycogen, 13–17, 19, 24
 lactose, 35–43, 115, 117, 119
 in liver, 48
Carbon dioxide transfer, 59
Carlson, Anton J., 22
Carleton, Mark, 101
Casein, 115, 117
Cattle, 123–130
 breeding, 127, 129, 130
 breeds, 124–130
 evaluation, 127
 genetic traits, 128
 numbers and productivity, 130
Cattle feed, conversion rate to food, 123
Cell
 lactating, 118, 121, 122
 shrinkage, 42
 "satiety," 24
Cereals
 per capita use, 214
 demand, 214
 production and yield, 217, 218, 227
Cerretelli, Paolo, 17
Cesium, 77
Chaikoff, Israel L., 147
Champagnat, Alfred, article by, 254–258
Chase, Sherret, 110
Chemicals in food, 153, 159, 203
Chlorella, 195, 202

INDEX

Chromatography, 29, 31
Chromosomes, 110
   damage from mercury, 84, 86
   of wheat, 95–99
Cinnabar, 87
Clark, Colin, 195
Clements, F. W. A., 70
Climate
   alteration of, 211–212
   and cattle breeds, 126
   for winegrowing, 169–170
Clisey, Kathryn H., 67
Coconut, 232
Codex Alimentarius, 159
Cohn, Edwin J., 27
Colombia, corn in, 248
Colors in food, 153–155
Connecticut Agricultural Experiment Station, 107
Conservation methods, 210
Continental shelf and slope, 148
Contraception, 230
Conversion rate (feed to food)
   in animals, 234
   poultry, 136
   cattle, 123
Cook, G. C., 37
Cori, Carl F., 27, 50
Corn, hybrid, 105–113
   biological basis, 105, 106
   breeding process, 106–110
   characteristics, 109
   cost, 107
   dangers, 110
   hybrid vigor, 107, 108, 110
   types, 110
   yield, 112, 206
Corn, high-lysine, 245–253
   amino acids in, 246
   breeding, 246–249
   endosperm, 247, 252, 253
   glutelin in, 247, 252
   lysine increase in, 247
   nutritional effects on pigs, 249–251
   nutritional effects on children, 251, 253
   proteins in, 245–253
   strains, 246, 247
Cottam, Clarence, 79
Cowan, Pauline M., 83
Craig, Lyman C., 30
Cretinism, 71
Crocker, E. C., 9, 10
Crustaceans as protein source, 234
Cuatecasas, Pedro, 37
Cyclamates, 153, 159
cysteine, 29, 119

Dairy products, 115
Darwin, Charles, 105
Davies, John, 54
DDT
   in biological cycle, 79
   effects of, 213
   in foodchains, 78
   in forest community, 72–73
   in man, 79
   in undeveloped countries, 227
Deevey, Edward S., Jr., article by, 189–195
Delgado, José M., 22
Diets, reducing, 51
Dill, D. B., 17
Dingle, A. Nelson, 74
Dublin, Louis J., 21
Durand, Paolo, 36

East, Edward M., 107

Ecosystem, 72, 76
Edema, 51
Edwards, H. T., 17
Egg production, 131, 207
Eijkman, Christiaan, 131
Emulsifiers, 157
Enzymes
   amylase, 164, 167
   in barley, 161
   biotin, 57–62
   lactase, 35–46
   lactose synthetase, 118, 122
   papain, 156
   in peptide synthesis, 32, 34
   trypsin, 212
Epiglottis, 11
Escherichia coli, 70
Ethylene, 153
Eutrophication, 213
Exercise and obesity, 26
Exhaustion, 19, 20

Fallout (radioactive)
   distribution, 76–77
   movement of, 72
   rainfall and, 74
Famine, 214
Fat droplet of milk, 114, 120
Fatty acids, 115, 117, 119
Fenton, Paul, 26
Fermentation
   of beer, 163–166
   and flavor changes, 8
   in rumen, 119
   of wine, 173–176
Fertilizer
   benefits, 212
   future demand, 212, 223
   hazards, 212–213
   use, 209–212
Fischer, Emil, 29
Fischer-Hofmeister hypothesis, 30
Fish catch
   average, 141
   by groups, 139
   maximum, 144
   potential, 145
   by species, 143
   U.S., 140, 145
Fish consumption, U.S., 140
Fishermen, annual income, 139
Fish farming, 233, 234, 238–244, 255
   artificial ponds, 241
   carp, 238, 242
   milkfish, 238, 240
   mullet, 239–240
   potential, 240
   rainbow trout, 241
Fish flour and meal, 139–141, 202, 219
Fish food, harvesting of, 150
Fishing areas
   continental shelf and slope, 148
   main, 140–141
   upwellings, 146
Fishing, International management of, 141–148, 150
Fishing powers, 141
Fishing research and engineering, 141–148, 150
Fishing powers, 141
Fishing research and engineering, 146–148, 151
Flavor
   fatty acids, 117
   milk, 117
   beer, 165, 166
   wine, 8

Flavor additives in food, 151, 153–154, 158
Flour, 157
Food
   calories, 200–201
   energy sources, 24
   enrichment, 201
   needs, 229–237, 230
   preservation methods, 200
   production, 205–214, 203–204
   resources of ocean, 139–151
   resources of fresh water, 238–244
   science and technology, 197
   synthetic, 202
Food additives, 153–159, 202, 203
Food adulteration, 153
Food and Agriculture Organization (FAO)
   Codex Alimentarius, 159
   and ionizing radiation, 157
   plan for world agriculture, 215–229
Food chain
   DDT in, 74–76
   fallout in, 72
   mercury in, 81, 84
Food intake rate, 13, 24, 44–51
Ford Foundation, 206
Forest community, DDT in, 72–73
Fossil fuel energy in agriculture, 207
France
   protein from petroleum, 254–258
   wine production in, 171
Fruton, Joseph S., article by, 27–34
Furth, Jacob, 25

Galactose, 35, 118
Galton, Francis, 105
Gamma rays, 77
Garnett, E. S., 45
Gatz, Donald F., 74
Genetics
   corn, 105–109
   haploid plants, 110
   hybrid vigor, 107, 108, 110, 113
   wheat, 95–96
   See also Breeding
Gerald, D. Robert, 243
Gillie, Bruce, article by, 63–71
Gillman, Joseph and Theodore, 53
Globulin, 115
Glucagon, 24
Glucose
   in brain, 45, 46
   in kidney, 49
   in liver, 46
   as metabolite, 18
   satiety cells and, 24
Glutamic acid, 29, 154
Glycerides, 117
Glycogen, 13, 15, 17–19, 24
Godell, John, 39
Goiter, 63–71
   in animals, 70
   goitrogenic substances, 67, 68, 69, 90
   history of, 63
   iatrogenic substances, 70
   prophylaxis, 67
Goldwater, Leonard J., article by, 80–86
Golgi apparatus, 120–122
Gossypol, 199
Grain
   consumption, 214
   production, 217, 227
   protein deficiency, 256
   yield, 218
Grape, 169–173
   breeding, 171
   composition, 171–173
   skin bloom, 173

varieties, 170, 171, 173
Gray, Asa, 105
Gray, Gary, 35
Greenberg, G. Robert, 61
Green revolution, 206
Green vegetables as protein source, 234
Griffin, B. J., 77
Gullet, 11
Guy-Lussac, Joseph L., 169, 178
György, Paul, 57, 58

Haagen-Smit, A. J., article by, 8–12
Hansen, E. C., 166
Hanson, Wayne C., 77
Harpstead, Dale D., article by, 245–253
Haploid plants, 110
Harberber, Arnold C., 195
Harington, Robert, 65
Harris, Stanton A., 59
Hayes, Herbert K., 108
Haze in beer, 165–168
Henderson, L. F., 9
Higgins, Elmer, 79
High-lysine Corn. *See* Corn
Hill, A. V., 17
Hirsch, Jules, 46
Hofmeister, Franz, 30
Holt, S. J., article by, 139–151
Holzel, Aaron, 36
Hops, 164, 165
Hormones
  ACTH, 26
  glucagon, 24
  insulin, 25, 26, 30, 34, 49
  during lactogenesis, 119
  oxytocin, 120
  thyroxine, 63, 65
Howland, John, 36
Hunger sensations, 22, 24
Hybrid corn. *See* Corn
Hybrid vigor, 107, 108, 110, 113
Hybrids. *See* Breeding, Corn, Genetics, Wheat
Hydrocarbons, 254
Hydrogen bond, 31, 34
Hygiene, influence on population, 229, 230
Hyperthyroidism, toxic, 67
Hypothalamus, 22–25

Incaparina, 201, 202
Indian Ocean, pelagic resources of, 147
Indicative World Plan for Agriculture (IWP), 215–228
Institute of Nutrition of Central America, 201
Insulin, 25, 26, 30, 34, 49
Integrated Global Ocean Station System (IGOSS), 147
International Atomic Energy Agency, 157
International Rice Research Institute, 206
Intestine, wall of, 38
Iodine deficiency, 63–71
Iodine fallout, 77
Ionizing radiation for food preservation, 156–157, 200
Irrigation
  in food preoduction, 210, 211
  small-scale, 210
  side effects, 211
  systems, 209, 223
Isaacson, Peter A., 79
Italy, import of hybrid corn, 112

Jacobi, Abraham, 36
Japan
  shellfish farming, 238, 239
  mariculture, 150–151

Jensen, Sören, 82
Jernelöv, Arne, 82
Johannsen, Wilhelm Ludwig, 100, 105, 106
Jones, Donald, 107
Just, Felix, 256

Kajubi, S., 37
Kanred, 101
Kermode, G. O., article by, 153–159
Ketones, 11, 46, 47, 48
Ketosis, 47
Kendall, Edward C., 65
Keys, Ancel, 44
Kidney, during starvation, 49
Kihara, H., 101
Kimball, O. P., 67
Kistiakowsky, G. B., 11
Kögl, Fritz, 57, 58, 59
Kossel, Albrecht, 29
Krebs, Hans A., 47
Kretschmer, Norman, article by, 35–43
Krill, 150, 243
Kulp, S. Lawrence, 72
Kunitz, Moses, 27
Kwashiorkor, 53–56
  areas of occurrence, 52–53
  clinical signs, 50, 51, 56
  prevention, 56

Lactase, 35–43
Lactate cycle, 50
Lactic acid
  formation, 13, 15, 19
  from milk, 118
  in wine, 126
Lactogenesis, 118, 119
Lactose
  formation, 35
  digestion, 39, 40
  intolerance, 31, 35, 37, 38, 41, 42
  molecular structure, 36
Land reform, 224
Larsson, Stig, 22
Lebenthal, Emanuel, 39
Leghorn, 135
Liebig, Justus von, 27, 171, 212
Linneus, Carolus, 8
Lipid synthesis, 118, 119
Lipmann, Fritz, 30
Liver
  biotin in, 58, 59
  fatty, in Kwashiorkor, 53, 55
  pathways of carbohydrates, 48
Lones, D. Peter, 61
Loosanoff, Victor, 241
Lynen, Feodor, 61
Lysine, 29, 245, 246, 254, 256

Mackenzie, Julia B. and Cosmo G., 67
Malnutrition
  effects on population, 197
  Kwashiorkor, 53–56
Malt, 161
Manatee, 233
Malthus, Thomas, 195, 215
Mammary gland, 115–121
Manpower in undeveloped countries, 224, 225
Mangelsdorf, Paul C., articles by, 94–103, 105–113
Marasmus, 44, 50
Margaria, Rodolfo, article by, 13–20
Mariculture, 150, 151
Marine farming, 238–244
Marine, David, 67
Marshall, Norman, 24
Martin, A. J. P., 29
Martin, Frederic T., 79

Matthiessen, G. C., 239
Maturing agents for flour, 157
Mauer, Jerome, 249
Mayer, Jean, article by, 21–26
Meat production by region, 130
Meat substitutes, 154, 214
Meier, Richard L., 195
Menthol, 10
Mercury, 80–86
  in biosphere, 81, 84
  cinnabar, 81
  compounds, use of, 82, 83
  in fish and shellfish, 80, 81
  in food, 84, 85
  in human body, 85, 86
  Minamata disease, 80
  poisoning, 80, 84, 85
  in waste, 80, 85
  use, 82, 84, 86
  world production, 82
Mertz, Edwin T., 246
Methemoglobinemia, 213
Methionine, 201, 254, 256
Mexico, breeding program in, 103, 112
Mickelson, Olaf, 26
Milk, 35–43, 115, 122
  biology, 115
  composition, 115, 116, 117
  digestion, 35–43
  evaporated, 117
  lipids, 115–117
  proteins, 115
  secretion, 120
  synthesis, 119, 120
  tissue, 121
  world production, 130, 205
Mineral production of ocean, 139
Mint, 10
Mirsky, Alfred E., 31
Mönckeberg, Fernando, 50
Mollusks as protein source, 234
Monosodium glutamate, 156, 161
Moore, Stanford, 29
Mortality rate, 21
Moruzzi, Gianni, 17
Müller, Paul Hermann, 213
Mulder, Gerard Johannes, 27
Muscular energy, sources of, 13–20
  alactic, 15, 17, 18
  lactic, 15, 16, 17
  measurements, 13–20
  oxygen debt, 19, 20
Mussels as protein source, 236

Nelson, Oliver E., 246
Neutralizing agents in food, 157
Nielssen, R., 57
Nigeria, lactose tolerance in, 39, 42
Nitrate, 213, 243
Nitrogen loss, 48, 49
Nono, 39
North Africa, wine production in, 171
Northrup, John, 27

Obesity, 21–26
  causes of, 22
  and confinement, 21
  and degenerative disease, 21
  and exercise, 21, 26
  glucagon, 24
  hereditary, 22, 25
  and hormones, 26
  and hypothalamus, 22, 23, 24, 25
  life expectancy, 21
  and satiety center, 23
  traumatic, 25, 26
Ocean, food resources of, 139–151

Odor
  classification, 8–9
  scale, 9
  fatigue, 9
  receptors, 8–9
  theories, 10
Oil, offshore, 139
Oleic acid, 117
Oilseed residues as protein source, 201, 234
Osborne, Thomas Burr, 246
Owen, Oliver E., 47

Palmer, H. E., 77
Palmitic acid, 117
Pasteur, Louis, 169, 178
  and beer, 166, 167
Pathogens in food, 156
Patton, Stuart, article by, 115, 122
Pauling, Linus, 31
Peptides, 30–32
Peru, as fishing power, 141, 146, 242
Pesticides, 72, 74, 77, 213, 227
Petroleum, proteins from, 254–258
  concentrate, 257
  fractions, 257
  quality, 257
  technical complications, 256, 257
  yield, 256, 258
Philippine Republic, milkfish farming in, 240
Phillips, Ralph W., article by, 123–130
Phosphagen, 13, 15, 17
Phosphates, 213, 243
Phosphoric acid, 13, 33
Phosphorus, 118, 212
Phytoplankton, 147, 239
Pickett, Richard A., 249
Pinchot, Gifford B., article by, 238–244
Pirie, N. W., 229
Population, human, 189–195
  checks on, 189, 191
  equilibrium, 189, 192, 195
  and food production, 216, 230
  growth, 189–192, 195, 205, 230
  life expectancy, 193
  maximum, 195
  mean age, 193
Pork production with high-lysine corn, 250, 251
Potassium, 24, 212
Poultry, 133–138, 219
  breeding, 132, 135, 138
  consumption, U.S., 131
  conversion, feed to food, 136
  disease control, 136
  economics, 138
  egg production, 131, 134, 135, 137
  feeding and housing, 135, 137
  strains, 132–133, 135
Poultry Science Association, 132
Pradilla, Alberto G., 257
Preservatives as food additives, 156
Progesterone during lactogenesis, 119
Protein, 27–34
  amino acids, 28–29, 30
  hydrogen bond, 31, 34
  hydrolysis, 29
  peptides, 30–32
  structures of, 30–32
  size, 28
Protein breakdown in muscle, 46
Protein-calorie ratio in food, 53–54
Protein contents of body, 27
Protein deficiency, 201, 213, 232, 256
Protein diet, 214
Protein manufacturing processes, 220
Protein, methods of analysis, 29–31

Protein, sources of
  animals, 255
  wild herbivores, 232–233
  high-lysine corn, 245–253
  ocean, 255, 233, 234, 236
  oilseed residue, 234
  petroleum, 254–258
  plants, 235, 255
  ruminants, 233
  soybeans, 154
  synthetic, 220
  yeast, 256
Purines, biosynthesis of, 60, 61

Rabinowitch, Eugene J., 195
Radioactive elements in environment, 72–79
Rainbow, Cyril, 61
Rainmaking, 212
Ramachandran, G. N., 27, 33
Rancidity, 157
Ransome-Kuti, Olikoye, 39
Ranson, S. W., 22
Rennin, 117
Rhoades, Marcus, 111
Rice, 206, 212
Richey, Frederick D., 110
Richter, Curt P., 67
Roberts, Herbert, 101
Rockefeller Foundation, 206
Roels, A., 243
Rose, Anthony H., article by, 160–168
Rosenzweig, Norton S., 37
Rothamsted Experimental Station, 234
Rumen, 118, 119
Ruminants, 117, 233
Ryther, John H., 239

Saccharin, 153, 159
Saccharomyces cerevisiae, 169
Sakamura, T., 97
Sanger, Frederick, 30
Satiety center, 23
Salinity. *See* Water table
Salmonella, destruction by radiation, 157
Saturated fatty acids in rumen, 119
Saunders, Charles, 101
Sax, Karl, 97
Schiemann, Elisabeth, 19
Schistosomiasis, 211
Schulert, Arthur R., 72
Scrimshaw, Nevin S., articles by, 44–51, 197–204
Sensory apparatus, 9–11
Sequestrants as food additives, 157, 158
Selye, Hans, 191
Senes, Jaques, 256
Shellfish farming
  fertilizer, 240, 241, 244
  mussels, 239
  shellfish, 147
  suspension cultures, 238–239, 240
  oysters, 238, 240
Shipping, 139
Shrimp, 139, 140
Shull, George H., 105, 106
Simmonds, Sofia, 33
Simoons, Frederick J., 42, 43
Skinner, B. F., 23
Smell, 8–12
Smell receptors, 10
Snail fever, 211
Social forces in population equilibrium, 192
Sodium benzoate, 156, 158
Sodium nitrite, 159
Sörensen, Sven P. L., 27
Soft palate, 11

Soil erosion, 209, 210
Solar energy, 195
Sorbic acid, 156
Soybeans, 154, 254
Speck, John F., 33
Stabilizers, 157, 158
Stakman, Elvin, 103
Starch. *See* Carbohydrates
Starvation, physiology of, 44–51
  breakdown of triglycerides, 46
  breakdown of skeletal muscle protein, 46, 48
  cell shrinkage, 46
  changes in metabolism, 46–47
  chemical needs of body, 45
  glucose use after fast, 47
  oxygen uptake after fast, 47
  semistarvation, 51
  survival without food, 44, 45
  water balance, 49
Stearic acid, 119
Stein, William H., 29
Steroid molecule, 11
Stomach contractions, 22, 24
[90]Strontium
  effect on body, 76
  distribution, 72, 73, 76–77
  half-life of, 74
Stunkard, Albert, 24
Sugar reserves in body, 24
Sulfite. *See* Sulfur dioxide
Sulfur dioxide
  as preservative, 156, 158
  treatment of wine, 174
Sunshine, Philip, 36, 39
Svedberg, T., 28
Sweetener, artificial, 153, 159
Sweet taste, 9, 11, 117, 118
Sweet substances, molecular structure of, 12
Synge, R. L. M., 29

Taiwan, milkfish farming in, 240
Taste, 8–12, 117, 118, 165
  bitter, 9, 11, 165
  blindness, 12
  buds, 9, 11
  groups, 11
  perception, 12
  receptors, 9
  salt, 9, 11
  sense, 11
  sour, 9, 11
  sweet, 9, 11, 117, 118
Texture agents, 157, 158
Thompson, T. J., 45
Thomson, Margaret, 54
Triticum. See Wheat
Threonine, 201
Thyroid gland
  activity, 69
  biosynthesis of hormones, 67
  feedback system, 63, 66
  hypertrophy, 63
Thyroxine, 63, 65
Tocopherols as antioxidants, 157
Tönnis, B., 57
Tongue, 9, 11
Toxicity of food additives, 159
Toxic substances in ecosphere, 72–79, 202–203
Traub, W., 61
Tricarboxylic acid cycle, 48
Tri-iodothyronine, 63
Treadmill, 19, 20, 26
Trowell, Hugh C., article by, 52–56
Trypsin, 202

INDEX

Tryptophan, 29, 246, 254, 256
Tswett, Michael, 29

Undeveloped countries
 agriculture, 129, 197–199, 216–225
 arable area, 222
 calories per capita, 226
 economic growth, 197, 199, 225, 226
 food demand, 220
 food preservation, 200
 help to, 203, 220, 224, 226, 228
 land reform, 224
 manpower, 216–221, 225
 population, 221
 protein deficiency, 201
 trade, 217, 231, 232
Upwelling areas
 artificial, 242, 243, 244
 fishing areas, 148
 natural, 242
 productivity, 239
U.S. cornbelt, 105
U.S. Food and Drug Administration, 158
U.S.S.R.
 agriculture, 197, 201
 as fishing power, 141
 river diversions, 211
 wheat breeding, 103
Unsaturated fatty acids, 119

Vanilla extract as food additive, 154, 156
Van Slyde, Donald D., 29
Vavilov, Nicolai, 97
Vegetables as protein source, 154, 214, 219
Vigneau, Vincent du, 58
Vitamins, 57–62, 58

Wakil, Salih J., 61
Wallace, Henry A., 108
Warburg, Otto, 27
Water
 desalination, 211
 diversion of rivers, 211
 eutrophication, 213
Watertable, raising of, 211
Weather Watch, 149
Weight loss, during starvation, 44, 49
West, Philip M., 57
Whales
 decline, 144
 farming of, 243
 regulations, 150
Wheat, 94–103, 206
 bread, 100
 breeding, 95, 103
 diseases, 103
 dwarf, 206
 evolution, 96, 97, 98, 99, 102
 groups, 95
 hybridization, 101–103
 nutritional value, 94
 species, 95–99
 U.S. varieties, 101–103
Williams, Cicely, 52
Wildiers, E., 57
Wilson, P. W., 57
Wilson, Wilbor O., article by, 131–138
Wine and wine production, 169–179
 aging, 171, 175, 177, 178
 bottling, 177
 clearing, 176, 177
 climate, 169–170
 composition, 169
 fining, 171, 177
 flavor, 8
 must, 170, 171
 regions and countries, 171, 178
 See also Fermentation, Grape
Winick, Myron, 50
Wishart, J. W., 70
Wolff, Jan, 67
Woods Hole Oceanographic Institution, 239
Woodward, John D., article by, 57–62
Woodwell, George M., article by, 72–79
World Health Organization
 Codex Alimentarius, 159
 estimate of food spoilage, 156
 evaluation of food colors, 155
 and ionizing radiation, 157
 tests for food additives, 159
World
 agriculture, plan for, 215–228
 arable area, 205, 222
 cattle production, 130
 cereal production, 116, 214
 fertilizer needs, 212
 fishery yields, 139, 144
 protein needs, 254
 Weather Watch, 147
 wine production, 178
Wort, 161, 165
Worzel, J. Lamar, 243
Würster, Jr., Charles F., 79

Yam, 231
Yeasts
 in beer brewing, 166, 168
 in petroleum, 256, 257
 in wine-making, 169, 174
Young, Vernon, R., article by, 44–51

Zebu, 124, 130
Zein, 246, 247, 252
Zooplankton, 147, 241
Zwaardemaker, H. C., 9, 10